McGraw-Hill Education

2,000 Review Questions for the CPA Exam

About the Authors

Denise M. Stefano, CPA, CGMA, MBA, is an associate professor of accounting and the accounting program chairperson with Mercy College. She serves as a board member to the New York State Society of Certified Public Accountants at the New York State level.

Darrel Surett, CPA, taught accounting, business law, and income tax courses for 25 years as an adjunct professor at Union County College. He is a partner in the CPA firm of Barry Surett & Co.

McGraw-Hill Education

2,000 Review Questions for the CPA Exam

Denise M. Stefano, CPA, CGMA, MBA
Darrel Surett, CPA

New York   Chicago   San Francisco   Athens   London   Madrid
Mexico City   Milan   New Delhi   Singapore   Sydney   Toronto

1 2 3 4 5 6 7 8 9   RHR   21 20 19 18 17 16

ISBN   978-1-25-958629-3
MHID   1-25-958629-4

e-ISBN   978-1-25-958630-9
e-MHID   1-25-958630-8

This publication is designed to provide accurate and authoritative information in regard to the subject matter covered. It is sold with the understanding that neither the author nor the publisher is engaged in rendering legal, accounting, securities trading, or other professional services. If legal advice or other expert assistance is required, the services of a competent professional person should be sought.

—From a Declaration of Principles Jointly Adopted by a Committee of the American Bar Association and a Committee of Publishers and Associations

McGraw-Hill Education books are available at special quantity discounts to use as premiums and sales promotions or for use in corporate training programs. To contact a representative, please visit the Contact Us pages at www.mhprofessional.com.

Darrel Surett dedicates this book to his father, Barry,
who taught college accounting for over 50 years.

Denise M. Stefano dedicates this book to her daughter, Catalina,
and all of her students, who collectively inspire her
to be the best educator she can be.

CONTENTS

INTRODUCTION

You've taken a big step toward CPA exam success by purchasing *McGraw-Hill Education: 2,000 Review Questions for the CPA Exam*. This book gives you 2,000 multiple-choice questions, combining theory and practice, and covering the most essential material for all four parts of the Uniform CPA Examination: Auditing and Attestation, Business Environment and Concepts, Financial Accounting and Reporting, and Regulation. Each question is clearly explained in the answer key. The questions will give you valuable independent practice to supplement your other studies.

You might be the kind of student who needs extra study a few weeks before the exam for final review. Or you might be the kind of student who puts off preparing until the last minute before the exam. No matter what your preparation style, you will benefit from reviewing these 2,000 questions, which closely parallel the content of the actual CPA exam. These questions and the explanations in the answer key are the ideal last-minute study tool for those final weeks before the test.

If you practice with all the questions and answers in this book, we are certain you will build the skills and confidence needed to excel on all sections of the CPA exam. Good luck!

PART I

AUDITING AND ATTESTATION

CHAPTER 1

PROPER USE OF THE TERM *AUDIT* AND AN OVERVIEW OF AUDITING

QUESTIONS 1–11

1. Which of the following standards-setting bodies has authority to issue auditing standards for financial statement audits of nonissuers?
   I. Auditing Standards Board
   II. Public Company Accounting Oversight Board

   A. I only
   B. II only
   C. Both I and II
   D. Neither I nor II

2. Whenever an independent expert is brought in to examine financial statements with hopes of adding credibility, that engagement and reporting process is known as an:
   I. audit
   II. attestation

   A. I only
   B. II only
   C. Both I and II
   D. Neither I nor II

3. A CPA performed the following engagements in February of Year 3. Which is considered an attestation engagement?
   I. Audit of Year 2 financial statements
   II. Examination of Year 4's proposed financial information

   A. I only
   B. II only
   C. Both I and II
   D. Neither I nor II

4. After an audit, the financial statements are the responsibility of:
   I. the independent auditor
   II. the management of the reporting company

   A. I only
   B. II only
   C. Both I and II
   D. Neither I nor II

5. According to the generally accepted auditing standards (GAAS), which of the following must be expressed in a standard auditor's report?
   I. The auditor's conclusion that consistent accounting principles were applied from period to period
   II. The auditor's opinion that the financial statement disclosures and footnotes are sufficient and appropriate in the circumstances

   A. I only
   B. II only
   C. Both I and II
   D. Neither I nor II

6. Lara is a covered member in an audit engagement. Which of the following cannot work in any capacity for a company being audited by Lara?
   I. Lara's spouse
   II. Lara's dependent daughter

   A. I only
   B. II only
   C. Both I and II
   D. Neither I nor II

7. Which of the following is correct regarding a covered member of an audit engagement?
   I. If the dependent child of a covered member owns $300 worth of stock in an audit client, the covered member would still be independent if the dependent child were under age five.
   II. If the spouse of a covered member owns an immaterial indirect financial interest in the audit client, the covered member would still be independent.

   A. I only
   B. II only
   C. Both I and II
   D. Neither I nor II

8. In which of the following situations regarding independence would the concept of materiality NOT apply?
   I. Auditing firm owns one share of stock in a publicly traded company under audit. The share is held in a brokerage account.
   II. Auditor's spouse owns one share in a mutual fund that owns shares in a client company. The client is a publicly traded company.

   A. I only
   B. II only
   C. Both I and II
   D. Neither I nor II

9. A violation of the profession's independence standards most likely would have occurred when:
   I. the daughter of a covered member is employed as a parking lot attendant and makes cash tips at the client under audit
   II. the CPA issued an unmodified opinion on the Year 2 financial statements when fees for the Year 1 audit were unpaid

   A. I only
   B. II only
   C. Both I and II
   D. Neither I nor II

10. In an audit of a nonissuer, if a generally accepted auditing standard is considered an "unconditional requirement," which of the following is correct?
   A. The auditor must comply with the standard in order for the auditor to complete an engagement in accordance with GAAS.
   B. The auditor is generally expected to comply with the standard but only if the client is being audited for the first time.
   C. The auditor should comply with the standard or must clearly document the reason for departure.
   D. Consideration of the standard is unconditional, but compliance with the standard is left to the auditor's judgment.

11. According to the clarified standards, the auditor is required to (must) comply with the standard in order for the auditor to complete the engagement in accordance with GAAS if the standard is deemed:
   I. presumptively mandatory
   II. unconditional

   A. I only
   B. II only
   C. Both I and II
   D. Neither I nor II

CHAPTER 2

AUDIT PLANNING AND RISK ASSESSMENT

12. Which of the following should be considered by a CPA prior to acceptance of an audit engagement of a nonissuer?
    I. The quality of the accounting records
    II. The future plans for the company

    A. I only
    B. II only
    C. Both I and II
    D. Neither I nor II

13. Inquiries of the predecessor auditor prior to acceptance of the engagement should include specific questions regarding:
    I. disagreements with management as to accounting principles and auditing procedures
    II. the integrity of management

    A. I only
    B. II only
    C. Both I and II
    D. Neither I nor II

14. A CPA should decide NOT to accept a new client for an audit engagement if:
    I. the CPA lacks an understanding of the client's industry and accounting principles prior to acceptance
    II. the client's management has unusually high turnover

    A. I only
    B. II only
    C. Both I and II
    D. Neither I nor II

15. Which of the following procedures would an auditor likely perform in the planning stage of a financial statement audit?
    I. Obtaining a signed engagement letter from the client's management
    II. Examining documents to detect violations of laws and regulations having a material effect on the financial statements

    A. I only
    B. II only
    C. Both I and II
    D. Neither I nor II

16. Which of the following procedures is likely to be performed in the planning stage of the audit?
    I. Determining the extent of involvement of specialists and internal auditors
    II. External confirmation of client accounts receivables

    A. I only
    B. II only
    C. Both I and II
    D. Neither I nor II

17. All of the following are correct regarding an auditor's understanding with a potential client prior to beginning an audit EXCEPT:

    A. the understanding should cover the responsibilities of the independent auditor.
    B. the understanding should cover the limitations of the engagement.
    C. the understanding should be in the form of an engagement letter in order to be in conformity with auditing standards.
    D. the understanding should list the audit fees and frequency of billing.

5

18. Management's responsibilities in the engagement letter include which of the following?
    I. Adjusting the financial statements to correct material misstatements
    II. Identifying and ensuring that the entity complies with laws and regulations
    III. Selecting and applying accounting policies

    A. I and II only
    B. II and III only
    C. I and III only
    D. I, II, and III

19. Which of the following is correct regarding the auditor's preliminary judgment about materiality?
    I. The auditor utilizes the results of the internal control questionnaire.
    II. The auditor utilizes annualized interim financial statements.

    A. I only
    B. II only
    C. Both I and II
    D. Neither I nor II

20. Which of the following procedures would an auditor likely perform in planning a financial statement audit?
    I. Selecting a sample of vendors' invoices for comparison to receiving reports
    II. Coordinating the assistance of entity personnel in data preparation
    III. Reading the current year's interim financial statements

    A. II only
    B. II and III only
    C. I, II, and III
    D. III only

21. Which of the following will cause the auditor to assess inherent risk as high?
    I. Complex transactions with third parties are discovered.
    II. No related-party transactions are discovered.
    III. Management relies heavily on estimates in the financial statements.

    A. I and II only
    B. I, II, and III
    C. I and III only
    D. III only

22. Inherent risk:
    I. would not be present if the company were not being audited
    II. is assessed by the auditor, but this assessment has no bearing on the actual amount of inherent risk present

    A. I only
    B. II only
    C. Both I and II
    D. Neither I nor II

23. Which of the following risks is assessed by the auditor in the planning stage?
    I. Inherent risk
    II. Control risk

    A. I only
    B. II only
    C. Both I and II
    D. Neither I nor II

24. Which of the following risks is assessed by the auditor but the auditor's assessment has no bearing on the actual amount of risk present?
    I. Control risk
    II. Inherent risk

    A. I only
    B. II only
    C. Both I and II
    D. Neither I nor II

25. Which of the following is a component of audit risk?
    I. Detection risk
    II. Inherent risk

    A. I only
    B. II only
    C. Both I and II
    D. Neither I nor II

26. An auditor can lower overall audit risk by reducing:

    A. inherent risk
    B. control risk
    C. detection risk
    D. all of the above

27. In an audit under GAAS, when an auditor increases the assessed level of control risk because certain control activities were determined to be ineffective, the auditor most likely would:

    A. lower detection risk
    B. decrease the extent of tests of details
    C. increase inherent risk
    D. perform tests of controls

28. Which of the following is correct?
    I. Control risk is not part of overall audit risk, although it is assessed by the auditor.
    II. Detection risk is part of overall audit risk, but it is not assessed by the auditor.

    A. I only
    B. II only
    C. Both I and II
    D. Neither I nor II

29. Inherent risk is:
    I. not influenced by the amount of work or other testing performed by the independent auditor
    II. a characteristic of the accounting system and the personnel who work in that system

    A. I only
    B. II only
    C. Both I and II
    D. Neither I nor II

30. Control risk is:
    I. influenced by the amount of work or other testing performed by the independent auditor
    II. mitigated by good internal controls

    A. I only
    B. II only
    C. Both I and II
    D. Neither I nor II

31. If an auditor assesses both the inherent risk and the control risk for a particular account to be high:
    I. the auditor must then set the acceptable level of detection risk for that account to a relatively low level
    II. the auditor will perform more substantive testing in that area

    A. I only
    B. II only
    C. Both I and II
    D. Neither I nor II

32. By gathering more evidence through substantive testing, an auditor can reduce:
    I. detection risk
    II. control risk
    III. inherent risk

    A. I and III only
    B. I and II only
    C. I only
    D. I, II, and III

33. With regard to overall audit risk, an auditor's decision to reduce detection risk ultimately reduces:
    I. control risk
    II. audit risk
    III. inherent risk

    A. I and II only
    B. II and III only
    C. I, II, and III
    D. II only

34. An auditor wants to reduce detection risk. To achieve this goal, the auditor can:
    I. do more substantive testing or can gather evidence of a better quality
    II. perform more testing earlier in the audit

    A. I only
    B. II only
    C. Both I and II
    D. Neither I nor II

35. On the basis of audit evidence gathered and evaluated, an auditor decides to increase the assessed level of control risk, and therefore the risk of material misstatement, from that originally planned. To achieve an overall audit risk level that is substantially the same as the planned audit risk level, the auditor would:

    A. decrease detection risk
    B. decrease substantive testing
    C. increase inherent risk
    D. increase materiality levels

36. In a financial statement audit, inherent risk is evaluated to help an auditor assess which of the following?

    A. The internal audit department's objectivity in reporting a material misstatement of a financial statement assertion it detects to the audit committee
    B. The risk that the internal control system will not detect a material misstatement of a financial statement assertion
    C. The susceptibility of the financial statements to a material misstatement, assuming there are no related controls
    D. The risk that the audit procedures implemented will not detect a material misstatement of a financial statement assertion

37. There is an inverse relationship between detection risk and the auditor's assessment of:
    I. inherent risk
    II. control risk

    A. I only
    B. II only
    C. Both I and II
    D. Neither I nor II

38. Which of the following is an example of fraudulent financial reporting?
    I. An employee steals inventory and the shrinkage is recorded in cost of goods sold.
    II. Company management changes inventory count tags and overstates ending inventory while understating cost of goods sold.

    A. I only
    B. II only
    C. Both I and II
    D. Neither I nor II

39. Which of the following is an example of fraudulent financial reporting?
    I. The treasurer stealing cash from the company
    II. The recording of false sales prior to year-end to help reach company sales forecasts

    A. I only
    B. II only
    C. Both I and II
    D. Neither I nor II

40. If a company incorrectly applies an accounting principle to a significant transaction, and the misstatement was other than intentional, which of the following could describe the misstatement?
    I. Error
    II. Fraud

    A. I only
    B. II only
    C. Both I and II
    D. Neither I nor II

41. Special consideration must be given to the possibility that fraud exists during which of the following phases of the audit?
    I. Assessment of inherent risk
    II. Assessment of control risk
    III. Substantive testing

    A. I and II only
    B. I, II, and III
    C. I and III only
    D. I only

42. Which of the following is a fraud risk factor?
    I. Unauthorized client transaction
    II. Unusual client delay

    A. I only
    B. II only
    C. Both I and II
    D. Neither I nor II

43. Which of the following should be viewed by the auditor as a fraud risk factor?
    I. Company officials have issued a report stating that they expect earnings per share to double in the current year.
    II. There have been no missing documents and no delays in delivering the documents.

    A. I only
    B. II only
    C. Both I and II
    D. Neither I nor II

44. Which of the following should be viewed by the auditor as a fraud risk factor?
    I. The threat of bankruptcy
    II. The absence of significant competition

    A. I only
    B. II only
    C. Both I and II
    D. Neither I nor II

45. Which of the following analytical procedures is likely to aid the auditor in evaluating the risk of improper revenue recognition due to fraud?
    I. Comparison of sales volume to production capacity
    II. Trend analysis of revenues and sales returns by month

    A. I only
    B. II only
    C. Both I and II
    D. Neither I nor II

46. Which of the following is a component of the fraud triangle?
    I. Ability to rationalize fraud
    II. Pressure to commit fraud

    A. I only
    B. II only
    C. Both I and II
    D. Neither I nor II

47. Which of the following is a fraud risk factor regarding fraudulent financial statements?
     I. Large amounts of cash are kept on hand overnight.
     II. The company is being audited for the first time in order to issue equity securities to the public.
     III. The company recently announced that it expects earnings per share to double.

     A. I and II only
     B. II only
     C. I, II, and III
     D. II and III only

48. Which of the following is a fraud risk factor regarding an opportunity to commit fraudulent financial statements?
     I. Significant, unusual, or highly complex transactions are recorded near the end of the year.
     II. A number of reported balances are based on significant estimations.

     A. I only
     B. II only
     C. Both I and II
     D. Neither I nor II

49. Which of the following is viewed as a fraud risk factor that indicates that management or other employees have the incentive to carry out fraudulent financial reporting?
     I. There is a high turnover of senior management.
     II. There are unreasonable demands on the independent auditor, such as time restraints.

     A. I only
     B. II only
     C. Both I and II
     D. Neither I nor II

50. Which of the following is viewed as a fraud risk factor that indicates that management or other employees have the incentive or pressure to carry out fraudulent financial reporting?
     I. Decline in customer demand
     II. Negative cash flows from operations
     III. Company plans to obtain additional debt financing

     A. I, II, and III
     B. II and III only
     C. I and II only
     D. I and III only

51. Which of the following would NOT heighten an auditor's concern about the risk of intentional manipulation of financial statements?
     I. Insiders recently purchased additional shares of the entity's stock.
     II. Management places substantial emphasis on meeting earnings projections.
     III. Management is dominated by several top executives.
     IV. Inventory is comprised mostly of small, high-dollar items.

     A. I only
     B. II and III only
     C. I, III, and IV only
     D. I and II only

52. At which stage of the audit may fraud risk factors for misappropriation of assets be identified?
     I. Planning
     II. Internal control
     III. Evidence gathering

     A. I and II only
     B. II and III only
     C. I and III only
     D. I, II, and III

53. Which of the following factors would most likely heighten an auditor's concern about the risk of fraudulent financial reporting?
     I. Large amounts of liquid assets that are easily convertible into cash
     II. Financial management's participation in the initial selection of accounting principles
     III. An overly complex organizational structure involving unusual lines of authority

     A. III only
     B. II and III only
     C. I, II, and III
     D. I and III only

54. The auditor's responsibility to detect fraud would change if the fraud was caused by:
     I. collusion
     II. management override of controls

     A. I only
     B. II only
     C. Both I and II
     D. Neither I nor II

55. Which of the following statements reflects an auditor's responsibility for detecting errors and fraud?

    A. An auditor is responsible for detecting employee errors and fraud, but not for discovering fraud involving employee collusion or management override.

    B. An auditor is not responsible for detecting errors and fraud unless the application of GAAS would result in such detection.

    C. An auditor should design the audit to provide reasonable assurance of detecting errors and fraud that are material to the financial statements.

    D. An auditor should plan the audit to detect errors and fraud that are caused by departures from GAAP.

56. If management or employees have high personal debts and company layoffs are anticipated, which leg of the fraud triangle would these fraud risk factors relate to?

    A. Incentive to commit fraudulent financial reporting

    B. Opportunity to commit misappropriation of assets

    C. Opportunity to commit fraudulent financial reporting

    D. Incentive to commit misappropriation of assets

57. Which of the following should be viewed as fraud risk factors that point to incentives or pressure for employees to misappropriate assets?

    I. Compensation levels inconsistent with expectations

    II. Inadequate segregation of duties

    A. I only

    B. II only

    C. Both I and II

    D. Neither I nor II

58. An auditor would likely assess inherent risk to be high in which of the following situations?

    I. Employees are not required to take vacations.

    II. Management does not have an adequate understanding of the information technology in use by the company.

    A. I only

    B. II only

    C. Both I and II

    D. Neither I nor II

59. If a company is planning on raising additional financial capital in the near future by issuing either bonds or shares of stock, the auditor would likely consider this a fraud risk factor for intentional manipulation because the company might want to increase its:

    I. reported net income

    II. debt-to-equity ratio

    A. I only

    B. II only

    C. Both I and II

    D. Neither I nor II

60. If brainstorming sessions reveal no significant fraud risk factors, which of the following is NOT likely to be included in an auditor's inquiry of management while obtaining information to identify the risks of material misstatement due to fraud?

    I. Does management have knowledge of fraud or suspect fraud?

    II. Does management have programs to mitigate fraud risk?

    A. I only

    B. II only

    C. Both I and II

    D. Neither I nor II

61. In every audit, regardless of the outcome of the brainstorming sessions, there exists a presumption of fraud risk in which of the following areas?

    I. Recognition of revenue

    II. Management override of internal control

    A. I only

    B. II only

    C. Both I and II

    D. Neither I nor II

62. Overstating ending inventory:

    I. results in an understatement of cost of goods sold

    II. results in an overstatement of net income

    A. I only

    B. II only

    C. Both I and II

    D. Neither I nor II

63. Which of the following is required on an audit?

    I. Make a legal determination of whether fraud has occurred

    II. Test appropriateness of adjusting journal entries

    A. I only

    B. II only

    C. Both I and II

    D. Neither I nor II

64. A basic premise underlying the application of analytical procedures is that:
    I. plausible relationships among data may reasonably be expected to exist and continue in the absence of known conditions to the contrary
    II. analytical procedures can substitute for tests of certain balances and transactions

    A. I only
    B. II only
    C. Both I and II
    D. Neither I nor II

65. Which of the following is NOT an analytical procedure?
    I. Developing the expected current year sales based on the sales trend of the prior five years
    II. Estimating payroll expense by multiplying the number of employees by the average hourly wage rate and number of hours worked

    A. I only
    B. II only
    C. Both I and II
    D. Neither I nor II

66. In which stage of the audit would analytical procedures NOT likely be performed?
    I. Overall review stage
    II. Planning stage

    A. I only
    B. II only
    C. Both I and II
    D. Neither I nor II

67. Which of the following is correct regarding Statements on Auditing Standards?
    I. Statements on Auditing Standards mostly apply to audits of issuers, but audits of nonissuers are permitted (but not required) to follow these standards also.
    II. Auditors will not be held responsible for a violation of Statements on Auditing Standards if the auditor was not aware of the standard.

    A. I only
    B. II only
    C. Both I and II
    D. Neither I nor II

CHAPTER 3

UNDERSTANDING AND TESTING OF INTERNAL CONTROL

QUESTIONS 68–98

---

68. Management's ability to foresee problems and take steps in advance to prevent problems is known as:
   I.   control environment
   II. control activities

   A. I only
   B. II only
   C. Both I and II
   D. Neither I nor II

69. Internal controls of all of a reporting entity's operating units and business functions is a primary concern of:
   I.   the entity's independent auditor
   II. the entity's management and those charged with governance

   A. I only
   B. II only
   C. Both I and II
   D. Neither I nor II

70. The auditor is likely to focus the assessment of control risk on the entity's:
   I.   reporting controls
   II. operational controls

   A. I only
   B. II only
   C. Both I and II
   D. Neither I nor II

71. The component of internal control that refers to adequate physical safeguards and segregation of duties is known as:
   I.   control environment
   II. risk assessment
   III. control activities

   A. II and III only
   B. I and III only
   C. III only
   D. I, II, and III

72. An auditor generally tests the segregation of duties by:
   I.   personal inquiry and observation
   II. analytical procedures
   III. inspecting and recalculating

   A. I only
   B. II and III only
   C. I and III only
   D. I and II only

73. In the internal control stage, an independent auditor searches for control activities to:
   I.   determine whether the opportunities to allow any person to both perpetrate and conceal fraud are minimized
   II. determine whether procedures and records concerning the safeguarding of assets are reliable

   A. I only
   B. II only
   C. Both I and II
   D. Neither I nor II

74. An entity's ongoing monitoring activities often include:
    I. the audit of the annual financial statements
    II. reviewing the payroll cycle

    A. I only
    B. II only
    C. Both I and II
    D. Neither I nor II

75. An auditor gains an understanding of the client's attempt to keep internal controls up to date. This ongoing process of keeping controls effective:
    I. refers to the monitoring component of internal control
    II. is often performed by the internal audit function

    A. I only
    B. II only
    C. Both I and II
    D. Neither I nor II

76. Which of the following is NOT one of the five components of internal control?
    I. Control activities
    II. Control group
    III. Control risk

    A. II only
    B. II and III only
    C. III only
    D. I and II only

77. Management's attitude toward aggressive financial reporting and its emphasis on meeting projected profit goals most likely would significantly influence an entity's control environment when:
    I. management is dominated by one individual who is also a shareholder
    II. a significant portion of management compensation is represented by stock options
    III. those charged with governance are active in overseeing the entity's financial reporting policies

    A. I and III only
    B. II and III only
    C. I only
    D. I and II only

78. In an audit in conformity with GAAS, an auditor gains an understanding of the client's internal controls. At this stage, what needs to be understood?
    I. The design of the client's system
    II. Whether the controls have been placed in operation

    A. I only
    B. II only
    C. Both I and II
    D. Neither I nor II

79. In an audit in accordance with GAAS, as part of understanding internal control, an auditor is required to:
    I. obtain knowledge about the operating effectiveness of internal control
    II. ascertain whether internal controls have been implemented

    A. I only
    B. II only
    C. Both I and II
    D. Neither I nor II

80. Which of the following describes the auditor's ultimate purpose of assessing control risk?
    I. Evaluate the risk of financial statement misstatement
    II. Make recommendations regarding the five components of internal control

    A. I only
    B. II only
    C. Both I and II
    D. Neither I nor II

81. Assessing control risk at a low level most likely would involve:
    I. identifying specific controls relevant to specific assertions
    II. performing more extensive substantive tests than originally planned

    A. I only
    B. II only
    C. Both I and II
    D. Neither I nor II

82. When an auditor chooses the substantive approach and increases the assessed level of control risk because certain control activities were determined to be ineffective, the auditor would most likely:
    I. increase the extent of tests of controls
    II. increase the extent of substantive procedures

    A. I only
    B. II only
    C. Both I and II
    D. Neither I nor II

83. After gaining an understanding of a client's internal control, an auditor chose to use the combined approach to further audit procedures. Which of the following would be a reason that the auditor chose the combined approach?
   I. Based on the auditor's assessment of internal control, the auditor thinks the controls are in place.
   II. The auditor would choose the combined approach if testing controls would reduce further substantive procedures.
   A. I only
   B. II only
   C. Both I and II
   D. Neither I nor II

84. After gaining and documenting an understanding of the components of internal control, the auditor should make a preliminary assessment of control risk. If the auditor's investigation indicates that internal control is probably weak, the auditor should:
   I. use the combined approach for further audit procedures
   II. emphasize substantive testing rather than test of controls
   A. I only
   B. II only
   C. Both I and II
   D. Neither I nor II

85. An auditor must obtain an understanding of the components of a client's internal control. Auditors often choose to use questionnaires to gain information because:
   I. each "no" response suggests a potential internal control weakness
   II. compared to flowcharting, both strengths and weaknesses are easier to determine with a questionnaire
   A. I only
   B. II only
   C. Both I and II
   D. Neither I nor II

86. An auditor's flowchart of the accounting system is a diagrammatic representation that shows the auditor's:
   I. understanding of the system
   II. assessment of control risk
   A. I only
   B. II only
   C. Both I and II
   D. Neither I nor II

87. To obtain audit evidence about control risk, an auditor seeks to test controls and test for segregation of duties. The auditor will likely test for segregation of duties by:
   A. inquiry
   B. observation
   C. confirmations
   D. preparing a questionnaire or flowchart

88. An auditor is performing tests of controls in hopes of assessing control risk to be low in order to reduce overall audit testing. After obtaining an understanding of the design of an individual system, the auditor should:
   I. seek to identify specific control activities within that system that would reduce control risk if they are operating effectively and efficiently, as intended
   II. analyze and confirm
   A. I only
   B. II only
   C. Both I and II
   D. Neither I nor II

89. An auditor would test controls to gather evidence about:
   I. whether a control is functioning as designed
   II. whether an account balance is fairly stated
   A. I only
   B. II only
   C. Both I and II
   D. Neither I nor II

90. The auditor should design "further audit procedures" before the assessment of:
   I. inherent risk
   II. control risk
   A. I only
   B. II only
   C. Both I and II
   D. Neither I nor II

91. In an audit of financial statements, the entity's management is responsible for:
   I. establishing, maintaining, and monitoring the entity's internal controls
   II. considering whether those controls are operating as intended
   A. I only
   B. II only
   C. Both I and II
   D. Neither I nor II

92. With regard to automated controls and manual controls, an auditor would expect to find manual controls when:
    I. judgment and discretion are required
    II. large, nonrecurring transactions are involved
    A. I only
    B. II only
    C. Both I and II
    D. Neither I nor II

93. An auditor would expect to find manual controls rather than automated controls when:
    I. potential misstatements are more difficult to predict
    II. transactions are high volume and recurring
    A. I only
    B. II only
    C. Both I and II
    D. Neither I nor II

94. Which of the following represents an inherent limitation of internal control?
    I. Collusion among employees
    II. Mistakes in judgment
    A. I only
    B. II only
    C. Both I and II
    D. Neither I nor II

95. Which of the following represents an inherent limitation of internal control?
    I. Management override
    II. Incompatible duties
    A. I only
    B. II only
    C. Both I and II
    D. Neither I nor II

96. Under US GAAS, which of the following is always necessary in a financial statement audit?
    I. An indication whether or not the financial statements agree with the accounting records
    II. Risk assessment procedures
    III. Testing of controls
    A. I, II, and III
    B. I and III only
    C. II and III only
    D. I and II only

97. In an audit performed under GAAS, which of the following should an auditor do when control risk is assessed at the maximum level?
    A. Perform fewer substantive tests of details
    B. Document the assessment
    C. Document the control structure more extensively
    D. Perform more tests of controls

98. Tests of controls must be performed:
    I. when the auditor's risk assessment is based on the assumption that controls are operating effectively
    II. when substantive procedures alone are insufficient
    A. I only
    B. II only
    C. Both I and II
    D. Neither I nor II

CHAPTER 4

AUDIT DOCUMENTATION, RELATED-PARTY TRANSACTIONS, AND SUBSEQUENT EVENTS

QUESTIONS 99–114

99. An auditor maintains a current file within the audit documentation. This file should:
  I. contain all of the evidential material gathered to support the opinion rendered by the auditor
  II. contain a working trial balance

  A. I only
  B. II only
  C. Both I and II
  D. Neither I nor II

100. Which of the following would be maintained in the permanent file?
  I. Copies of documents such as the reporting company's organization chart and long-term contracts
  II. The audit plan and management representation letter

  A. I only
  B. II only
  C. Both I and II
  D. Neither I nor II

101. The permanent file most likely would include copies of the:

  A. auditor's lead schedules
  B. client attorney's letters
  C. client bank statements
  D. client debt agreements

102. The permanent file of an auditor's working papers would NOT include:
  I. bond indenture agreements
  II. lease agreements
  III. lead schedules
  IV. working trial balances

  A. I and II only
  B. II and III only
  C. III only
  D. III and IV only

103. No deletions of audit documentation are allowed after the:

  A. client's year-end
  B. documentation completion date
  C. last date of significant fieldwork
  D. report release date

104. Which of the following factors would likely affect an auditor's judgment about the quantity, type, and content of the auditor's working papers?
  I. The assessed level of control risk
  II. The type of audit report issued

  A. I only
  B. II only
  C. Both I and II
  D. Neither I nor II

17

105. Which of the following is NOT a primary function of audit working papers?

   A. Assisting management in proving that the financial statements are in accordance with generally accepted accounting principles
   B. Assisting the audit team members responsible for supervision in reviewing the work of the audit staff
   C. Assisting auditors in planning engagements from one year to the next
   D. Providing the auditor with support for the opinion that was rendered on the financial statements

106. Which of the following is correct concerning related-party transactions?

   I. The audit procedures directed toward identifying related-party transactions should include considering whether transactions are occurring but are not given proper accounting recognition.
   II. An auditor should substantiate that related-party transactions were consummated on terms equivalent to those that prevail in arm's-length transactions.

   A. I only
   B. II only
   C. Both I and II
   D. Neither I nor II

107. Which of the following auditing procedures most likely would assist an auditor in identifying related-party transactions?

   I. Searching accounting records for recurring transactions recorded just after the balance sheet date
   II. Reviewing confirmations of loans receivable and payable for indications of loan guarantees

   A. I only
   B. II only
   C. Both I and II
   D. Neither I nor II

108. Which of the following is likely the auditor's biggest concern with regard to related-party transactions?

   A. Money is borrowed or lent at an interest rate different from the market rate.
   B. Property is sold or bought for amounts different from fair value.
   C. Loans are made with no set repayment schedule.
   D. Transactions with related parties are not given proper accounting treatment.

109. When investigating the possibility of related-party transactions, the auditor should look carefully for transactions that do not fit into patterns typically anticipated. Which of the following loans made by the client would make the auditor suspicious of a related-party loan?

   I. The loan was made without a fixed interest rate.
   II. The loan was made with no maturity date.
   III. The loan was made with a rate of interest that the auditor considers extremely low.

   A. I and II only
   B. I and III only
   C. I, II, and III
   D. II and III only

110. Just before the end of the year, a company sells several acres of land that had been held for a number of years. The sales price was significantly above the book value of the property so that a large gain was recognized. Neither this transaction nor any other transaction has been disclosed as a related-party transaction. Which of the following is correct?

   I. Since the sales price was significantly above the book value of the property, the auditor should be particularly suspicious that a related-party transaction has occurred.
   II. If the land had been sold involving an amount significantly different from its fair market value, the auditor likely would not suspect a related-party transaction.

   A. I only
   B. II only
   C. Both I and II
   D. Neither I nor II

111. Which of the following procedures would an auditor most likely perform to obtain evidence about the occurrence of subsequent events?

   I. Comparing the financial statements being reported on with those of the prior period
   II. Investigating personnel changes in the accounting department occurring after year-end

   A. I only
   B. II only
   C. Both I and II
   D. Neither I nor II

112. If the auditor believes that a client's financial statements need to be revised to reflect a subsequent event and management does not make the revision, the auditor should express which type of opinion?
    A. Unmodified with an other-matters paragraph
    B. Disclaimer or qualified
    C. Adverse or qualified
    D. Qualified or unmodified

113. Which of the following is correct regarding the auditor's responsibility for subsequent events?
    I. The auditor has an active responsibility to make continuing inquiries between the date of the financial statements and the date of the auditor's report.
    II. The auditor has an active responsibility to make continuing inquiries after the date of the auditor's report.

    A. I only
    B. II only
    C. Both I and II
    D. Neither I nor II

114. Which of the following statements is NOT true regarding the auditor's responsibility for subsequent events?
    A. The auditor has an active responsibility to make continuing inquiries between the date of the financial statements and the date on which sufficient appropriate audit evidence has been obtained.
    B. The auditor has an active responsibility to make continuing inquiries between the date of the financial statements and the date of the auditor's report.
    C. The auditor has an active responsibility to make continuing inquiries between the date of the auditor's report and the date on which the report is submitted.
    D. The auditor has no active responsibility to make continuing inquiries after the date of the auditor's report.

CHAPTER 5

AUDIT REPORTING

115. For an audit of a nonissuer, which of the following paragraphs is found in a standard unmodified audit report?
     I. Scope
     II. Introductory
     III. Management's responsibility
     IV. Auditor's responsibility

     A. I, II, III, and IV
     B. III and IV only
     C. I, II, and IV only
     D. II, III, and IV only

116. How many paragraphs are found in a standard unmodified audit report?

     A. 3
     B. 4
     C. 5
     D. 6

117. Put these paragraphs in the order they appear in a standard unmodified audit report:
     I. management's responsibility
     II. auditor's responsibility
     III. introductory
     IV. opinion
     V. scope

     A. III, II, I, IV
     B. III, V, I, II, IV
     C. III, V, II, I, IV
     D. III, I, II, IV

118. Under GAAS, in the auditor's responsibility paragraph, how does an auditor describe his or her responsibility regarding the client's internal controls?

     A. Examined internal controls
     B. Evaluated the overall internal controls
     C. Expressed an opinion on internal controls
     D. Considered internal controls

119. According to the opinion paragraph found in the standard unmodified audit report:
     I. the auditor has assessed the accounting principles and evaluated significant accounting estimates used by the reporting entity
     II. "present fairly" and US generally accepted accounting principles (GAAP) are specifically referenced

     A. I only
     B. II only
     C. Both I and II
     D. Neither I nor II

120. The auditor's standard report implies that the auditor is satisfied that the comparability of financial statements between periods:
     I. has not been materially affected by changes in accounting principles
     II. has been consistently applied between or among periods

     A. I only
     B. II only
     C. Both I and II
     D. Neither I nor II

121. An emphasis-of-matter paragraph is included in the auditor's report:
    I. when required by GAAS
    II. at the auditor's discretion

    A. I only
    B. II only
    C. Both I and II
    D. Neither I nor II

122. The inclusion of an emphasis-of-matter paragraph in the auditor's report:
    I. is used when referring to a matter that is not appropriately presented in the financial statements
    II. does not affect the auditor's opinion

    A. I only
    B. II only
    C. Both I and II
    D. Neither I nor II

123. Which of the following is correct regarding the adding of an emphasis-of-matter paragraph to an unmodified report?
    I. If the auditor decides to add a paragraph, the extra paragraph should go before the opinion paragraph.
    II. The emphasis paragraph should contain a statement that the auditor's opinion may need to be modified.

    A. I only
    B. II only
    C. Both I and II
    D. Neither I nor II

124. An other-matters paragraph is used:
    I. when required by GAAS
    II. at the auditor's discretion

    A. I only
    B. II only
    C. Both I and II
    D. Neither I nor II

125. Other-matters paragraphs refer to matters that are relevant to the user's understanding of the:
    I. financial statements
    II. auditor's responsibilities
    III. auditor's report

    A. II and III only
    B. II only
    C. I and II only
    D. I, II, and III

126. An auditor would express an unmodified opinion with an emphasis-of-matter paragraph added to the auditor's report for a:
    I. justified change in accounting principle
    II. material internal control weakness

    A. I only
    B. II only
    C. Both I and II
    D. Neither I nor II

127. The preparation and fair presentation of the financial statements requires:
    I. identification of the applicable financial reporting framework
    II. inclusion of an adequate description of the framework

    A. I only
    B. II only
    C. Both I and II
    D. Neither I nor II

128. If an auditor chooses an emphasis-of-matter paragraph to describe a going concern issue, which of the following is required language in that emphasis paragraph?
    I. "12 months from the balance sheet date"
    II. "Reasonable period of time"

    A. I only
    B. II only
    C. Both I and II
    D. Neither I nor II

129. Where does a group auditor make reference to a component auditor in a division of responsibility?
    I. Emphasis-of-matter paragraph
    II. Other-matters paragraph

    A. I only
    B. II only
    C. Both I and II
    D. Neither I nor II

130. When a group auditor decides to make reference to the examination of a component auditor:
    I. the group auditor's report should not make reference to the "component auditor" in the auditor's responsibility paragraph
    II. the introductory paragraph is the same whether the auditor divides responsibility or not

    A. I only
    B. II only
    C. Both I and II
    D. Neither I nor II

131. A typical auditor's report should include a reference to the country of origin of:
    I. the auditing standards the auditor followed in performing the audit
    II. the accounting principles used to prepare the financial statements
    A. I only
    B. II only
    C. Both I and II
    D. Neither I nor II

132. An auditor can issue an unmodified report without any reference to consistency when:
    I. the client changes from straight line depreciation to accelerated depreciation
    II. the client changes the useful life of an asset used to calculate depreciation expense
    A. I only
    B. II only
    C. Both I and II
    D. Neither I nor II

133. A group auditor chose to divide the responsibility for an audit with another firm. This other firm issued a qualified opinion on the financial statements of the subsidiaries that it audited. Which of the following is correct regarding the responsibility of the group auditor?
    I. The group auditor must render a qualified opinion on the consolidated financial statements.
    II. The group auditor may not render an unmodified opinion on the consolidated financial statements.
    A. I only
    B. II only
    C. Both I and II
    D. Neither I nor II

134. Which of the following correctly describes the effect on the auditor's otherwise unmodified report when a client changes an accounting principle that has a material effect on the financial statements but the auditor concurs with the change?
    I. An emphasis-of-matter paragraph preceding the opinion paragraph is required.
    II. If the previous accounting principle was NOT in conformity with GAAP, the emphasis-of-matter paragraph would still be required.
    A. I only
    B. II only
    C. Both I and II
    D. Neither I nor II

135. When an auditor qualifies an opinion because of a scope limitation, the wording in the opinion paragraph should indicate that the qualification pertains to:
    I. the possible effects on the financial statements
    II. the scope limitation itself
    A. I only
    B. II only
    C. Both I and II
    D. Neither I nor II

136. An auditor may issue a report that omits any reference to consistency when:
    I. the client changes from straight line to accelerated depreciation for property, plant, and equipment
    II. there is a change from an accounting principle that is NOT generally accepted to one that is generally accepted
    A. I only
    B. II only
    C. Both I and II
    D. Neither I nor II

137. If a publicly held company issues financial statements that purport to present its financial position and results of operations but omits the statement of cash flows, the auditor ordinarily will express:
    A. an unmodified opinion with an emphasis-of-matter paragraph
    B. a qualified opinion
    C. an unmodified opinion without an emphasis-of-matter paragraph
    D. a disclaimer of qualified opinion

138. When an auditor expresses an adverse opinion, the opinion paragraph should include:
    I. the substantive reasons for the financial statements being misleading
    II. a direct reference to a separate paragraph disclosing the basis for the opinion
    A. I only
    B. II only
    C. Both I and II
    D. Neither I nor II

139. An auditor would NOT issue a disclaimer of opinion for:
I. inadequate disclosure
II. an accounting principle change that the auditor does not agree with

A. I only
B. II only
C. Both I and II
D. Neither I nor II

140. After performing an audit, the independent CPA is still somewhat concerned that the financial statements are not free from all material misstatements. If, in the auditor's judgment, the misstatements were material but not pervasive, the opinion expressed is likely to be:

A. unmodified
B. adverse
C. disclaimer
D. qualified

141. When an auditor expresses a qualified opinion due to a material misstatement of the financial statements, the auditor's responsibility paragraph should be amended to state that the auditor believes that the audit evidence obtained is sufficient and appropriate to provide a basis for the auditor's:

A. opinion
B. modified opinion
C. qualified opinion
D. nonstandard opinion

142. Which of the following is an implicit representation when issuing the auditor's report on comparative financial statements under US auditing standards?
I. Obtaining evidence that is sufficient and appropriate
II. Consistent application of accounting principles

A. I only
B. II only
C. Both I and II
D. Neither I nor II

143. An auditor who is unable to form an opinion on a new client's opening inventory balances may NOT issue an unmodified opinion on the current year's:
I. balance sheet
II. income statement
III. statement of cash flows

A. I and III only
B. I only
C. III only
D. II and III only

144. When an auditor issues an adverse opinion or disclaimer on the financial statements taken as a whole, the auditor could still issue an unmodified opinion on just:
I. the income statement
II. property, plant, and equipment

A. I only
B. II only
C. Both I and II
D. Neither I nor II

CHAPTER 6
REVIEWS AND COMPILATIONS

145. SSARS applies to:
- **A.** compilations but not reviews
- **B.** reviews but not compilations
- **C.** compilations and reviews of publicly traded companies
- **D.** compilations and reviews of non-publicly traded companies

146. Which of the following audit procedures generally is NOT performed in a review engagement?
  - I. Going concern
  - II. Inquiries of the entity's outside legal counsel

- **A.** I only
- **B.** II only
- **C.** Both I and II
- **D.** Neither I nor II

147. Which of the following documentation would likely NOT be included in a review engagement of a nonissuer?
  - I. Procedures used to assess control risk
  - II. Inquiring about subsequent events

- **A.** I only
- **B.** II only
- **C.** Both I and II
- **D.** Neither I nor II

148. Which of the following procedures is likely to be performed in a compilation?
  - I. Analytical procedures
  - II. Inquiries

- **A.** I only
- **B.** II only
- **C.** Both I and II
- **D.** Neither I nor II

149. For a nonissuer, which of the following is required in a review engagement but NOT in a compilation engagement?
  - I. Communication with the predecessor who performed the engagement in the prior year
  - II. A basic knowledge of the accounting principles and practices of the industry in which the entity operates

- **A.** I only
- **B.** II only
- **C.** Both I and II
- **D.** Neither I nor II

150. An accountant who had begun a review of the financial statements of a nonissuer was asked to change the engagement to a compilation. If there is reasonable justification for the change, the accountant's report should include reference to the:
  - I. reason for the change
  - II. original engagement that was agreed to

- **A.** I only
- **B.** II only
- **C.** Both I and II
- **D.** Neither I nor II

151. If requested to perform a review engagement for a nonissuer in which an accountant has an immaterial direct financial interest, the accountant is:

    A. not independent and, therefore, may not issue a compilation
    B. not independent and, therefore, may not issue a review report, but may issue a compilation
    C. not independent and, therefore, may not be associated with the financial statements
    D. independent because the financial interest is immaterial and, therefore, may issue a review report

152. A review provides limited assurance that there are no material modifications that should be made to the financial statements in order for them to be in conformity with GAAP, whereas a compilation:

    A. provides limited assurance that the CPA followed SSARS and the client followed GAAP
    B. provides negative assurance that no material modifications need to be made to the financial statements, rather than reasonable assurance
    C. provides negative assurance that no material modifications need to be made to the financial statements, rather than limited assurance
    D. provides no assurance

153. Which of the following types of engagements tests for reasonableness of the financial statements?

    I. Compilations
    II. Reviews

    A. I only
    B. II only
    C. Both I and II
    D. Neither I nor II

154. If independence is compromised:

    A. the CPA can still express limited assurance on the financial statements
    B. the CPA can still perform a compilation engagement
    C. disclosing such lack of independence would not compensate for the lack of independence and, therefore, the CPA would need to withdraw from a compilation engagement
    D. None of the above

155. A review for a nonissuer that is prepared unmodified from the standard review report will contain how many paragraphs?

    A. 4
    B. 5
    C. 2
    D. 3

156. In a standard unmodified review report for a nonissuer, the second paragraph is known as the:

    A. opinion paragraph
    B. CPA's responsibility paragraph
    C. scope paragraph
    D. management responsibility paragraph

157. As part of the CPA's responsibilities in performing a review engagement for a nonissuer, which of the following is required evidence to be signed by the client?

    I. Engagement letter
    II. Management representation letter

    A. I only
    B. II only
    C. Both I and II
    D. Neither I nor II

158. As part of the CPA's responsibilities in performing a compilation, which of the following is required evidence to be signed by the client?

    I. Engagement letter
    II. Management representation letter

    A. I only
    B. II only
    C. Both I and II
    D. Neither I nor II

159. According to SSARS 21, in which of the following engagements are analytical procedures and inquiries performed by an independent CPA?

    I. Reviews of a nonissuer
    II. Compilations
    III. Preparation engagements

    A. I and II
    B. I and III
    C. I only
    D. None of the above

160. According to SSARS 21, a standard compilation report on historical financial statements prepared with footnotes by an independent CPA contains how many paragraphs?

    A. Four
    B. Three
    C. Two
    D. One

161. A compilation report presented without footnotes by a CPA who is NOT independent:

    A. cannot be performed, because the CPA is not independent
    B. cannot be performed, because the CPA lacks independence and the report lacks disclosures required under GAAP
    C. can be performed if the client is not a relative of the CPA and all instances of a lack of independence are provided
    D. can be performed provided the report discloses both the lack of independence and the fact that the disclosures are missing

162. According to SSARS 21, which of the following engagements may a CPA perform without issuing a report at the conclusion of the engagement?

    I. Compilation
    II. Review
    III. Preparation of financial statements

    A. I and III
    B. I only
    C. III only
    D. I, II, and III

163. With respect to SSARS 21, Preparation of Financial Statements, what may a practitioner deliver to a client without an accompanying report?

    A. A limit of one financial statement if footnotes and disclosures are excluded
    B. One or more financial statements, provided footnotes and disclosures are included
    C. One or more financial statements with or without footnotes
    D. One or more financial statements with or without footnotes, provided the practitioner is independent

164. Which of the following engagements provided by a CPA to a nonissuer requires the CPA to be independent even though no opinion will be expressed?

    I. Review engagements
    II. Compilations of financial statements that include footnotes

    A. I only
    B. II only
    C. Both I and II
    D. Neither I nor II

165. According to SSARS 21, a preparation of financial statements engagement is NOT subject to peer review if:

    A. the practitioner performs compilations but no audits or reviews
    B. the practitioner performs compilations and reviews but not audits
    C. the practitioner performs no audits, compilations, or reviews
    D. the practitioner has undergone peer review at least twice in the last five years

CHAPTER 7

REPORTING ON SPECIAL PURPOSE FRAMEWORKS AND OTHER REPORTING ISSUES

QUESTIONS 166–200

166. Reports on special purpose frameworks are issued in conjunction with:
   I. cash basis
   II. income tax basis
   III. regulatory basis of accounting

   A. I and III only
   B. I and II only
   C. II and III only
   D. I, II, and III

167. An auditor's report will contain an emphasis-of-matter paragraph alerting readers to a special purpose framework when the financial statements are prepared using the:
   I. income tax basis
   II. cash basis

   A. I only
   B. II only
   C. Both I and II
   D. Neither I nor II

168. When a CPA reports on financial statements prepared on the cash basis:
   I. the report will contain an emphasis-of-matter paragraph
   II. the opinion paragraph will evaluate the usefulness of the basis of accounting and compare it to GAAP

   A. I only
   B. II only
   C. Both I and II
   D. Neither I nor II

169. A report on special purpose framework financial statements prepared on the income tax basis should include an emphasis-of-matter paragraph:
   I. stating the basis of accounting used
   II. referring to the footnote in the financial statements that describes the basis of accounting
   III. indicating that it is a non-GAAP basis

   A. I only
   B. I, II, and III
   C. I and III only
   D. II and III only

170. Which of the following reports would contain restricted use language?
   I. A report on a client's compliance with a regulatory requirement, assuming the report is prepared based on a financial statement audit of the complete financial statements
   II. A report on financial statements prepared on the cash basis of accounting

   A. I only
   B. II only
   C. Both I and II
   D. Neither I nor II

171. An auditor's report on special purpose financial statements will contain a restricted use paragraph (other matters) when the financial statements are presented using the:
   I. cash basis
   II. income tax basis

   A. I only
   B. II only
   C. Both I and II
   D. Neither I nor II

172. Which of the following will be included in an auditor's report on special purpose financial statements NOT intended for general use?
  I. Emphasis-of-matter paragraph alerting the reader about the preparation in accordance with a special purpose framework
  II. Other-matters paragraph restricting the use of the auditor's report

  A. I only
  B. II only
  C. Both I and II
  D. Neither I nor II

173. A dual opinion on special purpose frameworks and GAAP would be required if the financial statements were prepared on which of the following frameworks?
  I. Income tax basis
  II. Cash basis

  A. I only
  B. II only
  C. Both I and II
  D. Neither I nor II

174. A CPA is asked to report on one financial statement and not the others. The auditor should do which of the following?

  A. Accept the engagement but disclaim an opinion because the complete set of financial statements was not audited
  B. Not accept the engagement, because it would constitute a violation of the profession's ethical standards
  C. Not accept the engagement, because reporting on one financial statement and not the others is not permitted unless the auditor is not independent
  D. Accept the engagement because such engagements merely involve special considerations in the application of US GAAS

175. Clyde, CPA, has been asked to report on the balance sheet of Western Company but not on the other basic financial statements. Which of the following is required of Clyde?
  I. When auditing a single financial statement, Clyde should perform procedures, as necessary, on interrelated items (sales/receivables, inventory/payables, fixed assets/depreciation).
  II. When auditing a single financial statement, Clyde may perform the audit as a separate engagement or in conjunction with an audit of an entity's complete set of financial statements.

  A. I only
  B. II only
  C. Both I and II
  D. Neither I nor II

176. Clyde, CPA, has been asked to report on the balance sheet of Western Company but not on the other basic financial statements. Which of the following is required of Clyde?
  I. When auditing a single financial statement, Clyde should determine materiality for the complete set of financial statements rather than for the single financial statement.
  II. When auditing a single financial statement, Clyde should obtain an understanding of the intended users of the statement.

  A. I only
  B. II only
  C. Both I and II
  D. Neither I nor II

177. Starkey, CPA, expressed an adverse opinion on the financial statements of Harrison Corp. Which of the following is required if Starkey wishes to express an unmodified opinion on a specific element of those financial statements?
  I. The specific element must not be a major part of the total financial statements.
  II. The report on the specific element must be shown together with the report on the complete financial statements.

  A. I only
  B. II only
  C. Both I and II
  D. Neither I nor II

178. Which of the following is correct with regard to an auditor's report on compliance?
    I. An auditor's report would be designated a report on compliance when it is issued in connection with compliance with aspects of regulatory requirements related to audited financial statements.
    II. An auditor's report on compliance does not involve the auditor giving positive assurance regarding compliance with regulatory requirements.

    A. I only
    B. II only
    C. Both I and II
    D. Neither I nor II

179. Which of the following is correct regarding an auditor's report on compliance?
    I. The auditor does not have to audit the client's complete financial statements in order to issue a report on compliance.
    II. The report on compliance could express positive or negative assurance on compliance.

    A. I only
    B. II only
    C. Both I and II
    D. Neither I nor II

180. Which of the following is correct regarding an auditor's report on compliance?
    I. Would contain negative assurance if material instances of noncompliance were discovered by the auditor
    II. Would express negative assurance if the auditor issued a disclaimer or adverse opinion on the complete financial statements

    A. I only
    B. II only
    C. Both I and II
    D. Neither I nor II

181. The auditor's report on compliance with a regulatory requirement:
    I. must be a separate report from the auditor's report on the financial statements
    II. contains a paragraph restricting the use of the report

    A. I only
    B. II only
    C. Both I and II
    D. Neither I nor II

182. An auditor's report on compliance would include a restriction of use if the report on compliance was:
    I. issued separately from the report on the financial statements
    II. included as an other-matters paragraph in a report on the complete financial statements

    A. I only
    B. II only
    C. Both I and II
    D. Neither I nor II

183. An auditor's report on compliance may contain negative assurance regarding instances of noncompliance when:
    I. the auditor's report on compliance is issued separately from the report on the complete financial statements
    II. the auditor's report on compliance is issued as an other-matters paragraph within the auditor's report on complete financial statements

    A. I only
    B. II only
    C. Both I and II
    D. Neither I nor II

184. Which is correct regarding the auditor's report on compliance issued as a separate report from the auditor's report on the complete financial statements?
    I. The date of the separate report should be later than the auditor's report on the complete financial statements.
    II. The separate report should contain a statement that the audit was not directed primarily toward obtaining knowledge regarding compliance.

    A. I only
    B. II only
    C. Both I and II
    D. Neither I nor II

185. An auditor's standard report on compliance issued as a separate report would contain how many paragraphs?
    A. 2
    B. 3
    C. 4
    D. 5

186. Reports on special purpose frameworks, also known as special reports, include auditor's reports on:
    I.   compliance with reporting requirements to be filed with a specific regulatory agency
    II. cash basis financial statements

    A. I only
    B. II only
    C. Both I and II
    D. Neither I nor II

187. Which of the following special reports provides negative assurance?
    I.   Report on cash basis financial statements
    II. Auditor's report on compliance with aspects of contractual agreements

    A. I only
    B. II only
    C. Both I and II
    D. Neither I nor II

188. If there are both emphasis-of-matter and other-matters paragraphs in an auditor's report, in what order should the various paragraphs be presented?

    A. Opinion paragraph, emphasis-of-matter paragraph, other-matters paragraph
    B. Emphasis-of-matter paragraph, other-matters paragraph, opinion paragraph
    C. Emphasis-of-matter paragraph, opinion paragraph, other-matters paragraph
    D. Opinion paragraph, other-matters paragraph, emphasis-of-matter paragraph

189. An auditor may report on summary financial statements that are derived from complete financial statements if the auditor:
    I.   indicates in the report whether the information in the summary financial statements is fairly stated in all material respects in relation to the complete financial statements from which it has been derived
    II. includes both the date of the report on the complete financial statements and the opinion expressed on those statements

    A. I only
    B. II only
    C. Both I and II
    D. Neither I nor II

190. Which of the following engagements should the auditor NOT accept unless the auditor also is engaged to audit the complete financial statements?
    I.   Report on compliance with a regulatory requirement
    II. Report on summary financial statements

    A. I only
    B. II only
    C. Both I and II
    D. Neither I nor II

191. When an entity is required by the Securities and Exchange Commission (SEC) to file a quarterly report:
    I.   an independent accountant must perform an audit of the interim financial information before the quarterly report is filed
    II. the CPA must follow Public Company Accounting Oversight Board (PCAOB) standards

    A. I only
    B. II only
    C. Both I and II
    D. Neither I nor II

192. Regarding fraud, as part of a review of interim financial information for a public entity, the accountant is required to inquire of management about its knowledge of:
    I.   suspected fraud
    II. allegations of fraud

    A. I only
    B. II only
    C. Both I and II
    D. Neither I nor II

193. Andriola, CPA, has been hired to perform an interim review of Prager Corp., an issuer. In a review on interim financial information for a public entity, Andriola's knowledge about Prager Corp.'s business and its internal control would influence Andriola's:
    I.   inquiries
    II.   analytical procedures performed
    III. timing of inventory observation

    A. I, II, and III
    B. II only
    C. I only
    D. I and II only

194. The annual financial statements of Hosana Inc., a publicly held company, have been audited and its interim financial statements have been reviewed. Both engagements were performed by Adams, Franklin, and Dickinson, CPAs. Which of the following is true about the application of professional standards to this review?
    I. Statements on Standards for Accounting and Review Services apply.
    II. PCAOB standards apply.

    A. I only
    B. II only
    C. Both I and II
    D. Neither I nor II

195. Which of the following is a required procedure in an engagement to review the interim financial information of a publicly held entity?
    I. Obtaining corroborating evidence about the entity's ability to continue as a going concern
    II. Inquiries of management about their knowledge of fraud or suspected fraud

    A. I only
    B. II only
    C. Both I and II
    D. Neither I nor II

196. Which of the following is an example of disaggregated data that a CPA is required to compare in a review of interim financial information for an issuer?
    I. Disaggregated revenue data for the current interim period with that of comparable prior periods
    II. Disaggregated revenue data for the entity with that of competitors in the industry

    A. I only
    B. II only
    C. Both I and II
    D. Neither I nor II

197. Salt, CPA, is performing an interim review of quarterly financial information of Peter Corp., an issuer. Inquiries of which of the following is required by Salt?
    I. Peter Corp.'s management
    II. Peter Corp.'s outside legal counsel

    A. I only
    B. II only
    C. Both I and II
    D. Neither I nor II

198. Which of the following procedures is required in a review of interim financial statements of an issuer?
    I. Inquiry regarding compliance with GAAP
    II. Management representation letter
    III. Engagement letter

    A. I and II only
    B. II and III only
    C. I and III only
    D. I, II, and III

199. Boyle Inc. is an issuer. Tanner, CPA, is performing a review of Boyle's interim financial information. As part of planning, Tanner reads the audit documentation from the preceding year's annual audit. Which of the following is likely to affect Tanner's review?
    I. Identified risks of material misstatement due to fraud
    II. Scope limitations that were overcome through acceptable alternative procedures

    A. I only
    B. II only
    C. Both I and II
    D. Neither I nor II

200. Which of the following is correct regarding a comfort letter?
    I. A comfort letter contains a restriction on the use of the report.
    II. In a comfort letter, negative assurance is provided on unaudited financial information.

    A. I only
    B. II only
    C. Both I and II
    D. Neither I nor II

CHAPTER 8

ATTESTATION ENGAGEMENTS OTHER THAN AUDITS OF HISTORIC FINANCIAL INFORMATION

QUESTIONS 201–230

201. Which of the following is correct regarding attestation standards?
  I. Sufficient evidence shall be obtained to provide a reasonable basis for the conclusion that is expressed in the report.
  II. The work shall be adequately planned, and assistants, if any, shall be properly supervised.
  III. A sufficient understanding of internal control shall be obtained to plan the engagement.

  A. I and III only
  B. II and III only
  C. II only
  D. I and II only

202. Which of the following is an essential principle of a trust engagement?
  I. Processing integrity
  II. Online privacy
  III. Confidentiality

  A. I and II only
  B. II and III only
  C. I and III only
  D. I, II, and III

203. A CPA reporting on which of the following types of trust engagements would need to follow Statements on Standards for Attestation Engagements (SSAE)?
  I. SysTrusts
  II. WebTrusts

  A. I only
  B. II only
  C. Both I and II
  D. Neither I nor II

204. Which of the following attestation engagements may a CPA perform that would allow the client to affix a seal of approval on the client's Internet site indicating, among other things, transaction integrity?

  A. WebGem
  B. WebTrust
  C. WebSys
  D. SysWeb

205. SSAE do NOT apply to:
  I. pro forma financial statements
  II. tax preparation services

  A. I only
  B. II only
  C. Both I and II
  D. Neither I nor II

206. SSAE do NOT apply to reports and services relating to:
  I. forecasts
  II. projections

  A. I only
  B. II only
  C. Both I and II
  D. Neither I nor II

207. SSAE do NOT apply to:
 I. audits of nonissuers
 II. compilations
 III. reviews of nonissuers

 A. I only
 B. II and III only
 C. II only
 D. I, II, and III

208. Which of the following is generally correct regarding an agreed-upon procedures engagement?
 I. Agreed-upon procedures engagements follow Statements on Standards for Agreed-Upon Procedures.
 II. The CPA need not be independent if the client chooses the procedures for the CPA to report on.

 A. I only
 B. II only
 C. Both I and II
 D. Neither I nor II

209. Which of the following is correct regarding agreed-upon procedures engagements?
 I. The CPA's report is limited in distribution.
 II. The CPA takes responsibility for the adequacy of the procedures selected.

 A. I only
 B. II only
 C. Both I and II
 D. Neither I nor II

210. In an agreed-upon procedures engagement, which of the following is correct?
 I. The CPA provides negative assurance in the report.
 II. The report is restricted in distribution.

 A. I only
 B. II only
 C. Both I and II
 D. Neither I nor II

211. Which of the following engagements requires the CPA to be independent even though no assurance is being provided?
 I. Review engagements of a nonpublic entity
 II. Agreed-upon procedures engagements

 A. I only
 B. II only
 C. Both I and II
 D. Neither I nor II

212. Which of the following engagements requires the CPA to be independent even though no opinion is being expressed?
 I. Review engagements of a nonpublic entity
 II. Agreed-upon procedures engagements

 A. I only
 B. II only
 C. Both I and II
 D. Neither I nor II

213. An examination of a financial forecast is a professional service that involves:
 I. assembling and compiling a financial forecast that is based on management's assumptions
 II. evaluating the preparation of a financial forecast and the support underlying management's assumptions

 A. I only
 B. II only
 C. Both I and II
 D. Neither I nor II

214. An accountant's report on a financial forecast should include a caveat that the prospective results of the financial forecast may NOT be achieved if the accountant:
 I. performed agreed-upon procedures regarding the client's forecast
 II. reviewed the client's forecast

 A. I only
 B. II only
 C. Both I and II
 D. Neither I nor II

215. A CPA in public practice is required to comply with the provisions of the SSAE when:
 I. compiling a client's financial projection that presents a hypothetical course of action
 II. compiling a client's historical financial statements

 A. I only
 B. II only
 C. Both I and II
 D. Neither I nor II

216. In an attestation engagement, use of the accountant's report should be restricted to specified parties:
 I. when reporting directly on the subject matter and a written assertion has not been provided
 II. when reporting on an agreed-upon procedures engagement
A. I only
B. II only
C. Both I and II
D. Neither I nor II

217. In an attestation engagement where the CPA examines and reports directly on subject matter, which of the following phrases would likely be in the report?
 I. "We have examined management's assertion"
 II. "We have examined the accompanying schedule"
A. I only
B. II only
C. Both I and II
D. Neither I nor II

218. Negative assurance may be expressed when an accountant reports on:
 I. compilation of prospective financial statements
 II. results of performing a review of management's assertion
A. I only
B. II only
C. Both I and II
D. Neither I nor II

219. Which of the following items should be included in prospective financial statements issued in an attestation engagement performed in accordance with SSAE?
 I. All significant assumptions used to prepare the financial statements
 II. Historical financial statements for the past three years
A. I only
B. II only
C. Both I and II
D. Neither I nor II

220. SSAE standards do NOT apply to reports and services relating to:
 I. internal control
 II. consulting
A. I only
B. II only
C. Both I and II
D. Neither I nor II

221. An accountant's report on a financial forecast should include a caveat that the prospective results of the financial forecast may NOT be achieved if the accountant:
 I. examined the client's forecast
 II. compiled the client's forecast
A. I only
B. II only
C. Both I and II
D. Neither I nor II

222. An accountant's report on a financial forecast should include:
 I. a restriction in distribution
 II. a limitation on the usefulness of the report
A. I only
B. II only
C. Both I and II
D. Neither I nor II

223. An auditor's letter issued on significant deficiencies relating to a nonissuer's internal control observed during a financial statement audit should:
 I. include a restriction on distribution
 II. indicate that the purpose of the audit was to report on the financial statements and report on internal control
A. I only
B. II only
C. Both I and II
D. Neither I nor II

224. Significant deficiencies in internal control noted during a financial statement audit should be communicated to:
 I. management
 II. those charged with governance
A. I only
B. II only
C. Both I and II
D. Neither I nor II

225. Management provides an assertion concerning the effectiveness of internal control as part of a financial statement audit of:
   I. a nonissuer
   II. an issuer

   A. I only
   B. II only
   C. Both I and II
   D. Neither I nor II

226. Which of the following is correct regarding a practitioner's examination and report on management's assertion about the effectiveness of the entity's internal control?
   I. The examination must be integrated with an audit of the entity's financial statements.
   II. The practitioner's report must be limited in distribution.

   A. I only
   B. II only
   C. Both I and II
   D. Neither I nor II

227. Clark is a CPA whose clients are nonissuers. Which of the following reports issued by Clark must be limited in distribution?
   I. A report on significant deficiencies in internal control noted during a financial statement audit
   II. A report on the examination of a client's assertion about the effectiveness of the entity's internal control

   A. I only
   B. II only
   C. Both I and II
   D. Neither I nor II

228. In the audit of a nonissuer, which of the following is required to assess and report on internal control?
   I. Management
   II. The independent auditor

   A. I only
   B. II only
   C. Both I and II
   D. Neither I nor II

229. Which of the following is an appropriate topic regarding an auditor's communication to those charged with governance?
   I. The fact that no material weaknesses were noted in internal control that would affect the financial statements
   II. The fact that a material misstatement was noted by the auditor on the financial statements and corrected by management

   A. I only
   B. II only
   C. Both I and II
   D. Neither I nor II

230. The auditor should ensure that those charged with governance are informed about:
   I. the basis for the auditor's conclusions regarding the reasonableness of sensitive accounting estimates
   II. disagreements with management in the application of accounting principles relating to asset impairment

   A. I only
   B. II only
   C. Both I and II
   D. Neither I nor II

CHAPTER 9
ASSERTIONS

231. With regard to the assertion category known as classes of transactions and events, which of the following assertions relate to whether all assets, liabilities, and equity interests that should be recorded in the financial statements are included?
  I. Completeness
  II. Occurrence

  A. I only
  B. II only
  C. Both I and II
  D. Neither I nor II

232. Which of the following is an assertion under the category of classes of transactions?
  I. Cutoff
  II. Completeness
  III. Occurrence

  A. II and III only
  B. I only
  C. I and III only
  D. I, II, and III

233. Within the assertion category known as classes of transactions, the cutoff assertion has a direct impact on which other assertions in that class?
  I. Completeness
  II. Occurrence

  A. I only
  B. II only
  C. Both I and II
  D. Neither I nor II

234. Which of the following is an assertion under the category of classes of transactions?
  I. Classification
  II. Accuracy
  III. Completeness

  A. III only
  B. I, II, and III
  C. II and III only
  D. I and III only

235. Which of the following is a financial statement assertion regarding account balances?
  I. Rights and obligations
  II. Valuation
  III. Existence

  A. I and II only
  B. I, II, and III
  C. II and III only
  D. III only

236. Which of the following is an assertion found under the category of account balances (balance sheet assertions)?
  I. Completeness
  II. Rights and obligations
  III. Existence
  IV. Valuation

  A. II, III, and IV only
  B. II and IV only
  C. III and IV only
  D. I, II, III, and IV

237. Accounts receivable affects one or more assertions. Which of the following assertions relates to accounts receivable?
   I. Existence
   II. Valuation
   III. Rights and obligations

   A. I, II, and III
   B. II and III only
   C. I and II only
   D. I and III only

238. Accounts receivable affects one or more assertions. Which of the following assertions relates to accounts receivable, net of allowance for doubtful accounts?
   I. Existence
   II. Valuation

   A. I only
   B. II only
   C. Both I and II
   D. Neither I nor II

239. Inventory that was bought right before the end of Year 1 was incorrectly recorded in Year 2 (the subsequent period). Which assertion is affected in Year 1?
   I. Completeness
   II. Existence

   A. I only
   B. II only
   C. Both I and II
   D. Neither I nor II

240. Completeness is an assertion found under the category of:
   I. classes of transactions
   II. account balances

   A. I only
   B. II only
   C. Both I and II
   D. Neither I nor II

241. Rights and obligations is an assertion found under the category of:
   I. classes of transactions and events
   II. account balances

   A. I only
   B. II only
   C. Both I and II
   D. Neither I nor II

242. Nadasky is the president of Johnson Corp. Karl is the auditor for Johnson Corp. Which assertion regarding account balances is affected if a debt owed by Nadasky was inappropriately reported on the balance sheet of Johnson Corp.?
   I. Completeness
   II. Rights and obligations

   A. I only
   B. II only
   C. Both I and II
   D. Neither I nor II

243. Nadasky is the president of Johnson Corp. Karl is the auditor for Johnson Corp. Which assertion regarding account balances is affected if a debt owed by Nadasky was inappropriately reported on the balance sheet of Johnson Corp.?
   I. Existence
   II. Rights and obligations

   A. I only
   B. II only
   C. Both I and II
   D. Neither I nor II

244. With regard to the existence/occurrence assertion, the auditor would test for:
   I. understatement of liabilities
   II. overstatement of revenue

   A. I only
   B. II only
   C. Both I and II
   D. Neither I nor II

245. Recalculation of invoice amounts and inspection of certain documents for authorization are audit procedures designed to test which of the following assertions?
   I. Cutoff
   II. Valuation

   A. I only
   B. II only
   C. Both I and II
   D. Neither I nor II

246. Luke, CPA, is the independent auditor for Nazareth Corp. Analee is the president of Nazareth Corp. Luke has decided that inventory is based on a variation of FIFO and LIFO that is not viewed as proper accounting according to US GAAP. Which assertion is impacted?

    I. Rights and obligations

    II. Valuation

    A. I only

    B. II only

    C. Both I and II

    D. Neither I nor II

247. The auditor has determined that inventory is overstated based on incorrect cutoff and a variation of FIFO and LIFO that is not viewed as proper accounting according to US GAAP. Which assertion is affected?

    I. Completeness

    II. Valuation

    A. I only

    B. II only

    C. Both I and II

    D. Neither I nor II

248. If inventory is understated based on incorrect cutoff and a variation of FIFO and LIFO that is not viewed as proper accounting according to US GAAP, which assertion is affected?

    I. Completeness

    II. Valuation

    A. I only

    B. II only

    C. Both I and II

    D. Neither I nor II

249. The reporting company records sales revenue and accounts receivable near the end of the year because a sales order has been received. However, the earnings process will not be complete until next period. Which assertion relates directly to the income statement in the year under audit being overstated for sales?

    I. Existence

    II. Occurrence

    A. I only

    B. II only

    C. Both I and II

    D. Neither I nor II

250. The reporting company records sales revenue and accounts receivable near the end of the year because a sales order has been received. However, the earnings process will not be complete until next period. Which assertion is affected in the current year?

    I. Occurrence

    II. Existence

    A. I only

    B. II only

    C. Both I and II

    D. Neither I nor II

251. Phillip is the auditor for the Andrinua Corp. A building is recorded by Andrinua Corp. for $750,000, which is the correct cost, but the building actually belongs to another company, Desimone Inc., and is only being used by Andrinua Corp. through an operating lease. Which assertion is impacted?

    I. Rights and obligations

    II. Completeness

    A. I only

    B. II only

    C. Both I and II

    D. Neither I nor II

252. Which of the following is an assertion found under the category of presentation and disclosure?

    I. Completeness

    II. Classification and understandability

    A. I only

    B. II only

    C. Both I and II

    D. Neither I nor II

253. Which of the following is an assertion found in all three categories of assertions?

    I. Completeness

    II. Rights and obligations

    A. I only

    B. II only

    C. Both I and II

    D. Neither I nor II

254. An asset is categorized as a fixed asset when it should have been recorded as inventory. Which assertion is affected?

    I. Rights and obligations

    II. Classification

A. I only

B. II only

C. Both I and II

D. Neither I nor II

255. Which of the following is NOT an assertion category?

    I. Presentation and disclosure

    II. Classes of transactions and events

    III. Completeness

A. I and II only

B. II and III only

C. III only

D. II only

CHAPTER 10

EVIDENCE GATHERING AND TRANSACTION CYCLES, PART 1

QUESTIONS 256–336

256. When an independent auditor uses professional judgment to make decisions about the "nature, extent, and timing" of audit procedures, what does the term *nature* refer to?

   I. The amount of testing to be performed
   II. The type of test to be performed

  A. I only
  B. II only
  C. Both I and II
  D. Neither I nor II

257. Which of the following involves a theft of receivables followed by a delay in the posting of credits to specific customer accounts?

   I. Kiting
   II. Lapping

  A. I only
  B. II only
  C. Both I and II
  D. Neither I nor II

258. Corey is the auditor for Arthur Inc. When a customer pays Arthur Inc. by check and mails the check to Arthur Inc., Carol, the secretary, gathers the customer checks from their envelopes. For good internal control, what should Carol NOT have the authority to do?

   I. Deposit the customer checks into Arthur Inc.'s bank account
   II. Prepare a listing of the checks received
   III. Post the credits to the individual customer's accounts

  A. I and III only
  B. III only
  C. I, II, and III
  D. II and III only

259. In a revenue cycle, which of the following departments prepares the sales order and approves the customer for credit?

	Preparation of Sales Order	Authorization of Credit
A.	Credit department	Credit department
B.	Credit department	Sales department
C.	Sales department	Credit department
D.	Sales department	Sales department

260. Prior to shipping, a copy of the sales order is:

   I. sent to the billings department to verify that the shipment is going to an approved customer who is not over any credit limit
   II. sent to the billings department to enable the billings department to prepare a bill of lading

  A. I only
  B. II only
  C. Both I and II
  D. Neither I nor II

261. In a revenue cycle, a copy of the approved sales order is sent to which department(s)?

   I. Billings
   II. Shipping

  A. I only
  B. II only
  C. Both I and II
  D. Neither I nor II

262. The billings department prepares the sales invoice after receiving a copy of which of the following documents?
    I. Purchase requisition
    II. Sales order
    III. Bill of lading

    A. II only
    B. II and III only
    C. I, II, and III
    D. III only

263. Within the revenue cycle, which of the following departments maintains a pending or open file but takes no action until a copy of both the sales order and the bill of lading are received?

    A. Sales department
    B. Billings department
    C. Credit department
    D. Warehouse department

264. In the revenue cycle, which of the following departments matches the information on the sales order and bill of lading and verifies that each is properly authorized?

    A. Credit department
    B. Sales department
    C. Warehouse department
    D. Billings department

265. Within a proper segregation of duties for the revenue cycle, which of the following departments represents an example of custody?

    A. Shipping department
    B. Billings department
    C. Receiving room
    D. Warehouse department

266. Within the revenue and purchasing cycle of an organization, which of the following departments normally has the authority to move goods only within the organization?
    I. Warehouse
    II. Shipping department
    III. Receiving room

    A. I and II only
    B. III only
    C. I only
    D. I and III only

267. Within a proper segregation of duties for the revenue cycle, which of the following departments serves an authorization function?

    A. Credit department
    B. Billings department
    C. Purchasing department
    D. Shipping department

268. Within the revenue cycle, for proper segregation of duties, which of the following departments normally prepares the bill of lading and the sales invoice?

	Bill of Lading	Sales Invoice
A.	Billings department	Sales department
B.	Billings department	Shipping department
C.	Shipping department	Sales department
D.	Shipping department	Billings department

269. For proper segregation of duties in the revenue cycle, the warehouse department delivers merchandise to the shipping department. Before accepting the goods, the shipping department should:
    I. inspect the goods for damage
    II. count the items and compare the number and other information to the sales order

    A. I only
    B. II only
    C. Both I and II
    D. Neither I nor II

270. For proper segregation of duties in a revenue cycle, the shipping department:
    I. prepares the bill of lading and sends a copy to inventory accounting to update the perpetual records
    II. sends a copy of the bill of lading to the billings department

    A. I only
    B. II only
    C. Both I and II
    D. Neither I nor II

271. In what order are these three forms usually generated in a credit sales system: bill of lading, sales invoice, sales order?

    A. Sales order, bill of lading, sales invoice
    B. Sales order, sales invoice, bill of lading
    C. Sales invoice, sales order, bill of lading
    D. Bill of lading, sales order, sales invoice

272. In a revenue cycle, which of the following departments does NOT prepare the sales order, the sales invoice, or the bill of lading?

   A. Sales department
   B. Warehouse department
   C. Shipping department
   D. Billings department

273. Shann, CPA, is performing an audit of Cove Corp., a wholesaler of consumer products. Shann begins with entries in the sales journal and makes sure that there is a sales invoice to support it. Which of the following is correct?

   I. This is a test of the existence/occurrence assertion.
   II. Shann is probably concerned with overstatement of revenue.

   A. I only
   B. II only
   C. Both I and II
   D. Neither I nor II

274. An auditor begins with a sample of bills of lading and traces forward into the accounting records. Which of the following is correct?

   I. The auditor is testing the completeness assertion for sales.
   II. If there is no sales invoice found for a particular bill of lading, the auditor fears that sales may be overstated.

   A. I only
   B. II only
   C. Both I and II
   D. Neither I nor II

275. An auditor begins with a sample of bills of lading and traces forward into the accounting records. If a sales invoice was not found for a particular shipment, the auditor could suspect that goods were shipped out:

   I. fraudulently
   II. on consignment

   A. I only
   B. II only
   C. Both I and II
   D. Neither I nor II

276. An auditor is concerned that the company is increasing reported net income by producing sales invoices for goods that were never ordered or shipped.

   I. The auditor should select a sample of sales invoices and verify that matching sales orders and bills of lading exist.
   II. If the auditor finds sales invoices with no related shipping documents, this would be a test of the occurrence assertion rather than the completeness assertion.

   A. I only
   B. II only
   C. Both I and II
   D. Neither I nor II

277. An auditor is concerned that sales are being made and shipped but are never billed or recorded. The auditor believes that employees may be stealing company assets in this way. Which of the following is correct?

   I. The auditor should select a sample of bills of lading and verify that sales invoices do exist.
   II. Shipments on consignment would not explain the missing sales invoices.

   A. I only
   B. II only
   C. Both I and II
   D. Neither I nor II

278. Tracing shipping documents to prenumbered sales invoices:

   I. provides evidence that shipments to customers were properly invoiced
   II. is a test for overstatement of sales rather than understatement

   A. I only
   B. II only
   C. Both I and II
   D. Neither I nor II

279. If an auditor starts with the entries in the sales journal and seeks supporting documentation to corroborate:

   I. the auditor is testing the completeness assertion
   II. the auditor would be looking for sales orders rather than shipping documents

   A. I only
   B. II only
   C. Both I and II
   D. Neither I nor II

280. If the objective of an auditor's test of details is to detect a possible understatement of sales, the auditor most likely would trace transactions from the:

    A. sales invoices to the shipping documents
    B. cash receipts journal to the sales journal
    C. shipping documents to the sales invoices
    D. sales journal to the cash receipts journal

281. Which of the following is a substantive test for accounts receivable in the subsequent period?
    I. Examining how much bad debt was written off shortly after year-end
    II. Examining how much cash was actually collected shortly after year-end

    A. I only
    B. II only
    C. Both I and II
    D. Neither I nor II

282. Which of the following substantive procedures provides evidence of the existence assertion for accounts receivable in the subsequent period?
    I. Examining how much bad debt was written off shortly after year-end
    II. Examining how much cash was actually collected shortly after year-end

    A. I only
    B. II only
    C. Both I and II
    D. Neither I nor II

283. Which assertion is being most directly addressed when an auditor selects a sample of sales invoices and compares it to the subsequent journal entries recorded in the sales journal?

    A. Occurrence
    B. Classification
    C. Accuracy
    D. Completeness

284. When an auditor gathers evidence within a revenue cycle, tracing sales invoices to the client's revenue account provides evidence that:
    I. approved spending limits are not exceeded
    II. sales are not understated

    A. I only
    B. II only
    C. Both I and II
    D. Neither I nor II

285. An auditor plans to confirm a sample of accounts receivable. An auditor confirms receivables primarily to obtain evidence about:
    I. the valuation assertion
    II. the existence assertion

    A. I only
    B. II only
    C. Both I and II
    D. Neither I nor II

286. To test the existence assertion for accounts receivable an auditor would:
    I. send accounts receivable confirmation requests to a sample of client customers
    II. inspect and verify the credit-granting policies of the client

    A. I only
    B. II only
    C. Both I and II
    D. Neither I nor II

287. An auditor is confirming receivables and was planning to use negative confirmations. The auditor assessed inherent risk and control risk and found them to be higher than anticipated.
    I. The auditor should consider switching from negative confirmations to positive confirmations.
    II. Positive confirmations are more likely to be used when the acceptable level of detection risk is especially low.

    A. I only
    B. II only
    C. Both I and II
    D. Neither I nor II

288. For good internal controls in a revenue cycle, which of the following correctly describes the credit manager's duties?
    I. Should report directly to the vice president of sales
    II. Should authorize a write-off of an uncollectible account

    A. I only
    B. II only
    C. Both I and II
    D. Neither I nor II

289. An auditor must know the relationship between inventory errors and the effect on net income. If a client's ending inventory is overstated:
    I. net income is overstated because gross profit is overstated
    II. cost of goods sold is understated

    A. I only
    B. II only
    C. Both I and II
    D. Neither I nor II

290. When an auditor examines a client's inventory, items shipped out on consignment by the client:
    I. belong to the client rather than the consignee
    II. are a concern to the auditor because of the rights and obligations assertion

    A. I only
    B. II only
    C. Both I and II
    D. Neither I nor II

291. In a purchasing cycle, the receiving room gets a copy of the:
    I. purchase requisition
    II. purchase order

    A. I only
    B. II only
    C. Both I and II
    D. Neither I nor II

292. How many different documents are generally involved in the purchasing cycle?

    A. 5
    B. 4
    C. 3
    D. 2

293. Put these documents in the order in which they appear in a purchasing cycle:
    I. purchase order
    II. receiving report
    III. purchase invoice
    IV. purchase requisition

    A. IV, I, II, III
    B. IV, II, III, I
    C. I, II, III, IV
    D. I, II, IV, III

294. In a purchasing cycle, which of the following departments reconciles the purchase order and receiving report and approves the purchase invoice for payment?

    A. Purchasing department
    B. Billings department
    C. Receiving room
    D. Accounts payable

295. In the purchasing cycle, which of the following departments does NOT receive a copy of the receiving report?
    I. Accounts payable
    II. The department that prepared the purchase requisition

    A. I only
    B. II only
    C. Both I and II
    D. Neither I nor II

296. Which of the following documents is NOT prepared by the purchasing department?
    I. Purchase order
    II. Purchase invoice
    III. Purchase requisition

    A. I and III only
    B. I and II only
    C. II and III only
    D. III only

297. Which of the following documents is prepared outside the organization?
    I. Purchase invoice
    II. Receiving report
    III. Voucher package

    A. I and III only
    B. I only
    C. III only
    D. I and II only

298. For effective internal control purposes, the vouchers payable department generally should:
    I. establish the agreement of the vendor's invoice with the receiving report and purchase order
    II. deliberately remove the quantity ordered on the receiving department copy of the purchase order

    A. I only
    B. II only
    C. Both I and II
    D. Neither I nor II

299. Within a client's purchasing cycle there are various departments. Which of the following departments approves the voucher for payment and which department pays the vendor?

	Approves the Voucher	**Pays the Vendor**
A.	Accounts payable	Accounts payable
B.	Accounts payable	Cash receipts
C.	Accounts payable	Cash disbursements
D.	Cash disbursements	Cash disbursements

300. In a purchasing cycle that uses a voucher system, which of the following forms is attached to the voucher and becomes part of the voucher package?
  I. Purchase order
  II. Receiving report
  III. Bill of lading

  A. I and II only
  B. I only
  C. I, II, and III
  D. II only

301. In the purchasing cycle, which of the following is correct regarding the voucher and the voucher package?
  I. The voucher is the document that acknowledges the liability and approves payment.
  II. The backup documentation (a copy of all four forms) is attached in what is called a voucher package.
  III. The voucher package is recorded in the voucher register and forwarded to cash disbursements for payment.

  A. I and II only
  B. II and III only
  C. I and III only
  D. I, II, and III

302. In a purchasing cycle that uses a voucher system, good internal control dictates that which of the following departments should be responsible for signing the check and mailing the check to the vendor?

	Signs the Check	**Mails the Check to the Vendor**
A.	Cash disbursements	Vouchers payable
B.	Vouchers payable	Cash disbursements
C.	Cash disbursements	Cash disbursements
D.	Vouchers payable	Vouchers payable

303. In a cash disbursements cycle that employs a voucher system, which of the following departments cancels or perforates the voucher package so that the voucher cannot be paid more than once and then mails the check to the vendor?

  A. Cash disbursements
  B. Vouchers payable
  C. Purchasing
  D. Receiving

304. In an audit, in the evidence-gathering stage of the purchasing cycle, the auditor would examine a sample of paid vouchers to gather evidence as to whether each voucher is:
  I. supported by a vendor invoice
  II. stamped "paid" by the check signer

  A. I only
  B. II only
  C. Both I and II
  D. Neither I nor II

305. To provide assurance that each voucher is submitted and paid only once, an auditor would examine a sample of paid vouchers and determine whether each voucher is:
  I. supported by a vendor invoice and purchase order
  II. stamped "paid" by the check signer

  A. I only
  B. II only
  C. Both I and II
  D. Neither I nor II

306. An auditor vouches a sample of entries in the voucher register to the supporting documents. Which assertion would this test most likely support?
  I. Existence or occurrence
  II. Completeness

  A. I only
  B. II only
  C. Both I and II
  D. Neither I nor II

307. In a properly designed internal control system, which department would match vendors' invoices with receiving reports and also recompute the calculations on vendors' invoices?
  I. Purchasing department
  II. Vouchers payable
  III. Cash disbursements

  A. I and II only
  B. II and III only
  C. I and III only
  D. II only

308. Which of the following documents is part of a purchasing cycle?
　I. Receiving report
　II. Bill of lading

　A. I only
　B. II only
　C. Both I and II
　D. Neither I nor II

309. If the auditor is testing the completeness assertion for accounts payable, a sample of which of the following documents would the auditor likely begin with?
　I. Purchase invoices
　II. Receiving reports

　A. I only
　B. II only
　C. Both I and II
　D. Neither I nor II

310. An auditor traced a sample of purchase orders and the related receiving reports to the purchases journal and the cash disbursements journal. The purpose of this substantive audit procedure most likely was to:
　I. determine that purchases were properly recorded
　II. test the existence or occurrence assertion for accounts payable

　A. I only
　B. II only
　C. Both I and II
　D. Neither I nor II

311. In the purchasing cycle, when the auditor is testing an existence or occurrence assertion, the auditor:
　I. starts with the supporting documents and looks to see if the transaction was in fact recorded
　II. starts with the recorded balances and works backward seeking support

　A. I only
　B. II only
　C. Both I and II
　D. Neither I nor II

312. Which of the following is an example of audit evidence generated by the client in the purchasing cycle?
　I. Bills of lading
　II. Receiving reports

　A. I only
　B. II only
　C. Both I and II
　D. Neither I nor II

313. Which of the following documents are examples of audit evidence generated by the client?
　I. Vendor invoices and packing slips
　II. Bills of lading and accounts receivable confirmations

　A. I only
　B. II only
　C. Both I and II
　D. Neither I nor II

314. An auditor selects transactions recorded in the voucher register for three days prior to the end of the fiscal year and compares each of these entries to the related receiving report and purchase invoice. Which of those two documents should indicate the FOB point when title changed hands, and which document should indicate the date the goods were received?

	Title Changed Hands	Receipt of the Goods
A.	Purchase invoice	Purchase invoice
B.	Purchase invoice	Receiving report
C.	Receiving report	Purchase invoice
D.	Receiving report	Receiving report

315. Which of the following procedures would an auditor most likely perform in searching for unrecorded liabilities?
　I. Trace a sample of accounts payable entries recorded just before year-end to the unmatched receiving report file
　II. Trace a sample of cash disbursements recorded just after year-end to receiving reports and vendor invoices

　A. I only
　B. II only
　C. Both I and II
　D. Neither I nor II

316. Observation of physical inventory counts provides evidence about which of the following assertions?
　I. Existence
　II. Completeness

　A. I only
　B. II only
　C. Both I and II
　D. Neither I nor II

317. As part of the process of observing a client's physical inventories, an auditor would be able to determine:
    I. any change in the method of pricing from prior years
    II. the existence of outstanding purchase commitments

    A. I only
    B. II only
    C. Both I and II
    D. Neither I nor II

318. With regard to inventory, the rights and obligations assertion might be tested by the auditor:
    I. inspecting consignment agreements and contracts
    II. confirming inventory held at outside locations

    A. I only
    B. II only
    C. Both I and II
    D. Neither I nor II

319. An auditor's observation procedures with respect to well-kept perpetual inventories that are periodically checked by physical counts may be performed at which of the following times?

    A. Before the end of the year
    B. At year-end
    C. After year-end
    D. All of the above

320. Which of the following are the most efficient and effective means of gathering evidence regarding a client's inventory held at a public warehouse?

	Most Efficient	Most Effective
A.	Observation	Observation
B.	Confirmation	Confirmation
C.	Confirmation	Observation
D.	Observation	Confirmation

321. Fritz is an auditor for Barbarino Corp., a manufacturing entity. Which of the following procedures would Fritz likely perform to determine whether slow-moving, defective, and obsolete items included in inventory are properly identified?
    I. Tour the manufacturing plant or production facility
    II. Compare inventory balances to anticipated sales volume

    A. I only
    B. II only
    C. Both I and II
    D. Neither I nor II

322. When observing inventory, which of the following is a purpose for the auditor taking test counts of the client's inventory?
    I. To help ensure the accuracy of the client unit count
    II. To aid later verification of final cost figures

    A. I only
    B. II only
    C. Both I and II
    D. Neither I nor II

323. The auditor should test the client's physical inventory report by tracing test counts taken by the auditor to the client's physical inventory count. Which assertion is affected by this test?

    A. Completeness
    B. Existence
    C. Rights and obligations
    D. Valuation

324. When gathering evidence regarding inventory, the auditor would begin with the client's physical inventory listing and compare to the auditor's test count. Which assertion would be tested by this procedure?

    A. Rights and obligations
    B. Existence
    C. Completeness
    D. Classification and understandability

325. When an auditor starts with the tags and compares the tags to the detailed inventory listings, he or she is testing for:
    I. existence
    II. completeness

    A. I only
    B. II only
    C. Both I and II
    D. Neither I nor II

326. Tracing from inventory tags to the inventory listing schedule verifies the:
    I. completeness of the schedule
    II. existence of the items

    A. I only
    B. II only
    C. Both I and II
    D. Neither I nor II

327. Tracing from the inventory schedule to the inventory tags verifies the:
    I. validity (existence) of the items
    II. completeness of the inventory schedule

    A. I only
    B. II only
    C. Both I and II
    D. Neither I nor II

328. Tracing from receiving reports and vendors' invoices to the perpetual inventory listing are procedures used to verify:
    I. completeness of the inventory listing
    II. existence of the inventory

    A. I only
    B. II only
    C. Both I and II
    D. Neither I nor II

329. The Lexy Corp. buys and sells handbags. In Year 1, the average number of days that it took to sell a handbag was 14. In Year 2, because of the downturn in the economy, the average number of days that it took to sell a handbag rose to 25.

    Which of management's assertions about the balance being reported as inventory on the company's balance sheet would be of most concern to the independent auditor?

    A. Presentation
    B. Valuation
    C. Existence
    D. Completeness

330. Alan is performing an audit of Berman Industries Inc. During the evidence-gathering phase for inventory, Alan would verify that certain inventory, owned by Berman Industries at year-end, is included in the count. Which of the following should be included in the year-end count?
    I. Inventory purchased FOB shipping point and still in transit at year-end
    II. Inventory shipped out on consignment by Berman Industries on December 31

    A. I only
    B. II only
    C. Both I and II
    D. Neither I nor II

331. When auditing inventories, an auditor would least likely verify that:

    A. the financial statement presentation of inventories is appropriate
    B. damaged goods and obsolete items have been properly accounted for
    C. all inventory owned by the client is on hand at the time of the count
    D. the client has used proper inventory pricing

332. Brunner is doing an audit of Tucker Corp. Tests designed to detect purchases made by Tucker before the end of the year that have been recorded in the subsequent year most likely would provide assurance about Tucker's assertion regarding:
    I. rights and obligations
    II. cutoff

    A. I only
    B. II only
    C. Both I and II
    D. Neither I nor II

333. Alex Corp. is a manufacturer. Under the category of presentation and disclosure, completeness is an assertion that relates to inventory disclosure. Which of the following inventory balances would Alex Corp. NOT be required to disclose?
    I. Work in process
    II. Raw materials

    A. I only
    B. II only
    C. Both I and II
    D. Neither I nor II

334. With regard to inventory, assertions about accuracy relate to:
    I. whether data related to recorded transactions have been included in the financial statements at appropriate amounts
    II. cutoff testing for purchases

    A. I only
    B. II only
    C. Both I and II
    D. Neither I nor II

335. Inventories should be reduced, when appropriate, to replacement cost or net realizable value, to support management's assertion of:

  I. valuation
 II. understandability
III. existence

  A. I and III only
  B. I only
  C. I and II only
  D. I, II, and III

336. Su is performing an audit of Allegra Corp. With regard to assertions relating to inventory, understandability and classification might be tested by:

  I. confirming inventories pledged under loan agreements
 II. examining drafts of the financial statements for appropriate balance sheet classification

  A. I only
  B. II only
  C. Both I and II
  D. Neither I nor II

CHAPTER 11

AUDIT SAMPLING

337. When using statistical sampling to estimate a rate (sampling for attributes):

I. the auditor is frequently assessing control risk

II. the auditor is concerned with overstatement of an account balance

A. I only
B. II only
C. Both I and II
D. Neither I nor II

338. In statistical sampling, which of the following factors regarding the population is considered in determining the sample size for a test of controls?

I. Expected error or deviation rate

II. Tolerable error or deviation rate

A. I only
B. II only
C. Both I and II
D. Neither I nor II

339. An auditor is sampling for attributes, that is, testing controls. Which of the following is correct regarding sample size when the auditor determines that the expected error rate is different from that originally expected?

A. If the expected error rate has risen, the sample size will be reduced.

B. If the expected error rate has fallen, the sample size will be increased.

C. If the expected error rate has risen, the sample size will be increased.

D. Both A and B

340. An auditor is estimating an error rate for a test of controls. The auditor must set a level of sampling risk that is viewed as acceptable. For some reason, the auditor decides to reduce the allowable level of sampling risk for a particular test. Which of the following statements is correct?

I. The auditor will likely select a smaller sample than originally anticipated.

II. If the auditor increases sample size, the chance that the sample will have characteristics different from the population goes down.

A. I only
B. II only
C. Both I and II
D. Neither I nor II

341. Wes is performing an audit of Turner Corp. Wes has identified a control activity that will reduce the assessment of control risk if it is operating effectively and efficiently. Wes has decided to perform sampling for attributes. Wes believes the actual error rate of this activity is 2 percent but can tolerate an error rate of up to 5 percent and still feel that the control is reliable. Wes wants to reduce sampling risk to a 10 percent level and be 90 percent sure that the sample is representative of the population. Which of the following statements is correct?
    I. If Wes were suddenly to change his assessment of the actual error from 2 percent to 3 percent, the sample size would have to be increased.
    II. If Wes wants to reduce the allowable level of risk from 10 percent to 5 percent, the sample size will have to be increased.

    A. I only
    B. II only
    C. Both I and II
    D. Neither I nor II

342. An auditor has identified a control activity that will reduce the assessment of control risk if it is operating effectively and efficiently. The auditor has decided to perform sampling for attributes. The auditor believes the actual error rate of this activity is 2 percent but can tolerate a rate of up to 5 percent. The auditor wants to reduce sampling risk to 10 percent. The appropriate sample size is determined and selected, and an error rate of 3 percent is discovered. A chart is examined that indicates that the upper deviation rate is 6.4 percent. Which of the following statements is correct?
    I. The allowance for sampling risk is 3.4 percent.
    II. The auditor should determine that the control is working effectively and reduce control risk, since the sample rate of 3 percent is below the tolerable rate of 5 percent.

    A. I only
    B. II only
    C. Both I and II
    D. Neither I nor II

343. The auditor believes the actual error rate of an activity is 2% but can tolerate a rate of up to 5 percent. The auditor wants to reduce sampling risk to 10 percent. The appropriate sample size is determined and selected, and an error rate of 3 percent is discovered. A chart is examined that indicates that the upper deviation rate is 4.4 percent. Which is correct?
    I. The auditor should assess the control activity as having too many errors.
    II. The tolerable rate is higher than the upper deviation rate.

    A. I only
    B. II only
    C. Both I and II
    D. Neither I nor II

344. The sample rate of deviation plus the allowance for sampling risk is equal to the:
    I. upper deviation rate
    II. tolerable deviation rate

    A. I only
    B. II only
    C. Both I and II
    D. Neither I nor II

345. The likelihood of assessing control risk too high relates to the:
    I. effectiveness of the audit
    II. efficiency of the audit

    A. I only
    B. II only
    C. Both I and II
    D. Neither I nor II

346. When an auditor is estimating an account balance, the auditor must set a level of sampling risk that is viewed as acceptable. For some reason, the auditor decides to reduce the allowable level of sampling risk for a particular test. Which of the following is correct?
    I. The auditor will have to select a larger sample than originally anticipated.
    II. This type of sampling is known as sampling for variables.

    A. I only
    B. II only
    C. Both I and II
    D. Neither I nor II

347. Which of the following illustrates the concept of sampling risk?
     I. A randomly chosen sample may not be representative of the population as a whole on the characteristic of interest.
     II. An auditor may select audit procedures that are not appropriate to achieve the specific objective.
     A. I only
     B. II only
     C. Both I and II
     D. Neither I nor II

348. When an auditor is estimating an account balance:
     I. the auditor must set a limit for the largest amount of discovered problem that can be tolerated before the account balance is considered not fairly presented
     II. as the amount of misstatement that an auditor can tolerate rises, the appropriate sample size will have to go up
     A. I only
     B. II only
     C. Both I and II
     D. Neither I nor II

349. In performing attribute sampling, which of the following would have a significant effect on the sample size?
     I. Number of items in the population
     II. Tolerable deviation rate
     A. I only
     B. II only
     C. Both I and II
     D. Neither I nor II

350. In performing variable sampling, which of the following would have a significant effect on the sample size?
     I. Number of items in the population
     II. Allowable level of risk
     A. I only
     B. II only
     C. Both I and II
     D. Neither I nor II

351. While performing a test of details during an audit, an auditor determined that the sample results supported the conclusion that the recorded account balance was materially misstated. It was, in fact, not materially misstated. This situation illustrates the risk of:
     A. assessing control risk too high
     B. assessing control risk too low
     C. incorrect rejection
     D. incorrect acceptance

352. While performing a test of details during an audit, an auditor determined that the sample results supported the conclusion that the recorded account balance was fairly presented in accordance with GAAP. It was, in fact, materially misstated. This situation illustrates the risk of:
     A. assessing control risk too high
     B. assessing control risk too low
     C. incorrect rejection
     D. incorrect acceptance

353. The expected balance of a client's accounts receivable is being estimated by the auditor. The expected rate of error in the account balance is 3 percent. The auditor has established a tolerable rate of 5 percent. The auditor would probably NOT use:
     A. stratified sampling
     B. variable sampling
     C. PPS sampling
     D. attribute sampling

354. In a probability proportional to size sample with a sampling interval of $9,000, an auditor discovered that a selected account receivable with a recorded amount of $6,000 had an audited value of $4,000. If this were the only misstatement discovered by the auditor, the projected misstatement of this sample would be:
     A. $2,000
     B. $3,000
     C. $4,000
     D. $6,000

CHAPTER 12

EVIDENCE GATHERING AND TRANSACTION CYCLES, PART 2

355. Which of the following is correct regarding the auditor's use of the standard bank confirmation?
  I. The usefulness of the standard bank confirmation request may be limited because the bank employee who completes the form may be unaware of all the financial relationships that the bank has with the client.
  II. The standard bank confirmation should request balances of all bank accounts, except for accounts that were closed during the year.

  A. I only
  B. II only
  C. Both I and II
  D. Neither I nor II

356. When auditing a client's year-end cash balance, which of the following is an auditor-prepared document specifically designed to detect kiting?
  I. Bank reconciliation
  II. Bank cutoff statement
  III. Bank transfer schedule

  A. I, II, and III
  B. II and III only
  C. III only
  D. I and III only

357. The auditor should obtain bank cutoff statements that include transactions for 10 to 15 days after year-end. The information on the bank cutoff statements should agree with:
  I. the outstanding checks at year-end on the bank reconciliation
  II. the deposits in transit at year-end on the bank reconciliation

  A. I only
  B. II only
  C. Both I and II
  D. Neither I nor II

358. When auditing cash, client checks dated after year-end would NOT be included in the:
  I. bank cutoff statement
  II. year-end outstanding check list

  A. I only
  B. II only
  C. Both I and II
  D. Neither I nor II

359. Which of the following is correct?
  I. A bank cutoff statement is used to verify the items appearing on a bank reconciliation.
  II. If a deposit in transit from the bank reconciliation is not recorded by the bank in a reasonable period of time, the auditor should be suspicious that the deposit was not really in transit.

  A. I only
  B. II only
  C. Both I and II
  D. Neither I nor II

360. Regarding reliability of audit evidence, municipal property tax bills prepared in the client's name are an example of:

    A. internal evidence
    B. external evidence
    C. evidence that is less reliable than internal evidence
    D. evidence that is more reliable than external evidence

361. Koko, CPA, is preparing an internal control questionnaire regarding equipment purchases during an audit of Conisha Corp. Which of the following questions would Koko likely include on an internal control questionnaire concerning the initiation and execution of equipment transactions?

    I. Are prenumbered purchase orders used for equipment and periodically accounted for?
    II. Are requests for purchases of equipment reviewed for consideration of soliciting competitive bids?

    A. I only
    B. II only
    C. Both I and II
    D. Neither I nor II

362. Which of the following explanations most likely would satisfy an auditor who questions management about significant debits to the accumulated depreciation accounts?

    I. The prior year's depreciation expense was erroneously understated.
    II. Plant assets were retired during the year.

    A. I only
    B. II only
    C. Both I and II
    D. Neither I nor II

363. Determining that proper amounts of depreciation are expensed provides assurance about management's assertion of:

    I. valuation, allocation, and accuracy
    II. existence

    A. I only
    B. II only
    C. Both I and II
    D. Neither I nor II

364. Testing to see whether equipment listed in the accounting records is physically present in the plant and still in service is an effective way to:

    I. test whether unrecorded disposals of equipment have occurred
    II. test whether depreciation was taken on each item of equipment during the year

    A. I only
    B. II only
    C. Both I and II
    D. Neither I nor II

365. When auditing property, plant, and equipment, which of the following would an auditor do to search for unrecorded additions?

    I. Examine the repairs and maintenance account
    II. Select certain items of equipment from the accounting records and locate them in the plant

    A. I only
    B. II only
    C. Both I and II
    D. Neither I nor II

366. An analysis of which of the following accounts would NOT aid in verifying that all fixed assets have been capitalized?

    I. Repair and maintenance
    II. Depreciation expense

    A. I only
    B. II only
    C. Both I and II
    D. Neither I nor II

367. When auditing equipment, an auditor would examine insurance records and tour the client's facility to:

    I. search for unrecorded disposals of assets
    II. search for assets that were erroneously charged to expense

    A. I only
    B. II only
    C. Both I and II
    D. Neither I nor II

368. Analyzing the repairs and maintenance account provides evidence that:

    I. obsolete plant and equipment assets were written off before year-end
    II. all recorded plant and equipment assets actually exist

    A. I only
    B. II only
    C. Both I and II
    D. Neither I nor II

369. An auditor who determines that proper amounts of depreciation are expensed provides assurance about management's assertion of:
    I. completeness
    II. rights and obligations

    A. I only
    B. II only
    C. Both I and II
    D. Neither I nor II

370. In testing for unrecorded retirements of equipment, an auditor most likely would:
    I. select items of equipment from the accounting records and then locate them during the plant tour
    II. scan the general journal for unusual equipment additions and excessive debits to repairs and maintenance expense

    A. I only
    B. II only
    C. Both I and II
    D. Neither I nor II

371. An auditor would expect to find significant debits to the accumulated depreciation account if, during the year, assets were:
    I. sold
    II. retired
    III. permanently impaired

    A. I, II, and III
    B. I and II only
    C. I and III only
    D. II and III only

372. Which is correct when testing notes payable or other long-term liabilities?
    I. An auditor should review the minutes of the meetings of the board of directors.
    II. A bank cutoff statement is reviewed as part of the auditor's search for unrecorded long-term liabilities.

    A. I only
    B. II only
    C. Both I and II
    D. Neither I nor II

373. When an auditor is searching for unrecorded liabilities, which assertion is directly impacted?
    I. Valuation
    II. Completeness
    III. Existence

    A. I only
    B. I and II only
    C. II only
    D. I, II, and III

374. The auditor will read which of the following to gather evidence regarding contingencies?
    I. The minutes of the board of directors meetings
    II. The management rep letter
    III. Letters from client's legal counsel

    A. I and II only
    B. II and III only
    C. I and III only
    D. I, II, and III

375. The auditor will read which of the following to gather evidence regarding contingencies?
    I. Client contracts that contain a liquidated damages clause
    II. Client loan agreements that contain debt covenants

    A. I only
    B. II only
    C. Both I and II
    D. Neither I nor II

376. With regard to contingent losses, some method has to be derived to corroborate the company's assessment of:
    I. the likelihood of each loss
    II. the estimated amount of each loss

    A. I only
    B. II only
    C. Both I and II
    D. Neither I nor II

377. Which of the following is considered a procedure involving the auditor's search for contingent liabilities?
    I. Reviewing a bank confirmation letter
    II. Reviewing a customer's response to a negative confirmation
    III. Examining client invoices received from professionals who have provided service

    A. I only
    B. I and III only
    C. I, II, and III
    D. III only

378. Information about unasserted claims should come to the auditor from the:
    I. client's attorney
    II. client

    A. I only
    B. II only
    C. Both I and II
    D. Neither I nor II

379. The primary source of information to be reported about litigation, claims, and assessments is the:

    A. client's lawyer
    B. court records
    C. client's management
    D. independent auditor

380. A lawyer's response to an auditor's inquiry concerning litigation, claims, and assessments may be limited to matters that are considered individually or collectively material to the client's financial statements. Which parties should reach an understanding on the limits of materiality for this purpose?

    A. The auditor and the client's management
    B. The client's audit committee and the lawyer
    C. The client's management and the lawyer
    D. The lawyer and the auditor

381. Which of the following procedures would accomplish the audit objective of searching for unrecorded long-term liabilities?
    I. Examining unusual and large cash receipts, especially near the end of the year
    II. Reconciling interest expense to the amount of long-term debt reported at year-end

    A. I only
    B. II only
    C. Both I and II
    D. Neither I nor II

382. An auditor must perform analytical procedures in the:
    I. planning stage of an audit
    II. internal control stage of an audit

    A. I only
    B. II only
    C. Both I and II
    D. Neither I nor II

383. Analytical procedures are required in which stage of the audit?
    I. Evidence-gathering stage
    II. Overall review stage

    A. I only
    B. II only
    C. Both I and II
    D. Neither I nor II

384. Which of the following payroll control activities would most effectively ensure that payment is made only for work performed?
    I. Require all employees to record arrival and departure by using the time clock.
    II. Require all employees to have their direct supervisors approve their time cards.

    A. I only
    B. II only
    C. Both I and II
    D. Neither I nor II

385. Segregation of duties between human resources and payroll departments is an important control to ensure that:
    I. only valid employees receive paychecks
    II. all payroll checks are printed unsigned

    A. I only
    B. II only
    C. Both I and II
    D. Neither I nor II

386. Which of the following activities performed by a department supervisor would be considered an incompatible function?
    I. Distributing paychecks directly to department employees
    II. Approving a summary of hours each employee worked during the pay period
    III. Setting the pay rate for departmental employees

    A. I and II only
    B. I and III only
    C. II and III only
    D. II only

387. The occurrence assertion as it relates to payroll transactions would correspond to which of the following audit objectives?
    I. To determine that all payroll checks were issued to valid employees for hours actually worked
    II. To determine if any payroll checks were missing
    A. I only
    B. II only
    C. Both I and II
    D. Neither I nor II

388. An auditor recomputes payroll deductions and verifies the preparation of the monthly payroll account bank reconciliation to provide evidence for which of the following assertions?
    A. Existence
    B. Completeness
    C. Accuracy
    D. Cutoff

389. Which of the following circumstances most likely would cause an auditor to assess control risk at a high level for payroll?
    I. Payroll checks generally are disbursed by the same person (or the same department) each payday.
    II. Employee time cards are approved by individual departmental supervisors.
    A. I only
    B. II only
    C. Both I and II
    D. Neither I nor II

390. The independent auditor makes an evaluation of the internal audit staff as a procedure in the assessment of control risk. Normally, the independent auditor will look at the internal auditor's:
    I. competency
    II. objectivity
    A. I only
    B. II only
    C. Both I and II
    D. Neither I nor II

391. In assessing the competence of internal auditors, an independent CPA most likely would obtain information about:
    I. where in the organization chart the internal audit staff reports
    II. the quality of the internal auditors' working paper documentation
    A. I only
    B. II only
    C. Both I and II
    D. Neither I nor II

392. Which of the following factors most likely would assist an independent auditor in assessing the objectivity of the internal auditor?
    A. The professional certifications of the internal audit staff
    B. The consistency of the internal audit reports with the results of work performed
    C. The appropriateness of internal audit conclusions in the circumstances
    D. The organizational status of the director of internal audit

393. During an audit an internal auditor may provide direct assistance to the independent auditor in:

	Performing Tests of Controls	Performing Substantive Tests
A.	No	Yes
B.	Yes	No
C.	No	No
D.	Yes	Yes

394. An internal auditor who is assessed by the independent auditor to be both competent and objective may assist the independent auditor in the assessment of:
    I. inherent risk
    II. control risk
    A. I only
    B. II only
    C. Both I and II
    D. Neither I nor II

395. For which of the following may an independent auditor share responsibility with an entity's internal auditor who is assessed to be both competent and objective?
    I. Materiality levels
    II. Evaluation of accounting estimates
    A. I only
    B. II only
    C. Both I and II
    D. Neither I nor II

396. Which of the following statements is correct about the independent auditor's use of the work of a specialist?

I. The appropriateness and reasonableness of methods and their application are the responsibility of the specialist.

II. The auditor is required to perform substantive procedures to verify the specialist's assumptions and findings.

A. I only
B. II only
C. Both I and II
D. Neither I nor II

397. When an independent auditor hires a specialist to perform certain substantive tests, an understanding should exist among which of the following parties as to the nature of the work to be performed?

I. The auditor
II. The client
III. The specialist

A. I and II only
B. I and III only
C. II and III only
D. I, II, and III

398. When an independent auditor hires a specialist to perform certain substantive tests and believes that the specialist's findings are reasonable in the circumstances:

I. the auditor would mention the specialist in the auditor's report

II. the auditor would either need to be capable of reperforming the specialist's procedures or hire a second specialist to corroborate the findings of the first specialist

A. I only
B. II only
C. Both I and II
D. Neither I nor II

399. When an independent auditor hires a specialist to perform certain substantive tests, which of the following will happen?

I. If the auditor believes that the specialist's findings are contrary to the client's assertions, the auditor would mention the specialist in the auditor's report.

II. If the specialist were related to the client, the auditor would not be able to use that specialist.

A. I only
B. II only
C. Both I and II
D. Neither I nor II

CHAPTER 13

ETHICS, SARBANES-OXLEY, AND THE COSO FRAMEWORK

QUESTIONS 400–451

400. According to the AICPA Code of Professional Conduct, Article IV, which of the following is correct regarding objectivity and independence?

A. Objectivity and independence apply to all services rendered.

B. Independence applies to all services rendered, but objectivity applies to attestation services only (e.g., audits, special reports, and reviews).

C. Objectivity applies to all services rendered, but independence applies to attestation services only (e.g., audits, special reports, and reviews).

D. None of the above

401. According to Rule 101 of the AICPA Code of Professional Conduct, independence will be impaired if a firm does which of the following?

I. Reports to the board on behalf of management

II. Makes operational but not financial decisions for the client

III. Performs nonattest services for an audit client

A. I and III only

B. II and III only

C. I, II, and III

D. I and II only

402. Which of the following is correct regarding the AICPA Code of Professional Conduct?

I. The AICPA Code of Professional Conduct governs a service that a member of the AICPA performs in the area of compilation and review.

II. The AICPA Code of Professional Conduct does not apply to audits of issuers, because Sarbanes-Oxley rules would apply.

A. I only

B. II only

C. Both I and II

D. Neither I nor II

403. The first three principles (articles) of the AICPA's code of conduct are responsibilities, public interest, and:

A. independence

B. objectivity

C. integrity

D. due care

404. According to AICPA and PCAOB standards, which of the following loans in the amount of $20,000 from a financial institution audit client to a CPA would impair the CPA's independence?

A. Cash advance of $20,000 collateralized by money market cash deposits in the same financial institution of $27,000

B. Auto loan of $20,000 from a financial institution audit client, made under normal lending policies

C. Cash advance from a financial institution of $20,000 to be repaid within 10 days, made under normal lending policies

D. All of the above

405. Which of the following bodies ordinarily would NOT have the authority to suspend or revoke a CPA's license to practice public accounting?

   I. A state CPA society

   II. The AICPA

   III. A state board of accountancy

A. I and II only

B. II and III only

C. I and III only

D. III only

406. A violation of the profession's ethical standards most likely would have occurred when a CPA:

   I. purchased a CPA firm's practice for a percentage of fees to be received over a three-year period

   II. issued an unmodified opinion on the Year 12 financial statements when fees for the Year 11 audit were unpaid

A. I only

B. II only

C. Both I and II

D. Neither I nor II

407. Under the ethical standards of the profession, which of the following secured loans is a "permitted loan" regardless of the date it was obtained?

   I. Home mortgage

   II. Automobile loan

A. I only

B. II only

C. Both I and II

D. Neither I nor II

408. When a CPA leaves his or her firm and joins a client within one year of disassociating from the firm, which of the following applies?

   I. Independence is impaired if a partner or professional employee leaves his or her firm and is employed by a client in a key position even if the individual is no longer in a position to influence or participate in the firm's business.

   II. Independence will be impaired unless the engagement is reviewed by a qualified professional to determine whether the engagement team members maintained the appropriate level of skepticism when evaluating the representations and work of the former firm member.

A. I only

B. II only

C. Both I and II

D. Neither I nor II

409. According to the AICPA code of professional conduct, if a firm is engaged to provide attest services to the public, what is the minimum percent ownership of the firm that must be held by CPAs?

A. 100%

B. Greater than 80%

C. Greater than 75%

D. Greater than 50%

410. According to the AICPA Code of Professional Conduct, Rule 201—General Standards, which of the following is NOT part of professional competence?

   I. Consulting with others

   II. Ability to supervise and evaluate work

A. I only

B. II only

C. Both I and II

D. Neither I nor II

411. Which of the following terms relates to the CPA exercising due professional care?

   I. Reasonably prudent person

   II. Critical review

A. I only

B. II only

C. Both I and II

D. Neither I nor II

412. A CPA is NOT allowed to have a fee contingent upon results in which of the following engagements?

   I. Examinations of prospective financial statements

   II. Reviews of historical financial statements

   III. Filing an original tax return, Form 1040

A. I, II, and III

B. II and III only

C. I and III only

D. I and II only

413. A contingent fee is permissible in which of the following situations?

   I. Review of a nonissuer's historical financial statements

   II. Compilations of financial statements expected to be used by third parties and lack of independence is disclosed in the compilation report

   III. Representation with a client on a previously filed tax return now being audited by the IRS

A. I and III only

B. II and III only

C. II only

D. III only

414. Which of the following statements best describes the ethical standard of the profession pertaining to advertising and solicitation?
    I. False, misleading, or deceptive advertising is not allowed.
    II. Advertising that is informative and objective is allowed.

    A. I only
    B. II only
    C. Both I and II
    D. Neither I nor II

415. Which of the following is an act discreditable to the profession?
    I. Failure to give working papers to the client after the client makes a demand
    II. Determination by a court or administrative agency of discrimination in public practice

    A. I only
    B. II only
    C. Both I and II
    D. Neither I nor II

416. Which of the following is considered an act discreditable to the profession?
    I. A CPA's failure to return client records to the client because the client has refused to pay the CPA's bill
    II. Disclosing confidential client information during a quality review of a professional practice by a team from the state society of CPAs

    A. I only
    B. II only
    C. Both I and II
    D. Neither I nor II

417. Which of the following would be considered an act discreditable to the profession?
    I. Arranging with a collection agency to collect fees owed by a client
    II. Using an off-site cloud storage server to store confidential client computer files

    A. I only
    B. II only
    C. Both I and II
    D. Neither I nor II

418. A CPA in public practice must be independent when providing which of the following services?
    I. Compilation of a personal financial statement
    II. Compilation of a financial forecast
    III. Attestation engagements

    A. I and III only
    B. II and III only
    C. I, II, and III
    D. III only

419. Under PCAOB, tax services may be provided to an issuer audit client:
    I. without preapproval from the audit committee
    II. provided the services do not include aggressive tax transactions

    A. I only
    B. II only
    C. Both I and II
    D. Neither I nor II

420. The AICPA Code of Professional Conduct would be violated if a member reveals confidential client information:
    I. as a result of a validly issued subpoena or summons
    II. as a result of a quality review of the CPA's practice

    A. I only
    B. II only
    C. Both I and II
    D. Neither I nor II

421. According to the Sarbanes-Oxley Act of 2002, only CPA firms registered with PCAOB are permitted to audit:
    I. privately held entities that do business with issuers of securities
    II. entities that are issuers of securities

    A. I only
    B. II only
    C. Both I and II
    D. Neither I nor II

422. PCAOB requires a registered CPA firm to:
    I. provide a concurring or second partner review of each audit report
    II. describe in the audit reports the extent of the testing of the issuer's internal control structure and procedures
    III. maintain audit documentation for a minimum of five years

    A. II only
    B. I and II only
    C. I and III only
    D. I only

423. Audit firms need to retain working papers relating to their audit clients for at least:
    I. seven years if the client is publicly held
    II. five years if the client is not publicly held

    A. I only
    B. II only
    C. Both I and II
    D. Neither I nor II

424. Under Sarbanes-Oxley, registered audit firms are required to report which of the following information to the audit committee of audited corporations?
    I. A schedule of unadjusted audit differences
    II. The treatment that the audit firm prefers regarding alternative accounting treatments discussed with the corporation's management

    A. I only
    B. II only
    C. Both I and II
    D. Neither I nor II

425. Under PCAOB, a cooling-off period of how many years is required before a member of an issuer's audit engagement team may begin working for the registrant in a key position?

    A. One year
    B. Two years
    C. Three years
    D. Four years

426. According to PCAOB, which of the following must be rotated off an audit engagement every five years?
    I. Lead partner
    II. Reviewing partner

    A. I only
    B. II only
    C. Both I and II
    D. Neither I nor II

427. With regard to auditing a nonissuer, which of the following standards requires lead auditor rotation?
    I. AICPA standards
    II. PCAOB standards

    A. I only
    B. II only
    C. Both I and II
    D. Neither I nor II

428. According to Title VI of Sarbanes-Oxley, which of the following is required as an enhanced financial disclosure?
    I. Any officer, director, or owner of more than 10 percent of any equity security must file a report indicating how many shares they own within 10 days after becoming an officer, director, or more than 10 percent owner.
    II. A change in ownership must be filed within seven days of such change.

    A. I only
    B. II only
    C. Both I and II
    D. Neither I nor II

429. According to the Sarbanes-Oxley Act of 2002, auditors are required to attest to management's assessment of the effectiveness of internal control over financial reporting in a:
    I. 10-K Annual Report
    II. 10-Q Quarterly Report

    A. I only
    B. II only
    C. Both I and II
    D. Neither I nor II

430. Firms registered with PCAOB are required to undergo:
    I. PCAOB inspection
    II. quality review inspection by a peer review panel from the state society

    A. I only
    B. II only
    C. Both I and II
    D. Neither I nor II

431. Under Sarbanes-Oxley, in an audit of a publicly traded company, the issuer must rotate every five years:
    I. their designated "financial expert"
    II. their auditing firm

    A. I only
    B. II only
    C. Both I and II
    D. Neither I nor II

432. According to Sarbanes-Oxley, an explanation would need to be attached to Forms 10-Q and 10-K if an issuer lacks which of the following?

I. A financial expert on its audit committee
II. A code of ethics for senior financial officers

A. I only
B. II only
C. Both I and II
D. Neither I nor II

433. According to Sarbanes-Oxley, audit partners NOT considered lead or reviewing partners must rotate off an audit engagement after _____ years and then must sit out for _____ years before returning to the engagement.

A. 5, 5
B. 7, 2
C. 5, 2
D. 7, 1

434. Under Sarbanes-Oxley, after rotating off an audit engagement, lead partners are required to take a "time-out" of how many years before returning to an audit engagement?

A. One year
B. Two years
C. Five years
D. Seven years

435. For a firm that is engaged to audit and is concerned about independence, tax services related to confidential or aggressive tax transactions would be a violation of:

I. AICPA standards
II. PCAOB/SEC standards

A. I only
B. II only
C. Both I and II
D. Neither I nor II

436. Which of the following standards prohibits the performance of financial information system design and implementation services for audit clients?

I. PCAOB standards relating to audits of issuers
II. AICPA standards relating to audits of nonissuers

A. I only
B. II only
C. Both I and II
D. Neither I nor II

437. Which of the following services is a CPA firm NOT allowed to provide to an audit client (issuer of securities), according to Sarbanes-Oxley?

I. Bookkeeping services
II. Income tax return preparation

A. I only
B. II only
C. Both I and II
D. Neither I nor II

438. According to Sarbanes-Oxley, which of the following statements is correct regarding an issuer's audit committee's financial expert?

I. The audit committee financial expert must be the issuer's audit committee chairperson to enhance internal control.
II. If an issuer does not have an audit committee financial expert, the issuer must disclose the reason why the role is not filled.

A. I only
B. II only
C. Both I and II
D. Neither I nor II

439. Which of the following is correct?

I. The PCAOB will inspect the public accounting firms that register with it. If not satisfied by the findings, the PCAOB can revoke the firm's registration so that it cannot audit publicly held companies.
II. The PCAOB was established to issue accounting standards for publicly traded companies.

A. I only
B. II only
C. Both I and II
D. Neither I nor II

440. Nonaudit services that do not exceed what percentage of total revenues from an audit client do NOT require audit committee preapproval?

A. 1
B. 2
C. 4
D. 5

441. The internal control provisions of Sarbanes-Oxley apply to which companies in the United States?

A. All public and nonpublic companies
B. All public companies
C. All issuers with more than 100 stockholders
D. All nonissuer companies

442. Regarding internal control, Sarbanes-Oxley requires a publicly traded company to:
   I. report on their own internal control
   II. make an assertion regarding the effectiveness of their own internal control

   A. I only
   B. II only
   C. Both I and II
   D. Neither I nor II

443. The most common management tool for evaluating internal control is the:

   A. Sarbanes-Oxley internal control framework
   B. COSO internal framework
   C. AICPA internal control framework
   D. SEC internal control framework

444. According to the COSO internal framework, there are how many components of internal control?

   A. 3
   B. 6
   C. 4
   D. 5

445. The COSO framework of evaluating internal control is recognized as appropriate by:
   I. PCAOB
   II. SEC

   A. I only
   B. II only
   C. Both I and II
   D. Neither I nor II

446. In management's report on internal control (required under Sarbanes-Oxley for a publicly traded company), there is a statement that:
   I. the company's independent auditor has issued an attestation report on management's assertion
   II. mentions COSO as the framework for evaluating internal control

   A. I only
   B. II only
   C. Both I and II
   D. Neither I nor II

447. Which of the following is required in management's report on internal control under Sarbanes-Oxley?
   I. A statement that management is responsible for internal control
   II. A statement that the independent auditor has assessed management's assertion
   III. Management's assertion of the effectiveness of their internal control

   A. I and III only
   B. I and II only
   C. II and III only
   D. I, II, and III

448. Which of the following is an interrelated component of internal control according to the COSO framework?
   I. Information and communication
   II. Control environment

   A. I only
   B. II only
   C. Both I and II
   D. Neither I nor II

449. Which is NOT one of the interrelated components of internal control according to the COSO framework?
   I. Control activities
   II. Risk assessment

   A. I only
   B. II only
   C. Both I and II
   D. Neither I nor II

450. Regarding internal control under Sarbanes-Oxley, which of the following must be reported to those charged with governance?
   I. All significant deficiencies
   II. All control deficiencies
   III. All material weaknesses

   A. I and III only
   B. II and III only
   C. I and II only
   D. I, II, and III

451. An auditor's communication of material weaknesses and significant deficiencies to those charged with governance should be done:

   A. during the audit and then again at the audit's completion
   B. at the completion of the audit
   C. during the audit
   D. during the audit or at the end of the audit

CHAPTER 14

INTERNATIONAL AUDITING STANDARDS, GOVERNMENT AUDITING STANDARDS, AND INFORMATION TECHNOLOGY

QUESTIONS 452–477

452. With regard to marketing professional services, the International Federation of Accountants (IFAC) indicates that:

A. direct marketing is prohibited
B. marketing is allowed if lawful
C. marketing should be honest and truthful
D. marketing of audit services is prohibited

453. In relation to the AICPA Code of Professional Conduct, the IFAC Code of Ethics for Professional Accountants:

A. has more outright prohibitions
B. has fewer outright prohibitions
C. has no outright prohibitions
D. applies only to professional accountants in business

454. Which of the following is NOT true about international auditing standards?

I. The location in which the auditor practices must be disclosed in the audit report.
II. External confirmation of accounts receivable is generally required.

A. I only
B. II only
C. Both I and II
D. Neither I nor II

455. Which is correct regarding international auditing standards?

I. When dating the audit report for a subsequent event, international standards require the dating of the report to be the amended date or a dual date.
II. If the client suddenly wishes to change the engagement and the auditor is unable to agree with the client as to the reason for the sudden change, the auditor should withdraw and consider whether there is an obligation to contact third parties.

A. I only
B. II only
C. Both I and II
D. Neither I nor II

456. Which of the following is permitted for an audit client with appropriate safeguards under the international code of ethics (IFAC) but not permitted under the AICPA code of professional conduct?

I. Investment banking
II. Legal services

A. I only
B. II only
C. Both I and II
D. Neither I nor II

457. Before reporting on the financial statements of a US entity that have been prepared in conformity with another country's accounting principles, an auditor practicing in the United States should:
    I. understand the accounting principles generally accepted in the other country
    II. be certified by the appropriate auditing or accounting board of the other country

    A. I only
    B. II only
    C. Both I and II
    D. Neither I nor II

458. With regard to internal audit outsourcing, which of the following is correct?
    I. Permissible under US GAAS for audit clients under certain conditions
    II. Not permissible under international auditing standards for audit clients under any conditions

    A. I only
    B. II only
    C. Both I and II
    D. Neither I nor II

459. Government Auditing Standards published by the US Government Accountability Office define standards associated with the following types of engagements:
    I. financial audits
    II. attest engagements
    III. performance audits

    A. I and III only
    B. I and II only
    C. II and III only
    D. I, II, and III

460. Which of the following is correct regarding reporting requirements in a compliance audit?
    I. The auditor must report on whether the entity has complied with applicable requirements.
    II. The auditor does not express an opinion on the effectiveness of internal control over compliance.

    A. I only
    B. II only
    C. Both I and II
    D. Neither I nor II

461. In performing an audit in accordance with Generally Accepted Government Auditing Standards (the "Yellow Book"), the auditor accepts greater reporting responsibilities than accepted under a GAAS audit, since the auditor must report on:
    I. compliance with laws, rules, and regulations, violations of which may affect financial statement amounts
    II. the organization's internal control over financial reporting

    A. I only
    B. II only
    C. Both I and II
    D. Neither I nor II

462. Compared to a typical GAAS audit for a for-profit entity, the audit of an entity that receives federal financial assistance requires:
    I. more fieldwork than a typical GAAS audit
    II. less reporting than a typical GAAS audit

    A. I only
    B. II only
    C. Both I and II
    D. Neither I nor II

463. Which of the following is a documentation requirement that an auditor should follow when auditing in accordance with Government Auditing Standards?
    I. Audit documentation should contain sufficient information so that supplementary oral explanations are not required
    II. Audit documentation should include the auditor's assessment of the material risk of noncompliance

    A. I only
    B. II only
    C. Both I and II
    D. Neither I nor II

464. The auditor's objectives in a compliance audit of a governmental entity include:
    I. minimizing control risk of noncompliance
    II. forming an opinion on whether the government complied in all material respects with applicable compliance requirements

    A. I only
    B. II only
    C. Both I and II
    D. Neither I nor II

465. Auditors engaged to perform a "single audit" of a major program must:
    I. obtain an understanding of internal control over compliance
    II. perform tests of controls

    A. I only
    B. II only
    C. Both I and II
    D. Neither I nor II

466. Auditors engaged to perform a single audit must perform procedures to obtain an understanding of internal control pertaining to the compliance requirements for federal programs sufficient to plan an audit and to support a low assessed level of control risk for:
    I. major programs
    II. nonmajor programs

    A. I only
    B. II only
    C. Both I and II
    D. Neither I nor II

467. Under the Single Audit Act, auditors are responsible for:
    I. understanding internal control
    II. reporting the results of their tests

    A. I only
    B. II only
    C. Both I and II
    D. Neither I nor II

468. In which of the following audits is the CPA required to prepare a written report on the auditor's understanding of internal control and the assessment of control risk?
    I. Audits performed in accordance with GAGAS
    II. Audits performed in accordance with GAAS

    A. I only
    B. II only
    C. Both I and II
    D. Neither I nor II

469. Reporting responsibilities under GAGAS are expanded to include:
    I. reports on compliance with laws, rules, and regulations
    II. reports on internal control over financial reporting

    A. I only
    B. II only
    C. Both I and II
    D. Neither I nor II

470. Which of the following is correct regarding program-specific audits under the Single Audit Act?
    I. Program-specific audits do not involve reporting on the financial statements of the entity spending federal financial assistance.
    II. If the entity spending federal financial assistance does not meet certain criteria, a program-specific audit must be performed rather than a single audit.

    A. I only
    B. II only
    C. Both I and II
    D. Neither I nor II

471. Which of the following best describes a single audit?

    A. An audit of federal financial assistance
    B. A report on fair presentation of financial statements
    C. A combined audit of both an entity's financial statements and federal financial assistance programs
    D. A program-specific audit

472. Which of the following is an engagement attribute for an audit of an entity that processes most of its financial data in electronic form without any paper documentation?
    I. Increased effort to search for evidence of management fraud
    II. Performance of audit tests on a continuous basis

    A. I only
    B. II only
    C. Both I and II
    D. Neither I nor II

473. Durka Company, a client of Corey, CPA, has recently automated its accounting system. While Corey has been the auditor of Durka for several years, this will be the first audit encompassing the new system. Which of the following is most likely a result of this change?
    I. Corey will need to take courses to develop an appropriate level of IT skill.
    II. Corey will need to revise his audit objectives from prior years to reflect the new situation.
    III. Corey will need to revise his audit program and audit procedures from prior years to reflect the new situation.

    A. III only
    B. I and II only
    C. II and III only
    D. I, II, and III

474. The Malkin Corp. has recently installed a new computerized payroll-processing program. Before the program is used to compute actual payroll checks for the employees, test data are going to be run through the computer to see how they would be processed. Which of the following is likely to be tested in this manner?
    I. Two checks requested for the same employee
    II. A check requested for an employee who hasn't worked for the company in two months

    A. I only
    B. II only
    C. Both I and II
    D. Neither I nor II

475. Which of the following controls involves dummy transactions being run simultaneously with live transactions in the client's computer system?
    I. Test data
    II. Integrated test facility

    A. I only
    B. II only
    C. Both I and II
    D. Neither I nor II

476. Which of the following is a computer-assisted audit technique that permits an auditor to insert the auditor's version of a client's program to process data and compare the output with the client's output?
    I. Test data
    II. Parallel simulation

    A. I only
    B. II only
    C. Both I and II
    D. Neither I nor II

477. An auditor would likely use generalized audit software to:
    I. construct parallel simulations
    II. assess IT control risk
    III. access client data files

    A. I and II only
    B. I and III only
    C. I, II, and III
    D. III only

CHAPTER 15

MANAGEMENT REPRESENTATION LETTER AND QUALITY CONTROL AT THE FIRM

478. Which of the following is true regarding the management representation letter under US GAAS and PCAOB?
  I. The date of the management rep letter should match the date of the auditor's report.
  II. Under certain circumstances, failure to obtain a management representation letter is not a scope limitation.

A. I only
B. II only
C. Both I and II
D. Neither I nor II

479. Under US GAAS, which of the following officers would need to sign the management rep letter?
  I. CEO
  II. CFO

A. I only
B. II only
C. Both I and II
D. Neither I nor II

480. With respect to the management rep letter, materiality would apply to management having made available to the auditor access to which of the following?
  I. Minutes of board meetings
  II. Records relating to revenue and expenses

A. I only
B. II only
C. Both I and II
D. Neither I nor II

481. In a typical management representation letter, management would acknowledge their responsibility for:
  I. fair presentation of financial statements
  II. internal control over financial reporting
  III. communicating to the audit committee any material disagreements with the auditor

A. I and II only
B. I, II, and III
C. I only
D. II only

482. Which of the following should be found in the management representation letter?
  I. The results of management's assessment of the risk that the financial statements may be materially misstated due to fraud
  II. A statement that all known or potential litigation has been disclosed to the auditor

A. I only
B. II only
C. Both I and II
D. Neither I nor II

483. The following quote is found in the current file from a communication pertaining to an audit of financial statements.

"... There are no material transactions that have not been properly recorded in the accounting records underlying the financial statements. ..."

Which communication is the quote likely to be taken from?

A. Management representation letter
B. Communication with predecessor auditor
C. Auditor's engagement letter
D. Auditor's report

484. The following quote is found in the current file from a communication pertaining to an audit of financial statements.

"... Fees for our services are based on our per diem rates plus travel expenses. ..."

Which communication is the quote likely to be taken from?

A. Auditor's report
B. Audit inquiry letter to legal counsel
C. Engagement letter
D. Management representation letter

485. The following quote is found in the current file from a communication pertaining to an audit of financial statements.

"... The objective of our audit is to express an opinion on the financial statements, although it is possible that facts or circumstances encountered may prevent us from expressing an unmodified opinion. ..."

Which communication is the quote likely to be taken from?

A. Engagement letter
B. Management representation letter
C. Auditor's inquiry to client's legal counsel
D. Communication with predecessor auditor

486. The following quote is found in the current file from a communication pertaining to an audit of financial statements.

"... There has been no fraud involving employees that could have a material effect on the financial statements. ..."

Which communication is the quote likely to be taken from?

A. Communication with audit committee
B. Audit inquiry letter to legal counsel
C. Management representation letter
D. Communication with the predecessor

487. The following quote is found in the current file from a communication pertaining to an audit of financial statements.

"... Are you aware of any facts or circumstances that may indicate a lack of integrity by any member of senior management? ..."

Which communication is the quote likely to be taken from?

A. Management representation letter
B. Engagement letter
C. Auditor's report
D. Communication with predecessor auditor

488. The following quote is found in the current file from a communication pertaining to an audit of financial statements.

"... There were unreasonable delays by management in permitting the start of the audit and in providing needed information. ..."

Which communication is the quote likely to be taken from?

A. External receivable confirmation
B. Auditor's engagement letter
C. Auditor's communication with audit committee
D. Management representation letter

489. The following quote is found in the current file from a communication pertaining to an audit of financial statements.

"... If this statement is not correct, please write promptly, using the enclosed envelope, and give details of any differences directly to our auditors...."

Which communication is the quote likely to be taken from?

A. External receivable confirmation
B. Management representation letter
C. Audit inquiry to legal counsel
D. Communication with predecessor

490. The following quote is found in the current file from a communication pertaining to an audit of financial statements.

"... The company has suffered recurring losses from operations and has a net capital deficiency that raises substantial doubt about its ability to continue as a going concern...."

Which communication is the quote likely to be taken from?

A. Audit inquiry letter to legal counsel
B. External receivable confirmation
C. Communication with predecessor
D. Auditor's report

491. Which of the following requires a CPA firm providing audit and attest services to adopt a system of quality control?
   I. AICPA
   II. IRS

A. I only
B. II only
C. Both I and II
D. Neither I nor II

492. Which of the following elements of quality control encompasses criteria for recruitment and hiring compensation and advancement?

A. Leadership responsibilities
B. Human resources
C. Risk assessment
D. Monitoring

493. Which of the following is NOT one of the interrelated elements of quality control at the firm?

A. Considering audit risk
B. Leadership responsibilities
C. Client acceptance and continuance
D. Monitoring

494. With regard to the elements of quality control at the firm, the category known as leadership responsibilities is essential because:
   I. the firm's leadership bears the ultimate responsibility for the firm's quality control systems
   II. the firm must be able to perform the engagement within the reporting deadlines

A. I only
B. II only
C. Both I and II
D. Neither I nor II

495. When measuring the quality control at a CPA firm, providing a means to resolve differences of opinion falls under the category of:

A. Performance
B. Leadership
C. Monitoring
D. Human resources

496. With regard to a firm's system of quality control, which component of quality control involves an ongoing consideration and evaluation of the design and effectiveness of the quality control system?

A. Performance
B. Leadership
C. Monitoring
D. Human resources

497. With regard to quality control, Sarbanes-Oxley requires for every public company audit:
   I. peer review to be conducted under the AICPA standards so that one firm may review another firm's quality control system
   II. a wrap-up or secondary partner review of the audit documentation by a partner not otherwise involved in the audit

A. I only
B. II only
C. Both I and II
D. Neither I nor II

498. A CPA firm that fails to maintain quality control standards:
   I. has not necessarily violated GAAS
   II. may still be in compliance with professional standards with respect to individual engagements

A. I only
B. II only
C. Both I and II
D. Neither I nor II

499. The CPA firm's size as well as cost-benefit consider-
ations should be taken into account when:
  I. determining independence with respect to a
     client
  II. developing quality controls at the CPA firm

  A. I only
  B. II only
  C. Both I and II
  D. Neither I nor II

500. Which of the following is correct regarding client
quality-control standards at the firm?
  I. Quality-control standards apply to auditing
     and attestation but not to accounting and
     review.
  II. A primary purpose of quality-control stan-
      dards is to minimize the likelihood of associ-
      ating with a client whose management lacks
      integrity.

  A. I only
  B. II only
  C. Both I and II
  D. Neither I nor II

Bonus Questions

501. The Dagger Corp. began the year with an acid test
ratio greater than 1. What is the effect on the acid test
ratio if the company declares and pays a dividend in
the amount of $5,400?

  A. Increase
  B. Decrease
  C. No effect
  D. Cannot be determined without knowing the
     exact acid test ratio at the beginning of the year

502. A company shipped merchandise (FOB destination)
to a customer on December 29, Year 5, and recorded
the sale but not the relief of inventory. The customer
received the inventory on December 30, Year 5.
What is the effect on the inventory turnover ratio?

  A. Increase
  B. Decrease
  C. No effect
  D. Cannot be determined without knowing
     whether the inventory turnover ratio began the
     year above or below 1

PART I ANSWERS AND EXPLANATIONS

Chapter 1: Proper Use of the Term *Audit* and an Overview of Auditing

1. **A.** I is correct. While the Public Company Accounting Oversight Board (PCAOB) sets the standards for audits of publicly traded entities, the Auditing Standards Board continues to set the standards with regard to audits of financial statements of nonissuers. Auditors of nonissuers are required to comply with Statements on Auditing Standards and should be prepared to justify any departures. II is wrong. PCAOB is empowered under the Sarbanes-Oxley Act of 2002 to set auditing standards with regard to publicly traded companies (issuers).

2. **B.** II is correct. Whenever an independent expert is brought in to examine financial statements with hopes of adding credibility, that engagement and reporting process is known as an attestation but NOT necessarily an audit, because there are several types of attestations. I is wrong. When an attestation is carried out on historic financial information, the attestation is known as an audit. There is no indication in the question that the financial statements are historic; therefore, the term *attestation* may be used but NOT the term *audit*. An audit is the highest level of attestation service a CPA may provide.

3. **C.** I is correct. When an attestation is carried out on historic financial information, the attestation is known as an audit. An audit is the highest level of attestation service a CPA may provide. It involves providing an opinion, and, therefore, the CPA must be independent. It is important to note that an audit is just one type of attestation. Use the term *audit* when the CPA is doing an attestation engagement involving historic financial statements. II is correct. While audits are attestations that look backward at historic financial information, examination engagements are attestations that look forward. Therefore, when the CPA examines in Year 3 what Year 4 may look like, this is an example of an attestation but not an audit. The CPA Exam expects a candidate to know the proper use of the word *audit*.

4. **B.** II is correct. Financial statements are the responsibility of the management of the reporting organization. The responsibility of the independent auditor is to express an opinion on those statements based on an audit. I is wrong. Even after the audit is completed and the opinion expressed, financial statements are still the responsibility of the management of the reporting organization. The responsibility of the independent auditor is to express an opinion on those statements based on an audit.

5. **D.** I is wrong. In the auditor's report, consistency of accounting principles from period to period is implied and only referred to explicitly if there is an inconsistency. For example, if the client used FIFO in Year 1 for inventory valuation, it's implied that he or she also used FIFO in Year 2. This would be consistent and, therefore, would NOT have to be expressed in the auditor's report. However, if the client used FIFO in Year 1 and Average Cost in Year 2, this would represent an inconsistency and would need to be expressed in the report. II is wrong. In an auditor's standard report the fact that client disclosures and footnotes are adequate need not be indicated. The auditor would mention disclosures and footnotes only if there were problems with them. Otherwise, it is implied in a standard audit report that client footnotes and disclosures are adequate.

6. **D.** I is wrong. Family members employed by the audit client do not automatically affect the independence of a covered member. A spouse of a covered member can work for the company under audit as long as there is no influence on the financial statements. II is wrong. A dependent child of a covered member can work for the client under audit, without impairing independence, provided there is no influence on financial statements. Jobs that would impair independence include accounting jobs like internal auditor or controller, or any job that influences the financial activities of the client.

7. **B.** II is correct. For covered members and their families, there are direct ownership rules and there are indirect ownership rules when it comes to owning stocks and bonds of the client company. Although direct ownership rules are very specific, indirect ownership rules are less specific. Indirect ownership results from owning shares in a mutual fund, and the mutual fund owns shares in the client company. If the spouse of a covered member owns an immaterial number of shares in a mutual fund, and the mutual fund happens to own shares of the client company, the indirect immaterial financial interest is OK and would not impair independence. I is wrong. Direct ownership rules are very specific and materiality is NOT a factor. If the spouse

or dependent of a covered member owns even one share of stock directly in the client company, independence is impaired regardless of the child's age. Independence would be impaired whether the shares were held in a brokerage account or in a safe-deposit box.

8. **A.** I is correct. Materiality would not apply, since the audit firm itself is considered a covered member and independence would be impaired. While ownership of one share is clearly immaterial, an audit firm is not allowed to own any shares of its client under audit. II is incorrect. Materiality would apply to indirect ownership of just a single share in a mutual fund. The spouse of a covered member may not directly own any shares, but, indirectly, through a mutual fund, an immaterial indirect ownership is allowed.

9. **B.** II is correct. An audit firm cannot have unpaid audit fees from the previous year when it issues an audit report for the current year. The audit can still take place and all the fieldwork can be done, but no opinion can be given until payment is received from the prior year's audit. I is wrong. If a dependent of a covered member is employed as a parking lot attendant of the client under audit, this would not by itself impair independence. Only if the spouse or immediate family member of a covered member were employed at the client in a position that could influence the financial statements would independence be impaired.

10. **A.** If a generally accepted auditing standard is considered an "unconditional requirement," the auditor would be required to comply with the standard in all cases in order to comply with GAAS. For example, the standard that requires an auditor to have training and professional competence in order to conduct an engagement in accordance with GAAS is an "unconditional requirement."

11. **B.** II is correct. According to the clarified standards, if a generally accepted auditing standard is deemed "unconditional," then the auditor is required to (must) comply with the standard in order for the auditor to complete an engagement in accordance with GAAS. Simply documenting the reason for departure would NOT be acceptable if the standard was deemed an "unconditional requirement." I is wrong. According to the clarified standards, if a standard is deemed "presumptively mandatory," the standard should also be complied with, and an auditor would need to comply with the standard or

clearly document the reason for departure in order to follow GAAS.

Chapter 2: Audit Planning and Risk Assessment

12. **C.** I is correct. The CPA needs to assess the auditability of the client by considering the adequacy of the accounting records. Lack of quality accounting records equals a scope limitation. Sometimes an auditor can work within the scope limitation, but the auditor would want to know about this before accepting the engagement. II is correct. The auditor needs to know the future plans for the company because they may impact the decision whether to accept the engagement. Before accepting an engagement, the auditor should determine why the company even needs an audit. For example, are they considering going public? Sometimes a bank demands an audit be performed in order to renew the client's loan or line of credit.

13. **C.** I is correct. Inquiries of the predecessor prior to acceptance of the audit engagement should include specific questions regarding facts that might bear on the integrity of management. II is correct. Inquiries of the predecessor prior to acceptance should include any disagreements that the predecessor had with management as to accounting principles and procedures. Other significant matters should be addressed with the predecessor auditor also, such as communications with those charged with governance regarding fraud, conforming with laws and regulations, and the predecessor's understanding as to the reasons for the change of auditors.

14. **D.** I is wrong. If a CPA lacks an understanding of the client's industry and accounting principles but feels confident that such information and knowledge can be obtained prior to commencement of the audit, the engagement can still be accepted. II is wrong. If the client's management has unusually high turnover, the engagement can still be accepted, although the high turnover would be considered a fraud risk factor.

15. **A.** I is correct. Obtaining a signed engagement letter from the client's management spelling out the understanding between the client and the CPA is essential in the planning stage. The engagement letter is the most common form of written understanding between client and CPA. II is wrong. Examining documents to detect illegal acts having a material effect on the financial statements is

considered evidence gathering. Evidence gathering is not likely to be done in the planning stage and is more likely to be done later in the audit. *Exam hint:* The Auditing and Attestation section of the CPA Exam often asks questions that involve audit procedures and when they are to be performed. This question asks about the planning stage and what procedures are to be performed during planning. The correct answer involves an engagement letter because a written understanding is a procedure to be performed in the planning stage. The incorrect answer is often a necessary audit procedure but performed in a different stage of the audit. There are many questions similar to this style throughout the Auditing and Attestation section where the wrong answer involves a correct audit procedure performed in a different part of the audit.

16. **A.** I is correct. Procedures likely to be performed in the planning stage of an audit include determining the extent of involvement, if any, of consultants, specialists, and internal auditors. II is wrong. External confirmation of accounts receivable balances is a substantive test, performed in the evidence-gathering stage of the audit.

17. **C.** Although an understanding with the audit client must be in writing, an engagement letter is not mandatory. An engagement letter is standard practice, but other formats may be used, provided all responsibilities of the auditor and management are clearly presented. Compare with review and compilation, where the understanding with the client must be in the form of an engagement letter. A is wrong. The responsibilities should cover the auditor's responsibilities, that the auditor is responsible for an opinion regarding the financial statements being prepared in conformity with the framework. B is wrong. Limitations of the engagement should be included in the understanding with the client. An example of limitations would be the following: "Our engagement is subject to the risk that material errors and fraud may exist and will not be detected." D is wrong. The written understanding should include the audit fee and frequency of billing to minimize misunderstandings.

18. **D.** I is correct. The engagement letter should state that management is responsible for the financial statements and for adjusting the financial statements to correct material misstatements identified by the auditor. II is correct. The engagement letter should state that management is responsible for compliance with laws and regulations. III is correct. The engagement letter should state that

management is responsible for selection and application of accounting policies. The engagement letter should also state that management is responsible for internal controls, making all financial records available to the auditor, and providing the auditor with a representation letter at the end of the audit.

19. **B.** II is correct. The auditor makes a preliminary judgment about materiality in the planning stage of the audit based on annualized interim financial statements, which the auditor reads during the planning stage. I is wrong. The auditor makes a preliminary judgment of materiality in the planning stage. An internal control questionnaire applies to the internal control stage of the audit, not the planning stage. *Exam hint:* The Auditing and Attestation section of the CPA Exam is centered around knowing which procedures are done in which stages of the audit. If it's a planning question, and the answer choice says something about an internal control procedure, it is the wrong answer. Internal control happens after the planning stage.

20. **B.** II is correct. Coordinating the assistance of entity personnel in data preparation is usually performed during the planning stage. III is correct. During planning, the auditor generally would read the current year's interim financial statements. I is wrong. Selecting a sample of vendors' invoices for comparison to receiving reports is performed during the evidence-gathering stage of the audit.

21. **C.** I is correct. Complex transactions would cause an auditor to assess inherent risk as high. For example, if it were difficult for the auditor to understand the point at which the earnings process is complete, the auditor would assess inherent risk as high. III is correct. Relying heavily on estimates allows management the opportunity to be biased in making those estimates. An auditor would likely assess inherent risk as high if many figures are based on estimates rather than actual figures. Estimations are less open to objective verification. Therefore, the possibility of a material misstatement occurring is usually greater for figures that must be estimated. When the auditor is evaluating an account where significant estimations are reported, the degree of inherent risk is usually assessed at a relatively high level. II is wrong. Many related-party transactions would cause an auditor to assess inherent risk as high. The auditor would rather discover that no related-party transactions have taken place because the auditor fears that management will disguise related-party transactions and make them appear

arm's-length. The more related-party transactions, the higher the assessed level of inherent risk.

22. **B.** II is correct. Inherent risk is assessed by the auditor, but this assessment has no bearing on the actual amount of inherent risk present and the auditor can do nothing to mitigate the amount of inherent risk that is present. I is wrong. Since the auditor's assessment of inherent risk has no bearing on the actual level of inherent risk, inherent risk exists independent of the financial statement audit. Inherent risk is a characteristic of the accounting system and the personnel who work in that system.

23. **A.** I is correct. Inherent risk is assessed by the auditor. Inherent risk represents the risk that there are material errors in the financial statements. An auditor assesses inherent risk as high or low based on factors such as transactions being complex and difficult for the auditor to understand. Other factors that have an impact on the auditor's assessment of inherent risk relate to whether there are many related-party transactions and client-prepared estimates substituting for actual amounts in the financial statements. Inherent risk is assessed early in the audit, in the planning stage. II is wrong. Control risk is assessed by the auditor in the internal control stage, not the planning stage. Control risk can be assessed as high if the auditor feels that the client's internal controls will not prevent or detect a material misstatement.

24. **C.** I is correct. Control risk is assessed by the auditor after coming to an understanding and documenting the five components of internal control. The auditor's assessment, although based on judgment, has no bearing on how good or bad the client's controls actually are. The more work that went into the auditor's assessment—testing controls and so on—the more likely that the auditor came to the correct assessment of control risk. However, the auditor's assessment of control risk has nothing to do with the amount of control risk present. The auditor's assessment of control risk does not affect the chance that the client's internal controls will fail to detect or prevent a material error from appearing on the financial statements. The auditor's assessment is simply the auditor's judgment of how much risk the auditor thinks he or she is facing. II is correct. Inherent risk is assessed by the auditor, and, once again, the auditor's assessment has no bearing on the actual amount of inherent risk present. Inherent risk is the risk posed by an error or omission in a financial statement due to a factor other than a failure of control. This risk is most likely to be high

when transactions are complex or where a high degree of judgment (e.g. estimates) is used in the reporting of transactions. The auditor's assessment is simply the auditor's judgment of how much risk the auditor thinks he or she is facing.

25. **C.** I is correct. Detection risk is a component of audit risk. Audit risk is made up of inherent risk, control risk, and detection risk. II is correct. Inherent risk is a component of audit risk.

26. **C.** If inherent risk and control risk are assessed as high by the auditor, this would result in the auditor thinking that he or she is facing high risk that the financial statements contain material misstatements. This would make it more difficult for the auditor to give reasonable assurance that the financial statements are presented in conformity with the framework. In that situation, the auditor's best chance of lowering overall audit risk would be to lower detection risk, being more careful when performing substantive testing. A and B are wrong. The auditor cannot reduce inherent risk or control risk, as the auditor only assesses inherent risk and control risk.

27. **A.** An increase in the assessed level of control risk means that the assessed risk of material misstatement has also increased, and this requires a corresponding decrease in detection risk to maintain the same (presumably low) level of overall audit risk. Increasing the extent of tests of details will result in a reduction in detection risk and thus reduce overall audit risk. B is wrong. If the auditor increased the assessed level of control risk, the result would be an increase in the extent of tests of details, not a decrease. C is wrong. An auditor cannot increase or decrease inherent risk; an auditor only assesses inherent risk. D is wrong. In an audit under GAAS, an auditor does not perform tests of controls if the assessed level of inherent risk is high.

28. **B.** II is correct. Detection risk is part of overall audit risk, but detection risk is not assessed by the auditor. Rather, detection risk is lowered or raised by the auditor. I is wrong. Control risk is part of overall audit risk, and control risk is assessed by the auditor.

29. **C.** I is correct. Inherent risk is a client characteristic that is evaluated by the auditor. The more work and testing done by the auditor, the better the chances that the evaluation will be accurate. II is correct. The quantity of work performed by the auditor will not impact the actual amount of inherent risk present within the reporting company; it is a characteristic

of the accounting system and the personnel who work in that system.

30. **B.** II is correct. Good internal controls at the client company can mitigate the client's control risk. I is wrong. The quantity of work performed by the auditor during the internal control stage of the audit will not impact the actual amount of control risk present within the reporting company. Control risk is a client characteristic that must be assessed by the auditor.

31. **C.** I is correct. The assessments of inherent and control risk will vary inversely with the level of detection risk that is considered to be acceptable. If inherent risk and control risk are both estimated as being high for a particular account or assertion, detection risk must be reduced to a level where overall audit risk is at an acceptable level. Only then would the auditor be able to provide reasonable assurance that the financial statements are in conformity with the reporting framework. II is correct. As a result of lowering detection risk, more substantive testing and more evidence gathering will be needed.

32. **C.** I is correct. The amount and type of evidence that is gathered by the auditor will influence the level of detection risk. More evidence will reduce the detection risk as will gathering evidence of a better quality. II and III are wrong. Inherent risk and control risk are company characteristics that are assessed by the auditor. They are not affected by the work performed by the auditor.

33. **D.** II is correct. The auditor's decision to reduce detection risk ultimately reduces overall audit risk. I is wrong. An auditor cannot reduce control risk. An auditor can only assess control risk. III is wrong. An auditor cannot reduce inherent risk. An auditor can only assess inherent risk.

34. **A.** I is correct. Testing that uses more sophisticated techniques or more experienced auditors will, indeed, generate evidence that is considered of a better quality. II is wrong. Evidence gathered closer to the end of the year will be considered superior to evidence obtained at an earlier point in time. This is because the auditor is rendering an opinion on the year-end balances, not balances at earlier times during the year. Therefore, evidence gathered at year-end is considered better evidence to support the auditor's opinion of year-end balances.

35. **A.** Overall audit risk is made up of the risk of material misstatement and detection risk. The risk of material misstatement is itself comprised of two separate risks, inherent risk and control risk. When the assessed level of control risk is increased, the risk of material misstatement also increases, and detection risk must be decreased to achieve an overall audit risk level that is substantially the same as the planned audit risk level. Therefore, B, C, and D are wrong.

36. **C.** Inherent risk is the susceptibility of a material misstatement, assuming there are no related controls. A is wrong. The auditor does not assess inherent risk in order to assist the internal auditor's communications to the audit committee. B is wrong. The risk that the internal control system will not detect a material misstatement of a financial statement assertion is known as control risk. D is wrong. The risk that the audit procedures implemented will not detect a material misstatement of a financial statement assertion is known as nonsampling risk.

37. **C.** I is correct. There is an inverse relationship between detection risk and the auditor's assessment of inherent risk. Detection risk needs to be lowered when inherent risk is assessed as high. The result of assessing inherent and control risk as high is that more substantive tests would be needed. II is correct. There is an inverse relationship between detection risk and the auditor's assessment of control risk. Detection risk needs to be lowered when control risk is assessed as high. The result is that more substantive tests would be needed. Detection risk has an inverse relationship with both inherent risk and control risk. If control risk and inherent risk are assessed as high, detection risk needs to be lowered. By lowering detection risk, the auditor would be attempting to be more careful than usual.

38. **B.** II is correct. Overstating ending inventory by changing count tags is an example of fraudulent financial reporting. I is wrong. Stealing assets is an example of misappropriation.

There are two types of fraud, fraudulent financial reporting and misappropriation. If the question asks about one type, make sure you don't choose the other. While both I and II are examples of fraud, the question asks which one is fraudulent financial reporting.

39. **B.** II is correct. The recording of false sales prior to year-end to help reach company sales forecasts is an example of fraudulent financial reporting. I is wrong. The treasurer stealing cash is fraud, but

stealing cash is an example of misappropriation of assets, not fraudulent financial reporting.

40. **A.** I is correct. An error is an unintentional mistake, whereas fraud is an intentional action that distorts the financial statements. The problem here with the application of the accounting principle seems to be unintentional and could have been caused by an accident. II is wrong. Fraud would be an intentional rather than unintentional misstatement. Knowledge of the intention behind the misstatement would be necessary to distinguish between an error and an act of fraud.

41. **B.** I, II, and III are all correct. Special consideration must be given to the possibility that fraud exists during the auditor's assessment of inherent risk and control risk and during the auditor's substantive testing.

42. **C.** I is correct. Unauthorized client transactions are a fraud risk factor. If the auditor finds unauthorized client transactions and other fraud risk factors, the auditor would raise the assessment of inherent risk, and, as a result, the auditor would possibly have to lower detection risk. II is correct. Unusual client delays is a fraud risk factor. If the client takes a significant amount of time responding to auditor inquiries, the auditor would have to increase the assessment of inherent risk and possibly have to lower detection risk. Fraud risk factors are situations or events that increase the possibility that fraud has occurred. Fraud may not be present, but the chances are elevated. Fraud risk factors include missing documents, unauthorized transactions, and unusual delays. If these factors are encountered, the auditor will probably have to do more extensive substantive procedures or more specialized testing.

43. **A.** I is correct. Whenever optimistic earnings forecasts are issued, company officials may feel pressure to achieve those projections. If net income does not materialize as anticipated, the company may revert to fraudulent financial reporting (such as the recording of false sales) to reach the amounts that were promised. II is wrong. The auditor expects all requests for documents to be delivered completely and timely; if not, this would be a fraud risk factor.

44. **A.** I is correct. The threat of bankruptcy is a fraud risk factor. The company may be engaging in hiding assets from creditors or stealing assets so that the assets won't become part of a bankruptcy estate. Another fraud risk factor in bankruptcy is fraudulent financial reporting to make the company's balance sheet appear better. II is wrong. The presence,

not the absence, of significant competition would represent a fraud risk factor.

45. **C.** I is correct. The auditor would test for improper revenue recognition due to fraud by possibly comparing sales volume with production capacity. An excess of sales over production capacity may be indicative of the recording of fictitious sales. II is correct. The auditor would test overstatement of revenue by comparing sales in one month with sales returns in the following month. Larger than average sales in one month compared to larger than average sales returns in the following month would be an indication of overstating revenue.

46. **C.** I and II are correct. The fraud triangle is comprised of three legs: (1) the incentive or pressure to commit fraud, (2) the opportunity to commit fraud, and (3) the ability to rationalize fraud. The more legs of the fraud triangle that are present in a given situation, the greater the risk of fraud.

47. **D.** II is correct. The decision to go public could easily result in additional pressure to commit fraudulent financial reporting in order to attract investors and receive the highest possible IPO price. III is correct. Whenever optimistic earnings forecasts are issued, company officials may feel pressure to achieve those projections. If net income does not materialize as anticipated, the company may resort to fraudulent financial reporting (such as the recording of false sales) to reach the amounts that were promised. I is wrong. Large amounts of cash would be a fraud risk factor regarding misappropriation, not fraudulent financial reporting.

48. **C.** I is correct. Significant, unusual, or highly complex transactions occurring near the end of the year provide an opportunity to commit fraudulent financial reporting. If determined, the auditor would likely reduce detection risk as a result and examine these transactions more carefully. II is correct. Having a number of reported balances based on significant estimations provides an opportunity to commit fraudulent financial reporting. If determined, the auditor would likely raise the assessed level of inherent risk. This doesn't mean that there is fraud, but management may be biased with the estimates, and the financial statements could be misstated as a result. The auditor would likely reduce detection risk as a result.

49. **D.** I is wrong. High turnover of senior management would create an opportunity to commit fraudulent financial reporting but would not be an incentive. Incentives to commit fraudulent financial reporting

would come from members of management or other employees facing pressures that make fraud more likely. For example, if employees are scheduled to receive bonuses based on the stock price or reported net income, they have an incentive to make the company results look especially good. Also, employees may have their own personal financial pressures. II is wrong. Unreasonable demands on the independent auditor is a fraud risk factor that indicates that individuals within the company have the attitude needed to commit fraud and are in a position to rationalize such false reporting. Unreasonable demands placed upon the auditor are not an incentive to commit fraudulent reporting.

50. **A.** I is correct. Declining demand and a shrinking industry result in lower sales and would add to the pressure or incentive to commit fraudulent financial reporting. II is correct. Negative cash flows from operations could also create pressure to commit fraudulent financial reporting. Inability to generate cash flows from operations while somehow reporting substantial earnings growth would be a fraud risk factor for fraudulent financial reporting. III is correct. If the company were seeking debt financing, higher interest rates would be charged if the company were shown to have a high risk for default. The incentive for fraudulent financial reporting would be increased in order to make the company look like a better credit risk.

51. **C.** I is correct. Insider buying of company shares would NOT heighten the auditor's concern about fraudulent financial reporting. Insider selling is more likely to be viewed as a fraud risk factor. III is correct. An auditor would expect management to be dominated by several top executives. If management were dominated by only one or two top executives, that could be a fraud risk factor as anytime one person can override internal controls, there is opportunity for fraud. IV is correct. Although small high-value inventory items create an opportunity to steal, the question asks about fraudulent financial reporting, not misappropriation of assets. II is wrong. If management placed substantial emphasis on meeting earnings projections, this would be a fraud risk factor relating to pressure to commit fraudulent financial reporting.

52. **D.** I is correct. The best place to start looking for fraud is in the planning stage, where the auditor first brainstorms with the audit team and begins to identify potential fraud and fraud risk factors. II is correct. During the internal control stage, the auditor can identify specific controls that can minimize

the risk from those fraud risk factors previously identified in the planning stage. Brainstorming sessions could continue to reveal fraud risk factors in the internal control stage. III is correct. An auditor will still be looking for fraud even as late as the evidence-gathering stage. Some fraud is very well hidden. The higher up the fraud exists, the more difficult it is for the auditor to detect.

53. **A.** III is correct. An overly complex organization structure involving unusual lines of authority provides an opportunity for fraudulent financial reporting that would heighten the auditor's concern. I is wrong. Large amounts of liquid assets that are easily convertible into cash would heighten an auditor's concern about misappropriation of assets, not about fraudulent financial reporting. II is wrong. Financial management is expected to participate in the selection of accounting principles. Perhaps if nonfinancial management participated in the selection of accounting principles, that might heighten the auditor's concern, but that is not what the question asks.

54. **D.** I is wrong. Although collusion makes fraud more difficult to detect, the audit should be designed to detect material errors and fraud, regardless of the cause. The presence of employee collusion does not change the auditor's responsibility, but it may affect certain audit procedures. II is wrong. An auditor is responsible for designing the audit to provide reasonable assurance of detecting material misstatement. This responsibility is the same regardless of the cause of the misstatement. Management override of controls might explain why a properly planned and executed audit did not result in the discovery of material fraud, but the presence of management override does not change the auditor's responsibility.

55. **C.** The auditor should assess the risk that errors and fraud may cause the financial statements to contain a material misstatement. Based on that assessment, the auditor should design the audit to provide reasonable assurance of detecting material errors and fraud. A, B, and D all contain exclusions that are incorrect.

56. **D.** These two situations are fraud risk factors that would indicate to the independent CPA that there is an incentive for employees or pressure on employees to misappropriate assets. High personal debts and layoffs would make employees feel more pressure to steal from the company to protect their families. As a result, companies sometimes screen

potential employees by asking questions regarding personal credit card debt. A is wrong. An incentive to commit fraudulent financial reporting would involve a company that is about to issue stock or bonds and that is feeling the pressure to "cook the books" for a lower interest rate or higher IPO price. B is wrong. An example of an opportunity to commit misappropriation of assets would be if a company lacked safeguards over assets. An auditor would be concerned about misappropriation if cash was left undeposited or small valuable inventory was within reach of employees without controls in place. C is wrong. An example of an opportunity to commit fraudulent financial reporting would be if management was dominated by one individual who could override all controls and make journal entries to record fake sales.

57. **A.** I is correct. Compensation levels inconsistent with expectations would relate to incentive or perhaps even rationalization to steal. II is wrong. Inadequate segregation of duties provides the opportunity for such theft. Inadequate segregation of duties is neither an incentive nor a pressure but an opportunity. Mandatory vacations can sometimes prevent or detect theft brought about by inadequate segregation of duties.

58. **C.** I is correct. If employees are not forced to take vacations, opportunity exists within a company for the misappropriation of assets. Mandatory vacation time would both prevent and detect theft, since less opportunity would exist if the individual already knows that his or her job will be performed by another individual during vacation. Without mandatory vacation policies, the auditor will probably assess inherent risk as high and have to perform additional substantive testing in order to reduce overall audit risk to the level viewed as acceptable. II is correct. If management lacks understanding of the IT used in the company, the auditor would assess inherent risk as high. For both of these situations, additional testing could include use of audit team members with specialized skills, reliance on more physical inspection, testing closer to the end of the fiscal year, and reliance on more sources of information outside of the reporting company.

59. **A.** I is correct. Fraudulent financial reporting refers to the purposeful manipulation of a company's financial statements. An auditor should be aware that company officials might be tempted to enter misstatements into the financial records to achieve the desired result. This type of purposeful manipulation of a company's financial statements is

sometimes referred to as "cooking the books" and is known on the CPA Exam as fraudulent financial reporting. II is wrong. A company would intentionally manipulate the financial statements to decrease the debt-to-equity ratio, not to increase it.

60. **D.** I is wrong. Even if the brainstorming sessions reveal no fraud risk factors, the auditor is still required to inquire regarding management's knowledge of actual or potential fraud. The auditor would inquire how management communicates to employees its views on acceptable business practices and whether there are any particular business segments for which a risk of fraud may be more likely to exist. II is wrong. Even if the brainstorming sessions reveal no fraud risk factors, the auditor is still required to inquire regarding management's programs to mitigate fraud risk.

61. **C.** I is correct. In every audit, regardless of the outcome of the brainstorming sessions, revenue recognition is an area considered high risk for fraud. The auditor fears that due to pressures and opportunities, false sales are being recorded or sales are being recorded prior to the earnings process being complete. Since sales have the biggest impact on the income statement, revenue recognition is always an area of concern for an auditor, and analytical procedures would help in this area. The auditor would also test journal entries and inquire about any unusual entries that were made at the end of the year. II is correct. In every audit, regardless of the outcome of the brainstorming sessions, management override of controls is a risk factor for fraudulent financial reporting. The auditor fears that top management could be making adjustments to the financial records that would create misstatements in order to make the company appear more profitable. An auditor would test journal entries for reasonableness and inquire about unusual entries made at year-end.

62. **C.** The easiest way for a client to overstate net income is to overstate ending inventory. An overstated ending inventory figure makes cost of goods sold lower than it should be. If cost of goods sold is lower than it should be, gross profit is immediately overstated. In the example that follows, sales are assumed to be $400. Notice how ending inventory being overstated by $20 leads to an overstatement of gross profit. An overstatement of gross profit would then result in an overstatement of net income.

	Correct Amount	Ending Inventory Overstated by $20
Beginning inventory	$0	$0
Purchases	$150	$150
Cost of goods available for sale	$150	$150
Less ending inventory	**$30**	**$50**
Cost of goods sold	**$120**	**$100**
Sales	$400	$400
Less cost of goods sold	**$120**	**$100**
Gross profit	**$280**	**$300**

63. **B.** II is correct. Auditors will test journal entries for reasonableness especially where estimates were used in place of actual figures. I is wrong. Making a legal determination of whether fraud occurred would require a legal license, an attorney, and a judge. CPAs do not normally possess such accreditation.

64. **C.** I is correct. Analytical procedures are based on the fact that plausible relationships among data may reasonably be expected to exist and continue in the absence of known conditions to the contrary—for example, payroll and payroll tax expense. If payroll increases from Year 1 to Year 2, payroll tax expense should increase also. If payroll increases and payroll tax expense declines, the auditor would want to know why. It could be that the company is behind on the payroll taxes. If so, the auditor would look for a liability on the balance sheet for unpaid payroll taxes. If no such liability exists, the client would be hiding debts. II is correct. Analytical procedures can sometimes substitute for tests of certain balances and transactions. In the case of bonds payable and interest expense, the auditor can perform analytical procedures to compare the expected amount of interest expense to the client's reported figure. In this way, an auditor can sometimes rely on analytical procedures in the evidence-gathering stage of an audit rather than performing a substantive test.

65. **D.** I is wrong. Analytical procedures are useful to detect unusual relationships. Analytical procedures consist of evaluations of financial information made by a study of expected relationships among both financial and nonfinancial data. An auditor could rely on a five-year sales trend to estimate sales for Year 6. Plausible relationships among data may reasonably be expected to exist and continue in the absence of known conditions to the contrary. II is wrong. If the auditor knows the number of employees and the average hourly wage, payroll figures can be estimated and then compared to the client-reported figure for reasonableness.

66. **D.** I is wrong. Analytical procedures are mandatory in the overall review stage (final moments) of the audit. II is wrong. Analytical procedures are mandatory in the planning stage of the audit. The only stage of the audit that analytical procedures are not likely to be done at all is the internal control stage, because the internal control stage does not involve numbers.

67. **D.** I is wrong. An auditor of a nonissuer is required to follow Statements on Auditing Standards and should be able to justify any departures. II is wrong. Lack of familiarity with a Statement on Auditing Standards is not a valid reason for departing from its guidance. On rare occasions, auditors may depart from an SAS but must be able to justify the departure.

Chapter 3: Understanding and Testing of Internal Control

68. **D.** I is wrong. The control environment does not relate to management's ability to foresee problems. The control environment relates to the tone at the top of an organization. Top management is charged with communicating and demonstrating ethical behavior, and there should be a code of ethics for top management. Those responsible for governance and management of the organization should demonstrate a commitment to ethics by example. II is wrong. The control activities component of internal control refers to safeguarding assets and segregation of duties. Management's ability to foresee problems and take steps to prevent problems describes the risk assessment component of internal control, not the control environment or the control activities.

69. **B.** II is correct. Internal controls of all of a reporting entity's operating units and business functions are a primary concern of the entity's management and those charged with governance, such as the audit committee and the board of directors. All of internal control is relevant to the entity, its operating units, and its business functions. I is wrong. While all of internal control is relevant to the entity, not all of a company's internal controls may be relevant to a financial statement audit. The independent auditor is interested in those controls that relate to financial statement assertions.

70. **A.** I is correct. An auditor's primary consideration in evaluating controls is whether specific controls affect the account balances on the client's financial statements, since ultimately the auditor must render an opinion on whether the financial statements are fairly presented. II is wrong. Operational controls are relevant to the entity, its operating units, and its business functions. Operational controls are not a primary concern of the independent auditor. The auditor is only concerned with controls that affect the financial statements.

71. **C.** III is correct. Control activities relate to segregation of duties and safeguarding assets. I is wrong. The control environment is the tone at the top of the organization charged with communicating and demonstrating ethical behavior. II is wrong. Risk assessment (as one of the five components of internal control) relates to the company's ability to foresee problems and take steps to prevent problems.

72. **A.** I is correct. Segregation of duties is tested by making sure that one person is not performing incompatible functions. Testing for segregation of duties does not involve paperwork or even an audit trail. An auditor will observe, inquire, and inspect to test for segregation of duties. II is wrong. This question is about internal control, and, like any other question on internal control, any answer choice to an internal control question that mentions "analytical procedures" is the wrong answer. Analytical procedures are not performed in the internal control stage of the audit. III is wrong. Inspecting and recalculating are substantive tests. The question is about internal control; with internal control questions, an answer choice that involves a substantive test is probably wrong.

73. **C.** I is correct. In the internal control stage, an independent auditor searches for control activities to determine whether the opportunities to allow any person to both perpetrate and conceal fraud are minimized. This choice relates to segregation of duties. If duties are properly segregated, the same person would not be able to both steal from the company and cover it up in the accounting records. II is correct. Control activities should be in place to safeguard assets. The auditor observes to make sure safeguards are in place. The auditor would raise his or her assessment of control risk should these safeguards not be found.

74. **B.** II is correct. Ongoing monitoring involves assessing the design and operation of controls on a timely basis and taking necessary corrective actions. Such an approach may be followed in reviewing one particular cycle at a time, the payroll cycle or purchasing cycle. I is wrong. Monitoring of internal control is internal, not external, so the annual audit is not considered a monitoring engagement of the client's internal controls.

75. **C.** I is correct. The monitoring component of internal control involves assessing the design and operation of controls on a timely basis and taking necessary corrective actions. The auditor looks to see if monitoring of internal control is a priority of the client company because this will impact the auditor's assessment of control risk. II is correct. The monitoring component of internal control involves assessing the design and operation of controls on a timely basis and taking necessary corrective actions. Monitoring is an internal function often performed by the client's internal audit department.

76. **B.** II is correct. Control group is not one of the five components of internal control. The control group is involved in internal control in an IT environment but is not a component of overall internal control. III is correct. Control risk is not one of the five components of internal control. Control risk is assessed by the auditor after coming to an understanding of all five components of internal control. The five components of internal control are control environment, risk assessment, control activities, information and communication, and monitoring.

77. **D.** I is correct. When management is dominated by one individual who is also a shareholder, there may be an opportunity for management to override control procedures. II is correct. Management's emphasis on meeting projected profit goals would significantly influence an entity's control environment when a significant portion of management compensation is represented by stock options, because management would then have a personal interest that might be at odds with accurate financial reporting. III is wrong. If those charged with governance were active in overseeing the entity's financial reporting policies, it would be less likely that management's attitude toward aggressive financial reporting would significantly influence an entity's control environment.

78. **C.** I and II are correct. As part of gaining an understanding of internal control, the auditor needs to know both the design of the system and whether the system has been put in place. The client could have designed a system of controls, described them in detail to the auditor, but never implemented them.

As a next step, the auditor may decide to test controls to see if the controls that have been designed and implemented are functioning as designed to detect and prevent material misstatements.

79. **B.** II is correct. As part of gaining an understanding of internal control, the auditor needs to know the design of the client's system and whether the controls have been placed into operation. I is wrong. The auditor is not required to obtain knowledge about the operating effectiveness of controls. Operating effectiveness of the client's internal controls is evaluated later, and only for those controls on which the auditor plans to rely.

80. **A.** I is correct. The ultimate purpose of assessing control risk is to determine the nature, extent, and timing of further audit procedures. II is wrong. While recommendations would ordinarily be made if appropriate, the primary reason for the auditor to assess control risk is to evaluate the risk of financial statement misstatement.

81. **A.** I is correct. An auditor can assess control risk as low for inventory or any other account balance if the auditor finds an internal control that is relevant and functioning as designed. II is wrong. If control risk is assessed as low, less substantive testing than planned would be performed, not more.

82. **B.** II is correct. When the auditor chooses the substantive approach, carefully designed substantive tests will substitute for tests of controls to gather sufficient competent evidence to support the opinion. I is wrong. When the auditor chooses the substantive approach, tests of controls are NOT performed. The auditor chooses the substantive approach when internal controls are poor or no time savings would come from testing controls.

83. **C.** I is correct. An auditor would choose to use the combined approach to further audit procedures if, based on the auditor's assessment of internal control, the auditor thinks the controls are in place. II is correct. An auditor would choose to use the combined approach to further audit procedures if, based on the auditor's assessment of internal control, the auditor thinks the controls are in place and testing controls could reduce substantive procedures.

84. **B.** II is correct. After gaining and documenting an understanding of the components of internal control, the auditor should make a preliminary assessment of control risk. If the auditor's investigation indicates that internal control is probably weak, the auditor should emphasize substantive testing rather than test of controls. I is wrong. If internal control is considered weak, the amount of substantive testing (performed to decrease detection risk) will be increased, not reduced. Therefore, if the auditor feels that controls are weak, nothing can be gained by testing the controls further. Additional testing of controls is carried out only if the overall amount of audit testing is likely to be reduced.

85. **C.** I is correct. In developing a questionnaire for a particular system or activity, the auditor considers (1) the general control activities that are applicable, and (2) specific control activities that should be utilized in this system. Then, for each of these anticipated controls, the auditor simply asks a question to see if the activity is actually present in the system. Thus, a "yes" answer means the expected control is included in the design whereas a "no" points up a potential problem. Both the strengths and weaknesses can be easily noted even by an inexperienced auditor. II is correct. Using a flowchart to identify strengths and weaknesses takes a certain amount of experience and expertise compared to a questionnaire, which is easier to use to identify internal control strengths and weaknesses. Because the auditor must gain an understanding of the five components of internal control, documentation is especially important to demonstrate that GAAS have been followed. The auditor can use any of several methods (such as a questionnaire, a flowchart, or a memorandum) to document the understanding of these components that is achieved.

86. **A.** I is correct. An auditor's flowchart of the accounting system is a diagrammatic representation that shows the auditor's understanding of the system. The auditor must document his or her understanding of the system, and the use of a flowchart is one of several alternatives to comply. II is wrong. While an auditor's flowchart of the accounting system is a diagrammatic representation that shows the auditor's understanding of the system, it does not show the auditor's assessment of control risk. Flowcharting aids the auditor's understanding of the system. The auditor's assessment of control risk is based on the auditor's professional judgment and is not documented graphically.

87. **B.** Observation of the activity itself is the auditor's best way to test for segregation of duties. For example, the auditor would observe that the same person is not both collecting cash and recording the collection in the accounting records. A is wrong. An auditor can inquire about segregation of duties, but a good auditor would want more than just

a response, which is why observation would be a better answer than inquiry regarding segregation of duties. C is wrong. Confirmations are not tests of controls; they are substantive tests. D is wrong. Preparing a flowchart or questionnaire is useful to gain an understanding of the system, but once the auditor decides to test the system, he or she needs to look for control activities that can relate to specific assertions and test those control activities if the auditor seeks to rely on those controls.

88. **A.** I is correct. The auditor is interested in discovering the presence of specific control activities that should reduce control risk. For example, if a questionnaire or flowchart shows that an independent party reconciles the cash account each week, that activity (if it is being performed properly) might well reduce the assessment of control risk in this area. II is wrong. Analyzing and confirming are substantive tests, not tests of controls.

89. **A.** I is correct. Testing controls is the auditor's best method to determine if controls are functioning as designed in order to rely on that control and possibly reduce substantive testing. II is wrong. The question asks about testing controls. Controls are tested in the internal control stage, whereas account balances are tested using substantive tests in the evidence-gathering stage, a later stage of the audit. The results of the test of controls would be to determine the nature, timing, and extent of substantive tests that, if carefully designed, can estimate account balances and help accomplish specific audit objectives.

90. **D.** I is wrong. By "further audit procedures," the auditor chooses either the combined approach or the substantive approach. The auditor doesn't know which approach to choose until the assessment of inherent risk is completed. II is wrong for the same reason. If control risk is assessed as high for a particular account or assertion, the substantive approach would be chosen.

91. **C.** I is correct. The external auditor is required to obtain sufficient knowledge of internal control, but he or she is not responsible for establishing, maintaining, and/or monitoring internal control. II is correct. The entity's management is responsible for establishing, maintaining, and monitoring the entity's internal controls, considering whether those controls are operating as intended, and modifying controls as conditions change

92. **C.** I is correct. Manual controls are internal controls performed by people and are more suitable when

judgment and discretion are required, such as when there are large, unusual, or nonrecurring transactions. II is correct for the same reason.

93. **A.** I is correct. When potential misstatements are more difficult to predict, judgment is needed. If judgment is needed, manual controls (humans) are needed rather than computers. Manual controls are internal controls performed by people and are more suitable when judgment and discretion are required, such as when there are large, unusual, or nonrecurring transactions. Such transactions make potential misstatements more difficult to predict. II is wrong. When transactions are high volume and recurring, the auditor expects to find automated controls rather than manual controls.

94. **C.** I is correct. Inherent limitations of internal control are limitations that are built in and cannot be entirely prevented. Collusion among employees is an inherent limitation because even when duties are properly segregated, the risk still exists that two or more individuals could combine to steal from the company. Thus, collusion is a built-in, inherent limitation that cannot entirely be prevented. II is correct. Judgments are made by people. Even well-trained employees with experience are not perfect and can make errors in judgment. Thus, errors in judgment are another inherent limitation of internal control.

95. **A.** I is correct. Management override of controls is an inherent limitation of internal control. An example of an inherent limitation would be if the CEO is the only employee who can request a check with no purchase order. II is wrong. Incompatible duties are internal control weaknesses but not inherent limitations. An inherent limitation is built in and cannot entirely be prevented. Incompatible duties can be corrected and, therefore, are not inherent limitations.

96. **D.** I is correct. In every audit, the audit documentation must contain an indication whether or not the financial statements agree with the accounting records. II is correct. Risk assessment procedures must be performed to assess the risk of material misstatement and to determine whether and to what extent further audit procedures are necessary. Risk assessment procedures are performed during the assessment of inherent risk and control risk. III is wrong. Tests of the operating effectiveness of controls are performed only when the auditor's risk assessment is based on the assumption that controls

are operating effectively or when substantive procedures alone are insufficient.

97. B. When an auditor assesses control risk at the maximum level, the assessment should be documented and the auditor should make decisions to potentially perform more substantive procedures. A is wrong. When the auditor assesses control risk at the maximum, the auditor would perform more substantive tests, not fewer. C is wrong. The documentation would not be more extensive when control risk is assessed at the maximum; the documentation would have to be more detailed when control risk is assessed below the maximum to explain why the assessment is lower than the maximum. The extra documentation would pertain to the controls that were found and how they were tested. D is wrong. Tests of controls are not performed in a GAAS audit unless the auditor believes that control risk is below the maximum.

98. C. I is correct. Tests of the operating effectiveness of controls are performed only when the auditor's risk assessment is based on the assumption that controls are operating effectively. II is correct. Tests of the operating effectiveness of controls are performed when substantive procedures alone are insufficient, such as when there is no audit trail in an IT environment.

Chapter 4: Audit Documentation, Related-Party Transactions, and Subsequent Events

99. C. I is correct. The current file is maintained to hold, organize, and document all of the evidence gathered so that the auditor can support this year's audit opinion. II is correct. A working trial balance is meant to resemble the financial statements without footnotes and includes additional columns for reclassifications and adjustments. A working trial balance pertains only to this year's audit, so it belongs in the current file.

100. A. I is correct. The permanent file is used to store relevant information that would NOT be expected to change significantly from year to year. Such items as contracts, organization charts, chart of account numbers, bond indentures, and the company charter should be kept in the permanent file for reference purposes. II is wrong. The audit plan and management representation letter pertain to the current year audit and should be stored in the current file, not the permanent file.

101. D. Debt agreements are not expected to change from year to year; therefore, they should be stored in the permanent file. A is wrong. Lead schedules are totals of the client's various accounts that are transferred to the working trial balance. Both the working trial balance and the lead schedule are stored in the current file. B and C are wrong. Attorney's letters and bank statements pertain to the current year audit and should be stored in the current file.

102. D. III is correct. The lead schedules relate to the current year opinion and are stored in the current file, not the permanent file. Lead schedules are totals of the client's various accounts that are transferred to the working trial balance. IV is correct. The working trial balance relates to the current year opinion and is stored in the current file, not the permanent file. The working trial balance contains all of the client's account balances on a single spreadsheet, with additional columns set up for adjustments and reclassifications. I and II are wrong. Bond indenture agreements and lease agreements are ongoing and would be stored in the permanent file, since they relate to more than just the current year audit. Bond indentures contain the stated rate of interest on the bond, the term of the debt agreement, and any covenants, such as the company being required to maintain a current ratio above 1:1 or the bonds being due immediately.

103. B. After the documentation completion date, no documents may be deleted. Even "auditor's professional judgment" is not an acceptable excuse for deletion of audit documentation once the documentation completion date has passed. Documents can always be added, but any documents that have been added must be noted. Prior to the documentation completion date, the auditor may change, delete, or discard superseded documents.

104. C. I is correct. Factors affecting the auditor's judgment regarding audit documentation about the quantity, type, and content of the auditor's working papers for a particular engagement include the type of audit report issued, the condition of the client's records, and the assessed level of control risk. II is correct. Factors affecting the auditor's judgment regarding audit documentation about the quantity, type, and content of the auditor's working papers for a particular engagement include the nature of the engagement and the type of report issued.

105. A. All audit documentation (working papers) is the property of the independent auditor and is not intended to assist the company's management. B and C are wrong. Audit documentation assists the auditor in both the planning and the supervision of the audit. D is wrong. Audit documentation serves to provide the principal support for the auditor's opinion. Audit working papers can assist the audit team in proving that the audit was conducted in accordance with professional standards.

106. **A.** I is correct. The audit procedures directed toward identifying related-party transactions should include considering whether transactions are occurring but are not given proper accounting recognition. II is wrong. If proper disclosures are made, related-party transactions are not required to be recorded on terms equivalent to arm's-length transactions. The auditor's biggest fear with related-party transactions is not about the terms but rather about disclosure. The auditor fears that the client is going to disguise a related-party transaction and make it appear as if it were arm's-length.

107. **B.** II is correct. Related parties sometimes guarantee the debts of affiliates; therefore, reviewing confirmations of loans receivable and payable for indications of loan guarantees would assist the auditor in identifying related-party transactions not previously disclosed. I is wrong. Undisclosed related-party transactions tend to be nonrecurring rather than recurring.

108. **D.** Auditors' biggest fear with regard to related-party transactions is that related-party transactions are occurring but are not given proper accounting recognition. The auditor is concerned that the client is recording the related-party transaction as if it were an arm's-length transaction. With related-party transactions, the auditor is primary interested in disclosure. A is wrong. The client could borrow or lend to a related-party at an interest rate different from the market rate provided it is disclosed as a related-party transaction. B is wrong. The client could buy or sell property from related parties for amounts different from fair value provided it is disclosed as a related party transaction. C is wrong. The client can make a loan to a related party with no set repayment schedule as long as it is disclosed as a related-party transaction.

109. **D.** II is correct. A loan with no maturity date would be more likely to suggest a related-party transaction because such terms are not typical. III is correct. A loan made by the client with an extremely low interest rate would be evidence of a related-party loan because again the terms are not typical. I is wrong.

Variable rate loans are very common and would not necessarily indicate the existence of a related-party transaction.

110. **D.** I is wrong. Selling any asset that has been held for an extended length of time for an amount different from book value is not unusual and would not necessarily indicate the presence of a related-party transaction. II is wrong. If the land had been sold for an amount different from its fair market value or if the payment terms had been unusual, the auditor would probably want to investigate further the possibility of a related-party sale that would need to be disclosed. Remember, the terms don't really matter; the primary auditor concern is that it is disclosed as a related-party transaction.

111. **D.** I is incorrect. Comparing the financial statements being reported on with those of the prior period is not a very good source of subsequent event information. II is incorrect. Changes in accounting personnel at any time would probably not result in any subsequent-event financial statement adjustment or disclosure.

112. **C.** If the auditor believes that the financial statements need to be revised to reflect a subsequent event and management does not make the revision, the auditor should express a qualified or adverse opinion, since the issue is known to the auditor to be GAAP related. A is wrong. If the auditor believes that the financial statements need to be revised to reflect a subsequent event and management does not make the revision, an unmodified opinion would not be appropriate; the opinion would need to be modified. Simply adding an other-matters paragraph would not be a valid substitute for a qualified or adverse opinion in this case. B is wrong. In this situation, a disclaimer would not be appropriate. Disclaimers are appropriate only in situations where an auditor lacks evidence to support an opinion. This scenario relates to evidence being present, not evidence missing. D is wrong. While a qualified opinion may be appropriate, an unmodified opinion would not be, since the auditor does not agree with management regarding revision of the financial statements. The auditor wants the financial statements revised in order to be fairly presented.

113. **A.** I is correct. The auditor has an active responsibility to make continuing inquiries between the date of the financial statements and the date of the auditor's report. II is wrong. The auditor has no active responsibility to make continuing inquiries between the date of the auditor's report and the

date on which the report is submitted. The auditor's active responsibility stops on the date of the auditor's report.

114. **C.** The auditor has no active responsibility to make continuing inquiries between the date of the auditor's report and the date on which the report is submitted. The auditor's active responsibility stops on the date of the auditor's report. A and B are wrong. The auditor has an active responsibility to make continuing inquiries between the date of the financial statements and the date of the auditor's report, which is the date on which sufficient appropriate audit evidence has been obtained. D is wrong. The auditor has no active responsibility to make continuing inquiries after the date of the auditor's report.

Chapter 5: Audit Reporting

115. **D.** The paragraphs found in a standard unmodified audit report for a nonissuer are introductory paragraph, management's responsibility paragraph, auditor's responsibility paragraph, and opinion paragraph. There is no more "scope" paragraph.

116. **B.** There are four paragraphs in a standard unmodified audit report: introductory paragraph, management's responsibility paragraph, auditor's responsibility paragraph, and opinion paragraph.

117. **D.** There are four paragraphs in a standard unmodified audit report and should appear in this order: introductory paragraph, management's responsibility paragraph, auditor's responsibility paragraph, and opinion paragraph. There is no more "scope" paragraph in an audit report.

118. **D.** The audit report does not state that the auditor evaluated the overall internal control. The correct statement is "In making those risk assessments, the auditor considers internal control relevant to the entity's preparation and fair presentation of the financial statements in order to design audit procedures that are appropriate in the circumstances, but not for the purpose of expressing an opinion on the effectiveness of the entity's internal control."

119. **B.** II is correct. In the opinion paragraph, the auditor uses the terms *present fairly* and *US GAAP*. I is wrong. It is in the auditor's responsibility paragraph, not the opinion paragraph, that the auditor mentions assessing the accounting principles and evaluating significant accounting estimates used by the reporting entity.

120. **C.** I is correct. The auditor's standard report implies that the auditor is satisfied that the comparability of financial statements between periods has not been materially affected by changes in accounting principles. II is correct. The auditor's standard report implies that the auditor is satisfied that the comparability of financial statements between periods has not been materially affected by changes in accounting principles and that such principles have been applied consistently between or among periods. Since the auditor has gathered sufficient evidence about consistency, no reference need be made in the report.

121. **C.** I is correct. An emphasis-of-matter paragraph is included in the auditor's report when required by GAAS. The emphasis-of-matter paragraph is required when the auditor concludes that there is substantial doubt about an entity's ability to continue as a going concern or when there is a justified change in accounting principles that has a material effect on the entity's financial statements. II is correct. An emphasis-of-matter paragraph is included in the auditor's report at the auditor's discretion anytime the auditor wants to emphasize a matter, possibly regarding uncertainty or related-party transactions.

122. **B.** II is correct. An inclusion of an emphasis-of-matter paragraph in the auditor's report does not affect the auditor's opinion. The auditor's opinion is still unmodified. I is wrong. An inclusion of an emphasis-of-matter paragraph in the auditor's report is used when referring to a matter that is appropriately presented in the financial statements.

123. **D.** I is wrong. The emphasis-of-matter paragraph should be placed after the opinion paragraph. The auditor can always emphasize a matter in connection with a set of financial statements by adding a paragraph after the opinion paragraph. This paragraph allows the auditor to draw the reader's attention to any specific information that might be deemed essential. II is wrong. The emphasis paragraph should state that the auditor's opinion is not modified.

124. **C.** I is correct. An other-matters paragraph is required when the auditor's report needs to be restricted. The restriction is placed in an other-matters paragraph immediately following any emphasis paragraph (after the opinion). II is correct. The auditor is always permitted to add an other-matters paragraph. Unlike the emphasis-of-matter paragraph, the other-matters paragraph is used to

describe something that is not already presented or disclosed in the financial statements and that is relevant to the user's understanding of the audit.

125. **A.** II and III are correct. Other-matters paragraphs refer to matters other than those presented or disclosed in the financial statements that are relevant to the user's understanding of the auditor's responsibilities. I is wrong. Other-matters paragraphs are relevant to the user's understanding of the audit, not to the user's understanding of the financial statements. The other-matters paragraph generally describes matters other than those presented or disclosed in the financial statements.

126. **A.** I is correct. An auditor would express an unmodified opinion with an emphasis-of-matter paragraph added to the auditor's report for a justified change in accounting principle. The emphasis-of-matter paragraph should be placed after the opinion paragraph. II is wrong. A material weakness must be reported to management and those charged with governance, but it would not be disclosed in an emphasis-of-matter paragraph added to an otherwise unmodified opinion.

127. **C.** I is correct. The preparation and fair presentation of the financial statements requires identification of the applicable financial reporting framework. II is correct. The preparation and fair presentation of the financial statements also requires an adequate description of the framework in the financial statements. While US GAAP is the likely framework, other frameworks are acceptable, such as IFRS.

128. **D.** I is wrong. Twelve months is not mentioned in the going concern paragraph, nor is any other amount of time. II is wrong. Reasonable period of time is not expressed in the emphasis-of-matter paragraph either. The two required phrases in an emphasis-of-matter paragraph relating to going concern are "reasonable doubt" and "going concern."

129. **D.** An auditor would generally issue an unmodified audit opinion without an emphasis-of-matter paragraph or other-matters paragraph when the auditor decides to make reference to the audit of a component auditor as a basis, in part, for the auditor's opinion. The auditor would modify his or her report but would not add a paragraph. The reference to the other auditor would be in the auditor's responsibility paragraph and opinion paragraph.

130. **B.** II is correct. The introductory paragraph does not change whether the auditor divides responsibility or assumes responsibility for the component auditor. I is wrong. In a division of responsibility, the group auditor would specify the amount of assets and revenues audited by the other firm (magnitude). This reference would be made in the auditor's responsibility paragraph.

131. **C.** I is correct. The auditor's report should include a reference to the country of origin of the auditing standards that the auditor followed in performing the audit. If US GAAS was followed in conducting the audit, the report should so indicate by mentioning the country as well as the standards. II is correct. The auditor's report should include a reference to the country of origin of the accounting principles used to prepare the financial statements. If US GAAP was used to prepare the financial statements, the report should mention the country as well as the standards.

132. **C.** I is correct. Change in useful life of an asset is a change in estimate, handled prospectively. Since the change in useful life is not considered a change in accounting principle, there is no consistency issue, so an unmodified opinion is proper. II is correct. Change in depreciation method is considered a change in principle, inseparable from a change in estimate, and is handled prospectively as a change in estimate. Since it is not considered a change in principle, consistency is not an issue; therefore, an unmodified opinion is proper.

133. **D.** Neither I nor II is correct. The principal may decide that the problem encountered by the other auditor is material to the consolidated statements. If that decision is made, a qualified opinion should be rendered by the principal. However, a problem that was material to a portion of the statements may not necessarily be material to the consolidated statements as a whole. The principal is not required to issue a qualified opinion. The auditor's professional judgment would be the final determinate.

134. **B.** II is correct. If the previous accounting principle was NOT in conformity with GAAP, the emphasis-of-matter paragraph would still be required. I is wrong. When a client changes an accounting principle that has a material effect on the financial statements but the auditor concurs with the change, an emphasis-of-matter paragraph would be required, but it would not need to go before the opinion. Rather, it would likely be placed after the opinion, since the opinion is still unmodified.

135. **A.** I is correct. When an auditor qualifies an opinion because of a scope limitation, the wording in

the opinion paragraph should indicate that the qualification pertains to the possible impact on the financial statements. II is wrong. When an auditor qualifies an opinion because of a scope limitation, the wording in the opinion paragraph should indicate that the qualification pertains to the scope limitation itself. The scope limitation is described in an additional paragraph, known as the basis for qualified opinion paragraph.

136. **A.** I is correct. A change in depreciation method is considered a change in accounting estimate and is accounted for prospectively. It does not affect comparability, so consistency would not be addressed in the report. II is wrong. Consistency would be a concern and need to be expressed with the use of an emphasis-of-matter paragraph when the previous accounting principle was not GAAP, because a change in accounting principle affects comparability.

137. **B.** If a company issues financial statements that purport to present financial position and results of operations but omit the related statement of cash flows, the auditor will normally conclude that the omission requires qualification of the opinion. A and C are wrong. The statement of cash flows is a required financial statement. Omitting the statement of cash flows would be an example of financial statements that are less than "fairly presented"; therefore, an unmodified opinion would not be allowed even with an emphasis paragraph. D is wrong. Disclaimers of opinion are not rendered when the financial statements are less than "fairly presented." Disclaimers are only rendered when evidence to support an opinion is lacking.

138. **B.** II is correct. The opinion paragraph in an adverse opinion should state that, in the auditor's opinion, because of the significance of the matters described in the basis for adverse opinion paragraph, the financial statements are not presented fairly. I is wrong. When an auditor expresses an adverse opinion, the opinion paragraph should not include the substantive reasons for the financial statements being misleading. The rationale for the adverse opinion should be found in an additional paragraph called the basis for adverse opinion paragraph.

139. **C.** I is correct. Inadequate disclosure is a GAAP problem. GAAP problems result in audit opinions that are qualified or adverse if not unmodified. II is correct. A change in accounting principle is a GAAP issue also resulting in an audit opinion that is qualified or adverse if not unmodified. Disclaimer is only

for GAAS-related issues, and the lack of evidence would have to be rather extreme.

140. **D.** If an auditor finds misstatements that are material but not pervasive, a qualified opinion is expressed. A is wrong. If an auditor finds misstatements that are material, the auditor would likely not issue an unmodified (clean) opinion but rather a qualified opinion. B is wrong. For an adverse opinion to be expressed, the misstatements would likely be pervasive (widespread) as well as material. C is wrong. A disclaimer would not be appropriate for a material misstatement. Disclaimers are issued for a lack of evidence.

141. **C.** When an auditor expresses a qualified opinion due to a material misstatement of the financial statements, the auditor's responsibility paragraph should be amended to state that the auditor believes that the audit evidence obtained is sufficient and appropriate to provide a basis for the auditor's qualified opinion.

142. **B.** II is correct. Consistent application of accounting principles is implied in the auditor's report. The auditor makes no mention of consistency unless there is an inconsistency in application of accounting principles. I is wrong. Under US GAAS, the auditor explicitly states in the auditor's responsibility paragraph of the opinion: "We believe that the audit evidence we have obtained is sufficient and appropriate to provide a basis for our audit opinion."

143. **D.** II and III are correct. If the auditor is unable to form an opinion on a new client's opening inventory balances, the auditor will issue an opinion on the closing balance sheet only and will issue a disclaimer of opinion on both the income statement and the statement of cash flows. I is wrong. If the auditor is unable to form an opinion on a new client's opening inventory balances, the auditor will issue an opinion on the closing balance sheet only. The auditor will then issue a disclaimer of opinion on the income statement, the statement of retained earnings, and the statement of cash flows.

144. **D.** I is wrong. When an auditor expresses an adverse opinion or disclaimer on a complete set of financial statements, the auditor's report should not also include an unmodified opinion on a single financial statement. II is wrong. When an auditor expresses an adverse opinion or disclaimer on a complete set of financial statements, the auditor's report should not also include an unmodified opinion on property, plant, and equipment or any other specific

element, account, or item of a financial statement. Issuing an unmodified opinion in these circumstances would contradict the adverse opinion or the disclaimer of opinion on the financial statements taken as a whole.

Chapter 6: Reviews and Compilations

145. **D.** SSARS applies to compilations and reviews of non–publicly traded companies. A and B are wrong. SSARS applies to both compilations and reviews. C is wrong. Public company reviews are governed by SAS.

146. **C.** I is correct. Gathering evidence regarding a client's ability to continue as a going concern is not considered part of a review engagement. II is correct. Inquiries of the entity's outside legal counsel are not performed in a review. In a review, inquiries tend to be internal; the auditor inquires within the organization, not to outside parties.

147. **A.** I is correct. An accountant is not required to assess control risk as part of a review engagement. Assessment of control risk would be appropriate for an audit engagement. II is wrong. Inquiring of management is the primary source of review evidence, so inquiring to management regarding subsequent events is an appropriate review procedure.

148. **D.** I is wrong. Analytical procedures are mandatory in a review engagement (and audit) but are not likely to be performed in a compilation. II is wrong. Inquiries are mandatory in a review engagement and audit but are not likely to be performed in a compilation. A compilation merely involves taking management information, creating financial statements, and issuing a compilation report. No assurance is given that the financial statements are in conformity with the reporting framework.

149. **D.** I is wrong. Communication with the predecessor who performed the engagement in the prior year is NOT required for a review or compilation (although it would be required for an audit). II is wrong. A basic knowledge of the accounting principles and practices of the industry in which the entity operates is required for both a review and compilation.

150. **D.** I and II are wrong. If the accountant concludes that there is reasonable justification to change the engagement, the accountant's report should NOT include reference to the original engagement, to any procedures that may have been performed, or

to the scope limitation that resulted in the changed engagement.

151. **B.** An accountant with an immaterial direct financial interest in a client is no longer independent with respect to that client. The accountant is precluded from issuing a review report on the financial statements of an entity with respect to which he or she is not independent. If the accountant is not independent, he or she may issue a compilation report, provided the accountant complies with the compilation standards. A and C are wrong. If requested to perform a review engagement for a nonissuer in which an accountant has an immaterial direct financial interest, the accountant cannot perform a review but may perform a compilation, provided lack of independence is disclosed, and the accountant can still be associated with the financial statements. D is wrong. If requested to perform a review engagement for a nonissuer in which an accountant has an immaterial direct financial interest, the accountant is not independent.

152. **D.** A review provides limited assurance that there are no material modifications that should be made to the financial statements in order for them to be in conformity with generally accepted accounting principles, whereas a compilation provides no assurance. A is wrong. A compilation does not provide limited assurance that the CPA followed SSARS, nor does a compilation provide limited assurance that the client followed GAAP. A compilation provides no assurance. B and C are wrong. A compilation does not provide negative or limited assurance; a compilation provides no assurance.

153. **D.** I is wrong. A compilation does not test for reasonableness of the financial statements. A compilation provides no assurance and includes no testing. A compilation often involves just reading the financial statements to consider whether they are free of obvious mistakes in the application of accounting principles. II is wrong. A review does not test for reasonableness of the financial statements. A review provides limited assurance that no material modifications need to be made to the financial statements. In a review, limited assurance is based on inquiry and analytical procedures.

154. **B.** An accountant who is not independent with respect to an entity may compile financial statements for such an entity and issue a report. The last paragraph of the report should disclose this lack of independence. The accountant is permitted, but not required, to disclose the reasons for the lack of

independence. A is wrong. If independence is compromised, a CPA cannot express limited assurance on the financial statements, because a CPA must be independent to perform such an engagement (review). C is wrong. The CPA does not have to be independent of the reporting entity when performing a compilation. If the CPA is not independent, the CPA would disclose the lack of independence in the compilation report, and thus there would be no need to withdraw from the engagement.

155. **A.** An unmodified review report under Statements on Standards for Accounting and Review Services (SSARS) for a nonissuer contains four paragraphs: (1) introductory paragraph, (2) management responsibility paragraph, (3) CPA's responsibility paragraph, and (4) limited assurance paragraph.

156. **D.** The second paragraph of the four paragraphs found in the standard review report for a nonissuer is known as the management responsibility paragraph. An unmodified review report under Statements on SSARS for a nonissuer contains four paragraphs in the following order: (1) introductory paragraph, (2) management responsibility paragraph, (3) CPA's responsibility paragraph, and (4) limited assurance paragraph.

157. **C.** I is correct. As part of a review for a nonissuer, an engagement letter is mandatory and needs to be signed by the client to minimize the risk of a misunderstanding regarding the responsibilities of the CPA and management. II is correct. As part of a review engagement for a nonissuer, a management representation letter is required because a review involves inquiries from the CPA that management normally responds to orally. The CPA needs to turn that oral evidence into written evidence by writing down management's responses and presenting them to management for signature as part of the final review evidence.

158. **A.** I is correct. As part of a compilation for a nonissuer, an engagement letter is mandatory. II is wrong. A management representation letter is not required as part of a compilation engagement for a nonissuer, since no inquiries are made in a compilation that involve written management responses.

159. **C.** I is correct. According to SSARS 21, a review involves an independent CPA performing inquiries and analytical procedures. II is wrong. A compilation is merely the production of financial statements from information given to the CPA by the client. No inquiries, no testing, not even analytical procedures are performed in a compilation engagement. The

CPA does NOT need to be independent to perform a compilation. III is wrong. A "preparation" engagement involves the CPA merely preparing adjusting entries into the client's accounting system and then printing out the financial statements. Prepared financial statements could then be distributed to the client or third party without a report, provided each page is marked "no assurance provided." An accountant need NOT be independent to perform a preparation engagement, and no inquiries or analytical procedures are performed by the CPA.

160. **D.** A standard compilation report previously contained three paragraphs: (1) introductory paragraph, (2) management responsibility paragraph, and (3) CPA's responsibility paragraph. In 2015, SSARS 21 changed the standard compilation to only require one paragraph so as not to confuse a compilation report with a review or audit report. Additional paragraphs may be needed in the compilation report if the CPA is not independent or if financial statement disclosures are purposely being omitted.

161. **D.** A compilation report presented without footnotes by a CPA who is not independent can be performed provided the report discloses both the lack of independence and the fact that the footnotes are missing. This would be accomplished by adding two paragraphs to the compilation report. The report would contain an additional paragraph for the lack of independence and another additional paragraph to mention the fact that required footnotes are missing. The report would have five paragraphs rather than three. A is wrong. Lack of independence is not a factor for a compilation as long as it's disclosed in a separate paragraph. B is wrong. A compilation can be performed even if the disclosures are omitted provided the lack of disclosure is mentioned in a separate paragraph. C is wrong. In a compilation in which the CPA lacks independence, the reason for lack of independence is not generally provided. If one reason for lack of independence is mentioned, then all instances of lack of independence must be disclosed.

162. **C.** III is correct. SSARS 21 created a new engagement known as a preparation of financial statements. According to SSARS 21, a "preparation" engagement is a nonattest service that the practitioner can perform as long as he or she is NOT also performing a review, compilation, or audit on the same financial statements. For a preparation engagement, although an engagement letter is required, an accountant's report is generally NOT permitted. I is

wrong. Although SSARS 21 revised the accountant's compilation report from three paragraphs to one paragraph, an accountant's report is still required for a compilation. II is wrong. Although SSARS 21 applies to review engagements, an accountant's report is required for a review engagement.

163. **C.** With respect to SSARS 21, Preparation of Financial Statements, a practitioner may deliver to a client, without an accompanying report, one or more financial statements, with or without additional disclosures (footnotes) and independence or lack thereof is not a factor.

164. **A.** I is correct. A review of a nonpublic entity requires independence, and the CPA provides limited assurance, not an opinion, that no material modifications need be made to the financial statements for them to be in accordance with the framework. II is wrong. The CPA need not be independent when performing a compilation. No procedures are performed in a compilation, so no assurance is provided. A compilation is often limited to reading the financial statements to consider whether they are free of obvious mistakes in the application of accounting principles. Whether or not the financial statements being reported on contained footnotes is irrelevant.

165. **C.** According to SSARS 21, the practitioner would be exempt from peer review if a preparation of financial statements is the only type of engagement he or she performs—no audits, compilations, or reviews.

Chapter 7: Reporting on Special Purpose Frameworks and Other Reporting Issues

166. **D.** I is correct. A special purpose framework is a financial basis of accounting other than GAAP that includes cash-basis financial reporting. II is correct. A special purpose framework is a financial basis of accounting other than GAAP that includes income tax basis financial reporting. III is correct. Reporting to comply with regulatory requirements fits a special purpose framework that deviates from traditional GAAP reporting.

167. **C.** I is correct. An auditor's report on financial statements prepared using the income tax basis will contain an emphasis-of-matter paragraph alerting the reader to a framework different from GAAP. II is correct. An auditor's report on the cash-basis financial statements will contain an emphasis-of-matter

paragraph alerting the reader to a framework different from GAAP.

168. **A.** I is correct. A report on special purpose framework financial statements should include an emphasis-of-matter paragraph stating the basis, referring to the footnote that describes it, and indicating that it is a non-GAAP basis. II is wrong. A report on special purpose framework financial statements does not include an evaluation of the usefulness of the basis of accounting.

169. **B.** I, II, and III are correct. A report on special purpose framework financial statements prepared on the income tax basis should include an emphasis-of-matter paragraph that (1) states the basis of accounting used, (2) refers to the footnote that describes the income tax basis, and (3) indicates that it is a non-GAAP basis.

170. **A.** I is correct. A report on a client's compliance with a regulatory requirement, assuming the report is prepared based on a financial statement audit of the complete financial statements, would contain restricted use language. II is wrong. A report on financial statements prepared in conformity with a special purpose framework (such as the cash basis) does not require a restriction on the use of the report.

171. **D.** I and II are wrong. Neither the cash basis nor income tax basis reporting requires the auditor to restrict the use of the report. Therefore, the auditor's report will NOT contain a restricted use paragraph (i.e., an other-matters paragraph).

172. **C.** I is correct. An auditor's report on special purpose financial statements prepared in accordance with a regulatory basis not intended for general use should include an emphasis-of-matter paragraph that indicates that the financial statements are prepared in accordance with the applicable special purpose framework. II is correct. An auditor's report on special purpose financial statements prepared in accordance with a regulatory basis not intended for general use should include an other-matters paragraph that restricts the use of the auditor's report to those within the entity, the parties to the contract or agreement, or the regulatory agencies to which the entity is subject.

173. **D.** I is wrong. A dual opinion on special purpose framework and GAAP would not be required if the financial statements were prepared on the income tax basis. II is wrong. A dual opinion on special purpose framework and GAAP would not be

required if the financial statements were prepared on the cash basis. A dual opinion would apply only to financial statements prepared on a regulatory basis that are intended for general use. Then and only then would the auditor have to give an opinion on both conformity with GAAP and also whether the statements present fairly in accordance with the special purpose framework designed by the regulatory agency.

174. D. An audit of a single financial statement is permitted under US GAAS. An audit of a single financial statement can be performed as a separate audit or in conjunction with an audit of the complete set of financial statements. An audit of a single financial statement is permitted under US GAAS, as it merely involves special considerations in the application of the standards. A is wrong. An audit of a single financial statement can be performed as a separate audit or in conjunction with an audit of the complete set of financial statements. B is wrong. Compliance with this request would not violate any ethical standards of the profession. C is wrong. The auditor must be independent to perform an audit.

175. C. I is correct. In auditing a single financial statement, the auditor should perform procedures, as necessary, on interrelated items. II is correct. The auditor can perform the audit as either a separate engagement or in conjunction with an audit of the complete set of financial statements.

176. B. II is correct. The auditor, when auditing a single financial statement, is required to understand the intended users of the financial statement. I is wrong. When auditing a single financial statement and not a complete set, the auditor should determine materiality for the single financial statement.

177. A. I is correct. An auditor who expresses an adverse opinion but still wishes to express an unmodified opinion on a specific element of those financial statements may do so if the specific element does not constitute a major portion of the entity's complete set of financial statements or the specific element is not based on net income or stockholders' equity. II is wrong. The report on the specific element would have to be a separate report and cannot accompany the auditor's report on the complete set of financial statements.

178. C. I is correct. An auditor's report would be designated a report on compliance when it is issued in connection with compliance with aspects of regulatory requirements related to audited financial statements. II is correct. It should be noted that a report on compliance in connection with audited financial statements provides negative assurance on compliance.

179. D. I is wrong. To issue a report on compliance, the auditor must have audited the client's financial statements. II is wrong. To issue a report on compliance, the auditor may only issue negative assurance on compliance.

180. D. I is wrong. If the auditor finds one or more instances of noncompliance, the report on compliance should describe the noncompliance rather than express negative assurance. II is wrong. If an adverse opinion or disclaimer is expressed on the financial statements, a report on compliance can be issued only when there are material instances of noncompliance. In this case, negative assurance would not be appropriate.

181. B. II is correct. The report, if separate, would contain a restricted use paragraph. I is wrong. The auditor's report on compliance with a regulatory requirement can be separate or combined as an other-matters paragraph in the auditor's report on the financial statements.

182. C. I is correct. The auditor's report on compliance should contain a restriction on the use of the report if the report is issued separately. II is correct. The auditor's report on compliance should include a restriction on the use of the report as an other-matters paragraph if the report on compliance is not issued separately but included as part of an auditor's report on complete financial statements.

183. C. I and II are correct. The auditor's report on compliance should contain negative assurance regarding compliance if no instances of noncompliance are found, whether the report was combined or separate.

184. B. II is correct. The auditor's report on compliance issued as a separate report should contain a statement that the audit was not directed primarily toward obtaining knowledge regarding compliance. In addition, a paragraph that restricts the use of the auditor's report to management, those charged with governance, others within the organization, the regulatory agencies, or the other parties to the contract should be included in a separate report on compliance. I is wrong. The auditor's report on compliance issued as a separate report should be dated the same as the auditor's report on the complete financial statements.

185. **B.** The auditor's standard report on compliance issued separately should contain three paragraphs: introductory paragraph, negative assurance paragraph, and restricted use paragraph.

186. **C.** I is correct. A special purpose framework is a financial basis of accounting other than GAAP that includes cash basis. Reporting to comply with cash basis fits a special purpose that deviates from traditional GAAP reporting. II is correct. A special purpose framework is a financial basis of accounting other than GAAP that includes reporting to comply with regulatory requirements.

187. **B.** II is correct. Negative assurance is provided in reports on compliance with aspects of contractual agreements and reports on regulatory requirements related to audited financial statements. Saying, "We are not aware of any instances of noncompliance" is considered giving negative assurance. I is wrong. Cash basis, tax basis, and other non-GAAP reports provide positive rather than negative assurance. The emphasis-of-matter paragraph in the report indicates that the financial statements (elements, accounts, items) were prepared in accordance with the applicable special purpose framework (positive assurance).

188. **A.** If there are both emphasis-of-matter and other-matters paragraphs in an auditor's report, the opinion paragraph would be followed by the emphasis-of-matter paragraph, which would be followed by the other-matters paragraph.

189. **C.** I is correct. An auditor may report on summary financial statements that are derived from complete financial statements if the auditor indicates in the report whether the information in the summary financial statements is fairly stated in all material respects in relation to the complete financial statements from which it has been derived. II is correct. An auditor may report on summary financial statements that are derived from complete financial statements if the auditor indicates in the report the date of the auditor's report and the type of opinion expressed on the complete financial statements.

190. **C.** I is correct. The auditor should not accept an engagement to report on compliance with a regulatory requirement unless the auditor also is engaged to audit the complete financial statements. II is correct for the same reason. The auditor needs to have been engaged to audit the complete financial statements if the auditor is to prepare a report on compliance or a report on summary financial statements.

191. **B.** II is correct. The CPA must follow PCAOB standards when associated with interim reporting required by the SEC. When an entity is required by the SEC to file a quarterly report, the SEC also requires that an independent accountant perform a review. The review also follows PCAOB standards. I is wrong. When an entity is required by the SEC to file a quarterly report, the SEC also requires that an independent accountant perform a review, not an audit, of the interim financial information.

192. **C.** I is correct. As part of a review, the accountant is required to inquire of management about suspected fraud. Internal inquiry is a large part of a review. II is correct. As part of a review, the accountant is required to inquire of management about allegations of fraud.

193. **D.** I is correct. An accountant's knowledge of an entity's business and its internal control influences the inquiries made. II is correct. An accountant's knowledge of an entity's business and its internal control influences the analytical procedures performed. III is wrong. An interim review does not involve observation of inventory. A review is primarily inquiry and analytical procedures, not evidence gathering.

194. **B.** II is correct. A review of the interim financial information of a publicly held company is conducted in accordance with Public Company Accounting Oversight Board (PCAOB) standards. I is wrong. Statements on Standards for Accounting and Review Services (SSARS) apply to reviews of the financial statements of nonissuers.

195. **B.** II is correct. As part of a review of interim financial information, the accountant is required to inquire of management about their knowledge of fraud, suspected fraud, or allegations of fraud. I is wrong. A review of interim financial information is not designed to provide information regarding an entity's ability to continue as a going concern.

196. **A.** I is correct. As part of a review, the accountant is required to compare disaggregated revenue data for the current interim period with that of comparable prior periods. Disaggregated data refers to data that are broken out from a total. An example of disaggregated data would include revenue by month and revenue by product line. Comparing disaggregated data of current and prior periods is an example of analytical procedures. II is incorrect. Benchmarking, or comparing amounts to industry standards, is an optional analytical procedure for a review but is not required.

197. **A.** I is correct. Internal inquiries, that is, inquiries of management, are required in a review of interim financial information of an issuer. II is wrong. External inquiries are permitted but not required.

198. **D.** I is correct. Inquiry regarding compliance with GAAP or another framework is required in a review of interim financial statements. II is correct. A written understanding in the form of a signed engagement letter is mandatory in a review of interim financial statements so that there is no misunderstanding regarding the responsibility being assumed by the CPA. In a review, a CPA doesn't want management to mistakenly think an audit is being performed. III is correct. A representation letter signed by management is required in a review of interim financial statements because a review consists primarily of inquiry (oral questions), and responses to inquiry are often oral responses. At the conclusion of the interim review, the CPA asks management to sign the rep letter. By having management sign the rep letter, the CPA is making sure that management understood the oral inquiry and that management still believe in their oral responses to the inquiry.

199. **A.** I is correct. Identified risks of material misstatement due to fraud help the accountant to identify the types of material misstatements that may occur in the interim financial information and to consider the likelihood of their occurrence. II is wrong. Scope limitations relate to problems in performing an engagement, but since they were overcome, they would bear little relationship to procedures performed in a review.

200. **C.** I is correct. A comfort letter is a letter for an underwriter from an auditor and contains a restriction of use. II is correct. In a comfort letter, the CPA gives negative assurance regarding unaudited information and positive assurance regarding audited information.

Chapter 8: Attestation Engagements Other than Audits of Historic Financial Information

201. **D.** I is correct. In an attestation, sufficient evidence should be obtained to provide a reasonable basis for the conclusion that is expressed in the report. An attestation is a very high level of service and requires both independence and evidence gathering to support the opinion being rendered. II is correct. In an attestation, the work needs to be planned and supervised. III is wrong. A sufficient

understanding of internal control is not required to be obtained in an attestation engagement involving an examination of forward-looking financial statements. *Exam hint:* If the question asks about attestation, ask yourself what the answer would be if the question were about an audit (which is a type of attestation). Usually the answer would be the same, unless the answer had something to do with internal control. An audit looks backward at historic financial information, whereas other attestations may look forward. Another difference between an attestation and an audit is that an audit requires internal control work while other attestations often do not.

202. **D.** I, II, and III are correct. Trust services are assurance and advisory services used to address the risks and opportunities of information technology. Security, availability, processing integrity, online privacy, and confidentiality are the five essential principles that guide a trust engagement.

203. **C.** I and II are correct. Trust services, whether WebTrust or SysTrust, follow attestation standards, since the CPA needs to be independent and an opinion will be rendered.

204. **B.** A WebTrust engagement is an attestation engagement designed to measure transaction integrity, information protection, and disclosure of business practices. When an unmodified report is issued, the client may add the CPA WebTrust Seal to its website, indicating that its site is a reasonably safe and private place for e-commerce.

205. **B.** II is correct. Statements on Standards for Attestation Engagements (SSAE) do not apply to tax preparation. I is wrong. SSAE apply to pro forma financial statements.

206. **D.** I is wrong. SSAE apply to forecasts, or forward-looking financial statements that are intended for general use. II is wrong. SSAE apply to projections, or forward-looking financial statements that are NOT intended for general use. Projections will contain a restriction on use, but the same standards apply. Other engagements for which SSAE apply include separate engagements regarding internal control, pro forma, compliance agreements, and agreed-upon procedures.

207. **D.** I is correct. SSAE do not apply to audits of non-issuers; Statements on Auditing Standards (SAS) would apply. II is correct. SSAE do not apply to compilations, because Statements on Standards for Accounting and Review Services (SSARS) apply

to compilations. III is correct. SSAE do not apply to reviews of nonissuers; rather, SSARS apply to reviews of nonissuers.

208. **D.** I is wrong. Agreed-upon procedures engagements follow SSAE. There is no such thing as Statements on Standards for Agreed-Upon Procedures. II is wrong. The CPA must be independent to perform agreed-upon procedures. In an agreed-upon procedures engagement, parties must agree to the procedures performed by the CPA, unlike an audit, where the auditor comes in with his or her own audit plan.

209. **A.** I is correct. Use of the report is restricted to the specified parties. II is wrong. In an agreed-upon procedures engagement, the client is responsible for the subject matter and its adequacy. The items being reported on must be measurable and result in reasonably consistent findings. Furthermore, evidence to support the report should be expected to exist. The parties need to agree to the procedures performed by the CPA.

210. **B.** II is correct. The agreed-upon procedures report is limited in distribution. I is wrong. In an agreed-upon procedures engagement, the CPA lists the procedures and the findings but does not provide any assurance.

211. **B.** II is correct. The CPA must be independent when applying agreed-upon procedures even though no assurance is provided. The report describes the procedures and the CPA's findings without providing any assurance. I is wrong. A review of a nonpublic entity requires independence, and the CPA provides limited assurance that no material modifications need be made to the financial statements for them to be in accordance with the framework.

212. **C.** I is correct. A review of a nonpublic entity requires independence, but the CPA expresses no opinion. Instead, the CPA provides limited assurance that no material modifications need be made to the financial statements for them to be in accordance with the framework. Note that in a review engagement, no opinion is expressed, and limited assurance is provided. II is correct. The CPA must be independent when applying agreed-upon procedures even though no opinion is provided. The report describes the procedures and the CPA's findings without providing any assurance.

213. **B.** II is correct. Examination of a financial forecast includes evaluating—and giving an opinion after evaluating—the preparation of a financial forecast and the support underlying management's assumptions, similar to an audit. I is wrong. Compiling involves a lower level of service with regard to the financial forecast. Compiling the forecast would not involve evaluating or gathering evidence to support the forecast.

214. **A.** I is correct. Whenever an accountant reports on prospective financial statements, the report should include a caveat that prospective results may not be achieved. II is wrong. A review of a forecast or projection is not an appropriate level of service for a forecast or projection. Review engagements look backward at historical financial information. Forecasts and projections are forward looking. *Exam hint:* Do not use the term *review* or *audit* unless the financial information is historic.

215. **A.** I is correct. Compilations of projections follow SSAE. II is wrong. Compilations of historical financial statements follow SSARS.

216. **C.** I is correct. Since a written assertion has not been provided, when reporting directly on subject matter, the report should be restricted to specified parties. II is correct. Use of the accountant's report should be restricted to specified parties when reporting on an agreed-upon procedures engagement.

217. **B.** II is correct. In an attestation engagement where the CPA examines and reports directly on subject matter, the report indicates what the subject matter was that the CPA examined. A report directly on the subject matter would say something like, "We have examined the accompanying schedule, the profit-sharing plan, for the purposes of determining if management is contributing sufficiently to the plan." Since the CPA is reporting directly on the subject matter, the CPA mentions the subject matter, that is, the accompanying schedule. I is wrong. In an attestation engagement where the CPA examines and reports directly on subject matter, the report indicates what the subject matter was that the CPA examined. The CPA would not mention any assertion made by management unless the CPA was hired to report on management's assertion. If the CPA was hired to report on management's assertion, the report might then say, "We have examined management's assertion that they have contributed the appropriate amount into the profit-sharing plan."

218. **B.** II is correct. Negative assurance may be expressed when an accountant reports on the results of performing a review of management's assertion. Review engagements lead to the CPA's giving negative assurance. Negative assurance includes using

phrases such as "Nothing came to our attention" or "We are not aware." Even in a review of historical financial statements, negative language is used, but in that one instance it is called limited assurance rather than negative assurance. I is wrong. Negative assurance is not provided in a compilation of prospective financial statements; no assurance is provided in a compilation of prospective financial statements.

219. **A.** I is correct. When performing an attestation engagement related to a client's prospective financial statements, the accountant should ensure that the client discloses all significant assumptions that are used for the prospective financial statements. II is wrong. Historical financial statements are not required in an attestation engagement related to prospective financial statements.

220. **B.** II is correct. Consulting engagements fall under the standards of Statements on Standards for Consulting Services. I is wrong. SSAE apply to engagements involving the auditor examining internal control, pro forma financial reporting, compliance, agreed-upon procedures, forecasts, and projections.

221. **C.** I and II are correct. Whenever an accountant reports on prospective financial statements, the report should include a limitation, a caveat that prospective results may not be achieved.

222. **B.** II is correct. An accountant's report on a financial forecast should include a limitation on the usefulness of the report. Since a forecast contains forward-looking financial information, the limitation is in the form of a caveat that the prospective results of the financial forecast may not be achieved. I is wrong. An accountant's report on a financial forecast need not include a restriction in distribution, since a forecast can be for general use. A projection, on the other hand, needs a restriction in distribution.

223. **A.** I and II are correct. An auditor's letter issued on significant deficiencies relating to a nonissuer's internal control observed during a financial statement audit should include a restriction on distribution and indicate that the purpose of the audit was to report on the financial statements and not on internal control.

224. **C.** I is correct. The auditor is required to communicate to management any significant deficiencies and material weaknesses that the auditor observes. II is correct. The auditor is required to communicate to those charged with governance (the audit committee) any significant deficiencies and material weaknesses in internal control that the auditor observes.

225. **B.** II is correct. Management provides an assertion concerning the effectiveness of internal control as part of a financial statement audit of an issuer. I is wrong. Management does not automatically provide an assertion concerning the effectiveness of internal control as part of a financial statement audit of a nonissuer. Management would provide such an assertion only in a separate engagement related to internal control.

226. **A.** I is correct. For a practitioner to examine and report on management's assertion about the effectiveness of an entity's internal control, the attestation engagement would have to be integrated with an audit of the entity's financial statements. This would mean that the practitioner would have to do both the audit of the financial statements and the internal control examination if the practitioner wanted to do the internal control examination. II is wrong. If the practitioner were to examine and report on management's assertion about the effectiveness of an entity's internal control, the attestation engagement report on internal control would not need to be restricted but could be made available for general distribution.

227. **A.** I is correct. In the report to governance regarding significant deficiencies found in internal control during the audit of a nonissuer, the report should state that the communication is intended solely for the use of management, those charged with governance, and others within the organization. II is wrong. If Clark were to examine and report on management's assertion regarding the effectiveness of an entity's internal control, the report on internal control would not need to be restricted but could be made available for general distribution. For Clark to examine and report on management's assertion about the effectiveness of an entity's internal control, the attestation engagement would have to be integrated with an audit of the entity's financial statements. This would mean that Clark would have to do both the audit of the financial statements and the internal control examination if he wanted to report on the nonissuer's assertion regarding the client's internal control. Clark's report should include a paragraph stating that because of inherent limitations, internal control may not prevent or detect material misstatements.

228. **D.** I is wrong. In the audit of a nonissuer, management is not required to assess and report on the client's internal controls. II is wrong. In the audit of a nonissuer, the auditor is not required to assess and report on the entity's internal controls. If the audit was being performed for an issuer, both management and the auditor would be required to assess and report on the entity's internal controls.

229. **B.** II is correct. If the auditor detects a material misstatement and management corrects it, this would be an appropriate topic for a communication between the auditor and those charged with governance. I is wrong. The auditor may not report the absence of significant deficiencies to those charged with governance, because that would imply that the auditor searched for such deficiencies.

230. **C.** I is correct. Since estimates are subject to bias, the auditor should ensure that those charged with governance are informed about the basis for the auditor's conclusions regarding the reasonableness of sensitive accounting estimates. II is correct. Disagreements in the application of accounting principles relating to asset impairment or any other accounting principle should be communicated to those charged with governance.

Chapter 9: Assertions

231. **A.** I is correct. With completeness, the client is asserting that all transactions and events that should have been recorded have been recorded. If some have not been recorded, the books are not complete. As always with completeness, the auditor's concern is understatement. With regard to classes of transactions, the auditor's concern is that transactions such as purchases and the related accounts payable may not have been recorded when they should have been. II is wrong. With occurrence, the client is asserting that whatever transactions and events have been recorded really did occur in the year under audit. With regard to the assertion category known as classes of transactions, the auditor's biggest concern with occurrence is overstatement of revenue. The assertions found under the category of classes of transactions are as follows: completeness—concern is understatement; occurrence—concern is overstatement; cutoff—concern is correct period; classification—concern is correct account; and accuracy—concern is correct amount.

232. **D.** I is correct. Cutoff is an assertion under classes of transactions. With the cutoff assertion, the client asserts that transactions and events have been recorded in the correct accounting period. Cutoff is closely linked with understatement and overstatement. II is correct. Completeness is another assertion under the category of classes of transactions. The assertion is that all transactions and events have been recorded. If some have not been recorded, the books are not complete. As always with completeness, the concern is understatement. Transactions may not have been recorded and they should have been, for example, purchases and accounts payable. If they were not recorded, liabilities and expenses are understated. The auditor will design tests for understatement in order to test the completeness assertion for classes of transactions. III is correct. Occurrence is the assertion that transactions and events that have been recorded have occurred and pertain to the company. The concern is overstatement. If the client recorded sales that have not yet occurred, the client has overstated. Since occurrence is an income statement assertion, the auditor's direct concern with occurrence is an overstatement of revenue on the income statement. The auditor will design tests for overstatement because an overstatement of revenue is presumed in every audit.

233. **C.** I is correct. Cutoff has a direct impact on completeness and understatement. The client asserts that the proper cutoff was applied to purchases. If purchases are not recorded at year-end because the goods have not been received but title has already passed, then the books are not complete. II is correct. Cutoff also has a direct impact on occurrence and overstatement. The client asserts that the proper cutoff to sales was applied. If the client fails to use year-end as the proper cutoff, sales may be recorded prior to the earnings process. If so, sales are overstated for the period under audit, and that would impact the occurrence assertion.

234. **B.** I is correct. Classification is an assertion under the category of classes of transactions and events. With classification, the client asserts that transactions have been recorded in the proper accounts—contra account and so on. For example, rather than debit sales, the company should use the contra account, sales returns, and allowances. II is correct. Accuracy is an assertion under the category of classes of transactions and events. With accuracy, the client asserts that transactions have been recorded for the proper amounts and data have been recorded accurately. III is correct. Completeness is an assertion under the category of classes of transactions. The assertion is that all transactions and events have been recorded. If some have not been recorded, the books are not complete.

235. **B.** I is correct. Rights and obligations is an assertion under the category of account balances. With the rights and obligations assertion, the company asserts that it holds or controls the rights to assets and the liabilities are the obligation of the company. II is correct. Valuation is an assertion under the category of account balances. With the valuation assertion, management asserts that the assets and liabilities are properly valued and appropriately recorded. (Inventory should be recorded at the lower of cost or market, accounts receivable at the net realizable value.) III is correct. Existence is an assertion under the category of account balances. With existence, the company asserts that the asset exists. The concern is overstatement. Existence is similar if not identical to the occurrence assertion found under classes of transactions.

236. **D.** I, II, III, and IV are all correct. Completeness, rights and obligations, existence, and valuation are all assertions found under the category of account balances. With completeness, the auditor's concern is understatement. The client asserts that all assets, liabilities, and equity interests that should have been recorded have been recorded. If some assets, liabilities, and equity interests have not been recorded when they should have been, the balance sheet is not complete. The auditor will perform various tests for understatement involving specific assets and liabilities to test the completeness assertion. With rights and obligations, the company asserts that it holds or controls the rights to assets and that the liabilities are the obligation of the company. The auditor's concern is that assets may be pledged as collateral and not properly disclosed. This would impact the rights and obligations assertion. The rights and obligations assertion applies to liabilities also. The client asserts that all liabilities listed are debts of the company. The auditor is concerned with the fact that a liability may be listed on the balance sheet when the liability belongs to the president of the company personally, rather than to the company itself. With existence, the client asserts that all assets, liabilities, and equity interests exist. With existence, the auditor's concern is overstatement. If assets are listed on the balance sheet when they don't exist, assets are overstated on the balance sheet and the existence assertion is affected. The auditor will test the existence assertion, testing for overstatement for specific assets. For example, when testing accounts receivable, the auditor will send confirmations to client customers to gather evidence regarding the existence of the customer. With valuation, the client asserts that assets, liabilities, and equity interests have been appropriately recorded at the proper amounts based on GAAP: inventory at the lower of cost or market, securities marked to market, and accounts receivable at the net realizable value. With valuation, the auditor's concern is that some or all of these assets may be valued incorrectly on the balance sheet; if so, the valuation assertion is affected. The auditor will test the valuation assertion with regard to specific assets and liabilities. With accounts receivable, the auditor needs to substantiate estimations regarding age of receivables and net realizable value of accounts receivable. The auditor will also gather evidence regarding credit-granting policies of the company because if the company extends credit to just anyone, the net realizable value of accounts receivable will be overstated.

237. **A.** I is correct. The existence assertion relates to the gross accounts receivable. The client asserts that all customers exist and none are fraudulent. To test the existence assertion, the auditor sends confirmations to the client's customers to ensure the existence of customer balances. II is correct. The valuation assertion relates to accounts receivable, net of the valuation allowance. The client asserts that accounts receivable is properly valued. To gather evidence to support the valuation assertion, the auditor will test the credit-granting policies of the company. The auditor wants to make sure that there is a control in place to grant credit only to approved customers and then test that control. III is correct. Rights and obligations is an assertion regarding accounts receivable. The company asserts that it has ownership rights over its accounts receivable. The auditor is concerned that some or all of the receivables have been pledged as collateral. If this has happened, the rights and obligations assertion is affected.

238. **B.** II is correct. The valuation assertion relates to accounts receivable, net of the valuation allowance. To gather evidence to support the valuation assertion, the auditor will test the credit-granting policies of the company. The auditor wants to make sure that there is a control in place to grant credit only to approved customers and then test that control. I is wrong. The existence assertion relates to the gross accounts receivable, not the net. To test the existence assertion, the auditor sends confirmations to ensure the existence of customer balances.

239. **A.** I is correct. If inventory was bought right before the end of Year 1 and incorrectly recorded in Year 2 (the subsequent period), the Year 1 books are not complete. In Year 1, the completeness assertion is impacted because of the understatement of inventory and related accounts payable (books are not complete). Completeness always relates to understatement. II is wrong. In the subsequent period (Year 2) there is an overstatement of inventory, which would affect the existence assertion. After Year 2, the error cancels itself out.

240. **C.** I is correct. Completeness is an assertion under the category of classes of transactions and events (income statement assertions). The assertion is that all transactions and events (sales and expenses) have been recorded. If some sales and purchases have not been recorded, the books are not complete. As always with completeness, the concern is understatement. With completeness, the auditor is concerned that expenses may not have been recorded when they should have been. The auditor will perform tests to find unrecorded items. II is correct. Completeness is an assertion found under the category of account balances. Again, the auditor's concern is understatement. The client asserts that all assets, liabilities, and equity interests that should have been recorded have been recorded. If some assets, liabilities, and equity interests have not been recorded when they should have been, the balance sheet is not complete. The auditor will perform various tests for understatement involving specific assets and liabilities to test the completeness assertion.

241. **B.** II is correct. Rights and obligations is an assertion found under the category of account balances (balance sheet assertions). The company asserts that it holds or controls the rights to assets and that the liabilities are the obligation of the company. The auditor's concern is that assets may be pledged as collateral and not properly disclosed. This would affect the rights and obligations assertion. The rights and obligations assertion applies to liabilities also. The client asserts that all liabilities listed are debts of the company. The auditor is concerned that a liability may be listed on the balance sheet when the liability belongs to the president of the company personally, rather than to the company itself. I is wrong. Rights and obligations are not found under the assertions about classes of transactions. Rights and obligations relate to assets and liabilities (balance sheet assertions). Assertions about classes of

transactions and events relate to income statement accounts.

242. **B.** II is correct. With the rights and obligations assertion, the company asserts that it holds or controls the rights to assets and that the liabilities are the obligation of the company. The rights and obligations assertion is affected in this question because the liability is listed on the balance sheet when in fact it belongs to the president of the company personally, rather than being an obligation of the company. I is wrong. While completeness is an assertion regarding account balances, completeness is a concern only when the auditor fears an understatement. In this question, the liabilities of the company are overstated, not understated, because the liability is not a corporate obligation. The rights and obligations assertion applies as does the existence assertion. The obligation should be taken off the balance sheet and not reported by the company.

243. **C.** I is correct. Existence is an assertion found under the category of account balances (balance sheet assertions). The client asserts that all assets, liabilities, and equity interests exist. With existence, the auditor's concern is overstatement. If assets are listed on the balance sheet when they don't exist, or don't pertain to the company, the existence assertion is affected because the liability is overstated. In this question, the liability appears on the balance sheet but doesn't exist from the standpoint of the entity, since it belongs to the company's president. Therefore, the overstatement of the liability affects the existence assertion. Existence will always relate to overstatement. II is correct. With the rights and obligations assertion, the company asserts that it holds or controls the rights to assets and that the liabilities are the obligation of the company. The rights and obligations are affected in this question because the liability is listed on the balance sheet when in fact it belongs to the president of the company personally, rather than being an obligation of the company.

244. **B.** II is correct. With regard to the existence/occurrence assertion, the auditor would test for overstatement of revenue because his or her concern is overstatement. I is wrong. With regard to existence/occurrence, the auditor would test for overstatement, not understatement. While the auditor would test for understatement of liabilities during the audit, any test for understatement would be in support of the completeness assertion.

245. B. II is correct. Recalculating (footing and cross-footing) invoices helps test valuation. Inspection of documents also assists with valuation because the auditor would look for authorization. For example, if the auditor sees that credit was checked before goods were shipped to a customer, accounts receivable is likely to be properly valued. The auditor will look for approvals on sales orders. I is wrong. Checking math accuracy will NOT help with cutoff testing. Examining transactions just before and just after the end of the year for proper accounting period recognition (to see when they were recorded) would be a cutoff test.

246. B. II is correct. Valuation is an assertion found under the category of account balances (balance sheet assertions). With this assertion, the client asserts that assets, liabilities, and equity interests have been appropriately recorded at the proper amounts based on GAAP. Therefore, if the auditor has decided that inventory is based on a variation of FIFO and LIFO that is not viewed as GAAP, then the inventory is not properly valued. I is wrong. Rights and obligations are also found under the category of account balances (balance sheet assertions). With the rights and obligations assertion, the company asserts that it holds or controls the rights to the assets and that the liabilities listed on the balance sheet are the obligation of the company. In this question, there is no evidence to suggest that the inventory is not that of the company.

247. B. II is correct. Valuation is an assertion found under the category of account balances (balance sheet assertions). The client asserts that assets, liabilities, and equity interests have been appropriately recorded at the proper amounts based on GAAP. If the auditor has decided that inventory is based on a FIFO and LIFO method that is not viewed as proper accounting, the inventory is not properly valued. I is wrong. While completeness is an assertion found under the category of account balances, completeness would affect inventory only if the inventory were understated based on incorrect cutoff. In this question the inventory is overstated based on incorrect cutoff. Therefore, the existence assertion would be affected rather than the completeness assertion.

248. C. I is correct. With completeness, the client asserts that all inventory and the related accounts payable have been recorded. If some inventory has not been recorded due to incorrect cutoff, the books are not complete. Since the incorrect cutoff led to the understatement, the completeness assertion is affected. II is correct. Valuation is an assertion found under the

category of account balances (balance sheet assertions). The client asserts that assets, liabilities, and equity interests have been appropriately recorded at the proper amounts based on GAAP. If the auditor has decided that inventory is based on a FIFO and LIFO method that is not viewed as proper accounting, the inventory is not properly valued; therefore, the valuation assertion is affected.

249. B. II is correct. Occurrence is an assertion found in the category known as classes of transactions and events (income statement assertions). With the occurrence assertion, the client asserts that transactions and events that have been recorded on the income statement have actually occurred. If the client recorded sales on the income statement but the sales have not yet occurred, the client has overstated sales and affected the occurrence assertion for sales. The concern with occurrence is an overstatement of revenue. The auditor will design tests for overstatement because an overstatement of revenue is presumed in every audit. I is wrong. Existence is a balance sheet assertion, not an income statement assertion. While recording sales prior to the earnings process being complete would affect the existence assertion due to an overstatement of accounts receivable at year-end, the question asks which income statement assertion is affected and existence is not an income statement assertion.

250. C. I is correct. Occurrence is an assertion found in the category known as classes of transactions and events (income statement assertions). With the occurrence assertion, the client asserts that transactions and events that have been recorded on the income statement have actually occurred. The concern is overstatement. If the client recorded sales on the income statement but they have not yet occurred, the client has overstated sales and the occurrence assertion for sales is affected. The auditor will test the occurrence assertion for sales because an overstatement of revenue is presumed in every audit. II is correct. Existence is an assertion found under the category of account balances (balance sheet assertions). The client asserts that all assets, liabilities, and equity interests exist. With existence, the auditor's concern is overstatement of assets. If assets are listed on the balance sheet but they don't exist, the existence assertion is affected. If the account receivable is recorded prior to the earnings process being complete, assets are overstated. Existence is similar to occurrence, as they both relate to overstatement, but existence relates to overstatement of assets (existence is a balance sheet assertion) whereas occurrence relates to overstatement of revenue (occurrence is an income statement assertion).

251. **A.** I is correct. Rights and obligations are an assertion found under the category of account balances (balance sheet assertions). With the rights and obligations assertion, the company asserts that it holds or controls the rights to the assets and that the liabilities listed on the balance sheet are the obligation of the company. In this question, the building recorded on the balance sheet of Andrinua Corp. belongs to Desimone Inc., so Andrinua Corp. has no rights of ownership and should not include the building on its balance sheet. Thus, the rights and obligations assertion is affected. II is wrong. Completeness is an assertion found under the category of account balances. Andrinua asserts that all assets that should have been recorded have been recorded. If some assets have not been recorded when they should have been recorded, the balance sheet is not complete. With completeness, the auditor's concern is understatement. In this question, however, the asset was recorded but should not have been. Therefore, overstatement is a concern, not understatement.

252. **C.** I is correct. Completeness is an assertion found under the category of presentation and disclosure. The client asserts that all disclosures are complete. If any material items that should have been disclosed were not disclosed, the footnotes are not complete. Once again with completeness, the concern is understatement. II is correct. Classification and understandability is an assertion under the category of presentation and disclosure. Liabilities that mature in less than one year should be classified as current liabilities rather than long term. Assets that are liquid should be classified as current assets. Assets that are not intended to be liquidated within a year should be reported as long term. Understandability relates to information being presented and described clearly. For example, related-party footnotes—including the nature of the relationship, who the parties are (buyer and seller), and the dollar amount of each related-party transaction—must be understood by nonaccountants. The assertions found under the category of presentation and disclosure are occurrence, rights and obligations, completeness, classification and understandability, and accuracy and valuation.

253. **A.** I is correct. Completeness is found in all three categories of assertions. With classes of transactions and events (income statement assertions), the client asserts that all revenue and expenses have been

recorded. If some have not, the income statement is not complete. With assertions regarding account balances (balance sheet assertions), the client asserts that all assets, liabilities, and equity accounts have been recorded. If some assets, liabilities, and equity accounts have not been recorded, the books are not complete. With the assertion category known as presentation and disclosure, the client asserts that the footnotes are complete. II is wrong. Rights and obligations is an assertion found under the category of account balances (balance sheet assertions) and also presentation and disclosure. It is not found under the assertion category known as classes of transactions and events (income statement assertions).

254. **B.** II is correct. Classification is an assertion under the category of classes of transactions and events (income statement assertions). With classification, the client asserts that the transactions were recorded using the correct accounts. If equipment was purchased and it was recorded as inventory, the classification assertion is affected. I is wrong. With rights and obligations, the concern is that the asset that was recorded is not owned by the company. In this question, the asset is owned by the company; it is just not classified properly.

255. **C.** III is correct. Completeness, while an assertion, is not an assertion category. Completeness is found in all three assertion categories: classes of transaction and events, account balances, and presentation and disclosure. I is wrong. Presentation and disclosure is an assertion category relating to footnotes and presentation of items in the financial statements. II is wrong. Classes of transactions and events is an assertion category, relating mostly to income statement accounts.

Chapter 10: Evidence Gathering and Transaction Cycles, Part 1

256. **B.** II is correct. In the phrase "nature, extent, and timing" of audit procedures, the term *nature* refers to the type of test performed, whether the test is a test of controls or perhaps a substantive test. I is wrong. In the phrase "nature, extent, and timing" of audit procedures, the term *nature* does not refer to the amount of testing. The term *extent* refers to the amount of testing.

257. **B.** II is correct. Lapping involves the theft of receivables by an employee. The employee then must cover the theft by giving credit to the customer

who paid. However, lapping results in a delay in the recording of specific credits to customer accounts because today's collection covers up yesterday's theft. Lapping can be prevented by proper segregation of duties. The same employee should not be able to both deposit customer checks and post the credits to the customer accounts. I is wrong. Kiting has nothing to do with receivables. Kiting involves cash that appears to be in two company bank accounts at the same time.

258. **B.** III is correct. The same employee should not be able to both deposit customer checks and post the credits to the customer accounts. If the same employee were able to do both, the employee could both steal from the company and cover up the theft in the accounting records. If one employee were in position to do both jobs, mandatory vacation would help prevent and detect such potential theft of receivables, known as lapping. I is wrong. The employee who opens the mail should deposit the customer checks into Arthur's bank accounts, but first the employee should prepare a listing of all checks received that day. II is wrong. The employee who opens the mail should prepare a listing of all checks received that day, known as a duplicate check listing.

259. **C.** In a revenue cycle, for proper segregation of duties, the sales department will prepare the initial sales order, quantity, price, color, and so on, but a separate department will authorize the customer's credit. Since most companies ship the goods to the customer prior to receiving payment, the independent auditor tests to see if there is a policy in place within the organization to verify customer credit before shipping goods. Therefore, answers A, B, and D are wrong.

260. **D.** I is wrong. Orders of merchandise should not lead directly to goods being shipped; some verification needs to be made of the credit worthiness of the customer. The credit department, not the billings department, will maintain a credit file for this purpose. The file will contain a credit report for the customer, the history of payments, and possibly financial statements if the customer buys large amounts. II is wrong. The billings department does not prepare the bill of lading; rather, the shipping department prepares the bill of lading. The billings department prepares the sales invoice.

261. **C.** I is correct. The shipping department needs a copy of the approved sales order to serve as authorization for shipment of the goods to the customer. II

is correct. The billings department needs a copy of the approved sales order to serve as authorization to prepare the sales invoice and send it to the customer so that the company can get paid. Payment won't happen until a copy of the bill of lading is received by the billings department to serve as evidence of the shipment.

262. **B.** II is correct. In the revenue cycle, the billings department prepares the sales invoice and sends a copy to the customer so the company can get paid. The sales invoice is prepared by the billings department but not before the billings department receives a copy of the sales order. III is correct. In the revenue cycle, the billings department prepares the sales invoice and sends a copy to the customer so the company can get paid. The sales invoice is prepared by the billings department but not before the billings department receives a copy of the bill of lading indicating that goods were shipped. I is wrong. The purchase requisition is not part of the revenue cycle; instead, purchase requisition is part of the purchasing cycle.

263. **B.** The billings department keeps a pending, or open, file. No action is taken by the billings department until a copy of both the sales order and the bill of lading are received. Then, the billings department compares the sales order to the bill of lading in a process called reconciliation. The billings department is an example of the accounting function. If the billings department determines that the shipment was authorized and the two documents reconcile, the billings department will prepare a sales invoice and send a copy to the customer so the entity can get paid. A is wrong. The sales department prepares the sales order but does not need a copy of the bill of lading. C is wrong. The credit department approves customer credit before shipment if the order is over a certain dollar amount, but the credit department would not need a copy of the bill of lading. D is wrong. The warehouse does not need a copy of the bill of lading. The warehouse department maintains custody of the goods and can only transfer the goods within the organization, usually to the shipping department. The shipping department, rather than the warehouse, prepares the bill of lading and ships the goods.

264. **D.** A copy of the sales order and bill of lading is sent to the billings department. The billings department is an accounting function. In this department, they match the information on the sales order with the bill of lading and verify that each is properly authorized. This process is called reconciliation. If

everything is in agreement, the billings department prepares the sales invoice and records the sales invoice into the sales journal. Therefore, A, B, and C are wrong.

265. **D.** Within a proper segregation of duties for the revenue cycle, the warehouse department is charged with custody of the merchandise until an approved sales order is received from the credit department. Then the warehouse department sends the ordered goods within the organization to the shipping department to ready the goods for transport. A is wrong. The shipping department is not charged with custody of the goods but rather with reconciliation and execution. Before shipping but after receiving the goods from the warehouse, the shipping department matches the sales order received from the warehouse with the sales order received from the credit department. This process is known as reconciliation. Only if the two sales orders agree on quantity and type of goods are the goods readied and shipped. B is wrong. The billings department is an example of accounting, not custody. Within the revenue cycle, the billings department prepares the sales invoice and records the sale. C is wrong. The receiving room is not part of the revenue cycle. The receiving room is part of the purchasing cycle.

266. **D.** I is correct. The warehouse department is charged with custody of the merchandise until an approved sales order is received from the credit department. Then the warehouse department normally transfers the goods within the organization to the shipping department to ready the goods for transport. III is correct. Within a purchasing cycle, the receiving room takes initial receipt of merchandise that arrives from the vendor. After making an independent count of the goods received, the receiving room normally transfers these newly received goods within the organization to the warehouse department. II is wrong. The shipping department will normally transport goods outside the organization.

267. **A.** Within a proper segregation of duties for the revenue cycle, the credit department is charged with authorization. In most companies, goods are shipped to the customer before the selling company gets paid. Therefore, only if the credit department approves the customer for credit should goods be transferred from the warehouse and shipped to the customer. If the credit department denies the customer's credit, the goods should not be transferred from the warehouse to the shipping department, or shipped to the customer. B is wrong. The billings

department is an accounting function. The billings department will prepare the sales invoice after receiving a copy of the approved sales order from credit and a copy of the bill of lading from shipping. If the two documents match, the sales invoice should be prepared by the billings department and sent to the customer so that the company can get paid. C is wrong. The purchasing department is not part of the revenue cycle. D is wrong. The shipping department is an example of reconciliation and execution, not authorization. Before shipping, the shipping department reconciles a copy of the approved sales order received from the credit department with the sales order received from the warehouse. If the two sales orders match, with the same amount and type of goods, then the goods are gathered and shipped to the customer.

268. **D.** Within the revenue cycle, for proper segregation of duties, the bill of lading, a shipping document, is prepared by the shipping department and the sales invoice is prepared by the billings or accounting department. Therefore, A, B, and C are wrong.

269. **C.** I is correct. Whenever any asset is conveyed within a company, the recipient should inspect the goods for damage. This procedure is an important internal control to detect mistakes and problems before the asset moves any further within the system. II is correct. Whenever any asset is conveyed within a company, the recipient should count and verify the description with the related documentation. This procedure is an important internal control to detect mistakes and problems before the asset moves any further within the system.

270. **C.** I is correct. A perpetual inventory system maintains a constant record of the inventory on hand. As goods are shipped, the inventory records should be reduced accordingly. Therefore, a copy of each bill of lading should be forwarded to the inventory department for this purpose. II is correct. The billings department needs a copy of the bill of lading in order to prepare the sales invoice. It is not enough for the billings department to have a copy of the approved sales order. A copy of the bill of lading is also needed to serve as evidence that the goods were shipped and that the sales order was not only approved but fully executed.

271. **A.** In a revenue cycle, the sales order is prepared first, followed by the bill of lading, and then the sales invoice. Therefore, B, C, and D are wrong.

272. **B.** The warehouse department does not prepare the sales order, the sales invoice, or the bill of lading. The warehouse prepares a warehouse receipt that serves as evidence that the warehouse transferred the goods ordered to the shipping department. The warehouse transfers goods only within the organization. The shipping department conveys merchandise to appropriate outside parties. Internal control is strengthened by having these departments independent of each other; thus, goods cannot be removed from the company without having two departments involved. This arrangement offers a system of checks and balances. A is wrong. The sales department prepares the sales order. C is wrong. The shipping department prepares the bill of lading. D is wrong. The billings department prepares the sales invoice.

273. **C.** I is correct. If the auditor begins with entries in the sales journal and makes sure that there is a sales invoice to support it, this would be a test of the occurrence or existence assertion. The auditor is testing for overstatement of sales. An auditor always begins with the event that has presumed to have taken place—in this case, that revenue was recorded—and moves to the event that is uncertain—that a sale actually occurred. II is correct. If an auditor begins with entries in the sales journal and makes sure that there is a sales invoice to support it, the auditor is searching for overstatement of revenue. If the auditor finds an entry in the sales journal with no supporting sales invoice, sales are overstated.

274. **A.** I is correct. If an auditor begins with a sample of bills of lading and traces forward into the accounting records, the auditor is testing completeness of sales, or understatement. The auditor always begins with the event that is assumed to have taken place—in this case, that goods were shipped—and moves to the event that is uncertain—that sales invoices were prepared. II is wrong. If there is no sales invoice found for a particular bill of lading, the auditor fears that sales may be understated, not overstated. For each bill of lading, the auditor expects to find a sales invoice and an entry in the sales journal that records that invoice. For any bill of lading where a sales invoice isn't found, the auditor suspects that the shipment was either a fraudulent shipment involving theft of goods or, possibly, a consignment shipment, in which case the client shipped goods to a potential customer but cannot record the sale until the potential customer resells the goods.

275. **C.** I is correct. For each bill of lading, the auditor expects to find a sales invoice and an entry in the sales journal that records that invoice. For any bill of lading where a sales invoice isn't found, the auditor suspects that the shipment may be a fraudulent shipment involving theft of goods. II is correct. For each bill of lading, the auditor expects to find a sales invoice and an entry in the sales journal that records that sales invoice. For any bill of lading where a sales invoice isn't found, the auditor suspects that the shipment was fraudulent or, possibly, a consignment shipment, in which case the client shipped goods to a potential customer but cannot record the sale until the potential customer resells the goods. Since a consignment shipment involves a transfer of possession but not title, no sales invoice would be found. The auditor would request a list of consignment shipments.

276. **C.** I is correct. The auditor wants to know, if a sales invoice is prepared, were the goods actually ordered and shipped? The auditor should start by selecting a sample from the sales invoices and look to see if there are shipping documents to support the sales invoices. The auditor always starts with the event that is assumed to have happened and moves to the event that is uncertain. II is correct. If the auditor finds sales invoices with no related shipping documents, this would be a test for overstatement of sales, rather than understatement. The occurrence assertion is affected rather than the completeness assertion when the fear is overstatement.

277. **A.** I is correct. The auditor wants to know, if goods are ordered and shipped, was an invoice sent and a record made? The auditor should select a sample of bills of lading and verify that corresponding sales invoices are properly prepared and recorded. II is wrong. Consignment shipments could explain why goods were shipped but not recorded as a sale, since consignment shipments involve a transfer of possession but not title.

278. **A.** I is correct. Starting with the source documents and tracing forward to the sales invoice means that the auditor is concerned with understatement—in this case, understatement of revenue. A shipment of merchandise where no sales invoice is found could be an indication of a fraudulent shipment. The concern with understatement of revenue is the possible theft of merchandise. II is wrong. Starting with the shipping documents and looking for sales invoices means that the auditor is concerned with understatement of revenue, not overstatement of

revenue. While the auditor will certainly perform audit procedures to gather evidence regarding overstatement of revenue, this test is for understatement of revenue. An auditor begins with the event that has presumed to have taken place—that goods were shipped—and moves to the event that is uncertain—that sales were recorded.

279. **D.** I is wrong. Any test looking for support for a recorded balance in a journal or ledger provides evidence about the existence or occurrence assertion, not completeness. When performing two-directional testing, an auditor begins with the event that is assumed to have taken place—that sales were recorded—and moves to the event that is uncertain—that goods were shipped. II is wrong. If an auditor starts with the entries in the sales journal and seeks supporting documentation to corroborate, the auditor would be more interested in finding shipping documents that correspond to the recorded sale, not just sales orders. Shipping documents are greater evidence that the sale was fully executed, while sales orders prove only that the customer intended to buy. Only if the credit department approves the customer should the sale be fully executed and shipped. Therefore, the auditor would want to find both the bill of lading and the sales order for even greater evidence that the sale occurred.

280. **C.** To detect a possible understatement of sales, an auditor would trace from the shipping documents to the sales invoice to see if the items shipped (and presumably sold) have been recorded. The auditor always begins a two-directional test by starting with the event that is presumed to have taken place—that goods were shipped—and moves to the event that is uncertain—that sales were recorded. In this case the auditor is testing forward. Any two-directional test that moves forward is a test for completeness, or understatement. A is wrong. Starting with the sales invoice and moving to the shipping documents is a backward-directional test. Testing backward is a test for occurrence or existence, that is, overstatement. B and D are wrong because moving from one journal to another is not a test for understatement or overstatement.

281. **C.** I is correct. In the subsequent period, the auditor looks at certain types of transactions because they can help to substantiate the balances reported on the financial statements. With accounts receivable, examining how much bad debt was written off shortly after year-end is a substantive test for accounts receivable in the subsequent period because it provides evidence as to valuation assertion for accounts receivable. Accounts receivable must have been overvalued at year-end by the amount written off early in January. II is correct. In the subsequent period, the auditor looks at certain types of transactions because they can help substantiate the balances reported on the financial statements. If a customer pays in January, the customer must have owed in December, which means the customer must have existed in December. Therefore, examining cash collections a few days after year-end provides evidence regarding the existence assertion for accounts receivable.

282. **B.** II is correct. In the subsequent period, the auditor looks at certain types of transactions because they can help to substantiate the balances reported on the financial statements. If a customer pays in January, the customer must have owed in December, which means the customer must have existed in December. Therefore, examining cash collections a few days after year-end provides evidence regarding the existence assertion for accounts receivable. I is wrong. In the subsequent period, the auditor looks at certain types of transactions because they can help substantiate the balances reported on the financial statements. With accounts receivable, examining how much bad debt was written off shortly after year-end provides evidence as to valuation assertion. However, it provides no evidence regarding existence of the customer, which is what the question asks about. To test the existence assertion for accounts receivable in the subsequent period, examine cash collections in January.

283. **D.** The completeness assertion is tested whenever the auditor tests forward. A test that starts with the sales invoice and moves to the sales journal is a test going forward because the sales invoice is created and then the sales invoice is recorded in the sales journal. In a two-directional test, an auditor starts with the event that is presumed to have taken place—in this case, that sales invoices were created—and then moves to the event that is uncertain—that sales invoices were recorded. A is wrong. The occurrence assertion would be tested if the auditor began with entries in the sales journal and looked for evidence that the sales occurred, the goods were shipped, and the sales were invoiced. This would be a test for overstatement. B is wrong. The classification assertion would be tested by the auditor looking to see if the client used a contra-account for sales returns and not just decreased the sales account for every sales return. C is wrong.

Accuracy would be tested if the auditor recomputed amounts on the sales invoices.

284. **B.** II is correct. Tracing sales orders to the revenue account provides evidence concerning the completeness assertion of the revenue account. The auditor begins with the event that is presumed to have taken place—that goods were ordered—and moves to the event that is uncertain—that sales were recorded. I is wrong. Tracing sales orders to the revenue account provides no evidence that approved spending limits are exceeded. If approved spending limits are exceeded, this would be the result of management override of internal control, but this would not be detected by the auditor tracing sales orders to the revenue account.

285. **B.** II is correct. External confirmations provide evidence to support the existence assertion. Confirmations are meant to ascertain that the balances shown on the company's records actually do exist; the customer is real and not fictitious. For this reason, the auditor mails confirmations to the client's customers and the customers are asked to respond directly to the auditor so that the client cannot intervene. I is wrong. External confirmations provide little evidence as to whether accounts will actually be collected and, therefore, are not particularly helpful in estimating net realizable value. Valuation assertion for accounts receivable is tested by checking the client's credit-granting policies and by reading contractual agreements regarding pledging of receivables as well as by examining bad write-offs in the subsequent period.

286. **A.** I is correct. External confirmations provide evidence to support the existence assertion. External confirmations are meant to ascertain that the balances shown on the company's records actually do exist; the customer is real and not fictitious. For this reason, the auditor mails the confirmations to the client's customers and the customers are asked to respond directly to the auditor so that the client cannot intervene. The auditor should be in charge of mailing the confirmations to ensure that they actually do get mailed. Either the auditor or the client can prepare the confirmations, but if the client is involved, the auditor should make a careful review. Because of confidentiality, a representative of the client must sign the confirmations, but all other actions are taken by the auditor, both the mailing and the receiving of the responses. II is wrong. Credit verification refers to the valuation of accounts receivable. By checking credit before shipping goods, the client is trying to minimize the

likelihood of selling goods and then having to write off the debt as uncollectible. Any question about accounts receivable that deals with the uncollectible accounts or the aging schedule deals with the valuation assertion rather than existence.

287. **C.** I is correct. Positive confirmations ask for a response in every case so that more tangible evidence is obtained. II is correct. Positive confirmations are more likely to be used when inherent and control risks have been assessed as high and the acceptable level of detection risk has been lowered. Negative confirmations are used when risks are low. Note that both positive and negative confirmations can be used in the same audit.

288. **D.** I is wrong. For good internal controls, the credit manager should be independent of the sales function. If the credit manager reported to the vice president of sales, the vice president of sales would be able to influence the credit manager to relax the standards and approve more customers for credit in order to increase sales. II is wrong. The credit manager should not authorize a bad debt write-off. The authorization for a bad debt write-off should come from a higher source, someone independent of the sales function. The treasurer normally authorizes a bad debt write-off, not the credit manager.

289. **C.** I and II are correct. As indicated by the following table, if ending inventory is overstated, cost of goods sold is understated; therefore, gross profit, and ultimately net income, is too high.

Beginning inventory	0
Purchases	10
Less ending inventory	**4**
Cost of goods sold	**6**
Sales	25
Less cost of goods sold	**6**
Gross profit	**19**

290. **C.** I is correct. Goods shipped out on consignment still belong to the consignor; that is, no title passes, only possession. II is correct. When an auditor examines a client's inventory, items shipped out on consignment by the client still belong to the client, so the rights and obligations assertion is affected. The client still has rights of ownership even after the consignment shipment.

291. **B.** II is correct. The receiving department gets a copy of the purchase order with the quantity ordered deliberately missing. The receiving department needs a copy of the purchase order to know what kind of goods to expect delivery of, but if the receiving room doesn't know how many units are

being delivered, the workers there are forced to perform a more accurate independent count. I is wrong. The receiving department does not need a copy of the purchase requisition. The purchase requisition is needed only so that someone within the organization cannot both authorize and execute a purchase of goods from outside the entity.

292. **B.** Four documents are involved in a typical purchasing cycle: purchase requisition, purchase order, receiving report, and purchase invoice. The purchase requisition could be prepared by anyone but then needs to be approved by that person's department head. The purchase order is prepared in the purchasing department. The receiving report is prepared by the receiving room. The purchase invoice is prepared outside the organization.

293. **A.** In a purchasing cycle, the first document prepared is the purchase requisition (IV). The requisition is prepared by someone in the company that is requesting an item and is first sent to that individual's supervisor for approval. The approved requisition is then sent to the warehouse to see if the item is in stock and can be transferred within the company from the warehouse to the department that requested the item. If the item is not in stock, the purchasing department gets involved and orders the item from outside the company. This department prepares the purchase order (I). When the purchased item arrives, a receiving report (II) is then prepared by the receiving room. Eventually, a purchase invoice (III) will arrive from the vendor.

294. **D.** A pending (or open) file is maintained in accounts or vouchers payable to gather the four documents: purchase requisition, purchase order, receiving report, and purchase invoice. When all are eventually received, they are matched by accounts payable and the authorizations are checked. Then, a voucher is prepared by accounts payable. The voucher is the approval for payment. A is wrong. The purchasing department prepares the purchase order but does not authorize payment. B is wrong. The billings department is not part of the purchasing cycle. The billings department is found in the revenue cycle and prepares the sales invoice. C is wrong. The receiving room prepares the receiving report but has no authorization to approve payment for goods.

295. **D.** I is wrong. If goods are accepted by the receiving room, receiving room personnel complete a receiving report to provide all information on the merchandise, the quantity received, and so on. A copy of the receiving report goes to accounts payable, which now gets its third document and keeps the file open with the three documents in it until the fourth document, the purchase invoice, is received. II is wrong. The department that originally requested the merchandise will also get a copy of the receiving report. Whatever department within the company originally requested the item needs to know that it came in so that the department can put it out for sale.

296. **C.** II is correct. The purchase invoice is prepared outside the organization by the vendor. III is correct. The purchase requisition is prepared by the department within the organization that requests an item be purchased. This is normally an item that needs to be purchased for resale. I is wrong. The purchase order is the only document prepared by the purchasing department.

297. **B.** I is correct. The purchase invoice is prepared outside the organization. This is important because documents generated outside the organization are generally considered to be more persuasive audit evidence than documents generated within the organization. II is wrong. The receiving report is prepared within the organization, in the receiving room, when the purchased items arrive. After the receiving department counts the items in, department personnel prepare the receiving report without knowing how many goods were ordered. III is wrong. The voucher package is prepared by the vouchers payable or accounts payable department. The voucher package contains copies of the purchase requisition, the purchase order, the receiving report, and the purchase invoice. Once accounts payable has all four documents, they can reconcile the documents and prepare the voucher package.

298. **A.** I is correct. The vouchers payable department approves vendors' invoices for payment. Before approval, the purchase invoice should be compared with the purchase order and receiving report, the supporting documents. If all documents match and are properly authorized, the vouchers or accounts payable department prepares the voucher, which is the approval for payment to the vendor. II is wrong. Deliberately removing the quantity ordered on the receiving department copy of the purchase order is a desirable internal control procedure, but it is typically performed by the purchasing department, not vouchers payable.

299. **C.** While vouchers payable typically prepares the approval for payment, called the voucher, the

voucher is then sent to the cash disbursements department for payment. The check to the vendor is ultimately cut in the cash disbursements department, not vouchers or accounts payable. This is an example of a segregation of duties between authorization and execution. Vouchers payable authorizes the payment; cash disbursements makes the payment. Therefore, A, B, and D are wrong.

300. **A.** I is correct. A copy of the purchase order is attached to the voucher and becomes part of the backup documentation. The voucher is the document that acknowledges the liability and approves payment. The backup documentation consists of copies of the purchase requisition, purchase order, receiving report, and purchase invoice. The four forms are attached in what is sometimes called a voucher package. The voucher package is sent to the cash disbursements department for payment. II is correct. A copy of the receiving report is attached to the voucher and becomes part of the backup documentation. III is wrong. The bill of lading is not a document in the purchasing cycle, but rather a document in the sales cycle.

301. **D.** I is correct. The voucher is the document that acknowledges the liability and approves payment. A company uses a voucher system as a control to prevent money from leaving the company without proper authorization. The voucher has to be prepared, signed, and forwarded to cash disbursements in order for payment to be made to the vendor. II is correct. The backup documentation (all four forms) is attached to the voucher in what is sometimes called a voucher package. III is correct. The voucher is recorded in the voucher register, which is summarized periodically for recording in the general ledger by general accounting. The voucher package is forwarded to the cash disbursements department for payment.

302. **C.** The cash disbursements department both signs the check and mails the check to the vendor. Good internal controls dictate that once a check is signed, it should be mailed immediately and not travel backward through the system. Vouchers payable prepares the voucher and forwards the voucher to the cash disbursements department. Usually the check is signed by the treasurer in the cash disbursements department. The check should be mailed out immediately once signed. Therefore, A, B, and D are wrong.

303. **A.** In the cash disbursements department, the check is signed and the voucher is perforated or marked as "paid" so that the voucher won't be paid twice. The check is recorded in the check register (or cash disbursements journal) and the check is quickly mailed after it has been signed. B is wrong. Vouchers payable prepares the voucher and records the voucher in the voucher register, but vouchers payable does not cancel or perforate the voucher. The department that pays the bill should cancel the voucher, and that department is cash disbursements. C is wrong. The purchasing department prepares the purchase order but does not prepare the voucher or perforate the voucher. D is wrong. The receiving department does not even get a copy of the voucher. Receiving gets a copy of the purchase order with the number of units ordered deliberately left blank to force an accurate count of the goods by receiving. Receiving is then forced to count the goods in and prepare a receiving report based on what was counted in.

304. **C.** I is correct. In an audit, in the evidence-gathering stage of the purchasing cycle, the auditor would examine a sample of paid vouchers to gather evidence as to whether each voucher is supported by a vendor invoice. Any paid voucher that is not supported by a vendor invoice could be a fraudulent payment and someone may be stealing from the company. II is correct. In an audit, in the evidence-gathering stage of the purchasing cycle, the auditor would examine a sample of paid vouchers to gather evidence as to whether each voucher is perforated or marked as paid so that the voucher will be paid only once.

305. **B.** II is correct. To provide assurance that each voucher is submitted and paid only once, an auditor would examine a sample of paid vouchers and determine whether each voucher is perforated or marked as paid. Once marked as paid, the voucher will not be paid again. I is wrong. While the auditor would examine a sample of paid vouchers to gather evidence as to whether each voucher is supported by a vendor invoice, making sure that each voucher is supported by a vendor's invoice would show authorization but not any evidence of double payment.

306. **A.** I is correct. When an auditor vouches a sample of entries in the voucher register to the supporting documents, this procedure is testing whether recorded entries are valid, that is, whether they did exist. The auditor always starts with the event that is presumed to have taken place—in this case, that a voucher was recorded—and moves to the event that is uncertain—that goods were ordered and received. II is wrong. When an auditor vouches

a sample of entries in the voucher register to the supporting documents, this procedure is testing whether recorded entries are valid, NOT whether valid entries were recorded. With completeness, the concern is understatement, but this question asks about overstatement.

307. **D.** II is correct. The accounts payable, or vouchers payable, department has the responsibility to prepare vouchers for payment. As part of that process, an employee in the vouchers payable (or accounts payable) department should check vendors' invoices for math accuracy by recomputing calculations and extensions, and should match the vendors' invoices with receiving reports and purchase orders for quantities, prices, and terms. Only after this reconciliation process should the voucher be prepared. I is wrong, the purchasing department selects the vendor and prepares the purchase order and ultimately executes the purchase. III is wrong, Cash disbursements takes the approved voucher from the vouchers payable department, signs the check, and then immediately mails the check to the vendor and cancels the voucher so that the voucher cannot be paid twice.

308. **A.** I is correct. In the purchasing cycle, the receiving report is prepared by the receiving room. II is wrong. The bill of lading is a document in the revenue cycle, not the purchasing cycle. In the revenue cycle, the bill of lading serves as evidence of a shipment of goods.

309. **C.** I is correct. In testing completeness for accounts payable, the auditor will choose a selection of purchase invoices and make sure that any obligation is recorded properly. The auditor starts with the supporting documentation and looks to see if the transaction was properly recorded. Any test that moves forward is testing completeness, or understatement. The auditor starts with the event that is assumed to have happened—in this case, that goods were purchased and a debt was incurred—and moves to the event that is uncertain—that the debt was recorded. II is correct. In testing completeness for accounts payable, the auditor will choose a selection of receiving reports and make sure that any goods received were recorded and any obligation is recorded properly. When the auditor starts with the supporting documentation and looks to see if the transaction was properly recorded, this is a test for understatement, or completeness.

310. **A.** I is correct. When an auditor traces a sample of purchase orders and the related receiving reports to

the purchases journal and the cash disbursements journal, the auditor is testing to see if transactions were recorded. The client asserts that all transactions that should have been recorded have been recorded. If some have not been recorded, the books are not complete. The auditor starts with the event that is assumed to have happened—that goods were purchased and received and a debt was incurred—and moves to the event that is uncertain—that the debt was recorded. II is wrong. When the auditor starts with the supporting documentation and looks to see if the transaction was properly recorded, this is a test for completeness (understatement), not existence.

311. **B.** II is correct. Testing the existence or occurrence assertion, the auditor starts with the general ledger balance and vouches backward, seeking support. The client asserts that all recorded transactions were valid. If any transactions that were recorded did not actually exist, the books are overstated. The auditor starts with the event that is assumed to have happened—in this case, that purchases were recorded—and moves to the event that is uncertain—that goods were ordered and received. I is wrong. In the purchasing cycle, when the auditor is testing the existence or occurrence assertion, he or she does not start with the supporting documents. Starting with the supporting documents is a test for completeness.

312. **B.** II is correct. Receiving reports are client-generated documents in the purchasing cycle. I is wrong. Bills of lading, although they may be generated by the client, are documents generated in the sales cycle, not the purchasing cycle.

313. **D.** I is wrong. Vendor invoices and packing slips are generated by vendors. II is wrong. Bills of lading may be generated by the client, but accounts receivable confirmations are not generated by the client. They are auditor generated. To be considered valid evidence, accounts receivable confirmations should be between the auditor and the client's customer.

314. **B.** The purchase invoice should indicate the FOB point when the title changed hands, and the receiving report should indicate the date of receipt of the goods. These documents would enable the auditor to determine the date on which the liability was incurred to ensure that it occurred in the period it was recorded in and that the inventory exists in the current period. A, C, and D are wrong.

315. **B.** II is correct. Unrecorded liabilities eventually become due and must be paid. A review of cash

disbursements after the balance sheet date is an effective procedure for detecting unrecorded liabilities. I is wrong. Starting with a sample of accounts payable entries recorded just before year-end will not provide evidence regarding what should have been recorded; rather, it would be helpful to gather evidence regarding what should not have been recorded.

316. **C.** I and II are correct. Observation of physical inventory counts provides evidence about both existence and completeness. Observing the inventory provides evidence that it physically exists; observing the actual count provides evidence regarding completeness (i.e., does it appear that the client is doing a careful, accurate, and complete job of counting all of the inventory?).

317. **D.** I is wrong. An auditor cannot determine whether there have been changes in pricing methods simply by observing a client's physical inventories. II is wrong. An auditor cannot determine whether outstanding purchase commitments exist simply by observing a client's physical inventories.

318. **C.** I and II are correct. Rights and obligations might be tested by examining paid vendors' invoices, by inspecting consignment agreements and contracts, or by confirming inventory held at outside locations.

319. **D.** An auditor's observation procedures with respect to well-kept perpetual inventories that are periodically checked by physical counts may be performed before, during, or after the end of the audit period. If, however, the assessed level of control risk for inventory is high, the observation procedures should be performed at year-end.

320. **D.** The auditor should observe the inventory count of goods held in a public warehouse if the inventory held there is significant; otherwise, confirmation of such inventory is sufficient. The auditor's personal observation is generally one of the most reliable and effective forms of evidence. Observing physical inventory counts provides reliable evidence that the inventory actually exists. It may be more efficient to confirm the inventory held at the public warehouse but not as effective as observation. A, B, and C are not the most efficient means.

321. **C.** I is correct. During a tour of the manufacturing plant or production facility, the auditor should be alert for items that appear to be old, obsolete, or defective. II is correct. Comparisons of inventory balances with anticipated sales volume might

indicate higher inventory levels than would be expected, perhaps due to slow-moving, defective, or obsolete inventory items.

322. **C.** I is correct. An auditor will make "test counts" of a client's inventory to be sure client count is accurate. II is correct. An auditor will make test counts of a client's inventory for later verification of final cost figures. In performing test counts, the auditor selects a sample of inventory items, counts them, and compares the result to the client's count.

323. **A.** The auditor should test the client's physical inventory report by tracing test counts taken by the auditor to the client's physical inventory count report, thereby verifying the completeness of the client count. B is wrong. If the auditor began with the client's physical inventory listing and compared it to the auditor's test count, this would verify existence and test for overstatement of inventory. C is wrong. The auditor would test the rights and obligations assertion for inventory by reading loan agreements and the minutes of meetings to see if any inventory has been pledged. Also, inquiring if any inventory is here on consignment would relate to rights and obligations. D is wrong. The valuation assertion can be tested by touring the facility and performing analytical procedures regarding inventory turnover. Comparing inventory balances with anticipated sales volume might indicate higher inventory levels than would be expected, perhaps due to slow-moving, defective, or obsolete inventory.

324. **B.** When the auditor begins with the client's physical inventory listing and compares it to the auditor's test count, this is to verify existence and test for overstatement of the client's inventory listing. Therefore, A, C, and D are wrong.

325. **B.** II is correct. Starting with the tags and testing forward to the detailed inventory listing is a test for completeness. The auditor starts with what is believed to have happened—in this case, that inventory was counted—and moves to the event that is uncertain—that inventory was recorded. This is a test for understatement (completeness assertion). I is wrong. If the auditor began with the client's detailed inventory listing and moved to the tags, this would be a test for overstatement, or existence. In a good inventory count, the client would use prenumbered tags. This ensures that every item in the warehouse is counted because the client puts a physical tag on each item as it is counted. It also ensures that the client doesn't count something twice or count something that shouldn't be counted.

326. **A.** I is correct. Tracing from inventory tags to the inventory listing schedule verifies the completeness of the schedule. II is wrong. Tracing from inventory tags to the inventory listing schedule verifies the completeness of the schedule, not the existence (or validity) of the items.

327. **A.** I is correct. Tracing from the inventory schedule to the inventory tags and the auditor's record count sheets verifies the validity (existence) of the items. II is wrong. Tracing from the inventory schedule to the inventory tags and the auditor's record count sheets verifies the validity of the items, not the completeness of the schedule.

328. **A.** I is correct. Tracing from receiving reports and vendors' invoices to the inventory listing are cut-off procedures used to verify completeness of the inventory listing. The auditor starts with the event that is believed to have taken place—that inventory was purchased and received—and moves to the event that is uncertain—that the inventory was recorded. II is wrong. For existence of the inventory, the auditor would begin with the inventory listing and move to see if there is support from a receiving report and vendor invoice. This would prove that the entries in the books for inventory are valid.

329. **B.** As inventory gets older, the chance that its value will fall below cost goes up. As goods get older, they tend to get damaged or show other signs of age that may require them to be sold at a reduced price. Inventory is reported at the lower of cost or market. The increase in age might be a cause for the market value to decline so that a reduction in the reported balance will be necessary. A, C, and D are wrong. While presentation, existence, and completeness all pertain to inventory, the question asked about the age of the inventory.

330. **C.** I is correct. Inventory purchased by Berman with terms FOB shipping point belongs to the buyer (Berman) while in transit. Therefore, this inventory should be counted at year-end even though it has not yet arrived. II is correct. Inventory shipped out on consignment by Berman still belongs to Berman until resold and should be counted at year-end.

331. **C.** Verifying that all inventory owned by the client is on hand at the time of the count is not an objective when auditing inventories. Purchased items still in transit at year-end belong to the client under FOB shipping point. Items sold with terms FOB destination still belong to the seller (the client). Inventory out on consignment should also be included in inventory. Since certain items of inventory owned by the client are not on hand at year-end, the auditor would therefore not need to verify that all inventory owned is on hand. A is wrong. An auditor would gather evidence regarding appropriate presentation of inventory on the balance sheet. B is wrong. An auditor would gather evidence whether damaged goods and obsolete items have been properly accounted for. D is wrong. The auditor would gather evidence regarding inventory pricing and whether or not the inventory is priced using a method that is generally acceptable, such as LIFO or FIFO.

332. **B.** II is correct. If purchases made before the end of the year have been recorded in the subsequent year, inventory will not be complete. The auditor uses cutoff tests to detect such situations and to determine that inventory quantities include all products owned by the company. (Note that the cutoff assertion is closely related to the completeness and occurrence assertions.) I is wrong. An auditor most likely would inspect loan agreements under which an entity's inventories are pledged to support the rights and obligations assertion for inventory.

333. **D.** I is wrong. The disclosures involving inventory require inventory balances to be disclosed for work in process inventory. II is wrong. The disclosures involving inventory require inventory balances to be disclosed for raw materials. Under the category of presentation and disclosure, completeness is an assertion relating to inventory disclosure. For a manufacturer, disclosures related to inventory are required as follows: inventory balances for raw materials, work in process, and finished goods all need to be disclosed or the presentation and disclosure for inventory is not complete.

334. **A.** I is correct. Assertions about accuracy deal with whether data related to recorded transactions have been included in the financial statements at appropriate amounts. II is wrong. Cutoff tests do not provide evidence related to the accuracy assertion for purchases, since accuracy assertion relates to what has been recorded, not what should have been recorded.

335. **B.** I is correct. Inventories should be reduced, when appropriate, to replacement cost or net realizable value. This is closely related to the valuation of inventory. II is wrong. Understandability for inventory is related to inventory disclosures. III is wrong. Existence assertion for inventory relates to overstating inventory by counting inventory that does not exist.

336. C. I is correct. Understandability and classification might be tested by confirming inventories pledged under loan agreements. The pledge or assignment of any inventory should be appropriately disclosed in the financial statements. II is correct. Understandability and classification might be tested by examining drafts of the financial statements for appropriate balance sheet classification.

Chapter 11: Audit Sampling

337. A. I is correct. There are two types of statistical sampling: sampling for attributes and sampling for variables. Sampling for attributes involves sampling to determine whether controls are functioning as designed. The auditor relies on sampling for attributes when assessing control risk. II is wrong. Sampling for variables, not sampling for attributes, is concerned with evidence regarding account balances.

338. C. I is correct. The first step in determining sample size for a test of controls is for the auditor to estimate the likely error rate in the population. II is correct. The second step in determining sample size for a test of controls is for the auditor to set a limit for how much error in the population the auditor could tolerate.

339. C. When an auditor sampling for attributes, that is, testing controls, determines that the error rate is higher than originally expected, the sample size must be increased. A, B, and D are wrong.

340. B. II is correct. The auditor fears that the sample will not be representative of the population as a whole. This risk is known as sampling risk or the allowable level of sampling risk. To lower that risk, the auditor needs to add more items to the sample. The larger the sample, the more likely it is to be representative of the population. I is wrong. To reduce sampling risk, the auditor will always have to sample a larger portion of the population.

341. C. I is correct. The more errors expected in the population, the larger the sample size must be. When the auditor expects more errors, the auditor needs to be more careful and look at a larger sample. II is correct. The lower the level of sampling risk, the larger the sample size must be. If the auditor wants to reduce sampling risk from 10% to 5%, this means that the auditor wants to go from being 90% sure to being 95% sure that the sample represents the population. Anytime the auditor wants to be more certain that the sample represents the population, the sample size must be increased.

342. A. I is correct. The sample showed a 3% error rate, but the population will always have a higher error rate than the sample. Given the parameters established by the auditor, the population error rate is calculated as 6.4%. The difference between the sample error rate and the upper deviation rate of the population is known as the allowance for sampling risk, 6.4 − 3 = 3.4. II is wrong. Since the upper deviation rate (new expected error rate of the population) is higher than the tolerable rate, the auditor would not find the control to be effective enough to lower the assessment of control risk.

343. B. II is correct. The tolerable rate, given as 5%, is higher than the upper deviation rate, given as 4.4%. Therefore, the auditor will likely view the control as reliable and lower his or her assessment of control risk, thus leading to less substantive testing in this area of the audit. I is wrong. Although there were errors, the sample error rate of 3% translated into an upper deviation rate of 4.4%. Therefore, the auditor would not conclude that there were too many errors, since the upper deviation rate of 4.4% error was lower than the tolerable error rate of 5%.

344. A. I is correct. The sample rate of deviation plus the allowance for sampling risk is equal to the upper deviation rate. The upper deviation rate is then compared to the tolerable deviation rate, and if the upper deviation rate is lower than the tolerable rate, the control is assessed as reliable. II is wrong. The tolerable deviation rate is equal to how much error the auditor can tolerate and still feel that the client's control is reliable. The auditor knows that some error is inevitable in any control or account balance. The tolerable deviation rate is set by the auditor.

345. B. II is correct. Risk of assessing control risk too high relates to the efficiency of the audit. When control risk is assessed too high, more substantive procedures than needed will have to be performed, making the audit inefficient. I is wrong. As for effectiveness, if the substantive tests were done properly, the audit opinion should not be affected by the fact that the auditor assessed control risk too high. The audit will still be effective, just not particularly efficient.

346. C. I is correct. To reduce sampling risk, the auditor will always have to sample a larger portion of the population. If the auditor selects more items, the chance that the sample will have characteristics different from the population goes down. II is correct.

When sampling for variables, an auditor is estimating an account balance.

347. **A.** I is correct. In every audit, there is a chance that a randomly chosen sample may not be representative of the population as a whole on the characteristic of interest. This concept is known as sampling risk. There will always be some element of sampling risk because an auditor does not examine 100% of the population. II is wrong. Selecting audit procedures that are not appropriate to achieve specific objectives relates to an error that could exist even if 100% of the population is examined (nonsampling risk). Audits are full of risk, both sampling risk as well as nonsampling risk.

348. **A.** I is correct. The auditor knows that there will probably be some error in every account balance. Therefore, the auditor must set a limit for the largest amount of discovered error that can be tolerated before the account balance is considered not fairly presented. This is referred to as the tolerable error rate. II is wrong. If the auditor can tolerate a higher error rate, or if the auditor can tolerate a bigger misstatement in the client balance, the auditor will need to sample fewer items. The more problems that the auditor can tolerate, the smaller the sample size can be.

349. **B.** II is correct. The tolerable deviation rate is one of three parameters needed to determine sample size. The other two parameters are the expected error rate of the population and the allowable level of sampling risk. I is wrong. In attribute sampling, the number of items in the population is not a factor in determining sample size.

350. **C.** I is correct. In variable sampling, which is done to test account balances, the number of items in the population is a significant factor in determining sample size. II is correct. In variable sampling, the allowable level of risk is an important parameter to determine sample size. The allowable level of risk refers to the risk that the auditor's sample has characteristics different from the population.

351. **C.** Incorrect rejection of the account balance is where sample results support the conclusion that the recorded account balance was materially misstated when, in fact, it was not. The risk that a sample is not representative of the population is known as the allowable level of risk. When performing substantive tests, the allowable level of risk is the risk that the auditor makes the wrong conclusion regarding the account balance based on the sample. The question tells us that the sample was bad, as it made the account balance appear to be misstated when it was not. Therefore, the auditor would have incorrectly rejected the entire account balance as "not fairly presented," based on the sample. For those reasons, A, B, and D are wrong.

352. **D.** Incorrect acceptance is when an auditor determines that the sample results support the conclusion that the recorded account balance is fairly presented, when in fact the account balance is materially misstated. The risk that a sample is not representative of the population is known as the allowable level of risk. When performing substantive tests, the allowable level of risk refers to the risk that the auditor makes the wrong conclusion regarding the account balance based on the sample. This question tells us that the sample made the account balance appear to be fairly presented when it was not. Therefore, the auditor would have incorrectly accepted the account balance. A, B, and C are wrong.

353. **D.** Attribute sampling is used when testing controls. A, B, and C are wrong. PPS sampling and stratified sampling are variable sampling techniques that help the auditor deal with variability in a population. These methods would be common when the auditor is sampling to gather evidence for a client's accounts receivable.

354. **B.** The sample error of $2,000 ($6,000 − $4,000) is projected to the entire interval through use of a tainting factor of 33% ($2,000/$6,000). 33% or 1/3 of $9,000 = $3,000.

Chapter 12: Evidence Gathering and Transaction Cycles, Part 2

355. **A.** I is correct. An auditor will confirm all client bank account balances. There is a standard bank confirmation form to expedite the process. The usefulness of the standard bank confirmation may be limited because the bank employee who completes the form may be unaware of all the financial relationships that the bank has with the client. II is wrong. The standard bank confirmation should request balances of all bank accounts, even those accounts that the client indicates were closed out during the year. The client may not have actually closed all of the accounts and may be using one to steal from the company.

356. **C.** III is correct. Kiting involves the client's cash appearing as though it were in two bank accounts at the same time. To detect kiting, the auditor should review all checks and deposits clearing the bank two weeks after the end of the year. If found, these transactions should be scheduled to ensure that both the deposit and withdrawal are recorded in the correct time period. The auditor should request a bank cutoff statement from the bank for this purpose and prepare a bank transfer schedule. I is wrong. A bank reconciliation is a process that explains the difference between the bank balance shown in an organization's bank statement, as supplied by the bank, and the corresponding amount shown in the organization's own accounting records at a particular point in time. While an auditor would examine the client's bank reconciliation, it would not assist the auditor in detecting kiting. II is wrong. A bank cutoff statement is a statement obtained from the bank by the auditor that contains client deposits and checks that occurred 7 to 14 days after year-end. A bank cutoff statement is useful to gather evidence regarding whether or not deposits in transit at year-end actually cleared the bank. All deposits in transit that were listed on the year-end bank reconciliation should be listed on the bank cutoff statement. While the auditor would request a bank cutoff statement, it is not an auditor-prepared document.

357. **C.** I is correct. The auditor should obtain bank cutoff statements that include transactions for 7 to 14 days after year-end. The outstanding checks at year-end on the bank reconciliation should have cleared the bank and be listed as a check on the bank cutoff statement. II is correct. The auditor should obtain bank cutoff statements that include transactions for 7 to 14 days after year-end. The deposits in transit at year-end on the bank reconciliation should have cleared the bank and be listed as a deposit in the bank cutoff statement.

358. **B.** II is correct. Checks dated after year-end would not be included in the year-end outstanding check list. I is wrong. Checks dated after year-end might be on the bank cutoff statement. Some of those checks dated after year-end could have cleared the bank a week or two into the new year. When auditing cash, the auditor requests a bank cutoff statement to examine transactions that cleared a week or two into the new year.

359. **C.** I is correct. A bank cutoff statement is used to verify the items appearing on a bank reconciliation. If theft has occurred, the fraud may be hidden by tampering with the information on the bank reconciliation. Therefore, the auditor should check the math on the reconciliation and verify all items that appear, such as the bank balance, deposits in

transit, and outstanding checks. Information about each of these three items will be found in a bank cutoff statement. II is correct. If a deposit in transit is not recorded by the bank in a reasonable period of time, the auditor should be suspicious that the deposit was not really in transit. Likewise, if checks do not clear when anticipated, the auditor may be concerned that they were not actually outstanding at year's end.

360. **B.** Municipal property tax bills prepared in the client's name are an example of external evidence that the client actually owns the property. If the question had asked about which assertion was affected by examining property tax bills, the rights and obligations assertion and existence assertion would be correct. A, C, and D are wrong.

361. **C.** I is correct. A question about the existence of prenumbered purchase orders would likely be included on the internal control questionnaire since prenumbering functions are an important control supporting the completeness assertion. II is correct. A question about controls related to competitive bids would likely be included on a questionnaire related to controls over the initiation and execution of equipment purchases.

362. **B.** II is correct. A debit to accumulated depreciation decreases the balance in that account. The retirement of plant assets necessitates the removal (decrease) of accumulated depreciation related to the retired asset by debiting accumulated depreciation. I is wrong. If the prior year's depreciation expense were understated (i.e., too low), the entry to correct the error would be a credit to accumulated depreciation.

363. **A.** I is correct. Determining that proper amounts of depreciation are expensed provides assurance with regard to valuation and allocation related to the asset and assures accuracy in terms of financial statement presentation. II is wrong. Verifying depreciation computations does not provide evidence with respect to existence or occurrence.

364. **A.** I is correct. Testing to see whether equipment listed in the accounting records is physically present in the plant and still in service is an effective way to test whether unrecorded disposals occurred. II is wrong. Reviewing whether depreciation is still being taken would not provide evidence about unrecorded fixed-asset disposals unless the auditor also performs a physical inspection of the assets being depreciated. Also, assets that are fully depreciated

yet still in service would not appear in depreciation records.

365. **A.** I is correct. The auditor should review the related repair and maintenance expense accounts to test for completeness of asset additions. The company may have recorded the payment but recorded it as an expense rather than an asset addition. The auditor is looking for items recorded as repairs that should have been capitalized, known as unrecorded additions. II is wrong. Testing to see whether equipment listed in the accounting records is physically still present in the plant and still in service is an effective way to test whether unrecorded disposals occurred but is not useful in finding unrecorded additions.

366. **B.** II is correct. An analysis of depreciation expense would not identify fixed assets that were not properly capitalized, since no depreciation would be included for items not already classified as assets. I is wrong. An analysis of the repairs and maintenance account would best aid the auditor in verifying that all fixed assets have been capitalized. This account is generally analyzed to test for completeness of asset additions (i.e., the auditor is looking for items recorded as repairs or maintenance that would more properly have been capitalized as improvements of an asset).

367. **A.** I is correct. To search for unrecorded disposals, the auditor would inspect the property ledger and the insurance and tax records, and then tour the client's facilities. II is wrong. Analysis of the repair and maintenance account is useful in identifying transactions that should have been capitalized versus expensed.

368. **D.** I is wrong. Analyzing the repairs and maintenance account does not provide evidence about obsolete assets. The auditor reviews repair and maintenance expense accounts to test for completeness of asset additions. II is wrong. Analyzing the repairs and maintenance account does not provide evidence about the existence of assets. The auditor might select recorded plant and equipment assets and then physically locate and observe them in order to verify existence.

369. **D.** I is wrong. Verifying depreciation computations does not provide evidence with respect to completeness but rather to valuation. II is wrong. Verifying depreciation computations does not provide evidence with respect to rights and obligations but rather to valuation.

370. **A.** I is correct. Selecting items from the accounting records and attempting to locate them (existence) will reveal unrecorded retirements when the item cannot be located. II is wrong. Scanning the general journal for recorded entries is unlikely to reveal unrecorded retirements of equipment.

371. **A.** I is correct. Accumulated depreciation is debited when an asset is sold. II is correct. The journal entry to retire an asset includes a debit to accumulated depreciation and a credit to the asset account. Accumulated depreciation is debited when an asset is retired. III is correct. Accumulated depreciation is debited when there is total and permanent impairment of an asset.

372. **A.** I is correct. In most companies, long-term debt cannot be incurred without the formal approval of the board of directors. Therefore, evidence of the authorization of such debt should be sought to determine if all long-term liabilities are being reported by the company. II is wrong. A bank cut-off statement provides information about cash transactions in a checking account for 7 to 14 days after the end of the year and is unrelated to long-term debt. Rather than a bank cutoff statement, the auditor should review all bank confirmations for evidence of such debt balances as well as information on maturity dates, interest rates, and security agreements.

373. **B.** I is correct. Contingencies often have little, if any, tangible documentation. A person, for example, simply may have made a threat against a company. Whenever physical evidence is lacking, the auditor will want to test the completeness assertion to ensure that no balances have been omitted. II is correct. With contingencies, the auditor should obtain evidence to support the valuation assertion. Uncertainty surrounds the outcome of any contingency so that the potential amount of loss may be difficult to assess, since it often involves anticipating the outcome of a court case. III is wrong. Existence relates to overstatement of liabilities, not understatement.

374. **D.** I is correct. The reporting company should provide a listing of all contingencies. However, the auditor needs to ensure that other contingencies have not been omitted. The auditor reads the minutes of the board of directors meetings for any discussions regarding contingent liabilities. II is correct. The reporting company should provide a listing of all contingencies. However, the auditor needs to ensure that other contingencies have not

been omitted. The management rep letter gives the auditor an opportunity to inquire about contingencies. III is correct. Litigation surrounds many contingencies so that a review of the correspondence with the company's attorneys might bring discussion of contingencies to light.

375. C. I is correct. Client contracts that contain a liquidated damages clause contain a contingent liability. A liquidated damages clause in a contract contains a specific dollar amount of damage, agreed to in advance, should that particular contract be breached. II is correct. Debt covenants contained in loan agreements sometimes allow the bank to call the loan due immediately in the event that the current ratio falls below a certain amount. For example, a typical debt covenant might allow the bank to call the client's loan due if the current ratio fell below 2:1. The auditor would read the bank confirmation letter because any debt covenant provides evidence of a contingent liability. The auditor would need to determine if a contingency exists at the balance sheet date from that particular loan being in breach of the debt covenant.

376. C. I is correct. With regard to contingent losses, some method has to be derived to corroborate the company's assessment of the likelihood of each loss. II is correct. With regard to contingent losses, some method has to be derived to corroborate the estimated amount of each loss. Traditionally, the evidence regarding both the likelihood of each loss and the estimated amount has been obtained by sending a list of these contingencies, along with the possibility and amount of loss, to the company's attorneys, who are asked to indicate disagreements with that information. Attorneys need only provide information about cases in which they have had substantial participation. For those cases, disagreements should be indicated to the auditor. Otherwise, the attorney must state that sufficient knowledge is not available to render any type of assessment.

377. B. I is correct. A primary objective when auditing liabilities is to determine that they are all properly included. Accordingly, the auditor has to search for liabilities that exist as of the balance sheet date. In searching for contingent liabilities, the auditor will typically review bank confirmation letters for any indication of direct or contingent liabilities. If the client's bank loan contained a debt covenant that required the current ratio to be 2:1 or better at all times, a direct or contingent liability would exist if the client were to fall below that ratio. III is correct. Examining invoices for professional services,

especially from attorneys who may be working on pending litigation, may provide evidence of contingent liabilities. II is wrong. Accounts receivable confirmations provide evidence regarding assets, not liabilities.

378. B. II is correct. If a claim has been omitted, in what's known as an unasserted claim, the lawyer should inform the client and suggest that the client disclose all details to the auditor. Information about unasserted claims must come from the client company. If that information is not subsequently conveyed by the client, the attorney should consider resigning. I is wrong. Information regarding unasserted claims would NOT come from the client's attorney. Information regarding unasserted claims would come from the client. Information regarding asserted (that is, not unasserted) claims would come from the client's attorney.

379. C. The primary source of information to be reported about litigation, claims, and assessments is the client's management; the client's attorney is a secondary source. A is wrong. The client's attorney is the primary source of corroboration of evidence, but the primary source of evidence regarding litigation, claims, and assessments is the client. B is wrong. Court records are not a primary source of information. Court records would be a secondary rather than a primary source of evidence regarding litigation, claims, and assessments. D is wrong. The independent auditor is not a source of evidence regarding litigation, claims, and assessments. The independent auditor is searching for such evidence.

380. D. The lawyer and the auditor should agree on materiality regarding litigation, claims, and assessments. A, B, and C are wrong. The client's management and governance should not get to decide what is material regarding such contingencies.

381. C. I is correct. Unusual and large cash receipts, especially near the end of the year, should be investigated. The company could have recently borrowed the money and purposely not recorded the debt yet. II is correct. Reconciling interest expense to the reported amount of long-term debt is an analytical procedure useful in searching for understated liabilities. A very common analytical procedure is the anticipation of interest expense because the degree of reliability should be quite high; it is basically a mathematical calculation. If interest expense is higher than the auditor expects, the possibility arises that long-term debt has been omitted from the financial records. The interest is being paid but the debt is not being reported or is being under-stated, perhaps on purpose.

382. **A.** I is correct. Analytical procedures and comparing auditor estimates to client actual amounts are required in the planning stage of an audit. II is wrong. Analytical procedures are not performed in the internal control stage. *Exam hint:* With an analytical procedures question, any answer choice that says "assess control risk" or "test controls" is the wrong answer because analytical procedures are not performed in the internal control stage.

383. **B.** II is correct. In the overall review stage of the audit, analytical procedures are mandatory to search for any unusual relationships that would signify that more evidence gathering is needed. I is wrong. Analytical procedures are not required in the evidence-gathering stage but are optional. Sometimes analytical procedures can be performed as a substitute for a particular substantive test in the evidence-gathering stage.

384. **B.** II is correct. A direct supervisor's approval of the time cards most effectively ensures that payment is paid for work performed, as the supervisor observes the employees and determines whether employees are present and working. I is wrong. Having employees record their arrival and departure by using the time clock does not ensure that the employees were actually present and/or working during the recorded time. Employees could clock in and then leave.

385. **A.** I is correct. Segregation of duties between human resources and payroll departments is an important control to ensure that only valid employees receive paychecks. II is wrong. While all payroll checks should be printed in the payroll department, they are not signed in the human resources department but rather in the treasury department.

386. **B.** I is correct. For effective internal control, the departmental supervisor should approve payroll and approve the hours that were worked prior to the payroll being processed. If the departmental supervisor distributed paychecks directly to departmental employees, then this would be incompatible functions, since the departmental supervisor would have access to assets (execution, distributing paychecks) and also authorization of the transaction (approval of payroll). The departmental supervisor could dismiss an employee and not notify human resources, keep the dismissed employee's paycheck, and forge an endorsement on the employee's check. III is correct. For effective internal controls, the pay

rate should be established by the human resources department, not the employee's department supervisor. If the departmental supervisor set the pay rates, then he or she could be in collusion with the employee and obtain a kickback for paying an employee more than an established rate. II is wrong. For effective internal control, the departmental supervisor should approve payroll and approve the hours that were worked prior to the payroll being processed.

387. **A.** I is correct. The occurrence assertion as it relates to payroll transactions would correspond to an audit objective to determine that payroll transactions actually occurred (i.e., that all payroll checks were issued to valid employees for hours actually worked). II is wrong. While an auditor would inspect prenumbered checks to see if any payroll checks were missing, inspecting evidence related to prenumbering of payroll checks would relate to the completeness assertion rather than existence or occurrence.

388. **C.** Recomputing payroll deductions and verifying the preparation of the monthly payroll account bank reconciliation would provide significant evidence for the accuracy assertion for payroll transactions. A, B, and D are wrong. These assertions would not be supported by recomputing payroll deductions and verifying the preparation of the monthly payroll account bank reconciliation.

389. **D.** I is wrong. Payroll checks generally are disbursed by the same person or the same department, a paymaster, each payday, and this would not cause the auditor to assess control risk as high or to suspect fraud. II is wrong. Time card approval by departmental supervisors is a standard practice and would not raise an auditor's suspicions of a payroll fraud scheme or assess control risk as high.

390. **C.** I and II are correct. In assessing the work of the internal audit staff, competency and objectivity are the two primary criteria for making an evaluation.

391. **B.** II is correct. The quality of the internal auditors' working paper documentation is likely to reflect their competence. I is wrong. Objectivity relates to how high up in the organization the internal audit staff report. The external auditor expects and hopes to see that the internal audit staff reports directly to the audit committee, and not to anyone within management, for maximum objectivity. No one in the organization should be able to intimidate the internal audit staff.

392. **D.** Objectivity is reflected by the organizational level to which the internal auditor reports. A, B, and C relate to the competence of the internal auditor, but the question asks about the objectivity of the internal auditor.

393. **D.** The internal auditor may assist the independent auditor in all three fieldwork standards: planning, internal control, and evidence gathering, usually in low-risk areas. The only areas of the audit where the internal auditor is excluded from any assistance are decisions requiring judgment and assessments.

394. **D.** I is wrong. Assessing inherent risk requires an auditor's professional judgment, and while a competent and objective internal auditor may assist the independent auditor in all three fieldwork standards—planning, internal control, and evidence gathering—he or she may not participate in areas that require judgment. II is wrong for the same reason. Assessing control risk requires an auditor's professional judgment. While a competent and objective internal auditor may assist the independent auditor in all three fieldwork standards, he or she may not assist in areas that require judgment.

395. **D.** I is wrong. Materiality levels require an auditor's professional judgment. The independent auditor may not subordinate his or her judgment to an internal auditor, even one who is competent and objective. II is wrong. Evaluating estimates made by management requires judgment. The independent auditor may not subordinate his or her judgment to an internal auditor, even one who is competent and objective.

396. **A.** I is correct. The appropriateness and reasonableness of methods used are the responsibility of the specialist. II is wrong. While the appropriateness and reasonableness of methods used are the responsibility of the specialist, the auditor should obtain an understanding of the methods or assumptions used in order to determine whether the findings, are suitable for corroborating the representations in the financial statements. However, the auditor is not required to perform substantive procedures to verify the specialist's assumptions and findings because the auditor, while highly trained in GAAS and GAAP, is often not capable of performing the same substantive tests that the specialist performed. If the auditor were able to perform those tests, there would have been no need for the specialist.

397. **D.** I, II, and III are correct. When an independent auditor hires a specialist to perform certain substantive tests, an understanding should exist among the auditor, the client, and the specialist as to the nature of the work to be performed.

398. **D.** I is wrong. When an independent auditor hires a specialist to perform certain substantive tests and believes that the specialist's findings are reasonable in the circumstances, the auditor would not mention the specialist in an unmodified opinion, because the use of a specialist is quite common. II is wrong. When an independent auditor hires a specialist to perform certain substantive tests and believes that the specialist's findings are reasonable in the circumstances, the auditor may consider performing substantive procedures to verify the specialist's findings, especially if the specialist is somehow related to the client, but is not required to do so.

399. **A.** I is correct. When an independent auditor hires a specialist to perform certain substantive tests and the auditor believes that the specialist's findings are contrary to the client's assertions, the auditor would mention the specialist in the auditor's report because the auditor's opinion would likely be affected. The auditor would mention the specialist in an emphasis paragraph. II is wrong. If the specialist were related to the client, the auditor may still be able to use that specialist, but the relationship would have an impact on the credibility of the findings.

Chapter 13: Ethics, Sarbanes-Oxley, and the COSO Framework

400. **C.** A CPA must always be objective; however, a CPA need not be independent, except when engaged in public practice such as audits, special reports, reviews. According to the AICPA's code of conduct, "A member should maintain objectivity and be free of conflicts of interest in discharging professional responsibilities. A member in public practice should be independent in fact and appearance when providing auditing and other attestation services."

401. **D.** I is correct. According to Rule 101 of the AICPA Code of Professional Conduct, independence will be impaired if a firm performs operational or financial decisions for clients. Performing one but not the other still impairs independence. II is correct. According to Rule 101, independence will be impaired if a firm performs management functions such as reporting to the board on behalf of management. III is wrong. Rule 101 also states that a firm may perform certain nonattest services for clients

and still be independent as long as the firm does not serve or appear to serve as a member of the client's management.

402. **A.** I is correct. The AICPA Code of Professional Conduct governs any service that a member of the AICPA performs. These services include audits, special reports, compilations, reviews, and services performed on financial forecasts and projections, as well as attestation engagements. II is wrong. Sarbanes-Oxley and its offspring, PCAOB, regulate publicly traded company audits and the firms that conduct those audits but do not replace the AICPA Code of Professional Conduct.

403. **C.** The first three articles of the AICPA Code of Professional Conduct are: Article 1, Responsibilities; Article II, Public Interest; and Article III, Integrity. Article III, Integrity, states, "To maintain and broaden public confidence, members should perform all professional responsibilities with the highest sense of integrity." Integrity addresses the question of what is right and just. A and B are wrong. Article IV of the AICPA Code of Professional Conduct is titled Objectivity and Independence. D is wrong. Article V of the AICPA Code of Professional Conduct is titled Due Care.

404. **C.** A cash advance from a financial institution of $20,000 to be repaid within 10 days made under normal lending policies would impair independence. A, B, and D are wrong. Certain loans made under normal lending policies do NOT impair independence. Automobile loans, loans of the surrender value under the terms of an insurance policy, borrowings fully collateralized by cash deposits at the same financial institution, and credit cards and cash advances on checking accounts with a total unpaid balance of $10,000 or less do NOT impair independence if made under normal lending policies.

405. **A.** I is correct. A state's society of CPAs is more of a social organization that promotes the profession through sponsored gatherings and committees and helps the CPA attain continuing education credits. It does NOT have the authority to revoke the CPA's license. II is correct. The AICPA is a standard-setting body that conducts hearings should a member violate the standards. If the member is found liable, the AICPA could recommend to the state board of accountancy that the CPA's license be suspended, but the AICPA has no power to revoke the CPA's license. III is wrong. The state board of accountancy has the power to revoke the CPA's license.

406. **B.** II is correct. Issuing an unmodified opinion on the Year 12 financial statements when fees for the Year 11 audit were unpaid would be an ethics issue. Since fees are outstanding, a loan exists to the client. Auditors are not allowed to loan money to their clients. I is wrong. Most firms are sold for a percentage of fees collected over a multiple-year time frame. This would not be an ethics issue at all.

407. **B.** II is correct. According to Rule 101, Independence, of the AICPA's code of conduct, a fully secured automobile loan with a financial institution client is permitted (regardless of the date obtained) and does not impair the independence rule. I is wrong. A home mortgage with an attestation client is not permitted; it would impair independence.

408. **B.** II is correct. When a CPA leaves a firm and joins a client within one year of disassociating from the firm, independence will be impaired unless the engagement is reviewed by a qualified professional to determine whether the engagement team members maintained the appropriate level of skepticism when evaluating the representations and work of the former firm member. I is wrong. In this situation, independence is impaired unless the individual is no longer in a position to influence or participate in the firm's business.

409. **D.** According to the AICPA code of professional conduct, a firm engaged to provide attest services to the public must be owned greater than 50% by CPAs. The non-CPA ownership of the firm must be held by active firm members, not by passive investors.

410. **D.** Professional competence includes the technical qualifications of the CPA and of the CPA's staff, the ability to supervise and evaluate work, and the knowledge of technical subject matter or the ability to obtain that knowledge by research or by consulting with others.

411. **C.** I is correct. The member must act as a reasonably prudent accountant would. II is correct. The CPA should exercise due professional care in the performance of professional services. The member must critically review work done by those assisting in the engagement at every level of supervision. The member must possess the same degree of skill commonly possessed by others in the field.

412. **A.** I is correct. Contingent fees are specifically prohibited for audits and reviews of financial statements. II is correct. Contingent fees are specifically prohibited for examinations of prospective financial

information. III is correct. A CPA is not allowed to have a fee contingent upon the size of a taxpayer's refund when filing an original tax return, Form 1040.

413. **B.** II is correct. Contingent fees are permitted for compilations of financial statements expected to be used by third parties only if the member includes a statement that the member is not independent. III is correct. A contingent fee is permitted when representing a client in an examination of a tax return by an IRS agent. Note that a contingent fee is not allowed when preparing the client's original tax return. I is wrong. A contingent fee is not permissible with a review engagement or any engagement that requires independence.

414. **C.** I is correct. False, misleading, or deceptive advertising is not allowed. II is correct. Advertising that is informative and objective is allowed.

415. **B.** II is correct. Determination by a court or administrative agency of discrimination or harassment in public practice is considered an act discreditable to the profession. I is wrong. Work papers belong to the auditor. Failure to return work papers is not a problem; failure to retain client records would be an act discreditable to the profession. Failure to return client records after the client makes demand could result in loss of license.

416. **A.** I is correct. Failure to retain client records would be an act discreditable to the profession under the AICPA Code of Professional Conduct. Failure to return client records after the client makes demand could result in loss of license even if the client has not yet paid the CPA's bill. If the CPA is still not paid after return of the client's original records, the CPA can seek legal or other collection remedies. II is wrong. A CPA may reveal confidential client information to a state CPA society quality review team. For a CPA to not reveal such information would require the CPA to cross out the client's name on every page and obliterate Social Security numbers, and this is not a requirement prior to sending financial statements and tax returns to the state review board for quality review purposes.

417. **D.** I is wrong. Arranging with a collection agency to collect fees owed from clients does not violate the profession's ethical standards. II is wrong. There is no prohibition against using a cloud-based server to store confidential client files.

418. **D.** III is correct. Independence is required for attestation engagements, audits, review engagements,

examinations, or agreed-upon procedures. I is wrong. Compilations of personal financial statements do not require CPA independence. II is wrong. Compilations of financial forecasts do not require CPA independence. Compilations in general do not require independence, but if the CPA is not independent, the report should so indicate.

419. **B.** II is correct. Tax services may be provided to an issuer audit client but cannot include aggressive tax transactions with uncertain chances of success. I is wrong. Tax services may be provided to an issuer audit client but would need to be preapproved by the audit committee.

420. **D.** I is wrong. The AICPA Code of Professional Conduct would NOT be violated if a member revealed confidential client information as a result of a validly issued subpoena or summons. A CPA must obey a court order. II is wrong. The AICPA Code of Professional Conduct would not be violated if a member revealed confidential client information as a result of a quality review of the CPA's practice. Quality review is still the standard for firms not registered with PCAOB. For registered firms that audit publicly traded companies, PCAOB takes care of quality review.

421. **B.** II is correct. According to the Sarbanes-Oxley Act of 2002, issuers must now be audited only by firms that register with PCAOB. I is wrong. Privately held companies can be audited by a CPA firm that is not registered with PCAOB even if the client does business with publicly traded companies.

422. **B.** I is correct. PCAOB requires a registered CPA firm to provide a concurring or second partner review of each audit report. II is correct. PCAOB requires a registered CPA firm to describe in audit reports the scope of the testing of the issuer's internal control structure and procedures. III is wrong. PCAOB requires a registered CPA firm to maintain audit documentation for seven years. Criminal penalties will apply for failure to retain work papers for at least seven years.

423. **C.** I is correct. Audit firms need to retain work papers relating to their audit clients for at least seven years if the client is publicly held. II is correct. Audit firms need to retain work papers relating to their audit clients for at least five years if the client is not publicly held.

424. **C.** I is correct. Registered firms must report to the audit committees of audited corporations any material written communications between the audit firm

and management, including a schedule of unadjusted audit differences. II is correct. Registered firms must report to the audit committee's alternative accounting treatments discussed with the corporation's management, the ramifications of the alternatives, and the treatment the firm prefers.

425. **A.** A cooling-off period of one year is required before a former member of an audit client engagement team can be employed in a financial oversight role for that same client. This requirement is necessary to preserve auditor (firm) independence. This is to reduce the chance of a conflict of interest.

426. **C.** I is correct. According to Sarbanes-Oxley, the lead auditor or coordinating partner auditing a publicly traded company must rotate off the audit every five years. II is correct. According to Sarbanes-Oxley, the reviewing partner involved in a publicly traded audit engagement must rotate off the audit every five years. Under PCAOB, these individuals must take a time-out of five years before returning to that same audit client.

427. **D.** I is wrong. The AICPA Code of Professional Conduct, which is followed when auditing non-issuers, does not require audit partner rotation. II is wrong. The PCAOB/SEC ethical standards that apply to the audits of issuers require that the lead partner rotate off the audit engagement after five years. PCAOB does not apply to the audit of a nonissuer.

428. **A.** I is correct. According to Title VI of Sarbanes-Oxley, any officer, director, or owner of more than 10% of any equity security must file a report indicating how many shares he or she owns within 10 days after becoming an officer, director, or more than 10% owner. II is wrong. According to Title VI of Sarbanes-Oxley, any officer, director, or owner of more than 10% of any equity security must file a report of change in ownership within two days of such change.

429. **C.** I is correct. According to Sarbanes-Oxley, auditors are required to attest to management's assessment of the effectiveness of internal control over financial reporting in a 10-K Annual Report. Form 10-K must include an internal control report stating management's responsibility for establishing an adequate internal control structure and procedure for financial reporting and an assessment of the effectiveness of the current year's control structure. II is correct. According to Sarbanes-Oxley, auditors are required to attest to management's assessment of the effectiveness of internal control over financial

reporting in a 10-Q Quarterly Report. Form 10-Q must include an internal control report stating management's responsibility for establishing an adequate internal control structure and procedure for financial reporting and an assessment of the effectiveness of the current year's control structure. Auditors are required to attest to management's assessment of the effectiveness of internal control over financial reporting.

430. **A.** I is correct. Firms registered with PCAOB are required to undergo PCAOB inspection. These inspections occur every three years or every year depending on how many publicly traded company audits are conducted by the firm. If the firm audits more than 100 publicly traded companies annually, PCAOB will inspect that firm every year. Otherwise, these inspections will occur every three years. II is wrong. Firms registered with PCAOB are required to undergo PCAOB inspection, not peer review. Peer review is for the firms not registered with PCAOB. Peer review evidently wasn't doing a good enough job inspecting the large firms prior to the accounting scandals that led up to the Sarbanes-Oxley Act of 2002. PCAOB has replaced peer review for the large firms.

431. **D.** I is wrong. Sarbanes-Oxley does NOT require rotation of the issuer's designated financial expert every five years. II is wrong. Sarbanes-Oxley does NOT require rotation of the issuer's auditing firm every five years. The issuer does not have to change audit firms, but the audit firm has to rotate lead partners every five years.

432. **C.** I is correct. The SEC requires each issuer to disclose in Forms 10-K and 10-Q whether or not they have an audit committee financial expert. If they do not have an audit committee financial expert, they must state their reasons why. II is correct. The SEC requires each issuer to disclose in Forms 10-K and 10-Q whether or not the entity has a code of ethics for senior financial officers. If there is no code, the entity must state its reasons why.

433. **B.** According to the Sarbanes-Oxley and the SEC, other audit partners should rotate off the audit engagement after no more than 7 years and must remain out for 2 years before returning to the engagement. These rules apply to partners who are NOT considered to be lead partners or reviewing partners on the engagement.

434. **C.** Under Sarbanes-Oxley, lead partners and concurring partners are subject to a five-year "time-out" period before returning to an engagement.

Other audit partners are subject to a two-year time-out period. These rules apply to audits of publicly traded companies. Rotation and time out are not required for audits of nonissuers.

435. **B.** II is correct. For audits of issuers, assisting the client in aggressive tax transactions would be a violation of independence. I is wrong. For audits of nonissuers, assisting the client in aggressive tax transactions would NOT be a violation of independence.

436. **C.** I and II are correct. Under both Sarbanes-Oxley and AICPA standards, auditor independence is impaired if any of the following nonaudit services are provided during the audit or during the professional engagement period: bookkeeping or other services related to the accounting records or financial statements of the audit client; financial information systems design and implementation; appraisal or valuation services; and actuarial services.

437. **A.** I is correct. According to Sarbanes-Oxley, accounting firms that audit publicly traded companies cannot perform certain services for those companies. Among the prohibited services are bookkeeping services. II is wrong. While many nonaudit services for an audit client are now prohibited under Sarbanes-Oxley, income tax return preparation is still allowed.

438. **B.** II is correct. If the audit committee doesn't designate a member as the financial expert on the audit committee, the audit process still goes on but the reason for lack of financial expert must be disclosed. I is wrong. Sarbanes-Oxley does not require that the audit committee chairperson be its financial expert.

439. **A.** I is correct. Among the powers of PCAOB is the ability to discipline the members of the profession involved with violations while auditing publicly traded companies. PCAOB can reprimand, fine, or suspend a member or member firm from auditing public companies. II is wrong. Accounting standards come from the Financial Accounting Standards Board (FASB). Auditing, quality control, and independence standards come from PCAOB.

440. **D.** Nonaudit services that do not exceed 5% of total revenues from an audit client do not require audit committee preapproval as long as the services are brought to the audit committee's attention and approved before the completion of the audit. The general rule is that all services must be preapproved by the audit committee. This would include tax services and other nonaudit services, even those performed on a recurring basis.

441. **B.** The internal control provisions of Sarbanes-Oxley apply to public companies only. Sarbanes-Oxley does not apply to private companies. Therefore, A, C, and D are wrong.

442. **C.** I is correct. Sarbanes-Oxley requires a publicly traded company to report on its own internal control. II is correct. Sarbanes-Oxley requires a publicly traded company to make an assertion regarding the effectiveness of its own internal control. This report must include a statement by management taking responsibility for the internal control and identifying the framework for evaluating the internal control.

443. **B.** Sarbanes-Oxley requires a publicly traded company to report on its own internal control and make an assertion regarding the effectiveness of its own internal control. This report must include a statement by management taking responsibility for the internal control and identifying the framework for evaluating the internal control. The most common management tool for evaluating internal control is the COSO internal framework. The COSO framework of evaluating internal control is recognized as appropriate by both the SEC and PCAOB. Management simply mentions this framework in its report on internal control. A, C, and D are wrong.

444. **D.** According to the COSO internal framework for evaluating internal control, the five components of internal control are (1) control environment, (2) risk assessment, (3) control activities, (4) information and communication, and (5) monitoring.

445. **C.** I and II are correct. The COSO framework of evaluating internal control is recognized as appropriate by both PCAOB and the SEC. Management simply mentions COSO as the framework in its report on internal control.

446. **C.** I is correct. In management's report on internal control (required under Sarbanes-Oxley for publicly traded companies), another component of the report is a statement that the company's independent auditor has issued an attestation report on management's assertion. II is correct. In management's report on internal control, management mentions COSO as the framework for reporting and evaluating its internal control.

447. **D.** I is correct. Management's report on internal control for a publicly traded company must include a statement that management is responsible

for internal control. II is correct. Management's report on internal control for a publicly traded company must include a statement that the "independent auditor has assessed management's assertion" regarding internal control. III is correct. Management's report on internal control for a publicly traded company must also include management's assertion regarding the effectiveness of the company's internal control.

448. **C.** I and II are correct. The five interrelated components of internal control, according to the COSO framework, are (1) control environment, (2) risk assessment, (3) control activities, (4) information and communication, and (5) monitoring.

449. **D.** Note that the question asks which are NOT part of the COSO framework. The other three components of the COSO framework are control environment, information and communication, and monitoring.

450. **A.** I is correct. The auditor must report to those charged with governance all significant deficiencies. Significant deficiencies are those control deficiencies that are discovered by the auditor and that the auditor considered significant enough to report. III is correct. The auditor must report to those charged with governance all material weaknesses. Material weaknesses are more severe than significant deficiencies. A material weakness can be a combination of significant deficiencies. II is wrong. Control deficiencies may be reported but are not required unless they are significant deficiencies or material weaknesses.

451. **D.** An auditor must communicate material weaknesses and significant deficiencies to those charged with governance. The timing is up to the auditor, so the communication could be done during the audit or at the audit's completion.

Chapter 14: International Auditing Standards, Government Auditing Standards, and Information Technology

452. **C.** According to the IFAC, marketing of professional services is allowed if the content of the marketing promotion is honest and truthful. A and D are wrong, because no particular form of marketing is prohibited. B is wrong because marketing must be honest and truthful as well as legal.

453. **B.** The international code of ethics for professional accountants has fewer outright prohibitions than the AICPA Code of Professional Conduct. For example, international standards do NOT outright prohibit internal audit outsourcing, actuarial services, and financial information system design and implementation. While the AICPA Code of Professional Conduct and Sarbanes-Oxley consider those nonaudit services to be a violation of independence, IFAC permits such services if appropriate safeguards exist. D is wrong because the IFAC code of ethics applies to all professional accountants.

454. **B.** II is correct. While PCAOB generally requires external confirmations of accounts receivable, international standards do NOT require external confirmations of receivables. I is wrong. Per international standards, the location in which the auditor practices must be disclosed in the audit report.

455. **B.** II is correct. Under international standards, if the client suddenly wishes to change the engagement and the auditor is unable to agree with the client as to the reason for the sudden change, the auditor should withdraw and consider whether there is an obligation to contact third parties. I is wrong. Under international audit standards, dual dating of audit reports is not allowed. When dating the audit report for a subsequent event, international standards require the dating of the report to be the amended date.

456. **C.** Under IFAC, both investment banking and legal services can be provided to an audit client provided appropriate safeguards are in place. Under the AICPA code of conduct, there are no appropriate safeguards to allow investment banking or legal services to be performed for audit clients.

457. **A.** I is correct. United States auditors will sometimes report on financial statements of a US entity that have been prepared in conformity with another country's accounting principles. The auditor can issue an unmodified opinion or any other opinion, but first the auditor needs to understand the accounting principles generally accepted in the foreign country. II is wrong. There is no need for the auditor to be certified in the foreign country. It is enough to have an understanding of the accounting principles used in that country.

458. **D.** I is wrong. Internal audit outsourcing services may not be provided to audit clients under US ethics standards. II is wrong. Under IFAC's code of ethics, an auditor may provide internal audit services if appropriate safeguards are put in place to limit or eliminate any threats to independence.

459. **D.** I, II, and III are correct. Government Auditing Standards define three types of engagements: financial audits, attest engagements, and performance audits.

460. **C.** I is correct. In a compliance audit, the auditor reports on whether the entity has complied with applicable requirements. II is correct. In a compliance audit the auditor does not express an opinion on the effectiveness of internal control over compliance.

461. **C.** I is correct. In performing an audit in accordance with GAGAS (the "Yellow Book"), the auditor accepts greater reporting responsibilities than accepted under a GAAS audit, since the auditor must report on compliance with laws, rules, and regulations, violations of which may affect financial statement amounts. II is correct. In performing an audit in accordance with GAGAS, the auditor must report on the organization's internal control over financial reporting.

462. **A.** I is correct. Compared to a typical GAAS audit, a government audit entails expanded internal control and testing requirements. A government audit involves a formal written report on the consideration of internal control and assessment of control risk. II is wrong. Compared to a typical GAAS audit, government audits require expanded reporting to include whether the federal financial assistance has been administered in accordance with laws and regulations.

463. **C.** I is correct. Per Government Auditing Standards, audit documentation should contain sufficient information so that supplementary oral explanations are not required. II is correct. Assessed risk of material noncompliance must be documented, including procedures performed and understanding of internal control. This can be in the form of a flowchart, questionnaire, or narrative, but it must be documented.

464. **B.** II is correct. An objective of a compliance audit of a governmental entity is to form an opinion on whether that government complied with applicable compliance requirements in all material respects. I is wrong. The auditor cannot minimize control risk of noncompliance, since control risk exists independently of the audit. The auditor can only assess control risk of noncompliance.

465. **C.** I is correct. Auditors engaged to perform a single audit must perform procedures to obtain an understanding of internal control pertaining to the compliance requirements for federal programs sufficient to plan an audit. II is correct. Auditors engaged to perform a single audit must perform procedures to support a low assessed level of control risk for major programs. Testing controls is the way to support a low assessed level of control risk.

466. **A.** I is correct. Auditors engaged to perform a single audit must perform procedures to obtain an understanding of internal control pertaining to the compliance requirements for federal programs sufficient to plan an audit and to support a low assessed level of control risk for programs considered to be major programs. II is wrong. Auditors have NO responsibility to obtain an understanding of internal control over compliance or perform related tests of compliance for any federal program deemed to be nonmajor.

467. **C.** I is correct. Under the Single Audit Act, auditors are responsible for understanding internal control. The auditor must understand internal control over financial reporting and over federal programs sufficient to plan the audit to support a low assessed level of control risk for major programs. II is correct. Under the Single Audit Act, auditors are responsible for reporting the results of their tests. Significant deficiencies and material weaknesses must be disclosed.

468. **A.** I is correct. GAGAS require a written report on the auditor's understanding of internal control and the assessment of control risk in all audits. II is wrong. GAAS require written communication only when significant deficiencies are noted. Significant deficiencies should be reported to specific legislative and regulatory bodies.

469. **C.** I is correct. When compared to GAAS audits, reporting responsibilities under GAGAS are expanded to include reports on compliance with laws, rules, and regulations, violations of which may affect financial statement amounts. II is correct. Responsibilities under GAGAS include reports on internal control over financial reporting.

470. **C.** I is correct. Program-specific audits do NOT include reports on the financial statements of the organization taken as a whole. Under certain circumstances, recipients of federal monies are allowed to have program-specific audits rather than a full single audit. II is correct. The Single Audit Act allows an entity that spends more than $500,000 per year to have an audit of each specific program rather than a single audit, but only if criteria are met.

471. **C.** A single audit represents a combined audit of both an entity's financial statements and its federal financial assistance programs. The single audit provides audited organizations with the opportunity to capitalize on the efficiency of satisfying their audit requirements with a single audit. Auditors are governed by the Single Audit Act and OMB Circular A-133.

472. **B.** II is correct. Continuous performance of tests of controls is required when financial data are processed electronically, without provision of paper documentation, to ensure that controls are operating effectively throughout the period under audit. I is wrong. Consideration of the risk of management fraud is required in all audits, regardless of the method used to process financial data or the adequacy of the paper documentation provided.

473. **A.** III is correct. The audit program will likely need to be revised to reflect the risks and capitalize on the strengths inherent in an automated system. For example, there will likely be a greater risk of unauthorized access, while there may also be greater opportunities for data analysis and review. I is wrong. If specialized IT skills are needed, the auditor is less likely to take IT courses and more likely to seek the assistance of an IT professional. II is wrong. Audit objectives are the same in a computerized environment as they are in a manual environment. The audit procedures to accomplish those objectives may need to change, but the objectives are the same.

474. **C.** I is correct. Using test data, an auditor is likely to test a request for two checks for the same employee, and the computer would be expected to print an error report. If the client's payroll program printed out two checks for the same employee, the auditor would assess control risk as high for payroll. II is correct. A request for a check to be paid to an employee who no longer works for the company should result in an error report. If the client's payroll program prints out the payroll check for the terminated employee, the auditor would assess control risk as high for payroll.

475. **B.** II is correct. Integrated test facility (ITF) allows dummy transactions to be run simultaneously with live transactions in the client's computer system. ITF is often programmed into the computer for this purpose. I is wrong. Test data are a set of dummy transactions developed by the auditor and processed through the client's computer system but not at the same time that the client is using the

computer for live transactions. Test data sometimes are performed by default because ITF was not programmed into the system.

476. **B.** II is correct. Parallel simulation is a computer-assisted audit technique that permits an auditor to insert the auditor's version of a client's program to process data and compare the output with the client's output. I is wrong. Test data are a set of dummy transactions developed by the auditor and processed through the client's computer system but not at the same time that the client is using the computer for live transactions.

477. **B.** I is correct. Generalized audit software would be used when constructing parallel simulations. Parallel simulation involves taking the client's data and reprocessing that data using the auditor's equipment and software. III is correct. The auditor would use generalized audit software or retrieval package software to access client data files. II is wrong. The assessment of control risk is based on auditor judgment. A computer cannot replace auditor professional judgment in assessing IT control risk.

Chapter 15: Management Representation Letter and Quality Control at the Firm

478. **A.** I is correct. The management rep letter is considered the final piece of audit evidence and, under both US GAAS and PCAOB standards, must be dated the same as the audit report. II is wrong. The management rep letter is a required piece of audit evidence. An auditor's failure to receive a signed rep letter would result in a scope limitation likely to result in a disclaimer or a withdrawal from the engagement.

479. **C.** I is correct. The CEO would be asked to sign the management rep letter because the CEO has control over operations. II is correct. The CFO would be asked to sign the rep letter because the CFO has control over financial matters. Note that members of management with responsibility over financial and operating matters would ordinarily sign the rep letter, and other officers may also be asked to sign the rep letter.

480. **D.** I is wrong. Materiality does not apply to the level of access that management has given to the auditor regarding access to minutes of board meetings. Either the auditor was given access or he or she wasn't. II is wrong. Materiality does not apply to the level of access that management has given to the auditor regarding records relating to revenue and

expenses. Once again, either the auditor was given access or he or she wasn't. In a management representation letter, materiality may or may not apply, and often it doesn't.

481. **A.** I is correct. In a typical management representation letter, management would acknowledge its responsibility for fair presentation of financial statements. II is correct. In a typical management representation letter, management would acknowledge its responsibility for internal control over financial reporting. III is wrong. In a typical management representation letter, management would NOT acknowledge its responsibility for communications with the audit committee. The management rep letter deals with communications between management and the auditor, not communications between management and the audit committee.

482. **C.** I is correct. In the management rep letter, management should disclose the results of its assessment of the risk that the financial statements may be materially misstated due to fraud. II is correct. In the management rep letter, management should acknowledge that all known or potential litigation has been disclosed to the auditor and accounted for and disclosed in the financial statements or footnotes in accordance with the applicable framework.

483. **A.** A statement such as "There are no material transactions that have not been properly recorded in the accounting records underlying the financial statements" most likely would be found in the management rep letter, which is stored in the current file. In the management rep letter, management acknowledges that the financial statements are complete and that all material transactions have been recorded. B is wrong. This excerpt would NOT be found in the communication with the predecessor. The first communication with the predecessor, prior to the engagement acceptance, would be concerned with the integrity of the client. A second, optional communication with the predecessor after the engagement has been accepted would be concerned with the client's opening balances. C is wrong. The engagement letter would be concerned with the responsibilities of management and responsibilities of the auditor. Further, the auditor never makes such a statement. D is wrong. This excerpt would not appear in the auditor's report. The auditor never makes such a statement. Instead, the auditor provides an opinion as to fair presentation of the financial statements in accordance with the framework.

484. **C.** The statement "Fees for our services are based on our per diem rates plus travel expenses" would be most likely found in the engagement letter. In the engagement letter, the auditor includes a section on fees and frequency of billing. The engagement letter is stored in the current file. A is wrong. This excerpt would NOT be found in the auditor's report. The auditor's report does not mention fees charged to the client by the auditor. B is wrong. This excerpt would NOT be found in the audit inquiry letter to legal counsel. The auditor's letter to legal counsel asks the client's lawyer to respond to questions regarding contingent liabilities. D is wrong. This passage would NOT be found in the management rep letter, as fees for the audit are not mentioned in the management rep letter. The management representation letter is where management acknowledges in writing its answers to various inquiries from the auditor.

485. **A.** The excerpt "The objective of our audit is to express an opinion on the financial statements, although it is possible that facts or circumstances encountered may prevent us from expressing an unmodified opinion" would most likely be found in the auditor's engagement letter. The engagement letter contains a section regarding limitations of the engagement. The fact that there are potential limitations to being able to express any opinion should be mentioned in the engagement letter. The engagement letter is stored in the current file. B is wrong. This passage would NOT be found in the management rep letter. The management representation letter is where management acknowledges in writing its answers to various inquiries from the auditor. C is wrong. This passage would NOT be found in the auditor's inquiry to the client's legal counsel. The auditor's letter to legal counsel asks the client's lawyer to respond to questions regarding contingent liabilities. D is wrong. This passage would NOT be found in the auditor's communication with the predecessor. The auditor's communication prior to the engagement acceptance would be concerned with the integrity of the client. A second, optional communication with the predecessor after the engagement has been accepted would be concerned with the client's opening balances.

486. **C.** The excerpt "There has been no fraud involving employees that could have a material effect on the financial statements" would be found in the management rep letter. In the rep letter at the end of the audit, the auditor asks the client to acknowledge that there has been no fraud involving employees

that could have a material effect on the financial statements. The management rep letter is stored in the current file. A is wrong. This statement would NOT be found in the auditor's communication with the audit committee. The auditor's communication with the audit committee might include instances of fraud observed or even suspected. B is wrong. This statement would NOT be found in the audit inquiry letter to legal counsel. The auditor's letter to legal counsel asks the client's lawyer to respond to questions regarding contingent liabilities. D is wrong. This statement would NOT be found in the audit communication with the predecessor auditor. The auditor's communication prior to the engagement acceptance would be concerned with the integrity of the client. A second, optional communication with the predecessor after the engagement has been accepted would be concerned with the client's opening balances.

487. **D.** The passage "Are you aware of any facts or circumstances that may indicate a lack of integrity by any member of senior management?" would likely appear in the auditor's communication with the predecessor auditor. The successor would want to know about any issues that would indicate that management of the potential new audit client lacks integrity. The communication with the predecessor would be stored in the current file. A is wrong. This passage would NOT be contained in the management rep letter. The management rep letter is where management acknowledges in writing its answers to various inquiries from the auditor. B is wrong. This passage would NOT be contained in the engagement letter. The engagement letter sets forth the agreement between the auditor and the client. The auditor would not ask the client about management integrity but would instead ask the predecessor auditor. C is wrong. This passage would NOT be contained in the auditor's report. The auditor's report provides an opinion as to fair presentation of the financial statements in accordance with the framework.

488. **C.** The excerpt "There were unreasonable delays by management in permitting the start of the audit and in providing needed information" would likely be found in the auditor's communication with the audit committee. The auditor would indicate these delays to the audit committee in receiving requested information. This communication with the audit committee would be stored in the current file. A is wrong. The passage would NOT be found in an accounts receivable confirmation. In

an accounts receivable confirmation (now called an external confirmation), the auditor asks the client's customers for information about the balances owed to the client. B is wrong. The passage would NOT be found in the auditor's engagement letter. The engagement letter is between the client and the auditor, not between the auditor and the audit committee. D is wrong. The passage would NOT be found in the management rep letter. The rep letter includes statements made by management to the auditor, not statements made by the auditor to the audit committee.

489. **A.** The excerpt "If this statement is not correct, please write promptly, using the enclosed envelope, and give details of any differences directly to our auditors" is most likely taken from an accounts receivable confirmation. In an accounts receivable confirmation (now called an external confirmation), the auditor asks the client's customers for information about the balances owed to the client. These responses should mailed back to the auditor directly, without client interference, and the auditor should store these responses in the current file. B is wrong. This statement would NOT be found in the management rep letter. The management rep letter includes statements made by management to the auditor, not evidence involving the client's customers. C is wrong. This statement would NOT be found in the audit inquiry to legal counsel. The auditor's letter to legal counsel asks the client's lawyer to respond to questions regarding contingent liabilities, not about balances owed to the client from customers. D is wrong. This statement would NOT be found in the auditor's communication with the predecessor. The auditor's communication with the predecessor prior to engagement acceptance would be concerned with the integrity of the client. A second, optional communication with the predecessor after the engagement has been accepted would be concerned with the client's opening balances. The auditor's communication with the predecessor is not concerned with specific customer balances owed to the client.

490. **D.** The excerpt "The company has suffered recurring losses from operations and has a net capital deficiency that raises substantial doubt about its ability to continue as a going concern" would most likely be found in the auditor's report. In the auditor's report, the auditor would include an emphasis-of-matter paragraph, after the opinion paragraph, to describe any matter that the auditor wanted to call to the user's attention. Going concern would be

an example of an issue that would receive such an emphasis paragraph. The auditor's report could still be unmodified even with the emphasis-of-matter paragraph. The auditor's report would be stored in the current file. A is wrong. This passage would NOT be found in the audit inquiry letter to legal counsel. The auditor's letter to legal counsel asks the client's lawyer to respond to questions regarding contingent liabilities. B is wrong. The passage would NOT be found in accounts receivable confirmations. In an accounts receivable confirmation (now called an external confirmation), the auditor asks the client's customers for information about the balances owed to the client. It would not mention recurring losses. C is wrong. This statement would NOT be found in the auditor's communication with the predecessor. The auditor's communication with the predecessor prior to engagement acceptance would be concerned with the integrity of the client. A second, optional communication with the predecessor after the engagement has been accepted would be concerned with the client's opening balances. Going concern has to do with the client's ending balances.

491. **A.** I is correct. The AICPA Code of Professional Conduct requires firms providing auditing, attestation, and accounting and review services to adopt a system of quality control. A quality control system consists of policies and procedures designed, implemented, and maintained to ensure that the firm complies with professional standards and also ensures that the reports that are issued by the firm are appropriate in the circumstances. II is wrong. The Internal Revenue Service does NOT require audit firms to adopt a system of quality control.

492. **B.** The human resources element of quality control (at the firm) deals with recruitment and hiring practices, assigning personnel to engagements, professional development, performance evaluation, compensation, and advancement. A is wrong. A CPA firm's leadership responsibilities for quality within the firm are essential because a firm's leadership bears the ultimate responsibility for the firm's quality control systems. The tone at the top of a firm influences attitudes throughout the firm. C is wrong. Risk assessment is NOT an element of quality control at the firm. D is wrong. Monitoring helps the firm determine whether the quality control system has been designed appropriately and implemented effectively.

493. **A.** Considering audit risk is NOT an element of quality control at the firm. The elements of quality control at the firm are client acceptance and continuance, human resources, ethical requirements, leadership, monitoring, and performance.

494. **A.** I is correct. A CPA firm's leadership responsibilities for quality within the firm are essential because a firm's leadership bears the ultimate responsibility for the firm's quality control systems. The tone at the top of a firm influences attitudes throughout the firm. II is wrong. While performing the engagement within its reporting deadlines is essential, it falls under the quality control category known as client acceptance and continuance.

495. **A.** When measuring the quality control at a CPA firm, providing a means to resolve differences of opinion falls under the category of performance. A firm should strive to achieve a consistently high level of performance. All audit work should be supervised and appropriately reviewed. Experts may need to be consulted for complex and unusual issues. B is wrong. Leadership relates to a CPA firm's tone at the top. The tone at the top of a firm influences attitudes throughout the firm. C is wrong. Monitoring helps the firm determine whether the quality control system has been designed appropriately and implemented effectively. D is wrong. The human resources element of quality control (at the firm) deals with recruitment and hiring practices, assigning personnel to engagements, professional development, performance evaluation, compensation, and advancement.

496. **C.** Monitoring helps the firm determine whether the quality control system has been designed appropriately and implemented effectively. A is wrong. Performance relates to the idea that all audit work should be supervised and appropriately reviewed. Experts may need to be consulted for complex and unusual issues. B is wrong. Leadership relates to a CPA firm's tone at the top. The tone at the top of a firm influences attitudes throughout the firm. D is wrong. The human resources element of quality control (at the firm) deals with recruitment and hiring practices, assigning personnel to engagements, professional development, performance evaluation, compensation, and advancement.

497. **B.** II is correct. Sarbanes-Oxley requires in every public company audit a "wrap-up" or secondary partner review of the audit documentation by a partner not otherwise involved in the audit. The primary purpose of this second partner review is to ensure that the financial statements are presented in accordance with the framework. I is wrong. Peer review is an attempt at self-regulation as one firm reviews another. The purpose of peer review is to

determine whether the CPA firm being reviewed has developed adequate policies and procedures for the elements of quality control and is following them in practice. While firms that are members of the AICPA get peer reviewed every three years, Sarbanes-Oxley ended self-regulation for firms that audit public companies. PCAOB now regulates the larger audit firms, and those firms are no longer peer reviewed.

498. C. I is correct. A firm that fails to maintain quality control standards has NOT necessarily violated GAAS. Quality control standards relate to the conduct of a firm's entire practice, whereas professional standards such as GAAS relate to the conduct of an individual engagement. II is correct. While the adoption of quality control standards does increase the likelihood of compliance with professional standards on individual engagements, quality control standards relate to the conduct of a firm's entire practice, whereas professional standards such as GAAS relate to the conduct of an individual engagement.

499. B. II is correct. The CPA firm's size and cost-benefit considerations should be taken into account with regard to the nature and extent of the firm's quality-control policies and procedures. I is wrong. The CPA firm's size and cost-benefit considerations have nothing to do with independence.

500. B. II is correct. Quality-control policies and procedures should provide the CPA firm with reasonable assurance that the likelihood of associating with clients whose management lacks integrity is minimized. Within quality-control standards is a component dedicated to engagement acceptance and continuance. I is wrong. Quality-control standards apply to auditing and attestation as well as accounting and review services.

Bonus Questions

501. B. The acid test ratio will decrease when a cash dividend is declared and paid because current assets (numerator) decreases while current liabilities (denominator) remain the same.

502. A. The effect on the inventory turnover ratio is an increase because as a result of the journal entry, the (numerator) cost of goods sold increased and the (denominator) inventory decreased. The entry that the company needs to book is a debit to cost of goods sold and a credit to inventory. The entry is needed because the shipping terms were FOB destination and the customer received the merchandise prior to year-end.

PART II

BUSINESS ENVIRONMENT AND CONCEPTS

CHAPTER 16

OPERATIONS MANAGEMENT

QUESTIONS 1–119

1. Which of the following performance measures is/are nonfinancial?
   I. Gross margin
   II. Number of days missed due to workplace accidents

   A. I only
   B. II only
   C. Both I and II
   D. Neither I nor II

2. Measures of nonfinancial performance include:
   I. total productivity ratios
   II. partial productivity ratios

   A. I only
   B. II only
   C. Both I and II
   D. Neither I nor II

3. Which of the following measures of nonfinancial performance would be considered internal benchmarks?
   I. Control charts
   II. Total productivity ratios

   A. I only
   B. II only
   C. Both I and II
   D. Neither I nor II

4. Which of the following measures of nonfinancial performance would be considered internal benchmarks?
   I. Fishbone diagrams
   II. Pareto diagrams

   A. I only
   B. II only
   C. Both I and II
   D. Neither I nor II

5. Which of the following nonfinancial measures would monitor the performance of a particular process in relation to acceptable upper and lower limits of deviation?
   I. Control chart
   II. Fishbone diagram

   A. I only
   B. II only
   C. Both I and II
   D. Neither I nor II

6. An international theme park is having problems with amusement rides that are temporarily closed during peak operations. Quality control wants to begin by repairing the ride that has had the most shutdowns over the previous two months, fix that specific ride, and then move on to the ride with the next most frequent shutdowns. Which diagram or chart would likely be used to determine which ride needs attention first?

   A. Control chart
   B. Pareto diagram
   C. Fishbone diagram
   D. All of the above

7. Honest John Inc. is a large retailing chain that attempts to offer the lowest possible price on consumer goods. What is the marketing practice that best describes Honest John's approach?

   A. Interaction-based relationship marketing
   B. Network marketing
   C. Transaction marketing
   D. Database marketing

8. Wickatunk Bike Shop is a retailer that believes that sales advance relationships, thereby driving more sales. Wickatunk Bike Shop is practicing:

   I. database marketing
   II. interaction-based relationship marketing
   III. transaction marketing

   A. II and III
   B. I only
   C. I, II, and III
   D. II only

9. Competitive commission plans tend to emphasize which type of performance compensation?

   I. Future compensation
   II. Current compensation

   A. I only
   B. II only
   C. Both I and II
   D. Neither I nor II

10. Inventoriable costs include:

    I. product costs
    II. period costs

    A. I only
    B. II only
    C. Both I and II
    D. Neither I nor II

11. Inventoriable costs include which of the following?

    I. Direct materials
    II. Indirect materials

    A. I only
    B. II only
    C. Both I and II
    D. Neither I nor II

12. Cost drivers:
    I. are activities that cause costs to increase as the activity increases
    II. can be financial as well as nonfinancial

    A. I only
    B. II only
    C. Both I and II
    D. Neither I nor II

13. Falk Manufacturing is attempting to calculate total overhead applied. For the current year, budgeted direct labor hours were 20,000 hours. In addition, budgeted factory overhead was $75,000. Actual costs and hours for the year were as follows:

    | Direct labor hours | $18,000 |
    | Direct labor costs | $103,000 |
    | Machine hours | $30,000 |

    For a particular job, 1,200 direct labor hours were used. Using direct labor hours as the cost driver, what amount of overhead should be applied to this job?

    A. $5,190
    B. $4,500
    C. $5,730
    D. $6,500

14. In developing a predetermined factory overhead application rate for use in a process costing system, which of the following could be used in the numerator?

    I. Actual factory overhead
    II. Estimated factory overhead

    A. I only
    B. II only
    C. Both I and II
    D. Neither I nor II

15. In developing a predetermined factory overhead application rate for use in a process costing system, which of the following would generally be used in the denominator?

    I. Actual machine hours
    II. Estimated machine hours

    A. I only
    B. II only
    C. Both I and II
    D. Neither I nor II

Use the following facts to answer **Questions 16–17**.

Anita Corp. has two major categories of factory overhead: indirect labor and replacement parts for factory machinery. The costs expected for these categories for the coming year are as follows:

Indirect labor	$90,000
Replacement parts for factory machinery	$70,000

Anita currently applies overhead based on direct labor hours. The estimated direct labor hours are 40,000 per year. The plant manager is asked to submit a bid for a potential job and assembles the following data:

Direct materials	$4,000
Direct labor (2,000 hours)	$16,000

16. Which amount reflects the prime costs for the job?

- A. $4,000
- B. $16,000
- C. $20,000
- D. $28,000

17. What is the total estimated product cost on the proposed job?

- A. $28,000
- B. $32,000
- C. $24,000
- D. $20,000

18. In the relevant range, fixed costs are:

- A. constant in total but decrease per unit as production levels increase
- B. constant in total but increase per unit as production levels increase
- C. constant in total but decrease per unit as production levels decrease
- D. constant per unit but increase in total as production levels increase

19. Variable costs:

- I. per unit remain unchanged in the relevant range
- II. increase in total as unit volume increases

- A. I only
- B. II only
- C. Both I and II
- D. Neither I nor II

Use the following facts to answer **Questions 20–25**.

Hercules Corp. had the following inventories at the beginning and end of March:

	3/1	3/31
Finished goods	$120,000	$110,000
Work in process	$230,000	$250,000
Direct materials	$134,000	$124,000

The following additional manufacturing data were available for March:

Direct materials purchased	$190,000
Purchase returns and allowances	$1,000
Transportation in	$2,000

Direct labor was $200,000, and factory overhead is applied at a rate of 40% of direct labor cost. Actual factory overhead was $165,000.

20. How much direct materials were used during March?

- A. $325,000
- B. $223,000
- C. $199,000
- D. $201,000

21. What were Hercules' total prime costs for March?

- A. $200,000
- B. $400,000
- C. $401,000
- D. $435,000

22. How much did Hercules incur in total manufacturing costs for March?

- A. $566,000
- B. $525,000
- C. $711,000
- D. $481,000

23. Total manufacturing costs available in March were:

- A. $566,000
- B. $525,000
- C. $711,000
- D. $481,000

24. How much was Hercules' cost of goods manufactured for March?

- A. $481,000
- B. $461,000
- C. $501,000
- D. $485,000

25. How much was Hercules' cost of goods sold for March?

    A. $451,000
    B. $461,000
    C. $471,000
    D. $481,000

26. For a manufacturing entity, cost of goods sold is equal to cost of goods manufactured:

    A. plus beginning finished goods minus ending finished goods
    B. plus ending finished goods minus beginning finished goods
    C. plus beginning finished goods minus ending work in process
    D. plus ending work in process minus beginning finished goods

27. The cost of goods manufactured differs from the total manufacturing costs in that the cost of goods manufactured:

    A. adds beginning work in process and subtracts ending finished goods
    B. adds beginning work in process and subtracts beginning finished goods
    C. adds ending work in process and subtracts beginning work in process
    D. adds beginning work in process and subtracts ending work in process

28. Ending finished goods inventory is subtracted and beginning finished goods inventory added when attempting to calculate:

    A. cost of goods manufactured
    B. total manufacturing costs
    C. overhead applied
    D. cost of goods sold

29. Micki Corp. uses a job-order cost system and applies manufacturing overhead to jobs using a predetermined overhead rate based on direct labor dollars. The rate for the current year is 200% of direct labor dollars. This rate was calculated last November and will be used throughout the current year. During September, direct labor added to jobs was as follows:

	Job #1	Job #2	Job #3
Direct labor	$1,000	$4,500	$2,000

Actual manufacturing overhead for the month of September was $17,500. For September, manufacturing overhead was:

    A. overapplied by $2,500
    B. underapplied by $2,500
    C. correctly applied
    D. underapplied by $1,000

30. In a job costing system, issuing indirect materials to production increases which account(s)?
    I. Factory overhead applied
    II. Factory overhead control

    A. I only
    B. II only
    C. Both I and II
    D. Neither I nor II

31. When doing process costing using the weighted average method, what is the first step in determining equivalent units?

    A. Determining ending inventory units
    B. Determining what percentage of the ending inventory units are complete
    C. Determining costs per unit started but not completed
    D. Determining units completed during the period

Use the following facts to answer **Questions 32–37**.

Andrews Manufacturing uses a process costing system to manufacture homogeneous products. The following information summarizes operations during the quarter ending March 31:

Work in process, January 1	100 units
Started during the quarter	500 units
Completed during the quarter	400 units
Work-in-process inventory, March 31	200 units

32. Beginning work-in-process inventory was 50% complete for direct materials. Ending work-in-process inventory was 75% complete for direct materials. If the actual costs were $650,000 for the current period and $32,000 for the beginning inventory, calculate the equivalent units to be included in the cost per equivalent unit calculation using the weighted average method, with regard to materials for the quarter ended March 31.

A. 400 units
B. 500 units
C. 550 units
D. 600 units

33. Beginning work-in-process inventory was 50% complete for direct materials. Ending work-in-process inventory was 75% complete for direct materials. If the actual costs were $650,000 for the current period and $32,000 for the beginning inventory, how much cost needs to be included in the cost per equivalent unit calculation using the weighted average method, with regard to materials for the quarter ended March 31?

A. $32,000
B. $682,000
C. $650,000
D. $511,500

34. Beginning work-in-process inventory was 50% complete for direct materials. Ending work-in-process inventory was 75% complete for direct materials. If the actual costs were $650,000 for the current period and $32,000 for the beginning inventory, what is the cost per equivalent unit of production using the weighted average method, with regard to materials for the quarter ended March 31?

A. $1,240
B. $1,182
C. $1,300
D. $1,364

35. Beginning work-in-process inventory was 50% complete for direct materials. Ending work-in-process inventory was 75% complete for direct materials. If the actual costs were $650,000 for the current period and $32,000 for the beginning inventory, calculate the equivalent units to be included in the cost per equivalent unit calculation using the FIFO method, with regard to materials for the quarter ended March 31.

A. 400 units
B. 500 units
C. 550 units
D. 600 units

36. Beginning work-in-process inventory was 50% complete for direct materials. Ending work-in-process inventory was 75% complete for direct materials. If the actual costs were $650,000 for the current period and $32,000 for the beginning inventory, how much cost needs to be included in the calculation of cost per equivalent unit using the FIFO method, with regard to materials for the quarter ended March 31?

A. $32,000
B. $682,000
C. $650,000
D. $511,500

37. Beginning work-in-process inventory was 50% complete for direct materials. Ending work-in-process inventory was 75% complete for direct materials. If the actual costs were $650,000 for the current period and $32,000 for the beginning inventory, calculate the cost per equivalent unit of production using the FIFO method, with regard to materials for the quarter ended March 31.

A. $1,240
B. $1,300
C. $1,083
D. $1,364

38. In process costing, which of the following would be included in total costs when calculating cost per equivalent unit under the weighted average assumption?
   I. Costs of units completed during the period
   II. Costs of beginning inventory

A. I only
B. II only
C. Both I and II
D. Neither I nor II

39. In process costing, when determining cost per equivalent unit, the number of equivalent units in the denominator will include *beginning inventory units* if the cost flow assumption being used is:
  I. weighted average
  II. FIFO

  A. I only
  B. II only
  C. Both I and II
  D. Neither I nor II

40. In process costing, which of the following would be included in the numerator when calculating cost per equivalent unit under the FIFO assumption?
  I. Current costs
  II. Beginning inventory costs

  A. I only
  B. II only
  C. Both I and II
  D. Neither I nor II

41. Under process costing, which of the following cost flow assumptions would include ending inventory times the percentage of completion in the calculation for the number of equivalent units?
  I. Weighted average
  II. FIFO

  A. I only
  B. II only
  C. Both I and II
  D. Neither I nor II

42. Under process costing, when determining cost per unit, which of the following methods would consider beginning inventory units but NOT beginning inventory costs?
  I. Weighted average
  II. FIFO

  A. I only
  B. II only
  C. Both I and II
  D. Neither I nor II

43. Which of the following describes a system that accumulates all costs of overhead for each of the departments or activities of the organization and then allocates those overhead costs based on causal factors?

  A. Process costing
  B. Job-order costing
  C. Activity-based costing
  D. None of the above

44. What benefits can management expect from activity-based costing?
  I. It provides management with a more thorough understanding of product costs and product profitability for strategies and pricing decisions.
  II. It leads to a more competitive position by evaluating cost drivers.
  III. It uses a common departmental or factory-wide measure of activity, such as direct labor hours or dollars, to distribute manufacturing overhead to products.

  A. I and II
  B. I and III
  C. II and III
  D. I, II, and III

45. Eliminating all cost drivers would eliminate which of the following?
  I. Value-adding activities
  II. Non–value-adding activities

  A. I only
  B. II only
  C. Both I and II
  D. Neither I nor II

46. Which of the following can be used to allocate production costs to products and services by averaging the cost over the total units produced?
  I. Job-order costing
  II. Process costing
  III. Activity-based costing

  A. I only
  B. I and II
  C. II and III
  D. II only

47. Activity-based costing includes:
  I. using cost drivers as application bases to increase the accuracy of reported product costs
  II. using several machine cost pools to measure product costs on the basis of time in a machine center
  III. using application rates that are plant-wide rather than incurring the cost of detailed allocations

  A. I and III
  B. I and II
  C. II only
  D. I, II, and III

48. Which of the following would be an appropriate costing method for internal but NOT external reporting?
    I. Activity-based costing
    II. Job-order costing
    III. Process costing

    A. I only
    B. II and III
    C. I, II, and III
    D. None of the above

49. Tammy Manufacturing uses direct costing. At the end of its first year of operations, 2,000 units of inventory are on hand. Fixed manufacturing costs are $40 per unit. Which of the following statements is/are correct?
    I. The use of absorption costing, rather than variable costing, would result in a higher net income.
    II. The use of absorption costing, rather than variable costing, would result in a higher ending inventory.

    A. I only
    B. II only
    C. Both I and II
    D. Neither I nor II

50. Which of the following could be used to refer to the contribution approach?
    I. Direct costing
    II. Full absorption costing
    III. Variable costing

    A. III only
    B. I and III
    C. I only
    D. I, II, and III

51. Direct costing can be used for financial reporting that is:
    I. internal
    II. external

    A. I only
    B. II only
    C. Both I and II
    D. Neither I nor II

52. Under absorption costing, costs are broken down between which of the following?
    I. Fixed and variable
    II. Product and period

    A. I only
    B. II only
    C. Both I and II
    D. Neither I nor II

53. Under variable costing:
    I. all fixed factory overhead is treated as a period cost and is expensed in the period incurred
    II. cost of goods sold includes only variable costs

    A. I only
    B. II only
    C. Both I and II
    D. Neither I nor II

54. Under variable costing, which of the following would be expensed in the period incurred?
    I. Fixed selling, general, and administrative expenses
    II. Fixed factory overhead

    A. I only
    B. II only
    C. Both I and II
    D. Neither I nor II

55. Which of the following would appear in ending inventory under absorption costing but NOT under direct costing?

    A. Fixed selling and administrative costs
    B. Variable selling and administrative costs
    C. Fixed manufacturing costs
    D. Variable manufacturing costs

Use the following facts to answer **Questions 56–58**.

In Year 1, its first year of operation, Pecorino Manufacturers had the following manufacturing costs when it produced 100,000 and sold 75,000 units of its only product:

Fixed costs	$195,000
Variable costs	$160,000

56. Under direct costing, how much fixed manufacturing cost will be expensed in Year 1?

    A. $0
    B. $48,750
    C. $146,250
    D. $195,000

57. Under full absorption costing, how much fixed manufacturing cost will be expensed in Year 1?

    A. $0
    B. $48,750
    C. $146,250
    D. $195,000

58. What is the difference in net income between absorption costing and direct costing?

    A. $0
    B. $48,750
    C. $146,250
    D. $195,000

59. Which of the following is/are correct regarding the relationship between direct costing and full absorption costing as it relates to production and sales?

    I. When production exceeds sales, net income under absorption costing is higher than net income under direct costing.
    II. When sales exceed production, absorption costing net income is less than variable costing net income.

    A. I only
    B. II only
    C. Both I and II
    D. Neither I nor II

60. Selected information concerning Owen Industries Inc. for the year ended December 31 is as follows:

Units produced	40,000
Units sold	37,000
Direct materials used	$180,000
Direct labor incurred	$140,000
Fixed factory overhead	$150,000
Variable factory overhead	$124,000
Fixed selling and administrative expenses	$160,000
Variable selling and administrative expenses	$19,000

    Work-in-process inventories at the beginning and end of the year were zero. What was Owen Industries' finished goods inventory cost at December 31 under the direct (variable) costing method?

    A. $33,300
    B. $44,550
    C. $47,250
    D. $49,360

61. Under the contribution approach, which of the following would contain only variable costs?

    I. Ending inventory
    II. Cost of goods sold

    A. I only
    B. II only
    C. Both I and II
    D. Neither I nor II

62. Under direct costing, which of the following is subtracted from sales to calculate contribution margin?

    A. All variable costs
    B. Variable overhead but not variable selling expenses
    C. Variable selling expenses but not variable overhead
    D. Variable overhead and fixed overhead

63. Under direct costing, variable overhead is included in the calculation of which of the following?

    I. Contribution margin
    II. Cost of goods sold

    A. I only
    B. II only
    C. Both I and II
    D. Neither I nor II

64. Under the contribution approach, variable selling and general expenses are included in the calculation of which of the following?

    I. Contribution margin
    II. Cost of goods sold

    A. I only
    B. II only
    C. Both I and II
    D. Neither I nor II

65. Under direct costing, when calculating contribution margin:

    A. variable manufacturing costs are included as well as fixed manufacturing costs
    B. variable manufacturing costs are included as well as variable selling and general expenses
    C. variable selling and general expenses are included as well as fixed selling and general expenses
    D. variable manufacturing costs are included but not variable selling and general expenses

66. The following information pertains to Tatum Corp.:

Sales	$750,000
Manufacturing costs	$210,000 (fixed), $140,000 (variable)
Selling and administrative costs	$300,000 (fixed), $45,000 (variable)

    If Tatum produces and sells 30,000 units, how much is the contribution margin?

    A. $565,000
    B. $410,000
    C. $355,000
    D. $265,000

Use the following facts to answer **Questions 67–68**.

Ridge Corp. is a manufacturer. One of its products, "chip," is used as a spare part for military and civilian vehicles. This product has the following financial structure per unit in Year 1:

Selling price	$160
Direct materials	$20
Direct labor	$15
Variable manufacturing overhead	$12
Fixed manufacturing overhead	$30
Shipping and handling—freight out	$3
Fixed selling and administrative costs	$10
Total costs	$90

67. How much is the contribution margin for one unit of product "chip"?

   A. $110
   B. $113
   C. $120
   D. $150

68. If total sales are 18,000 units and sales returns are $80,000, what is the total contribution margin for Year 1?

   A. $2,000,000
   B. $1,980,000
   C. $1,900,000
   D. $900,000

69. Barry Inc. is a manufacturer. Which of the following would increase for Barry if production and sales were to increase?
   I. Variable costs per unit
   II. Contribution margin per unit

   A. I only
   B. II only
   C. Both I and II
   D. Neither I nor II

70. The following information relates to Griffin Corp., which produced and sold 55,000 units during Year 1:

Sales	$750,000
Fixed manufacturing costs	$310,000
Variable manufacturing costs	$130,000
Fixed selling and administrative costs	$200,000
Variable selling and administrative costs	$45,000

For Year 2, if production and sales are expected to be 60,000 units, Griffin should anticipate a contribution margin per unit of:

   A. $10.45
   B. $11.73
   C. $12.09
   D. $13.29

71. Homer Company developed its business plan based on the assumption that units would sell at a price of $400 each. The variable costs for each unit were projected at $200, and the annual fixed costs were budgeted at $80,000. Homer's after-tax profit objective was $160,000; the company's effective tax rate is 30%. If no changes are made to the selling price or cost structure, determine the number of units that Homer must sell in order to break even.

   A. 400
   B. 367
   C. 350
   D. 250

72. Island Ridge Manufacturing has variable costs of 20% of sales and fixed costs of $30,000. What is Island Ridge's breakeven point in sales dollars?

   A. $60,500
   B. $30,500
   C. $24,500
   D. $37,500

Use the following facts to answer **Questions 73–76**.

In Year 1, Scully Manufacturing sells products for $7.50 each. Variable costs of manufacturing are $2.25 per unit.

73. The company needs to sell 20,000 units to break even. How much are fixed costs?

   A. $45,000
   B. $105,000
   C. $150,000
   D. Need more information to solve

74. In Year 2, Scully Manufacturing expects the units to sell for $9. Variable manufacturing costs are expected to increase by one-third, and fixed costs are expected to increase by 20%. How much is the new contribution margin per unit for Year 2?

    A. $9
    B. $6.75
    C. $6
    D. $4.50

75. In Year 2, Scully Manufacturing expects the units to sell for $9. Variable manufacturing costs are expected to increase by one-third, and fixed costs are expected to increase by 20%. How much does Scully expect total fixed costs to be in Year 2?

    A. $105,000
    B. $115,500
    C. $125,000
    D. $126,000

76. In Year 2, Scully Manufacturing expects the units to sell for $9. Variable manufacturing costs are expected to increase by one-third, and fixed costs are expected to increase by 20%. How many units does Scully need to sell to break even in Year 2?

    A. 20,750
    B. 20,000
    C. 21,000
    D. 22,000

Use the following facts to answer **Questions 77–79**.

Franco Company manufactures helmets with direct material costs of $10 per unit and direct labor of $7 per unit. A regional freight company charges Franco $5 per unit to make deliveries. Sales commissions are paid at 10% of the selling price. Helmets are sold for $100 each. Indirect factory costs and administrative costs are $5,000 and $20,200 per month, respectively.

77. How much are total variable costs per unit?

    A. $17
    B. $22
    C. $32
    D. $37

78. How much are Franco's fixed costs?

    A. $5,000
    B. $20,200
    C. $25,200
    D. None of the above

79. How many helmets must Franco produce to break even?

    A. 371
    B. 421
    C. 547
    D. 631

80. Musk Corp. developed its business plan based on the assumption that products would sell at a price of $400 each. The variable costs for each product were projected at $200, and the annual fixed costs were budgeted at $100,000. Musk's profit objective was $240,000. If no changes are made to the selling price or cost structure, determine the number of units that Musk must sell to achieve its profit objective.

    A. 4,500
    B. 3,500
    C. 1,700
    D. 2,500

81. Gold Manufacturing makes mini solar panels and has the following cost structure:

Direct materials	$3.25
Direct labor	$4
Freight out	$0.75
Total fixed costs	$100,000

How many panels must Gold Manufacturing sell to earn a profit of $50,000 before taxes if the selling price is $20 per unit?

    A. 8,333
    B. 12,500
    C. 14,166
    D. 15,000

82. Harbor Manufacturing earned a profit in Year 1 of $95,000 before tax. The tax rate for Year 1 was 30%. In Year 2, Harbor desires an after-tax profit of $100,000, and the tax rate for Year 2 is 35%. How much pretax profit does Harbor need to earn to reach its desired after-tax profit goal?

    A. $122,564
    B. $153,846
    C. $150,000
    D. $164,346

Use the following facts to answer **Questions 83–84**.

Spotswood Corp. is a manufacturer with the following information for Year 1:

Sales	$200,000
Contribution margin	$120,000
Fixed costs	$70,000
Income taxes	$10,000

83. How much is breakeven in dollars?

    A. $90,000
    B. $124,444
    C. $81,665
    D. $116,667

84. How much is the margin of safety?

    A. $50,000
    B. $70,000
    C. $82,667
    D. $83,333

85. Breakeven analysis assumes that over the relevant range which of the following will occur?
    I. Variable cost per unit will change with volume.
    II. Fixed cost will remain constant.

    A. I only
    B. II only
    C. Both I and II
    D. Neither I nor II

86. Breakeven analysis assumes that which of the following would be constant on a per unit basis?
    I. All variable costs
    II. Revenue

    A. I only
    B. II only
    C. Both I and II
    D. Neither I nor II

87. When considering a special order, a manufacturer would accept the order if the sales price were in excess of which of the following?

    A. Variable costs
    B. Opportunity costs
    C. Relevant costs
    D. Fixed costs

88. At full capacity, relevant costs of accepting a special order include which of the following?
    I. Contribution margin in dollars that will be forfeited to produce the special order
    II. Variable costs

    A. I only
    B. II only
    C. Both I and II
    D. Neither I nor II

89. Mosca Company has considerable excess manufacturing capacity. A special job order's cost sheet includes the following applied manufacturing overhead costs:

Fixed costs	$11,000
Variable costs	$23,000

The fixed costs include a normal $2,700 allocation for in-house design costs, although no in-house design will be done. Instead the job will require the use of external designers costing $8,750. What is the total amount to be included in the calculation to determine the minimum acceptable price for the job?

    A. $31,750
    B. $34,000
    C. $37,050
    D. $44,000

90. Which of the following assumptions underlie(s) cost-volume-profit analysis?
    I. Total variable costs are directly proportional to volume over a relevant range.
    II. Selling prices are to remain unchanged.

    A. I only
    B. II only
    C. Both I and II
    D. Neither I nor II

91. Norcross Corp. is offered a one-time special order for its product and has the capacity to take this order without losing current business. Variable costs per unit and fixed costs in total will be the same. The gross profit for the special order will be 20%, which is 10% less than the usual gross profit. What impact will this order have on total fixed costs and operating income?

    A. Total fixed costs increase, and operating income increases.
    B. Total fixed costs do not change, and operating income increases.
    C. Total fixed costs decrease, and fixed costs per unit increase.
    D. Total fixed costs do not change, and operating income does not change.

92. What is the term for the potential benefit lost by selecting a particular course of action?

    A. Contribution margin
    B. Variable cost per unit
    C. Opportunity cost
    D. Breakeven point in units

93. When deciding on whether to accept a special order, if idle space has no alternative use, which of the following would be correct?
    I. Opportunity cost would be zero.
    II. The special order would be accepted if the selling price was more than the variable cost per unit.

    A. I only
    B. II only
    C. Both I and II
    D. Neither I nor II

94. Whether to make or purchase a product is NOT influenced by fixed costs that are:
    I. avoidable
    II. unavoidable

    A. I only
    B. II only
    C. Both I and II
    D. Neither I nor II

95. Howard Corp. has a factory with idle space and is deciding whether to build more units or rent out the space. Opportunity cost is equal to the:

    A. combined value of the opportunity selected and the next best use
    B. difference between the best alternative and the next best alternative
    C. most profitable use of the factory space
    D. value of the next best alternative

96. Tillman Corp. had an opportunity to use its capacity to produce an extra 4,000 units with a contribution margin of $5 per unit or to rent out the space for $15,000. What was the opportunity cost of using the capacity?

    A. $20,000
    B. $5,000
    C. $15,000
    D. $35,000

97. The relevance of a particular cost to a decision is determined by which of the following?
    I. Potential effect on the decision of the particular cost
    II. The number of decision alternatives

    A. I only
    B. II only
    C. Both I and II
    D. Neither I nor II

98. Fascination Corp. is a clothing manufacturer. In a decision analysis situation, which of the following costs would be relevant to a decision?
    I. Avoidable cost
    II. Incremental cost

    A. I only
    B. II only
    C. Both I and II
    D. Neither I nor II

99. The operational decision method, referred to as marginal analysis, is used when analyzing business decisions such as which of the following?
    I. The introduction of a new product
    II. Whether to change output levels of existing products

    A. I only
    B. II only
    C. Both I and II
    D. Neither I nor II

100. The operational decision method, referred to as marginal analysis, would NOT be useful when analyzing which of the following business decisions?
    I. Accepting or rejecting special orders
    II. Making versus buying a product or service

    A. I only
    B. II only
    C. Both I and II
    D. Neither I nor II

101. When considering alternatives, such as make or buy, costs that will change under different alternatives:
    I. are known as relevant costs
    II. should be considered by management unless they vary with production

    A. I only
    B. II only
    C. Both I and II
    D. Neither I nor II

102. Which of the following costs would NOT be considered in a decision to sell or process further?
    I. Joint costs
    II. Separable costs

    A. I only
    B. II only
    C. Both I and II
    D. Neither I nor II

Use the following facts to answer **Questions 103–104**.

Hathaway Corp. manufactures two products from a joint process. The two products developed are product "Quo" and product "Rael." A standard production run incurs joint costs of $150,000 and results in 30,000 units of Quo and 60,000 units of Rael. Each Quo sells for $3 per unit; each Rael sells for $6 per unit.

103. Assuming no further processing work is done after the split-off point, how much joint cost should be allocated to product Rael based on total quantity of units produced?

    A. $50,000
    B. $100,000
    C. $150,000
    D. None of the above

104. Each Quo sells for $3 per unit; each Rael sells for $6 per unit. If there are no further processing costs incurred after the split-off point, how much joint cost should be allocated to Rael using the relative sales value method?

    A. $30,000
    B. $60,000
    C. $90,000
    D. $120,000

105. Manning Corp. produced two products, product A and product B. A standard production run resulted in joint cost of $400,000. At the split-off point, Manning anticipates 30,000 units of product A and 20,000 units of product B. If Manning sold all of the products at the split-off point, product A would sell for $5.50 and product B for $7. If there are no further processing costs incurred after the split-off point, how much of the joint cost should Manning allocate to product A on a physical quantity allocation basis?

    A. $200,000
    B. $300,000
    C. $240,000
    D. $350,000

106. In a decision analysis situation, relevant costs include:
    I. incremental costs
    II. prime costs

    A. I only
    B. II only
    C. Both I and II
    D. Neither I nor II

107. Fanny Manufacturing is deciding whether to keep or drop a segment of its business. Which costs and benefits are compared in reaching that decision?

    A. The cost of contribution margin lost is compared to unavoidable fixed costs.
    B. Avoidable fixed costs are compared to the profit or loss from the segment.
    C. Profit or loss from the segment is compared to profit or loss for the entire company.
    D. The cost of contribution margin lost is compared to avoidable fixed costs.

108. A regression equation is based on an estimate of the _____ based on changes in the _____.

    A. independent variable, dependent variable
    B. dependent variable, independent variable
    C. dependent variable, dependent variable
    D. independent variable, independent variable

109. Which of the following measures the strength of the relationship between the dependent variable and the independent variable in a number between −1.0 and 1.0?

    A. Total cost
    B. Correlation coefficient
    C. Learning curve
    D. Linear regression equation

Use the following facts to answer **Questions 110–113**.

Assume the regression analysis results for Rayon Manufacturing Corp. can be shown as: $y = 80x + 25$.

110. What does y represent?

    A. Fixed costs
    B. Total costs
    C. Variable costs
    D. The independent variable

111. What does the 25 represent?

    A. Fixed costs
    B. Total costs
    C. Variable costs
    D. The independent variable

112. If the budget calls for producing 150 units, which of the following could be a correlation coefficient for the relationship between volume and total cost?

    A. 0.85
    B. −0.79
    C. 0
    D. 2.0

113. If the budget calls for producing 150 units, and the coefficient of variation is 85%, which of the following would be correct?
    I. Total cost is equal to $12,000.
    II. The coefficient of determination measures the proportion of the total variation in "y"—or total cost—that is explained by the total variation in the independent variable, x, or variable costs.

    A. I only
    B. II only
    C. Both I and II
    D. Neither I nor II

114. Sayre Corp. uses the coefficient of correlation to measure the strength of the cost volume relationships used in planning. Which of the following would be correct regarding costs and volume with respect to the coefficient of correlation?
    I. Cost volume relationships are not only positive but also assumed to be proportional.
    II. A coefficient of correlation of zero would NOT be expected for fixed costs.

    A. I only
    B. II only
    C. Both I and II
    D. Neither I nor II

115. When selecting cost drivers or independent variables, management would LEAST likely select a cost driver with a correlation coefficient of:

    A. −1.0
    B. 1.0
    C. 0.005
    D. 0.50

116. When forecasting total cost, management would likely select a cost driver or independent variable if the correlation coefficient were which of the following?
    I. Positive
    II. Negative
    III. Zero

    A. I only
    B. I and III
    C. II and III
    D. I and II

117. Which of the following would NOT be used to classify costs as either fixed or variable?
    I. High-low method
    II. Regression analysis method

    A. I only
    B. II only
    C. Both I and II
    D. Neither I nor II

Use the following facts to answer **Questions 118–119.**

Meadows Corp. applied the high-low estimation for customer order data from July 1 through December 31 of Year 8.

Period	Volume	Cost
July	420	$7,260
Aug.	470	$7,840
Sept.	370	$6,935
Oct.	364	$6,834
Nov.	410	$7,110
Dec.	520	$8,350

118. How much was variable cost per order?

    A. $8.80
    B. $9.72
    C. $10.40
    D. $10.88

119. How much was fixed cost for December?

    A. $3,754
    B. $3,296
    C. $2,814
    D. $2,645

CHAPTER 17

PLANNING AND BUDGETING

QUESTIONS 120–188

120. Participative budgeting can be characterized by which of the following?
    I. Increased motivation
    II. More time consuming
    III. Decreased acceptance

    A. I and II
    B. II and III
    C. I and III
    D. I, II, and III

121. Which of the following types of budgets would NOT be contained in the master budget?
    I. Operating budgets
    II. Financial budgets

    A. I only
    B. II only
    C. Both I and II
    D. Neither I nor II

122. Which of the following would be found in the operating rather than the financial budget?
    I. Pro forma income statement
    II. Capital expenditures budget

    A. I only
    B. II only
    C. Both I and II
    D. Neither I nor II

123. Which of the following budgets is/are generally produced BEFORE the sales budget?
    I. Production budget
    II. Cash budget

    A. I only
    B. II only
    C. Both I and II
    D. Neither I nor II

124. A manufacturer wants to improve its staging process and compares this process against the check-in process for a major airline. In doing so, the tool the manufacturer is using is:

    A. Six Sigma
    B. economic value-added
    C. benchmarking
    D. total quality management

125. Which of the following budgets is prepared independently of the sales budget?

    A. Production budget
    B. Selling and administrative budget
    C. Cash budget
    D. Capital expenditures budget

126. Which of the following budgets are appropriate for planning because they involve both fixed and variable costs?
    I. Flexible budgets
    II. Static budgets

    A. I only
    B. II only
    C. Both I and II
    D. Neither I nor II

127. A static budget:
    I. is based on costs at one level of output
    II. includes budgeted costs for actual and budgeted output

    A. I only
    B. II only
    C. Both I and II
    D. Neither I nor II

128. The annual business plan typically begins with operating budgets driven by which of the following?

    A. Financial budgets
    B. Production budgets
    C. Personnel budgets
    D. Sales budgets

129. Of the four budgets listed, what is the proper order in which they are prepared?
    I. Cash disbursements budget
    II. Production budget
    III. Direct materials budget
    IV. Sales budget

    A. IV, II, III, I
    B. IV, I, III, II
    C. III, II, IV, I
    D. I, II, III, IV

130. What are sales forecasts based upon?
    I. Past patterns of sales
    II. Changes in the firm's prices
    III. Results of market research studies

    A. I and II
    B. I, II, and III
    C. II and III
    D. I and III

131. What is the required unit production level given the following factors?

Projected sales	2,000
Beginning inventory	185
Desired ending inventory	220
Prior-year beginning inventory	30

    A. 1,965 units
    B. 2,035 units
    C. 1,995 units
    D. 1,935 units

132. A company's controller is adjusting next year's budget to reflect the impact of an expected 4% inflation rate. Listed are selected items from next year's budget before the adjustment:

Salaries expense	$210,000
Insurance expense	$120,000
Supplies expense	$60,000

After adjusting for the 4% inflation rate, what is the company's total budget for the selected items before taxes for next year?

    A. $380,000
    B. $395,800
    C. $401,200
    D. $405,600

133. A company's controller is adjusting next year's budget to reflect the impact of an expected 4% inflation rate. Listed are selected items from next year's budget before the adjustment:

Salaries expense	$210,000
Insurance expense	$120,000
Supplies expense	$60,000
Depreciation expense	$25,000
Interest expense on 10-year fixed rate bonds	$27,000

After adjusting for the 4% inflation rate, what is the company's total budget for the selected items before taxes for next year?

    A. $459,680
    B. $458,680
    C. $458,350
    D. $457,600

134. Rascal Company plans to produce 100,000 toy fire trucks during July. Planned production for August is 150,000 trucks. Sales are forecasted at 90,000 trucks for July and 110,000 trucks for August. Each truck has eight wheels. Rascal's policy is to maintain 5% of the next month's production in inventory at the end of a month. How many wheels should Rascal purchase during July?

    A. 860,000
    B. 820,000
    C. 810,000
    D. 780,000

135. Mallard Inc. is in the process of preparing its annual budget. The following beginning and ending inventory levels (in units) are planned for the year ending December 31, Year 4:

	Beginning Inventory	Ending Inventory
Raw material	30,000	40,000
Work in process	20,000	20,000
Finished goods	60,000	40,000

Two units of raw material are needed to produce each unit of finished product. If Mallard plans to sell 380,000 units during Year 4, how many units would it have to manufacture during the year?

A. 400,000 units
B. 360,000 units
C. 350,000 units
D. 325,000 units

136. The sales budget for Wagner Industries shows quarterly sales for the next year as follows:

Quarter	Units
1	11,000
2	9,000
3	12,000
4	16,000

Wagner's policy is to have a finished goods inventory at the end of each quarter equal to 10% of the next quarter's sales. What would budgeted production for the second quarter of the next year be?

A. 8,700 units
B. 9,300 units
C. 9,550 units
D. 9,900 units

137. Yanna Corp. manufactures computer tables. The tabletops are manufactured by Yanna, but the keyboard draw is purchased from an outside supplier. The assembly department takes a manufactured table and attaches the keyboard draw. It takes 30 minutes of labor to assemble a keyboard draw to a table. The company follows a policy of producing enough tables to ensure that 30% of next month's sales are in the finished goods inventory. Yanna also purchases sufficient raw materials to ensure that raw materials inventory is 55% of the following month's

scheduled production. Yanna's sales budget in units for the fourth quarter of Year 1 follows:

October	2,400
November	3,000
December	2,100

Yanna's ending inventories in units for September 30, Year 1, are:

Finished goods	1,600
Raw materials (keyboard draws)	3,800

What is the number of computer tables to be produced during November in Year 1?

A. 1,825 tables
B. 2,210 tables
C. 2,340 tables
D. 2,730 tables

138. Tucker Tool and Dye has developed the following production plan:

Month	Units
January	11,000
February	13,000
March	8,000
April	10,000

Each unit contains 3 pounds of raw material. The desired raw material ending inventory each month is 120% of the next month's production, plus 500 pounds. (The beginning inventory meets this requirement.) Tucker has developed the following direct labor standards for production of these units:

	Department 1	Department 2
Hours per unit	3.0	0.5
Hourly rate	$6.75	$10

Tucker's total budgeted direct labor dollars for March usage should be:

A. $162,000
B. $122,000
C. $202,000
D. $192,000

139. Inputs in calculating a cost of goods manufactured budget include which of the following?
    I. Overhead applied
    II. Material usage

A. I only
B. II only
C. Both I and II
D. Neither I nor II

140. Inputs in calculating a cost of goods manufactured budget include which of the following?
    I. Finished goods inventory
    II. Work-in-process inventory

    A. I only
    B. II only
    C. Both I and II
    D. Neither I nor II

141. The selling and administrative expense budget can be correctly described as:
    I. a financial rather than an operational budget
    II. dependent upon sales

    A. I only
    B. II only
    C. Both I and II
    D. Neither I nor II

142. Stirling Corp. is preparing a Year 1 cash budget for the purchase of merchandise. Budgeted data are:

    | Cost of goods sold for Year 1 | $200,000 |
    | Accounts payable, Jan. 1, Year 1 | $20,000 |
    | Inventory, Jan. 1, Year 1 | $30,000 |
    | Inventory, Dec. 31, Year 1 | $43,000 |

    Purchases will be made in 12 equal monthly amounts and paid for in the following month. What is Stirling's Year 1 budgeted cash payment for purchases of merchandise?

    A. $210,750
    B. $215,250
    C. $226,250
    D. $245,000

143. The cash budget shows itemized cash receipts and disbursements during the period, including the:
    I. financing activities
    II. beginning cash balances

    A. I only
    B. II only
    C. Both I and II
    D. Neither I nor II

144. Which of the following is/are correct regarding a cash budget?
    I. The cash budget shows the availability of funds for repayment of debt.
    II. The cash budget is usually NOT broken down into monthly periods.

    A. I only
    B. II only
    C. Both I and II
    D. Neither I nor II

145. Singer Company budgeted sales on account of $200,000 for October, $250,000 for November, and $275,000 for December. Collection experience indicates that 70% of the budgeted sales will be collected the month after the sale, 26% the second month, and 4% will be uncollectible. The cash receipts from accounts receivable that should be budgeted for December would be:

    A. $198,250
    B. $199,700
    C. $147,700
    D. $191,712

146. Levin Inc. is preparing a schedule of cash receipts and disbursements for Year 4. Which of the following items should be included?
    I. Borrowing funds from a bank on a note payable taken out in August Year 4 and agreeing to pay the principal and interest in July Year 5
    II. Dividends declared in October Year 4 to be paid in January Year 5 to shareholders of record as of December Year 4

    A. I only
    B. II only
    C. Both I and II
    D. Neither I nor II

147. Which of the following would NOT be included in a statement of cash receipts and disbursements for KingPin Corp. in Year 2?
    I. A purchase order issued in December Year 2 for items to be delivered in January Year 3
    II. The amount of uncollectible customer accounts for Year 2

    A. I only
    B. II only
    C. Both I and II
    D. Neither I nor II

148. Norris Company forecasted first quarter sales of 10,000 units, second quarter sales of 15,000 units, third quarter sales of 14,000 units, and fourth quarter sales of 17,000 units at $4 per unit. Past experience has shown that 70% of the sales will be in cash and 30% will be on credit. All credit sales are collected in the following quarter, and none are uncollectible. What amount of cash is forecasted to be collected in the second quarter?

    A. $54,000
    B. $42,000
    C. $30,000
    D. $28,500

149. Which of the following budgeted (pro forma) financial statements is prepared first?

    A. Pro forma statement of cash flows
    B. Pro forma income statement
    C. Pro forma balance sheet
    D. May be prepared in any order

150. Flexible budgeting is limited because it is highly dependent upon an accurate identification of:
    I. fixed cost
    II. variable cost per unit

    A. I only
    B. II only
    C. Both I and II
    D. Neither I nor II

151. Planned additions of capital equipment from the capital budget are added to the:
    I. pro forma balance sheet
    II. cash budget

    A. I only
    B. II only
    C. Both I and II
    D. Neither I nor II

152. A flexible budget would NOT be appropriate for:
    I. service industries
    II. a direct labor usage budget

    A. I only
    B. II only
    C. Both I and II
    D. Neither I nor II

153. When calculating net income using flexible budgeting, which of the following would be assumed constant within a relevant range?
    I. Variable cost per unit
    II. Total fixed cost
    III. Selling price per unit

    A. II only
    B. I and II
    C. II and III
    D. I, II, and III

154. A flexible budget contains:

    A. budgeted costs for budgeted output
    B. actual costs for budgeted output
    C. budgeted costs for actual output
    D. actual costs for actual output

Use the following facts to answer **Questions 155–156.**

Hyson Inc. manufactures and sells products. The master budget and the actual results for July are as follows:

	Actual July Sales	Master Budget
Unit sales	12,000	10,000
Sales	$132,000	$100,000
Variable costs	$70,800	$60,000
Contribution margin	$61,200	$40,000
Fixed costs	$30,000	$25,000
Operating income	$31,200	$15,000

155. If flexible budgeting is used, how much is contribution margin per unit based on actual sales of 12,000 units?

    A. $4.00
    B. $5.10
    C. $4.55
    D. None of the above

156. How much is the operating income for Hyson Inc. using a flexible budget for July?

    A. $31,200
    B. $21,000
    C. $23,000
    D. $15,000

Use the following facts to answer **Questions 157–158.**

Gilbert Watches sells a line of wrist wear. Gilbert's performance report for March Year 4 follows:

	Actual	Static Budget
Watches sold	500	600
Sales	$24,000	$30,000
Variable costs	$14,500	$18,000
Contribution margin	$9,500	$12,000
Fixed costs	$8,100	$8,800

157. If Gilbert Watches uses a flexible budget to analyze its performance, the variable cost flexible budget variance for March is

    A. $500 unfavorable
    B. $500 favorable
    C. $3,500 unfavorable
    D. $3,500 favorable

158. The fixed cost variance for March is:
    A. $700 unfavorable
    B. $700 favorable
    C. $2,500 favorable
    D. $300 unfavorable

159. The initial budget forecast for Jayson Corp. was production of 10,000 units during the year with a variable cost of $10 per unit. Jayson produced 9,000 units during the year. Actual variable manufacturing costs were $89,000. What is Jayson's flexible budget variance for the year?
    A. $1,000 unfavorable
    B. $11,000 favorable
    C. $1,000 favorable
    D. $11,000 unfavorable

160. Which of the following would NOT be a purpose for identifying manufacturing variances and assigning their responsibility to a person or department?
    I. To promote learning and improve operations
    II. To provide useful information about pricing of finished goods

    A. I only
    B. II only
    C. Both I and II
    D. Neither I nor II

161. A company budgeted the need for 10,000 materials at a price of $30 per unit. The actual units needed turned out to be 11,400 at a price of $28.50 per unit. What is the company's materials price variance?
    A. $15,000 unfavorable
    B. $17,100 unfavorable
    C. $17,100 favorable
    D. $15,000 favorable

162. For the current period production levels, Imhoff Company budgeted 12,300 board feet of production and purchased 15,000 board feet. The material cost was budgeted at $7 per foot. The actual cost for the period was $9.50 per foot. What was Imhoff's material price variance for the period?
    A. $37,500 favorable
    B. $30,750 favorable
    C. $30,750 unfavorable
    D. $37,500 unfavorable

163. The difference between standard hours at standard wage rates and actual hours at standard rates is referred to as:
    A. indirect labor variance
    B. direct labor rate variance
    C. direct labor rate
    D. direct labor efficiency variance

164. Romeo Manufacturing has relevant information for material Tyrisis as follows:

Quantity purchased	3,500 pounds
Standard quantity allowed	3,000 pounds
Actual price	$4.80
Standard price	$5

What was the direct material price variance for material Tyrisis?
    A. $700 unfavorable
    B. $600 unfavorable
    C. $600 favorable
    D. $700 favorable

165. The direct labor efficiency variance:
    I. could be unfavorable as a result of an unfavorable material usage variance
    II. is calculated by using the standard wage rate rather than the actual wage rate

    A. I only
    B. II only
    C. Both I and II
    D. Neither I nor II

166. When analyzing unfavorable variances, inadequate supervision may explain the reason behind an unfavorable:
    I. material price variance
    II. labor usage variance

    A. I only
    B. II only
    C. Both I and II
    D. Neither I nor II

167. The purchase of higher than standard quality material would likely result in:
    A. an unfavorable material price variance and a favorable material usage variance
    B. a favorable material price variance but an unfavorable material efficiency variance
    C. an unfavorable material price variance and an unfavorable material usage variance
    D. a favorable material usage variance and a favorable material price variance

Use the following facts to answer **Questions 168–169**.

Mojo Inc. manufactures backup generators and uses a standard cost system. The following information is available for the month of September:

80,000 direct labor hours were budgeted.
A total of 84,000 direct labor hours were worked at a total cost of $840,000.
The standard direct labor rate is $9 per hour.
The standard direct labor time per unit is four hours.

168. The direct labor price variance for September was

A. $84,000 favorable
B. $84,000 unfavorable
C. $79,000 unfavorable
D. $79,000 favorable

169. Mojo planned on producing 25,000 generators, but only 20,000 were actually produced. What was the direct labor efficiency variance for September?

A. $36,000 unfavorable
B. $36,000 favorable
C. $40,000 unfavorable
D. $40,000 favorable

Use the following facts to answer **Questions 170–171**.

Barlow Enterprises uses a standard cost system. The standard cost information regarding materials needed to manufacture one unit is 60 pounds of material at $1.70 per pound. The standard cost for labor needed to manufacture one unit of Tull is three hours at $12 per hour. During October, Barlow produced 1,750 units of Tull compared to a normal capacity of 1,900 units. The actual costs per unit of materials and labor were as follows:

Materials purchased
   and used   59 pounds at $1.85 per pound
Labor   3.5 hours at $12.50 per hour

170. Barlow's material price variance for October is

A. $15,750 unfavorable
B. $15,488 favorable
C. $15,750 favorable
D. $15,488 unfavorable

171. Barlow's labor rate variance for October is

A. $875 unfavorable
B. $875 favorable
C. $3,063 unfavorable
D. $3,063 favorable

172. Gabriel Corp. uses a standard costing system. At the end of the current year, the company provides the following overhead information:

Actual direct labor hours	10,000
Actual overhead incurred	$80,000 (variable), $52,000 (fixed)
Budgeted fixed overhead	$55,000
Variable overhead rate (per direct labor hour)	$9
Standard hours allowed for actual production	11,000

What is Gabriel's variable overhead efficiency variance?

A. 0
B. $9,000 unfavorable
C. $9,000 favorable
D. $19,000 favorable

173. Ryan Corp. budgeted sales of 5,250 at $13 per unit but sold 4,000 at $16 per unit. Ryan would compute a selling price variance of:

A. $3,750 unfavorable
B. $12,000 favorable
C. $15,750 favorable
D. $4,250 favorable

174. Harper Company has gathered the following information from a recent production run:

Standard variable overhead rate	$20
Actual variable overhead rate	$16
Standard process hours	44
Actual process hours	50

What is the company's variable overhead spending variance?

A. $200 favorable
B. $200 unfavorable
C. $176 favorable
D. $176 unfavorable

175. Which of the following can occur when the quantity budgeted to be sold differs from the quantity actually sold?

I. Sales price variance
II. Sales volume variance

A. I only
B. II only
C. Both I and II
D. Neither I nor II

176. Which of the following can be used to monitor the purchasing manager's performance?

    A. Direct material usage variance

    B. Direct labor rate variance

    C. Indirect material usage variance

    D. Direct material price variance

177. Benchmarking can be best defined as:

    A. the complete redesign of a process within an organization

    B. the development of the most effective methods of completing tasks in a particular industry

    C. a technique that examines product and process attributes to identify areas for improvements

    D. the comparison of existing activities with the best levels of performance in other, similar organizations

178. Which of the following could be used as an example of responsibility accounting?

    I. Cost center

    II. Profit center

    III. Investment center

    A. I and III

    B. II and III

    C. I and II

    D. I, II, and III

179. Strategic business units (SBUs) are classified into different types based on the responsibility levels assigned to their managers. Put the following SBUs in order from least responsibility to greatest responsibility.

    I. Profit SBU

    II. Cost SBU

    III. Revenue SBU

    IV. Investment capital SBU

    A. II, IV, I, III

    B. II, I, III, IV

    C. II, III, I, IV

    D. IV, II, I, III

180. The balanced scorecard reports management information regarding organizational performance as defined by "critical success factors." These critical success factors are often classified as:

    I. human resources

    II. business process

    III. customer satisfaction

    IV. financial performance

    A. I, III, and IV

    B. I, II, and IV

    C. II, III, and IV

    D. I, II, III, and IV

181. Responsibility accounting defines a "profit center" as being responsible for:

    I. revenues

    II. costs

    III. invested capital

    A. I and III

    B. I, II, and III

    C. I only

    D. I and II

182. How does responsibility accounting define and describe an investment center?

    I. An investment center is responsible for revenues, expenses, and invested capital.

    II. An investment center is similar to an independent business.

    A. I only

    B. II only

    C. Both I and II

    D. Neither I nor II

183. Which of the following would be contained in a performance report for a cost center?

    I. Controllable costs

    II. Controllable revenues

    A. I only

    B. II only

    C. Both I and II

    D. Neither I nor II

184. The financial perspective of a balanced scorecard is concerned with which of the following?

    I. Capture of increased market share

    II. Employee satisfaction and retention measures

    A. I only

    B. II only

    C. Both I and II

    D. Neither I nor II

185. The "internal business" perspective of the balanced scorecard measures:

    I. results of business operations through improved efficiencies

    II. nonfinancial performance such as employee satisfaction and retention

    A. I only

    B. II only

    C. Both I and II

    D. Neither I nor II

186. Which section of the balanced scorecard would focus on results of operations and utilization of assets?
    I. Customer
    II. Financial
    III. Learning and innovation

    A. II only
    B. I and II
    C. II and III
    D. I, II, and III

187. Sales less variable costs less controllable fixed costs is referred to as the:

    A. contribution margin
    B. controllable margin
    C. overhead efficiency variance
    D. volume variance

188. Which of the following is/are correct regarding controllable margins?
    I. Controllable margins are specifically defined as contribution margin less controllable fixed costs.
    II. The reporting objective of controllable margin is to most clearly define those margins for which a manager is responsible.

    A. I only
    B. II only
    C. Both I and II
    D. Neither I nor II

CHAPTER 18

FINANCIAL MANAGEMENT

189. In evaluating costs for decision-making, a company would consider which of the following as relevant?
  I. Differential costs
  II. Incremental costs
  III. Avoidable costs

  A. I and III
  B. I, II, and III
  C. II and III
  D. I and II

190. In evaluating costs for decision-making, a company would NOT generally consider which of the following as relevant?
  I. Discretionary costs
  II. Opportunity costs
  III. Sunk costs

  A. I and III
  B. II and III
  C. III only
  D. I, II, and III

Use the following facts to answer **Questions 191–194**.

Battaglia Corp. is considering the acquisition of a new machine. The machine can be purchased for $100,000; it will cost $4,000 to install and $7,000 to transport to Battaglia's plant. It is estimated that the machine will last 10 years, and it is expected to be worth $4,000 after it's fully depreciated. Over its 10-year life, the machine is expected to produce 3,000 units per year with a selling price of $300 and combined material and labor costs of $250 per unit. Federal tax regulations permit machines of this type to be depreciated using the straight-line method over 7 years with no consideration for salvage value. Battaglia has a marginal tax rate of 30%.

191. What is the net cash outflow at the beginning of the first year that Battaglia Corp. should use in a capital budgeting analysis?

  A. $100,000
  B. $107,000
  C. $111,000
  D. $97,500

192. How much depreciation should Battaglia include in the calculation of after-tax cash flow in its capital budgeting analysis for Year 2?

  A. $15,857
  B. $13,059
  C. $11,500
  D. $11,100

193. What is the net cash flow for the second year that Battaglia should use in a capital budgeting analysis?

  A. $150,000
  B. $109,757
  C. $134,143
  D. $40,243

194. What is the net cash flow for Year 10 of the project that Battaglia should use in a capital budgeting analysis?

  A. $105,000
  B. $107,800
  C. $109,800
  D. $109,000

195. Crellin Inc. is considering purchasing a new machine to replace an older, inefficient model. The new machine has a cost of $320,000. The old machine has a value of $9,500. Which of the following costs would NOT be included in a capital budgeting analysis as part of the net cash outflow of the new machine?

  I.   Transportation cost of the new machine
  II. Installation cost of the new machine
  III. Depreciation expense times the tax rate

  A. III only
  B. I and III
  C. II and III
  D. None of the above

196. Herbie's Auto Shop purchased an asset for $90,000 that has no salvage value and a 10-year life. Herbie's effective income tax rate is 30 percent, and it uses the straight-line depreciation method for income tax reporting purposes. For book purposes, Herbie will also depreciate this asset using the straight-line method, and there is an expected salvage value of $10,000. Herbie's annual depreciation tax shield from the asset would be

  A. $9,000
  B. $2,700
  C. $6,300
  D. $2,400

197. The cash management technique that focuses on cash disbursements is:

  A. depository transfer checks
  B. a lockbox system
  C. zero-balance accounts
  D. concentration banking

198. In equipment replacement decisions, which of the following costs are relevant?

  I.   Original fair market value of the old equipment
  II. Current salvage value of the old equipment
  III. Operating costs of the new equipment
  IV. Cost of the new equipment

  A. I, II, III, and IV
  B. II and III
  C. I, III, and IV
  D. II, III, and IV

199. Olney Company owns land that could be developed in the future. Olney estimates it can sell the land to Ritter Inc. for $950,000 net of all selling costs. If the land is not sold, Olney will continue with its plans to build three single-family homes on the land. If Olney decided to develop the property, what type of cost would the potential selling price of the land represent in Olney's decision?

  A. Sunk
  B. Incremental
  C. Opportunity
  D. Variable

Use the following facts to answer **Questions 200–201.**

Aron Company is trying to decide whether to keep an existing machine or replace it with a new machine. The old machine was purchased just 2 years ago for $40,000 and had an expected life of 12 years. It now costs $1,300 a month for maintenance and repairs. A new machine is being considered to replace it at a cost of $50,000. The new machine is more efficient, and it will cost only $120 a month for maintenance and repairs. The new machine has an expected life of 12 years.

200. In deciding to replace the old machine, which of the following is a sunk cost?

  A. $50,000
  B. $1,300 per month
  C. $120 per month
  D. $40,000

201. Which of the following factors would Aron consider when deciding whether to replace the machine?

  I.   Any estimated salvage value of the old machine
  II. The lower maintenance cost of the new machine
  III. The estimated salvage value of the new machine

  A. I and II
  B. I, II, and III
  C. II and III
  D. I and III

202. Capell Corp. makes an investment of $250,000 with a useful life of 10 years (no salvage value) and expects to use this investment to generate $370,000 in sales with $290,000 in incremental operating costs. If the company operates in an environment with a 40% tax rate, what are the expected after-tax cash flows that Capell will use to evaluate the capital investment decision?

A. $10,000
B. $23,000
C. $48,000
D. $58,000

Use the following facts to answer **Questions 203–204.**

Cace Corp. is deciding whether to replace an asset. A new asset costing $50,000 can be purchased to replace the existing asset that originally cost the company $40,000 and has accumulated depreciation of $32,000. A vendor of Cace has offered $13,300 for the old asset.

203. Assuming a tax rate of 30%, which of the following would be relevant when making the decision whether to replace the old asset?
   I. Purchase price of new asset
   II. Purchase price of old asset
   III. Accumulated depreciation of old asset

A. I, II, and III
B. I only
C. I and III
D. I and II

204. How much of the gain on the sale of the old asset is relevant to the decision of replacing the old asset?

A. $1,590
B. $5,300
C. $3,710
D. $13,300

205. When applying cash flows with discounting to business decisions, the calculation of annual net cash inflow:
   I. includes the cash inflow times 1 minus the tax rate
   II. includes depreciation expense times 1 minus the tax rate

A. I only
B. II only
C. Both I and II
D. Neither I nor II

206. Which of the following methods of capital budgeting would require managers to evaluate the dollar amount of return?

A. Net present value
B. Internal rate of return
C. Payback method
D. All of the above

207. Which of the following would be an advantage of using the net present value method of analyzing capital budgeting decisions?
   I. The net present value method can be used when there is a different rate of return for each year of the project.
   II. The net present value method indicates whether an investment will earn the hurdle rate of return.

A. I only
B. II only
C. Both I and II
D. Neither I nor II

208. The Truncale Company is planning a $210,000 equipment investment that has an estimated five-year life with no estimated salvage value. The present value of an annuity due for five years is 6.109. The company has projected the following annual cash flows for the investment:

Year	Projected Cash Flows	Present Value of $1
1	$120,000	0.91
2	$60,000	0.76
3	$40,000	0.63
4	$40,000	0.53
5	$40,000	0.44
Total	$300,000	3.27

The net present value for this investment is:

A. ($3,800)
B. $8,800
C. $2,548
D. ($800)

209. If the net present value of a project is positive, it would indicate that:
    I. the rate of return for the project is less than the discount percentage rate (hurdle rate) used in the net present value computation
    II. the present value of cash outflows is less than the present value of cash inflows

    A. I only
    B. II only
    C. Both I and II
    D. Neither I nor II

210. Weiskoff Company is considering a project that yields annual net cash inflows of $430,000 for Years 1 through 5, and a net cash inflow of $90,000 in Year 6. The project will require an initial investment of $1,750,000. Weiskoff's cost of capital is 10%. Present value information is:

    Present value of $1 for five years at 10% is 0.65.
    Present value of $1 for six years at 10% is 0.59.
    Present value of an annuity of $1 for five years at 10% is 3.83.

    What is Weiskoff's expected net present value for this project?

    A. $5,400
    B. ($50,000)
    C. $53,100
    D. $50,000

211. Dean Inc. is investing in a machine with a three-year life. The machine is expected to reduce annual cash operating costs by $40,000 in each of the first two years and by $30,000 in the third year. Which of the following is/are correct?
    I. To calculate the present value of the savings for Years 1 and 2, the factor for the present value of an annuity of $1 for two periods is used.
    II. To calculate the present value of the savings for Year 3, the factor for the lump sum of a present value of $1 for three periods is required.

    A. I only
    B. II only
    C. Both I and II
    D. Neither I nor II

212. The discount rate where the present value of the inflows is equal to the outflows is known as the:

    A. net present value
    B. internal rate of return
    C. profitability index
    D. All of the above

213. Which of the following is/are correct regarding the internal rate of return?
    I. The internal rate of return method determines the present value factor and related interest rate that yields a net present value equal to zero.
    II. The internal rate of return focuses the decision maker on the discount rate at which the present value of the cash inflows equals the initial investment.
    III. Projects with an internal rate of return greater than the hurdle rate should be rejected.

    A. I and III
    B. I and II
    C. I, II, and III
    D. I only

214. Which of the following would be an advantage of the payback method?
    I. It is easy to understand.
    II. It does NOT consider the time value of money.

    A. I only
    B. II only
    C. Both I and II
    D. Neither I nor II

215. In discounted cash flow analysis, which of the following would illustrate a difference between the net present value method and the internal rate of return?
    I. When using the net present value method, different hurdle rates can be used for each year of the project.
    II. The net present value method uses discounted cash flows and the internal rate of return does NOT.

    A. I only
    B. II only
    C. Both I and II
    D. Neither I nor II

216. In evaluating a capital budget project, the use of the net present value model is NOT generally affected by the:
    I. project's tax depreciation allowance
    II. amount of added working capital needed for operations during the term of the project

    A. I only
    B. II only
    C. Both I and II
    D. Neither I nor II

217. The discounted cash flow model is considered the best for long-term decisions. Which of the following are discounted cash flow methods?
    I. Net present value
    II. Internal rate of return
    III. Profitability index

    A. I, II, and III
    B. I and II
    C. I and III
    D. II and III

218. Bill Mann is an analyst who is looking to calculate the cost of Labriola Corp.'s common stock. In doing so, Bill evaluates the risk-free rate, the beta coefficient, and rate of return on Labriola's common stock, as well as the rate of return on the market portfolio. The valuation model that Bill Mann is using is the:

    A. capital asset pricing model
    B. constant growth model
    C. net present value model
    D. weighted marginal cost of capital model

219. If the profitability index of a project is exactly 1.0, which of the following is correct?

    A. The present value of the outflows is greater than the present value of the inflows.
    B. The present value of the inflows is greater than the present value of the outflows.
    C. The present value of the inflows is equal to the present value of the outflows.
    D. None of the above

220. Pry Inc. is evaluating a capital investment proposal for a new machine. The investment proposal shows the following information:

Initial cost	$600,000
Life	4 years
Annual net cash inflows	$220,000
Salvage value	$100,000

    If acquired, the machine will be depreciated using the straight-line method. What is the payback period for this investment?

    A. 2.27
    B. 2.73
    C. 2.84
    D. 3.0

221. Which of the following methods of analyzing investment alternatives ignore(s) cash flows after the initial investment has been recovered?
    I.   Payback method
    II. Discounted payback method
    III. Net present value

    A. II only
    B. I, II, and III
    C. I only
    D. I and II

222. Limitations of the net present value method and the internal rate of return include which of the following?
    I. They rely on the forecasting of future data.
    II. They consider the time value of money.

    A. I only
    B. II only
    C. Both I and II
    D. Neither I nor II

223. Alden Corp. purchases equipment for $46,000. The salvage value of the equipment is $6,000. Pertinent information follows:

Year	Net Cash Flows	Present Value
1	$9,000	0.943
2	$15,000	0.841
3	$19,000	0.776
4	$25,000	0.719

    What is the discounted payback period in years?

    A. 3.484 years
    B. 3.217 years
    C. 3.692 years
    D. 3.564 years

224. Which of the following is often calculated using trial and error by dividing the investment by the cash inflows to equal a desired present value factor?

    A. Net present value
    B. Internal rate of return
    C. Payback method
    D. Accounting rate of return

225. Which of the following describe the net present value method?
    I. It assumes that positive cash flows are reinvested at the hurdle rate.
    II. It measures the value of capital investments in dollars and considers the time value of money.
    III. It uses the accrual basis, not the cash basis.

    A. II and III
    B. I and III
    C. I, II, and III
    D. I and II

226. Which of the following methods would NOT be useful for determining total project profitability?
    I. Discounted payback method
    II. Net present value

    A. I only
    B. II only
    C. Both I and II
    D. Neither I nor II

227. The profitability index:
    I. is used to rank investments
    II. is calculated by taking the total investment and dividing by annual cash flows
    III. expresses the net present value in terms of a percentage

    A. I and II
    B. I, II, and III
    C. II and III
    D. I and III

Use the following facts to answer **Questions 228–229**.

Blauser Corp. is considering purchasing a machine that costs $90,000 and has a $15,000 salvage value. The machine will provide net annual cash inflows of $20,000 per year and a net income of $12,000 per year. It has a five-year life. The corporation uses a discount rate of 9%. The discount factor for the present value of a single sum five years in the future is 0.618. The discount factor for the present value of an annuity for five years is 3.847.

228. What is the present value of the cash inflows?
    A. $76,940
    B. $86,210
    C. $90,000
    D. $82,428

229. How much is the net present value of the machine?
    A. $15,210
    B. $9,270
    C. ($22,330)
    D. ($3,790)

230. Mullin Company is considering the purchase of a new machine that costs $560,000. The new machine will generate net cash flow of $125,000 per year and net income of $90,000 per year for five years. Mullin's desired rate of return is 7%. The present value factor for a five-year annuity of $1, discounted at 7%, is 4.698. The present value factor of $1, at compound interest of 7% due in five years, is 0.789. What is the new machine's net present value?
    A. $27,250
    B. ($27,250)
    C. ($137,180)
    D. $18,250

231. Dupree Corp. is evaluating its potential investment in a piece of equipment with a four-year life and no salvage value. The tax rate is 35%. Discounted pretax cash flows are $399,874, undiscounted after-tax cash flows are $286,600, and discounted after-tax cash flows are $237,992. The company's hurdle rate is 9%, and it anticipates that pretax cash flows in each of the three years will equal 25%, 30%, and 50%, respectively, of the investment's face value. If the investment costs $244,500, what is the net present value of the investment?
    A. ($6,508)
    B. $6,508
    C. ($42,100)
    D. None of the above

232. Kendrick Corp. is evaluating an investment in a piece of equipment with a four-year life and no salvage value. The equipment has a cost of $218,340. Kendrick anticipates that pretax cash flows in each of the four years will equal 10%, 32%, 40%, and 30%, respectively, of the investment's face value. The tax rate is 30%. Pretax cash flows, discounted at 9.5%, are $387,655, undiscounted after-tax cash flows are $262,171, and after-tax cash flows, discounted at 9.5%, are $218,340. Calculate the internal rate of return.
    A. 9.5%
    B. 10%
    C. 11.5%
    D. Cannot be determined from the information given

233. In this form of capital budgeting, project cash flows are discounted based upon a predetermined discount rate and compared to the investment in the project to arrive at a positive or negative dollar amount.

   I. Net present value
   II. Internal rate of return
   III. Accounting rate of return

  A. I and II
  B. I, II, and III
  C. II and III
  D. I only

234. Which of the following is correct regarding operating leverage?

  A. Operating leverage is defined as the degree to which a firm uses fixed operating costs as opposed to variable operating costs.
  B. Operating leverage is defined as the degree to which a firm uses variable operating costs as opposed to fixed operating costs.
  C. Operating leverage results from the use of both fixed operating costs and fixed financing costs to magnify returns to the firm's owners.
  D. Operating leverage is defined as the degree to which a firm uses debt to finance the firm.

235. A firm's degree of operating leverage is calculated by which of the following formulas?

  A. Percent change in sales divided by percent change in earnings before interest and taxes
  B. Percent change in earnings before interest and taxes divided by percent change in sales
  C. Percent change in earnings per share divided by percent change in earnings before interest and taxes
  D. Percent change in earnings before interest and taxes divided by percent change in earnings per share

236. A firm's degree of financial leverage is calculated by which of the following formulas?

  A. Percent change in sales divided by percent change in earnings before interest and taxes
  B. Percent change in earnings before interest and taxes divided by percent change in sales
  C. Percent change in earnings per share divided by percent change in earnings before interest and taxes
  D. Percent change in earnings before interest and taxes divided by percent change in earnings per share

237. When a firm has a relatively high degree of operating leverage:

   I. a small increase in sales can lead to a large increase in profit because fixed costs remain the same over a relevant range
   II. variable operating costs are high relative to fixed operating costs

  A. I only
  B. II only
  C. Both I and II
  D. Neither I nor II

238. Which of the following can be defined as the degree to which a firm uses debt to finance the firm?

   I. Financial leverage
   II. Operating leverage

  A. I only
  B. II only
  C. Both I and II
  D. Neither I nor II

239. Vista Company has a degree of operating leverage of 4 after experiencing a 24% increase in earnings before interest and taxes as a result of earning additional revenue. What percentage of additional revenue did Vista Company earn in order to experience a 24% increase in earnings before interest and taxes?

  A. 20%
  B. 96%
  C. 4%
  D. 6%

240. Company A experiences an increase in sales of 6% and an increase in earnings before interest and taxes of 18%. Company B experiences an increase in earnings before interest and taxes of 10% after a 5% increase in sales. Which of the following would be correct?

   I. Company A has a higher degree of operating leverage than company B.
   II. Company A has relatively lower variable operating costs and higher fixed operating costs compared to company B.

  A. I only
  B. II only
  C. Both I and II
  D. Neither I nor II

241. Which of the following is/are correct regarding operating leverage?
    I. If a firm has high operating leverage, a relatively small decrease in sales will have a potentially greater decrease in shareholder value.
    II. The higher the firm's operating leverage, the higher the potential profit.

    A. I only
    B. II only
    C. Both I and II
    D. Neither I nor II

242. Combined financial leverage is calculated by:

    A. adding total operating leverage plus financial leverage
    B. multiplying operating leverage times financial leverage
    C. dividing the percent change in earnings before interest and taxes by percent change in sales
    D. dividing the percent change in earnings per share by percent change in earnings before interest and taxes

243. Which of the following would be defined as the degree to which a firm uses debt to finance the firm?
    I. Financial leverage
    II. Operating leverage
    III. Combined leverage

    A. I and II
    B. I only
    C. I and III
    D. I, II, and III

244. The capital structure of Royce Corp. includes bonds with a coupon rate of 11% and an effective interest rate of 13%. The corporate tax rate is 40%. What is Royce's net cost of debt?

    A. 6.6%
    B. 5.2%
    C. 7.1%
    D. 7.8%

Use the following facts to answer **Questions 245–248**.

Anderson's debt is 30% of its capital structure, its preferred stock is 10%, and common stock is the remainder. The cost of common stock is 10%; preferred stock and debt have a cost of 10% each. Anderson's marginal tax rate is 25%.

245. How much is Anderson's weighted average cost of debt capital?

    A. 7.5%
    B. 2.25%
    C. 5.25%
    D. 3%

246. How much is Anderson's weighted average cost of its preferred stock?

    A. 1.2%
    B. Less than 1%
    C. More than 2% but less than 3%
    D. 1%

247. How much is Anderson's weighted average cost of common stock?

    A. 6%
    B. 10%
    C. 7.5%
    D. 4.5%

248. How much is Anderson's weighted average cost of capital?

    A. 7%
    B. 8.25%
    C. 9.25%
    D. 12%

249. The weighted average cost of capital is the average cost of which of the following given a firm's existing assets and operations?
    I. Debt financing
    II. Equity financing

    A. I only
    B. II only
    C. Both I and II
    D. Neither I nor II

250. Which of the following would be correct regarding the optimal capital structure and the weighted average cost of capital (WACC)?
    I. The optimal cost of capital is the ratio of debt to equity that produces the lowest WACC.
    II. If the debt to equity ratio increases, investors will likely demand a greater return.

    A. I only
    B. II only
    C. Both I and II
    D. Neither I nor II

251. Strat-O-Matic is a wholesaler and retailer of board and computer games. Using the capital asset pricing model (CAPM), how much is the required rate of return for Strat-O-Matic assuming a beta of 0.95 when the market return is 12% and the risk-free rate is 5%?

    A. 7%
    B. 13%
    C. 11.65%
    D. 10.95%

252. Valley Corp. is issuing debt to raise capital. Which of the following would be correct regarding the cost of debt capital to Valley?
    I. If market interest rates are higher than the coupon rate of the bond, Valley's cost of debt capital will be reduced.
    II. Because interest expense is a tax deduction, the cost to Valley is lower than the market yield rate on debt.

    A. I only
    B. II only
    C. Both I and II
    D. Neither I nor II

253. Webster Inc. is planning to use retained earnings to finance anticipated capital expenditures. The beta coefficient for Webster's stock is 1.2, the risk-free rate of interest is 7%, and the market return is estimated at 12.4%. Using the capital asset pricing model (CAPM), Webster's cost of using retained earnings to finance the capital expenditures is:

    A. 13.48%
    B. 6.48%
    C. 18.48%
    D. 8.48%

254. Which of the following methods could be used to calculate the cost of common equity capital?
    I. Capital asset pricing model
    II. Discounted cash flow model

    A. I only
    B. II only
    C. Both I and II
    D. Neither I nor II

255. The stock of Norbert Inc. is selling for $50. The next annual dividend is expected to be $4 and is expected to grow at a rate of 6%. The corporate tax rate is 40%. What is the firm's cost of common equity?

    A. 14%
    B. 8.4%
    C. 5.6%
    D. 8%

256. Which of the following defines the current ratio?

    A. Current assets less current liabilities
    B. Current assets divided by current liabilities
    C. Current liabilities divided by current assets
    D. Current liabilities less current assets

257. Which of the following would have no effect on the current ratio?
    I. Sale of equipment
    II. Declaration of a stock dividend

    A. I only
    B. II only
    C. Both I and II
    D. Neither I nor II

258. During Year 5, Andolini Company's current assets increased by $100,000, current liabilities decreased by $35,000, and net working capital:

    A. increased by $65,000
    B. decreased by $65,000
    C. increased by $135,000
    D. decreased by $135,000

259. Return on investment is calculated as the ratio of:

    A. operating income to year-end operating assets
    B. operating income to beginning operating assets
    C. operating income to average operating revenue
    D. operating income to average operating assets

260. The following information pertains to Baines Corp.:

	Year 4	Year 5
Operating revenues	$700,000	$900,000
Operating expenses	$550,000	$700,000
Operating assets	$900,000	$1,300,000

What percentage represents the return on investment for Year 5?

A. 15.38%
B. 18.18%
C. 15.9%
D. 16.7%

261. When calculating return on investment for two different companies, which of the following should be used to value the average assets (denominator) so as to minimize the effect of the age of each company's assets and different depreciation methods used?

A. Replacement cost
B. Net book value
C. Gross book value
D. Liquidation value

262. Which of the following methods of calculating investment return in dollars involves taking net income per the income statement and comparing it to the required rate of return?

  I. Return on investment
 II. Residual income

A. I only
B. II only
C. Both I and II
D. Neither I nor II

263. Berg Company has two divisions known as J and K. J division has operating income of $150 and total assets of $1,000. K division has operating income of $300 and total assets of $1,200. The required rate of return for Berg is 9%. Residual income for the Berg Company would be:

A. $450
B. $252
C. $198
D. $0

264. Ray is the divisional manager of the Henley Corp.. Ray receives a bonus based on 25% of the residual income from the division. The results of the division include: divisional revenues, $1,000,000; divisional expenses, $600,000; and divisional assets, $2,000,000. The required rate of return is 15%. How much is Ray's bonus?

A. $25,000
B. $30,000
C. $75,000
D. $100,000

265. Which of the following is/are correct regarding economic value added (EVA)?

  I. It is similar to the residual income method in that it measures return in dollars based on net income less required return.
 II. With EVA, management can set the hurdle rate or the weighted average cost of capital may be used as the hurdle rate.

A. I only
B. II only
C. Both I and II
D. Neither I nor II

266. The ratio that would be most appropriate to use to compare the profitability of two manufacturing companies that differ in size would be the:

A. current ratio
B. quick (acid-test) ratio
C. asset turnover ratio
D. return on assets ratio

267. Investments that provide a return that exceeds which of the following should continuously add to the value of the firm?

  I. Internal rate of return
 II. Weighted average cost of capital (WACC)

A. I only
B. II only
C. Both I and II
D. Neither I nor II

268. Which of the following would cause a firm to increase the debt in its financial structure?

  I. Decreased economic uncertainty
 II. Increase in corporate tax rates

A. I only
B. II only
C. Both I and II
D. Neither I nor II

269. Which of the following is/are correct regarding the WACC?
    I. The optimal capital structure is the mix of financing instruments that produces the lowest WACC.
    II. The company's borrowing rate is NOT a component of the WACC.
    A. I only
    B. II only
    C. Both I and II
    D. Neither I nor II

270. Which of the following would lead to a reduction in average inventory?
    I. A decrease in the cost of carrying inventory
    II. An increase in customer demand
    A. I only
    B. II only
    C. Both I and II
    D. Neither I nor II

271. Liquidity measurements focus on the ability of the company to meet obligations as they come due. Which of the following can be used to measure liquidity?
    I. Quick ratio
    II. Average collection period
    A. I only
    B. II only
    C. Both I and II
    D. Neither I nor II

272. Assume a company has a quick (acid-test) ratio of 2.0, current assets of $5,000, and inventory of $2,000. What is the amount of current liabilities?
    A. $6,000
    B. $3,500
    C. $2,500
    D. $1,500

273. Wolfert Corp. has current assets and current liabilities of $400,000 and $500,000 respectively. Which of the following transactions would increase the current ratio?
    A. Collecting $100,000 of accounts receivable
    B. Paying $100,000 of accounts payable
    C. Refinancing $100,000 of a long-term obligation with short-term debt
    D. Purchasing $100,000 of inventory on accounts payable

274. Light Year Company sells 20,000 high-quality refractor telescopes on credit, per annum, for $25,000 each. Light Year's average accounts receivables and average inventory are $30,000,000 and $40,000,000, respectively. Light Year's average accounts receivable collection period (using a 365-day year) approximates:
    A. 61 days
    B. 29 days
    C. 22 days
    D. 17 days

275. The target capital structure of Kowalski Company is 40% debt, 20% preferred equity, and 40% common equity. The interest rate on debt is 6%, the yield on the preferred is 9%, the cost of common equity is 12%, and the tax rate is 30%. Kowalski does not anticipate issuing any new stock. What is Kowalski's WACC?
    A. 10.7%
    B. 9%
    C. 8.3%
    D. 9.8%

276. A company's debt to total capital ratio includes which of the following in the denominator?
    I. Interest-bearing debt
    II. Noninterest-bearing debt
    A. I only
    B. II only
    C. Both I and II
    D. Neither I nor II

277. Which of the following actions would have no effect on a company's quick ratio?
    I. Purchasing inventory through the issuance of long-term notes
    II. Selling inventory at a loss
    A. I only
    B. II only
    C. Both I and II
    D. Neither I nor II

278. A corporation obtains a loan of $180,000 at an annual rate of 11%. The corporation must keep a compensating balance of 20% of any amount borrowed on deposit at the bank but normally does not have a cash balance account with the bank. What is the effective cost of the loan?
    A. 11%
    B. 13.5%
    C. 13.75%
    D. 14%

279. Which of the following would NOT be needed to estimate the cost of equity capital for use in determining a firm's WACC?

   I. Current dividends per share
   II. Expected growth rate in earnings per share
   III. Current market price per share of common stock

   A. I only
   B. II and III
   C. I and II
   D. II only

280. Using the discounted cash flow method, estimate the cost of equity capital for a firm with a stock price of $20, an estimated dividend at the end of the first year of $2 per share, and an expected growth rate of 11.5%.

   A. 19.5%
   B. 11.5%
   C. 13.5%
   D. 21.5%

281. The sale of property, plant, and equipment for an amount of cash less than net book value would result in which of the following?

   A. An increase in working capital and an increase in net income
   B. An increase in working capital and a decrease in net income
   C. A decrease in working capital and a decrease in net income
   D. A decrease in working capital and an increase in net income

282. To measure inventory management performance, the Galkin Company monitors its inventory turnover ratio. Listed are selected data from the company's accounting records:

	Current Year	Prior Year
Sales	$2,375,000	$2,455,000
Cost of goods sold	$1,500,000	Not given
Ending inventory	$350,500	$259,100

If short-term interest rates are 4%, what was Galkin Company's inventory turnover at the end of the current period?

   A. 5.45
   B. 4.92
   C. 7.93
   D. 6.31

283. Crown Corp.'s budgeted sales and budgeted cost of sales for the coming year are $7,500,000 and $3,800,000, respectively. Short-term interest rates are expected to average 6%. If Crown could increase inventory turnover from its current seven times per year to nine times per year, its expected cost savings in the current year would be:

   A. $18,236
   B. $9,712
   C. $7,238
   D. $25,333

284. Linden Stove Inc. is a manufacturer. The terms of trade are 4/10, net 30 with a particular supplier of raw materials. What is the cost on an annual basis of NOT taking the discount? Assume a 360-day year.

   A. 75.06%
   B. 18.00%
   C. 57.07%
   D. 37.03%

285. Fleming Corp., a clothing designer, is considering forgoing discounts in order to delay using its cash. Supplier credit terms are 3/10, net 30. Assuming a 360-day year, what is the annual cost of credit if the cash discount is not taken and Fleming pays net 30?

   A. 18.00%
   B. 20.25%
   C. 35.50%
   D. 55.62%

286. Which of the following working capital systems arranges for the direct mailing of customers' payments to a bank's post office box and subsequent deposit?

   A. Concentration banking
   B. Lockbox banking
   C. Zero balance account banking
   D. Compensating balances

287. Nadasky Inc. is considering implementing a lockbox collection system at a cost of $50,000 per year. Annual sales are $80 million, and the lockbox system will reduce collection time by three days. If Nadasky can invest funds at 9%, should it use the lockbox system? Assume a 360-day year.

   A. No, it produces a loss of $10,000 per year.
   B. No, it produces a loss of $50,000 per year.
   C. Yes, it produces a savings of $60,000 per year.
   D. Yes, it produces a savings of $10,000 per year.

288. Bly Corp. is considering a new cash management system that it estimates can add three days to the disbursement schedule. Average daily cash outflows are $1 million for Bly. Assuming Bly earns 6% on excess funds, how much should Bly be willing to pay per year for this cash management system?

A. $300,000
B. $180,000
C. $90,000
D. $1,000,000

289. A company's cash conversion cycle is calculated as the:

A. sum of the inventory conversion period plus the receivable collection period
B. sum of the inventory conversion period plus the receivable collection period less the payables deferral period
C. inventory conversion period less the receivable collection period
D. receivable collection period less the payables deferral period

290. From one year to the next, which of the following would indicate that a company's cash conversion cycle is improving?

I. Decrease in inventory conversion period
II. Decrease in receivable collection period
III. Decrease in payables deferral period

A. I and II
B. II and III
C. I and III
D. I, II, and III

291. Gateway 26 Corp. is trying to maintain inventory for its amusement centers. The CFO noticed that the inventory turnover was higher in Year 2 compared to Year 1 because of a lower average inventory in Year 2 compared to Year 1. This would indicate that the:

A. inventory conversion period is declining, which is a positive
B. inventory conversion period is rising, which is a positive
C. inventory conversion period is declining, which is a negative
D. inventory conversion period is rising, which is a negative

292. The amount of inventory that a company would tend to hold in stock would decrease as the:

I. cost of running out of stock increases
II. length of time that goods are in transit decreases

A. I only
B. II only
C. Both I and II
D. Neither I nor II

293. Anita's Hallmark Basket needs to determine its reorder point. What is the reorder point if Anita's average sales of Hallmark Cards are 50,000 cards per year, lead time is four weeks, and a safety stock of 750 cards is maintained? Assume Anita's is closed for two weeks during the month of August.

A. 1,750
B. 4,000
C. 4,250
D. 4,750

294. Which of the following are correct regarding a switch from a traditional inventory system to a just-in-time inventory system?

I. Just-in-time systems maintain a much smaller level of inventory when compared to traditional systems.
II. Inventory turnover increases with a switch from traditional to just-in-time inventory.
III. Inventory as a percentage of total assets increases with a switch to just-in-time inventory.

A. II and III
B. I and II
C. I and III
D. I, II, and III

295. In inventory management, which of the following would decrease safety stock?

I. Carrying costs increase
II. Lower stockout costs

A. I only
B. II only
C. Both I and II
D. Neither I nor II

296. The optimal level of inventory is affected by:
  I. the time required to receive inventory
  II. the cost per unit of inventory
  III. the cost of placing an order
  IV. the current amount of inventory

  A. II and III
  B. I and II
  C. I, II, III, and IV
  D. I, II, and III

297. Which of the following would be correct regarding the economic order quantity (EOQ)?
  I. Economic order quantity is a method of inventory control that anticipates orders at the point where carrying costs are nearest to restocking costs.
  II. The objective of EOQ is to minimize total inventory costs.

  A. I only
  B. II only
  C. Both I and II
  D. Neither I nor II

298. The decision to factor receivables would have which of the following effects?
  I. Increased accounts receivable
  II. Decreased accounts receivable turnover ratio

  A. I only
  B. II only
  C. Both I and II
  D. Neither I nor II

299. A company has ending accounts receivable of $13,000, sales of $105,000, and beginning accounts receivable of $15,000. Cash decreased in the period by $1,900. If total expenses are $20,000, what is the accounts receivable turnover ratio?

  A. 7.50
  B. 8.80
  C. 7.00
  D. 7.05

300. Which of the following is an assumption of the EOQ formula?
  A. The purchase price per unit can differ due to quantity discounts.
  B. Periodic demand for the goods is known with certainty.
  C. Carrying costs per unit vary with quantity ordered.
  D. Order costs vary with the quantity ordered.

301. Which of the following would NOT be relevant to EOQ?
  I. Purchase price per unit
  II. Annual sales volume

  A. I only
  B. II only
  C. Both I and II
  D. Neither I nor II

302. The Sneaker Barn sells athletic footwear. One particular model, the Wright Model #5, sells an average of 200 pairs per month and costs $35 per pair. Ordering costs are $50 per order. The carrying cost per unit is $3, which covers insurance on stored goods. The $3 also covers the opportunity costs of carrying the sneakers. Sneaker Barn wishes to minimize ordering and carrying costs. How much is the ideal order level of Wright Model #5 sneakers?

  A. 178 pairs
  B. 283 pairs
  C. 375 pairs
  D. 421 pairs

CHAPTER 19

INFORMATION TECHNOLOGY

QUESTIONS 303–362

303. An exception report can be described as:
  I. a specific report produced when an error or exception condition occurs
  II. a report that does not currently exist but that needs to be created on demand without having to get a software developer involved

  A. I only
  B. II only
  C. Both I and II
  D. Neither I nor II

304. In batch processing, grandfather, father, and son files can be used to:
  I. recover from processing problems
  II. retain files off-site for disaster recovery

  A. I only
  B. II only
  C. Both I and II
  D. Neither I nor II

305. Which of the following is correct regarding batch processing and online real-time processing?

  A. For batch processing, stored data are constantly current.
  B. Online real-time transactions are processed on a periodic basis.
  C. For online real-time processing data to be current, no changes can be made since the last batch update.
  D. There is no greater level of control necessary for batch processing versus online real-time (online) processing.

306. Which of the following is/are correct regarding an accounting information system (AIS)?
  I. An AIS is best suited to solve problems where there is certainty along with clearly defined reporting requirements.
  II. The first step in an AIS is that transaction data from source documents are entered into the AIS by an end user.

  A. I only
  B. II only
  C. Both I and II
  D. Neither I nor II

307. Of the steps listed, which of the following is the last step in an AIS?

  A. The original paper source documents are filed.
  B. Trial balances are prepared.
  C. Financial reports are generated.
  D. The transactions are posted to the general and subsidiary ledgers.

308. An entity would most likely include which of the following procedures in its disaster recovery plan?
  I. Storing duplicate copies of essential files at an off-site location, and away from the location where the file information is actually processed
  II. Encrypting data for storage purposes
  III. Maintaining a list of all employee passwords with the chief technology officer

  A. II and III only
  B. I only
  C. I and II only
  D. I, II, and III

309. Centralized processing has which advantage(s) over decentralized processing?
    I. Decreased local accountability
    II. Increased power and storage needs at the central location

    A. I only
    B. II only
    C. Both I and II
    D. Neither I nor II

310. Business information systems allow a business to perform which of the following functions?
    I. Initiate data
    II. Process data

    A. I only
    B. II only
    C. Both I and II
    D. Neither I nor II

311. A business information system has which of the following components?
    I. Software
    II. Reports
    III. Hardware
    IV. Data
    V. People

    A. I, II, III, and IV
    B. I and III
    C. I, III, IV, and V
    D. I, II, III, IV, and V

312. Kessler Corp. intended to order 200 units of product AX1397, but inadvertently ordered 200 units of product AX1379, which was a nonexistent product number. A control that would detect this error is:

    A. a hash total
    B. a closed-loop verification
    C. a check digit verification
    D. a limit check

313. Which of the following would NOT be correct regarding production data and test data?
    I. Production and test data are normally stored in the same database.
    II. Access to production data can be considerably less open than access to test data.

    A. I only
    B. II only
    C. Both I and II
    D. Neither I nor II

314. A general ledger chart of accounts that assigns revenue to the 3000 series and expenses to the 4000 series would be an example of what type of coding?

    A. Sequential coding
    B. Block coding
    C. Group coding
    D. None of the above

315. Activities that would most likely be performed in the information systems department include which of the following?
    I. Conversion of information to machine-readable form
    II. Initiation of changes to existing applications
    III. Initiation of changes to master files

    A. II and III only
    B. I only
    C. I and III only
    D. II only

316. A major function of transaction processing is:
    I. data storage
    II. data analysis

    A. I only
    B. II only
    C. Both I and II
    D. Neither I nor II

317. Which of the following is/are correct regarding extensible business reporting language (XBRL)?
    I. The Securities and Exchange Commission (SEC) requires public companies to present financial statements and related exhibits using XBRL.
    II. Extensible business reporting language is specifically designed to exchange financial information over the Web.

    A. I only
    B. II only
    C. Both I and II
    D. Neither I nor II

318. Which of the following would NOT be correct regarding program modification control software?
   I. Program modification controls include controls that attempt to prevent changes by unauthorized personnel.
   II. Program modification controls track program changes so that there is an exact record of what versions of what programs were running in production at any specific point in time.

   A. I only
   B. II only
   C. Both I and II
   D. Neither I nor II

319. In an IT environment, which of the following duties should NEVER be combined?
   I. Application programmer and systems analyst
   II. Application programmer and systems programmer

   A. I only
   B. II only
   C. Both I and II
   D. Neither I nor II

320. For software purchased from an outside vendor, which of the following is correct regarding maintenance of the software versus software support?

   A. Maintenance refers to keeping the system up and running.
   B. Maintenance includes monitoring the system, determining that a problem has occurred, and fixing or getting around the problem.
   C. Support refers to keeping the system up and running.
   D. Support is keeping the system "up to date" with new releases from time to time.

321. Which of the following systems would enable programming teams to work independently on different programs within the same system?
   I. Structured system
   II. Management reporting system
   III. Interactive system

   A. I and II
   B. II only
   C. I and III
   D. I only

322. Which person sets up and configures computers?
   A. User
   B. Software developer
   C. Network administrator
   D. Hardware technician

323. Which of the following is a decision support system that uses a what-if technique that asks how a given outcome will change if the original estimates of the model are changed?
   A. Scenario analysis
   B. Sensitivity analysis
   C. Database query applications
   D. Financial modeling applications

324. Which of the following represents a security risk in an IT environment?
   I. Web crawler
   II. Trojan horse
   III. Backdoor

   A. I and II
   B. II and III
   C. II only
   D. I, II, and III

325. Which of the following would be responsibilities of the network administrator?
   I. Network maintenance
   II. Design and control of a firm's database
   III. Wireless access

   A. I and II
   B. I and III
   C. I, II, and III
   D. I only

326. An application programmer is responsible for:
   I. writing application programs
   II. maintaining application programs
   III. controlling data entry

   A. I and II
   B. II and III
   C. I only
   D. I, II, and III

327. For better segregation of duties involving the computer program, which of the following IT jobs is an example of an authorization role that should be segregated from the custody role?

   A. Librarian
   B. Computer operator
   C. Programmer
   D. Systems analyst

328. Which of the following computer programmers would be responsible for installing, supporting, monitoring, and maintaining the operating system?

  I. Application programmer
  II. System programmer

  A. I only
  B. II only
  C. Both I and II
  D. Neither I nor II

329. Within the control objectives for information and related technology (COBIT) framework, which of the following would best describe the "reliability" criteria?

  I. To be reliable, the information must be available currently and in the future, and resources must be safeguarded.
  II. To be reliable, information needs to be appropriate to operate the entity.

  A. I only
  B. II only
  C. Both I and II
  D. Neither I nor II

330. Within the COBIT framework, which of the following would best describe the "integrity" criteria?

  I. Information needs to be accurate, complete, and valid.
  II. Information needs to be low cost without compromising effectiveness.

  A. I only
  B. II only
  C. Both I and II
  D. Neither I nor II

331. Which of the following are among the five areas for IT governance identified by the COBIT framework?

  I. Strategic alignment
  II. Resource management
  III. Risk management
  IV. Performance measurement

  A. I, III, and IV
  B. II, III, and IV
  C. I, II, and III
  D. I, II, III, and IV

332. Monitoring, evaluating, and modifying a system is a process known as:

  A. systems maintenance
  B. systems implementation
  C. a systems feasibility study
  D. systems analysis

333. Under the COBIT framework, the "monitor and evaluate" domain relates to:

  I. ensuring that directions are followed
  II. providing feedback to information criteria

  A. I only
  B. II only
  C. Both I and II
  D. Neither I nor II

334. The application environment of database management systems includes which of the following characteristics?

  I. Ease of data sharing
  II. Increased data redundancy
  III. Data definition is independent of any one program

  A. I, II, and III
  B. I and II only
  C. I only
  D. I and III only

335. With regard to internal controls, which of the following would remain the same when switching from a manual system to an automated system?

  I. Objectives
  II. Principles
  III. Implementation

  A. I and II
  B. II and III
  C. III only
  D. I, II, and III

336. Which of the following would normally take responsibility for training staff to use recently purchased software that is being integrated with the company's existing software?

  A. Computer programmer
  B. Network administrator
  C. Systems analyst
  D. IT supervisor

337. Which of the following types of transaction processing systems would eliminate the need for reconciliation of control accounts and subsidiary ledgers?
    I. Manual systems
    II. Automated systems

    A. I only
    B. II only
    C. Both I and II
    D. Neither I nor II

338. Executive support systems:
    I. provide managers and other users with reports that are typically predefined by management and used to make daily business decisions
    II. process and record routine daily transactions necessary to conduct business

    A. I only
    B. II only
    C. Both I and II
    D. Neither I nor II

339. In an IT environment, which of the following is/are charged with developing long-range plans and directing application development and computer operations?

    A. Steering committee
    B. Systems analyst
    C. System programmers
    D. End users

340. The Zehra Corp. recently purchased a new payroll program and has finished installing it. Which of the following control actions should be taken by the organization to reduce the risk of incorrect processing due to the implementation of a new system?
    I. Segregating transaction authorization, record-keeping, and asset custodial duties
    II. Ensuring that overtime is properly authorized
    III. Parallel processing transactions for independent verification

    A. I and III
    B. II and III
    C. III only
    D. I, II, and III

341. Which of the following involves using a password or a digital key to scramble a readable (plain text) message into an unreadable (cipher text) message?

    A. Validity check
    B. Encryption
    C. Decryption
    D. Echo check

342. Which of the following would NOT be a form of data security?
    I. Password management
    II. Data encryption
    III. Digital certificates

    A. II only
    B. I only
    C. III only
    D. None of the above

343. Which of the following is true regarding transmitting transactions over a value-added network (VAN) versus over the Internet?

    A. Transactions transmitted over a VAN are batch processed.
    B. In the event of disaster recovery, VANs typically do not archive the data for more than 48 hours.
    C. Transactions transmitted over the Internet are not processed as they occur.
    D. All of the above

344. The Lara Corp. has developed an internal system of managing customer accounts better in order to simplify marketing and sales, provide improved service, and cross-sell products more effectively. Which of the following describes Lara's internal system?

    A. Customer relationship management
    B. Electronic data interchange
    C. Decision support systems
    D. Public key infrastructure

345. An operating procedure that would mitigate the risk of an entity's exposure to computer viruses includes which of the following?
    I. Encrypting data files
    II. Less frequent backup of files
    III. Downloading public-domain software from electronic bulletin boards

    A. I only
    B. I and II only
    C. I, II, and III
    D. None of the above

346. Which of the following is/are correct regarding electronic data interchange (EDI)?
   I. The cost of sending EDI transactions using a VAN is greater than the cost of using the Internet.
   II. Electronic data interchange requires strict adherence to a standard data format.

   A. I only
   B. II only
   C. Both I and II
   D. Neither I nor II

347. Which of the following is characteristic of business-to-business (B2B) e-commerce?
   I. Decreased inventory levels
   II. Increased costs for information technology infrastructure
   III. Increased market efficiency

   A. II and III only
   B. I and III only
   C. I, II, and III
   D. III only

348. In an EDI environment, encoding of data for security purposes is known as:

   A. decoding
   B. mapping
   C. encryption
   D. translation

349. Audit trails in an electronic data interchange (EDI) system should include:
   I. activity logs of failed transactions
   II. network and sender/recipient acknowledgments

   A. I only
   B. II only
   C. Both I and II
   D. Neither I nor II

350. Compared to an EDI environment under a VAN, e-commerce transactions over the Internet are:

   A. faster, less expensive, and more secure
   B. slower, more expensive, and more secure
   C. slower, less expensive, and less secure
   D. faster, less expensive, and less secure

351. Which of the following involves having virtual servers available over the Internet for storing hardware and software?

   A. Domain name warehousing
   B. Secure socket layer
   C. Hypertext transfer protocol (HTTP)
   D. Cloud computing

352. Which of the following is the risk of choosing inappropriate technology?

   A. Strategic risk
   B. Operating risk
   C. Financial risk
   D. Information risk

353. Which of the following statements is/are correct regarding threats in a computerized environment?
   I. In a denial-of-service attack, one computer bombards another computer with a flood of information intended to keep legitimate users from accessing the target computer or network.
   II. Phishing is a program that appears to have a useful function but that contains a hidden and unintended function that presents a security risk.

   A. I only
   B. II only
   C. Both I and II
   D. Neither I nor II

354. Which of the following passwords would be the most difficult to crack?

   A. Matt99
   B. 45561212
   C. y9y9y4j2
   D. 2456dtR5!

355. Which of the following are input controls?
   I. Limit tests
   II. Validity checks

   A. I only
   B. II only
   C. Both I and II
   D. Neither I nor II

Use the following facts to answer **Questions 356–358.**

Check #	Hours	Employee ID #	Net Pay
201	40	943-56-9087	$887.54
202	32	948-65-0901	$612.54
203	10	949-09-4545	$340.32
204	24	991-04-0909	$478.90
205	40	998-01-9002	$567.90
1,015	146		$2,887.20

356. Which of the following control totals represents the batch total?

   A. 5
   B. 146
   C. 1,015
   D. $2,887.20

357. Which of the following control totals represents the record count?

   A. 5
   B. 146
   C. 1,015
   D. $2,887.20

358. Which of the following control totals represents the sum of the fifth digit of all five employee ID numbers?

   A. Batch total
   B. Hash total
   C. Record count
   D. None of the above

359. Electronic access controls include:
   I. passwords
   II. firewalls

   A. I only
   B. II only
   C. Both I and II
   D. Neither I nor II

360. Adler Inc. is preparing a business continuity plan in the event of disaster. Which of the following represents empty floor space where Adler can install whatever hardware is needed in one to three days because the space already contains all electrical requirements?

   A. Warm site
   B. Hot site
   C. Cold site
   D. Purple site

361. A likely benefit of engaging in EDI includes which of the following?
   I. Reduced likelihood of stockouts
   II. Guaranteed payments from customers
   III. Decreased liability as it relates to protecting business data

   A. I, II, and III
   B. I only
   C. I and III only
   D. I and II only

362. Which of the following is a privately sponsored form of electronic communication normally used for organizational communications?

   A. Internet
   B. Intranet
   C. Database management system
   D. Compiler

CHAPTER 20

ECONOMICS CONCEPTS

363. Gross domestic product (GDP) includes:
   I. the value of used goods that have been resold
   II. foreign-owned factories operating within the United States

   A. I only
   B. II only
   C. Both I and II
   D. Neither I nor II

364. Which of the following would remove the effect of inflation as it measures the value of all national output?
   I. Real GDP
   II. Nominal GDP

   A. I only
   B. II only
   C. Both I and II
   D. Neither I nor II

365. Fluctuations in economic activity vary in:

   A. severity and growth
   B. duration and recession
   C. duration and expansion
   D. severity and duration

366. The peak period of economic growth marks the end of one economic phase and the beginning of another. The peak marks the end of _____ and the beginning of _____.

   A. contraction, growth
   B. expansion, inflation
   C. contraction, expansion
   D. expansion, contraction

367. Which of the following economic cycles is characterized by a rise in demand for goods, a stabilization of corporate profits, and an increase in economic activity?

   A. Peak
   B. Contraction
   C. Expansion
   D. Recovery

368. Which of the following economic cycles is characterized by significant excess production capacity?

   A. Peak
   B. Trough
   C. Expansion
   D. Contraction

369. In a typical recession:
   I. potential output exceeds actual output
   II. real gross domestic product is rising

   A. I only
   B. II only
   C. Both I and II
   D. Neither I nor II

370. Which of the following would be evidence of a potential or even actual recession?
   I. Increasing aggregate demand
   II. Rising unemployment
   III. Falling GDP

   A. I, II, and III
   B. II and III
   C. II only
   D. III only

371. Real GDP will rise as a result of:
    A. decreasing government purchases
    B. increasing taxes
    C. increasing government purchases
    D. Both A and B

372. Which of the following would be considered expansionary fiscal policy?
    I. An increase in taxes
    II. A decrease in government spending

    A. I only
    B. II only
    C. Both I and II
    D. Neither I nor II

373. An increase in wealth and an increase in overall confidence about the economic outlook will cause:
    A. an increase in the cost of capital
    B. a shift in the aggregate demand curve to the left
    C. a shift in the aggregate demand curve to the right
    D. Both A and B

374. As aggregate demand rises:
    I. unemployment decreases
    II. real GDP increases

    A. I only
    B. II only
    C. Both I and II
    D. Neither I nor II

375. In the short run, which of the following would be correct regarding the aggregate supply curve and aggregate demand curve?
    I. Quantity demanded is inversely related to the price level.
    II. Quantity supplied is upward sloping.

    A. I only
    B. II only
    C. Both I and II
    D. Neither I nor II

376. A nation's long-term aggregate supply curve is dependent on:
    I. price levels
    II. technology and capital available
    III. labor and materials available

    A. I, II, and III
    B. II and III
    C. I only
    D. None of the above

377. Large decreases in input costs such as direct labor and direct materials would result in:
    A. real GDP increasing
    B. real GDP decreasing
    C. an increase in price levels
    D. the aggregate supply curve shifting to the left

378. Real GDP per capita is:
    I. the measure often used to compare standards of living across countries
    II. calculated by taking real GDP and dividing by population

    A. I only
    B. II only
    C. Both I and II
    D. Neither I nor II

379. If the US dollar falls in value:
    I. net exports will fall
    II. supply of foreign goods in the United States would decrease

    A. I only
    B. II only
    C. Both I and II
    D. Neither I nor II

380. When inflation occurs:
    I. purchasing power is reduced
    II. those with a fixed obligation are hurt

    A. I only
    B. II only
    C. Both I and II
    D. Neither I nor II

381. Inflation does NOT:
    I. help those on a fixed income
    II. increase the price level

    A. I only
    B. II only
    C. Both I and II
    D. Neither I nor II

382. An increase in aggregate demand causes:
    A. output to rise and the price level to rise
    B. output to rise and the price level to fall
    C. output to fall and the price level to rise
    D. output to fall and the price level to fall

383. A decrease in aggregate supply causes:
    A. output to fall and the price level to fall
    B. output to rise and the price level to rise
    C. output to rise and the price level to fall
    D. output to fall and the price level to rise

384. Mismatch of skills and jobs in the economy is an example of what type of unemployment?

    A. Structural unemployment
    B. Cyclical unemployment
    C. Frictional unemployment
    D. Seasonal unemployment

385. Which of the following is correct regarding the type of unemployment and its corresponding cause?

    A. Frictional unemployment is caused by seasonal demand for labor.
    B. Structural unemployment is caused by a time lag that individuals experience between jobs.
    C. Cyclical unemployment is caused by business cycles.
    D. Seasonal unemployment is caused by a mismatch between worker skills and available employment.

386. Unemployment caused by an entire industry being rendered obsolete due to a new invention is known as:

    A. seasonal unemployment
    B. structural unemployment
    C. frictional unemployment
    D. cyclical unemployment

387. Gross domestic product can be calculated by the:
    I. expenditures approach
    II. income approach
    III. net assets approach

    A. I only
    B. I and II
    C. II only
    D. I, II, and III

388. When calculating GDP, the expenditures approach uses:
    I. net exports
    II. capital investment

    A. I only
    B. II only
    C. Both I and II
    D. Neither I nor II

389. Business profits and employee compensation are used to calculate GDP under which of the following approaches?
    I. Expenditures approach
    II. Income approach

    A. I only
    B. II only
    C. Both I and II
    D. Neither I nor II

390. Who sets the discount rate that the central bank charges for loans?

    A. Commercial banks
    B. Savings and loans
    C. Investment banks
    D. Federal Reserve

391. If government expenditures are $12, imports are $4, exports are $7, investments are $30, and consumption is $16, how much is the GDP, assuming all numbers shown are in the billions?

    A. $69 billion
    B. $61 billion
    C. $58 billion
    D. $41 billion

392. Using the income approach, calculate GDP for the country of Griffania from the following information:

Consumer spending	$306 billion
Profits to proprietors	$83 billion
Profits to corporations	$119 billion
Employee wages	$305 billion
Net imports	$91 billion
Rental income	$19 billion
Interest income	$80 billion

    A. $912 billion
    B. $606 billion
    C. $697 billion
    D. $515 billion

393. The nation of Pradera wants to measure the value of all final goods and services produced by its residents whether produced within the borders of Pradera or outside Pradera's borders. Which of the following would determine that measure?

    A. Gross domestic product
    B. Net domestic product
    C. Net national product
    D. Gross national product

394. Which of the following measures the rate of increase in the overall price level in the economy?

    A. Prime rate
    B. Discount rate
    C. Nominal rate
    D. Inflation rate

395. Which of the following is a measure of the overall cost of a fixed basket of goods and services purchased by an average household?

    A. Gross domestic product
    B. Gross national product
    C. Consumer price index
    D. Producer price index

396. The consumer price index jumps from 121 in Year 2 to 133.5 in Year 3. What is the annual inflation rate?

    A. 12.5%
    B. 10.33%
    C. 9.36%
    D. 5%

397. Conducting competitor analysis includes which of the following?

    I. Understanding and predicting the behavior of the competition
    II. Determining the type of market structure and the number of competitors
    III. Evaluating the market structure to predict when new competitors are expected to enter the market

    A. II and III only
    B. I only
    C. I, II, and III
    D. I and II only

398. The Federal Reserve's powers include the ability to directly:

    I. raise or lower reserve requirements
    II. buy or sell government securities

    A. I only
    B. II only
    C. Both I and II
    D. Neither I nor II

399. Which of the following actions, if taken by the Federal Reserve, would stimulate the economy and expand the money supply?

    I. Reduce the discount rate
    II. Increase reserve requirements
    III. Purchase government securities

    A. I, II, and III
    B. I and II
    C. I and III
    D. II and III

400. Expansionary monetary policy affects the economy through which chain of events?

    A. Interest rates fall, aggregate demand increases, and real GDP increases.
    B. Interest rates rise, aggregate demand decreases, and real GDP decreases.
    C. Interest rates rise, aggregate demand increases, and real GDP increases.
    D. Interest rates fall, aggregate demand decreases, and real GDP decreases.

401. Nonmonetary assets whose values increase with inflation include:

    A. gold and silver
    B. corporate bonds
    C. state and local government bonds
    D. common stock

402. Which of the following is/are correct regarding perfect competition?

    I. Customers have no real preference about which firm they buy from.
    II. The level of a firm's output is large relative to the industry's total output.

    A. I only
    B. II only
    C. Both I and II
    D. Neither I nor II

403. Which of the following might be a strategy for a company competing in a purely competitive marketplace?

    I. Process reengineering
    II. Development of a brand name
    III. Lean manufacturing

    A. II only
    B. I and III
    C. I only
    D. I, II, and III

404. A firm in which of the following industries would produce products up to a point where marginal cost equals marginal revenue?

    I. An industry with monopolistic competition
    II. An industry with perfect competition

    A. I only
    B. II only
    C. Both I and II
    D. Neither I nor II

405. Significant barriers to entry and few firms in the marketplace are typical of:
    I. monopolistic competition
    II. an oligopoly
    III. perfect competition
    A. II only
    B. I only
    C. I and II
    D. II and III

406. A measure of how sensitive the demand for or the supply of a product is to a change in its price is known as:
    A. marginal cost
    B. gross domestic product
    C. elasticity
    D. producer price index

407. If demand is price inelastic, an increase in price will:
    A. have no effect on total revenue
    B. decrease total revenue
    C. increase total revenue
    D. None of the above

408. Inelastic demand would be exhibited by which of the following scenarios?
    A. A 4% increase in price results in a 2% decrease in quantity demanded.
    B. A 4% increase in price results in a 6% decrease in quantity demanded.
    C. A 4% increase in price results in a 4% decrease in quantity demanded.
    D. A 2% decrease in price results in a 4% increase in the quantity demanded.

409. When demand for a product is unit elastic, which of the following would be correct?
    I. A price increase will decrease total revenue.
    II. A price decrease will increase total revenue.
    A. I only
    B. II only
    C. Both I and II
    D. Neither I nor II

410. Supply is price inelastic if the absolute price elasticity of supply is:
    A. less than 1
    B. greater than or equal to 1
    C. less than or equal to 1
    D. exactly 1

411. If the elasticity of demand for a normal good is estimated to be 1.23, then a 10% increase in its price would cause:
    A. an increase in quantity demanded of 12.3%
    B. total revenue to fall by 10%
    C. total revenue to rise by less than 10%
    D. a decrease in quantity demanded of 12.3%

412. Which of the following business functions is NOT part of a company's value chain?
    A. Marketing
    B. Research and development
    C. Accounting
    D. Customer service

413. Which of the following would increase the bargaining power of the customer?
    I. Customers are aware that they make up a large volume of a firm's business.
    II. There is much information available to customers about products in the marketplace.
    III. The buyers have high switching costs.
    A. I and III
    B. I and II
    C. I only
    D. I, II, and III

414. Competitive advantage can be defined as which of the following?
    I. Product differentiation
    II. Cost leadership
    A. I only
    B. II only
    C. Both I and II
    D. Neither I nor II

415. Which of the following competitive advantage strategies would fail as a result of brand loyalty?
    I. Differentiation
    II. Cost leadership
    A. I only
    B. II only
    C. Both I and II
    D. Neither I nor II

416. Supply chain management focuses on which of the following?
    A. Improving quality
    B. Sharing of information with suppliers and customers
    C. Process redesign
    D. Strategic alliances

417. In a supply chain operations reference (SCOR) model, what type of decision is the selection of vendors?

    A. Plan
    B. Source
    C. Deliver
    D. Make

418. Assume that product B is a substitute of product A. The fundamental law of demand holds that there is an inverse relationship between the:

    I. price of product A and quantity demanded for product B
    II. price of product A and quantity demanded for product A
    III. price of product A and price of product B

    A. I and III
    B. II and III
    C. II only
    D. I, II, and III

419. Sales of company Q's product R increased 11% after company A increased its price on product B from $8 to $9.50. Product R and product B are:

    A. complementary goods
    B. substitute goods
    C. independent goods
    D. inferior goods

420. Which of the following would result in an increase in the price of a product?

    A. Increase in quantity demanded and increase in quantity supplied
    B. Increase in quantity demanded and decrease in quantity supplied
    C. Decrease in quantity supplied and decrease in quantity demanded
    D. Decrease in quantity demanded and increase in quantity supplied

421. Goods that are considered normal goods:
    I. have a negative elasticity of demand
    II. will increase in demand as income increases

    A. I only
    B. II only
    C. Both I and II
    D. Neither I nor II

422. Demand for a product tends to be price inelastic if:
    I. few good substitutes are available for the product
    II. a decline in price results in an increase in total revenue

    A. I only
    B. II only
    C. Both I and II
    D. Neither I nor II

423. If the admission price for a basketball game is raised from $25 to $30, causing attendance to drop from 60,000 to 40,000, the price elasticity of the demand for attending the basketball game is:

    A. −2.20
    B. −1.67
    C. 0.60
    D. 2.20

424. When a good is demanded, no matter what the price, demand is described as:

    A. perfectly elastic
    B. unit elastic
    C. perfectly inelastic
    D. complementary

425. In a SWOT analysis, which of the following would be correct?
    I. Strengths and weaknesses generally focus on internal factors.
    II. Opportunities and threats generally relate to external factors.

    A. I only
    B. II only
    C. Both I and II
    D. Neither I nor II

426. Which of the following suggests that even if one of two regions is absolutely more efficient in the production of every good than is the other, if each region specializes in the products in which it has greatest relative efficiency, trade will be mutually profitable to both regions?

A. Comparative advantage
B. Economies of scale
C. Law of diminishing returns
D. High-low method

427. Porter's five forces affecting a firm's performance include:

I. intensity of firm rivalry
II. threat of substitute goods
III. threat of new competitors

A. I and II
B. I, II, and III
C. I and III only
D. II and III only

CHAPTER 21

GLOBALIZATION AND PERFORMANCE, PROCESS, AND RISK MANAGEMENT

QUESTIONS 428–471

428. A just-in-time inventory system focuses on:
  I. minimizing storage costs
  II. eliminating non-value-added operations
  III. creating specialized labor

  A. I and II
  B. II and III
  C. I, II, and III
  D. I and III

429. A dumping pricing policy would be exhibited by which of the following?

  A. A Japanese company selling its goods in Japan at a price less than cost
  B. A Japanese company selling its goods in the United States at a price less than cost
  C. A Japanese company selling its goods in the United States as a price greater than cost
  D. A Japanese company selling its goods in Japan at a price greater than cost

430. Which of the following is/are correct regarding conformance and nonconformance costs?
  I. Conformance costs include both prevention and appraisal.
  II. Nonconformance costs include internal and external failure.

  A. I only
  B. II only
  C. Both I and II
  D. Neither I nor II

431. Conformance costs found under the category of prevention include:
  I. maintenance
  II. repair
  III. inspection

  A. I and II
  B. I and III
  C. III only
  D. I, II, and III

432. Internal failure costs include:
  I. product repair and warranty costs
  II. tooling changes and rework costs

  A. I only
  B. II only
  C. Both I and II
  D. Neither I nor II

433. Which of the following would NOT be a failure cost but a conformance cost?
  I. Repair
  II. Rework

  A. I only
  B. II only
  C. Both I and II
  D. Neither I nor II

434. Which of the following would be a way of seeking radical change by ignoring the current process and instead starting from the beginning to design a different way of achieving the end goal and/or product?

    I. Process management
    II. Process reengineering

A. I only
B. II only
C. Both I and II
D. Neither I nor II

435. Within project management, which of the following is responsible for project administration on a day-to-day basis, including identifying and managing internal and external stakeholder expectations?

A. Project sponsor
B. Project manager
C. Steering committee
D. Project members

436. Within project management, the project manager reports to the:

A. project sponsor
B. project members
C. steering committee
D. board of directors

437. Futures contracts contain which of the following distinguishing features?

    I. The contract is never speculative.
    II. The parties to the contract know each other.

A. I only
B. II only
C. Both I and II
D. Neither I nor II

438. Within project management, the project sponsor should communicate project needs to the:

    I. executive steering committee
    II. board of directors

A. I only
B. II only
C. Both I and II
D. Neither I nor II

439. Which of the following is known as the increased dispersion and integration of the world's economies and is often objectively measured as the growth in world trade as a percentage of gross domestic product?

A. Outsourcing
B. Off-shore activities
C. Globalization
D. Exports as a percentage of imports

440. Compared to long-term financing, short-term financing:

    I. increases credit risk
    II. decreases profitability

A. I only
B. II only
C. Both I and II
D. Neither I nor II

441. *Diversifiable risk* may also be referred to as:

    I. unique risk
    II. unsystematic risk

A. I only
B. II only
C. Both I and II
D. Neither I nor II

442. Which of the following is correct regarding default and credit risk?

A. The lender's default risk is based on the borrower's default risk.
B. The lender's default risk is based on the borrower's credit risk.
C. The lender's credit risk is based on the borrower's default risk.
D. The lender's credit risk is based on the lender's default risk.

443. Which of the following relates to purchasing power risk?

A. The fluctuation in the value of a "financial asset" when interest rates change
B. The risk that price levels will change and affect asset values
C. The ability to sell a temporary investment in a short period of time without significant price concessions
D. A general category of risk that includes default risk and interest rate risk

444. Wildwood Corp. issued bonds four years ago. If the _____ interest rate _____, the market value of each Wildwood corporate bond will _____.

A. coupon, increases, decrease
B. market, increases, increase
C. market, increases, decrease
D. market, decreases, decrease

445. If a US company has net cash outflows in a foreign currency, which of the following is correct?

    A. The US company would benefit from a drop in value of the foreign currency.
    B. The US company would benefit from an increase in value of the foreign currency.
    C. The US company would suffer a loss from a decrease in value of the foreign currency.
    D. The appreciation or depreciation of the foreign currency would be irrelevant.

446. A US firm that has cash flows in a foreign currency will suffer an economic loss if:

    I. the foreign currency appreciates and the US firm has net cash inflows
    II. the US firm has net cash outflows and the foreign currency depreciates

    A. I only
    B. II only
    C. Both I and II
    D. Neither I nor II

447. The decision to exercise a call option would NOT be based on:

    I. strike price
    II. call premium
    III. market price of the underlying security

    A. I and II
    B. II and III
    C. II only
    D. I only

448. Compared to US Treasury bonds, equity securities and corporate bonds, respectively, are:

    A. more risky, less risky
    B. less risky, more risky
    C. less risky, less risky
    D. more risky, more risky

449. Which of the following would result when the exchange rate of the US dollar significantly declines?

    I. US imports will be hurt.
    II. US exports will benefit.
    III. Foreign goods will be less expensive for US consumers.

    A. II only
    B. I and II only
    C. II and III only
    D. I and III only

450. Which of the following would happen if the price of the British pound were to increase relative to the US dollar?

    I. The British pound would buy more British goods.
    II. The British pound would buy more US goods.

    A. I only
    B. II only
    C. Both I and II
    D. Neither I nor II

451. As a general rule, which of the following domestic entities would be subject to foreign currency translation risk?

    I. A US entity whose foreign operations are limited to exporting goods to Canada
    II. A US entity who owns a Japanese subsidiary

    A. I only
    B. II only
    C. Both I and II
    D. Neither I nor II

452. Wright International is a US firm that typically exports goods to Japan. Since the international receivables are denominated in yen, they are subject to fluctuating currency rates. To mitigate this risk, Wright sometimes purchases put options to protect against loss from a decline in the yen. The put premium is NOT relevant to the:

    I. decision to exercise the option
    II. calculation of gain or loss on the exercise of the put option

    A. I only
    B. II only
    C. Both I and II
    D. Neither I nor II

453. Olympic Enterprises Inc. owns recreation centers with virtual reality games. The entity constantly needs to upgrade its arcades and fun centers with the latest releases. The bank requires a compensating balance of 15% on a $100,000 loan. If the stated annual interest rate is 6%, what is the effective cost of the loan to Olympic Enterprises?

    A. 7.05%
    B. 6.69%
    C. 6%
    D. 7.8%

454. Hayes Corp. is a US manufacturer of musical instruments. Which of the following risks is Hayes subject to if it uses its own cumulative earnings in capitalizing its operations?
   I. Financial risk
   II. Business risk
   III. Interest rate risk

   A. I only
   B. II only
   C. I and II
   D. I, II, and III

455. The required rate of return is generally computed as the risk-free rate of return plus a number of risk premium adjustments, including the maturity risk premium. Which of the following is/are correct regarding the interest rate risk?
   I. Interest rate risk is an adjustment to the risk-free rate of return and is the additional compensation demanded by lenders for bearing the risk that the issuer of the security will fail to pay the interest or fail to repay the principal.
   II. Interest rate risk is an adjustment to the risk-free rate of return and is the compensation investors demand for bearing risk.
   III. Interest rate risk is directly related to the term to maturity.

   A. I, II, and III
   B. III only
   C. II and III
   D. II only

456. Donruss Corp. is considering investing in a new project known as the Topps project. To evaluate the Topps project, Donruss management has developed the following cash flow projections and related probabilities:

Present Value of Future Cash Flows	Probability of Occurrence
$100,000	0.1
$600,000	0.3
$900,000	0.2
$300,000	0.4

   What is the expected return for the Topps project?

   A. $180,000
   B. $220,000
   C. $490,000
   D. $480,000

457. Surett Corp. is looking to implement a new in-house payroll processing system, and would like to determine the loss that might be anticipated as a result of user error. Surett estimates the probability of user error to be 80%, and also estimates the range of error (distributed evenly) to be between $5,000 and $20,000 for the year. Based on this information, what amount of loss might Surett expect for the year?

   A. $6,000
   B. $8,000
   C. $10,000
   D. $12,000

458. Which of the following would generally result when a corporation, about to issue new bonds, agrees to a debt covenant?
   I. The coupon rate of new corporate bonds would be increased.
   II. The company's bond rating would be lowered.

   A. I only
   B. II only
   C. Both I and II
   D. Neither I nor II

459. Immediately after raising capital, what is the effect (increase or decrease) on the debt equity ratio if the capital raised is from the sale of long-term bonds versus the sale of common stock?

	Long-Term Bonds	Common Stock
A.	Increase	Decrease
B.	Increase	Increase
C.	Increase	No effect
D.	Decrease	Increase

460. Factors that would likely cause a country's currency to appreciate on the foreign exchange market assuming exchange rates are allowed to fluctuate freely include:
   I. A low rate of inflation relative to other countries
   II. Lower domestic real interest rates than real interest rates abroad
   III. Slow growth rate to income compared to other countries, which results in net negative imports (imports less than exports)

   A. I only
   B. II only
   C. I and III only
   D. II and III only

461. Which of the following is/are correct regarding the P/E ratio?
    I. The P/E ratio measures the amount that investors are willing to pay for each dollar of earnings per share.
    II. Lower P/E ratios generally indicate that investors are anticipating more growth and are bidding up the price of the shares in advance of performance.

    A. I only
    B. II only
    C. Both I and II
    D. Neither I nor II

462. Sudbury Education Inc. has a payout of 30% and a forecasted growth rate of 9%. If investors require a 11% rate of return on their investment, what is the estimated P/E multiple on this stock?

    A. 14×
    B. 15×
    C. 17×
    D. 19×

463. Imposing a tariff on imported goods would produce which of the following effects?
    I. Increase domestic prices on the imported goods
    II. Reduce domestic production of the imported goods
    III. Produce a ban on the imported goods

    A. I only
    B. I and II only
    C. III only
    D. II only

464. Which of the following is/are correct regarding the constant growth dividend discount model?
    I. The stock price will grow at a faster rate than the dividend.
    II. The growth rate is less than the discount rate.

    A. I only
    B. II only
    C. Both I and II
    D. Neither I nor II

465. An investor is considering purchasing shares in a company with a dividend of $4 per share. If a zero growth model is used and 10% represents the desired return, how much should the stock sell for?

    A. $40
    B. $160
    C. $16
    D. $80

466. Assume that Aragona Corp. pays a dividend of $4 per share on its common stock and is expected to grow at 5% per year. Prager, an investor, wants to invest in Aragona and earn a 20% annual return. How much is Prager willing to pay for Aragona stock today?

    A. $15
    B. $21.25
    C. $25.50
    D. $28

467. Orange Corp. has a P/E ratio of 20 and its earnings in the current year are $10 per share. In the coming years, earnings of $18 per share are expected. What is the anticipated share price of Orange?

    A. $200
    B. $360
    C. $420
    D. $480

468. The effect from opening markets to foreign investments includes which of the following?
    I. An increase in investment growth rates
    II. An increase in local firms' cost of capital
    III. A decrease in the correlation of emerging stock markets with world markets

    A. I only
    B. I and II only
    C. III only
    D. I, II, and III

469. _____ is the type of risk faced by global companies, who deal with political and financial risks of conducting business in a particular foreign region.

    A. Inflation risk
    B. Business risk
    C. Country risk
    D. Interest rate risk

470. Which of the following ratios would NOT be meaningful if there were a loss or if earnings were extremely small?
    I. P/E ratio
    II. Price to sales ratio

    A. I only
    B. II only
    C. Both I and II
    D. Neither I nor II

471. According to behavioral finance, what is a financial manager suffering from if the manager believes that his or her actions will cause earnings to increase and market prices to remain in proportion to increased earnings?

   I. Confirmation bias

  II. Excessive optimism

 III. Illusion of control

A. I and II

B. II and III

C. III only

D. I and III

CHAPTER 22
CORPORATE GOVERNANCE

QUESTIONS 472–500

472. The Sarbanes-Oxley Act of 2002 addresses the problems related to inadequate board oversight by requiring public companies to have an:
  I. audit committee
  II. annual audit for all issuers

  A. I only
  B. II only
  C. Both I and II
  D. Neither I nor II

473. The board of directors of a corporation generally does NOT have the authority to do which of the following?

  A. Declare dividends
  B. Add or repeal bylaws
  C. Determine executive compensation
  D. Manage daily operations

474. According to the Sarbanes-Oxley Act of 2002, corporate responsibility for financial reports includes the chief executive officer (CEO) and chief financial officer (CFO) certifying that they have reviewed the report and that the report does NOT:
  I. contain untrue statements
  II. omit material information

  A. I only
  B. II only
  C. Both I and II
  D. Neither I nor II

475. Under the Sarbanes-Oxley Act of 2002, which of the following services would an auditor be permitted to perform for its public client?
  I. Tax compliance services
  II. Bookkeeping services
  III. Legal services

  A. II and III only
  B. II only
  C. I and III only
  D. I only

476. Under the Sarbanes-Oxley Act of 2002, which of the following are enhanced disclosures required in periodic reports?
  I. All correcting adjustments identified by the independent auditor
  II. Relationships with unconsolidated subsidiaries
  III. Material off–balance sheet transactions

  A. I and II
  B. I and III
  C. II and III
  D. I, II, and III

477. The Sarbanes-Oxley Act of 2002 requires that the management report on internal control include:
   I. a statement of management's responsibilities for establishing and maintaining adequate internal controls
   II. a conclusion about the effectiveness of the company's internal controls
   III. a statement that there are no disagreements between management and the auditor as to the effectiveness of internal controls

   A. I, II, and III
   B. III only
   C. I and II only
   D. II and III only

478. Under the Sarbanes-Oxley Act of 2002, an audit committee expert must have an understanding of which of the following?

   A. Federal tax law
   B. Corporate governance rules and procedures
   C. Generally accepted auditing standards
   D. Generally accepted accounting principles

479. The Sarbanes-Oxley Act of 2002 requires that the officers of a corporation be held accountable to a code of ethics. According to the act, codifications of ethical standards should include provisions for:
   I. full, fair, accurate, and timely disclosure in periodic financial statements
   II. honest and ethical conduct

   A. I only
   B. II only
   C. Both I and II
   D. Neither I nor II

480. According to the Sarbanes-Oxley Act of 2002, which of the following statements would be correct regarding an issuer's audit committee financial expert?
   I. The issuer's current outside CPA firm's audit partner would be a good choice to be the audit committee financial expert.
   II. The audit committee financial expert should be the issuer's audit committee chairperson to enhance internal control.

   A. I only
   B. II only
   C. Both I and II
   D. Neither I nor II

481. Benefits to establishing an enterprise risk management (ERM) system within an organization include all of the following EXCEPT:

   A. more effective capital allocation
   B. the ability to respond to opportunities expediently
   C. the ability to avoid all risks posed to the organization
   D. the ability to anticipate potential events

482. Which of the following is best suited to establish and execute risk procedures for a particular department in accordance with the Committee of Sponsoring Organizations (COSO) and as part of the ERM process?

   A. Internal audit department personnel
   B. The chief executive officer
   C. The audit committee
   D. A manager within that department

483. According to the COSO, principles relating to the control environment include:
   I. board of directors oversight of internal control
   II. commitment to attracting and retaining competent individuals
   III. evaluating and communicating internal control deficiencies

   A. I and II only
   B. II and III only
   C. I and III only
   D. I, II, and III

484. According to the Sarbanes-Oxley Act, which of the following individuals would be considered automatically qualified for the position of audit committee financial expert?
   I. Anyone with a CPA certificate
   II. A full-time tenured professor of accounting at a well-known university who has already earned a PhD

   A. I only
   B. II only
   C. Both I and II
   D. Neither I nor II

485. In accordance with its ERM process, Catalina Corp. identifies events and analyzes risks. The company wants to assess its risk after management's response to the risk. This type of risk is indicative of which of the following?

A. Residual risk
B. Detection risk
C. Inherent risk
D. Control risk

486. For compensation and promotion purposes, Fessler Corp. evaluates employees who are responsible for financial reporting on how well they fulfill those responsibilities. The company's policies support the idea that:

I. human resources practices should be designed to facilitate effective internal control over financial reporting
II. management's philosophy and operating style support achieving effective internal control over financial reporting

A. I only
B. II only
C. Both I and II
D. Neither I nor II

487. The existence of a published code of ethics and a periodic acknowledgment that ethical values are understood is evidence of:

I. the development of ethical values and ensuring that those values are understood and taken seriously
II. the board of directors understanding and exercising oversight responsibility related to financial reporting and related internal control

A. I only
B. II only
C. Both I and II
D. Neither I nor II

488. Broad Corp. has a corporate compliance program that allows employees the option of anonymously reporting violations of laws, rules, regulations, or policies or other issues of abuse through a hotline. Reported issues are reviewed by the internal auditor and either immediately forwarded to the CEO or summarized and reported to the CEO each month. The program also provides opportunities to report through supervisory channels and includes a biannual training class that all employees must complete. The corporate compliance program demonstrates which of the following?

I. Sound integrity and ethical values are developed and understood and set the standard of conduct for financial reporting.
II. Management and employees are assigned appropriate levels of authority and responsibility to facilitate effective internal control over financial reporting.

A. I only
B. II only
C. Both I and II
D. Neither I nor II

489. Active engagement by an audit committee in representing the board of directors relative to all matters of internal and external audits is evidence of:

I. the board's understanding of its oversight responsibility over financial reporting
II. the need for an organizational structure to support effective internal control over financial reporting

A. I only
B. II only
C. Both I and II
D. Neither I nor II

490. All of the following are techniques for identifying events in an ERM program EXCEPT for:

A. internal analysis
B. leading event indicators
C. probability and expected value analysis
D. process flow analysis

491. According to the COSO framework, variance analysis primarily supports:

A. internal control information
B. external control communication
C. internal control communication
D. effective financial reporting

492. Cohen Corp. recently relocated its manufacturing plan to a region that will allow the company to reduce its tax liability. However, this new region is also prone to tornadoes. In order to insure the plant from tornado losses, Cohen purchased a property and casualty insurance policy. Cohen employed what type of risk response when purchasing this insurance policy?

A. acceptance
B. avoidance
C. reduction
D. sharing

493. Which component of the COSO ERM framework addresses a corporation's risk management philosophy and risk appetite?

A. Risk assessment
B. Control (internal) environment
C. Information and communication
D. Control activities

494. According to the COSO ERM framework, which of the following would involve the determination of the likelihood and impact of events on the achievement of objectives?

A. Control activities
B. Risk assessment
C. Inherent risk
D. Residual risk

495. A response to risk that involves the diversification of product offerings rather than the elimination of product offerings is called risk:

A. acceptance
B. avoidance
C. reduction
D. sharing

496. According to the COSO, reporting that triggers prompt exception resolution, root cause analysis, and control updates illustrates the principle of:

A. internal control information
B. financial reporting information
C. internal communications
D. external communications

497. According to the COSO, which of the following would be an operations objective?
   I. Maintaining adequate staffing to keep overtime and benefit costs within budget
   II. Maintaining direct labor cost variances within published guidelines
   III. Maintaining accounting principles that conform to US GAAP

A. I and III
B. I, II, and III
C. II and III
D. I and II

498. The control activities component of the ERM framework includes key elements that relate to:
   I. the policies and procedures that ensure appropriate responses to identified risks
   II. integrity and ethical values

A. I only
B. II only
C. Both I and II
D. Neither I nor II

499. Which of the following is NOT typically included in a corporation's articles of incorporation?
   I. Number of authorized shares of a company's stock
   II. Procedure for electing the board of directors
   III. The corporation's purpose

A. I and III only
B. II only
C. I, II, and III
D. II and III only

500. The Institute of Internal Auditors' International Standards for the Professional Practice of Internal Auditing do NOT include which of the following sections of standards?

A. Attribute Standards
B. Independence Standards
C. Performance Standards
D. Implementation Standards

■ PART II ANSWERS AND EXPLANATIONS

Chapter 16: Operations Management

1. **B.** II is correct. Nonfinancial measures include number of days missed due to workplace accidents, an example of nonfinancial performance. Nonfinancial measures are attention getters without the use of dollar figures. Another example of a nonfinancial performance measure would be the number of defective goods manufactured. I is wrong. Gross margin is a measure of financial performance.

2. **C.** I and II are correct. Total productivity ratios are nonfinancial measures. Total productivity ratios compare the value of all output to the value of all input. Partial productivity ratios are also nonfinancial measures. Partial productivity ratios compare the value of all output to the value of just some input—for example, the value of all output to the value of direct materials input. A different partial productivity ratio would compare the value of all output with the value of just direct labor input. Productivity ratios measure outputs achieved in relation to the inputs of production. Productivity ratios measure efficiency.

3. **A.** I is correct. A control chart is a measure of nonfinancial performance that is considered an internal benchmark (see Figure 1). A control chart shows the performance of a particular manufacturing process in relation to acceptable upper and lower limits of error, or deviation. Control charts show if there is a trend of improved quality performance or if there is a trend of more error. II is wrong. A total productivity ratio is a measure of nonfinancial performance and is considered an external rather than an internal benchmark.

4. **C.** I and II are correct. Fishbone diagrams are considered internal benchmarks (see Figure 2). Fishbone diagrams describe a process, the contributions to the process, and the potential problems that could occur at each phase of the process. Fishbone diagrams identify a quality control problem and track the defect back to the source. A Pareto diagram also is considered an internal benchmark (see Figure 3). A Pareto diagram is used to determine quality control problems that occur most frequently so they can receive the more urgent attention and be corrected first. Then the next most frequent problem can be corrected.

5. **A.** I is correct. A control chart shows the performance of a particular process in relation to acceptable upper and lower limits of deviation. Processes are designed to ensure that performance consistently falls within the acceptable range of error. II is wrong. A fishbone diagram describes a process, the contributions to the process, and the potential

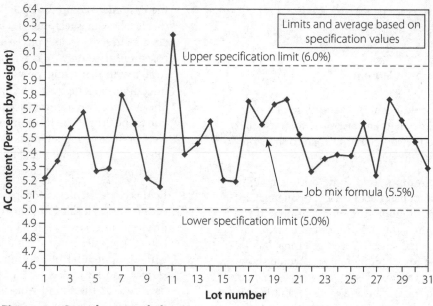

Figure 1   Sample control chart

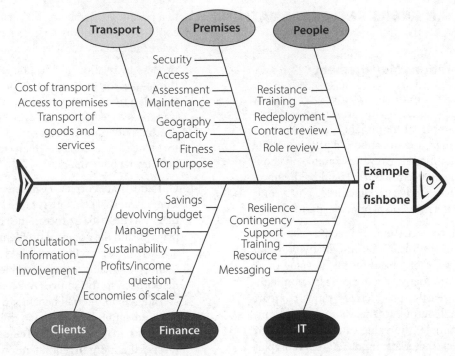

Figure 2   Sample fishbone diagram

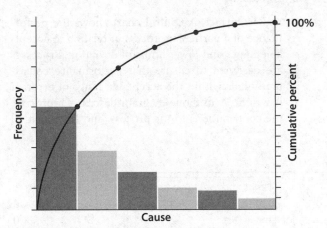

Figure 3   Sample Pareto diagram

problems that could occur at each phase of a process. The fishbone diagram attempts to track the problem back to the source rather than to show the upper and lower limits of acceptable error.

6. **B.** A Pareto diagram is used to determine quality control problems that occur most frequently so they can receive the more urgent attention and be corrected first; then the next most frequent problem can be corrected, and so on. A is wrong. While the control chart for an individual ride would show if there is a trend of improved quality performance for that ride or if there is a trend of more shutdowns with that specific ride, the control chart would not show which ride had the most shutdowns. C is wrong. The fishbone diagram would describe the amusement ride and attempt to track the shutdown back to the source. Was it a software problem or equipment malfunction? A fishbone diagram would not show which ride had the most shutdowns.

7. **C.** Honest John Inc. uses a transaction marketing practice. A transaction marketing practice emphasizes a single sale with no further interaction with the customer required. A retailer like Honest John that is following such practices believes that customers are attracted to low prices and will likely return based on price only. A is wrong. Interaction-based relationship marketing views the sale as the beginning of an ongoing relationship with the customer. The customer will return, thus providing more revenue to the firm as the relationship grows. B is wrong. Network marketing attempts to build sales through referrals. D is wrong. Database marketing involves targeting ads to specific customer profiles.

8. **D.** II is correct. Interaction-based relationship marketing says that sales further relationships, thereby driving more sales. With interaction-based marketing, the sale is just the start of the relationship with the potential of continued revenue through service and parts. I is wrong. Database marketing uses data as the foundation for identifying target markets. III is wrong. Transaction marketing says

that customers are attracted to low prices and will return based only on price.

9. **B.** II is correct. Competitive commission plans tend to emphasize current compensation; the employee can take the commission or bonus and leave. I is wrong. Future compensation involves stock options since the employee needs to continue in employment into the future to earn the shares represented by the options.

10. **A.** I is correct. Product costs are inventoriable. They are assets and remain on the balance sheet until the product is sold. II is wrong. Period costs are expensed immediately in the period incurred.

11. **C.** Inventoriable costs include direct materials and direct labor. Both costs would remain on the balance sheet until the product is sold.

12. **C.** I and II are correct. Activities that cause costs to increase as the activity increases are known as cost drivers. Cost drivers can be financial or nonfinancial. An example of a nonfinancial cost driver is the number of direct labor hours. As employees work more hours, more overhead cost is incurred in the factory. Machine hours are another example of a nonfinancial cost driver used to allocate overhead to a product. As the machinery runs, utility cost is being generated in the factory.

13. **B.** Using direct labor hours, the overhead applied calculation is as follows:

$75,000 budgeted overhead ÷ 20,000 budgeted direct labor hours = $3.75 per direct labor hour

Overhead applied to the job = $3.75 × 1,200 actual direct labor hours, or $4,500

Overhead is applied using budgeted figures rather than actual.

14. **B.** II is correct. A predetermined factory overhead rate is based on estimates. Estimated figures are used because actual cost figures are not known at the beginning of a period. Estimated variable overhead costs divided by estimated activity level equals the predetermined factory overhead rate. The numerator is the estimated dollar amount of overhead; the denominator may be estimated machine hours or estimated direct labor hours. Therefore, the predetermined factory overhead rate is based on estimates rather than actual figures.

15. **B.** A predetermined factory overhead rate is based on estimates. Estimated figures are used because actual cost figures are not known at the beginning

of a period. A predetermined factory overhead rate could be obtained by dividing estimated variable overhead costs by the number of estimated machine hours.

16. **C.** Prime costs are the sum of direct labor and direct materials:

Direct labor	$16,000
Direct materials	+ $4,000
Prime costs	$20,000

17. **A.** Total product costs are the sum of direct materials, direct labor, and factory overhead applied. To estimate the total product costs on the proposed job, prime costs were already calculated in Question 16 as the sum of direct labor and direct materials:

Direct labor	$16,000
Direct materials	+ $4,000
Prime costs	$20,000

Add in overhead applied of $8,000, calculated as follows (the estimated overhead application rate is calculated from the budgeted information given):

Indirect labor	$90,000
Replacement parts for factory machinery	+ $70,000
Total budgeted overhead	$160,000

$160,000 ÷ Cost driver = Applied overhead

The cost driver for this question is the direct labor hours for the proposed job, or 40,000 hours.

$160,000 ÷ 40,000 hours = $4 per direct labor hour

For every hour of direct labor, $4 is applied to overhead.

2,000 hours × $4 rate	$8,000
Prime costs	+ $20,000
Total estimated product cost of the job	$28,000

18. **A.** In the relevant range, fixed costs are constant in total but decrease per unit as production levels increase. The relevant range refers to the short term rather than the long term. In the short term, costs can be broken down between fixed and variable. Variable costs change with production. In the long term, all costs are considered variable because even fixed costs like rent eventually become variable (e.g., leases eventually expire).

19. **C.** I and II are correct. Variable costs per unit remain unchanged in the relevant range. Variable costs increase in total as unit volume increases.

20. **D.** The amount of direct materials used is calculated as follows:

Beginning inventory, direct materials	$134,000
Purchases during March	+ $190,000
Purchase returns and allowances	– $1,000
Transportation in	+ $2,000
Total direct materials available	$325,000
Ending inventory, direct materials	– $124,000
Direct materials used during March	$201,000

21. **C.** Prime costs are calculated as follows:

Step 1—Compute direct materials used.

Beginning inventory, direct materials	$134,000
Purchases during March	+ $190,000
Purchase returns and allowances	– $1,000
Transportation in	+ $2,000
Total direct materials available	$325,000
Ending inventory, direct materials	– $124,000
Direct materials used during March	$201,000

Step 2—Add direct labor.

Direct labor	+ $200,000
Total prime costs	$401,000

22. **D.**

Step 1—Compute direct materials used.

Beginning inventory, direct materials	$134,000
Purchases during March	+ $190,000
Purchase returns and allowances	– $1,000
Transportation in	+ $2,000
Total direct materials available	$325,000
Ending inventory, direct materials	– $124,000
Direct materials used during March	$201,000

Step 2—Add direct labor.

Direct labor	+ $200,000
Total prime costs	$401,000

Step 3—Apply overhead.

$0.40 × $200,000 direct labor dollars	+ $80,000
Total manufacturing costs incurred for March	$481,000

Note that actual overhead of $165,000 is irrelevant (until year-end).

23. **C.** The calculation is as follows:

Step 1—Compute direct materials used.

Beginning inventory, direct materials	$134,000
Purchases during March	+ $190,000
Purchase returns and allowances	– $1,000
Transportation in	+ $2,000
Total direct materials available	$325,000
Ending inventory, direct materials	– $124,000
Direct materials used during March	$201,000

Step 2—Add direct labor.

Direct labor	+ $200,000
Total prime costs	$401,000

Step 3—Apply overhead.

$0.40 × $200,000 direct labor dollars	+ $80,000
Total manufacturing costs incurred	$481,000

Step 4—Add beginning work in process.

Beginning work in process	+ $230,000
Total manufacturing costs available for March	$711,000

Note that manufacturing costs available differs from manufacturing costs incurred by the amount of beginning work-in-process inventory of $230,000.

24. **B.** Cost of goods manufactured is $461,000, calculated as follows:

Step 1—Compute direct materials used.

Beginning inventory, direct materials	$134,000
Purchases during March	+ $190,000
Purchase returns and allowances	– $1,000
Transportation in	+ $2,000
Total direct materials available	$325,000
Ending inventory, direct materials	– $124,000
Direct materials used during March	$201,000

Step 2—Add direct labor.

Direct labor	+ $200,000
Total prime costs	$401,000

Step 3—Apply overhead.

$0.40 × $200,000 direct labor dollars	+ $80,000
Total manufacturing costs incurred	$481,000
Beginning work in process	+ $230,000
Total manufacturing costs for March	$711,000
Ending work in process	– $250,000
Cost of goods manufactured	$461,000

25. **C.** The first step in calculating cost of goods sold for a manufacturer is to calculate cost of goods manufactured. Cost of goods manufactured is $461,000, calculated as follows:

Step 1—Compute direct materials used.

Beginning inventory, direct materials	$134,000
Purchases during March	+ $190,000
Purchase returns and allowances	– $1,000
Transportation in	+ $2,000
Total direct materials available	$325,000
Ending inventory, direct materials	– $124,000
Direct materials used during March	$201,000

Step 2—Add direct labor.

Direct labor	+ $200,000
Total prime costs	$401,000

Step 3—Apply overhead.

$0.40 × $200,000 direct labor dollars	+ $80,000
Total manufacturing costs incurred	$481,000
Beginning work in process	+ $230,000
Total manufacturing costs for March	$711,000
Ending work in process	– $250,000
Cost of goods manufactured	$461,000

Once cost of goods manufactured is known, cost of goods sold can easily be determined by adding beginning finished goods and subtracting ending finished goods.

$461,000 + $120,000 (beginning finished goods) – $110,000 (ending finished goods) = $471,000 (cost of goods sold)

26. **A.** For a manufacturing operation, cost of goods sold is equal to cost of goods manufactured plus beginning finished goods minus ending finished goods.

27. **D.** A simple example to calculate cost of goods manufactured from total manufacturing costs is as follows:

Total manufacturing costs	10
Beginning work in process	+ 1
Ending work in process	– 5
Cost of goods manufactured	6

28. **D.** Cost of goods manufactured plus beginning finished goods less ending finished goods equals cost of goods sold.

29. **B.** Since manufacturing overhead is applied on the basis of direct labor dollars, the total of the direct labor dollars for September must first be determined:

$1,000 + $4,500 + $2,000 = $7,500

Manufacturing overhead is applied at the rate of 200%, so $15,000 was applied for the month of September (200% × $7,500 = $15,000). Actual manufacturing overhead for September was $17,500, so manufacturing overhead was underapplied by $2,500 ($17,500 – $15,000). In a factory overhead control T account, actual costs are debits. Overhead applied is credited. A debit balance at the end means underapplied actual costs were higher. In this case actual costs were higher than budget by $2,500.

Factory Overhead Control	
Actual	Applied
$17,500	$15,000

Ending balance $2,500

30. **B.** II is correct. The cost of indirect materials used increases the factory overhead control account and decreases materials control. All actual overhead costs are debited to the overhead control T account. I is wrong. Overhead applied is based on estimates, not actual costs. If the estimates are higher than actual costs, a credit balance remains in the factory overhead control account.

31. **D.** The first step under the weighted average method is to determine the units completed during the period. Then calculate the percentage complete using the ending inventory units. Adding those two numbers together equals equivalent units. The second step is to determine cost per (equivalent) unit.

32. **C.** The question asks how many units would be included in the calculation of cost per equivalent unit under the weighted average method. To calculate cost per equivalent unit using the weighted average method, start with units completed for the period and then add the units still in ending inventory multiplied by the percent that they are complete.

Units completed during the period	400
Ending inventory units × 75%	
complete (200 × 0.75)	+150
Equivalent units in ending inventory	550

33. **B.** To calculate cost per equivalent unit using the weighted average method, the numerator includes both current costs and beginning inventory costs as follows:

$650,000 current costs + $32,000 beginning inventory costs = $682,000

34. **A.** The cost per equivalent unit of material production is calculated as follows:

$682,000 ÷ 550 units = $1,240

To calculate cost per equivalent unit using the weighted average method, the numerator includes both current costs and beginning inventory costs as follows:

Current costs	$650,000
Beginning inventory costs	+ $32,000
	$682,000

To calculate cost per equivalent unit using weighted average, the denominator starts with units completed for the period and then adds the ending inventory units times the percent complete.

Units completed during the period	400
Ending inventory units, 75% complete (200 × 0.75)	+ 150
Equivalent units in ending inventory	550

35. **B.** Under the FIFO method, 500 equivalent units are calculated as follows: To calculate cost per equivalent unit using FIFO, start with beginning inventory units:

100 units, 50% complete (100 × 0.50)	50 units
Units completed for the period	+ 400 units
Beginning inventory	− 100 units
Subtotal	350 units
Ending inventory units × the percent complete (200 × 0.75)	+ 150 units
Equivalent units	500 units

36. **C.** To calculate cost per equivalent unit using FIFO, the numerator includes current costs only: current costs $650,000.

37. **B.** To calculate cost per equivalent unit using FIFO, the first step is to calculate the equivalent units for the period (denominator). Using the FIFO method, 500 equivalent units are calculated as follows:

Beginning inventory units (50% complete, 100 units work this period)	50 units
Units completed for the period	+ 400 units
Beginning inventory	− 100 units
Subtotal	350 units
Ending inventory units × the percent complete (200 units × 0.75)	+ 150 units
Equivalent units using FIFO	500 units

In determining costs per equivalent unit, the second step is to calculate the numerator, or total costs. To calculate cost per equivalent unit using FIFO, the numerator includes current costs only, or $650,000. To calculate cost per equivalent unit using FIFO, the final step is to divide costs by equivalent units calculated.

$650,000 total costs ÷ 500 units = $1,300 cost per equivalent unit

38. **C.** I and II are correct. To calculate equivalent cost per unit using weighted average, use both current costs and beginning inventory cost in the numerator and divide by the number of equivalent units.

39. **B.** II is correct. Regardless of the method used, the formula for cost per equivalent unit is total costs divided by number of equivalent units. Using FIFO, the number of equivalent units (denominator) includes beginning inventory units. I is wrong.

Using weighted average, the starting point for the calculation of number of equivalent units (denominator) is the number of units completed and transferred out during the period. Using weighted average, the beginning inventory units are not considered in the calculation of equivalent units.

40. **A.** I is correct. To calculate cost per equivalent unit using FIFO, use only current costs in the numerator. II is wrong. To calculate cost per equivalent unit using FIFO, use current costs, *not* beginning inventory costs, in the numerator.

41. **C.** I and II are correct. When calculating equivalent units, treatment of ending inventory by the FIFO and weighted average methods is identical.

42. **B.** II is correct. Using process costing, FIFO considers beginning inventory units (in the denominator) but not beginning inventory costs (in the numerator) when determining cost per equivalent unit. I is wrong. Weighted average does not consider beginning inventory units (in the denominator) when calculating cost per equivalent unit, but weighted average does consider beginning inventory costs (in the numerator).

43. **C.** Activity-based costing describes a system that accumulates all costs of overhead for each of the departments or activities of the organization and then allocates those overhead costs based on causal factors, factors that caused the department or activity to incur overhead. Conversely, traditional costing allocates overhead for all departments of an organization by use of a single company-wide overhead allocation rate. For this reason, activity-based costing is considered a more sophisticated and accurate method of applying overhead than traditional costing methods. A is wrong. Process costing is a method of allocating production costs to products and services by averaging the costs over the total units produced. B is wrong. Job-order costing is a method of allocating production costs to products and services that are identifiable as separate units, custom-made goods that require different amounts of labor and materials to complete.

44. **A.** I and II are correct. By using more than one cost driver, activity-based costing provides management with a more thorough understanding of product costs and product profitability. In addition, activity-based costing leads to a more competitive position by evaluating cost drivers. In activity-based costing, cost reduction is accomplished by identifying and eliminating non–value-adding

activities. Reducing and eliminating non–value-adding activities will lower overall cost. III is wrong. The benefit that management can expect from traditional costing (not activity-based costing) includes using a common departmental or factory-wide measure of activity, such as direct labor hours or dollars, to distribute manufacturing overhead to products.

45. **C.** I and II are correct. Eliminating non–value-adding activities would reduce costs, which is one of the objectives of activity-based costing systems. Eliminating all cost drivers would eliminate all activity. Since most activities add value, management would only want to eliminate non–value-added activities. Value-added activities have their costs, but they are necessary, as they add value.

46. **D.** II is correct. Process costing is a method of allocating production costs to products and services by averaging the cost over the total units produced. Costs are usually accumulated by department rather than by job. I is wrong. Job-order costing accumulates costs per job. III is wrong. Activity-based costing allocates overhead on the basis of multiple cost drivers, rather than just a single cost driver.

47. **B.** I and II are correct. Activity-based costing involves using cost drivers as application bases to increase the accuracy of reported product costs. In addition, activity-based costing involves using several machine cost pools to measure product costs on the basis of time in a machine center. III is wrong. Plant-wide application rates applied to machine hours is a traditional costing approach, not an activity-based costing approach. Activity-based costing involves the more detailed and accurate cost allocations that are now preferred in manufacturing.

48. **A.** I is correct. Activity-based costing uses cause-and-effect relationships to capitalize costs to inventory. This is not acceptable for external reporting but useful to management for internal reporting. II is wrong. Job-order costing (a simple accumulation of costs associated with a specific job) is acceptable for both internal and external purposes. III is wrong. Process costing is acceptable for both internal and external purposes. Process costing involves an averaging of actual costs.

49. **C.** I and II are correct. The difference between variable and absorption costing is the manner in which fixed manufacturing costs are treated. Using variable costing, only variable costs are included in inventory. Consequently, the difference in net income using variable costing versus absorption costing is the amount of fixed manufacturing costs (accounted for in inventory using absorption costing) multiplied by the change in inventory. An increase in inventory indicates that a portion of the fixed costs associated with inventory using absorption costing is expensed using variable costing. Absorption costing, therefore, produces greater income than variable costing, as inventory levels increase as follows:

Change in inventory (increase)	2,000 units
Fixed manufacturing cost per unit (absorbed into inventory, excluded from cost of goods sold)	$40
Higher net income using absorption costing	$80,000

50. **B.** I and III are correct. Other terms for the contribution approach are *direct costing* and *variable costing*. II is wrong. Full absorption costing is the opposite of the contribution approach. The direct, or variable, costing or contribution margin approach excludes fixed costs from product (inventoried) costs. Full absorption costing includes those fixed costs in ending inventory.

51. **A.** I is correct. Direct (sometimes called variable) costing can be used for internal purposes only; GAAP prefers absorption costing. II is wrong. Direct costing is not used for the benefit of external users. Variable costs exclude fixed costs from product (inventoried) costs and thereby produce an income statement based on contribution margin, highly useful to internal managers in computing breakeven points and analyzing performance but not useful for external reporting.

52. **B.** II is correct. Using absorption costing, costs are broken down between product and period.

53. **C.** I and II are correct. Using variable costing, all fixed factory overhead is treated as a period cost and is expensed in the period incurred. The cost of inventory includes only variable manufacturing costs. Using variable costing, the cost of goods sold includes only variable costs. Also, the variable selling, general, and administrative expenses are part of total variable costs.

54. **C.** I and II are correct. Fixed selling, general, and administrative costs are always period costs whether direct costing or full absorption costing is used. Using variable costing, all fixed factory overhead is treated as a period cost and is expensed in the period incurred. The cost of inventory includes

only variable manufacturing costs, so the cost of goods sold includes only variable costs. Also, the variable selling, general, and administrative expenses are part of total variable costs.

55. **C.** The difference between variable costing and full absorption costing is the treatment of fixed manufacturing costs. Full absorption costing treats fixed manufacturing costs as product costs, while variable costing expenses these as period costs.

56. **D.** The difference between variable costing and full absorption costing is the treatment of fixed manufacturing costs. Full absorption costing treats fixed manufacturing costs as product costs, while variable costing expenses fixed manufacturing as period costs. Variable costing treats all fixed costs as period costs, expensing the costs regardless of sales.

57. **C.** The difference between variable costing and full absorption costing is the treatment of fixed manufacturing costs. Full absorption costing treats fixed manufacturing costs as product costs, while variable costing expenses these as period costs. Using full absorption costing:

Fixed manufacturing costs $195,000 ÷ 100,000 units produced = $1.95 per unit produced

$1.95 fixed manufacturing costs per unit × 75,000 units sold = $146,250 fixed manufacturing costs expensed (through cost of goods sold) using full absorption costing

Using full absorption costing, the remaining fixed manufacturing costs of $48,750 ($195,000 − $146,250) remain in inventory as product costs.

58. **B.** Variable costing treats all fixed costs as period costs and would expense $195,000 in the period incurred regardless of sales. Thus, the difference in net income would be the amount of fixed manufacturing costs inventoried using absorption costing ($195,000 − $146,250 = $48,750). Using full absorption costing:

Fixed manufacturing costs $195,000 ÷ 100,000 units produced = $1.95 per unit produced

$1.95 fixed manufacturing costs per unit × 75,000 units sold = $146,250 fixed manufacturing costs expensed (through cost of goods sold) using full absorption costing

Using full absorption costing, the remaining fixed manufacturing costs of $48,750 ($195,000 − $146,250) remain in inventory as product costs.

59. **C.** I and II are correct. When production exceeds sales, inventory increases. As inventory increases, net income using absorption costing benefits from fixed manufacturing overhead that is recorded in inventory instead of recognized in cost of goods sold. When sales exceed production, inventory falls. As inventory falls, net income using absorption costing is reduced by cost of goods sold that includes fixed manufacturing overhead from prior periods that had been recorded in inventory. As a result, when sales exceed production, absorption costing net income is less than variable costing net income.

60. **A.** The ending finished goods inventory computed using direct costing is calculated by allocating the total costs capitalized in inventory using direct (variable) costing to ending inventory as follows:

Direct materials used	$180,000
Direct labor incurred	+ $140,000
Variable factory overhead	+ $124,000
Total production	$444,000

$444,000 ÷ 40,000 units produced = $11.10 per unit
$11.10 per unit × 3,000 units on hand = $33,300

61. **C.** I and II are correct. Using variable costing, all fixed factory overhead is treated as a period cost and is expensed in the period incurred. The cost of inventory includes only variable manufacturing costs, so the cost of goods sold includes only variable costs.

62. **A.** Contribution margin is calculated as sales less all variable costs, even variable selling, general, and administrative costs.

63. **C.** I and II are correct. Contribution margin is calculated as sales less all variable costs. Cost of goods sold includes only *product costs* that are variable, not variable selling and general expenses. Variable selling and general expenses would be a period cost and not part of cost of goods sold, although they would be included in the calculation of contribution margin.

64. **A.** I is correct. Contribution margin includes *all* variable costs, while cost of goods sold includes only product costs that are variable.

65. **B.** The calculation of contribution margin is for internal purposes and includes sales less all variable costs.

66. A. The contribution margin is calculated as follows:

Sales – Variable costs = Contribution margin

Sales	$750,000
Variable manufacturing costs	– $140,000
Variable selling and general costs	– $45,000
Contribution margin	$565,000

67. A. Contribution margin can be calculated as selling price less all variable costs:

Sales	$160
Direct materials	– $20
Direct labor	– $15
Factory overhead	– $12
Shipping and handling	– $3
Variable cost per unit	$50
Contribution margin	$110

68. C. Contribution margin can be calculated as selling price less all variable costs:

Sales	$160
Direct materials	– $20
Direct labor	– $15
Factory overhead	– $12
Shipping and handling	– $3
Variable cost per unit	$50
Gross sales	
($160 per unit × 18,000 units)	$2,880,000
Sales returns and allowances	– $80,000
Net sales	$2,800,000
Variable costs	– $900,000*
Contribution margin	$1,900,000

69. D. I and II are wrong. Variable costs vary in total with production and sales, but on a per unit basis, variable costs per unit do *not* change with production. Contribution margin is made up of variable costs (subtracted from sales). Since variable costs per unit do not change with production and sales, contribution margin per unit does not change with production and sales.

70. A. The contribution margin is calculated as follows:

Sales	$750,000
Variable manufacturing costs	– $130,000
Variable selling and administrative costs	– $45,000
Contribution margin	$575,000

$575,000 ÷ 55,000 units = $10.45 contribution margin per unit

Note that variable costs per unit are assumed to remain unchanged from year to year.

---

*$900,000 = $50 variable costs per unit × 18,000 units

71. A. Four hundred units must be sold to break even. To find the breakeven point, divide the total fixed cost ($80,000) by the contribution margin per unit ($200).

72. D. Breakeven analysis can be used to calculate the required sales dollars to break even using the following formula:

Sales = Fixed costs ÷ Contribution margin ratio (contribution margin expressed as a percentage of revenue)

The fact pattern indicates that variable costs are 20% of sales. By extension, contribution must be 80% of sales (100% – 20%). The breakeven in sales dollars is computed using the formula based upon fixed costs given at $30,000:

$30,000 fixed costs ÷ 80% contribution margin = $37,500

73. B. Fixed costs can be calculated as follows:

Selling price is given at $7.50.
Variable costs are given at $2.25.
Contribution margin is $5.25/unit.
Breakeven in units is given at 20,000.

Fixed costs can then be calculated as follows:

Fixed costs ÷ $5.25 = 20,000 units to break even
20,000 × $5.25 = $105,000

74. C. Selling price per unit less variable cost per unit equals contribution margin per unit.

$9 – $3 variable costs = $6 contribution margin per unit

New variable cost is calculated by multiplying old variable cost by 1.333.

$2.25 × 1.333 = $3 variable cost per unit
$9 – $3 = $6

75. D. Fixed costs were calculated for Year 1 at $105,000, so just multiply by 1.2; fixed costs for Year 2 are $126,000.

76. C. Breakeven in units equals fixed costs divided by contribution margin per unit. Year 2 fixed costs were calculated in Question 75 at $126,000. Contribution margin per unit in Year 2 is $6.

$126,000 ÷ $6 = 21,000 units

77. C. Total variable costs include:

Direct materials	$10
Direct labor	+ $7
Delivery charges	+ $5
Commission ($100 × 10%)	+ $10
Total variable costs per unit	$32

78. C. Fixed costs include indirect factory costs and administrative costs, or $5,000 and $20,200 every month.

79. A. The breakeven point in units (helmets) is computed as fixed costs divided by contribution margin per unit. Contribution margin is computed as the difference between selling price and variable costs. Variable costs include the following:

Direct materials	$10
Direct labor	+ $7
Delivery charges	+ $5
Commission ($100 × 10%)	+ $10
Total variable costs per unit	$32

Contribution margin = $100 sales price − $32 = $68

Fixed costs comprise the following:

Indirect factory costs	$5,000
Administrative costs	+ $20,200
Total fixed costs	$25,200

Breakeven point in units is computed as follows:

$25,200 fixed costs ÷ $68 contribution margin per unit = 371 helmets required to break even

80. C. The number of units is calculated as follows:

$240,000 desired profit + $100,000 fixed cost = $340,000

$340,000 ÷ $200 contribution margin = 1,700 units required to earn desired profit

81. B. The 12,500 units are calculated as follows:

Price	$20
Direct materials	− $3.25
Direct labor	− $4
Freight out	− $0.75
Total variable cost	$8
Contribution margin	$12
Fixed costs	$100,000
Pretax profit desired	+ $50,000
Total fixed costs	$150,000

$150,000 total fixed costs ÷ $12 contribution margin per unit = 12,500 units required to achieve $50,000 pretax profit.

82. B. The pretax profit is calculated as follows:

Targeted profit before tax = targeted profit after tax ÷ 1 − tax rate

$100,000 ÷ 0.65 = $153,846

83. D. The breakeven is calculated as follows:

Breakeven in sales dollars = $70,000 fixed costs ÷ contribution margin ratio

Breakeven in sales dollars = $70,000 ÷ ($120,000 ÷ $200,000) = $70,000 ÷ 0.60 = $116,667 breakeven in sales dollars

84. D. The margin of safety is the difference between current sales and breakeven in sales. Breakeven sales is calculated by dividing fixed costs by the contribution margin ratio:

Breakeven in sales = $70,000 fixed costs ÷ contribution margin ratio

Breakeven in sales = $70,000 ÷ ($120,000 ÷ $200,000)

$70,000 ÷ 0.60 = $116,667 breakeven in sales

$200,000 current sales − $116,667 breakeven in sales = $83,333 margin of safety

85. B. II is correct. Breakeven analysis assumes that fixed costs in total are constant over a relevant range. I is wrong. While variable costs vary in total with production, breakeven analysis assumes that all variable costs and revenues are constant on a per unit basis.

86. C. I and II are correct. Breakeven analysis assumes that all variable costs and revenues are constant on a per unit basis and linear over a relevant range.

87. C. When considering a special order, a manufacturer would accept the special order if the sales price were in excess of the relevant costs. Relevant costs differ depending upon whether the manufacturer is already at full capacity. If already at full capacity, the relevant costs include not just all variable costs but opportunity costs as well. If there is excess capacity in the factory, relevant costs include only variable costs.

88. C. I and II are correct. At full capacity, relevant costs include variable costs and opportunity costs. Opportunity costs are the forfeited profits that will be sacrificed in order to produce the special order.

89. A. The minimum acceptable selling price should include only the incremental costs associated with the order: $23,000 variable costs + $8,750 external designers costs = $31,750. Note that this is a special order (won't affect regular sales) and there is already idle capacity.

90. **C.** I and II are correct. Using breakeven analysis, total variable costs are directly proportional to volume over a relevant range, and selling prices are to remain unchanged if breakeven analysis is to be utilized.

91. **B.** Total fixed costs do not change and operating income increases. Adding a job with a positive contribution margin within idle capacity will increase operating income. The company will still make a profit for the special order even though the gross profit percent will be lower. The question states that fixed costs in total will be the same (fixed costs are assumed to be the same if the company is operating within the relevant range). Variable costs *per unit* will be the same. Note that fixed costs per unit decrease with increased production. A and C are wrong. Fixed costs will not change within the relevant range, and fixed cost per unit would decrease, not increase. D is wrong. Operating income will increase since the new job has a positive margin and is utilizing otherwise idle capacity.

92. **C.** Opportunity cost is the potential benefit lost by selecting a particular course of action.

93. **C.** I and II are correct. Opportunity cost is the potential benefit lost by selecting a particular course of action. If idle space has no alternative use, there is no benefit forgone; opportunity cost is zero. In addition, when deciding on special orders with no opportunity cost, the order would be accepted if the selling price per unit was higher than the variable cost per unit.

94. **B.** II is correct. When deciding between make or buy, fixed costs should be ignored unless those fixed costs would be avoided by purchasing the product instead of making the product.

95. **D.** The opportunity cost is the next best use of the productive capacity, not the total of the two or the difference between the two. Opportunity cost is the value of the road *not* traveled.

96. **C.** The opportunity cost is $15,000, the value of the next best use of the space. The alternative selected carries a contribution margin of $20,000, and the next best use is renting the space for $15,000. The opportunity cost is *not* $35,000, the combined value of the alternative selected and the next best use. The opportunity cost is the next best use of the productive capacity ($15,000), not the difference between the best and next best alternatives ($20,000 – $15,000).

97. **A.** I is correct. The relevance of a particular cost to a decision is determined by the potential effect that the cost has on the decision. Relevant costs are expected future costs that vary with the action taken. II is wrong. Whether a cost is relevant to a particular decision has nothing to do with the number of decision alternatives.

98. **C.** I and II are correct. Avoidable costs would be relevant and so would incremental costs. Costs are relevant costs if they change with the decision to produce an additional amount of the unit over the present output.

99. **C.** I and II are correct. The operational decision method, referred to as marginal analysis, is used when analyzing business decisions such as the introduction of a new product. Operational decision analysis is also used when analyzing business decisions such as acceptance or rejection of special orders, making versus buying a product or service, and adding or dropping a segment. Marginal analysis is also used in deciding whether to change output levels of existing products.

100. **D.** I and II are wrong. Note that this is a NOT question. The operational decision method, referred to as marginal analysis, *is* used when analyzing business decisions such as acceptance or rejection of special orders and making versus buying a product or service.

101. **A.** I is correct. Costs that change using different alternatives are known as relevant costs. The relevance of a particular cost to a decision is determined by its potential effect on the decision. Relevant costs are expected future costs that vary with the action taken. II is wrong. If the cost varies with production of the next unit, it is a relevant cost and should be considered by management.

102. **A.** I is correct. Joint costs are sunk costs, incurred already, and are *not* relevant to the sell or process further decision. Joint costs occur when two (or more) main products start from the same process and then eventually become different identifiable products. All the costs up to the point that the products become identifiable are known as joint costs. The point where the two distinct products can be identified is known as the split-off point. II is wrong. Separable costs are the costs incurred after the split-off point. The sell or process further decision would need to take into consideration separable costs because separable costs may not need to be incurred if the identifiable product can be sold once the split-off point occurs. Conversely, if the identifiable product cannot be sold

or cannot be sold for much money at the split-off point, then separable costs may need to be incurred to increase the value of the joint product.

103. **B.** The question requires allocation based on quantity of units produced, as follows:

Total units Quo	30,000 units (30/90 = 1/3)
Rael	+ 60,000 units (60/90 = 2/3)
Total units	90,000

Allocation of joint costs:

Quo	1/3 × $150,000 = $50,000
Rael	2/3 × $150,000 = $100,000

Notice that the selling price per unit was not needed, because the joint cost allocation was to be based on physical quantity only. There is another method of allocating joint costs based on relative selling price. (See answer to Question 104.)

104. **D.** The joint cost to be allocated to Rael is calculated as follows:

Quo	30,000 units × $3 = $90,000
Rael	60,000 units × $6 = $360,000
Quo	$90,000 ÷ $450,000 = 20%
Rael	$360,000 ÷ $450,000 = 80%
Joint costs allocated to Quo	20% × $150,000 = $30,000
Joint costs allocated to Rael	80% × $150,000 = $120,000

105. **C.** The joint cost to be allocated is calculated as follows:

30,000 units of product A + 20,000 units of product B = 50,000 total units

A physical quantity allocation basis ignores selling price at the split-off point and just pro-rates based on physical quantity. Therefore, 30,000 units of product A divided by 50,000 units equals 60%.

60% × $400,000 of joint cost = $240,000 of joint cost allocated to product A

106. **C.** I and II are correct. Incremental costs are relevant costs. Incremental costs are relevant because they include costs that vary with the decision to produce an additional amount of the unit over the present output. Prime costs (direct materials and direct labor) are incremental costs and would be relevant because they too vary with the decision to produce an additional amount of the unit over the present output.

107. **D.** The decision to drop a segment is based on a comparison of cost and benefit. The benefit of

dropping the segment is the avoidable fixed costs associated with ejecting the segment. The benefit of avoidable fixed costs is compared with the contribution margin lost.

108. **B.** A regression equation estimates the dependent variable based on changes in the independent variable.

109. **B.** The correlation coefficient measures the strength of the relationship between the dependent variable and the independent variable. The correlation coefficient is always a number between −1 and +1. If the relationship is strong, it will have a coefficient near +1 or −1, depending on the slope of the relationship. D is wrong. Linear regression analysis is a statistical method that fits a line to the data by the least squares method. It is the most accurate way to classify costs of an object as either fixed or variable.

110. **B.** The total cost formula is the formula where total cost, the dependent variable (y), is equal to volume times the independent variable (variable costs [x]) plus a constant (fixed costs).

111. **A.** The total cost formula is the formula for a line where total cost, the dependent variable (y), is equal to volume times the independent variable (variable costs [x]) plus a constant (fixed costs).

112. **A.** The correlation coefficient is always a number between −1 and +1. If the relationship is strong, it will have a coefficient near +1 or −1, depending on the slope of the relationship. Change in total cost is almost totally dependent on volume; therefore, the relationship between the two will be a positive number close to 1.0. As volume goes up, total cost goes up; the slope is positive. C is wrong. A correlation coefficient of zero would indicate no relationship between volume and total cost.

113. **B.** II is correct. The coefficient of determination measures the total variation in "y"—or total cost—that is explained by the total variation in the independent variable, x, or variable costs. I is wrong. The plan is to produce 150 units, so total cost, y, is computed as follows:

y = $80 variable cost per unit × 150 units = $12,000 + $25 fixed costs = $12,025

114. **A.** I is correct. Cost volume relationships are not only positive but also assumed to be proportional since total cost increases with volume. II is wrong. A coefficient of correlation of zero indicates no relationship between costs and volume. We would expect this relationship for fixed costs, not variable costs.

115. **C.** Management will choose a cost driver or independent variable based on a number close to 1.0 or even –1.0. This would indicate that a lot of the change in the dependent variable is determined by the independent variable, and that would be considered a good regression model, full of useful information. On the other hand, if the coefficient of correlation is zero or close to zero, there is little or no relationship between the dependent variable and the independent variable, so that cost driver would be *least* likely chosen.

116. **D.** I and II are correct. When choosing independent variables like cost drivers, management would choose the cost driver with the highest coefficient of correlation, either positive or negative. III is wrong. If the coefficient of correlation is zero or close to zero, there is little or no relationship between the dependent variable and the independent variable, so that cost driver would be *least* likely chosen.

117. **D.** I and II are wrong. The high-low method is a simplified approach to classifying costs as fixed and variable. The high-low method uses only the points of highest and lowest activity. Regression analysis is a statistical method that is the most accurate way to classify costs of an object as either fixed or variable because the regression method considers every point of activity, not just the highest and lowest points.

118. **B.** The calculation for the high-low method is as follows:

Volume (520 – 364) 156 units
Dollars ($8,350 – $6,834) $1,516

Using the high-low method, the variable cost per unit is equal to the change in dependent variable divided by the change in independent variable, or $1,516 ÷ 156 = $9.72 variable cost per unit. Therefore, $9.72 of cost is added for each additional unit produced.

119. **B.** Since variable costs are $9.72 per unit, $9.72 times 520 units produced in December equals $5,054 variable costs for December. Since total costs for December were $8,350, just subtract variable costs for December of $5,054, and fixed costs for December must have been $3,296.

Chapter 17: Planning and Budgeting

120. **A.** I and II are correct. Participative budgeting allows for increased motivation because it seeks input from multiple parties and spreads the decision-making process over multiple layers of managers and individuals. Implementing participative budgeting is also more time consuming because it requires input from multiple parties and spreads the decision-making process over multiple layers of managers and individuals. III is wrong. Implementing participative budgeting is more time consuming but allows for wider acceptance because more people are involved.

121. **D.** I and II are wrong. Note that this question asks what would *not* be contained in the master budget. The annual business plan, the master budget, includes operating budgets. The operating budget process includes all budgets except cash and capital purchases budgets. The operating budget also includes the pro forma income statement. The annual business plan also includes financial budgets. The financial budget process includes cash and capital purchases budgets, the balance sheet, and the statement of cash flows. With both operating budgets and financial budgets, the annual business plan is prepared in anticipation of achieving a single level of sales volume for a specific period.

122. **A.** I is correct. The operating budget process includes the pro forma income statement and all budgets except the cash budget and capital purchases. II is wrong. The financial budget process includes cash and capital purchases budgets, the budgeted balance sheet, and the statement of cash flows.

123. **D.** I and II are wrong. The budgeting process usually begins with the sales budget, then the production budget, and toward the end of the budgeting process, the cash budget is prepared.

124. **C.** Benchmarking is a continuous improvement process that compares levels of performance of an entity to best levels of performance. It involves searching for and implementing best practices. There are different types of benchmarking, including competitive benchmarking (benchmark against an organization in the same industry), process benchmarking (looking at operations of organizations with similar processes regardless of industry), strategic benchmarking (searching for successful competitive strategies), and internal benchmarking (applying best practices in one area of an organization to another area of that same organization). The type of benchmarking addressed in this question is process benchmarking. A is wrong. Six Sigma is a quality improvement statistical measure that expresses how close a product comes to its quality goal. It is focused on reducing the number of defects

in a mass-production process. B is wrong. Economic value added, or EVA, is a financial performance measurement that is computed as follows: after-tax operating income (initial investment × weighted average cost of capital). D is wrong. Total quality management (TQM), like Six Sigma, is a quality improvement tool that focuses on managing an organization to excel in quality in all types of products and services for customers. It is the continuous pursuit of quality in every aspect of an organization's activities.

125. **D.** The capital expenditures budget is developed independently but must take into account the cash available. The production budget is based on the sales budget, with adjustments for any changes in planned inventory levels.

126. **C.** I and II are correct. A flexible budget provides cost allowances (adjustments) for different levels of activity. A static budget provides fixed and variable costs for one level of activity. Both flexible and static budgets include both variable and fixed costs and, therefore, are appropriate for planning purposes. While the question didn't ask this, a flexible budget is better than a static budget for evaluating performance since it can be adjusted to the actual production level.

127. **A.** I is correct. A static budget is based on costs at one level of output. Static budgets include budgeted costs for budgeted, not actual, output. II is wrong. Static budgets are not based on or adjusted for actual performance.

128. **D.** The annual business plan process typically begins with operating budgets that are driven by sales budgets that, in turn, provide the required variables for production and personnel budgets. After those budgets are prepared, then the financial budgets can be prepared, including the cash budget.

129. **A.** The order of budget preparation begins with the sales budget, which leads to the production budget (to support sales), which, in turn, leads to the direct material purchases budget (to support production), from which the cash disbursements budget is derived.

130. **B.** I, II, and III are correct. Sales budgets are based upon sales forecasts, which are based on multiple independent variables like opinions of sales staff, past patterns of sales, general economic conditions, changes in the firm's prices, results of market research studies, and advertising and sales promotions.

131. **B.** The calculation is as follows:

Budgeted sales	2,000 units
Ending inventory	+ 220 units
Beginning inventory	− 185 units
Desired level of production	2,035 units

Ignore prior-year beginning inventory.

132. **D.** A 4% inflation rate would impact salary, health care costs, and rent expense. The budget would be computed as follows:

Salary expense ($210,000 × 1.04)	$218,400
Insurance expense ($120,000 × 1.04)	+ $124,800
Supplies expense ($60,000 × 1.04)	+ $62,400
Total budget for select items	$405,600

133. **D.** A 4% inflation rate would impact salary, health care costs, and rent expense. The budget would be computed as follows:

Salary expense ($210,000 × 1.04)	$218,400
Insurance expense ($120,000 × 1.04)	+ $124,800
Supplies expense ($60,000 × 1.04)	+ $62,400
Depreciation expense ($25,000 × 1.0)	+ $25,000
Interest expense on 10-year fixed rate bonds	+ $27,000
Total budget for select items	$457,600

The depreciation and interest expense on fixed rate bonds would not be affected by inflation.

134. **B.** Rascal should anticipate purchasing 820,000 wheels in July. Rascal would purchase enough wheels for 100,000 toy trucks planned for production as adjusted for 5,000 already on hand in anticipation of July production plus 7,500 purchased in anticipation of August production as follows:

July production (trucks)	100,000
Beginning inventory (5% × 100,000)	− 5,000
Ending inventory (5% × 150,000)	+ 7,500
Total trucks produced	102,500
Wheels per truck	× 8
Total purchases of wheels	820,000

135. **B.** As calculated below, 360,000 units would need to be manufactured during Year 4 to support sales of 380,000 units:

Projected sales (units)	380,000
Desired ending inventory	+ 40,000
Required units	420,000
Beginning inventory	− 60,000
Required units to manufacture	360,000

136. **B.** Production needs to cover the current budgeted sales for the current quarter while also taking into account desired inventory levels, as shown:

Second quarter sales	9,000
Desired ending inventory (10% × 12,000)	+ 1,200
Total units required	10,200
Beginning inventory (10% × 9,000)	− 900
Budgeted production	9,300 units

137. **D.** In Year 1, 2,730 tables are to be produced during November, calculated as follows:

Budgeted sales for November	3,000
Desired ending inventory, Nov. 30	
(30% × 2,100 Dec. sales)	+ 630
Total required	3,630
Beginning inventory, Nov. 1	
(30% × 3,000 Nov. sales)	− 900
Production	2,730

138. **C.** The $202,000 budgeted direct labor dollars for March is calculated as follows:

8,000 units × 3.0 hours × $6.75 = $162,000
8,000 units × 0.5 hour × $10 = $40,000

Total budgeted direct labor dollars for March
$202,000

139. **C.** I and II are correct. Overhead applied and material usage are inputs to the cost of goods manufactured. Direct labor is another input in cost of goods manufactured.

140. **B.** II is correct. Work-in-process inventory affects both inputs (for beginning work in process) and outputs (for ending work in process). I is wrong. Finished goods inventory is not necessary for determining cost of goods manufactured but is necessary for calculating cost of goods sold. The calculation of a cost of goods manufactured budget includes materials, labor, and overhead applied.

141. **B.** II is correct. The selling and administrative expense budget is dependent upon sales. I is wrong. The selling and administrative expense budget is operational, not financial. The selling and administrative expense budget represents the fixed and variable nonmanufacturing expenses anticipated during the budget period.

142. **B.** Purchases in Year 1 should be budgeted to cover both the planned sales (cost = $200,000) and the desired increase in inventory ($13,000), for a total of $213,000. Accounts payable at Jan. 1, Year 1, will be paid in Year 1. Accounts payable at Dec. 31, Year 1, of $17,750 ($213,000 ÷ 12) will not be paid until Year 2. The total for Year 2 is calculated as follows:

Purchases	$213,000
Accounts payable paid in Year 1	+ $20,000
December purchase	− $17,750
Paid in Year 2	$215,250

143. **C.** I and II are correct. The cash budget shows itemized cash receipts and disbursements during the period, including the financing activities and the beginning and ending cash balances. The main reason for preparing a cash budget is to anticipate cash flows so that excess cash can be invested and also to minimize the need for interim financing.

144. **A.** I is correct. The cash budget helps show the availability of funds for repayment of debt. II is wrong. The cash budget is usually broken down into monthly periods.

145. **B.** The cash receipts can be calculated as follows:

October sales ($200,000 × 26%)	$52,000
November sales ($211,000 × 70%)	+ $147,700
Budgeted accounts receivable	
for December	$199,700

146. **A.** I is correct. Borrowing funds on a note in August Year 4 would be a cash inflow in Year 4 and would have to be included in a schedule of cash receipts and disbursements for Year 4. The repayment would be a cash outflow in Year 5. II is wrong. Dividends declared are a noncash item until paid in Year 5.

147. **C.** I and II are correct. A purchase order is a commitment but not a cash event. Uncollectible accounts are a noncash item.

148. **A.** Cash collections for the second quarter comprise second quarter cash sales and collections of first quarter credit sales:

Second quarter cash sales	
(15,000 units × $4 × 70%)	$42,000
Collections of first quarter credit sales	
(10,000 units × $4 × 30%)	+ $12,000
Second quarter cash collections	$54,000

149. **B.** The pro forma income statement is the first budgeted financial statement prepared. The budgeted income statement produces (anticipated) accrual basis net income or loss and is added to beginning owners' equity to generate the owners' equity section of the budgeted balance sheet. The budgeted statement of cash flows is usually the last pro forma financial statement prepared because so many things affect cash. Cash flow cannot be projected until everything else has been estimated.

150. **C.** I and II are correct. The limitation of flexible budgeting is that flexible budgeting is highly dependent on an accurate identification of fixed cost and the variable cost per unit within the relevant range. The benefit of flexible budgeting is that, given the actual output, management can budget what revenue and expenses will be.

151. **C.** I and II are correct. Planned additions of capital equipment and related debt from the capital budget are added to the pro forma balance sheet. Planned financing expenses and principal repayments on capital equipment additions are included as disbursements on the cash budget.

152. **D.** A flexible budget is a budget prepared at different levels of operating activity. It is appropriate for all industries and any activity that has variable costs and direct labor.

153. **D.** I, II, and III are correct. The selling price per unit, the variable cost per unit, and the total fixed cost remain constant regardless of volume within the relevant range. Since the selling price and variable costs remain constant, the contribution margin per unit will also remain the same regardless of volume within the relevant range. Flexible budgeting answers the question: What should revenue and expenses be, given an output change from the master budget? When starting with a master budget, the flexible number of units must be multiplied by the selling price per unit, the variable cost per unit, and the contribution margin per unit in order to convert from the master budget to the flexible budget.

154. **C.** A master budget is an overall budget, consisting of many smaller budgets, that is based on one specific level of production. A flexible budget is a series of budgets based on different activity levels within the relevant range. A flexible budget contains budgeted costs for actual output.

155. **A.** Contribution margin per unit equals $40,000 divided by 10,000 units, or $4 per unit. Flexible budgeting begins with a master budget, a static budget. Flexible budgeting converts from the master budget, the selling price per unit, the variable cost per unit, and the contribution margin per unit times the flexible number of units because the selling price per unit, the variable cost per unit, and the contribution margin per unit remain the same regardless of volume within the relevant range.

156. **C.** The operating income can be calculated as follows:

July units (12,000 units × $4/unit contribution margin)	$48,000
Fixed costs (from master budget)	– $25,000
Operating income for July per flexible budget	$23,000

The primary feature of flexible budgets is the ability to adjust to actual volume based on established relationships between revenue and variable costs from the master budget.

157. **B.** Variable costs are $14,500 and the variance is $500 favorable. Start by calculating budgeted variable costs per unit: $18,000 divided by 600 units equals $30/unit. Then multiply $30 per unit variable costs by the 500 actual units sold to equal $15,000 total (flexible) budgeted variable costs. Then $15,000 less actual variable costs of $14,500 equals $500 net favorable difference. This $500 difference represents $500 fewer dollars spent on variable costs than budgeted, which represents a favorable variance.

158. **B.** The fixed cost variance is calculated as follows:

Actual fixed costs	$8,100
Budgeted fixed costs	– $8,800
Variance	$700 (favorable since actual fixed cost is less than budget)

159. **C.** The flexible budget variance represents the difference between actual performance and the budget at the achieved volume. To calculate the variance, actual costs of $89,000 are compared to the flexible budget at actual volume levels, 9,000 units. Flexible budget is calculated by taking variable cost per unit from the original master budget of $10 per unit (given) and multiplying that by the actual level of volume, 9,000 units, equals $90,000. Therefore, $90,000 is the flexible budget variable cost. Actual costs incurred of $89,000 are compared to the forecasted costs of $90,000, which results in a $1,000 favorable flexible budget variance. The variance is favorable because actual expenses are less than the computed (flexible) budget.

160. **B.** II is correct. Selling prices of finished goods depend on market prices of competitors, not costs. I is wrong. Identifying manufacturing variances and assigning their responsibility to a person or department does promote learning and improvement of operations through cost control measures.

161. **C.** The price variance must be favorable because the actual cost is less than the standard cost, calculated as follows:

Price variance = (Standard price – Actual price) × Actual units

Price variance = ($30 standard – $28.50 actual) × 11,400 actual units needed

Price variance = $1.50 × 11,400 = $17,100 favorable

162. **D.** Imhoff Company experienced an unfavorable direct materials price variance for the current period. The materials price variance formula is calculated as follows:

Materials price variance = Actual quantity × (Actual price – Standard price)

Materials price variance = 15,000 × ($9.50 – $7)

Materials price variance = 15,000 × $2.50 = ($37,500) unfavorable

163. **D.** The difference between the standard hours at standard wage rates and actual hours at standard wage rates is referred to as the direct labor efficiency variance or labor usage variance.

164. **D.** Material Tyrisis experienced a favorable direct materials price variance for the current period. The materials price variance formula is calculated as follows:

Materials price variance = Actual quantity × (Actual price – Standard price)

Materials price variance = 3,500 × ($4.80 – $5)

Materials price variance = $700 favorable

The materials price variance is favorable since less money was actually spent than the standard.

165. **C.** I and II are correct. An unfavorable direct labor efficiency variance could be caused by an unfavorable material usage variance. Poor quality materials could mean unfavorable material usage and cause inefficient labor usage. In addition, the actual hours at the standard rate compared to the standard hours at the standard rate is referred to as the direct labor efficiency variance.

166. **B.** II is correct. Inadequate supervision pertains to management of employees and materials and results in usage variances. I is wrong. Price variances would not be caused by inadequate supervision but rather by purchasing from suppliers other than those offering the most favorable terms, purchasing nonstandard or uneconomical lots, and failing to correctly forecast price increases.

167. **A.** The purchase of higher than standard quality material would likely result in an unfavorable

material price variance (the better material costs more) and a favorable material usage variance (the better material causes less waste).

168. **B.** The direct labor price variance is calculated as follows:

Actual labor price = $840,000 ÷ 84,000 hours =	$10/hour
Standard labor price	– $9/hour
Variance per hour	$1/hour unfavorable
Direct labor hours worked × 84,000	
Direct labor price variance	$84,000 unfavorable

169. **A.** It is an unfavorable direct labor efficiency variance:

Actual direct labor hours worked	84,000
Standard direct labor hours (20,000 actual generators × 4 standard hours)	– 80,000
Excess labor hours	4,000

$9 standard labor rate × 4,000 excess hours = ($36,000) unfavorable direct labor efficiency variance

The variance is unfavorable since more hours were worked than budgeted.

170. **D.** The variance can be calculated as follows:

Standard price	$1.70
Actual price	– $1.85
Difference	$0.15 unfavorable since more was paid than the standard

$0.15 × 59 lbs. actual quantity purchased × 1,750 actual units produced = $15,488 unfavorable

171. **C.** The variance can be calculated as follows:

Standard labor rate	$12 per hour
Actual labor rate	$12.50 per hour

Difference of $0.50 per hour unfavorable
0.5 hour × 3.5 hours per unit × 1,750 actual units = $3,063 variance, unfavorable since Barlow paid more for labor than the standard amount

172. **C.** Overhead is being applied based on a cost driver of $9 per direct labor hour. The overhead efficiency variance compares the amount of the variable overhead applied using standard rates to the amount of variable overhead that would have been applied at actual. If more was applied than would have been incurred, the results are favorable.

Standard hours allowed	11,000
Application rate	× $9
Total standard hours cost	$99,000
Actual hours	10,000
Application rate	× $9
Total actual hours cost	$90,000

9,000 favorable overhead efficiency variance

173. **B.** Selling price variance is the actual selling price less the budgeted selling price times the actual number of units.

    $16 actual selling price – $13 budgeted selling price = $3 favorable selling price

    $3 × 4,000 actual units sold = $12,000 favorable selling price variance

174. **A.** Harper Company's variable overhead spending variance is $200 favorable. Both variable overhead rates are multiplied by the actual cost driver of 50 process hours. The actual overhead rate of $16 times the cost driver of 50 hours equals $800. Next, the standard overhead rate of $20 is multiplied by the actual cost driver of 50 hours to equal $1,000. The actual amount charged to the overhead account ($800) is less than the amount applied ($1,000), so the $200 variance is favorable.

175. **B.** II is correct. Sales volume variance arises when the quantity budgeted to be sold differs from the quantity sold. I is wrong. The sales price variance is based on the actual number of units sold and does not take into account the number of units budgeted to be sold.

176. **D.** The direct materials price variance could be used to monitor the purchasing manager's performance. A and C are wrong. The materials usage variance relates to the amount of materials used and would be influenced most significantly by the production manager, not the purchasing manager. B is wrong. The direct labor rate variance is influenced not by the purchasing manager but by the human resources department.

177. **D.** Benchmarking is a continuous improvement process that compares levels of performance of an entity to best levels of performance. Thus, benchmarking can be best defined as the comparison of existing activities with the best levels of performance in other, similar organizations. A is wrong. Process reengineering involves the complete redesign of a process within an organization. B is wrong. Best practices involves developing the most

effective methods of completing tasks in a particular industry. C is wrong. Continuous improvement is a technique that examines product and process attributes to identify areas for improvements.

178. **D.** I, II, and III are correct. Cost centers are responsible for costs only. Profit centers are responsible for revenues and expenses. Investment centers are responsible for revenues, expenses, and invested capital. Responsibility accounting is a system of accounting that recognizes various responsibility or decision centers throughout an organization and reflects the plans and actions of each of these centers by assigning particular revenues and costs to the one having the responsibility for making decisions about those revenues and costs.

179. **C.** From least to greatest responsibility, the correct order is cost, revenue, profit, and investment capital. Managers in a cost SBU only have responsibility to cut costs, and that is just one dimension of financial performance. Profit SBUs represent a greater responsibility than either cost or revenue SBUs. Profit SBUs require the manager to maintain control of revenues, costs, *and* the relationship between the two. Investment SBUs represent the highest level of responsibility. Managers consider not only cost, revenues, and their relationship, but also the relationship between assets invested and profits generated.

180. **D.** The balanced scorecard demonstrates that no single dimension of organizational performance can be relied upon to evaluate success. The critical success factors are often classified as human resources, business process, customer satisfaction, and financial performance.

181. **D.** I and II are correct. Responsibility accounting defines a profit center as being responsible for both revenues and costs. III is wrong. An investment center is responsible for revenues, costs, and invested capital.

182. **C.** I and II are correct. An investment center is most like an independent business because investment centers are responsible for revenues, expenses, and invested capital.

183. **A.** A performance report shows the budgeted and actual amounts and the variances between these amounts of key financial results appropriate for the type of responsibility center involved. I is correct. Controllable costs, as well as noncontrollable costs, are contained in a performance report for a cost center. II is wrong. Cost centers do not generate

revenues and, therefore, would not have any revenues to include in a performance report.

184. **A.** I is correct. The financial perspective of a balanced scorecard is concerned with the capture of increased market share. II is wrong. The learning and growth (advanced learning and innovation) perspective of a balanced scorecard is concerned with employee satisfaction and retention measures. The balanced scorecard demonstrates that no single dimension of organizational performance can be relied upon to evaluate success; thus, having financial and nonfinancial success factors makes it a "balanced" scorecard.

185. **A.** I is correct. The "internal business" perspective of the balanced scorecard measures results of business operations by improvements in measures of efficiency. II is wrong. Employee satisfaction and retention measures are measured using the "learning and growth" perspective of the balanced scorecard. Employee satisfaction typically correlates with productivity, employee effectiveness, and retention.

186. **A.** II is correct. Measures of financial performance would focus on results of operations and utilization of assets. I is wrong. The customer section of the balanced scorecard would focus on the company's defining its value in the marketplace. III is wrong. Learning and innovation would focus more on the effective use of personnel in improving business processes and linking rewards with recognition.

187. **B.** Controllable margin is computed as contribution margin net of controllable costs. Controllable costs represent those fixed costs that managers can impact in less than one year.

188. **C.** I and II are correct. Controllable margins are specifically defined as contribution margin less controllable fixed costs, and the reporting objective of controllable margin is to clearly define those margins for which a manager is responsible.

Chapter 18: Financial Management

189. **B.** I, II, and III are correct. Differential and incremental costs represent the change in costs associated with two separate courses of action and are considered relevant. Avoidable costs represent the costs that can be averted by selecting different courses of action and are also considered relevant.

190. **C.** III is correct. Sunk costs are unavoidable regardless of whatever alternative is ultimately selected. Since they have already been incurred, sunk costs are not relevant. I is wrong. Discretionary costs arise from periodic budgeting decisions; a company's decision to spend more on research and development is discretionary. Discretionary costs can change, so they are relevant. II is wrong. Opportunity costs are associated with forgoing the next best alternative when making a business decision; therefore, opportunity costs are relevant.

191. **C.** The $111,000 net cash outflow at the beginning of the first year is calculated as follows:

Purchase price	$100,000
Transportation cost	+ $7,000
Installation cost	+ $4,000
Net cash outflow at the beginning of the first year	$111,000

192. **A.** The depreciation can be calculated as follows:

Purchase price	$100,000
Transportation cost	+ $7,000
Installation cost	+ $4,000
Net cash outflow at the beginning of the first year	$111,000

$111,000 \div 7$ years = $15,857

Notice that the asset was depreciated using 7 years rather than 10 years. In capital budgeting decisions, tax depreciation rather than book depreciation is considered relevant because tax depreciation reduces the taxable income, thereby reducing the cash payments for taxes.

193. **B.** The net cash flow can be calculated as follows:

Cash inflow from selling (3,000 units × $300 per unit)	$900,000
Cash outflow for materials and labor (3,000 units × $250 per unit)	– $750,000
Cash inflow from operations	$150,000
Depreciation expense ($111,000 ÷ 7 years)	– $15,857
Taxable income	$134,143
Tax rate	× 30%
Tax to be paid	$40,243
Net cash flow in Year 2 after taxes ($150,000 – $40,243)	$109,757

194. **B.** The net cash flow for Year 10 can be calculated as follows:

Cash inflow from selling	
(3,000 units × $300 per unit)	$900,000
Cash outflow for materials and labor	
(3,000 units × $250 per unit)	– $750,000
Cash inflow from operations	$150,000
Taxes paid at 30%	– $45,000
Cash inflow from operations after taxes	$105,000
Salvage value of equipment in Year 10	$4,000
Taxes paid at 30%	– $1,200
Cash inflow from sale of equipment	
after tax	+ $2,800
Total cash inflow after taxes	
($105,000 + $2,800)	$107,800

The machine is fully depreciated in Year 10 because it was depreciated over a seven-year life. The tax basis of the machine is zero on the date Battaglia receives $4,000 salvage value for the machine. The gain on the machine of $4,000 ($4,000 salvage value – $0 basis) is taxed at 30%, or $1,200 in total tax outflow for the gain. The net inflows on the salvage is $2,800. Therefore, the total after-tax cash flows in Year 10 for the new machine would be $105,000 plus $2,800, or $107,800.

195. **A.** III is correct. Note the question is asking for which is *not* part of net cash outflow. The tax savings from depreciation expense is not a net cash outflow. I and II are wrong. The net cash outflow does include the purchase price, transportation cost, and installation cost.

196. **B.** The tax shield can be calculated as follows:

Cost of the asset	$90,000
Estimated life	÷ 10 years
Annual depreciation	$9,000
Annual depreciation tax shield	
($9,000 × 0.3 tax rate)	$2,700

197. **C.** The zero balance account technique is a cash management technique for cash disbursements whereby, at the end of each day of processing, the bank transfers just enough funds from an entity's master account to cover all checks presented against the zero balance account that day. This allows an entity to maintain higher cash balances in its master account, which can be used for short-term investing. A is wrong. Depository transfer checks are checks used by a designated collection bank for depositing the daily receipts of an entity from multiple locations. They are used in connection with concentration banking, which is a cash

management technique. B is wrong. A lockbox system is a cash receipts technique that expedites the funds availability of customer payments received by an entity. It involves having customers remit their payments to a post office box that is managed and maintained by a bank, whose personnel remove envelopes from the mailbox and immediately deposit the check payments in the entity's account. This is a particularly useful technique for entities that do business nationwide. D is wrong. Concentration banking is a cash receipts technique whereby payments from customers are routed to a firm's local branch offices rather than to the firm's headquarters. The branch office deposits the checks at a local bank, and then surplus funds are transferred to the firm's primary bank periodically. This technique helps expedite the collection of customer payments.

198. **D.** The original fair market value of the old equipment is a sunk cost that is irrelevant since it does not affect equipment replacement decisions. The items listed in II, III, and IV do affect the decision process.

199. **C.** Opportunity cost is the potential benefit lost by selecting a particular course of action. If the land is developed rather than sold, giving up the potential selling price of the land is an opportunity cost. A is wrong. Sunk costs are those costs that have already been incurred, are unavoidable in the future, and are not relevant in the decision. B and D are wrong. Incremental costs and variable costs are costs of production that change in total as more units are produced.

200. **D.** The original cost of the old machine, $40,000, is a sunk cost that will not change regardless of the decision that is made. Sunk costs are not relevant and would not be considered by Aron as part of the decision to keep or replace the current machine.

201. **B.** I, II, and III are correct. The estimated salvage value of the old machine is relevant to the decision to keep or replace the machine. The salvage value will be realized if the machine is replaced but not realized if the machine is not replaced. The lower maintenance cost of the new machine is also relevant to the decision to keep or replace the old machine. The maintenance cost of the new machine will impact the comparative operating costs of the company and would be considered in the decision. Finally, the estimated salvage value and estimated useful life of the new machine would be relevant to the decision to keep or replace the old machine.

202. D. The calculation is as follows:

Sales	$370,000
Variable costs	− $290,000
Cash inflows	$80,000
Tax rate 40%	− $32,000
Cash inflows net of tax	$48,000
Initial investment	$250,000
Useful life	10 years
Depreciation expense ($25,000 × 40%)	$10,000*

Cash inflows of $48,000 plus depreciation tax shield of $10,000 equals after-tax cash inflows of $58,000.

203. C. I and III are correct. The decision to replace the old asset will result in the company paying the purchase price of the new asset, receiving the disposal price of the old asset, and recognizing a gain and paying taxes on the sale of the old asset based on cost less accumulated depreciation. II is wrong. Costs are deemed to be relevant if they change as a result of selecting different alternatives. The cost of the old asset will not change based on the decision to replace it. The cost of the old asset is a sunk cost and is not relevant to the decision on whether to replace it.

204. A. The gain is calculated as follows:

Selling price	$13,300
Cost of the old asset less accumulated depreciation ($40,000 − $32,000)	− $8,000
Gain	$5,300
Multiplied by tax rate of 30%	= $1,590

With a tax rate of 30%, the additional taxes of $1,590 paid on the gain would be relevant to the decision whether to buy the new asset.

205. A. I is correct. The annual net cash inflow includes the dollar amount of cash inflow times 1 minus the tax rate. II is wrong. Annual net cash inflow includes the depreciation expense times the tax rate. Although depreciation expense is not a cash expense, there is a cash inflow from depreciation. The depreciation expense on the tax return times the tax rate equals the annual depreciation tax shield, which is an additional cash inflow.

206. A. The net present value method of capital budgeting requires managers to evaluate the dollar amount of return rather than years to recover principal (payback method) or percentages of return (internal rate of return) as a means to screen investments. B is wrong. The internal rate of return focuses the

*Tax shield from noncash expense

decision maker on the discount rate at which the present value of the cash inflows equals the initial investment. C is wrong. The payback method takes the total investment in a project and divides it by its annual cash flows to determine the number of years it will take to gain a return of the initial investment.

207. C. I and II are correct. Net present value is flexible and can be used when there is a different rate of return for each year of the project. If the cash inflows were not the same each year, the cash inflows would have to be multiplied by the present value of $1 (rather than the present value of an annuity). Although the net present value method does not provide the true rate of return on the investment, the net present value method indicates whether an investment will earn the hurdle rate of return. A positive net present value dollar amount indicates that the investment will earn the hurdle rate of return and the investment should be made. A negative net present value dollar amount indicates that the investment will *not* earn the hurdle rate and the project should be rejected.

208. B. The net present value is calculated as follows:

Year	Cash Inflows		Present Value Factor		Net Present Value
1	$120,000	×	0.91	=	$109,200
2	$60,000	×	0.76	=	$45,600
3	$40,000	×	0.63	=	$25,200
4	$40,000	×	0.53	=	$21,200
5	$40,000	×	0.44	=	$17,600
Total					$218,800

$218,800 present value of cash inflows − $210,000 initial outlay = $8,800 net present value

The present value of $1 is used rather than the present value of an annuity because the annual cash flows are not the same.

209. B. II is correct. If the present value of cash outflows is less than the present value of cash inflows, then the net present value is positive and the rate of return for the project is more than the discount percentage rate (hurdle rate). I is wrong. If the net present value of a project is positive, it would indicate that the rate of return for the project is greater than the discount percentage rate (hurdle rate) used in the net present value computation.

210. **B.** Net present value is computed as the difference between project inflows and outflows, discounted to present value as follows:

Inflows Years 1 through 5:
   $430,000 × 3.83 = $1,646,900
Year 6 inflow: $90,000 × 0.59 = $53,100

Present value of all inflows	$1,700,000
Outflow (today, discount factor of 1.0)	− $1,750,000
Net present value	($50,000)

211. **C.** I and II are correct. When the cash flows are the same for both years, use an annuity factor. To calculate the present value of the savings for Years 1 and 2, the factor for the present value of an annuity of $1 for two periods is used. To calculate the present value of the savings for Year 3, the factor for the lump sum of a present value of $1 for three periods is required because an annuity factor cannot be used for Year 3 since the amount of savings is not the same as Years 1 and 2.

212. **B.** The internal rate of return method determines the present value factor and related interest rate that yields a net present value equal to zero. The internal rate of return focuses the decision maker on the discount rate at which the present value of the cash inflows equals the initial investment. A is wrong. Net present value is computed as the difference between project inflows and outflows, discounted to present value. C is wrong. The profitability index is used for capital rationing. The profitability index is the ratio of the present value of the cash inflows to the present value of the net initial investment. Limited capital resources are applied in order of the index until either resources are exhausted or the investment required by the next project exceeds remaining resources.

213. **B.** I and II are correct. The internal rate of return method determines the present value factor and related interest rate that yields a net present value equal to zero. In addition, the internal rate of return focuses the decision maker on the discount rate at which the present value of the cash inflows equals the initial investment. III is wrong. Projects with an internal rate of return greater than the hurdle rate should be accepted, as they add value to the firm.

214. **A.** I is correct. One of the major strengths of the payback method is that it is easy to understand. The payback method takes the total investment in a project and divides it by its annual cash flows to determine the number of years it will take to gain a return of the initial investment. II is wrong. The payback method does *not* consider the time value of money and, while that is a characteristic of the payback method, it is viewed as a limitation of the payback method and *not* an advantage.

215. **A.** I is correct. When using the net present value method of capital budgeting, different hurdle rates can be used for each year of the project. II is wrong. Both the net present value method and the internal rate of return model are discounted cash flow methods.

216. **D.** I and II are wrong. The tax depreciation allowance will provide a tax savings, sometimes called a tax shield, that impacts cash flow and must be considered in the net present value analysis. Added working capital requirements will affect cash flow. If supplies need to be purchased to support a new machine, this would reduce cash flow.

217. **A.** I, II, and III are correct. The discounted cash flow model is the best for long-term decisions. Discounted cash flow methods include the net present value, internal rate of return, and profitability index. The profitability index is most useful when funds are limited and projects must be selected based on highest returns.

218. **A.** The capital asset pricing model is one method for estimating the cost of common equity and is computed using the risk-free interest rate, the stock's beta coefficient, and the estimated return on the market: risk-free rate + (estimated rate of return on the market − risk-free rate) × the beta coefficient. B is wrong. The constant growth model is used to determine the intrinsic value of common stock based on a future series of dividends that grow at a constant rate. It requires three inputs: dividends per share, growth rate in dividends, and required rate of return. C is wrong. The net present value model is not one used for calculating the cost of common stock; rather, it is a model used to assist in making decisions about what investment projects should and should not be accepted or pursued based on an evaluation of the initial investment and the present value of net cash savings or inflows expected over the life of the project. D is wrong. The weighted marginal cost of capital is not a method for calculating the cost of common stock. Instead it presents a weighting of the cost (to an entity) to raise one additional dollar of each different form of capital (e.g., debt, common stock, preferred stock).

219. B. Profitability index is measured as:

Present value of net future cash inflows ÷ Present value of net initial investment

Companies hope that this ratio will be higher than 1.0, which means that the present value of the inflows is greater than the present value of the outflows. The profitability index is useful when funds are limited and capital rationing needs to be considered.

220. B. With even cash flows, payback period is calculated as initial cost divided by annual net cash inflows, or $600,000 ÷ $220,000 = 2.73.

221. D. I and II are correct. The payback period computation ignores cash flows after the initial investment has been recovered. The payback method focuses on liquidity and the time it takes to recover the initial investment. The discounted payback period considers the time value of money, but, like any other payback method, it ignores cash flows after the initial investment has been recovered. III is wrong. The net present value method measures the amount of absolute return and, as a result, focuses on cash flows both before and after payback.

222. A. I is correct. The common disadvantage of all capital budgeting models is their reliance on an uncertain future. Capital financing relates to longer periods of time that are subject to greater levels of uncertainty than other, short-term budgeting decisions. II is wrong. The net present value method and internal rate of return do consider the time value of money, and because this is a characteristic of the net present value method and internal rate of return, this is considered an advantage of those methods rather than a limitation.

223. D. The discounted payback period is computed as follows:

Year	Net Cash Flows	Factor	PV	Cumulative Payback
1	$9,000	0.943	$8,487	$8,487
2	$15,000	0.841	$12,615	$21,102
3	$19,000	0.776	$14,744	$35,846
4	$25,000	0.719	$17,975	$53,821

Note that the cumulative payback after Year 3 is $35,846. The portion of the fourth year needed to fully pay back the $46,000 cost is computed as the ratio of the amount remaining to be recovered to the amount collected in the fourth year as follows:

$46,000 − $35,846 = $10,154
$10,154 ÷ $17,975 = 0.564

The discounted payback period is:

Years 1–3	3 years
Year 4	+ 0.564 year
Total	3.564 years

224. B. The internal rate of return is often calculated using trial and error by dividing the investment by the cash inflows to equal a desired present value factor. The internal rate of return is the present value factor that will equate cash inflows to cash outflows. A is wrong. The net present value is calculated by subtracting cash outflows from cash inflows; the net present value would only be zero if the cash inflows equal the cash outflows. C is wrong. The payback method is not a discounted cash flow method. This method focuses on liquidity and the time it takes to recover the initial investment. D is wrong. Accounting rate of return is not a discounted cash flow method. Based on accrual income rather than cash flows, it does not consider the time value of money and is considered inferior to the discounted cash flow methods.

225. D. I and II are correct. The net present value method assumes that positive cash flows are reinvested at the hurdle rate, thereby considering compounding. The net present value method also measures the value of capital investments in dollars and considers the time value of money. III is wrong. Net present value uses the cash basis, not the accrual basis.

226. A. I is correct. The payback (and discounted payback) method neglects total project profitability. Payback methods simply look at the time required to recover the initial investment; subsequent cash flows are ignored. II is wrong. The net present value method is useful in calculating the total project profitability. Simply subtract the cash outflows (often just the initial investment) from the present value of the cash inflows.

227. D. I and III are correct. Taking the total investment and dividing by annual cash flows is useful to determine the payback period. The profitability index can be calculated by dividing the present value of total net future cash inflows by the present value of net cash outflows.

228. B. The calculation is as follows:

Salvage value expected cash inflow ($15,000 × 0.618)	$9,270
Operating expected cash inflows ($20,000 × 3.847)	+ $76,940
Present value total cash inflows	$86,210

The present value of the cash inflows is $86,210. Cash flows received annually and evenly are discounted using the present value of an annuity, while single cash inflows are discounted using the present value of $1.

229. D. Net present value is computed as the difference between the present value of the initial cash outflows of the investment and the present value of the cash inflows from the project. Cash flows received annually and evenly are discounted using the present value of an annuity, while single cash inflows are discounted using the present value of $1. Net present value is calculated as follows:

Salvage value ($15,000 × 0.618)	$9,270
Annual cash inflows ($20,000 × 3.847)	+ $76,940
Present value total cash inflows	$86,210
Present value cash outflow	− $90,000
Total net present value	($3,790)

This investment would *not* add value to the firm and should be rejected. Note that present value figures ignore net income and instead focus on cash flow information.

230. A. The net present value is $27,250 with no salvage value. The only cash flows that are relevant are:

$125,000 × 4.698 present value of five-year annuity discounted at 7% = $587,250

$587,250 − $560,000 investment = $27,250 net present value

The net present value is positive, so the asset should be acquired, as it is expected to add value to the firm.

231. A. The net present value of an investment is equal to the discounted after-tax cash flows from the investment minus the initial cost of the investment. In this question, the discounted cash flows are $237,992 and the investment was $244,500, yielding a negative (unsatisfactory) net present value of $6,508.

232. A. The internal rate of return is the rate that provides a zero net present value. The internal rate of return is equal to the discount rate at which the net present value of the investment is equal to zero. The $218,340 present value of after-tax cash flows

associated with the investment discounted at 9.5% is equal to the cost of the investment, also given at $218,340. The internal rate of return, therefore, is 9.5% because at a rate of 9.5%, the investment neither makes money nor loses money on a cash flow basis. Note that often the internal rate of return needs to be calculated by trial and error, but in this question, as often happens on the exam, enough information to find the answer is given, although several distracting pieces of useless information were also included.

233. D. I is correct. Advance determination of management's required return is integral to the development and evaluation of net present value. Project cash flows are discounted based upon a predetermined rate and compared to the investment in the project. The difference is expressed as a positive or negative amount. II is wrong. Internal rate of return is evaluated in relation to management's required hurdle rate after the computation of net present value is done. III is wrong. The accounting rate of return computes a percentage return based upon accrual basis data and does not require a predetermined discount rate.

234. A. Operating leverage is defined as the degree to which a firm uses fixed operating costs as opposed to variable operating costs. A firm that has high operating leverage has high fixed operating costs and relatively low variable operating costs. A firm with high operating leverage (high fixed costs) must produce enough revenue to cover all those fixed costs. Once a firm with high operating leverage covers those high fixed costs, additional revenue should go straight to operating income since variable costs are so low. B is wrong. Operating leverage is defined as the degree to which a firm uses fixed operating costs as opposed to variable operating costs. C is wrong. Combined (total) leverage (not operating leverage) results from the use of both fixed operating costs and fixed financing costs to magnify returns to the firm's owners. D is wrong. Financial leverage (not operating leverage) is defined as the degree to which a firm uses debt to finance the firm.

235. B. A firm's degree of operating leverage is calculated by dividing the percentage change in earnings before interest and taxes (EBIT) by percentage change in sales. Operating leverage is defined as the degree to which a firm uses fixed operating costs as opposed to variable operating costs. A firm that has high operating leverage has high fixed operating costs and relatively low variable operating costs and uses this cost structure to amplify the financial results of each additional dollar in sales. For example: If a firm experiences a 33% increase in EBIT as a result of an 11% increase in sales, the firm's operating leverage is 3. When a firm has high operating leverage, a small increase in revenue can lead to a large increase in profit since fixed costs remain the same.

236. **C.** A firm's degree of financial leverage is calculated by taking the percent change in earnings per share divided by the percent change in earnings before interest and taxes. Financial leverage is defined as the degree to which a firm uses debt to finance the firm. B is wrong. A firm's degree of operating leverage, not financial leverage, is calculated by dividing the percentage change in EBIT by the percentage change in sales.

237. **A.** I is correct. When a firm has a relatively high degree of operating leverage, a small increase in sales can lead to a large increase in profit because fixed costs remain the same over a relevant range. II is wrong. When a firm has a relatively high degree of operating leverage, variable operating costs are low, not high, relative to fixed operating costs; therefore, a small increase in sales could lead to a large increase in profit because fixed costs would be covered already.

238. **A.** I is correct. Financial leverage is defined as the degree to which a firm uses debt to finance the firm. II is wrong. Operating leverage is defined as the degree to which a firm relies on fixed operating costs as opposed to variable operating costs.

239. **D.** The formula for calculating operating leverage is:

Percent change in earnings before interest and taxes divided by the percent change in sales

From the information given:

$24 \div x$ = degree of operating leverage of 4
x = 6% increase in sales revenue

240. **C.** I and II are correct. Company A has a higher degree of operating leverage than company B. Company A has lower variable operating costs and higher fixed operating costs compared to company B. Calculation of degree of operating leverage for company A = 3:

Increase in EBIT 18 divided by increase in sales 6

Degree of operating leverage for company B = 2

Calculated as:

Increase in EBIT 10 divided by increase in sales 5

241. **C.** I and II are correct. A high degree of operating leverage implies that a relatively small change in sales, an increase or decrease, will have a greater effect on profits and shareholder value. The higher the firm's degree of operating leverage, the greater its potential profitability, but also the greater the risk because it must cover a high fixed cost just to break even. But once it breaks even, sales mean profits!

242. **B.** Multiplying the operating leverage times the financial leverage equals the combined leverage. Another way of calculating combined leverage is to divide percent change in earnings per share by percent change in sales. A is wrong. Multiply (don't add) the operating leverage times the financial leverage to get total combined leverage. C is wrong. Dividing the percent change in earnings before interest and taxes by percent change in sales will result in the operating leverage. D is wrong. Dividing the percent change in earnings per share by the percent change in EBIT is the financial leverage.

243. **B.** I is correct. Financial leverage is defined as the degree to which a firm uses debt to finance the firm. II is wrong. Operating leverage is defined as the degree to which a firm uses fixed operating costs as opposed to variable operating costs. III is wrong. Combined (total) leverage results from the use of both fixed operating costs and fixed financing costs to magnify returns to the firm's owners.

244. **D.** The cost of debt capital is computed on an after-tax basis because interest expense is tax deductible. The cost of debt is computed on an after-tax basis using the effective interest rate instead of the coupon rate:

Effective interest rate 13% × 0.6* = 7.8%

245. **B.** The calculation is as follows:

Weighted average cost of debt capital = 30% weight × 10% interest cost

0.1 × (1 − 0.25) = 7.5% × 30% weight = 2.25% cost of debt capital

The optimal cost of capital is the ratio of debt to equity that produces the lowest weighted average cost of capital (WACC). Required rates of return by debt and equity holders fluctuate as the ratio of debt to equity changes.

246. **D.** Weighted average cost of 10% preferred stock × 10% weight = 1%.

247. **A.** Weighted average cost of common stock is equal to its 60% weight × 0.1 = 6%.

*1 − 0.4 tax rate = 0.6

248. **C.** The weighted average cost of capital is 9.25 percent, calculated as follows:

Weighted average cost of debt capital = 30% weight × 10% interest cost

$0.1 × (1 − 0.25) = 7.5\% × 30\%$ weight = 2.25% cost of debt capital

Weighted average cost of 10% preferred stock × 10% weight = 1%

Weighted average cost of common stock is equal to its 60% weight × 0.1 = 6%

Total weighted average cost of capital = 9.25%

To maximize shareholder wealth, the company will most likely establish a hurdle rate that will limit acceptance of projects to only those with minimum returns greater than the WACC of 9.25%.

249. **C.** I and II are correct. The weighted average cost of capital is the average cost of debt plus the average cost of equity financing given the firm's existing assets and operations. The weighted average cost of capital is determined by weighing each specific type of capital by its proportion to the firm's total capital structure.

250. **C.** I and II are correct. The optimal cost of capital is the ratio of debt to equity that produces the lowest WACC. Required rates of return by debt and equity holders fluctuate as the ratio of debt to equity changes. At some point as total debt increases in relation to equity, investors will demand a greater return because the risk of default on the debt increases. With that risk, the creditors will demand a premium in the form of higher returns.

251. **C.** The risk-free rate is 5%, and the market return is 12%. If you invested in the stock market, you would demand a premium of 7% beyond the risk-free rate, but the 7% market premium is only correct if the stock had a beta equal to the overall market, 1.0. Since the beta for this stock is less than 1.0, multiply the beta for the stock, which is 0.95, by the market risk premium of 7%, and 6.65% is the market risk premium for this stock. Then add the risk-free rate of 5%; the appropriate rate of return for this stock is 11.65%.

$5\% + 0.95 (12\% − 5\%)$
$= 5\% + (0.95 × 7\%)$
$= 5\% + 6.65\% = 11.65\%$

252. **B.** II is correct. Interest expense is a tax deduction; therefore, the cost to Valley Corp. is lower than the market yield rate on debt. I is wrong. If market interest rates increase, then Valley's bonds would have to be offered at a discount to stay competitive with the market. This discount would increase (not lower) Valley's cost of debt.

253. **A.** The risk-free rate is 7% and the market return is estimated at 12.4%. If you invested in the stock market, you would demand a premium of 5.4%, but a 5.4% premium is not good enough for this stock because the beta for this stock is 1.2. Multiply the 5.4% market risk premium by the 1.2 beta; the appropriate risk premium for this stock is 6.48%. Take the 6.48% and add the risk-free rate of 7%; the appropriate rate of return for this stock is 13.48%.

Cost of retained earnings = $0.07 + 1.2 (0.124 − 0.07)$
$1.2 × 0.054 = 0.0648$
$0.07 + 0.0648 = 13.48\%$

254. **C.** I and II are correct. The capital asset pricing model is used to calculate cost of retained earnings (cost of common equity). The discounted cash flow model also is used to calculate the cost of common equity. The forecasted dividend is divided by the current market price and then a growth rate is added.

255. **A.** 14%. Using the discounted cash flow (DCF) method, the cost of equity is computed as follows:

Cost of equity = Expected dividend ÷ Current share price + Growth rate

$(\$4 ÷ \$50) + 0.06 = 0.08 + 0.06 = 0.14$

Note that the cost of equity is not computed on an after-tax basis. Dividends are not tax deductible. Also, if the dividend given was the "current dividend" rather than the "next dividend," then to determine the numerator, the current dividend would need to be multiplied by the dividend growth rate of 6% because the numerator is the forecasted dividend rather than the current dividend.

256. **B.** The current ratio is found by dividing current assets by current liabilities. The result is a measure of a firm's ability to pay short-term obligations as they become due. When a firm cannot meet current obligations as they become due, the firm can be forced into bankruptcy by its creditors. For this reason, the current ratio is seen as a critical measure of a firm's liquidity.

257. **B.** II is correct. Declaring a stock dividend would only impact the stockholders' equity section of the balance sheet. I is wrong. The current ratio is current assets divided by current liabilities. The sale of equipment would increase cash and, therefore, increase current assets without increasing current

liabilities. As a result, the sale of equipment would increase the current ratio.

258. **C.** Net working capital is the difference between current assets and current liabilities. Current assets went up $100,000, so working capital increases. Current liabilities went down by $35,000, also increasing working capital. The net effect is an increase in net working capital of $135,000.

259. **D.** Return on investment (ROI) is the ratio of operating income to average operating assets. The denominator is beginning operating assets plus ending operating assets divided by 2. Although simple to calculate, ROI is not the best measure of investment performance, because ROI sometimes encourages shortsighted behavior that defers or avoids investment with a (low) positive return for the sake of current ROI performance.

260. **B.** Return on investment for Year 5 is equal to:

Operating income for Year 5
($200,000* ÷ $1,100,000**)   18.18%

261. **A.** When calculating return on investments (ROI), the higher the denominator, the lower the return. In calculating ROI, the denominator is average assets. Using replacement cost to value average assets will better compare company A to company B because replacement cost ignores age of assets and method of depreciation. B is wrong. Per GAAP rules, the net book value can be used, but that would be skewed by age of assets and method of depreciation. A company using accelerated depreciation would have a lower book value and, therefore, higher return. C is wrong. Gross book value would ignore the method of depreciation but still would be skewed by age of assets. A company with fully depreciated older assets would have a lower denominator and, therefore, a higher return. D is wrong. You should probably use liquidation value if the companies are going bankrupt, but there is no evidence that these companies are going bankrupt.

262. **B.** II is correct. Using the residual income method, net income per the income statement is compared to the required rate of return. The result is the dollar amount of residual income. Residual income is the excess of net income over the desired amount of return for the project or investment center. I is

wrong. Return on investment (ROI) calculates a percentage return, not a dollar amount of return. Although ROI is simple to calculate, there is a weakness of using it to evaluate the performance of investment center managers. The weakness is that ROI may lead to managers rejecting projects that yield positive cash flows yet have a low ROI percentage. Profitable investment center managers might be reluctant to invest in projects that might lower their ROI (especially if their bonuses are based only on their investment center's ROI), even though those projects might generate positive cash flows for the company as a whole. This characteristic is often known as the "disincentive to invest." Therefore, a different method of rating an investment center manager's performance, known as the residual income method, is often used instead of ROI.

263. **B.** Residual income is the difference between net income and the required return. The required return is net book value (total assets) times the hurdle rate (required rate of return). The calculations are as follows:

Division	Operating Income	Total Assets x Required Rate	Residual Net Income
J	$150	$1,000 × 0.09 = $90	$60
K	$300	$1,200 × 0.09 = $108	$192
Totals	$450	$198	$252

264. **A.** The calculation is as follows:

Divisional revenues	$1,000,000
Divisional expenses	− $600,000
Divisional income	$400,000
Division assets	$2,000,000
Required return	× 15%
Hurdle	($300,000)
Residual income	$100,000
Bonus rate	× 25%
Bonus amount	$25,000

265. **A.** I is correct. Economic value added (EVA) is essentially similar to the residual income method, as both measure investment performance in terms of dollars rather than percentages using net income minus the desired return. The difference between the two is what is being used as the hurdle rate to determine desired return. II is wrong. Using EVA, the hurdle rate must be the weighted average cost of capital. Note that EVA makes for a more objective measure of investment performance than residual

---

*$900,000 − $700,000 = $200,000

**$1,100,000 is average operating assets, calculated as ($900,000 + $1,300,000) ÷ 2 = $1,100,000

income, because using the residual income method, the hurdle rate can be set by management or management can use the weighted average cost of capital as the hurdle rate. Using residual income, judgment may need to be used if the hurdle rate set by management is too high or too low. The weakness of residual income compared to EVA is that if management sets the hurdle rate, management needs to use judgment to set a hurdle rate that is achievable to motivate the investment manager. Using EVA, this is not a problem, because EVA relies on WACC as the hurdle rate, and WACC is more objective for determining the hurdle rate than simply allowing management to set the hurdle rate.

266. **D.** The return on assets ratio measures the percentage return (income) generated on the available assets. It is, therefore, a measure that would be most appropriate to compare the profitability of two manufacturing (or other profit-generating) companies that differ in size. A is wrong. The current ratio is a measure of short-term liquidity computed by dividing current assets by current liabilities. It is not a profitability measure. B is wrong. The quick (acid-test) ratio is also a short-term liquidity measure, although a more stringent one than the current ratio. Its computation is similar to the current ratio but subtracts inventory from current assets in the numerator. C is wrong. Asset turnover is an activity ratio that measures the efficiency with which a firm uses its assets.

267. **C.** I and II are correct. The WACC is frequently used as the hurdle rate within capital budgeting techniques. Investments that provide a return that exceeds the WACC should continuously add value to the firm. WACC is most commonly compared to the internal rate of return to evaluate whether to make an investment. The internal rate of return is the rate of return that sets cash outflows to cash inflows.

268. **C.** I and II are correct. Increased economic uncertainty would cause a firm to decrease debt (and interest cost), so decreased economic uncertainty would provide the incentive for firms to borrow more. An increase in the corporate income tax rate might cause a firm to increase the debt in its financial structure because interest is tax deductible, while dividends are not.

269. **A.** I is correct. The optimal capital structure is the mix of financing instruments that produces the lowest WACC. A company with a low WACC is attractive to potential shareholders. II is wrong. The

company's borrowing rate is a component of the WACC, along with the cost of common stock, preferred stock, and retained earnings. At some point as the debt to equity ratio increases, investors will demand a greater return as leverage becomes more pronounced and debtors will require compensation for the high level of default risk.

270. **D.** I and II are wrong. Not a decrease but rather an increase in the cost of carrying inventory would lead to a reduction in average inventory. For example, dairy products are required to be refrigerated so that they will not spoil. If electricity prices are rising, management would prefer to have a lower inventory of fresh dairy products on hand because of the electricity (i.e., carrying) cost of the items. Increased demand would likely increase average inventory to avoid the cost of running out of desired items, known as stockout costs.

271. **C.** I and II are correct. A quick ratio is a measure of a firm's liquidity. Quick ratio is current assets minus inventory divided by current liabilities. Quick ratio recognizes the fact that inventory cannot be used to pay bills. Quick ratio is a better measure of liquidity than current ratio because it shows how a firm can satisfy current obligations without packaging up inventory and sending it to creditors to settle debts. A company's average collection period is used to evaluate the liquidity of the firm through the calculation of the cash conversion cycle.

272. **D.** The quick (acid-test) ratio is a measure of short-term liquidity and is computed as follows: (current assets − inventory) ÷ current liabilities. Therefore, if a company had a quick (acid-test) ratio of 2.0, and its current assets and inventory were $5,000 and $2,000, respectively, its current liabilities (solving for x) would have to be $1,500 ([$5,000 − $2,000] ÷ x) = 2.0; x = $1,500).

273. **D.** The current ratio = current assets divided by current liabilities. A transaction that produces an equal increase in both the numerator and denominator of a current ratio that is less than 1.0 increases the current ratio. In this question, the existing current ratio is $400,000 (current assets) divided by $500,000 (current liabilities), which is 0.8 (less than 1.0). Thus, purchasing $100,000 of inventory on accounts payable, which increases both the current assets (purchase of inventory increases current assets) and current liabilities (purchasing inventory on accounts payable increases accounts payable and, therefore, current liabilities) in an equal amount, increases the current ratio. This

can be further displayed in the following computation: new current assets = $400,000 + $100,000 (inventory purchase) = $500,000; new current liabilities = $500,000 + $100,000 (additional accounts payable) = $600,000; $500,000 ÷ $600,000 = 0.83. which is greater than the initial 0.8 current ratio measure.

274. **C.** The average accounts receivable collection period (also referred to as days' sales outstanding in receivables) can be calculated as follows: 365 days ÷ accounts receivable turnover. The accounts receivable turnover calculation = net credit sales ÷ average accounts receivable. In order to derive Light Year's accounts receivable collection period, the company's accounts receivable turnover must first be computed. Net credit sales = 20,000 × $25,000 = $500,000,000; $500,000,000 ÷ $30,000,000 (average accounts receivable) = 16.67. This measures the number of times Light Year turned over (or converted its accounts receivable to cash) in the year. Light Year's average accounts receivable collection period is, therefore, 22 days: 365 days ÷ 16.67 = 21.90 days (which can be rounded to 22 days). This measure represents the number of days between the time of sale and receipt of payment for the telescopes.

275. **C.** The calculation for WACC is:

Preferred equity 20% weight, 9% yield	1.8%
Common equity 40% weight, 12% yield	+ 4.8%
Debt 40% × 6% × (1 − 0.3)	+ 1.7%
WACC	8.3%

276. **A.** I is correct. A company's debt to total capital ratio includes in the denominator interest-bearing debt plus equity. II is wrong. Non–interest-bearing debt is not included in the denominator of the debt to total capital ratio. Debt to total capital ratio equals debt divided by interest-bearing debt plus equity.

277. **A.** I is correct. The quick ratio is current assets minus inventory divided by current liabilities. Purchasing inventory through the issuance of long-term notes would have no impact on the quick ratio. Inventory is excluded from the numerator of the quick ratio, and long-term debt is excluded from the denominator of the quick ratio. II is wrong. Selling inventory would increase the quick ratio. The addition of cash would increase the numerator with no impact on current liabilities.

278. **C.** The calculation is as follows:

$180,000 × 0.11 = $19,800 interest paid

$19,800 interest paid ÷ $180,000 loan × 0.8 net of 20% compensating balance = $144,000 net proceeds.

Therefore $19,800 ÷ $144,000 = 13.75%.

When a bank requires a 20% compensating balance, the net proceeds are only 80% of the loan.

279. **D.** II is correct. The growth rate of earnings is *not* part of the calculation of cost of equity. Three elements are needed to calculate the cost of equity capital: current dividends, market price of stock, and growth rate in dividends (not growth rate in earnings). A firm's cost of equity represents the compensation that the market demands in exchange for bearing the risk of ownership.

280. **D.** The calculation for cost of equity capital is:

$2 expected dividend next period ÷ $20 stock price	10%
Growth rate	+ 11.5%
Cost of equity capital	21.5%

281. **B.** The current ratio is current assets divided by current liabilities. The sale of property, plant, and equipment would increase cash and, therefore, current assets without increasing current liabilities. This would increase the current ratio. Furthermore, the sale of equipment at a loss would decrease net income.

282. **B.** Average inventory is computed as the sum of beginning and ending inventory divided by 2, as follows:

($350,500 + $259,100) ÷ 2 = $304,800

Inventory turnover is the ratio of cost of goods sold to average inventory, computed as follows:

Cost of Goods Sold	Average Inventory	Inventory Turnover
$1,500,000	÷ $304,800	= 4.92

283. **C.** Cost savings would be calculated by dividing cost of goods sold by actual inventory turnover and then by desired inventory turnover, as follows:

$3,800,000 ÷ 7 =	$542,857
$3,800,000 ÷ 9 =	− $422,222
Inventory decrease	$120,635
Interest rate	× 6%
Cost savings	$7,238

284. A. Annual percentage cost of not taking the discount is equal to 360 divided by the (total pay period minus the discount period) times discount divided by (100% minus discount).

$360/(30 - 10) \times 4\%/(100\% - 4\%)$
$= 360/20 \times 4\%/(96\%)$
$= 18 \times 4.17\% = 75.06\%$

Note that the formula to determine the cost of not paying within the discount period appears above. The formula would be the same if calculating the cost of offering a discount to customers in exchange for their quick payment.

285. D. Annual cost of not taking the discount is equal to 360 divided by the (total pay period minus the discount period) times discount divided by (100% minus discount).

$360/(30 - 10) \times 3\%/(100\% - 3\%)$
$= 360/20 \times 3.09\%$
$= 18 \times 3.09\% = 55.62\%$

The formula to determine the cost of not paying within the discount period would be the same if calculating the cost of offering a discount.

286. B. A lockbox system generally relates to expediting deposits over a specific group of transactions. The technique arranges for the direct mailing of customers' remittances to a bank's post office box and subsequent deposit. A is wrong. Concentration banking is the method by which a single bank is designated as a central bank. Concentration banking improves controls. Having all bank accounts in a single bank makes it easier to keep track of inflows and outflows. C is wrong. Zero balance banking doesn't control cash receipts; instead it represents an account that maintains a zero balance like a payroll account that receives money from a master account in time for employees to be paid and otherwise contains a zero balance. Zero balance banking serves to maximize the availability of idle cash, not control receipts. D is wrong. Compensating balances do not establish better control over cash receipts. Compensating balances are minimum balances maintained by a customer of a bank to avoid bank charges or eliminate fees for credit lines.

287. D. Using the lockbox produces a savings of $10,000 per year, as calculated below:

Lockbox cost	– $50,000
Investment income	+ $60,000*
Savings per year	$10,000

---
*$60,000 = (3 days ÷ 360 days) × $80,000,000 × 0.09

With a lockbox system, customers of the firm mail checks directly to the bank. Banks will charge a fee. The benefit is that the money immediately begins earning interest. A lockbox is a way to get paid sooner, but only use a lockbox if the interest income exceeds the bank fees.

288. B. The calculation is as follows:

Average daily cash outflows	$1,000,000
Days added to disbursement schedule	× 3
Excess funds	$3,000,000
Interest rate on excess funds	× 6%
Maximum allowable cost	$180,000

289. B. A company's cash conversion cycle is the average number of days to create cash from core operations. The formula for cash conversion cycle is number of days to sell inventory (low number!) plus number of days to collect (hopefully another low number!) minus the number of days to pay vendor (high number!). The cash conversion cycle is the sum of the inventory conversion and receivable collection periods minus the payables deferral period. A lower cash conversion cycle is better than a higher cycle.

290. A. I and II are correct. Decreasing inventory conversion and accounts receivable collection periods indicate that cash is being collected more quickly than last year from sales of inventory and from faster collections of accounts receivable. III is wrong. An increasing deferral period on payables indicates that the cash disbursements are being deferred (held as long as possible).

291. A. A higher inventory turnover from one year to the next means a lower inventory conversion. That is a positive since it takes fewer days in Year 2 to move inventory compared to Year 1. In the following example, all numbers are in millions:

Year 1	Cost of goods sold 27 ÷ 5 average inventory
Inventory turnover	5.4×
Year 1 conversion	365 days ÷ 5.4× = 67.6 days to sell inventory in Year 1

Year 2—For turnover to be higher in Year 2, let's say average inventory falls to $4 million from $5 million.

Cost of goods sold	$27
Average inventory	$4

Result would be a higher annual turnover of 6.75× (good news) and a lower inventory conversion period, 365 ÷ 6.75 = 54.07. This means that it took only 54 days to sell inventory in Year 2 compared to 67 days in Year 1; that's a positive. The goal is to minimize inventory but not too low. Inventory needs to be high enough to meet demand but no higher, because excess inventory adds no value to a firm; it only adds costs.

292. **B.** II is correct. The amount of inventory a company would tend to hold in stock would decrease as the length of time that goods are in transit decreases. If goods ordered could arrive the next day, for example, inventory levels could be minimized and resupplied quickly. I is wrong. The amount of inventory a company would tend to hold in stock would decrease as the cost of running out of stock decreases. If stockout costs were high, inventory would be higher, not lower.

293. **D.** The 50,000 cards sold per year divided by 50 weeks equals an average of 1,000 cards being sold per week. Then, 1,000 cards sold per week times four weeks lead time equals 4,000 cards sold during the time it takes to place and receive an order from Hallmark. If the safety stock is 750 cards, the reorder point is 4,750.

294. **B.** I and II are correct. In a just-in-time system, products are produced just-in-time to be sold. Therefore, just in time systems maintain a much smaller level of inventory when compared to traditional systems. Inventory turnover (cost of goods sold divided by average inventory) increases with a switch to just in time. III is wrong. Inventory as a percentage of total assets decreases rather than increases with a switch from a traditional to a just-in-time inventory system.

295. **C.** I and II are correct. High carrying costs would decrease safety stock. Lower stockout costs would decrease safety stock.

296. **D.** I, II, and III are correct. The optimal level of inventory is affected by the time required to receive inventory. If lead times become more variable, the amount of safety stock needed to reduce the risk of stockouts will increase. The optimal level of inventory is affected by the cost per unit of inventory, which will have a direct impact on inventory carrying costs. The cost of placing an order impacts order frequency, which affects order size and, therefore, affects optimal inventory levels. IV is wrong. The current amount of inventory has no impact on the optimal level.

297. **C.** I and II are correct. The EOQ method of inventory control anticipates orders at the point where carrying costs are nearest to restocking costs. The objective of EOQ is to minimize total inventory costs.

298. **D.** I and II are wrong. A reduction in accounts receivable would serve to improve (increase) the turnover ratio. Factoring (selling) receivables would serve to reduce the amount of accounts receivable (indicating more rapid collections). Factoring receivables would increase (improve) the company's accounts receivable turnover ratio. The accounts receivable turnover ratio is expressed as sales divided by accounts receivable.

299. **A.** Accounts receivable turnover is calculated as sales divided by average receivables.

$105,000 ÷ $14,000 = 7.5

Average receivables is calculated as beginning accounts receivable plus ending accounts receivable divided by 2.

$15,000 + $13,000 = $28,000
$28,000 ÷ 2 = $14,000

300. **B.** The EOQ is a formula that allows managers to calculate the ideal quantity of inventory to order for a given product. The calculation is designed to minimize ordering and carrying costs. There are a number of assumptions associated with use of the EOQ formula. They are as follows: unit costs (order costs and carrying costs) of items ordered are constant, no quantity discounts are allowed, and demand or production is uniform (occurs at constant rate and is known with certainty). A is wrong. Unit costs (purchase price) is constant; thus, there can be no quantity discounts. C and D are wrong, because order and carrying costs are assumed constant—they do not vary.

301. **A.** I is correct. The question asked which of the following would *not* be relevant to EOQ. The purchase price per unit is not a component of EOQ but rather the cost per purchase order. II is wrong. Annual sales volume *is* a key variable in the EOQ formula. The components of the EOQ formula include demand in units for the product, the ordering cost per purchase order, and the carrying cost for one unit.

302. B. The calculation is as follows:

$$EOQ = \frac{}{\sqrt{(2 \times \text{annual demand} \times \text{ordering costs})} \div \text{carrying costs}}$$

$$= \sqrt{(2 \times 2{,}400 \times (\$50))} \div 3$$

$$EOQ = \sqrt{(\$240{,}000 \div 3)} = \$80{,}000$$

$$EOQ = \sqrt{\$80{,}000}$$

$$EOQ = 282.84 \text{ (rounded to 283)}$$

Notice that the $35 price per pair is not used in the EOQ calculation since EOQ is based on cost per order, not cost per unit.

Chapter 19: Information Technology

303. A. I is correct. An exception report is a report produced when a specific condition or "exception" occurs. II is wrong. An ad hoc report is a report that does not currently exist but that needs to be created on demand without having to get a software developer involved.

304. C. I and II are correct. Grandfather, father, and son files can be used to recover from processing problems by reverting back to files prior to when they became corrupt. Grandfather, father, and son files can be used to retain files off-site for disaster recovery. As the most recent file is stored, the oldest is killed off.

305. D. There is no greater level of control necessary for batch processing versus online real-time (online) processing. Online processing (online, real-time [OLRT] processing) is an immediate processing method in which each transaction goes through all processing steps (data entry, data validation, and master file update) before the next transaction is processed. These OLRT files are always current, and error detection is immediate. A and C are wrong. For batch processing, stored data would only be current if no changes to the data have been made since the last batch update. B is wrong. Online real-time transactions are processed in real time, *not* on a periodic basis.

306. C. I and II are correct. An AIS is best suited to solve problems where there is certainty along with clearly defined reporting requirements. The first step in an AIS is that transaction data from source documents are entered into the AIS by an end user. While AIS systems generally have similar capabilities, the applications implemented for a particular business are generally modified to meet the specific needs of that business. For example, the requirements of a retail warehouse club would be different from those of a CPA firm.

307. C. The final step is the financial reports are generated. The steps in an AIS are:

The transaction data from source documents are entered into the AIS by an end user.

The original paper source documents are filed.

These transactions are recorded in the appropriate journal.

The transactions are posted to the general and subsidiary ledgers.

Trial balances are prepared.

Financial reports are generated.

308. B. I is correct. The objective of a disaster recovery plan is to be able to regain access to data, communications, work areas, and other business processes as quickly as possible in the event of a disaster. Storing duplicate copies of essential files at an off-site location and away from the location where the file information is processed protects those files from disaster at the computing site. Those undisrupted files can then be used to back up key data so that business operations can resume in a timely fashion. II is wrong. Encrypting data in the files protects them from unauthorized use, but not from being destroyed in the event of a disaster at the computing site. III is wrong. Maintaining a list of all employee passwords with the chief technology officer protects against the loss of passwords by employees, but it has no relevance if the files employees need to access are destroyed.

309. D. I and II are wrong. While a decrease in local accountability is a characteristic of centralized processing, this is *not* an advantage but a disadvantage of centralized processing. Increased power and storage needs at the centralized location are other disadvantages of centralized processing.

310. B. II is correct. Business information systems allow a business to collect data, process data, store and transform data, and distribute data. Hardware, software, network, people, and data are components of a business information system. I is wrong. Data initiation is not part of a business information system.

311. C. I, III, IV, and V are correct. The business information system includes software, hardware, data, and people. Reports are *not* one of the components of a business information system. Network, also a part of a business information system, was not listed in the question.

312. **C.** A check digit verification is an input control that could be used to detect miscoding of a product number on a customer order. A check digit is an extra digit added to an identification number (e.g., a product number) to detect certain types of data transmission errors, such as dropped and transposed digits. The computer calculates the correct check digit based on an algorithm that is applied to the (for example) product number, and then compares that to the check digit. A is wrong. A hash total is a batch processing control that calculates the sum of a numeric field, which has no meaning by itself but can provide a check and balance to ensure that the records that should have been processed were processed. It would not necessarily identify transmission errors such as dropped or transposed digits. Rather it might identify a record that did not get processed. B is wrong. In a closed-loop verification, data input is transmitted, processed, and displayed back to the data entry clerk to verify the input. For example, bank tellers process customer deposits by entering the customer account number noted on the deposit slip, and after doing so, verify the customer information displayed back on the screen against the deposit slip to ensure the correct customer account is being updated. D is wrong. A limit check is a control that tests the reasonableness of a field of data, where based on known limits for the given data, certain entries might be rejected. For instance, regular hours worked per week cannot exceed 40 hours. If 50 hours were inadvertently entered, the system would reject the entry. This control would not, however, reject dropped or transposed digits in data input, unless doing so falls outside of the limit established. For instance, if the hours worked were 21 hours, and this was, instead, entered as 12 hours, the system would not reject the error because it is still within the 40-hour limit.

313. **A.** I is correct. The question asked which of the following is *not* correct. Production and test data are stored in different databases. II is wrong. Access to production data is less open than access to test data. Since this is a true statement, II is an incorrect choice.

314. **B.** Block coding represents assignment of blocks of numbers to broad categories of items (e.g., a general ledger chart of accounts that assigns stockholders' equity to the 2000 series of account numbers, revenue to the 3000 series of account numbers, expenses to the 4000 series, and so on). A is wrong, as sequential coding simply numbers documents, transactions, or other items in order (sequence). A

stack of preprinted checks is an example of sequential coding; the first check is #101, the next is #102, and so on. C is wrong. Group coding embeds intelligence into the identification numbers associated with a particular item. A driver's license number, for example, contains intelligence about the driver's name and eye color and whether the driver wears glasses.

315. **B.** I is correct. Converting information into machine-readable format is necessary for data input and is an activity the information systems department would typically perform. II is wrong. The information systems department would not typically initiate changes to existing applications. While the information systems department might assist with facilitating those changes, it would not initiate the changes, as this would present an internal control deficiency. The initiation of the changes should come from the appropriate user group. III is wrong. Initiating changes to master files would not be performed by the information systems department. This should be performed by those who are independent of the change processing in order to maintain a system of effective internal control.

316. **A.** I is correct. Data storage is a major function of transaction processing along with data input, data processing, and information output. II is wrong. Analysis of data is not a major function of transaction processing. Analysis is typically performed after transaction processing.

317. **C.** I and II are correct. The SEC's Interactive Data Rule requires public companies to present financial statements and related exhibits using XBRL, which is specifically designed to exchange financial information over the Web.

318. **D.** I and II are wrong. Program modification controls include controls that attempt to prevent changes by unauthorized personnel. In addition, program modification controls track program changes so that there is an exact record of what versions of what programs were running in production at any specific point in time.

319. **B.** II is correct. The duties of systems programmers and application programmers should be segregated. The duties of systems analysts and application programmers are often combined, which is fine.

320. **C.** Support is keeping the system up and running. Support includes monitoring the system, determining that a problem has occurred, and fixing or getting around the problem. A is wrong. Maintenance

refers to keeping the system "up to date" with new releases from time to time. B is wrong. Support (not maintenance) includes monitoring the system, determining that a problem has occurred, and fixing or getting around the problem. D is wrong. Maintenance refers to keeping the system "up to date" with new releases from time to time.

321. **D.** I is correct. In a structured system, each program within a system is independent of other programs within the system. This enables programming teams to work independently on different programs within the same system. II is wrong. Management reporting systems provide managers with the information needed for day-to-day decision-making. III is wrong. Interactive systems are computer-based information systems that provide interactive support to managers or others during the decision-making process.

322. **D.** A hardware technician sets up and configures computers. A is wrong. Users are any workers who enter data into a system or who use the information processed by the system. Users could be employees as well as outside consultants such as accountants, auditors, etc. B is wrong. A software developer designs the systems and writes the programs to collect, process, store, transform, and distribute the data and information entered by the users. C is wrong. A network administrator sets up and configures a computer network so that multiple computers can share the same data and information.

323. **B.** Sensitivity analysis is a decision support system that uses a "what-if" technique that asks how a given outcome will change if the original estimates of the model are changed. A is wrong. Scenario analysis allows an analyst or manager to look at possible outcomes and predict a value given the probability of each outcome occurring. C is wrong. Database query applications read and reorganize data to management's specifications but do not allow alterations of the data. D is wrong. A financial modeling application is used to assist management in evaluating financing alternatives.

324. **B.** II and III are correct. A Trojan horse poses a security risk. A Trojan horse is software that appears to have a useful function but contains a hidden and unintended function that presents a security risk when the computer program is run. A backdoor represents a security risk because a backdoor is a means of access to a program or system that bypasses normal security measures and therefore should be eliminated. I is wrong, as a web crawler

poses no security risk. A web crawler is a program that browses the Internet to create copies of visited web pages for later processing by a search engine.

325. **B.** I and III are correct. Network maintenance and wireless access are both responsibilities of the network administrator. II is wrong. A database administrator designs the firm's database and controls it. His or her duties generally include maintaining security measures.

326. **A.** An application programmer is the person responsible for writing and/or maintaining application programs and should not be responsible for controlling or handling data.

327. **D.** A systems analyst designs the overall application system. The systems analyst is authorized to design the system, and that role should be segregated from the custody of the program, which will belong to the librarian. A is wrong. The librarian has a custodian role over the program, not an authorization role. B is wrong. A computer operator has a record-keeping job rather than authorization. C is wrong. Programmers have a record-keeping function rather than an authorization function.

328. **B.** II is correct. A system programmer is responsible for installing, supporting, monitoring, and maintaining the operating system. I is wrong. An application programmer is responsible for writing or maintaining application programs.

329. **B.** II is correct. The reliability business requirement for information includes the criterion that information be appropriate to operate the entity. I is wrong. The business requirement known as availability includes the criteria that information be available currently and in the future and that resources be safeguarded. The control objectives for information and related technology (COBIT) framework identifies seven information criteria: integrity, confidentiality, efficiency, reliability, availability, compliance, and effectiveness.

330. **A.** I is correct. The integrity business requirement for information includes the criteria that information be accurate, complete, and valid. II is wrong. Within the context of business requirements for information, efficiency concerns delivery of information through the optimal use of resources (e.g., low cost without compromising effectiveness). The control objectives for information and related technology (COBIT) framework identifies seven information criteria: integrity, confidentiality,

efficiency, reliability, availability, compliance, and effectiveness.

331. **D.** Along with value delivery, the focus areas identified by the control objectives for information and related technology (COBIT) framework for IT governance include:

Strategic alignment
Resource management
Risk management
Performance measurement

332. **A.** Systems maintenance involves monitoring the system, after the system becomes operational, to ensure ongoing performance. Evaluating the system to assess its efficiency and effectiveness is also part of this process. Additionally, redesigning the system (as necessary) to ensure it meets the needs of users and to correct any flaws is also a maintenance function. B is wrong. Systems implementation is a process that includes training users, converting over to the new system, and testing the system to ensure it is operational. C is wrong. A systems feasibility study is conducted to assess the need for a new system, what technology it will require, what economic resources need to be committed, and what operational impact the system will have. D is wrong. Systems analysis involves conducting a user needs assessment, as well as an assessment of the current system, and further identifying gaps between the required system and the current system.

333. **C.** The monitor and evaluate domain relates to ensuring that directions are followed and providing feedback to information criteria.

334. **D.** I is correct. One characteristic of database management systems is that data sharing between individuals and applications is relatively easy and can be used concurrently by multiple users. II is wrong. Because of the manner in which data is structured in database management systems, information is recorded in only one place, which makes updating the data that much easier. Data redundancy is, therefore, minimized, not increased. III is correct. In database management systems, the data are defined independently of the needs of any one program. Consequently, data can be used relatively easily by differing applications.

335. **A.** I and II are correct. When changing from a manual system to a computer system, internal control objectives and principles do not change. Whether using a manual or computerized system, the objectives and principles are still safeguarding assets and segregating duties. III is wrong. While safeguarding

assets and segregating duties remain the same, the implementation of the principles is different. Specific controls will need to change when switching from a manual system of controls to a computerized system.

336. **C.** A systems analyst would take on the role of learning a purchased software application and would have the job of integrating it into any existing software. The systems analyst would also take responsibility for training staff.

337. **D.** I and II are wrong. Automated systems do not eliminate the need to reconcile control accounts and subsidiary ledgers. If a reconciliation were needed in a manual system, it would still be needed in a computerized system.

338. **D.** I and II are wrong. I describes management information systems, not executive support systems. Executive support systems provide senior executives information to assist the executives in strategic issues such as nonroutine decisions that may involve analysis of cyclical data, acquisitions, and competitor behavior. II describes transaction processing rather than executive support systems.

339. **A.** Within an IT system, the steering committee is charged with developing long-range plans and directing application development and computer operations. B is wrong. A systems analyst is generally responsible for designing systems, preparing specifications for programmers, and serving as an intermediary between users and programmers. C is wrong. System programmers would be involved in the selection of system software and would be responsible for maintaining system software, including operating systems, network software, and the data management system. D is wrong. End users are typically responsible for maintaining control over the completeness, accuracy, and distribution of input and output, not the systems analyst.

340. **C.** The independent verification of payroll transactions that typically occurs using parallel processing of transactions represents one of the most effective methods to reduce the risk of incorrect processing of transactions in a newly installed payroll system. Payroll should be processed by the new system and by another system, possibly the old system, and results should be compared. I is wrong. While segregation of duties ensures that the same person cannot both perpetrate and conceal fraud, it does not minimize the risk of incorrect processing due to implementation of a new system. II is wrong. Authorization of transactions is a strong control

over the validity or legitimacy of overtime but does not reduce the risk of incorrect processing due to implementation of a new system.

341. **B.** Encryption involves using a password or a digital key to scramble a readable (plain text) message into an unreadable (cipher text) message. Data encryption is based on the concept of keys. The length of the key is extremely important in data encryption. The longer the key, the harder it is to crack.

342. **D.** All three choices are forms of data security. Password management is a method of preventing intrusion since it regulates system access. Data encryption also is a method of preventing intrusion since it uses a password or a digital key to scramble any readable data into a message unreadable to the potential hacker. Data encryption is, in fact, based on the concept of keys. However, the length of the key is extremely important in data encryption. The longer the key, the harder it is to crack. The algorithm is important, but the length of the key is more important. Finally, digital certificates are forms of data security. Digital certificates are electronic documents created and digitally signed by a trusted party that certifies the identity of the owners of a particular public key.

343. **A.** Transactions sent over a VAN are batched periodically rather than as they occur. B is wrong. A VAN is superior to the Internet in terms of disaster recovery because records of EDI transactions may be kept for months or years, which can aid in the disaster recovery process. C is wrong. The Internet permits EDI transactions to be sent to trading partners as transactions occur.

344. **A.** The objectives of customer relationship management (CRM) systems are to increase customer satisfaction and, therefore, increase revenue. A CRM enables the entity to analyze the behavior of customers. B is wrong. EDI is the computer-to-computer exchange of business data in structured format that allows direct processing of the data by the receiving system. It is not an internal communication but always between two separate businesses. C is wrong. Decision support systems (DSS) are computer-based information systems that provide interactive support to managers or others during the decision-making process. D is wrong. Public key infrastructure (PKI) refers to the system and processes used to issue and manage asymmetric keys and digital certificates.

345. **D.** I is wrong. Encrypting data files includes converting those files into a cipher text that cannot be easily understood by unauthorized people. Encryption is a control that prevents unauthorized access to the data but would not necessarily mitigate the risk of exposure to viruses, which are typically spread through the distribution of computer programs and/or via e-mail attachments or other file downloads. II is wrong. Neither more nor less frequent backup of files would mitigate the risk of an entity's exposure to viruses. Viruses are typically spread through e-mail attachments and/or other file downloads, and backing up existing files would not prevent this from occurring. III is wrong. Downloading public-domain software from electronic bulletin boards would increase, not mitigate, the risk of exposure to viruses, since this software could be contaminated with a virus and infect the entity's computer system when downloaded.

346. **C.** I and II are correct. The cost of sending EDI transactions using a value-added network is greater than the cost of using the Internet. In addition, EDI requires strict adherence to a standard data format. Translation software is required to convert internal company data to the strict standard format. This translation software must either be purchased or be internally developed.

347. **C.** I, II, and III are correct. Decreased inventory levels, increased costs for informational technology infrastructure, and increase market efficiency are all characteristic of B2B (business-to-business) e-commerce. B2B e-commerce provides for more effective coordination of delivery of inventory and can, therefore, make better use of inventory. B2B e-commerce also allows companies to connect directly with suppliers to obtain easy access to price quotes from various suppliers and, consequently, receive better pricing. Finally, implementing B2B e-commerce does require significant investment in equipment, software, and training.

348. **C.** Encryption is the encoding of data for security purposes. A is wrong. Decoding is the process used by the recipient of encoded information to decipher the message with use of an electronic "key." B is wrong. Mapping is the process of determining the correspondence between elements in a company's format and elements in standard EDI format. D is wrong. Translation is the conversion of data from one format to another. Once the mapping has been completed, translation software can be developed to convert transactions from one format to the other.

349. **C.** I and II are correct. The two most important controls in an electronic data interchange

(EDI) environment are activity trails of failed transactions and network and sender recipient acknowledgments.

350. **D.** Internet transactions are faster, less expensive, and less secure than EDI transactions over a VAN. This is because the VAN is more secure and there is a price to pay for those controls.

351. **D.** Cloud computing involves having virtual servers available over the Internet for storing hardware and software. This allows a company to expand its IT capabilities. Cost savings are expected over the long term. A is wrong. Domain name warehousing is the practice of obtaining control over domain names for possible future use. B is wrong. Secure socket layer is what encrypts certain data in conjunction with HTTP; for example, credit card data must be encrypted. C is wrong. Hypertext transfer protocol allows for sound, video, and images to be transferred over the Internet.

352. **A.** The risk of choosing inappropriate technology is known as strategic risk. B is wrong. Operating risk is the risk of doing the right thing but in the wrong sequential order. C is wrong. Financial risk includes the risk of having assets wasted, stolen, or lost. D is wrong. Information risk includes the risk of lost data, computer crashes, and hackers.

353. **A.** I is correct. In a denial-of-service attack, one computer bombards another computer with a flood of information intended to keep legitimate users from accessing the target computer or network. II is wrong. A Trojan horse, not phishing, is a program that appears to have a useful function but that contains a hidden and unintended function that presents a security risk. Phishing represents phony e-mails sent to recipients in order to gain access to the unknowing recipient's banking information.

354. **D.** No password is perfect, but of the passwords listed, 2456dtR5! is the most difficult to crack because it contains a combination of small letters, capital letters, numbers, and other characters, known as ascii.

355. **C.** I and II are correct. Limit tests set a numeric limit, a ceiling for processing, such as no payroll check allowed more than $5,000. The limit is $5,000, and any payroll check requested in excess of $5,000 should *not* be processed, but rather an exception report should be generated. A validity check is an input control that would prevent or detect an unauthorized transaction. For example, all employees should be on an electronic valid database. Any

attempt to pay an employee not on the valid list should be rejected, and only attempts to pay valid employees should be accepted. Any attempt to pay an invalid employee should generate an exception report. Either the employee doesn't exist at all, or he or she is simply no longer working for the company.

356. **B.** The total hours worked, 146, would be a batch total. Payroll is run in a batch, and the batch total would be the total hours worked during the period, which is represented as the total of column 2.

357. **A.** The record count is five, as there are five paychecks or five employees to pay.

358. **B.** A hash total attempts to detect if numbers that are not normally added (such as Social Security numbers or employee ID#s) have been processed incorrectly. An example of a hash total is the sum of the fifth digit of all employees' Social Security numbers. This amount is already predetermined and can function as a control that no employees have been added to the system.

359. **C.** I and II are correct. Passwords are electronic access controls that authenticate user access to a system and its applications and data. A firewall is an electronic access control that prevents unauthorized access to a system and its applications and data.

360. **C.** A cold site is an off-site location that has all the electrical connections and other physical requirements for data processing but does not have the actual hardware or software. A is wrong. A warm site may contain some or all of the hardware found in the original computer center but is not set up to function as an immediate backup center. B is wrong. A hot site will have hardware already installed at the alternate site. This hardware resembles the hardware at the original computer center and is already configured, or can be configured, to be the same as the company is using in its normal operations. D is wrong. The term *purple site* does not exist.

361. **B.** I is correct. Because EDI facilitates the communication of data directly from one entity's computer to another entity's computer, ordering goods from suppliers can be expedited, and inventory management can be enhanced. Thus, the likelihood of stockouts is reduced through the use of EDI. II is wrong. Although EDI can facilitate the electronic processing of customer payments and, therefore, reduce amounts receivable, it does not guarantee those payments. III is wrong. There is an increased, not decreased, liability as it relates to protecting

business data when using EDI. EDI transactions are subject to the same risks as any other electronic communications, and information transmitted may be insecure. Protecting business data is, therefore, a major consideration when using EDI.

362. **B.** Intranets can be thought of as private, company-owned Internets. While the same Web browser can be used for both the Internet and an intranet, intranets are privately sponsored forms of electronic data sharing normally used for organizational communications, not for public display. A is wrong. While the Internet is a public information highway, intranets tend to be private. C is wrong. A database management system is software that is in charge of providing data from a database to an application program and writing it back to disk. D is wrong. A compiler is a language processor, software that translates source code (human readable) to object code (machine readable).

Chapter 20: Economic Concepts

363. **B.** II is correct. GDP includes all final goods and services produced by resources within a country regardless of who owns the resources. Final US GDP would include output from a car factory in Detroit whether it's a factory owned by a US car company or a factory owned by a Japanese car company. I is wrong. GDP includes all final goods and services. Used goods that are resold would be excluded from GDP because they were already counted once when they were final.

364. **A.** I is correct. Real GDP measures the value of all goods and services produced within a nation's borders in constant dollars. Real GDP is adjusted to account for changes in the price level and removes the effect of inflation by using a price index. Real GDP can be used to compare economic performance over time; nominal GDP cannot be used for that purpose, because nominal GDP doesn't adjust for inflation. II is wrong. Nominal GDP is unadjusted for inflation. Nominal GDP measures the value of all final goods and services in current prices; therefore, it is not the best measure of economic performance.

365. **D.** Economic activity is characterized by fluctuations, which vary in severity and duration. Severity refers to how deep a recession is or how widespread a recovery may be. Duration refers to time—how many quarters a recession lasts or how many years of growth until inflation.

366. **D.** The peak marks the end of the expansionary phase and the beginning of the contraction phase. In the peak, firms are likely to face input shortages, leading to higher overall costs, and as a result of higher costs, profits begin to fall.

367. **D.** During a recovery phase, economic activity begins to increase and return to its long-term growth trend. Demands for goods and services begin to rise, and company profits, no longer falling, begin to stabilize. A is wrong. A peak is the high point of economic activity and marks the end of expansion and the beginning of the contraction phase. At a peak, profits are at their highest level. B is wrong. Firm profits are likely to be falling during contraction, not stabilizing. C is wrong. During expansion, economic activity is rising beyond its average long-term growth trend.

368. **B.** A trough is a low point of economic activity. Firm profits are at their lowest level, so cost cutting is essential for survival. Since jobs have been cut, demand for products is low and excess capacity would be expected.

369. **A.** I is correct. During a recession, potential output will exceed actual output. II is wrong. During a recession, prices are falling, employment is low, and real gross domestic product is falling.

370. **B.** II and III are correct. In a recession, GDP falls as unemployment rises. Rising unemployment and falling GDP are evidence of a recession. I is wrong. An increase in aggregate demand is not evidence of a recession. In a recession, GDP will fall if unemployment rises and there is a decrease in aggregate demand or a decrease in aggregate supply.

371. **C.** Increasing government purchases (government spending) will cause an increase in demand. An increase in demand causes real GDP to rise and unemployment to fall. B is wrong. Decreasing taxes, rather than increasing taxes, will cause real GDP to rise. Increasing taxes will cause GDP to fall.

372. **D.** I and II are wrong. Increasing taxes is an example of contracting rather than expansionary fiscal policy. A decrease in government spending is also an example of contracting fiscal policy rather than expansionary fiscal policy. Expansionary fiscal policy involves increasing government purchases and/or decreasing taxes. Expansionary fiscal policy would cause real GDP (output) to increase.

373. **C.** An increase in wealth and an increase in the general level of confidence shifts the aggregate demand curve to the right. Shifts in the aggregate demand

curve occur due to factors other than price. Prices would cause a change in the quantity demanded along the same aggregate demand curve, but price would not be enough to cause a shift in the curve. A shift to the right (good news) would occur as a result of reasons other than price, including factors such as increases in wealth (stock market gains), reductions in interest rates, and increases in consumer confidence. A is wrong. An increase in wealth and an increase in overall confidence about the economic outlook does not increase the cost of capital.

374. **C.** I and II are correct. As aggregate demand rises, output is up, GDP is up, and the employment rate goes up, which means unemployment decreases.

375. **C.** I and II are correct. The aggregate demand curve is downward sloping because quantity demanded (QD) is inversely related to the price level. For example, as prices rise, QD falls. Slope is a measure of sensitivity—in this case, sensitivity of the dependent variable (quantity demanded) to the change in the independent variable, price level. The short-run aggregate supply curve is upward sloping because quantity supplied is directly related to the price level. In the short run, if prices rise, sellers will want to sell more (a positive slope). In this case, slope is measuring the sensitivity of the dependent variable (quantity supplied) to the change in the independent variable, price. Note that in the long run, the aggregate supply curve is not about price but about resources available such as labor, materials, and capital.

376. **B.** II and III are correct. A nation's long-term aggregate supply curve represents the potential output of a nation, and long-run output is dependent on infrastructure, including available technology, capital, labor, and raw materials within the country. I is wrong. A nation's long-run aggregate supply curve is *not* dependent upon price levels; only the short-run aggregate supply curve is dependent upon price levels.

377. **A.** If a company's input costs go down, the company could make more money by increasing production. When supply goes up, output goes up and GDP goes up. When supply goes up, price per unit will go down. Therefore, a decrease in input costs like direct material and direct labor would shift the aggregate supply curve to the right, resulting in an increase in real GDP and a decrease in the overall price level.

378. **C.** I and II are correct. Real GDP per capita is typically used to compare standards of living across countries. Real GDP per capita is real GDP divided by population. By dividing real GDP by population, this measure adjusts for differences in the size of countries and differences in sizes of population over a period of time.

379. **B.** II is correct. If the US dollar falls in value, the supply of foreign goods in the United States should decrease as imports become more expensive due to a falling dollar's not being able to purchase as much overseas. I is wrong. If the dollar falls in value, net exports will gain as US goods become less expensive overseas.

380. **A.** I is correct. Inflation erodes purchasing power. II is wrong. Inflation actually helps anyone who has to make a fixed payment. While those making a fixed payment are helped, inflation hurts those who are receiving that same fixed payment.

381. **A.** I is correct. Note the question asks what inflation does *not* do. I is right because inflation does not help those on a fixed income. It actually hurts those on a fixed income but helps those with a fixed obligation. II is wrong because it's a true statement. Inflation will increase the price level.

382. **A.** An increase in aggregate demand causes output to rise and the price level to rise. If there are many buyers, price levels and output will rise, which will cause GDP and employment to rise. *Alternatively,* if there were few buyers, a decrease in aggregate demand would cause output to fall and the price level to fall.

383. **D.** A decrease in aggregate supply causes output to fall and the price level to rise. A decrease in aggregate supply will lead to fewer goods being created, which could lead to shortages. If goods are scarce, the price will rise. Alternatively, an increase in aggregate supply would cause output to rise and the price level to fall, since more goods are being created. More goods created could lead to a surplus, which leads to lower prices.

384. **A.** A mismatch of skills and jobs in the economy is an example of structural unemployment. B is wrong. Cyclical unemployment is caused by business cycles. Cyclical unemployment tends to rise during a recession and fall during an expansion. C is wrong. Frictional unemployment is a term for the time lag that individuals experience between jobs. D is wrong. Seasonal unemployment is caused by seasonal demand for labor.

385. C. Cyclical unemployment is caused by business cycles. Cyclical unemployment tends to rise during a recession and fall during an expansion. A is wrong. Frictional unemployment is a term for the time lag that individuals experience between jobs. B is wrong. Structural unemployment is caused by a mismatch of skills and jobs in the economy. D is wrong. Seasonal unemployment is caused by seasonal demand for labor.

386. B. If a new invention renders an entire industry obsolete, this leads to structural unemployment. When an industry is rendered obsolete, the labor that had been working in that industry needs to be retrained before those workers can be matched to a new industry.

387. B. I and II are correct. Gross domestic product can be calculated using the expenditures approach or the income approach. III is wrong. There is no such thing as the net assets approach.

388. C. I and II are correct. The expenditures approach to calculating GDP includes:

Net exports
Capital investment
Consumption
Government expenditures

389. B. II is correct. Business profits and employee compensation are used in the income approach for computing GDP. The income approach follows the acronym PRIDE:

Profits to corporations and small business
Rental income
Interest income
Depreciation
Employee pay (wages)

I is wrong. The expenditures approach does not use business profits and employee compensation. The expenditures approach to calculating GDP is as follows:

Investment—capital investment by private business
Consumption—consumer spending
Exports—net of imports
Government expenditures

390. D. The discount rate is set by the Federal Reserve and refers to the interest rate established for short-term (often overnight) loans the central bank makes to member banks.

391. B. The GDP, using the expenditures approach, is calculated as follows (all numbers are in the billions):

Government spending	$12
Net exports	+ $3*
Investments	+ $30
Consumption	+ $16
GDP—Expenditures approach	$61

392. B. The GDP of $606 billion is calculated as follows:

Profits to proprietors	$83 billion
Profits to corporations	+ $119 billion
Rental income	+ $19 billion
Interest income	+ $80 billion
Depreciation†	
Employee wages	+ $305 billion
GDP—Income approach	$606 billion

Consumer spending and net imports would only be used under the expenditures approach.

393. D. Gross national product (GNP) is the sum of all final goods and services produced by residents of Pradera whether produced within Pradera's borders or produced by Pradera residents working outside Pradera's borders. A is wrong. Gross domestic product measures the value of all final goods and services produced within Pradera's borders whether produced by Pradera residents or produced by foreigners working in Pradera. B is wrong. Net domestic product is equal to GDP minus depreciation. C is wrong. Net national product is equal to GNP less economic depreciation. Economic depreciation measures the losses in the value of capital goods due to age and wear.

394. D. The inflation rate measures the rate of increase in the overall price level in the economy. A is wrong. The prime rate is an interest rate charged by banks to their best credit risk borrowers. B is wrong. The discount rate is set by the Federal Reserve and refers to the interest rate established for short-term (often overnight) loans it makes to member banks. C is wrong. The nominal rate (of GDP) measures the level of economic output without taking into account the overall price level or inflation rate.

395. C. The consumer price index (CPI) is primarily used to compare relative price changes over time. The CPI is a measure of the overall cost of a fixed basket of goods and services purchased by an average urban household.

---

*Exports of $7 less imports of $4 equals net exports of $3.

†Not applicable in this question, but Depreciation is part of the PRIDE acronym.

396. **B.** The annual inflation rate is calculated as follows:

$$133.5 - 121 = 12.5$$
$$12.5 \div 121 = 10.33\%$$

397. **B.** I is correct. Competitor analysis involves gathering information about competitors' strategies, capabilities, and objectives and then using that information to understand and predict competitor behavior. II is wrong. Determining the type of market structure and the number of competitors is a function of industry analysis, not competitor analysis. III is wrong. Evaluating the market structure to predict when new competitors are expected to enter the market is an aspect of industry analysis and industry environment assessment.

398. **C.** I and II are correct. Reserve requirements relate to how much money banks must keep in reserve rather than loan out to customers. The Federal Reserve can raise a bank's reserve requirements or lower it. Raising the reserve requirement dampens the economy; lowering the reserve requirement stimulates the economy. The Federal Reserve would most likely purchase government securities if the goal were to stimulate the economy. Purchasing these securities increases the money supply and expands the economy. On the other hand, were the Federal Reserve to sell government securities, this would take money out of the economy.

399. **C.** I and III are correct. Reducing the discount rate will make it easier and cheaper to borrow and will expand the supply of money and stimulate the economy. When interest rates fall, aggregate demand increases and real GDP increases—the economy grows! Purchasing of government securities by the Federal Reserve puts more money into the market and stimulates the economy. II is wrong. Increasing reserve requirements makes it harder for banks to lend, since banks would be forced to keep more on reserve. This contracts the supply of money and slows the economy.

400. **A.** When the Federal Reserve has an expansionary monetary policy, interest rates fall, which stimulates the desired levels of business investment and personal and household consumption. Increases in desired investment and consumption cause an increase in aggregate demand and in GDP.

401. **A.** Precious metals are nonmonetary assets whose values increase with inflation. B and C are wrong. Bonds pay a fixed income to the investor, and fixed incomes suffer the most during a period of rising interest rates. D is wrong. As interest rates rise, the dividends and earnings may not keep up with inflation, making precious metals like gold and silver a better investment than common stock if inflation is expected.

402. **A.** I is correct. In a perfectly competitive marketplace, customers are indifferent about which firm they buy from and will buy from the cheapest firm. II is wrong. In a perfectly competitive market, the level of a firm's output is small (not large) relative to the industry's total output. The lawn-cutting industry is a good example of a perfectly competitive market. With no brand loyalty, customers would switch based solely on price. Firms would not be able to charge more than the competition or they would lose sales.

403. **B.** I is correct. In a purely competitive market, a large number of sellers with virtually identical products or services compete, with no one seller being able to impact the market price. While there are few purely competitive markets, an example of one such market would be commodities. The key to being successful in this type of market is to be a cost leader. Process reengineering is a cost leadership strategy, which involves major redesign of critical processes to achieve improvements in performance, the result of which is cost reduction. It is, therefore, a strategy that might be employed by a company competing in a purely competitive marketplace. II is wrong. Developing a brand name is a product differentiation strategy whose ultimate goal is to command a higher price for a product or products. In a purely competitive market, no one seller is able to impact price, so a product differentiation strategy like developing a brand name would not be effective. III is correct. Lean manufacturing is a technique that focuses on elimination of waste in the production process. It is a cost leadership/reduction strategy that would be effective in a purely competitive market.

404. **C.** I and II are correct. Firms produce up to the point where marginal cost equals marginal revenue, whether the markets are perfectly competitive or imperfectly competitive. In any industry, expanding production will increase profits up to the point that marginal revenue equals marginal cost. Marginal revenue is the additional revenue generated from selling one more unit of product. Marginal cost is the additional cost generated from producing one more unit. Regardless of the industry, firms will produce up to the point where marginal revenue equals marginal cost.

405. A. II is correct. Oligopoly market conditions are characterized by the following:

Few firms in the market
Significant barriers to entry
Little or no variability in pricing

The international oil industry is an example of an oligopoly. It is run by OPEC and there are significant costs to compete, few firms, and so on. In an oligopoly, the other firms in the market will match any price reduction so they do not lose market share, but they will not automatically match a price increase of an individual firm. Therefore, the demand curve is said to be "kinked" for a firm competing in an oligopoly. I is wrong. Monopolistic competition involves many firms, few barriers to entry, and at least some differentiation among competitors' products. III is wrong. In perfect competition, there are many competitors, there are no real barriers to entry, and customers have no real preference about which firm they buy from.

406. C. Elasticity of demand or supply is a measure of how sensitive the demand for or the supply of a product is to a change in its price. A is wrong. Marginal cost is defined as the total cost of producing one additional unit of output. D is wrong. The producer price index is another measure of inflation in addition to the consumer price index. B is wrong. Gross domestic product is the most common measure of economic activity; it measures the total output of all final goods and services produced within a nation's borders over a particular time period.

407. C. If demand is price inelastic, an increase in price will result in an increase in total revenue. An example of a product with inelastic demand is a Super Bowl ticket. A 10% increase in price would result in a decrease in demand of far less than 10%, so total revenue would increase as a result of an increase in price. This is probably why Super Bowl tickets increase in price by at least 10% every year.

408. A. Demand elasticity measures the sensitivity of demand to a change in price. It is computed by dividing the percentage change in quantity demanded by the percentage change in price. If the result is less than 1, demand is deemed to be inelastic (or not sensitive to price changes). A result yielding a greater than 1 ratio indicates elastic demand (demand is sensitive to price changes). In the case where the result is exactly 1, demand is deemed to be unitary (not sensitive or insensitive to changes in price). If a 4% increase in price results in a 2% decrease in quantity demanded, the result is 0.5 or

less than 1, indicating inelastic demand. B is wrong. This scenario results in a ratio greater than 1, which indicates elastic demand. C is wrong. The ratio here is exactly 1, which indicates neither sensitivity or insensitivity to the price change, or unitary demand. D is wrong. If a 3% decrease in price results in a 5% increase in quantity demanded, a ratio greater than 1 is derived, which indicates demand sensitivity to the price change or elastic demand.

409. D. I and II are wrong. When demand for a product is unit elastic, elasticity is equal to 1. Any price change would be offset by an equal change in demand, so a price increase would be offset by an equal drop in demand, resulting in no change in total revenue. In addition, when demand for a product is unit elastic, elasticity is equal to 1. Any price change would be offset by an equal change in demand, so a price decrease would be offset by an equal increase in demand, resulting in no change in total revenue.

410. A. Supply is price inelastic if the absolute price elasticity of supply is less than 1. B, C, and D are wrong. If the absolute price elasticity of supply is greater than 1, supply is elastic, rather than inelastic. Supply is unit elastic if the absolute price elasticity is equal to 1. Price elasticity of supply is determined by dividing change in quantity supplied by change in price. Any number greater than 1 is said to be supply price elastic and more sensitive to a change in price. As price goes up, quantity supplied should go up, but the question is by how much. If a firm has idle capacity, it would be willing and able to produce more as output prices rise, but if it were already at full capacity, the higher selling price would have less of an impact.

411. D. If the elasticity of demand for a normal good is estimated to be 1.23, then a 10% increase in its price would cause a decrease in quantity demanded of 12.3% (10% × 1.23 elasticity of demand = 12.3%). If price rises, quantity demanded falls, and in this case, total revenue would fall since demand for this item is sensitive to a price increase because the estimated elasticity is 1.23 (greater than 1). Any number greater than 1 is considered more sensitive to a price change. As quantity demanded falls, revenue falls. In this case, revenue would drop by 12.3% along with quantity demanded.

412. C. A company's value chain consists of internal processes or activities that are required to deliver a product or service to market, including the following: research and development, design, production, marketing, distribution, and customer service. Accounting is a back office function that is not required to deliver a product or service to market and, therefore, is not part of a company's value chain. A, B, and D are all wrong. Marketing, research and development, and customer service are all part of a company's value chain.

413. **B.** I and II are correct. Factors that increase the bargaining power of the customer include awareness by customers that they make up a large volume of a firm's business. Such awareness gives customers the power to dominate negotiations. More information available about dealer costs and substitute products in the marketplace gives customers increased bargaining power as well. III is wrong. A low, rather than high, switching cost would give customers more bargaining power.

414. **C.** I and II are correct. Competitive advantage is generally defined as either differentiation or cost leadership. Differentiation advantage may be best obtained by a firm that builds market share or increases its price. A firm enjoys a competitive advantage as a cost leader when it's able to match the prices of its rivals or has a cost structure that is lower than its competition.

415. **B.** II is correct. Brand loyalty will cause cost leadership strategies to fail. If customers are loyal to a particular brand, a price decrease by a competitor would be offset by brand loyalty. The best cost strategy is a combination of the benefits of cost leadership and differentiation strategies.

416. **B.** Supply chain management is a process used by companies to improve operations and manage relations with suppliers. Supply chain management is also focused on improving processes to reduce time, defects, and costs throughout the supply chain. Thus, the sharing of information with suppliers and customers is a major area of focus of supply chain management. A is wrong. Improving quality and applying quality principles to all company activities is an objective of total quality management (TQM). C is wrong. Process redesign is associated with the cost leadership strategy of process reengineering, which involves the major redesign of existing processes to achieve significant improvements in performance. D is wrong. Strategic alliances focus on an entity creating agreements with other outside companies (such as joint ventures or other collaborative agreements) with the goal of supplementing internal capabilities and activities with access to needed resources or processes from those companies.

417. **B.** Selecting vendors is a source decision. A is wrong. Planning relates to the necessary infrastructure needed to properly balance aggregate demand and aggregate supply within the goals and objectives of the firm. C is wrong. The deliver stage includes all the activities related to getting the finished product into the hands of the ultimate consumers. D is wrong. The make stage refers to production sites and methods.

418. **C.** II is correct. The fundamental law of demand holds that there is an inverse relationship between price of the product and the quantity demanded. If the price of A goes up, the quantity demanded for A should fall. I is wrong. If A and B are true substitutes and the price of A rises, the quantity demanded of B should rise, not fall. III is wrong. If A and B are true substitutes, then if the price of A rises, demand for B should rise as customers choose B. The price of A and the price of B are not necessarily related at all. An increase in the price of A does not result in an automatic increase in the price of B.

419. **B.** If goods are substitutes, as the price of one goes up, the demand for the other increases as consumers seek the lower-priced substitute good. A is wrong. Complementary goods move together; as the price of steak goes up, the demand for steak sauce drops. C is wrong. Independent goods have no relationship; as the price of wood increases, the demand for laundry detergent is not impacted. D is wrong. Demand for inferior (low-end) goods declines as wages increase.

420. **B.** If supply decreases, the product becomes scarce and prices will increase. If quantity demanded for a product goes up, this drives price up also.

421. **C.** I and II are correct. The elasticity of demand for a good is calculated by measuring the change in quantity demanded over the change in price. The elasticity of demand for a normal good is always negative—as prices rise, demand falls. The demand for normal goods will increase as income rises.

422. **A.** I is correct. If demand is inelastic, few good substitutes are available for the product. NFL play-off and Super Bowl tickets are inelastic because there are few if any substitutes for these products. Those who want to see the games in person will pay. A ticket price increase will bring additional revenue. II is wrong. If demand is inelastic, a decline in price will not result in an increase in total revenue. Instead, if demand is inelastic, a decline in price would lead to a decrease in total revenue.

423. **A.** Price elasticity of demand is calculated by dividing the percentage change in quantity demanded by the percentage change in price, using the average values of both.

    Step 1—Divide change in quantity by average quantity.
    $(40,000 - 60,000) \div 50,000 =$
    $-20,000 \div 50,000 = -0.4$

    Step 2—Divide change in price by average price.
    $\$5 \div \$27.50 = 0.1818$

    Step 3—Divide change in quantity by change in price.
    $-0.4 \div 0.1818 = -2.20$

    Any number greater than 1 (in absolute terms) indicates elastic demand rather than inelastic demand. This means that although the result is negative, −2.20, rather than 2.20, any number greater than 1 indicates elastic demand rather than inelastic demand.

424. **C.** When a good is demanded, no matter what the price, demand is described as perfectly inelastic. A newborn baby requiring milk and formula is an example of perfectly inelastic demand. Insulin for diabetics is another example of perfectly inelastic demand.

425. **C.** I and II are correct. Strengths and weaknesses focus on internal factors. Opportunities and threats relate to external factors. A SWOT analysis is the study of strengths, weaknesses, opportunities, and threats (SWOT). Evaluation of internal and external factors contributing to an organization's success is referred to as a SWOT analysis.

426. **A.** Comparative advantage suggests that even if one of two regions is absolutely more efficient in the production of every good than is the other, if each region specializes in the products in which it has greatest relative efficiency, trade will be mutually profitable to both regions. Comparative advantage leads to globalization. A characteristic of globalization is increased specialization. B is wrong. With economies of scale, firms may experience increasing returns because they operate more efficiently. With growth may come specialization of labor and related production efficiencies that reduce average costs. C is wrong. With the law of diminishing returns, a firm gets too large in the short run and an increase in labor or capital beyond a certain point causes a less than proportionate increase in production. D is wrong. The high-low method enables managers to estimate variable and fixed costs based

on the highest and lowest levels of activity during the period.

427. **B.** I, II, and III are correct. Porter's five forces affecting a firm's performance are intensity of firm rivalry, threat of substitute goods, threat of new competitors, bargaining power of customers, and bargaining power of suppliers. Intensity of firm rivalry is the first and most important factor affecting a firm's performance. The intensity of rivalry depends on the other four factors. The threat of substitute goods limits a firm's pricing power since consumers will switch to another product if the price differential becomes too high. If entry into an industry is relatively easy, firms within the industry face competition from new entrants if prices become too high and excess profits are earned. If customers hold bargaining power, there is a limit to price increases. In addition, a firm's cost structure and profitability are affected by the bargaining power of suppliers.

Chapter 21: Globalization and Performance, Process, and Risk Management

428. **A.** I and II are correct. Storage costs add no value to a firm, so a just-in-time system seeks to minimize storage costs, thus reducing non–value-added operations like storage. The just-in-time system focuses on expediting the production process by having materials available as needed without having to store them prior to usage. III is wrong. *Just in time* means that employees with multiple skills are used more efficiently and will not specialize in merely one job or task.

429. **B.** A dumping pricing policy involves the sales of goods by a company in one country in another country at a price that is lower than its cost. Thus, a Japanese company selling its goods in the United States at a price that is less than its cost would exhibit such a policy. A is wrong. A Japanese company selling its goods in its own country would not qualify as a dumping pricing policy regardless of the fact that the goods are being sold at lower than cost. C is wrong. For this to qualify as a dumping pricing policy, the goods would have to be sold at a price less than cost, not more than cost. D is wrong. In a dumping pricing policy, the goods are sold at an amount less than cost (not more than cost) and by a company in one country to another country, not the same country.

430. **C.** I and II are correct. Conformance costs include prevention and appraisal. The term *conformity*

describes goods that agree with manufacturing specifications. Conformance costs relate to investing a little extra money in the front end to make sure there are few or no problems later. The theory is that if a company spends a little extra on conformance, the result is a better-quality product and less failure. Prevention refers to training and preventive maintenance. Appraisal refers to inspection, and appraisal costs help discover and remove a defect before it's shipped to the customer or to the next department. Testing is an example of appraisal. Nonconformance costs include internal and external failures. The term *nonconformity* is a synonym for *failure*. The cost of failure is high, often resulting in lost customers and damaged reputation. Failure costs are referred to as nonconformance costs.

431. **B.** I and III are correct. Maintenance of machinery and inspection of final product are conformance costs found under the category of prevention cost. The two categories of conformance cost are prevention and appraisal. Prevention includes maintenance of equipment and inspection. Appraisal includes testing and inspection. Conformance costs are incurred to minimize nonconformance. II is wrong. Repair is a nonconformance (failure) cost. It is an external failure cost. Failure (nonconformance) is expensive; the real price is often lost customers and damaged reputation. Therefore, the theory is that higher conformance costs should lead to lower nonconformance costs, or less failure.

432. **B.** II is correct. There are external failure costs as well as internal failure costs. The question asked for an internal failure cost. Internal failure costs are discovered by the next department within the company rather than by the customer. When Department #2 sends back the product to Department #1 for rework and Department #1 needs to retool in order to do the rework, these are examples of internal failure costs. I is wrong. Product repair (warranty) is an external failure cost. When nonconforming products are detected by customers, the failure is considered external and warranty costs start to be incurred.

433. **D.** I and II are wrong. Repair is an external failure cost, discovered by customers. When nonconformance (failure) is discovered by customers, the costs are considered external failure costs. Rework is an internal failure cost. When the nonconformance (failure) is discovered within the company, the costs are considered internal failure costs. Rework and repair are nonconformance costs.

434. **B.** II is correct. Business process reengineering seeks radical change by ignoring the current process and instead starting from the beginning to design a different way of achieving the end goal and/or product. I is wrong. Business process management seeks incremental change by fine-tuning and tweaking the existing process and design. The advantage of incremental change (process management) is that if the change goes badly, the company is still left with a process that works.

435. **B.** The project manager is responsible for project administration on a day-to-day basis, including identifying and managing internal and external stakeholder expectations. A is wrong. The project sponsor is the party ultimately responsible for the success or failure of the project. The project sponsor is a member of top management that secures the funding and resources for the project. The sponsor interfaces between the organization and the project team itself but does not manage the project daily. C is wrong. The steering committee has oversight but does not manage the project on a daily basis. The project sponsor is the chair of the steering committee, and the remainder of the steering committee may be from within or outside the organization. D is wrong. The project members carry out the work and produce the final output known as the product "deliverables," but they do not manage the project on a day-to-day basis.

436. **A.** From top to bottom, the order is:

Board of Directors
↓
Steering Committee
↓
Project Sponsor (has ultimate responsibility)
↓
Project Manager
↓
Project Members

Within project management, the project manager is supervised by the project sponsor. The project sponsor reports to the steering committee, and the steering committee reports to the board of directors.

437. **D.** I is wrong. Future contracts, are a type of derivative instrument that can be used to either hedge an investment or for speculative purposes. A futures contract is a contractual arrangement to buy or sell a particular commodity or financial at a predetermined price in the future. They are standardized to facilitate trading on a futures exchange, which acts as a marketplace between buyers and sellers.

Futures contracts are marked to market at the close of each day, which helps mitigate their default as any profits or losses on the contracts must be received or paid each day through a clearinghouse. II is wrong. A futures contract is not a negotiated contract between parties (as is a forward contract). Futures contracts are standardized to facilitate trading on a futures exchange, and consequently, the counterparty to the contract is not known.

438. **A.** I is correct. The project sponsor should communicate project needs to the executive steering committee, not to the board of directors. II is wrong. The project sponsor does not approach the board of directors. Instead, the steering committee will approach the board of directors if the project sponsor can first convince the steering committee that the project is in the best interest of the company.

439. **C.** Globalization represents the increased dispersion and integration of the world's economies. It is often objectively measured as the growth in world trade as a percentage of gross domestic product. Globalization is frequently associated with comparative advantage and increased specialization.

440. **A.** I is correct. Short-term financing has increased credit risk since financing has not been secured long term; there is an increased risk that credit will be denied once the short-term debt matures. II is wrong. Short-term financing typically results in lower cost than long-term financing. Lower costs translate into higher profits. Therefore, short-term financing results in higher profitability (not lower profitability) than long-term financing. The reason that long-term financing results in higher costs than short-term financing is the higher interest rate risk for the lender associated with fixed long-term rates. The lender wants to be compensated for assuming a fixed rate of interest for a longer period of time. Short-term financing has as its advantage lower cost of borrowing, thus increasing profitability. Disadvantages with short-term borrowing include increased interest rate risk, since no long-term rate was locked in. Less potential credit available in the future is another disadvantage of short-term borrowing. Long-term financing involves securing a rate for longer periods of time. Long-term financing is more expensive than short-term financing, which results in lower profits, but long-term financing has as an advantage: less interest rate risk and less credit risk.

441. **C.** I and II are correct. Diversifiable risk includes unique risk, firm-specific risk of that particular investment. Since the risk is firm specific, it can be diversified away in a portfolio of investments of different risks. II is also correct. Diversifiable risk includes unsystematic risk. Unsystematic risk has less to do with the system and more to do with the stock itself. Since the risk is more stock than stock market, it also can be diversified away in a portfolio of investments of different risks.

442. **B.** The lender's default risk is based on the borrower's credit risk. Default risk impacts lenders. Lenders are exposed to default risk to the extent that it's possible that its borrowers will not repay the principal or interest due. Credit risk impacts borrowers. Exposure to credit risk includes a company's inability to secure financing or secure favorable credit terms as a result of poor credit ratings.

443. **B.** Purchasing power risk is the risk that price levels will change and affect asset values (mostly real estate). A is wrong. Interest rate risk is the fluctuation in the value of a "financial asset" when interest rates change. C is wrong. Liquidity risk is associated with the ability to sell the temporary investment in a short period of time without significant price concessions. D is wrong. Financial risk is a general category of risk that includes default risk and interest rate risk along with purchasing power risk, market risk, and liquidity risk.

444. **C.** If the market rate of interest increases, the value of the bond will decrease. This is true because the coupon rate is fixed, and if investors can do better elsewhere, the price of Wildwood Corp. bonds will drop.

445. **A.** If the foreign currency depreciates, the domestic currency appreciates. Since the US company has net cash outflows, a drop in value of the foreign currency would benefit the US company because such a drop means a drop in liabilities to the US company. Any drop in liabilities is considered a positive.

446. **D.** I and II are wrong. If the foreign currency appreciates and there are net cash inflows, that is positive for the US company because it will be paid in inflated dollars. If the foreign currency depreciates and the US company has net cash outflows, that's also positive for the US company because when the foreign currency depreciates, the domestic currency appreciates. If the foreign currency appreciates, the US company wants to have net cash inflows. Net cash outflows would be good if the foreign currency depreciates.

447. **C.** II is correct. The decision to exercise a call option would *not* be based on the amount paid for the call premium. The amount paid for the call, the call premium, would represent a sunk cost. Sunk costs are *not* relevant in decision-making. I is wrong. The decision to exercise a call option would be based on the strike price. The strike price is the price at which the shares represented by the call options could be purchased. III is wrong. The decision to exercise a call option would be based on the market price of the stock. If the strike price were below market price, the options would likely be exercised. However, if the market price were below the strike price, the decision would likely be made to let the call options expire.

448. **D.** Compared to US Treasury securities, equity securities and corporate bonds are both more risky. US Treasury securities are considered the least risky securities on the planet since they are backed by the full faith and credit of the US Treasury, which, so far, has never defaulted.

449. **B.** I is correct. If the exchange rate of the US dollar significantly declines, imported items will become more costly in the United States. Therefore, the exchange rate decline will hurt US imports. II is correct. US exports will benefit since the exchange rate decline in the US dollar will make exports less expensive outside of the United States. III is wrong. Foreign goods will be more, not less, expensive to US consumers if the exchange rate of the US dollar significantly declines.

450. **B.** II is correct. When the price of the pound rises, the price of British goods will also increase, and the pound will buy the same amount of British goods but more US goods. I is wrong. If the price of the pound increases relative to the US dollar, it will buy the same amount of British goods, not more.

451. **B.** II is correct. Having a foreign subsidiary subjects the domestic entity to foreign currency translation risk because when the US firm ultimately converts those financial statements from the Japanese currency back to the parent's currency, there could be big changes in amounts—especially if the local currency is not stable. I is wrong. No translation exposure exists, since there is no foreign investment or foreign subsidiary. The US entity exporting goods to Canada would be subject to foreign currency transaction risk but not subject to foreign currency translation risk, unless it makes an investment in a foreign entity or has a foreign subsidiary.

452. **A.** I is correct. The premium for the put option is a sunk cost and is not relevant to the decision on whether to exercise the put option. II is wrong. The premium paid for the put option is relevant to determining the total amount of asset value preserved.

453. **A.** Total interest for the loan is $100,000 × 0.06 = $6,000.

15% × $100,000 = $15,000 compensating balance
$85,000 net proceeds
$6,000 ÷ $85,000 = 7.05%

454. **B.** II is correct. Business risk represents the risk associated with the unique circumstances of a particular company. For example, if Hayes Corp. attempted to capitalize its operations using only its cumulative earnings, this could affect shareholder value significantly if the economy were to take a downturn and business were to slow. Therefore, relying solely on earnings for sustainability and growth is known as business risk. I is wrong. If an entity uses only its own cumulative earnings in capitalizing its operations, it's *not* exposed to the risk of defaulting on loans, which is known as financial risk. III is wrong. If an entity uses only its own cumulative earnings, then it is neither borrowing nor lending, so it's not exposed to the risks that the value of its financial instruments will change as a result of changes in interest rates, which is known as interest rate risk.

455. **C.** II and III are correct. Interest rate risk, otherwise known as maturity risk premium, is an appropriate risk adjustment to the risk-free rate of return and is the compensation investors demand for bearing risk. Maturity risk premium, or interest rate risk, increases with the term to maturity—the longer the term to maturity, the greater the maturity risk premium. I is wrong. Default risk premium, not interest rate risk, is an appropriate risk adjustment to the risk-free rate of return and is the additional compensation demanded by lenders for bearing the risk that the issuer of the security will fail to pay the interest or fail to repay the principal.

456. **C.** The expected return is calculated by summing the outcomes weighted by their probability of occurrence:

$100,000 × 0.1	$10,000
$600,000 × 0.3	+ $180,000
$900,000 × 0.2	+ $180,000
$300,000 × 0.4	+ $120,000
Expected return	$490,000

457. **C.** In order to determine the dollar loss from user error when the loss is distributed evenly over a range of dollars, the following computation is required: (low end of the range + high end of the range)/2, or ($5,000 + $20,000)/2 = $12,500. In the question, Surett Corp. estimates that there is an 80% chance that an error will occur; therefore, Surett can expect a $10,000 loss: $12,500 × 80% = $10,000.

458. **D.** I and II are wrong. A corporation about to issue new bonds agreeing to a debt covenant is generally good for potential bondholders and for the issuing corporation. It would probably reduce the coupon rate on the bonds being sold since the covenant generally serves to protect the bondholder's interests by placing restrictions on the issuing debtor. Such a covenant might raise, not lower, a company's bond rating because there would be less risk. A debt covenant is a provision in a bond indenture (contract between the bond issuer and the bondholders) that the bond issuer will refrain from doing what it otherwise has a legal right to do or possibly do something that it otherwise would not be required to do. Maintaining better than a 2:1 current ratio at all times is an example of a debt covenant. Violating a debt covenant would have consequences; for example, the entire debt could be due and payable immediately if the firm drops below the 2:1 current ratio. A debt covenant would normally increase the value of the bonds and lower the coupon rate due to decreased risk.

459. **A.** The sale of bonds to raise capital involves an immediate increase in cash but requires specific fixed payments and increases debt. Issuing bonds increases the debt equity ratio. The sale of common stock to raise capital does not require any payment and does not mature, and, because it increases equity while having no effect on debt, it decreases the debt equity ratio.

460. **C.** I is correct. A low rate of inflation would strengthen a country's currency and would, therefore, cause the currency to appreciate on the foreign currency market. II is wrong. Lower domestic real interest rates compared to real interest rates abroad would produce less demand for the currency for investment and, consequently, cause the domestic currency to depreciate, not appreciate, on the foreign exchange market. III is correct. A slow growth rate in a country's income relative to other countries, which produces a lesser amount of imports versus exports, means that there would be more demand for the country's currency (from other countries) in order to pay for the country's goods.

This would result in an appreciation of the country's currency on the foreign exchange market.

461. **A.** I is correct. The P/E ratio measures the amount that investors are willing to pay for each dollar of earnings per share. II is wrong. Higher P/E ratios generally indicate that investors are anticipating more growth and are bidding up the price of the shares in advance of performance.

462. **B.** The P/E multiple is calculated as follows:

K = Required rate of 11%
G = Forecasted growth rate of 9%
The estimated P/E multiple = Payout ÷ (K − G)
0.3 ÷ (0.11 − 0.09)
= 0.3 ÷ 0.02 = 15×

463. **A.** I is correct. A tariff (or protective tariff) adds to the purchase of imported goods and, therefore, increases domestic prices on the imported goods. II is wrong. Because a tariff increases the domestic price of imported goods, the demand for domestic goods increases. As a result, a tariff would produce an increase, not a decrease (or reduction), in the production of domestic goods. III is wrong. An embargo, not a tariff, is a total ban on the importation of specific goods.

464. **B.** II is correct. The constant growth model assumes that the growth rate is less than the discount rate. I is wrong. An underlying assumption of the constant growth model is the idea that the stock price will grow at the same rate as the dividend, thereby producing a constant growth rate.

465. **A.** The share price is calculated as follows:

Dividend ÷ desired return
$4 ÷ 10% = $40

The stock should sell for $40 per share to return 10% because $40 × 0.1 = $4 dividend per share. A zero growth model assumes that the next dividend is equal to the current dividend.

466. **D.** The price an investor is willing to pay today does not depend on what the dividend is today but on what the dividend is likely to be one year from now. The growth rate is 5%, so take today's $4 dividend and multiply by 1.05. Next year's dividend is expected to be $4.20; $4.20, next year's dividend, is the numerator. The denominator is the required rate of return, 20% minus the growth rate of 5%, so 15% is the denominator. Therefore, an investor is willing to pay for this stock today: $4.20 ÷ 0.15 = $28 per share. Common stock is valued based on next year's dividend; preferred stock is based on a dividend that is fixed. Common stock is valued based on growing dividends, while preferred stockholders receive a fixed dividend.

467. **B.** The P/E ratio is 20; therefore, the price is equal to the price divided by earnings anticipated for the coming year:

Price ÷ $18 = 20
Price = $360

468. **A.** I is correct. If markets are opened to foreign investments, there will undoubtedly be more investments made. Therefore, an increase in investment growth rates would result. II is wrong. Opening markets to foreign investment would have a decreasing, not increasing, effect on a local firm's cost of capital. III is wrong. The correlation of emerging markets with world markets would increase, not decrease, as a result of opening markets to foreign investments.

469. **C.** Country risk is the collection of risks/overall risk (such as political and financial risks) that a company faces when investing and doing business in a foreign country. A is wrong. Inflation risk is the risk of loss of future purchasing power associated with an investment. It is the risk that inflation will undermine the performance of that investment. B is wrong. Business risk (also called operations risk) is the risk of fluctuations in a company's earnings (operating income or EBIT), or the risk that a company will incur losses rather than earn profits as a result of various business/operational uncertainties (e.g., increased competition, changes in consumer preferences). D is wrong. Interest rate risk (also referred to as maturity risk) is the risk that a debt security/investment (e.g., loan or bond) will decline in value (before its maturity) due to an increase in interest rates.

470. **A.** I is correct. The P/E ratio is not meaningful if earnings are extremely small or if there is a loss. By name, the P/E ratio implies that there are earnings. Without sufficient earnings, the P/E ratio could not be used to determine a valuation of the company, whether the stock is selling for a fair price. Therefore, without sufficient earnings, the P/E ratio would not be used and a different measure of valuation like price to sales might be used instead. II is wrong. Price to sales ratio projection approaches can provide meaningful information in the event that net earnings are negative because even an entity with zero earnings still may command a certain valuation, especially if sales are expected to grow exponentially, which may generate the anticipation of profits.

471. **C.** III is correct. Financial managers that believe their actions will cause earnings to increase and impact the marketplace are suffering from an illusion of control. I is wrong. Confirmation bias occurs when managers use data that confirm their conclusions and ignore data that challenge their ideas. II is wrong. Excessive optimism is a manager's belief that results will generally be positive.

Chapter 22: Corporate Governance

472. **A.** I is correct. The Sarbanes-Oxley Act requires public companies to establish an audit committee that is directly responsible for the appointment, compensation, and oversight of the auditor. II is wrong. An annual audit provides meaningful information about financial reporting but does not address the issue of board oversight.

473. **D.** The board of directors of a corporation does not have the authority to directly manage the daily operations of a corporation; rather, the board maintains an oversight role and guides corporate management, whose responsibility it is to manage the corporation's daily operations. A, B, and C, are wrong since the declaration of dividends, adding or repealing bylaws, and determining executive compensation (as well as selecting and removing corporate officers) are all responsibilities that do fall under the board of directors' authority.

474. **C.** I and II are correct. The CEO and CFO must assert that they have reviewed the annual report and that there are no untrue statements and that no material information has been omitted.

475. **D.** I is correct. Under Section 201 of the Sarbanes-Oxley Act of 2002, audit firms may provide tax compliance, as well as certain other non-audit-related services to public audit clients, provided the activity is approved in advance by the client's audit committee. II is wrong. Under Section 201 of the Sarbanes-Oxley Act of 2002, performing bookkeeping or other services related to the client's accounting records or financial statements is prohibited as this could impair auditor objectivity in the conduct of the audit. III is wrong. Legal and expert services unrelated to the audit are not permitted to be provided by the auditor for its public client in accordance with Section 201 of the Sarbanes-Oxley Act of 2002. Other services that would be prohibited include internal auditing services, actuarial or valuation type services, and management consulting/

management functions–related services (e.g., human resources).

476. **D.** I, II, and III are correct. All correcting adjustments noted by the independent auditor need to be disclosed as an enhanced disclosure. In addition, with unconsolidated financial statements (equity method), related party transactions should be fully disclosed. Disclosures would put the readers on notice of the relationship because it increases the risk of investing in the company. Finally, enhanced disclosures include off–balance sheet financing. All material off–balance sheet financing transactions like operating leases must be disclosed.

477. **C.** I and II are correct. The Sarbanes-Oxley Act requires that the management report on internal control include management's assumption of responsibility for internal control. The act also requires that the management report on internal control include management's assessment of internal control effectiveness. III is wrong. Management does not describe disagreements, if any, between management and the auditor in its report on internal control as required by Sarbanes-Oxley. Instead that report should disclose and include a statement that addresses management's assumption of responsibility for internal control, management's assessment of internal control effectiveness, and that the auditor has reported on management's evaluation of internal control.

478. **D.** As prescribed by the Sarbanes-Oxley Act, in order for an audit committee member to be considered a financial expert, he or she must have an understanding of generally accepted accounting principles (US GAAP). The audit committee member does not need to have an understanding of federal tax law, corporate governance rules and procedures, or generally accepted auditing standards (GAAS). Thus, answers A, B, and C are wrong.

479. **C.** I and II are correct. The act specifically requires that the code of ethics include provisions for full, fair, accurate, and timely disclosure in periodic financial statements and that the code of ethics include provisions for honest and ethical conduct.

480. **D.** I and II are wrong. The partner in charge of the audit firm engaged to do the audit should not be the financial expert on the audit committee. Under the Sarbanes-Oxley Act, one member of the audit committee needs to be named the financial expert. However, no real hard rules for who must be named the financial expert exist under the act.

481. **C.** Enterprise risk management (ERM) is a process (effected by an entity's board of directors, management, and other personnel) that is designed to help an entity identify potential events that pose both risk and opportunities to the entity. In doing so, ERM allows the entity to effectively cope with the uncertainty presented by those events. Major capabilities of ERM include helping the entity align its risk appetite with strategy, reduce operational surprises and losses by improving the entity's ability to anticipate potential events and develop timely responses to those events, manage cross-enterprise risk and provide integrated responses to multiple risks, respond to and seize opportunities, improve the entity's deployment of capital, and enhance risk response decisions, which may include the decision to avoid, reduce, share, or accept risk. Thus, ERM does not provide an entity the ability to avoid all risks but rather provides a framework by which those risks may be identified and then responded to within the entity's risk appetite linked to its strategy. A, B, and D are wrong since more effective capital allocation and the ability to respond to opportunities timely, as well as anticipate potential events, are all benefits derived from implementing an ERM system.

482. **D.** The manager of a department—who is closest to, and most knowledgeable about, the department's day-to-day activities—is best suited to establish and execute risk procedures for a particular department. A, B, and C are incorrect since the internal audit department personnel, the chief executive officer, and the audit committee would typically assume more of an oversight, not execution-type, role over the implementation of risk procedures in a specific department of an entity.

483. **A.** I and II are correct. The control environment is a major component of COSO, which consists of a set of standards, processes, and structures that lay the foundation for affecting a system of internal control throughout, and across, an organization. The control environment includes the following principles: (1) the organization demonstrates a commitment to integrity and ethical values, (2) *the board* demonstrates independence from management and *exercises oversight of internal control*, (3) management establishes, with board oversight, structures, reporting lines, and authorities and responsibilities, (4) the organization demonstrates a *commitment to attract, develop, and retain competent individuals* in alignment with objectives, and (5) the organization holds individuals accountable for their internal

control responsibilities in pursuit of objectives. III is wrong. Evaluating and communicating internal control deficiencies is a principle embodied in the monitoring component of COSO.

484. **D.** I and II are wrong. While achieving a CPA certificate is an outstanding personal accomplishment, it would not automatically qualify an individual to serve as an audit committee financial expert. While a full-time tenured professor of accounting at a major university with a PhD would be expected to know the GAAP rules, this would not automatically qualify the individual to serve as an audit committee financial expert. The Sarbanes-Oxley Act does not provide any guidance on who would automatically qualify to serve as financial expert. Someone with academic success may still lack the experience needed to be a financial expert on an audit engagement. Audit committee members should use their judgment in all cases to determine who would qualify.

485. **A.** Residual risk is the "remaining" risk associated with an event after considering management's risk response. Put another way, it is the risk left over after natural or inherent risks have been reduced by risk controls. B is wrong. Detection risk is not a risk related to ERM. Rather, it is the risk that the auditor fails to detect a material misstatement in an entity's financial statements when conducting an audit of those statements. C is wrong. Inherent risk is risk that is already present before management does anything to alter the risk likelihood or impact. For example, there is an inherent collectability risk associated with selling goods on account (e.g., accepting accounts receivable). D is wrong. Control risk is the risk that a material financial misstatement could occur but may not be detected and corrected, or prevented, by an entity's system of internal controls.

486. **A.** I is correct. The regular evaluation of employees for their competence in financial reporting is an important link between human resources policies and the achievement of financial reporting objectives. II is wrong. Management's operating style relates more to work ethic and commitment to effective financial reporting than the recruitment, retention, and evaluation of employees.

487. **A.** I is correct. The existence of a published code of ethics and a periodic acknowledgment that ethical values are understood is evidence of a development of ethical values and a commitment to ensuring that those values are understood and taken seriously. II

is wrong. Board oversight relates more to overall leadership than to the specifics of ethical behavior.

488. **A.** I is correct. The existence of a compliance program that includes both ethics training and a hotline for anonymous reporting is evidence of the development of ethical values and ensuring that those values are understood and taken seriously. II is wrong. Appropriate delegation relates to the organization's assignment of duties rather than to the specifics of ethical behavior.

489. **A.** I is correct. Active engagement by an audit committee in representing the board of directors relative to all matters of internal and external audits is evidence of the board's understanding of its oversight responsibility over financial reporting. II is wrong. The organizational structure principle typically involves the appropriate alignment of reporting relationships to ensure that controls are not undermined (e.g., internal auditors should not report to the CFO but rather to the audit committee).

490. **C.** Probability and expected value analysis is not a technique used for identifying events in an ERM program. Instead, this type of analysis provides an assessment of the likelihood of probable outcomes of a particular event or decision. A is wrong. Internal analysis is a technique used for identifying events in an ERM program and involves using information gathered from stakeholders such as customers and suppliers. B is wrong. Leading event indicators is a technique that involves monitoring data associated with events to determine when the event is likely to occur and is used to identify events in an ERM program. D is wrong. Process flow analysis is a technique used to identify events in an ERM program by dissecting processes into inputs, tasks, responsibilities, and outputs to identify events that might impact the process in an adverse manner.

491. **A.** Variance analysis specifically supports internal control information, not financial reporting, internal communications, or external communications generally.

492. **D.** Risk sharing involves transferring some loss potential to another party. Some techniques for sharing risk include purchasing insurance, hedging, outsourcing, and entering into joint ventures. A is wrong. No action is taken when an entity responds to risk by accepting (or retaining) that risk. An entity that "self-insures" against possible catastrophes or disasters employs a risk acceptance response. B is wrong. Risk avoidance involves exiting the activity that gives rise to the risk. For

instance, an entity that would like to avoid the risk of customer nonpayments might decide not to sell goods and/or services on account, but rather require cash payment for those goods and/or services. C is wrong. Risk reduction involves taking action to lower the risk associated with an activity. For instance, implementing internal controls in an entity's cash collection process such as segregating the custodial, recording, and authorization responsibilities associated with that process is an example of a technique that can be used to reduce the risk of asset misappropriation.

493. **B.** The control (internal) environment component of the COSO ERM framework sets an entity's overall environment tone and reflects its risk management philosophy, risk appetite, ethical values, and integrity. A is wrong. The risk assessment component of the COSO ERM framework involves determining the likelihood and impact of events on the achievement of an entity's objectives. The assessment considers inherent risk and residual risk. C is wrong. The information and communication component of the COSO ERM framework identifies, captures, and communicates relevant and timely information. D is wrong. Under the COSO ERM framework, control activities consist of an entity's policies and procedures established and used to implement the response to risk.

494. **B.** According to the COSO framework, risk assessments involve the determination of the likelihood and impact of events on the achievement of objectives. A is wrong. Control activities are the methods used to implement the response to risk. Sometimes the control activity is also, effectively, the risk response. C is wrong. Inherent risk is the risk to an entity in the absence of any actions management might take to alter either the risk's likelihood or impact. Risk responses are developed to deal with inherent risk. D is wrong. Residual risk is the risk that still remains after management responds to the risk and the control activities are in place.

495. **C.** A response to risk that involves the diversification of product offerings rather than the elimination of product offerings is called risk reduction.

496. **A.** According to COSO, reporting that triggers prompt exception resolution, root cause analysis, and control updates illustrates the principle of internal control information. Internal control information is needed to facilitate the function of control components in a timely manner that enables personnel to fulfill their responsibilities. B is wrong.

Financial reporting information principles anticipate that information is identified, captured, used at all levels of the company, and distributed in a manner that supports the achievement of financial reporting objectives. C is wrong. Internal communications anticipate that communications enable and support understanding and execution of internal control objectives, processes, and individual responsibilities. D is wrong. External communications anticipate that matters affecting the achievement of financial reporting are communicated with outside parties.

497. **D.** I and II are correct. According to the COSO, maintaining adequate staffing to keep overtime and benefit costs within budget is an operational objective. In addition, maintaining direct labor cost variances within published guidelines is an operational objective. III is wrong. According to COSO, maintaining accounting principles that conform to US GAAP is a reporting objective rather than an operational objective.

498. **A.** I is correct. The control activities component of the ERM framework includes key elements that relate to the policies and procedures that ensure appropriate responses to identified risks, not to ethical values. II is wrong. The internal environment component (rather than the control activities component) of the ERM framework includes foundational elements such as organizational structure, assignment of authority and responsibility, integrity and ethical values, risk management philosophy, commitment to competence and human resources standards, and similar issues that influence the tone of the organization.

499. **B.** II is correct. The procedure for electing the board of directors is normally included in the bylaws of the corporation, not its articles of incorporation. The articles of incorporation must contain the name of the corporation and its initial address, the purpose and powers of the corporation, the name of the registered agent of the corporation, the name and address of each incorporator, and the number of authorized shares of the corporation's stock, as well as the type of stock. Thus, I and III are both wrong, as these are not exceptions, but rather are required to be included in the articles of incorporation.

500. **B.** Independence Standards is not a section of the Institute of Internal Auditor's International Standards for the Professional Practice of Internal Auditing. The internal auditing standards are

broken down into attribute standards (those related to the characteristics of the internal audit activity) and performance standards (those related to the quality of internal audit activities). The standards also include implementation standards that expand upon the attribute and performance standards. Thus, A, C, and D are wrong as they are sections of the Institute of Internal Auditor's International Standards for Professional Practice of Internal Auditing.

PART III

FINANCIAL ACCOUNTING AND REPORTING

CHAPTER 23

ACCOUNTING THEORY AND FINANCIAL REPORTING

QUESTIONS 1–37

1. Which of the following are included in the Accounting Standards Codification?
   I. Financial Accounting Standards Board (FASB) statements of financial accounting standards
   II. International Financial Reporting Standards (IFRS)
   A. I only
   B. II only
   C. Both I and II
   D. Neither I nor II

2. The objectives of financial reporting for business enterprises, as set forth by the FASB conceptual framework, are based on:
   A. SEC reporting requirements
   B. generally accepted accounting principles (GAAP)
   C. the needs of users of the information
   D. materiality

3. According to the FASB and International Accounting Standards Board (IASB) conceptual framework, relevance includes which of the following qualitative characteristics?
   I. Predictive value
   II. Confirmatory value
   A. I only
   B. II only
   C. Both I and II
   D. Neither I nor II

4. According to the FASB and IASB conceptual framework, neutrality is a component of:
   I. faithful representation
   II. relevance
   A. I only
   B. II only
   C. Both I and II
   D. Neither I nor II

5. Which of the following is a fundamental qualitative characteristic of financial reporting?
   I. Relevance
   II. Faithful representation
   A. I only
   B. II only
   C. Both I and II
   D. Neither I nor II

6. According to the FASB and IASB conceptual framework, which of the following is an enhancing (rather than fundamental) qualitative characteristic of financial reporting?
   I. Comparability
   II. Verifiability
   A. I only
   B. II only
   C. Both I and II
   D. Neither I nor II

7. According to the FASB and IASB conceptual framework, both timeliness and understandability are:

A. enhancing qualitative characteristics of useful financial information
B. fundamental qualitative characteristics of useful financial information
C. characteristics of relevance
D. characteristics of faithful representation

8. An entity's revenue might result from which of the following according to the FASB conceptual framework?

A. A decrease in a liability from primary operations
B. A decrease in an asset from primary operations
C. An increase in a liability from ancillary transactions
D. An increase in an asset from ancillary transactions

9. Which of the following is a correct statement regarding deferred revenue?

A. Deferred revenue result from services that have not yet been billed, but have been performed.
B. Deferred revenue reported on the books of one company to a transaction mirror accrued expenses reported on the books of the other party to the transaction.
C. Deferred revenue is reported as a liability until the services have been performed.
D. Deferred revenue represent amounts that have not yet been received in cash, but have been earned.

10. Accordingly to the FASB conceptual framework, essential characteristics of an asset include which of the following?

I. An asset is intangible.
II. Claims to the asset's benefits are legally enforceable.
III. An asset provides future benefits.

A. II and III only
B. III only
C. II only
D. I, II, and III

11. The underlying concept that governs gain contingencies under GAAP is:

A. conservatism
B. consistency
C. materiality
D. faithful representation

12. Which of the following is an element of comprehensive income?

A. Prepayments
B. Administrative expenses
C. Shareholder investments
D. Dividends

Use the following facts to answer **Questions 13–14:**

During January of Year 3, Durka Corp. agreed to sell the assets and product line of its Arelco division. The sale was completed on January 15, Year 4, and resulted in a gain on disposal of $900,000. Arelco's operating losses were $600,000 for Year 3 and $50,000 for the period January 1 through January 15, Year 4.

13. If the tax rate is 30%, what amount of net gain (loss) should be reported in Durka's Year 3 income statement under US GAAP?

A. $420,000
B. ($420,000)
C. ($600,000)
D. $0

14. Assuming a 30% tax rate, what amount of net gain (loss) should be reported in Durka's Year 4 income statement under US GAAP?

A. $850,000
B. $900,000
C. $595,000
D. $255,000

15. The Pastorini Corp. reported the following items on the income statement. Which of the following items would be reported as income from continuing operations?

I. Large loss from a foreign currency transaction
II. A union strike that shuts down operations for three months
III. Damage to a factory from a flood in an area that never had flood damage before

A. III only
B. II and III only
C. I and II only
D. I, II, and III

16. Which of the following accounting changes would receive prospective treatment in the income statement?
    I. Change in depreciation method
    II. Change in useful life of an asset

    A. I only
    B. II only
    C. Both I and II
    D. Neither I nor II

17. Which of the following accounting changes is treated as a change in accounting principle?
    I. a change from first in–first out inventory valuation to average cost
    II. a change from the direct write-off method of recognizing bad debt expense to the allowance method

    A. I only
    B. II only
    C. Both I and II
    D. Neither I nor II

18. On January 1, Year 8, Ashbrook Corp. changed from one IFRS method to another. The change in principle better presents the financial information of Ashbrook Corp. Under the old method the pretax accounting income was $600,000. Had Ashbrook Corp. been using the new method, pretax accounting income would have been $900,000. Ashbrook Corp.'s effective tax rate is 30%. How should Ashbroook Corp. report the cumulative effect of a change in accounting principle for Year 8?

    A. $300,000 additional income on the income statement
    B. $210,000 additional income on the income statement
    C. $300,000 increase to beginning retained earnings balance
    D. $210,000 increase to beginning retained earnings balance

19. An accounting change whose cumulative effect on prior periods is impracticable to determine should be accounted for:

    A. as a prior period adjustment
    B. on a prospective basis
    C. as a cumulative effect change on the income statement
    D. as an adjustment to retained earnings in the earliest period presented

20. Which of the following are reported as adjustments to the beginning balance of retained earnings for the earliest period presented?
    I. correction of an error in a period that is not being presented
    II. cumulative effect of a change in inventory from FIFO to weighted average

    A. I only
    B. II only
    C. Both I and II
    D. Neither I nor II

21. Rex Corp. changed from straight line depreciation to double declining balance, resulting in an additional expense of $20,000 after tax for Year 5. Also in Year 5, Rex Corp. failed to accrue bad debt expense of $30,000 (after tax) in its income statement. What amount should Rex Corp. report as a prior period adjustment in Year 5?

    A. $20,000
    B. $30,000
    C. $50,000
    D. $0

22. In its consolidated financial statements in the current year, Benson Corp. included a subsidiary it acquired several years ago that was appropriately excluded from consolidation last year. How should this be reported?

    A. By note disclosure only
    B. Currently and prospectively
    C. Currently with note disclosure of pro forma effects of retrospective application
    D. By retrospective application of all prior periods presented

23. The cumulative effect of which of the following accounting changes would be presented as an adjustment to the beginning balance of retained earnings for the earliest period presented?
    I. A change in the amount of mineral expected to be recoverable from an underground mine
    II. A change in the expected useful life of a machine from 7 years to 4 years

    A. I only
    B. II only
    C. Both I and II
    D. Neither I nor II

24. On October 31, Year 8, Kingman Corp. decided to change from the completed contract method to the percentage of completion method. Kingman Corp. is a calendar year corporation and used US GAAP. If comparative financial statements are NOT being presented, the cumulative effect of this change is:

A. shown as of October 31, Year 9
B. shown as of January 1, Year 9
C. not shown
D. shown as of December 31, Year 9

25. Which of the following is correct regarding the reporting of comprehensive income?
    I. Comprehensive income can be presented together with the income statement as a single financial statement.
    II. Comprehensive income may be shown separately on its own financial statement.

A. I only
B. II only
C. Both I and II
D. Neither I nor II

26. Which of the following standard setting bodies requires that a description of significant policies be included as an integral part of the financial statements?
    I. US GAAP
    II. IFRS

A. I only
B. II only
C. Both I and II
D. Neither I nor II

27. Which of the following should be disclosed in a footnote called "summary of significant accounting policies"?
    I. Basis of profit recognition on long-term construction contracts
    II. Criteria for measuring cash equivalents

A. I only
B. II only
C. Both I and II
D. Neither I nor II

28. Footnote disclosure of significant judgments and estimates is a requirement under which of the following standards?
    I. US GAAP
    II. IFRS

A. I only
B. II only
C. Both I and II
D. Neither I nor II

29. As it relates to financial reporting qualitative characteristics, which of the following is emphasized through the preparation of interim financial statements?

A. Timeliness over reliability
B. Comparability over neutrality
C. Materiality over completeness
D. Reliability over relevance

30. Which of the following accounting standards requires a statement in the footnotes that financial statements are presented in accordance with the reporting framework?
    I. US GAAP
    II. IFRS

A. I only
B. II only
C. Both I and II
D. Neither I nor II

31. Cimmino, Ltd. reported the following selected information for Year 2:

Foreign currency translation loss	$2,000
Distributions to owners	$10,000
Net income	$135,000
Unamortized prior service cost on pension plan	$15,000
Deferred gain on an effective cash flow hedge	$12,000

What amount should Cimmino report as other comprehensive income/(loss) for Year 2?

A. $145,000
B. $130,000
C. $118,000
D. ($5,000)

32. Which is correct regarding interim financial reporting?
    I. Interim financial reporting is not required under GAAP.
    II. Permanent inventory declines incurred during interim periods should NOT be recorded at the time of their decline, but rather should be reported at year-end.
    III. Revenues and expenses should be allocated evenly over interim reporting periods, regardless of when they actually occurred.

A. I only
B. II only
C. I and II only
D. I, II, and III

33. Which of the following is correct regarding the US Securities and Exchange Commission (SEC) reporting standards for a large accelerated filer?
    I. Form 10-K must be filed within 90 days of the close of the fiscal year.
    II. Form 10-Q must be filed within 40 days of the close of the first three fiscal quarters.

    A. I only
    B. II only
    C. Both I and II
    D. Neither I nor II

34. Which of the following is correct regarding forms 10-K and 10-Q for US registered companies?

    A. They must be prepared using US GAAP.
    B. Form 10-Q must be prepared using US GAAP, but Form 10-K can be prepared using US GAAP or IFRS.
    C. They can be prepared using either US GAAP or IFRS.
    D. Form 10-K must be prepared using US GAAP, but Form 10-Q may be prepared using IFRS.

35. Privately held companies are exempt from reporting which of the following?
    I. Earnings per share (EPS)
    II. Business segment information

    A. I only
    B. II only
    C. Both I and II
    D. Neither I nor II

The following information pertains to Cricket Corp.'s segments for Year 13:

Segment	Sales to Unaffiliated Customers	Intercompany Sales	Total Revenue
Travis	$6,000	$4,000	$10,000
Bass	$9,000	$5,000	$14,000
Lead	$4,000	$1,000	$5,000
Capo	$45,000	$18,000	$63,000
Combined	$64,000	$28,000	$92,000
Elimination		$28,000	$28,000
Consolidated	$64,000		$64,000

36. If Cricket uses the revenue test to determine reportable segments, which of the following is correct?
    I. Bass would NOT be a reportable segment in Year 13, since its revenue from sales to unaffiliated customers of $9,000 is less than 10% of $92,000.
    II. Lead would NOT be a reportable segment in Year 13, since its combined revenue of $5,000 is less than 10% of $92,000.

    A. I only
    B. II only
    C. Both I and II
    D. Neither I nor II

37. Wershing Corp., a publicly held corporation, is subject to the requirements of segment reporting. In its income statement for December 31, Year 12, Wershing Corp. reported revenues of $60,000,000, operating expenses of $58,000,000, and net income of $2,000,000. $40,000,000 of Wershing Corp. sales were to external customers. External revenues reported by operating segments must be at least how much for Year 12?

    A. $45,000,000
    B. $6,000,000
    C. $4,000,000
    D. $30,000,000

CHAPTER 24

REVENUE AND EXPENSE RECOGNITION

QUESTIONS 38–69

38. Which of the following requirements must be met for revenue to be recognized under US generally accepted accounting principles (GAAP)?
  I. There must exist persuasive evidence of an arrangement or contract.
  II. Services have been rendered or delivery of goods has occurred.
  III. At least 10% of the cash consideration must be received.

  A. I only
  B. I and II
  C. I, II, and III
  D. II only

39. Advantage Voice and Data LLC develops hardware and software for the telecom industry. On September 22, Year 2, Advantage signs a multiple element arrangement with Voicenext LLC, where Advantage will sell a phone system to Voicenext, train Voicenext staff, and offer post-sales customer support to Voicenext staff through December 31 of Year 3. The total value of the contract is $250,000. The phone system is installed on December 1 of Year 2; the employees' training is completed as of December 31 of Year 2. Although the contract is not substantially complete, Advantage would like to recognize revenue in Year 2 for the elements of the contract that have been completed thus far, including the installation of the system and training of the staff. Which of the following is a condition that must exist for Advantage to recognize revenue from separate elements of this contract prior to the completion of the entire agreement?

  I. The element has value on a stand-alone basis.
  II. The element can be sold separately.

  A. I only
  B. II only
  C. Both I and II
  D. Neither I nor II

40. According to the concept of accrual accounting, which of the following describes a deferral?
  I. Deferral of revenues will occur when cash is received but is NOT recognizable for financial statement purposes.
  II. Deferral typically results in the recognition of a liability or prepaid expense.

  A. I only
  B. II only
  C. Both I and II
  D. Neither I nor II

41. Abel, Inc. entered into a royalty agreement with Barreiro Corp. under which Abel will pay royalties for the assignment of patent for seven years. When should Abel expense the royalty payments?

  A. At the commencement date of the royalty agreement
  B. In the period the royalty expense is incurred
  C. In the period the royalty is paid
  D. The royalty expense should be deferred until the royalty agreement expires

42. Brace Inc. prepaid an annual insurance policy on August 1, Year 10, in the amount of $3,000. The entry to adjust the prepaid expense account at December 31, Year 10, would include:

    A. credit of $1,250 to prepaid insurance
    B. debit of $1,750 to insurance expense
    C. credit of $1,750 to prepaid insurance
    D. debit of $1,250 to prepaid insurance

43. Perry's Gift Shop, a retail store, sold gift certificates that are redeemable in merchandise. On November 1, Year 12, a customer buys $6,000 of gift certificates from Perry's Gift Shop. The gift certificates lapse 1 year after the date of issuance. Which of the following is correct?

    A. On November 1, Year 12, Perry would record a credit to revenue for $6,000.
    B. On November 1, Year 12, Perry would record a credit to deferred revenue for $6,000.
    C. On December 31, Year 12, Perry would record a credit to revenue for the months of November and December in the amount of $1,000.
    D. On November 1, Year 12, Perry would record a debit to prepaid expense for $6,000.

44. With regard to cash received in advance for gift certificates, the deferred revenue account would decrease by which of the following?

    I. Lapse or expiration of certificates
    II. Redemption of certificates

    A. I only
    B. II only
    C. Both I and II
    D. Neither I nor II

45. Which of the following is correct regarding cash basis and accrual basis revenue as related to accounts receivable?

    I. A decrease in accounts receivable from the beginning of the year to the end of the year generally represents cash collections.
    II. Under the cash basis, revenue is recognized when the receivable is initially recorded.

    A. I only
    B. II only
    C. Both I and II
    D. Neither I nor II

46. When adjusting service revenue from cash basis to accrual basis, which of the following items would be added to cash fees collected?

    I. The ending balance of accounts receivable
    II. The beginning balance of accounts receivable

    A. I only
    B. II only
    C. Both I and II
    D. Neither I nor II

47. International financial reporting standards require which revenue recognition method when the outcome of rendering services cannot be estimated reliably?

    A. Installment sales method
    B. Cost recovery method
    C. Completed contract method
    D. Percentage of completion method

48. The ending balance of unearned fees represents:

    I. cash received in advance and NOT yet earned during the period
    II. the decrease in accounts receivable for the period

    A. I only
    B. II only
    C. Both I and II
    D. Neither I nor II

49. Evanko Co. is analyzing its prepaid expense account balance at December 31, Year 2, and noted the following items composing that balance: $1,500 associated with a $3,000 annual insurance policy Evanko paid for that commenced on July 1, Year 1; a $2,000 advance rent payment Evanko paid on November 1, Year 1, in connection with a new building lease (the lease commences on January 1, Year 3); and $3,200 of supplies Evanko prepaid for on October 15, Year 2. A physical count of the prepaid supplies noted $2,000 of those supplies still on hand at December 31, Year 2. What amounts should Evanko report as prepaid expense in its December 31, Year 2, balance sheet, and as expense in its income statement for the year ended December 31, Year 2?

    A. $4,000 prepaid expense; $2,700 expense
    B. $5,200 prepaid expense; $1,500 expense
    C. $3,667 prepaid expense; $3,033 expense
    D. $2,000 prepaid expense; $4,700 expense

50. On January 2, Year 1, Maximus Corp. hired a chief technology officer and entered into an employment agreement to pay this officer $50,000 in Years 4, 5, and 6, as long as the officer is still employed by Maximus through December 31, Year 3. Maximus should report compensation expense under this agreement in which of the following ways?

    A. $25,000 in each of Years 1 through 6
    B. $50,000 in each of Years 1 through 3
    C. $150,000 in Year 1 when the employee agreement is executed
    D. $150,000 at the beginning of Year 4

51. When adjusting service revenue from cash basis to accrual basis, which of the following items would be added to cash fees collected?
    I. beginning unearned fees
    II. ending unearned fees

    A. I only
    B. II only
    C. Both I and II
    D. Neither I nor II

52. Moss, a consultant, keeps her accounting records on a cash basis. During Year 10 she collected $100,000 in fees from clients. At December 31, Year 9, she had accounts receivable of $40,000. At December 31, Year 10, she had accounts receivable of $60,000 and unearned fees of $4,000. On the accrual basis, what was her service revenue for Year 10?

    A. $120,000
    B. $180,000
    C. $116,000
    D. $124,000

53. Storage Inc. owns a warehouse and leases space under a variety of agreements. Some customers pay in advance, and others fall behind on their rent. Storage Inc.'s financial records contained the following data:

	Year 1	Year 2
Rent receivable	$7,600	$8,200
Unearned rent	$28,000	$21,000

During Year 2, Storage Inc. received $60,000 cash from tenants. What amount of rental revenue should Storage Inc. record for Year 2?

    A. $60,000
    B. $67,600
    C. $52,400
    D. $68,240

Use the following facts to answer **Questions 54–55:**

Millet Inc. uses the percentage of completion method to account for long-term construction contracts. On January 3, Year 12, Millet signed a 3-year contract with the state of New Jersey to build a road. The contract was for $2,000,000. Costs incurred in Year 12 amounted to $300,000, and total costs remaining on the contract were expected to be $1,200,000. Millet collected $200,000 from the state in advance at the time the contract was signed and another $150,000 at the end of Year 12. In Year 13, another $900,000 was spent, and it was estimated that an additional $400,000 of costs would be spent in Year 14.

54. How much profit from the contract should Millet Inc. recognize in Year 12?

    A. $0
    B. $100,000
    C. $350,000
    D. $500,000

55. How much profit from the contract should Millet Inc. recognize in Year 13?

    A. $300,000
    B. $400,000
    C. $100,000
    D. $200,000

56. For a long-term construction contract being accounted for using the percentage of completion method, the construction in progress account is debited for:
    I. construction costs incurred
    II. profit from the construction contract recognized to date

    A. I only
    B. II only
    C. Both I and II
    D. Neither I nor II

57. Everlast Construction Inc. uses the percentage of completion method to account for long-term construction contracts. The account "progress billings" is credited by Everlast Construction Inc. when:

    A. bills that have been sent to customers are returned with payment
    B. construction costs are paid
    C. profit is recorded
    D. bills are mailed to customers

58. With regard to profit recognition from long-term construction contracts accounted for on the percentage of completion method:

    A. progress billings impact profit, but cash collections do not
    B. cash collections impact profit, but progress billings do not
    C. both cash collections and progress billings impact profit recognition
    D. neither cash collections nor progress billings impact profit recognition

59. The completed contract method of accounting for long-term construction projects:

    A. is no longer permitted under US GAAP
    B. is to be used when the degree of completion can be determined with reasonable accuracy
    C. recognizes losses in the year they are apparent even if the project is not substantially completed
    D. is essentially a cash basis rather than accrual basis method

60. Olney Contracting is hired by the state of Arizona on January 1, Year 13, to build a section of a new highway. The contract will take several years to complete. The sales price is $50 million, and the company estimates that the work will cost $44 million. During Year 13, $11 million is spent. During Year 14, another $20 million is spent, and engineers expect that the project will require additional costs of $15 million after Year 14. Olney Corp. must use the percentage of completion method to account for this contract if the buyer has the ability to fulfill its obligations and Olney has the ability to:

    I. estimate the degree of completion with reasonable accuracy
    II. complete the job

    A. I only
    B. II only
    C. Both I and II
    D. Neither I nor II

Use the following facts to answer **Questions 61–62:**

The Buxton Corp. sold an asset on March 1 of Year 13 for the amount of $100,000. The cost of the asset was $60,000. Buxton was unable to estimate how much of the $100,000 they may collect; therefore, they chose to account for the sale under the installment method. In Year 13, $20,000 was collected in connection with this sale, and in Year 14, $10,000 more was collected.

61. How much gross profit from the sale should be realized by Buxton Corp. on the December 31, Year 13, income statement?

    A. $0
    B. $8,000
    C. $6,667
    D. $40,000

62. How much gross profit from the sale should be deferred by Buxton Corp. on December 31, Year 13?

    A. $32,000
    B. $60,000
    C. $40,000
    D. $92,000

63. Which of the following is considered a cash basis rather than an accrual basis method of revenue recognition?

    I. Percentage of completion
    II. Completed contract
    III. Installment method

    A. II and III
    B. III only
    C. II only
    D. I only

Use the following facts to answer **Questions 64–65:**

In Year 13, Russell Inc. uses the cost recovery method to account for a $5,000 sale with a total cost of $2,500. During Year 13, Russell collects $2,000 and then collects $3,000 in Year 14.

64. Using the cost recovery method, how much will Russell report as gross profit in Year 13?

    A. $2,500
    B. $1,000
    C. $500
    D. $0

65. Using the cost recovery method, how much will Russell report as gross profit in Year 14?

A. $500
B. $2,500
C. $1,500
D. $0

66. If Russell Inc. had used the installment method rather than cost recovery, how much gross profit would have been realized in Year 13?

A. $0
B. $2,000
C. $2,500
D. $1,000

67. During Year 1, Denni Stevens, Ltd. recorded a new classic rock album and signed an agreement with Kristin Records, Inc. to receive royalties of 30% on future album sales. At December 31, Year 2, Stevens reported royalties receivable of $75,000 from Kristin, and during Year 3 it received royalty payments from Kristin in the amount of $200,000. Also during Year 3, Kristin reported revenues of $1,000,000 from sales of the album. What amount of royalty revenue should Stevens report in its Year 3 income statement?

A. $500,000
B. $300,000
C. $275,000
D. $200,000

68. Mann Pharmaceuticals acquires patent rights to certain surgical equipment from various medical companies. In exchange, Mann, in some cases, pays royalties in advance for those rights, and in other cases pays royalties within 60 days from its December 31 year-end. A review of Mann's accounting records disclosed prepaid royalties in the amount of $60,000 and $50,000 at December 31, Year 1 and Year 2, respectively, and royalties payable in the amount of $95,000 and $90,000 at December 31, Year 1 and Year 2, respectively. During Year 2, Mann paid royalties of $300,000. What amount of royalty expense should Mann report in its Year 2 income statement?

A. $330,000
B. $310,000
C. $305,000
D. $295,000

69. Dartam Publishing created a board game called "Visit New York" and sold it to Parker Brothers for royalties of 10% of sales. Royalties are payable semi-annually on March 31 (for July through December sales of the previous year) and on September 30 (for January through June sales of the same year). On September 30, Year 4, Dartam Publishing received their first royalty check from Parker Brothers in the amount of $10,000. On March 31, Year 5, Dartam Publishing received a royalty check in the amount of $20,000. On September 30, Year 5, Dartam Publishing received a royalty check for $30,000. Dartam Publishing estimated that board game sales of "Visit New York" would total $180,000 for the second half of Year 5. How much royalty revenue should Dartam Publishing report for the year ended December 31, Year 5?

A. $48,000
B. $68,000
C. $21,000
D. $50,000
D. $55,000

CHAPTER 25

CASH, RECEIVABLES, AND INVENTORY

QUESTIONS 70–122

Use the following facts to answer **Questions 70–72:**

The Romanoff Company offers trade discounts of 30% and a sales discount of 2/10 net 30 on its sales. A customer bought items with a list price of $70,000 on April 1.

70. If all the preceding terms apply and Romanoff uses the gross method, which of the following is correct regarding the entry made on April 1?
   A. Sales will be credited for $70,000.
   B. Accounts receivable will be debited for $49,000.
   C. Trade discounts will be debited for $21,000.
   D. Cash discounts taken will be debited for $980.

71. If all of the preceding terms apply, and assuming the buyer pays within the discount period, the journal entry to record the collection would include a:
   A. credit to accounts receivable for $48,020
   B. credit to sales discounts taken for $980
   C. debit to sales discounts taken for $980
   D. debit to cash for $49,000

72. If the buyer paid after the 10-day discount period, which of the following is correct?
   A. Sales discounts not taken would be credited for $980.
   B. Sales discounts not taken would be debited for $980.
   C. Accounts receivable would be credited for $49,000.
   D. Cash would be debited for $48,020.

73. For financial statement reporting purposes, which of the following methods of recognizing bad debts is consistent with US GAAP since it provides for matching of revenues with expenses incurred to generate those revenues in the same accounting period?
   I. Direct write-off method
   II. Allowance method

   A. I only
   B. II only
   C. Both I and II
   D. Neither I nor II

74. Current assets are assets that are reasonably expected to convert into cash, be sold, or consumed:
   A. within one year
   B. within one year or one operating cycle, whichever is shorter
   C. within one operating cycle
   D. within one year or one operating cycle, whichever is longer

75. Besides cash, demand deposits, and money market accounts, highly liquid investments that are readily convertible into cash can be shown on the balance sheet as cash or cash equivalent if the investments have a maturity of 90 days or less:
   I. from the date the investment is acquired
   II. from the balance sheet date

   A. I only
   B. II only
   C. Both I and II
   D. Neither I nor II

76. Which of the following could NOT be reported as cash or cash equivalents?

    A. Money market accounts
    B. Demand deposits
    C. US treasury bills with an original maturity of 60 days from date purchased
    D. Legally restricted deposits held as compensating balances against borrowing arrangements with a lending institution

77. Turner has two items in the safe on December 31, Year 13. Which of these items should be included in Turner Corp.'s cash or cash equivalents on December 31, Year 13?
    I. A check payable to Turner Corp. in the amount of $600 dated January 2, Year 14, that Turner has on hand December 31 waiting to be deposited
    II. A US Treasury bill in the amount of $1,000 purchased December 1, Year 13, that matures February 15, Year 14

    A. I only
    B. II only
    C. Both I and II
    D. Neither I nor II

78. The Early Corp. had a cash balance in the ledger at December 31, Year 13, of $15,000. Included in the $15,000 balance were the following two items:
    I. a check in the amount of $1,800 that was written to Snell Corp. The check was dated December 31, Year 13, but was not mailed out to Snell Corp. until January 7, Year 14.
    II. a check payable to Early Corp. from a customer was deposited December 24, Year 13, and was returned for insufficient funds. The check was for $500 and was redeposited by Early Corp. January 2, Year 14, and cleared January 7, Year 14.

    How much cash should Early report in the December 31, Year 13, balance sheet?

    A. $15,000
    B. $13,200
    C. $14,500
    D. $12,700

79. A receives cash of $250,000 as a result of factoring its receivables "without recourse" to B. Which of the following best describes the transaction?
    I. The risk of uncollectible receivables remains with A.
    II. A has, in effect, obtained a loan from B for $250,000.

    A. I only
    B. II only
    C. Both I and II
    D. Neither I nor II

80. At January 1, Year 6, Edgar Co. had a credit balance of $250,000 in its allowance for uncollectible accounts. Based on past experience, 2% of Edgar's credit sales have been uncollectible. During Year 6, Edgar wrote off $315,000 of uncollectible accounts. Credit sales for Year 6 were $8,000,000. In its December 31, Year 6, balance sheet, what amount should Edgar report as allowance for uncollectible accounts?

    A. $160,000
    B. $315,000
    C. $250,000
    D. $95,000

Use the following facts to answer **Questions 81–82**:

Costas Corp. is an accrual based taxpayer and had written off $15,000 from a customer regarding a receivable deemed worthless in Year 12. In Year 13, Costas Corp. recovers 40% of the receivable from the customer's bankruptcy trustee.

81. The entry in Year 12 to record the write-off of the $15,000 considered worthless:
    I. increases the allowance for uncollectible accounts
    II. decreases net income
    III. decreases accounts receivable

    A. I, II, and III
    B. I and III
    C. III only
    D. II and II

82. In Year 13 when Costas Corp. recovers 40% of the receivable from the bankruptcy trustee, this results in:
    I. an increase in net income
    II. an increase in the allowance for doubtful accounts

    A. I only
    B. II only
    C. Both I and II
    D. Neither I nor II

Use the following facts to answer **Questions 83–84:**

Hondo received from a customer a 1-year $400,000 note bearing annual interest of 10%. After holding the note for 6 months, Hondo discounted the note at Second Republic Bank at an effective interest rate of 13%.

83. How much is the maturity value of the note?

   A. $440,000
   B. $452,000
   C. $497,200
   D. $400,000

84. How much cash did Hondo receive from the bank?

   A. $440,000
   B. $402,800
   C. $371,400
   D. $411,400

Use the following facts to answer **Questions 85–88:**

On December 31, Year 5, the Hackett Corp. had a credit balance of $700 in its allowance for doubtful accounts prior to consideration of the following aging schedule that was prepared at year-end.

Age	Amount	Estimated Uncollectible
0–30 days	$50,000	3%
31–60 days	$10,000	6%
Over 60 days	$5,000	$2,500

85. What amount should Hackett Corp. report as the ending balance in the allowance account at December 31, Year 5?

   A. $4,600 credit
   B. $4,600 debit
   C. $3,900 credit
   D. $5,300 credit

86. How much should Hackett Corp. record for bad debt expense in Year 5?

   A. $4,600
   B. $3,900
   C. $5,300
   D. $700

87. Assuming the allowance account had a previous balance prior to adjustment of $500 debit balance rather than $700 credit, how much should Hackett Corp. record for the ending allowance account balance at December 31, Year 5?

   A. $4,100
   B. $4,600
   C. $5,100
   D. $0

88. Assuming the allowance account had a previous balance prior to adjustment of $500 debit balance rather than $700 credit, how much should Hackett Corp. record for bad debt expense in Year 5?

   A. $4,100
   B. $4,600
   C. $5,100
   D. $0

89. When a company uses the allowance method to account for bad debts, what effect does a collection of a previously written off account have on bad debt expense and allowance for doubtful accounts?

   A. Bad debt expense, no effect; allowance for doubtful accounts, increase
   B. Bad debt expense, increase; allowance for doubtful accounts, decrease
   C. Bad debt expense, decrease; allowance for doubtful accounts, no effect
   D. Bad debt expense, no effect; allowance for doubtful accounts, no effect

90. Miller Corp. adjusted its allowance for doubtful accounts at December 31, Year 11. The general ledger balances for accounts receivable and the related allowance account were $2,000,000 and $75,000 respectively. In addition, sales on credit for Year 11 were $3,000,000. Miller uses a balance sheet approach to estimate its bad debt expense, and for Year 11 estimates that 4% of accounts receivable will be uncollectible. What amount should Miller record as an adjustment to its allowance for doubtful accounts at December 31, Year 11?

   A. $5,000
   B. $45,000
   C. $120,000
   D. $3,000

91. The Lubrano Corp. uses the income statement approach to estimating bad debt expense. In Year 13, sales on credit amounted to $2,000,000. Sales returns and allowances were $200,000. Lubrano Corp. estimates that 2% of net credit sales will be uncollectible. The allowance for doubtful accounts had a balance at the beginning of Year 13 of $25,000. How much should Lubrano Corp. charge to bad debt expense in Year 13?

A. $40,000
B. $36,000
C. $11,000
D. $15,000

92. At year-end, the previous balance in the allowance account is ignored for purposes of determining bad debt expense when using the:
I. income statement (percent of sales) approach
II. balance sheet approach (percent of receivables) approach

A. I only
B. II only
C. Both I and II
D. Neither I nor II

93. The following facts apply to Kaput Corp. in Year 13. If the allowance for doubtful accounts had a beginning balance of $55,000 and an ending balance of $45,000, and during the year, $15,000 of accounts receivable were written off as worthless, what amount should be recorded as bad debt expense for Year 13 under US GAAP?

A. $10,000
B. $15,000
C. $5,000
D. $25,000

94. Which of the following is included within the category known as cash and cash equivalents?
I. Cash in checking accounts
II. Petty cash
III. Cash in bond sinking fund

A. I, II, and III
B. I and III
C. I and II
D. I only

95. Cone Corp. is a calendar year corporation. Within the category of cash and cash equivalents is a postdated check received from one of Cone's customers dated seven days after the balance sheet date. Cone has possession of the check as of December 31 and should classify the check as:
I. cash
II. cash equivalent

A. I only
B. II only
C. Both I and II
D. Neither I nor II

96. Which of the following is treated as a sale of receivables?
I. Factoring without recourse in exchange for cash
II. Pledging receivables in exchange for a loan

A. I only
B. II only
C. Both I and II
D. Neither I nor II

97. On June 1, Year 13, the Barnes Corp. factored $100,000 of its accounts receivable without recourse to the Rohn Corp. Rohn Corp. retained 15% of the accounts receivable as an allowance for sales returns and charged a 5% commission on the gross amount of factored receivables. How much cash did Barnes Corp. receive from factoring the receivables?

A. $85,000
B. $95,000
C. $100,000
D. $80,000

98. In a period of falling prices, which of the following inventory valuation methods would report the highest cost of goods sold and the highest inventory valuation?

	Cost of Goods Sold	Ending Inventory
A.	LIFO	FIFO
B.	LIFO	LIFO
C.	FIFO	FIFO
D.	FIFO	LIFO

99. In a period of rising prices, which of the following would be higher under LIFO rather than FIFO?

   I. Cost of goods sold

  II. Net income

 III. Ending inventory

  A. I only

  B. II only

  C. Both I and II

  D. I, II, and III

100. Olympic Fascination Corp. has inventory with a FIFO cost of $16,730, net realizable value of $16,850, replacement cost of $16,490, and net realizable value less normal profit of $16,545. What amount should Olympic report as ending inventory in its balance sheet at year-end?

  A. $16,730

  B. $16,850

  C. $16,490

  D. $16,545

101. For Year 13, the Franklin Corp. has beginning inventory of $41,875 and ending inventory of $32,109. Purchase returns and freight in are $20,200 and $24,360, respectively. Purchases are $112,800 and freight out is $5,733. How much is cost of goods sold for Year 13?

  A. $126,726

  B. $158,835

  C. $134,475

  D. $118,406

102. If LIFO is being used to account for ending inventory and cost of goods sold for tax purposes, which of the following accounting standards would then require LIFO to be used for financial statement purposes under what is known as the LIFO conformity rule?

   I. US GAAP

  II. IFRS

  A. I only

  B. II only

  C. Both I and II

  D. Neither I nor II

Use the following facts to answer **Questions 103–110:**

Atlantic Corp. had beginning inventory in January of Year 13 of 10,000 units costing $1 each. On February 10, 11,200 units were purchased costing $3 each. On March 20, 11,800 units were sold. On December 30, 11,600 more units were purchased at $6 each.

103. How much is the cost of goods available for sale on December 31, Year 13, using FIFO, assuming Atlantic Corp. uses a periodic inventory system?

  A. $69,600

  B. $113,200

  C. $70,200

  D. $34,200

104. Under FIFO, what amount should Atlantic Corp. report as cost of goods sold, assuming it uses a periodic inventory system?

  A. $15,400

  B. $43,000

  C. $70,200

  D. $97,800

105. Under FIFO, what amount should Atlantic Corp. report as ending inventory, assuming it uses a periodic inventory system?

  A. $15,400

  B. $43,000

  C. $70,200

  D. $97,800

106. How much is cost of goods available for sale on December 31, Year 13, using LIFO, assuming Atlantic Corp. uses a periodic inventory system?

  A. $113,200

  B. $43,000

  C. $79,000

  D. $34,200

107. Under LIFO, what amount should Atlantic Corp. report as cost of goods sold, assuming it uses a periodic inventory system?

  A. $43,000

  B. $70,200

  C. $34,200

  D. $79,000

108. Under LIFO, what amount should Atlantic Corp. report as inventory at December 31, Year 13, assuming Atlantic uses a periodic inventory system?

A. $79,000
B. $43,000
C. $70,200
D. $34,200

109. Under LIFO, what amount should Atlantic Corp. report as cost of goods sold at December 31, Year 13, assuming Atlantic uses a perpetual inventory system?

A. $70,200
B. $43,000
C. $34,200
D. $79,000

110. Under LIFO, what amount should Atlantic Corp. report as ending inventory at December 31, Year 13, assuming it uses a perpetual inventory system?

A. $34,200
B. $79,000
C. $43,000
D. $70,400

Use the following facts to answer **Questions 111–113:**

Lesnik Corp. had beginning inventory in January of Year 13 of 10,000 units costing $1 each. On January 14, 4,000 units were purchased costing $3 each. On March 20, 8,000 units were sold. On December 22, 6,000 more units were purchased at $6 each.

111. If Lesnik Corp. uses a periodic inventory system, how much is the average cost per unit for Lesnik Corp. under the weighted average inventory valuation method?

A. $2.90
B. $2.00
C. $3.33
D. $4.00

112. If Lesnik Corp. uses a periodic system, Lesnik Corp. would report cost of goods sold using the weighted average method in the amount of:

A. $8,000
B. $34,800
C. $42,000
D. $23,200

113. If Lesnik Corp. uses a periodic system, Lesnik Corp. would report ending inventory using the weighted average method in the amount of:

A. $23,200
B. $34,800
C. $54,000
D. $16,000

114. In the calculation of ending inventory for Shula Corp. at December 31, Year 13, which of the following should be included?

  I. Goods sold to Langer Corp. on December 28, Year 13, terms FOB shipping point, still in transit at December 31, Year 13
  II. Goods purchased from Mandich Corp. December 29, Year 13, terms FOB destination, arrived January 2, Year 14

A. I only
B. II only
C. Both I and II
D. Neither I nor II

115. Which of the following is correct regarding the inventory rights and obligations associated with goods on consignment?

A. The consignor of the goods should include the goods in ending inventory.
B. The consignee of the goods should include the goods in ending inventory.
C. Shipping costs incurred by the consignor in transferring the goods to the consignee is an expense of the consignee.
D. Shipping costs incurred by the consignor in transferring the goods to the consignee is an expense of the consignor.

116. Beginning inventory for Frozen Foods Inc. is incorrectly stated at $13,000, and ending inventory is incorrectly stated as $10,000. Assuming purchases for the year are correctly stated at $5,000, which of the following inventory errors would result in an understatement of cost of goods sold?

  I. Beginning inventory is understated by $1,000.
  II. Ending inventory is overstated by $2,000.

A. I only
B. II only
C. Both I and II
D. Neither I nor II

117. Fenn Corp. adopted the dollar-value LIFO inventory method as of January 1, 2015. At that time, Fenn's inventory was valued at $575,000. The entire inventory constitutes a single inventory pool. Using a relevant price index of 1.10, Fenn determined that its December 31, 2015, inventory was $660,000 at current-year cost and $600,000 at base-year cost. Fenn's dollar-value LIFO inventory at December 31, 2015 is:

A. $600,000
B. $602,500
C. $627,500
D. $660,000

118. Loring Company's accounting records indicate the following information:

Inventory, January 1, 2015 $400,000
Purchases during 2015 $3,100,000
Sales during 2015 $2,500,000

A physical inventory taken on December 31, 2015, resulted in an ending inventory of $1,400,000. Loring's gross profit on sales has remained constant at 20% in recent years. Loring suspects some inventory may have been taken by a new employee. At December 31, 2015, what is the estimated cost of the missing inventory?

A. $25,000
B. $100,000
C. $200,000
D. $400,000

119. On December 23, 2015, Kenney, Inc. purchased inventory from Mann Corp. on FOB shipping terms. Additional costs incurred in connection with this purchase included the following:

Freight-in $3,000
Special handling costs   2,000
Insurance on shipment   500

What amount of these additional costs are inventoriable, and by which party, Kenney or Mann, would they be reported?

A. $5,500; Kenney
B. $2,500; Mann
C. $3,000; Kenney
D. $2,000; Mann

Use the following facts to answer **Questions 120–121:**

The Sanchez Corp. had beginning inventory of 1,200 units in January 1, Year 10. The following information pertains to the month of January.

Inventory Units	Unit Cost	Total Cost	Units on Hand
1/1/10 1,200	$1	$1,200	1,200
1/11 Purchase 800	$3	$2,400	2,000
1/19 Sold 1,000			1,000
1/30 Purchase 600	$5	$3,000	1,600

120. Under the moving average method, what amount should Sanchez Corp. report as inventory under US GAAP at January 31?

A. $3,600
B. $3,000
C. $4,200
D. $4,800

121. Under the moving average method, Sanchez Corp. would price the next sale of inventory at which of the following costs?

A. $1.80
B. $3.00
C. $5.00
D. $3.45

122. In Year 12, a hurricane destroyed much of the inventory records of Sandy Corp., but the following information was rescued from the accounting department:

Sales for Year 12 $200,000
Beginning Inventory 1/1/12 $25,000
Ending Inventory 12/31/12 $10,000

If Sandy's gross margin normally is 20%, how much represents purchases for Year 12?

A. $145,000
B. $170,000
C. $160,000
D. $15,000

CHAPTER 26

MARKETABLE SECURITIES AND INVESTMENTS

123. Under US generally accepted accounting principles (GAAP), investment securities should be classified into categories based on the intent of the purchaser. Which of the following is one of the acceptable classifications?

   I. Available for sale
  II. Mark to market
 III. Trading
 IV. Held to maturity

  A. I, II, III, and IV
  B. I and III
  C. I, III, and IV
  D. III and IV

124. According to US GAAP, both debt and equity securities may be classified as:

   I. available for sale
  II. trading
 III. held to maturity

  A. I and III
  B. I and II
  C. II only
  D. II and III

125. Tilly Company has provided the following information related to its investments in marketable equity securities:

	Cost	Market value Year 2	Market value Year 1
Trading	$150,000	$155,000	$100,000
Available for sale	$150,000	$130,000	$120,000

Based on the information provided, what amount should Tilley report as unrealized holding gain in its Year 2 income statement?

  A. $65,000
  B. $60,000
  C. $55,000
  D. $50,000

126. On January 1 of the current year, Fords Co. paid $800,000 to purchase two-year, 7%, $1,000,000 face value bonds that were issued by another publicly traded corporation. Fords Co. plans to sell the bonds in the first quarter of the following year. The fair value of the bonds at the end of the current year was $1,030,000. At what amount should Fords report the bonds in its balance sheet at the end of the current year?

  A. $1,000,000
  B. $1,030,000
  C. $870,000
  D. $800,000

127. Which is correct regarding unrealized gains and losses on marketable securities held for investment?
    I. Unrealized gains on trading securities should NOT be reported on the income statement if the security has not been sold.
    II. Unrealized losses on available-for-sale securities should NOT be reported on the income statement unless the loss is considered "other than temporary."

    A. I only
    B. II only
    C. Both I and II
    D. Neither I nor II

Use the following facts to answer **Questions 128–129:**

Azur Corp. purchases marketable securities in Green Corp. during Year 1. At the end of Year 1, the fair value of Green Corp. stock has dropped below its cost. Azur Corp. considered the decline in value to be temporary as of December 31, Year 1. The security is classified as an available-for-sale asset.

128. What should be the effect on Azur Corp.'s financial statements at December 31, Year 1?

    A. Decrease in available-for-sale assets and decrease in net income
    B. No effect on available-for-sale assets and decrease in net income
    C. No effect on net income and decrease on available-for-sale assets
    D. Decrease in available-for-sale assets and decrease in other comprehensive income

129. Assume in Year 2 that the value of the security has not changed, but Azur Corp. now considers the drop to be permanent. What should be the effects of the determination that the decline was other than temporary on Azur's Year 2 net available-for-sale assets and net income?

    A. Decrease in net available-for-sale assets and no effect on net income
    B. No effect on net available-for-sale assets and decrease in net income
    C. No effect on both net available-for-sale assets and net income
    D. Decrease in both net available-for-sale assets and net income

130. With regard to marketable securities held as available for sale, which of the following are reported in comprehensive income?
    I. Unrealized temporary losses
    II. Unrealized losses considered other than temporary
    III. Unrealized gains

    A. I and II
    B. I and III
    C. II and III
    D. I, II, and III

131. Trixie Corp. had the following items in the current year:

Loss on early extinguishment of bonds	$4,000
Realized gain on sale of available-for-sale securities	$31,000
Unrealized loss on available-for-sale securities	$16,000

    Which of the following amounts would the statement of comprehensive income report as other comprehensive income or loss?

    A. $15,000 other comprehensive income
    B. $20,000 other comprehensive loss
    C. $11,000 other comprehensive loss
    D. $16,000 other comprehensive loss

132. With regard to investments in securities, which of the following is correct regarding the cost (fair value) method?
    I. The investment in investee account is adjusted for investee earnings.
    II. The investment in investee is adjusted to fair value at the end of the reporting period.

    A. I only
    B. II only
    C. Both I and II
    D. Neither I nor II

133. Koontz, Inc. purchased 15% of Lamme Co.'s 50,000 outstanding shares of common stock on January 2, Year 5 for $100,000. On December 31, Year 5, Koontz purchased an additional 10,000 shares of Lamme for $175,000. Lamme reported earnings of $80,000 for Year 5. There was no goodwill as a result of either acquisition, and Lamme had not issued any additional stock during Year 5. There was no unrealized holding gain or loss reported in other comprehensive income for this investment. What amount should Koontz report in its December 31, Year 5 balance sheet as investment in Lamme?

    A. $275,000
    B. $287,000
    C. $291,000
    D. $300,000

134. Which of the following if received from the investee will affect the income reported by an investor, using the equity method?

    I. Cash dividend

    II. Stock dividend

    A. I only
    B. II only
    C. Both I and II
    D. Neither I nor II

135. Woodley Inc. became a 4% owner of Jensen Inc. by purchasing 5,000 shares of Jensen Inc.'s stock on March 1, Year 13. Woodley Inc. received a stock dividend of 1,000 shares on September 1, Year 13, when the market value of Jensen Inc. was $20 per share. Jensen Inc. paid a cash dividend of $3 per share on November 1, Year 13, to shareholders of record on October 1, Year 13. In its Year 13 income statement, what amount would Woodley Inc. report as dividend income?

    A. $15,000
    B. $18,000
    C. $25,000
    D. $32,000

136. Rochelle Corp. acquired 40% of Clark Inc.'s voting common stock on January 2, Year 13, for $400,000. The carrying amount of Clark's net assets at the purchase date totaled $900,000. Fair values equaled carrying amounts for all items except equipment, for which fair values exceeded carrying amounts by $100,000. The equipment has a 5-year life. During Year 13, Clark reported net income of $150,000. What amount of income from this investment should Rochelle Corp. report in its Year 13 income statement?

    A. $56,000
    B. $60,000
    C. $52,000
    D. $68,000

137. Singer Co. uses the equity method to account for its January 1, Year 1, purchase of Kaufman Inc.'s common stock. On January 1, Year 1, the fair values of Kaufman's FIFO inventory and land exceeded their carrying amounts. Which of these excesses of fair values over carrying amounts will reduce Singer's reported equity in Kaufman's Year 1 earnings?

    I. Inventory excess

    II. Land excess

    A. I only
    B. II only
    C. Both I and II
    D. Neither I nor II

138. A marketable debt security is transferred from available-for-sale to held-to-maturity securities. At the transfer date, the security's carrying amount exceeds its market value. What amount is used at the transfer date to record the security in the held-to-maturity portfolio?

    A. Cost, if the decline in market value below cost is temporary
    B. Market value, regardless of whether the decline in market value below cost is considered permanent or temporary
    C. Cost, regardless of whether the decline in market value below cost is considered permanent or temporary
    D. Market value, only if the decline in market value below cost is considered permanent

139. On January 2, Year 5, Henry Corp. purchased 10% of Einhorn, Inc.'s outstanding common shares for $400,000. Henry is the largest single shareholder in Einhorn, and Henry's officers represent a majority of Einhorn, Inc.'s board of directors. During Year 5, Einhorn reported net income of $500,000 and paid dividends of $150,000. What amount should Henry report as investment in Einhorn in its December 31, Year 5, balance sheet?

    A. $385,000
    B. $400,000
    C. $435,000
    D. $450,000

CHAPTER 27

FIXED ASSETS, INTANGIBLES, AND NONMONETARY EXCHANGES

QUESTIONS 140–202

140. Nickki Corp. purchased equipment by making a down payment of $2,000 and issuing a note payable for $16,000. A payment of $4,000 is to be made at the end of each year for 4 years. The applicable rate of interest is 7%. The present value of an ordinary annuity factor for 4 years at 7% is 4.18, and the present value for the future amount of a single sum of 1 dollar for 4 years at 7% is 0.645. Installation charges were $1,000. What is the capitalized cost of the equipment?

- **A.** $18,720
- **B.** $19,720
- **C.** $12,255
- **D.** $11,255

141. Mustafa, Inc. uses IFRS to prepare its financial statements. On January 1, Year 3, Mustafa acquired an aircraft for $150 million, which consisted of three main components each with its own assigned cost and useful life: the frame $80 million, the engine $50 million, and the interior components $20 million. Mustafa estimates the aircraft to have a 20-year useful life and estimates the three main components to have differing useful lives as well: the frame 20 years, the engine 16 years, and the interior components 10 years. Mustafa uses the straight-line method to depreciate its assets. How much depreciation expense should Mustafa record for Year 3?

- **A.** $4,000,000
- **B.** $7,500,000
- **C.** $9,125,000
- **D.** $11,250,000

142. Lavroff Corp. is purchasing an asset for use in its meat packaging business. Which of the following costs associated with the machine's purchase needs to be capitalized rather than expensed?
  - I. Cost of shipping the machine to Lavroff's plant
  - II. Cost of readying the machine for its intended use

- **A.** I only
- **B.** II only
- **C.** Both I and II
- **D.** Neither I nor II

143. At the end of Year 1, Buck Inc. had a class of assets with a carrying value of $1,200,000 and recorded a revaluation gain of $150,000. On December 31, Year 2, the assets had a carrying value of $900,000 and a recoverable amount of $720,000. Under the IFRS, what amount of impairment loss will Buck Inc. report on its December 31, Year 2, income statement?

- **A.** $190,000
- **B.** $150,000
- **C.** $40,000
- **D.** $30,000

144. A company has a parcel of land to be used for a future production facility. The company applies the revaluation model under IFRS to this class of assets. In Year 3, the company acquired the land for $80,000. At the end of Year 3, the carrying amount was reduced to $70,000, which represented the fair value at that date. At the end of Year 4, the land was revalued and the fair value increased to $85,000. How should the company account for the Year 4 change in fair value?

   A. By recognizing $15,000 in other comprehensive income
   B. By recognizing $10,000 on the income statement and $5,000 in other comprehensive income
   C. By recognizing $15,000 on the income statement
   D. By recognizing $10,000 in other comprehensive income

145. Fixed assets can be revalued upward from the asset's carrying amount if the reporting framework is:
   I. US generally accepted accounting principles (GAAP)
   II. IFRS

   A. I only
   B. II only
   C. Both I and II
   D. Neither I nor II

146. When replacing an asset in which the cost of the old asset is known:
   I. replace the old carrying value with the capitalized cost of the new asset
   II. reduce accumulated depreciation of the asset class to increase book value

   A. I only
   B. II only
   C. Both I and II
   D. Neither I nor II

147. If an old asset's life is extended but not improved, and the carrying value of the specific old asset is NOT known, what happens to the amount spent to extend the life of the old asset?
   I. Reduces accumulated depreciation of the asset class
   II. Gets capitalized

   A. I only
   B. II only
   C. Both I and II
   D. Neither I nor II

148. Under US GAAP, if a hurricane causes damage to property, and extraordinary repairs are made that result in extending the life of the old property but not improving the old property:
   I. the cost should be recorded as an asset
   II. accumulated depreciation of the old asset should be reduced

   A. I only
   B. II only
   C. Both I and II
   D. Neither I nor II

149. Baker Corp. purchases land for use as a future plant site. An old building on the site needs to be razed and the scrap materials will be sold. Legal fees will need to be paid to record ownership, and title insurance will need to be acquired. Which of the following should be capitalized rather than expensed in connection with the acquisition?
   I. Title insurance
   II. Legal fees for recording ownership
   III. Razing of old building less proceeds from sale of scrap

   A. I and II
   B. II and III
   C. III only
   D. I, II, and III

150. Which of the following costs would NOT be capitalized to the land account?
   I. Filling in dirt to level the property prior to excavation
   II. Excavating costs

   A. I only
   B. II only
   C. Both I and II
   D. Neither I nor II

151. Which of the following is correct regarding land improvements?
   I. Costs incurred to construct sidewalks and fences would be capitalized to land improvements rather than to land.
   II. Land improvements can be depreciated.

   A. I only
   B. II only
   C. Both I and II
   D. Neither I nor II

152. Vijay Fitness Inc. purchased land with the intention of building its new administrative headquarters on the site. Assuming the following can be debited to either land, land improvement, or building, which of the following should be charged to land improvements?
    I. Clearing of trees and grading
    II. Architect's fee
    III. Installation of a septic system

    A. I, II, and III
    B. II and III
    C. I and III
    D. III only

153. Cucinell Corp. acquired a fixed asset with an estimated five-year useful life and no residual value on January 1, Year 1. The asset is sold at the end of Year 2. How would using the sum of the years' digits method instead of the double declining balance method affect a gain or loss on the sale of the fixed asset?

	Gain	Loss
A.	Decrease	Decrease
B.	Decrease	Increase
C.	Increase	Decrease
D.	Increase	Increase

154. The Fleer Corp. spends $100,000 for land and building. The land was recently appraised for $20,000, but the building was appraised for $120,000. If only $100,000 is spent, how much is allocated to the land?

    A. $14,280
    B. $16,160
    C. $20,000
    D. $15,840

155. Downey Co. purchased an office building and the land on which it is located for $800,000 cash and an existing $200,000 mortgage. For realty tax purposes, the property is assessed at $944,000, 65% of which is allocated to the building. At what amount should Downey record the building?

    A. $944,000
    B. $613,600
    C. $520,000
    D. $650,000

156. Under IFRS, assets are classified as investment property on the balance sheet if they are:
    I. held for rental income
    II. to be sold for a quick profit

    A. I only
    B. II only
    C. Both I and II
    D. Neither I nor II

157. LaRue Corp. is a Canadian corporation that uses IFRS. LaRue Corp. has the following account balances as of December 31, Year 5:

Land used in manufacturing operations	$11,000,000
Land held for rental income	$4,000,000
Buildings used in manufacturing operations	$10,500,000
Goods held for resale	$2,500,000
Buildings held for capital appreciation	$3,000,000

    Under IFRS, what will LaRue Corp. report as investment property on its December 31, Year 5, balance sheet?

    A. $4,000,000
    B. $7,000,000
    C. $28,500,000
    D. $18,000,000

158. Which of the following statements regarding the accounting for investment property under IFRS is correct?
    I. If the entity elects the fair value method, no depreciation expense will be taken.
    II. Gains and losses from fair value adjustments on investment property are reported on the income statement.

    A. I only
    B. II only
    C. Both I and II
    D. Neither I nor II

159. Under IFRS, revaluation gains are reported on the income statement when the asset is classified as:
    I. investment property
    II. property plant and equipment

    A. I only
    B. II only
    C. Both I and II
    D. Neither I nor II

160. Medina Corp. is constructing a warehouse for use in manufacturing operations. The capitalization of interest cost is appropriate during a construction delay that is:
  I. intentional
  II. related to permit processing or inspections

  A. I only
  B. II only
  C. Both I and II
  D. Neither I nor II

161. During the current year, Hodge Corp. constructed machinery for its own use and constructed machinery for sale to customers in the ordinary course of business. The Acme Credit Company financed these assets both during construction and after construction was complete. Hodge Corp. should capitalize interest during construction rather than expense it if the interest is related to the machinery built for which of the following?
  I. Hodge's own use
  II. Sale to customers

  A. I only
  B. II only
  C. Both I and II
  D. Neither I nor II

162. Capitalization of interest cost is appropriate to finance the cost of items held for resale (inventory) if the assets are:
  I. self-constructed
  II. acquired in the open market

  A. I only
  B. II only
  C. Both I and II
  D. Neither I nor II

163. Interest cost after construction is completed is capitalized if the asset being constructed is:
  I. built to use
  II. built to sell

  A. I only
  B. II only
  C. Both I and II
  D. Neither I nor II

164. Frimette Fabricating Corp. was constructing fixed assets that qualified for interest capitalization and had the following outstanding debt issuance during the entire year of construction:

$5,000,000 face value, 7% interest
$7,000,000 face value, 10% interest

None of the borrowings were specified for the construction of the qualified fixed asset. Average expenditures for the year were $800,000. What interest rate should Frimette Fabricating Corp. use to calculate capitalized interest on the construction?

  A. 7%
  B. 8.7%
  C. 8.5%
  D. 10%

165. Which of the following is a required disclosure regarding interest cost?
  I. Total interest cost incurred for the period
  II. Total capitalized interest cost for the period, if any

  A. I only
  B. II only
  C. Both I and II
  D. Neither I nor II

166. Which of the following is correct regarding capitalized interest?
  I. Capitalized interest is reduced by income received on the unexpended portion of the construction loan.
  II. The amount of capitalized interest is the lower of actual interest cost incurred or computed capitalized interest.

  A. I only
  B. II only
  C. Both I and II
  D. Neither I nor II

167. Posner Inc. began constructing a building for its own use in January of Year 4. During Year 4, Posner incurred interest of $62,000 on specific construction debt related to this building and $22,000 on various other debt issued prior to Year 4. Interest computed based on the weighted average amount of accumulated expenditures for the building during the year was $37,000. Posner should capitalize what amount of interest in Year 4?

  A. $37,000
  B. $59,000
  C. $62,000
  D. $84,000

168. An asset is purchased April 1, Year 1, for $75,000 and has an estimated useful life of 7 years. The asset has a salvage value of $5,000. For tax purposes, the asset is being depreciated based on a 10-year life. For GAAP purposes, how much is straight line depreciation expense on the income statement dated December 31, Year 1?

- **A.** $10,000
- **B.** $7,500
- **C.** $7,000
- **D.** $5,250

Use the following facts to answer **Questions 169–170:**

Chef Giant Inc. uses the sum of the year's digits depreciation. In early January of Year 12, Chef Giant Inc. purchased and began depreciating a machine that cost $50,000 and had an estimated salvage value of $5,000. The machine had an estimated life of 5 years.

169. How much depreciation expense should be taken on the December 31, Year 12, income statement?

- **A.** $16,667
- **B.** $15,000
- **C.** $7,500
- **D.** $12,000

170. How much is the carrying value of the machine on the balance sheet dated December 31, Year 13 (the asset's second year)?

- **A.** $50,000
- **B.** $35,000
- **C.** $27,000
- **D.** $23,000

171. On July 15 of the current year, Pep Power Beverage Corp. purchased a drink color dispersing component to be attached to its assembly line. The cost of this component was $110,000. Pep also incurred the following costs in connection with the installation of this new component: installation costs $26,000; costs associated with rearranging and overhauling the assembly line $16,000. Adding the drink color dispersing component and rearranging the assembly line to incorporate the component into the manufacturing process did not increase the life of the assembly line, but it did help increase productivity and efficiency in the manufacturing process. What amount of these costs should be capitalized?

- **A.** $110,000
- **B.** $126,000
- **C.** $136,000
- **D.** $152,000

172. A depreciable asset has an estimated 10% salvage value. Under which of the following methods, properly applied, would the accumulated depreciation equal the original cost at the end of the asset's estimated useful life?

- I. Sum of the years' digits
- II. Double declining balance
- III. Straight line

- **A.** I and II
- **B.** II and III
- **C.** II only
- **D.** None of the above

173. Bruder Inc. bought a battery (plug-in) truck at a cost of $70,000 in January of Year 1, and it is being depreciated using the units of production method. The truck had an estimated useful life of 10 years and a battery with an estimated total capacity of 200,000 miles. In Year 1, the truck is driven 12,000 miles. The salvage value of the truck is $10,000. How much depreciation should be taken in Year 1 based on the units of production method?

- **A.** $6,000
- **B.** $3,600
- **C.** $4,200
- **D.** $7,000

174. A company uses cost depletion to allocate the cost of removing natural resources. Which of the following is correct?

- I. Depletion base is the cost to purchase the property minus the estimated net residual value.
- II. If the number of units produced exceeds the number of units sold, the depletion expense would be equal to the number of units produced.

- **A.** I only
- **B.** II only
- **C.** Both I and II
- **D.** Neither I nor II

175. Which of the following is correct regarding impairment losses under US GAAP?

- I. Impairment losses are typically reported before tax if the impairment loss is related to discontinued operations.
- II. Impairment losses reduce the carrying value of an asset due to a decline in book value below fair value.

- **A.** I only
- **B.** II only
- **C.** Both I and II
- **D.** Neither I nor II

176. Which of the following is correct regarding patent costs under US GAAP?
  I. Fees to acquire a patent from a third party are expensed.
  II. Most costs incurred to internally generate a patent are expensed.
  III. Costs associated with either a successful or unsuccessful patent defense should be capitalized.

  A. I only
  B. I and II only
  C. I, II, and III
  D. II only

177. Two years ago, Labriola, Ltd. acquired a trademark for $40,000 and estimated its useful life to be 40 years. The carrying amount of the trademark at the beginning of the current year was $38,000. At that time, Labriola determined that the cash flow to be derived from the trademark will be generated indefinitely at the trademark's current level. What amount should Labriola report as amortization expense for the current year?

  A. $0
  B. $1,000
  C. $2,667
  D. $38,000

178. All research and development costs are expensed as incurred under which of the following accounting standards?
  I. US GAAP
  II. International Financial Reporting Standards (IFRS)

  A. I only
  B. II only
  C. Both I and II
  D. Neither I nor II

179. Which of the following is correct regarding costs associated with goodwill?
  I. Costs of developing and maintaining goodwill are NOT capitalized.
  II. Goodwill is capitalized when incurred in the purchase of another entity and then amortized using the straight line method.

  A. I only
  B. II only
  C. Both I and II
  D. Neither I nor II

180. Which of the following is correct regarding capitalization and amortization of intangible assets under US GAAP?
  I. Intangible assets with infinite lives such as goodwill should be capitalized but NOT amortized.
  II. Intangible assets with finite lives such as patents, franchises, and covenants not to compete should be capitalized and amortized.

  A. I only
  B. II only
  C. Both I and II
  D. Neither I nor II

181. Intangible assets may be reported under the revaluation model (fair value) rather than the cost model under which of the following standards?
  I. US GAAP
  II. IFRS

  A. I only
  B. II only
  C. Both I and II
  D. Neither I nor II

182. During Year 1, Guidry Co. incurred $300,000 of research and development costs in its laboratory to develop a product for which a patent was granted on July 1, Year 1. Legal fees and other costs associated with the patent totaled $72,000. The estimated economic life of the patent is 12 years. What amount should Guidry capitalize for the patent on July 1, Year 1, under US GAAP?

  A. $72,000
  B. $300,000
  C. $372,000
  D. $0

183. If a company incurs costs to develop computer software, the company will expense all costs rather than capitalize them if the software is developed for:
  I. internal use only
  II. sale to customers
  A. I only
  B. II only
  C. Both I and II
  D. Neither I nor II

184. In Year 13, Gigabyte Logic incurred the following computer software costs for the development and sale of computer software programs:

Planning costs	$40,000
Design of software	$120,000
Substantial testing of the project's initial stages	$64,000
Production and packaging costs for the first month's sales	$72,000
Producing product masters after technological feasibility was established	$180,000

What amount of these software costs should NOT be expensed by Gigabyte Logic as research and development?

A. $0
B. $180,000
C. $252,000
D. $224,000

185. Costello Corp. produces software for sale and also for internal uses. During the current year, Costello Corp. incurred the following costs:

Research and development costs contracted out to third parties	$40,000
Design production and testing of preproduction prototypes	$120,000
Testing in search for new products	$25,000
Quality control	$13,000

In the current year income statement, what amount should Costello Corp. expense as research and development under US GAAP?

A. $198,000
B. $160,000
C. $65,000
D. $185,000

186. On January 2, Year 13, Scotti purchased a Subway franchise with a useful life of 20 years for $90,000. An additional franchise fee of 4% of sales must be paid each year to Subway world headquarters. Sales in Year 13 for Scotti's new Subway amounted to $300,000. In its December 31, Year 13, balance sheet, what amount should Scotti report as an intangible asset franchise?

A. $4,500
B. $85,500
C. $16,500
D. $90,000

187. On December 31, Benning Inc. analyzed a patent with a net carrying value of $500,000 for impairment. The entity determined the following:

Fair value	$485,000
Undiscounted future cash flows	$498,000

What is the impairment loss that will be reported on the December 31 income statement under US GAAP?

A. $15,000
B. $2,000
C. $17,000
D. $0

188. On December 31, Year 4, Plant Co. had capitalized costs for a new computer software product with an economic life of 10 years. Sales for Year 5 were 20% of expected total sales of the software. At December 31, Year 5, the software had a net realizable value equal to 60% of the capitalized cost. What percentage of the original capitalized cost should be reported as the net amount on Plant's December 31, Year 5, balance sheet?

A. 90%
B. 80%
C. 60%
D. 10%

189. Which of the following is considered monetary rather than nonmonetary?

 I. Accounts receivable
 II. Allowance for doubtful accounts

A. I only
B. II only
C. Both I and II
D. Neither I nor II

190. Which of the following is considered nonmonetary rather than monetary?

 I. Equipment
 II. Accumulated depreciation-equipment

A. I only
B. II only
C. Both I and II
D. Neither I nor II

191. Under US GAAP, a nonmonetary exchange is recognized at fair value of the assets exchanged unless:

A. the exchange has commercial substance
B. fair value is not determinable
C. the assets are similar in nature
D. the assets are dissimilar in nature

192. The Drexel Corp. exchanged equipment with an appraised value of $60,000 and an original cost of $52,000, and received from Dartmouth Corp. equipment with a fair value of $64,000. Under US GAAP, how much is the gain on the exchange for Drexel Corp., assuming that the transaction has commercial substance?

A. $0
B. $8,000
C. $4,000
D. $12,000

193. On January 1, Year 9, Hayley Corp. traded delivery trucks with Dylan Corp. and paid $5,000 cash to Dylan Corp. Hayley Corp.'s truck had a fair value of $95,000 and accumulated depreciation of $75,000 on the date of exchange. Hayley Corp.'s asset had an original cost of $130,000. Hayley estimated that the value of Dylan Corp.'s truck was $90,000 on the date of exchange. The book value of Dylan Corp.'s truck on January 1, Year 9, was $70,000. The transaction had commercial substance. Under US GAAP, what amount of gain should be recorded by Hayley Corp.?

A. $0
B. $35,000
C. $40,000
D. $55,000

194. Under US GAAP, losses in connection with nonmonetary exchanges are deferred when the exchange is said to:
    I. lack commercial substance
    II. have commercial substance

A. I only
B. II only
C. Both I and II
D. Neither I nor II

195. Under US GAAP, nonmonetary exchanges that lack commercial substance could possibly result in which of the following NOT being recognized immediately?
    I. Losses
    II. Gains

A. I only
B. II only
C. Both I and II
D. Neither I nor II

Use the following facts to answer **Questions 196–197**:

Durant Corp. exchanged equipment that cost $480,000 and had a fair value of $380,000 for a warehouse owned by Jordan Corp. Future cash flows will significantly change as a result of the exchange. On the date of exchange, the equipment had accumulated depreciation of $80,000, and Durant Corp. had to pay $5,000 in cash.

196. How much gain or loss should be reported by Durant Corp.?

A. $0
B. $5,000 loss
C. $20,000 gain
D. $20,000 loss

197. After the exchange, how much is the basis of the warehouse to Durant Corp. under US GAAP?

A. $480,000
B. $380,000
C. $385,000
D. $400,000

198. Under which of the following standards are nonmonetary exchanges characterized as exchanges of similar assets and exchanges of dissimilar assets?
    I. IFRS
    II. US GAAP

A. I only
B. II only
C. Both I and II
D. Neither I nor II

199. As it relates to long-lived assets with finite lives, in order for an impairment loss to be recognized, which of the following conditions must be present?
    I. The asset's carrying amount is irrecoverable.
    II. The asset's carrying amount is less than its fair value.

A. I only
B. II only
C. Both I and II
D. Neither I nor II

200. When testing an asset for impairment that is held for disposal as a part of a discontinued operation rather than held for use:

   I. the asset's carrying amount is first compared to the undiscounted cash flows to see if any impairment has occurred

   II. if an impairment has occurred, the discounted cash flows (asset's fair value) is compared to the asset's carrying amount

   A. I only
   B. II only
   C. Both I and II
   D. Neither I nor II

201. Manyindo Co. has a long-lived asset with a carrying amount of $160,000, expected future cash flows of $150,000, present value of expected future cash flows of $130,000, and a market value of $135,000. The impairment loss Manyindo should report is equal to:

   A. $35,000
   B. $30,000
   C. $25,000
   D. $0

202. For fixed assets, no reversal of an impairment loss is permitted when the asset is held for use under:

   I. US GAAP

   II. IFRS

   A. I only
   B. II only
   C. Both I and II
   D. Neither I nor II

QUESTIONS 203–253

---

203. Current liabilities are obligations with maturities:
  A. within 1 year
  B. within 1 year or one operating cycle, whichever is shorter
  C. within 1 year or one operating cycle, whichever is longer
  D. within one operating cycle

204. Dragon Corp. is a calendar year corporation. Which of the following should be recorded as current liabilities at December 31, Year 5?
  I. Dividends in arrears that the board of directors plans to declare in January of Year 6 and pay by March 15 of Year 6
  II. A bonus of $25,000 to a corporate executive expected to be paid February 5, Year 6

  A. I only
  B. II only
  C. Both I and II
  D. Neither I nor II

205. When recording trade accounts payable under the net method, which of the following is correct regarding the payment or settlement date?
  I. A purchase discount lost account would be debited if the payment date is after the discount period.
  II. A purchase discount would be debited if the buyer pays within the discount period.

  A. I only
  B. II only
  C. Both I and II
  D. Neither I nor II

206. When purchases are made, the purchase is recorded as a credit to accounts payable:
  A. as if the discount is going to be taken, if using the gross method
  B. without regard for the discount, if using the net method
  C. as if the discount is going to be taken, if using the net method
  D. as if the discount is going to be taken, using either the gross or net method

207. When recording accounts payable, a purchase discount is recorded:
  A. if using the net method
  B. if using the gross method, but only if the payment is made during the discount period
  C. if using the net method, provided the payment is made during the discount period
  D. if using the gross method, but the purchase discounts are reduced by any purchase discounts lost

208. Under state law, Randolph pays 3% of eligible gross wages for unemployment. Eligible gross wages are defined as the first $10,000 of gross wages paid to each employee. Randolph had three employees, each of whom earned $20,000 during the current year. In its December 31 balance sheet, what amount should Randolph report as accrued liability for unemployment?
  A. $900
  B. $300
  C. $1,800
  D. $600

209. On September 30, Graphnet Corp. borrowed $1,000,000 on a 9% note payable quarterly. Graphnet Corp. paid the first of four quarterly payments of $264,200 when due on December 30. How much of the first payment serves to reduce the principal?

    A. $264,200
    B. $90,000
    C. $241,700
    D. $758,300

210. Normally, interest is imputed when no, or an unreasonably low, rate is stated. An exception exists for receivables and payables arising from transactions with customers or suppliers in the normal course of business when the trade terms do NOT exceed:

    A. 1 year
    B. 9 months
    C. 6 months
    D. 3 months

211. Which of the following is correct regarding the discount resulting from the determination of a note payable's present value?
    I. The discount is NOT a separate account from the note payable account.
    II. The note payable is reported on the balance sheet at the net of the note payable face value less the unamortized discount.

    A. I only
    B. II only
    C. Both I and II
    D. Neither I nor II

212. The New Era Bank operates a savings and loan division and also a mortgage division. When loans are made, origination fees are either deducted from the loan or collected up front. How are loan origination fees accounted for by a mortgage company or lending institution?
    I. The amount collected up front is included in income in the year of receipt.
    II. The amount deducted from the loan proceeds is deferred and recognized over the life of the loan as additional income.

    A. I only
    B. II only
    C. Both I and II
    D. Neither I nor II

213. Sundance Inc. borrowed $1,000,000 by selling bonds and had to sign a debt covenant. Which of the following is correct regarding the debt covenant?
    I. A debt covenant may restrict Sundance Inc. from doing whatever it chooses with the proceeds of the bond issuance.
    II. The debt covenant may require Sundance Inc. to maintain a certain minimum working capital.

    A. I only
    B. II only
    C. Both I and II
    D. Neither I nor II

214. Which of the following is correct regarding a typical debt covenant associated with a loan agreement?
    I. A typical debt covenant may restrict companies from disposing of certain assets, but it cannot restrict the payment of dividends to stockholders, since only the board of directors can make decisions with regard to dividend declaration.
    II. Violation of a debt covenant results in technical default of the loan, and the lender could call the entire loan due and payable immediately.

    A. I only
    B. II only
    C. Both I and II
    D. Neither I nor II

215. Hall Corp. is obligated to pay a bonus to its CEO equal to 10% of the company's income after deduction of the bonus but before income tax. Hall's income before the bonus and income tax was $75,000. Hall's income tax rate is 40%. What amount should Hall accrue for the CEO's bonus?

    A. $4,773
    B. $5,250
    C. $6,818
    D. $7,500

216. Victor Co. includes coupons in the packages of its products. These coupons can be presented at retail stores to obtain discounts of other Victor products. Victor reimburses the retailers for the face amount of the coupons redeemed plus 5% of that amount for handling costs. Victor honors requests for coupon redemption by retailers up to six months after the coupon expiration date. Victor estimates that 80% of all coupons issued will ultimately be redeemed. Information regarding the coupons Victor issued during Year 1 is as follows:

Coupon expiration date	December 31, Year 1
Total face amount of coupons issues	$550,000
Total payments to retailers as of December 31, Year 1	$225,000

What amount should Victor report as a liability for unredeemed coupons in its December 31, Year 1 balance sheet?

- A. $0
- B. $237,000
- C. $325,000
- D. $462,000

217. During Year 1, Blacker, Inc., a golf supplies manufacturer, introduced a new golf club carrying a two-year warranty against defects. Blacker estimated the warranty costs to be 3% within 12 months following sale, and 6% in the second 12 months following sale. Blacker's accounting records reported sales in Years 1 and 2, of $750,000 and $1,000,000, respectively, and actual warranty expenditures of $10,000, and $30,000 for Years 1 and 2, respectively. Based on this information, what should Blacker report as an estimated warranty liability at December 31, Year 2?

- A. $30,000
- B. $40,000
- C. $117,500
- D. $157,500

218. Weis Co. borrowed $125,000 on November 1, Year 1, and signed a two-year note bearing interest of 10% on that date. Interest is compounded annually and is payable in full at the note's maturity date of March 31, Year 3. What amount of liability for interest should Weis have accrued as of December 31, Year 2?

- A. $14,791
- B. $12,500
- C. $2,083
- D. $0

219. For the month of January, Year 1, Catalina Corp. reported gross wages paid to employees in the amount of 20,000 and federal income tax withheld from those wages of $3,500. These wages were also subject to social security (FICA) tax withholding at 7% of gross wages, which Catalina Corp. must match. Payroll taxes are remitted to the appropriate taxing authority on the 15th of the month following withholding. What amount should Catalina Corp. report as both a liability and expense for payroll taxes as of, and for the month ended, January, Year 1?

- A. $3,500 payroll tax liability; $2,800 payroll tax expense
- B. $4,900 payroll tax liability; $2,800 payroll tax expense
- C. $4,900 payroll tax liability; $1,400 payroll tax expense
- D. $6,300 payroll tax liability; $1,400 payroll tax expense

220. At December 31, Year 1, Martinez, Ltd. reported a balance in accounts payable in the amount of $450,000. This balance included a $60,000 debit related to an advance payment Martinez had paid to a vendor for goods to be manufactured and delivered in Year 2, and $50,000 of checks written to vendors and recorded on December 30, Year 1, but not mailed until January 10, Year 2. Martinez should report accounts payable at what amount in its December 31, Year 1 balance sheet?

- A. $340,000
- B. $390,000
- C. $450,000
- D. $560,000

221. Under US GAAP, provision for a loss contingency relating to pending or threatened litigation is recorded if the:
  I. loss is considered reasonably possible
  II. amount can be reasonably estimated

- A. I only
- B. II only
- C. Both I and II
- D. Neither I nor II

222. The Dodo Corp. has guaranteed the indebtedness of the Squonk Corp. The Dodo Corp. can reasonably estimate the loss amount within a range of between $50,000 and $150,000. Which of the following is correct?
    I. US GAAP requires that the best estimate of the loss be accrued.
    II. If no estimated amount is considered better than any other, $150,000, the maximum amount in the range, should be accrued.
    A. I only
    B. II only
    C. Both I and II
    D. Neither I nor II

223. Minte Corp. is determining whether to record a contingent loss from claims and assessments. Minte will record a contingent liability if the loss is probable and the amount can be reasonably estimated under:
    I. US GAAP
    II. IFRS
    A. I only
    B. II only
    C. Both I and II
    D. Neither I nor II

224. Ulacia Corp. is obligated to repurchase receivables that have been sold and needs to record a loss contingency. Ulacia Corp. has estimated a range of losses between $75,000 and $150,000. Which of the following is correct?
    I. Under US GAAP, if no amount in the range is a better estimate than any other amount, the minimum amount, $75,000, should be accrued as the contingent loss.
    II. Under IFRS, the maximum amount of the range, $150,000, should be recorded.
    A. I only
    B. II only
    C. Both I and II
    D. Neither I nor II

225. During Year 4, Denny Corp. became involved in a tax dispute with the Internal Revenue Service (IRS). At December 31, Year 4, Denny's tax advisor believed that an unfavorable outcome was probable. A reasonable estimate of additional taxes was $400,000, but could be as much as $500,000. After the Year 4 financial statements were issued, Denny Corp. received and accepted an IRS settlement offer of $415,000. Under US GAAP, what amount of accrued liability should Denny Corp. have reported in its December 31, Year 4, balance sheet?
    A. $415,000
    B. $400,000
    C. $500,000
    D. $450,000

226. Stabler Corp. is discounting a note receivable at the First Alameda Bank. The contingent liability for this note receivable being discounted must be disclosed in the notes to the financial statements at its face amount if sold to the bank:
    I. with recourse
    II. without recourse
    A. I only
    B. II only
    C. Both I and II
    D. Neither I nor II

227. Under US GAAP, an example of a loss contingency that would be recorded if probable would include:
    I. a note discounted "with recourse"
    II. tax disputes with a state taxing agency
    A. I only
    B. II only
    C. Both I and II
    D. Neither I nor II

228. On February 19, Year 3, a Dunn Corp. truck was in an accident with an auto driven by Aaron. On January 16, Year 4, Dunn received notice of a lawsuit seeking $500,000 in damages for personal injuries suffered by Aaron. Dunn Corp.'s counsel believes it is reasonably possible that Aaron will be awarded an estimated amount in the range between $150,000 and $300,000, and that $220,000 is a better estimate of potential liability than any other amount. Dunn's accounting year ends on December 31, and the Year 3 financial statements were issued on March 8, Year 4. What amount of loss should Dunn accrue at December 31, Year 3?
    A. $150,000
    B. $220,000
    C. $300,000
    D. $0

229. Under US GAAP, a gain contingency:
   I. should be disclosed in the notes unless the likelihood of the gain being realized is remote
   II. can be recorded as revenue but only if the likelihood of realization is probable

   A. I only
   B. II only
   C. Both I and II
   D. Neither I nor II

230. A potential gain contingency in the amount of $350,000 as of December 31, Year 2, is settled out of court on March 12, Year 3, for $275,000. The financial statements for Year 2 were issued on March 1, Year 3. Which of the following is correct regarding the gain contingency and its recognition and disclosure in Year 2?

   A. No disclosure in the footnotes, since gain contingencies are not recognized until realized
   B. Loss of $75,000 should be recorded on the income statement since the settlement was for less than the contingency
   C. Gain of $275,000 should be recorded in the Year 2 income statement
   D. Footnote disclosure only in Year 2

231. Electric Motorcycles Inc. is currently involved in two lawsuits. One is a class action suit in which consumers claim that one of Electric's bestselling bikes caused severe burn injuries. It is reasonably possible that Electric will lose the suit and have to pay $16 million in damages. Electric Motorcycles Inc. is suing another company for false claims against Electric. It is probable that Electric Motorcycles will win the suit and be awarded $4 million in damages. What amount should Electric report on its financial statements as a result of these two lawsuits?

   A. $4 million income
   B. $0
   C. $12 million expense
   D. $16 million expense

232. Triano Corp. settled litigation on February 22, Year 5, for an event that occurred during Year 4. An estimated liability was determined as of December 31, Year 4. This estimate was significantly less than the final settlement. The transaction is considered to be material. The financial statements for year-end Year 4 have not been issued. How should the settlement be reported in Triano's year-end Year 4 financial statements?
   I. Disclosure
   II. Accrual

   A. I only
   B. II only
   C. Both I and II
   D. Neither I nor II

233. With regard to deferred taxes, use of the installment sales method for tax purposes would typically result in a:
   I. deferred tax asset
   II. deferred tax liability

   A. I only
   B. II only
   C. Both I and II
   D. Neither I nor II

234. The reporting of which of the following would typically result in a deferred tax liability?
   I. Warranty expense
   II. Bad debt expense

   A. I only
   B. II only
   C. Both I and II
   D. Neither I nor II

235. Which of the following is a true statement regarding the reporting of deferred taxes in financial statements prepared under US GAAP and IFRS?

   A. Under US GAAP, deferred tax assets are classified as current and deferred tax liabilities classified as noncurrent.
   B. Under IFRS, deferred tax assets and liabilities are netted if they relate to the same taxing authority or jurisdiction, and there is a legal right to offset the amounts.
   C. Under IFRS, deferred tax assets can never be netted against deferred tax liabilities.
   D. Under US GAAP, deferred tax assets and liabilities may only be classified as current.

236. Station Toy Train Co., a cash basis taxpayer, prepares accrual basis financial statements. In its Year 13 balance sheet, Station's deferred income tax liabilities increased compared to Year 12. Which of the following changes during Year 13 would cause this increase in deferred income tax liabilities?
    I. An increase in prepaid insurance
    II. An increase in rent receivable
    III. An increase in liability for warranty obligations

    A. II and III
    B. I only
    C. I and II
    D. III only

237. Which is correct regarding current and deferred income tax expense?
    I. Deferred income tax expense is equal to the change in deferred tax liability (or asset) on the balance sheet from the beginning of the year to the end of the year.
    II. Current income tax expense is equal to the income taxes payable on the corporate tax return, assuming no estimated tax payments were made.

    A. I only
    B. II only
    C. Both I and II
    D. Neither I nor II

238. The Ginger Corp. operates its business in two international jurisdictions, Greece and Italy, and prepares its taxes based on taxing authority. Ginger also has the legal right to offset taxes in these jurisdictions. Ginger's accounting records at December 31, Year 2, report the following deferred tax assets and liabilities, their amounts, and taxing jurisdictions:

    Deferred tax liability; $10,000; Italy
    Deferred tax asset; $25,000; Greece
    Deferred tax liability; $15,000; Greece

    Assuming Ginger prepares its financial statements in accordance with IFRS, how should Ginger present its deferred taxes in its December 31, Year 2, financial statements?

    A. $25,000 deferred tax asset and a $25,000 deferred tax liability
    B. $15,000 deferred tax asset and a $15,000 deferred tax liability
    C. $10,000 deferred tax asset and a $10,000 deferred tax liability
    D. $0 deferred tax asset and a $0 deferred tax liability

239. Fusco, Inc. reported the following amounts of taxable income (operating loss) for its first three years of operations:

    | Year 1 | $100,000 |
    | Year 2 | ($200,000) |
    | Year 3 | $400,000 |

    For each year, Fusco had no temporary differences, and its effective income tax rate was 40%. In its Year 2 income tax return, Fusco did not elect to forgo the carryback of its loss for Year 2. Additionally, Fusco determined that it was more likely than not that it would realize the full benefit of any loss carryforward. What amount should Fusco report as total income tax expense in its Year 3 income statement?

    A. $40,000
    B. $80,000
    C. $120,000
    D. $160,000

Use the following facts to answer **Questions 240–243**:

The Aragona Corp. reports net income on its Year 13 financial statements before income tax expense of $400,000. Aragona Corp. has been profitable in the past and expects to continue to be profitable. The company expensed warranty costs in Year 13 on the books for $35,000 that is expected to impact the tax return in Year 16. Aragona Corp. also had $60,000 in revenue that will not be taxed until Year 15. Aragona Corp. has a tax rate for Year 13 of 30% and an enacted rate of 40% beyond Year 13. In addition, Aragona Corp. made four estimated tax payments of $25,000 each in Year 13.

240. How much will Aragona Corp. report as taxable income on its income statement for December 31, Year 13?

    A. $375,000
    B. $495,000
    C. $425,000
    D. $400,000

241. How much would Aragona Corp. report as current year tax income tax expense on the December 31, Year 13, income statement?

    A. $150,000
    B. $112,500
    C. $12,500
    D. None of the above

242. How much would Aragona Corp. report as deferred income tax expense on the December 31, Year 13, income statement?

   A. $0
   B. $10,000
   C. $14,000
   D. $24,000

243. How much would Aragona Corp. report as total income tax expense on the December 31, Year 13, income statement?

   A. $112,500
   B. $10,000
   C. $122,500
   D. None of the above

244. Bruford Corp., a newly organized company, reported pretax financial income of $100,000 for the current year. Among the items reported in Bruford's income statement are the following:

   Premium on officer's life insurance with
      Bruford as owner and beneficiary $5,000
   Interest received on municipal bonds $10,000

   The enacted tax rate for the current year is 25% and 30% thereafter. In its December 31 balance sheet, Bruford should report a deferred income tax liability of:

   A. $3,000
   B. $3,750
   C. $2,500
   D. $0

   Use the following facts to answer **Questions 245–248:**

   Pecorino Corp. had a pretax financial income of $125,000 in Year 13. To compute the provision for federal income taxes, the following information was provided:

   Interest income received on state
      of Florida bonds $18,000
   Tax depreciation in excess of
      financial statement amount $8,000
   Rent received in advance $14,000
   Corporation tax rate   30% in Year 12
           35% in Year 13
           40% in Year 14
           45% in Year 15

   Pecorino made four installments of corporate estimated tax in the amount of $9,000 each during Year 13.

245. How much permanent difference between book income and taxable income existed at December 31, Year 13?

   A. $26,000
   B. $18,000
   C. $40,000
   D. $14,000

246. What amount of taxable income should be reported for Pecorino in Year 13?

   A. $131,000
   B. $139,000
   C. $147,000
   D. $113,000

247. What amount of current income tax expense should be reported in Pecorino's December 31, Year 13, income statement?

   A. $39,550
   B. $45,200
   C. $50,850
   D. $33,900

248. What amount of current income tax payable should be reported in Pecorino's December 31, Year 13, balance sheet?

   A. $0
   B. $39,550
   C. $36,000
   D. $3,550

249. The Shea Corp. has a temporary difference in Year 1 that is from a noncurrent liability and expected to reverse in Years 2, 3, and 4. In Year 1 the tax rate is 30%. In Years 2, 3, and 4, the enacted rate is 40%. Under US GAAP, the deferred tax liability is based on which of the following tax rates?

   A. Tax rate for Year 1
   B. Enacted rate for Years 1 and 2 divided by two
   C. Enacted rate for Years 1, 2, 3, and 4 divided by four
   D. Enacted rate for Years 2, 3, and 4

250. In Year 1, its first year of operations, Mack Industries has temporary differences resulting from the following two items. Which of the following differences should be reported as current deferred tax assets/liabilities on the Year 1 balance sheet?

   I. Depreciation expense
   II. Warranty expense

  A. I only
  B. II only
  C. Both I and II
  D. Neither I nor II

251. Trevellyan Corp. received cash in the amount of $20,000 that was included in its Year 1 financial statements, of which $12,000 will not be taxed until Year 2. Trevellyan's enacted tax rate is 30% for Year 1, and 25% for Year 2. What amount should Trevellyan report in its Year 1 balance sheet for deferred income tax liability?

  A. $3,600
  B. $3,000
  C. $2,400
  D. $2,000

252. On June 20, Year 1, Benson Corp. leased a building and received a rental payment in the amount of $42,000. The payment was for the rental period beginning July 1, Year 1, through July 1, Year 2. Benson's tax rates are 25% for Year 1, and 30% for Year 2. Assuming no other temporary differences, and that rental income is taxable when received, what amount of deferred tax asset should Benson report in its Year 1 balance sheet?

  A. $5,250
  B. $6,300
  C. $10,500
  D. $12,600

253. Among the items reported on Fisk Corp.'s income statement for Year 13 were the following:

Income	
Life insurance proceeds on death of officer	$500,000
Expenses	
Estimate for future warranty expense	$25,000
Estimate for bad debt expense	$18,000

What is the total amount of temporary differences for Fisk Corp. in Year 13?

  A. $543,000
  B. $500,000
  C. $43,000
  D. $18,000

CHAPTER 29

ACCOUNTING FOR LEASES AND PENSIONS

QUESTIONS 254–286

254. Which of the following criteria must be met for a lease to be accounted for as a capital lease?

I. The lease contains a bargain purchase option.

II. The lease transfers title to the lessee at the expiration of the lease.

III. The lease term is 75% or greater than the life of the asset.

IV. The present value of the lease payments is 90% or more of the fair value of the leased asset at the inception of the lease.

A. All four of the criteria

B. Any three of the criteria

C. Any two of the criteria

D. Any one of the criteria

255. The ADTC Group leases an asset from Mahan Corp. for 8 years. The life of the asset is expected to be 10 years. If the lease does NOT contain a bargain purchase option or a transfer of title, which of the following is correct?

A. The leased asset would be accounted for by the ADTC Group as an operating lease.

B. The leased asset would be depreciated by the ADTC Group over 8 years.

C. The leased asset would be depreciated by the ADTC Group over 10 years.

D. The leased asset would be depreciated using the same method for book purposes as for tax purposes.

256. An 8-year capital lease entered into on December 31, Year 1, specified equal minimum annual lease payments. Part of this payment represents interest and part represents a reduction in the net lease liability. The portion of the minimum lease payment in the 6th year applicable to the reduction of the net lease liability should be:

A. less than in the 5th year

B. more than in the 5th year

C. the same as in the 7th year

D. more than in the 7th year

257. For a lessor, which of the following is correct regarding the difference between a direct financing lease and a sales type lease?

I. The total amount of profit will be less if the lease is accounted for as a direct financing lease rather than a sales type lease, because in a direct financing lease the lessor recognizes only interest income.

II. If the lessor is either a manufacturer or dealer, the lease would be recorded as a sales type lease rather than direct financing.

A. I only

B. II only

C. Both I and II

D. Neither I nor II

258. In Year 2, Messing Corp. sold an asset for $1,000,000 to Susserman Corp. and simultaneously leased it back for 3 years. The asset's remaining life was 34 years, and the carrying amount at the time of sale was $350,000. The annual lease payments were $150,000 per year. How much gain should be recognized by Messing Corp. in Year 2?

   A. $650,000
   B. $500,000
   C. $200,000
   D. $0

259. The following information pertains to a sale and leaseback of equipment by Brennan Co. on December 31, Year 2:

Sales price	$300,000
Carrying amount	$210,000
Monthly lease payment	$3,550
Present value of lease payments	$37,800
Estimated remaining life	20 years
Lease term	1 year
Implicit rate	10%

   What amount of deferred gain on the sale should Brennan report at December 31, Year 2, under US generally accepted accounting principles (GAAP)?

   A. $90,000
   B. $9,000
   C. $52,200
   D. $0

260. The East Jersey Finance Corp. leased an asset to Mountainview Inc. on January 2, Year 13, for payments of $1,500 per month for 5 years. The lease included a provision that Mountainview Inc. would receive the first 6 months free. The lease is being accounted for as an operating lease. How much rent expense should Mountainview Inc. record in Year 13?

   A. $8,100
   B. $9,000
   C. $16,200
   D. $18,000

261. Diamonds Cardworld signs an operating lease to pay monthly rent at a fixed amount of $10,000 per month on the first $500,000 of monthly sales. The lease contains a contingent rent agreement that stipulates that Diamonds must pay additional rent of 2% of sales over $500,000 in any month. Which of the following is correct?
   I. If sales for the month were $800,000, rent expense for the month would be $16,000.
   II. If sales for the month were below $500,000, rent expense would NOT be less than $10,000.

   A. I only
   B. II only
   C. Both I and II
   D. Neither I nor II

262. Anita's Plaque Factory Inc. signed a 10-year operating lease for $80,000 per year on January 1, Year 1. The lease included a provision for contingent rent of 5% of annual sales in excess of $500,000. Sales for the year ended December 31, Year 1, were $600,000. Anita's Plaque Factory also paid a $20,000 bonus for the lease. Rent expense for the year ended December 31, Year 1, was:

   A. $80,000
   B. $82,000
   C. $85,000
   D. $87,000

263. Which of the following would be evidence that a lease should be accounted for by the lessee as an operating lease rather than a capital lease?
   I. The lease contains a bargain purchase option.
   II. The lease is for 8 years, and the asset's estimated life is 10 years.

   A. I only
   B. II only
   C. Both I and II
   D. Neither I nor II

264. When accounting for a 10-year operating lease that began January 2, Year 1, which of the following is a required footnote disclosure on December 31, 3?
   I. The full amount of the remaining lease obligation
   II. The total annual obligation for each of the next 3 succeeding years

   A. I only
   B. II only
   C. Both I and II
   D. Neither I nor II

265. On January 1, Year 13, Bowman Inc. entered into a 12-year operating lease for a factory. The annual minimum lease payments are $23,000. In the December Year 13 balance sheet, how much liability should be shown for the lease obligation?
    A. $23,000
    B. $276,000
    C. $253,000
    D. $0

266. Sherman Inc. is leasing a building from Crabtree Inc. The space was formerly a bank, and now Sherman Inc. needs to pay for improvements to convert the premises to an indoor sports training facility. These leasehold improvements will include the removal of drop ceilings and the installation of special flooring and new walls with safety padding. The costs of these improvements are capitalized if Sherman Inc. is accounting for the lease as
    I. an operating lease
    II. a capital lease
    A. I only
    B. II only
    C. Both I and II
    D. Neither I nor II

Use the following facts to answer **Questions 267–269:**

On November 30, Year 11, Summit leased office space to Edison Inc. for 15 years at a monthly rental of $25,000. On the same date, Edison paid Summit Inc. the following amounts:

First month's rent	$25,000
Refundable security deposit	$63,000
Last month's rent	$25,000
Installation of drop ceiling	$20,000
Installation of new walls	$30,000
Installation of flooring and lighting	$10,000

The life of the leasehold improvements is estimated to be 20 years. Edison Inc. is a calendar year corporation and accounting for this lease as an operating lease. There is no option to renew the lease.

267. Which of the following is correct?
    I. Leasehold improvements will be capitalized for $60,000.
    II. On Edison Inc.'s Year 11 balance sheet, the account "leasehold improvements" is listed under prepaid expenses, current assets.
    A. I only
    B. II only
    C. Both I and II
    D. Neither I nor II

268. Using the same facts, which of the following is correct?
    I. Edison Inc. will amortize the leasehold improvements over 20 years.
    II. The $25,000 for last month's rent will NOT be expensed on Edison Inc.'s Year 11 income statement.
    A. I only
    B. II only
    C. Both I and II
    D. Neither I nor II

269. The total expense recorded by Edison Inc. for Year 11 as a result of this lease is
    A. $25,333
    B. $25,000
    C. $29,000
    D. none of the above

Use the following facts to answer **Questions 270–273:**

On January 2, Year 13, Queen Corp. signs a noncancelable lease agreement with King Corp. The lease was for 5 years and called for Queen Corp. to make payments of $100,000 starting December 31, Year 13. The present value of the lease payments are $371,600 based on an interest of 10%.

270. If Queen Corp. is accounting for this lease as a capital lease and the first lease payment is made December 31, Year 13, what amount should Queen record as interest expense at December 31, Year 13?
    A. $10,000
    B. $50,000
    C. $27,160
    D. $37,160

271. What is the balance of the lease obligation that should be recorded by Queen Corp. on the December 31, Year 13, balance sheet?
    A. $198,760
    B. $371,600
    C. $308,760
    D. $334,440

272. If Queen Corp. is accounting for this lease as a capital lease and the first lease payment is made January 2, Year 13, what amount should Queen record as interest expense at December 31, Year 13?
    A. $37,160
    B. $27,160
    C. $10,000
    D. $50,000

273. What is the balance of the lease obligation that should be recorded by Queen Corp. on the December 31, Year 13, balance sheet?

    A. $198,760
    B. $371,600
    C. $308,760
    D. $334,440

Use the following facts to answer **Questions 274–275:**

Advantage Corp. leases equipment for 5 years with the first payment due immediately to customers and records the transaction as a direct financing lease under US GAAP. Advantage structures the payment to earn 7% annually. On January 2, Year 13, Advantage enters into a lease with Bussell Corp. for equipment with a fair value of $105,000. There is no bargain purchase option, and the equipment has no residual value at the end of the lease. Assume that the present value factors are as follows:

The present value of an annuity due for 5 years at 7% is 4.2.
The present value of an ordinary annuity for 5 years at 7% is 3.89.

274. How much are the annual lease payments to be received by Advantage?

    A. $25,000
    B. $26,993
    C. $21,000
    D. None of the above

275. How much interest revenue will Advantage Corp. earn over the life of the lease?

    A. $7,351
    B. $8,750
    C. $20,000
    D. None of the above

276. Golf Finance Corp. leased equipment to Fair Oaks Country Club Inc. on January 1, Year 13, and properly recorded the sales type lease. The first of eight annual lease payments of $300,000 are due at the beginning of each year. Golf Finance Corp. had purchased the equipment for $1,100,000 and had a list price of $1,480,000. The present value of the lease payments is $1,700,000. The imputed interest rate on the lease was 11%, and Fair Oaks Country Club Inc. had an incremental borrowing rate of 10%. What amount of profit on the sale should Golf Finance Corp. report in its Year 1 income statement?

    A. $380,000
    B. $600,000
    C. $220,000
    D. None of the above

277. Which of the following methods of accounting for pension expense is considered generally accepted under US GAAP?
    I. pay-as-you-go method
    II. terminal funding method

    A. I only
    B. II only
    C. Both I and II
    D. Neither I nor II

278. Easy Corp. amended its defined benefit pension plan on January 1, Year 13, granting a total credit of $64,000 to four employees for services rendered prior to the plan's adoption. The employees, Adam, Bridget, Chester, and Drudge, are expected to retire from the company as follows:

Adam will retire after 6 years.
Bridget will retire after 8 years.
Chester and Drudge will retire after 10 years.

What is the amount of prior service cost amortization for Easy Corp. in Year 13 under US GAAP?

    A. $8,000
    B. $6,400
    C. $16,000
    D. $64,000

279. The following information pertains to American Bottle Co.'s pension plan:

Actuarial estimate of projected benefit obligation at beginning of Year 9	$93,000
Assumed discount rate	10%
Service costs	$11,000
Pension benefits paid during the year	$5,000

If no change in actuarial estimates occurred during the year, the projected benefit obligation at December 31, Year 9, is:

A. $108,300
B. $99,000
C. $118,300
D. $104,000

280. Under US GAAP, the separate components of net periodic pension cost are presented in which of the following ways on the income statement?

A. The separate components of net periodic pension cost must be shown separately on the income statement.

B. The separate components of net periodic pension cost can be shown separately or aggregated and shown as one amount on the income statement.

C. The separate components of net periodic pension cost can be aggregated on the income statement and shown as one amount if the pension plan is overfunded, but must be shown separately on the income statement if the plan is underfunded.

D. The separate components of net periodic pension cost must be aggregated on the income statement and shown as one amount.

281. The Bollestro Corp.'s pension plan began Year 5 with a fair value of plan assets of $1,000,000. The entity contributed $50,000 into the plan during the year. They paid benefits to retirees in the amount of $20,000 in Year 5, and the fair value of plan assets at December 31, Year 5, was $1,300,000. How much was the actual return on the plan assets in Year 5?

A. $200,000
B. $270,000
C. $300,000
D. $370,000

282. Lexington Corp. established a defined benefit pension plan on January 1, Year 5. The following information was available at December 31, Year 7:

Accumulated benefit obligation	$14,000,000
Projected benefit obligation	$18,500,000
Unfunded accrued pension cost	$300,000
Plan assets at fair market value	$9,000,000
Unrecognized prior service cost	$2,658,000

If the expected return on plan assets is 7% and the discount rate is 5%, what amount represents the funded status of the pension plan at December 31, Year 7?

A. $9,500,000 underfunded
B. $9,500,000 overfunded
C. $5,000,000 underfunded
D. $2,252,000 underfunded

283. Under US GAAP, when calculating the present value of future retirement payments, which of the following is taken into consideration by the projected benefit obligation but NOT taken into consideration by the accumulated benefit obligation?

A. Current salary levels
B. Past salary levels
C. Past and current salary levels
D. Future salary levels

284. Which of the following is correct regarding net periodic pension cost?

I. Under US GAAP, interest cost included in the net pension cost recognized for a period by an employer sponsoring a defined benefit pension plan represents the increase in the projected benefit obligation due to the passage of time.

II. The increase in the projected benefit obligation resulting from employee services in the current period is known as the current service cost.

A. I only
B. II only
C. Both I and II
D. Neither I nor II

Use the following facts to answer **Questions 285–286:**

Century Corp. had service cost of $30,000 and interest cost of $20,000 related to its defined benefit pension plan for the year ended December 31, Year 13. The company's unrecognized prior service cost was $240,000 on December 31, Year 12, and the average remaining service life of employees was 15 years. Plan assets earned an expected and actual return of 12% in Year 13. The company made contributions to the plan of $35,000 and paid benefits of $40,000 in Year 13. Century Corp. had assets with a fair value of $350,000 at December 31, Year 12. The pension benefit obligation was $410,000 at December 31, Year 12, and $450,000 at December 31, Year 13.

285. What is the funded status of Century Corp.'s pension plan at December 31, Year 13?

   A. $105,000 underfunded
   B. $63,000 overfunded
   C. $105,000 overfunded
   D. $63,000 underfunded

286. How much prior year service cost is amortized to pension expense in Year 13?

   A. $12,000
   B. $44,000
   C. $16,000
   D. $30,000

CHAPTER 30

BONDS AND OTHER NONCURRENT LIABILITIES

QUESTIONS 287–314

287. Zaran Corp. issues bonds with a stated rate of 5%. If the market rate for comparable bonds is 6%, which of the following is correct?

A. Zaran Corp. will collect a premium.
B. Zaran Corp. will have to sell the bonds at a discount.
C. Zaran Corp. will sell the bonds at face value.
D. The amount of interest paid by Zaran Corp. to investors each period is based on the market rate of 6% rather than the stated rate of 5%.

288. Anna Inc. issues bonds with a stated rate of 5%. These bonds will sell at a premium if:
  I. the market rate of interest is above 5%
  II. the bonds pay interest semiannually rather than annually

A. I only
B. II only
C. Both I and II
D. Neither I nor II

289. With regard to a 5-year $1,000 bond issued at 102 on January 1, Year 10, that pays interest semiannually on June 30 and December 31, the stated interest rate of 8% is used to calculate the:

A. amount of interest payment
B. market price of the bond
C. selling price of the bond
D. actual amount of interest expense

290. On August 1, Year 4, Blue Corp. purchased 500 of Karl Corp.'s 10% $1,000 bonds at 98 plus accrued interest. The bonds are dated May 1 and mature on May 1, Year 14. Interest is payable semiannually on May 1 and November 1. What amount did Karl Corp. receive on the bond issuance?

A. $502,500
B. $496,250
C. $500,000
D. $483,750

Use the following facts to answer **Questions 291–292:**

On January 2, Year 1, Brunner Corp. issued 9% bonds with a face amount of $1,000,000 that mature on January 2, Year 7. The bonds pay interest semiannually on June 30 and December 31. The bonds were issued to yield 12%, which resulted in a discount of $140,000.

291. If Brunner uses the straight line method to amortize the discount, the amount of interest expense for the first interest payment date of June 30, Year 1, would be determined by:

A. subtracting the bond discount amortization for the period from the amount of cash interest paid
B. adding the bond discount amortization for the period to the amount of cash interest paid
C. multiplying the stated rate of interest by the par value of the bonds
D. multiplying the market rate of interest by the par value of the bonds

292. If Brunner uses the effective interest method to amortize the discount, the amount of interest expense for the first interest payment date of June 30, Year 1, would be determined by:
   A. subtracting the bond discount amortization for the period from the amount of cash interest paid
   B. multiplying the par value of the bonds by the stated rate of interest
   C. multiplying the carrying amount of the bonds by the market rate of interest
   D. multiplying the par value of the bonds by the market rate of interest

Use the following facts to answer **Questions 293–294:**

On July 1, Year 1, Truncale Corp. issued 8% bonds in the amount of $500,000, which mature on July 1, Year 11. The bonds were issued for $468,500 to yield 10%. Interest is payable annually on June 30. Truncale Corp. uses the effective interest method to amortize the discount.

293. How much interest expense should Truncale Corp. record on December 31, Year 1?
   A. $46,850
   B. $40,000
   C. $20,000
   D. $23,425

294. How much is the carrying value of the bonds on December 31, Year 1?
   A. $471,925
   B. $468,500
   C. $500,000
   D. $475,350

295. A bond is issued on May 1 of the current year and has interest payment dates of March 1 and September 1. The accrual for bond interest expense at December 31 would be for a period of:
   A. 8 months
   B. 10 months
   C. 4 months
   D. 6 months

296. Reynolds Corp. issued $200,000 worth of 11% bonds for par on January 31, Year 5. The bonds are dated December 31, Year 1, and pay interest semiannually on June 30 and December 31. What amount of accrued interest payable should Reynolds Corp. report in its September 30, Year 5, balance sheet?
   A. $5,500
   B. $7,333
   C. $11,000
   D. $1,833

297. Which of the following describe(s) unsecured bonds issued by a corporation that mature on different dates?
   I. Term bonds
   II. Serial bonds
   III. Debentures

   A. I and II
   B. I, II, and III
   C. I and III
   D. II and III

Use the following facts to answer **Questions 298–300:**

On August 1, Year 13, Tucker Corp. issued $800,000 worth of 7% bonds at par with interest payment dates of June 1 and December 1.

298. How much accrued interest should be recorded on August 1, Year 13?
   A. $0
   B. $4,667
   C. $9,333
   D. None of the above

299. How much accrued interest should be recorded at December 31, Year 13?
   A. $0
   B. $4,667
   C. $9,333
   D. None of the above

300. In its income statement for the current year ended December 31, Year 13, what amount of total interest expense should Tucker Corp. report?
   A. $4,667
   B. $23,333
   C. $9,333
   D. $32,667

Use the following facts to answer **Questions 301–302:**

The Holden Corp. issued 10-year bonds at 102 with a maturity value of $1,000,000. The bonds pay interest semiannually. The stated interest rate of the bonds was 6%.

301. The entry the Holden Corp. uses to record the original issue should include which of the following?

  A. Credit to bond premium for $2,000
  B. Credit to bonds payable for $1,020,000
  C. Debit to cash for $1,000,000
  D. Credit to bond premium for $20,000

302. The amortization of the bond premium each period would impact the financial statements in which of the following ways?

  A. Interest expense being greater than the amount of cash paid for interest
  B. Cash paid for interest being greater than interest expense
  C. Interest expense and cash paid being equal if the premium was being amortized using the straight line method
  D. None of the above

303. Which of the following is correct regarding convertible bonds at issuance?
  I. Under US GAAP, no value is assigned to the conversion feature.
  II. Under the IFRS, both a liability and an equity component should be recognized when the bonds are issued.

  A. I only
  B. II only
  C. Both I and II
  D. Neither I nor II

304. All costs associated with the issuance of a bond are:

  A. expensed in the period incurred
  B. capitalized but NOT amortized
  C. capitalized and amortized over the outstanding term of the bonds
  D. capitalized and amortized over 5 years

305. The Thunder Corp. issues bonds and warrants simultaneously for $1,000,000 at par. Thunder Corp. would be required to account for the value of the warrants separately on the date the bonds are originally issued if the warrants are:
  I. nondetachable
  II. detachable

  A. I only
  B. II only
  C. Both I and II
  D. Neither I nor II

306. On March 1, Year 1, Marco Corp. issued $500,000 worth of 10% nonconvertible bonds at 102, due on February 28, Year 21. Each $1,000 bond was issued with 20 detachable stock warrants, each of which entitled the holder to purchase, for $60, one share of Marco's $10 par common stock. On March 1, Year 1, the market price of each warrant was $5. By what amount should the bond issue proceeds increase stockholders' equity?

  A. $0
  B. $10,000
  C. $100,000
  D. $50,000

307. Which of the following is correct regarding a bond sinking fund?
  I. Sinking fund accounts that are considered to offset current bond liabilities can be included within current assets.
  II. A bond sinking fund is an example of an appropriation of retained earnings.

  A. I only
  B. II only
  C. Both I and II
  D. Neither I nor II

308. Which of the following is correct regarding troubled debt restructuring?
  I. For the creditor, the objective is to minimize the recovery of the investment.
  II. Concessions made by the creditor normally include reduced interest rates.

  A. I only
  B. II only
  C. Both I and II
  D. Neither I nor II

309. With regard to troubled debt restructuring, creditors typically make which of the following concessions to minimize the risk of bad debt write-off?

    I. Extension of maturity dates

    II. Reduction of accrued interest

  A. I only

  B. II only

  C. Both I and II

  D. Neither I nor II

Use these facts to answer **Questions 310–311:**

Livingston Corp. transferred land to Vette Corp. pursuant to a troubled debt restructuring. The transfer was made in full liquidation of Livingston's liability to Vette Corp. Information pertaining to the land is as follows:

Carrying amount of land transferred	$140,000
Fair value of land transferred	$80,000
Carrying amount of liability liquidated	$165,000

310. What amount should Livingston report as ordinary gain (loss) on transfer of land?

  A. ($60,000)

  B. $0

  C. ($85,000)

  D. $60,000

311. What amount should Livingston report as a pretax gain (loss) on restructuring of payables under US GAAP?

  A. $25,000

  B. $0

  C. $60,000

  D. $85,000

312. If a current liability is expected to be refinanced on a long-term basis, the liability may be reclassified as long term on the balance sheet under which of the following standards?

    I. US GAAP

    II. IFRS

  A. I only

  B. II only

  C. Both I and II

  D. Neither I nor II

313. In December of Year 13, Carpenter Inc. had a note payable scheduled to mature on February 23, Year 14. On December 30, Year 13, Carpenter Inc. signed a binding agreement with Summit Bank to refinance the existing note, and the refinancing commenced on January 2, Year 13. The financial statements were issued on February 15, Year 14. Under US GAAP, how should Carpenter Inc. report the note payable in its December 31, Year 13, income statement?

  A. Long-term liability

  B. Short-term liability

  C. Short-term note receivable

  D. Long-term note receivable

314. Simone Corp. reported the following liabilities at December 31, Year 4:

Accounts payable	$500,000
Mortgage payable (current portion, $150,000)	$2,000,000
Bank loan (matures May 31, Year 5)	$800,000

The $800,000 bank loan was refinanced with a 10-year loan on January 9, Year 5, with the first principal payment due in the amount of $100,000 on January 2, Year 6. Simone Corp.'s Year 4 audited financial statements were issued February 26, Year 5. What amount should Simone Corp. report as current liabilities at December 31, Year 4?

  A. $650,000

  B. $750,000

  C. $1,450,000

  D. $3,300,000

CHAPTER 31

QUESTIONS 315–352

315. A corporation has common stock with a $10 par value. A new share of this stock is issued for $13 to an investor. Which of the following is correct?
   I. The company will debit common stock for the par value of $10.
   II. The company will debit cash for $13 and credit gain on sale of stock for $3 if the purchaser of the stock was already a stockholder and is simply buying additional shares.

   A. I only
   B. II only
   C. Both I and II
   D. Neither I nor II

316. A company has common stock with a $10 par value and fair market value of $15. The company exchanges 1,000 shares of this common stock for an acre of land.
   I. The land will be debited for $10,000.
   II. The common stock account will be credited for $10,000 and no additional paid-in capital will be recorded.

   A. I only
   B. II only
   C. Both I and II
   D. Neither I nor II

317. A company was organized in January, Year 6, with authorized capital of $10 par value common stock. On February 1, Year 6, 2 shares were issued at par for cash. On March 1, Year 6, the company's attorney accepted 5,000 shares of the common stock in settlement for legal services with a fair value of $60,000. Additional paid-in capital would increase on:
   I. February 1, Year 6
   II. March 1, Year 6

   A. I only
   B. II only
   C. Both I and II
   D. Neither I nor II

318. Yoko Corp. issues 2,000 shares of its $5 par value common stock to Klein as compensation for 500 hours of trust services performed. Klein usually bills $180 per hour for similar services. On the date of issuance, the Yoko Corp. stock was traded on a public exchange at $100 per share. The journal entry to record the stock issued to Klein would include a:
   I. credit to common stock for $10,000
   II. credit to additional paid-in capital for $190,000

   A. I only
   B. II only
   C. Both I and II
   D. Neither I nor II

319. Mr. A subscribes to buy 1,000 shares of the common stock of Company Z for $22 per share, although the par value is only $10 per share. He pays $4 per share immediately and will pay the remaining $18 per share later. Which of the following is correct?

    I. Additional paid-in capital is increased at the time of the subscription by $4,000.

    II. On the day of the subscription, a common stock subscribed account is increased for the $10 par value of the stock.

    A. I only
    B. II only
    C. Both I and II
    D. Neither I nor II

320. Which is correct regarding the rights of common and preferred stockholders?

    I. Preferred stock has no set rights; the rights must be defined in the stock certificate.

    II. All common stocks issued by companies incorporated within a state typically will have the same legal rights because they are established by the laws of that state.

    A. I only
    B. II only
    C. Both I and II
    D. Neither I nor II

321. Which is correct regarding cumulative preferred stock?

    I. *Cumulative* means that if the preferred stock dividend is not declared, it will have to be paid before holders of common stock can receive any dividend payment.

    II. The issuing company reports a liability on the balance sheet for the dividends that are in arrears.

    A. I only
    B. II only
    C. Both I and II
    D. Neither I nor II

Use the following facts to answer **Questions 322–323:**

On February 1, Year 13, Matte Corp. issued 5,000 shares of $100 par convertible preferred stock for $110 per share. One share of preferred stock can be converted into 2 shares of Matte Corp.'s $10 par value common stock at the option of the preferred shareholder. On December 31, Year 14, when the market value was $40 per share, all of the preferred stock was converted.

322. What amount should be credited to additional paid-in capital-preferred stock on February 1, Year 13?

    A. $500,000
    B. $125,000
    C. $50,000
    D. $0

323. How much should be credited to additional paid-in capital from common stock as a result of the conversion on December 31, Year 14?

    A. $0
    B. $100,000
    C. $350,000
    D. $450,000

324. With regard to dividends paid from one corporation to another, retained earnings of the corporation paying the dividend is debited on which of the following dates?

    A. Date of declaration and the date of record
    B. Date of declaration and the date of payment
    C. Date of declaration only
    D. End of the fiscal year

325. With regard to dividends, which of the following result in a reduction of retained earnings at the date of declaration?

    I. Cash dividends

    II. Property dividends

    A. I only
    B. II only
    C. Both I and II
    D. Neither I nor II

Use the following facts to answer **Questions 326–328:**

Stefano Inc. was organized on January 2, Year 13, with $50,000 authorized shares of $5 par common stock. During Year 13, the company had the following capital transactions:

January 14	issued 20,000 shares at $11 per share
July 28	repurchased 5,000 shares at $16 per share
December 5	reissued the 5,000 shares held in treasury for $19 per share

326. Under US GAAP, how much additional paid-in capital is recorded by Stefano Inc. on January 14?

 A. $550,000
 B. $220,000
 C. $100,000
 D. $120,000

327. Assuming Stefano, Inc. uses the cost method to account for treasury stock, under US GAAP, how much (and what would be the entry) to record treasury stock on July 28, Year 13?

 A. $80,000 credit
 B. $80,000 debit
 C. $25,000 credit
 D. $25,000 debit

328. Assume Stefano Inc. uses the cost method to account for its treasury stock transactions. Under US GAAP, the entry to record the reissuance of the 5,000 treasury shares on December 5, Year 13, would include a credit to:

 A. gain on sale in the amount of $15,000
 B. retained earnings in the amount of $15,000
 C. additional paid-in capital in the amount of $15,000
 D. treasury stock in the amount of $95,000

Use the following facts to answer **Questions 329–335:**

Handy Inc. was organized on January 2, Year 13, with 40,000 authorized shares of $10 par value common stock. During Year 13, Handy Inc. had the following capital transactions:

January 2, Year 13	issued 20,000 shares at $15 per share
June 7, Year 13	repurchased 5,000 shares at $18
December 29, Year 13	reissued the 5,000 shares held in treasury for $30 per share

329. How much additional paid-in capital was recorded on January 2, Year 13?

 A. $300,000
 B. $150,000
 C. $200,000
 D. $100,000

330. Assume Handy Inc. uses the par value method of accounting for treasury stock transactions. Under US GAAP, how much is recorded for treasury stock on June 7, Year 13?

 A. $50,000
 B. $90,000
 C. $25,000
 D. $40,000

331. Assume Handy Inc. uses the par value method to account for treasury stock transactions. Under US GAAP, how much is recorded for additional paid-in capital on June 7, Year 13?

 A. $0
 B. $40,000 debit
 C. $25,000 debit
 D. $50,000 debit

332. Assume Handy Inc. uses the par value method to account for treasury stock transactions. Under US GAAP, the journal entry on June 7, Year 13, would impact retained earnings in which of the following ways?

 A. No effect
 B. Debit of $15,000
 C. Debit of $40,000
 D. Credit of $15,000

333. Assume Handy Inc. uses the par value method to account for treasury stock transactions. Under US GAAP, the journal entry on December 29, Year 13, would impact treasury stock in the amount of:

    A. $150,000 debit
    B. $150,000 credit
    C. $50,000 debit
    D. $50,000 credit

334. Assume Handy Inc. uses the par value method to account for treasury stock transactions. Under US GAAP, the journal entry on December 29, Year 13, to reissue the treasury stock would impact additional paid-in capital in the amount of:

    A. $100,000
    B. $150,000
    C. $50,000
    D. $0

335. Assuming Handy Inc. uses the par value method to account for treasury stock transactions, how much is the ending balance of additional paid-in capital on December 31, Year 13?

    A. $100,000
    B. $150,000
    C. $175,000
    D. $200,000

336. On January 6, Year 13, Theo Corp. issues a stock dividend to investors of record on February 3, Year 13. When determining how to account for this stock dividend, which of the following factors is the most important factor to Theo Corp.?

    A. The par value of the shares
    B. The market value of the shares
    C. The number of shares authorized
    D. The size of the stock dividend

Use the following facts to answer **Questions 337–338:**

The Reisig Corp. has 200,000 shares of $10 par value common stock outstanding on December 31, Year 12. On January 2, Year 13, it declares a stock dividend of 10,000 shares when the fair market value is $18. On the date of record, February 3, Year 13, the share price is $15. The shares are issued on March 1, Year 13, when the market value of the shares is $25.

337. When Reisig Corp. records the journal entry for the stock dividend, retained earnings will be debited for the number of new shares multiplied by which of the following amounts?

    A. Par value of the shares
    B. Market value of the shares on January 2, Year 13
    C. Market value of the shares on February 3, Year 13
    D. Market value of the shares on March 1, Year 13

338. When recording the journal entry to distribute the stock dividend, Reisig Corp. will credit additional paid-in capital for:

    A. $80,000
    B. $100,000
    C. $50,000
    D. $150,000

Use the following facts to answer **Questions 339–340:**

On June 25, Year 13, Allegra Corp. issues a 30% stock dividend on its 200,000 shares of $10 par value common stock. The shares will be issued on July 8, Year 13. The market price of Allegra Corp. stock is $15 per share on June 25, and on the date the shares are distributed, the stock is selling for $12 per share.

339. The journal entry to record the declaration of the stock dividend on June 25, Year 13, will include a:

    A. debit to retained earnings for $600,000
    B. debit to retained earnings for $900,000
    C. credit to additional paid-in capital for $300,000
    D. credit to additional paid-in capital for $200,000

340. The journal entry on June 25, Year 13, will include a credit to common stock distributable in the amount of:

    A. $200,000
    B. $300,000
    C. $600,000
    D. $900,000

341. On July 8, Year 13, the additional paid-in capital account is credited for:

    A. $300,000
    B. $200,000
    C. $600,000
    D. $0

342. Which of the following dividends will result in a decrease to total stockholders' equity?
    I. Large stock dividend
    II. Cash dividend
    III. Small stock dividend

    A. I, II, and III
    B. II and III
    C. II only
    D. III only

343. The Toro Corp. is splitting its 10,000 shares of $20 par value common stock 2:1. Common stock is currently $200,000, additional paid-in capital is $500,000, and retained earnings is $1,000,000. In connection with a stock split, the Toro Corp. will:

    A. increase total stockholders' equity
    B. decrease total stockholders' equity
    C. decrease retained earnings
    D. make no journal entry

344. Which of the following is a corporation likely to attempt to reduce its number of shares outstanding and increase its market price and par value of its stock?
    I. Stock dividend of 20% or less
    II. Stock split
    III. Reverse stock split

    A. I, II, and III
    B. II and III
    C. III only
    D. I and III

345. When issuing stock options to employees, which of the following factors is most relevant in determining the accounting treatment under US GAAP?

    A. The par value of the shares issued
    B. The market value of the shares issued
    C. The authorized number of shares
    D. Whether the stock options are issued in lieu of salary

346. Under a compensatory stock option plan, the expense to the corporation is:

    A. not booked until the options are exercised
    B. booked on the date the options are granted to employees
    C. determined on the date the options are granted to employees
    D. equal to the cash paid for the shares by the employee upon exercise

347. When accounting for the expense related to compensatory stock options, which of the following is decreased?
    I. Net income
    II. Retained earnings
    III. Total stockholders' equity

    A. I, II, and III
    B. I and II
    C. I only
    D. I and III

348. When accounting for compensatory stock options, when the employees exercise their options and purchase the shares for an amount above par but below the market price, the journal entry will include a:

    A. credit to additional paid-in capital-stock options
    B. debit to additional paid-in capital-common stock
    C. credit to common stock for the difference between the strike price and the market price
    D. debit to additional paid-in capital-stock options

349. Losses due to write-downs of assets under a quasi-reorganization would affect which of the following under US GAAP?
    I. Retained earnings
    II. Income statement

    A. I only
    B. II only
    C. Both I and II
    D. Neither I nor II

350. Working capital can be defined as:

    A. current assets divided by current liabilities
    B. cash plus net receivables plus marketable securities divided by current liabilities
    C. current assets minus current liabilities
    D. all of the above

351. The quick ratio includes which of the following in the numerator?
    I. Net receivables
    II. Short-term marketable securities
    III. Inventory
    IV. Prepaid rent

    A. I, II, and III
    B. I, II, III, and IV
    C. I and II
    D. I, II, and IV

352. Total current liabilities is used as the denominator in which of the following ratios?
    I. Current ratio
    II. Quick ratio

    A. I only
    B. II only
    C. Both I and II
    D. Neither I nor II

CHAPTER 32

EARNINGS PER SHARE

353. According to US generally accepted accounting principles (GAAP), which of the following entities are NOT required to present earnings per share (EPS) on the face of the income statement?
  I. Private entities that have yet to go public or make a filing for a public offering
  II. Entities whose shares are traded on a US securities exchange

A. I only
B. II only
C. Both I and II
D. Neither I nor II

354. A company can report basic EPS and not have to report diluted EPS if it has:
  I. common stock outstanding, no preferred stock, and options that are convertible into common stock
  II. common stock outstanding, no preferred stock, and bonds that are convertible into common stock

A. I only
B. II only
C. Both I and II
D. Neither I nor II

355. For purposes of calculating basic EPS, income available to common shareholders is determined by:
  I. deducting dividends declared in the period on noncumulative preferred stock (regardless of whether they have been paid)
  II. deducting dividends accumulated in the period on cumulative preferred stock (regardless of whether they have been declared)

A. I only
B. II only
C. Both I and II
D. Neither I nor II

356. At December 31, Year 11 and Year 10, Baum Inc. had 60,000 shares of common stock and 10,000 shares of preferred stock outstanding. The preferred stock was 5% $100 par value cumulative preferred stock, and no dividends were paid on any class of stock for the past 5 years. Net income for Year 11 was $1,400,000. For 2011, basic EPS amounted to:

A. $23.33
B. $22.50
C. $25.50
D. $31.90

357. When calculating the weighted average number of shares outstanding during the period, which of the following is treated as if it were outstanding since the beginning of the year?

    I. Stock dividends declared in July and paid in September

    II. Stock issued above par in August

    A. I only
    B. II only
    C. Both I and II
    D. Neither I nor II

358. Sadie Co., Inc. reported the following for Year 3:

    1/1, Year 3 common shares outstanding: 300,000
    7/1, Year 3 additional shares issued: 50,000

    During Year 3, Sadie also had outstanding stock options to purchase 40,000 shares of common stock at $15 per share. The average market price of Sadie's common stock was $20 per share during Year 3. What is the number of shares that Sadie should use in computing diluted EPS for Year 3?

    A. 365,000
    B. 360,000
    C. 335,000
    D. 325,000

359. When calculating basic EPS, which of the following is correct regarding the calculation of weighted average common shares outstanding?

    I. Include the convertible preferred shares that were converted during the period in the calculation of weighted average common shares outstanding, and time-weight them.

    II. Ignore convertible preferred shares unless they are converted.

    A. I only
    B. II only
    C. Both I and II
    D. Neither I nor II

360. How do dividends in arrears from Year 1 relate to a Year 2 basic EPS calculation when attempting to compute net income available to common shareholders?

    I. Year 1 dividends in arrears are subtracted from Year 2 net income along with Year 2 unpaid dividends if the preferred stock is cumulative.

    II. Year 1 dividends in arrears are added to a Year 2 net loss if the preferred stock is cumulative.

    A. I only
    B. II only
    C. Both I and II
    D. Neither I nor II

361. For the current year, Year 1, Frenzy, Inc. reports net income of $500,000 and pays its preferred stockholders cash dividends of $60,000. There are 100,000 shares of common stock outstanding so that basic EPS to be reported is $4.40. During Year 1, Frenzy also had 10,000 convertible bonds outstanding. Each bond was sold at face, pays $7 in interest each year, and can be converted into two shares of common stock. Frenzy has a tax rate of 30%. What amount should Frenzy report as diluted EPS for Year 1?

    A. $3.08
    B. $3.26
    C. $4.08
    D. $4.25

362. Which of the following is correct regarding a net loss for the period as it related to net income available to the common shareholders, the numerator of the EPS calculation?

    I. In the event of a net loss for the period, declared dividends on noncumulative preferred stock are added to the net loss even if the dividend was not paid.

    II. In the event of a net loss for the period, current year dividends on cumulative preferred stock are added to the net loss regardless of whether the dividends have been declared.

    A. I only
    B. II only
    C. Both I and II
    D. Neither I nor II

363. Everest Co., Ltd. had EPS of $15.00 for Year 2 before considering the effects of any convertible securities, which included convertible preferred stock and stock options. No conversion or exercise of the convertible securities occurred during Year 2. However, possible conversion of the preferred stock would have the effect of reducing EPS by $0.75. The effect of possible exercise and conversion of the common stock options would increase EPS by $0.10. What amount should Everest report as diluted EPS for Year 2?

    A. $14.25
    B. $14.35
    C. $15.00
    D. $15.10

364. Debt that was converted into common shares during the period would be included in the denominator to calculate weighted average common shares outstanding for the computation of:
  I. basic EPS
  II. diluted EPS

  A. I only
  B. II only
  C. Both I and II
  D. Neither I nor II

365. Lansing Corp. had 60,000 shares of common stock outstanding at January 1, Year 13. On July 1, Year 13, it issued 10,000 additional shares of common stock. What is the number of shares that Lansing Corp. should use to calculate Year 13 EPS?

  A. 60,000
  B. 70,000
  C. 65,000
  D. None of the above

366. On December 1 of the current year, Hackett Corp. declared and issued a 3% stock dividend on its 70,000 shares of outstanding common stock. There was no other common stock activity during the year. Net income for the current year was $100,000. What number of shares should Hackett use in determining basic earnings per common share for the current year?

  A. 70,000
  B. 72,100
  C. 70,175
  D. None of the above

367. The following information pertains to Conover Inc.'s outstanding shares for Year 13:

Preferred stock $10 par 5% cumulative 1,000 shares outstanding 1/1/Year 13

Common stock $1 par value:
Shares outstanding 1/1/13	10,000
2:1 stock split 3/1/13	10,000
Shares issued 10/1/13	5,000

What is the weighted average number of shares that Conover Inc. should use to calculate Year 13 EPS?

  A. 25,000
  B. 23,333
  C. 21,250
  D. 19,583

368. Gordon Corp. had 360,000 shares of common stock issued and outstanding at December 31, Year 12, and 100,000 shares of nonconvertible preferred stock. On January 2, Year 13, Gordon Corp. issued 100,000 more shares of nonconvertible preferred stock. Gordon Corp. declared and paid $45,000 cash dividends on the common stock and $20,000 on the preferred stock during Year 13. Net income for the year ended December 31, Year 13, was $290,000. What should be Gordon Corp.'s Year 13 earnings per common share?

  A. $0.75
  B. $0.81
  C. $0.63
  D. $0.59

Use the following facts to answer **Questions 369–371:**

At December 31, Year 12, Chaucer Corp. had 100,000 common shares outstanding along with 10,000 shares of preferred stock. Each share of preferred stock is convertible into 2 shares of Chaucer common stock. During Year 12, Chaucer Corp. paid dividends of $30,000 on its preferred stock. Chaucer also had 1,000, 9% convertible bonds outstanding. Each bond is convertible into 30 shares of Chaucer common stock. Both the debt and the preferred stock would be potentially dilutive if converted. Net income for Year 12 is $750,000. Assume that the income tax rate is 30%.

369. The preferred dividend would be subtracted from Chaucer Corp.'s net income to calculate Year 12:
  I. basic EPS
  II. diluted EPS

  A. I only
  B. II only
  C. Both I and II
  D. Neither I nor II

370. Calculate Chaucer Corp.'s basic EPS for Year 12.

  A. $7.50
  B. $7.80
  C. $7.20
  D. $7.02

371. Calculate Chaucer Corp.'s diluted EPS for Year 12.

  A. $5.42
  B. $5.00
  C. $6.78
  D. $5.77

CHAPTER 33

PARTNERSHIPS AND FAIR VALUE ACCOUNTING

QUESTIONS 372–396

372. Person and Wolinsky formed a partnership, each contributing assets to the business. Mr. Person contributed equipment with a current market value in excess of its carrying amount. Mr. Wolinsky contributed land with a carrying amount in excess of its current market value. Which of the following should be recorded at fair value?

I. Equipment

II. Land

A. I only

B. II only

C. Both I and II

D. Neither I nor II

373. Dauber and Zuckerman formed the DZ partnership on November 13 and contributed the following: Dauber contributed cash of $40,000. Zuckerman contributed land with a fair market value of $60,000 subject to a mortgage of $25,000, which is assumed by the partnership. Zuckerman's basis in the land was $43,000. The partners agree to share profits and losses equally. Zuckerman's capital on November 13th would be:

A. $43,000

B. $60,000

C. $35,000

D. $22,000

374. The partnership of Michael and Ivan has $180,000 worth of net assets. The partnership would like to add Tim as a partner with an exact one-fifth interest in capital. How much does Tim need to contribute to receive an exact one-fifth interest?

A. $45,000

B. $50,000

C. $36,000

D. $90,000

375. The partnership of Heaslip and Shapiro are considering adding Kenneth as a partner. When admitting Kenneth into the partnership, Kenneth's capital account equals the amount of his actual contribution under which of the following methods?

I. Bonus method

II. Goodwill method

A. I only

B. II only

C. Both I and II

D. Neither I nor II

376. Waldo, Weissman, and Broskie are partners in a partnership. Broskie wishes to retire. Which of the following methods of accounting for his retirement could increase the individual partners' capital accounts without changing total net assets of the partnership?

I. Goodwill method

II. Bonus method

A. I only

B. II only

C. Both I and II

D. Neither I nor II

377. Acquilino and Rudnick are partners in a partnership with capital balances of $45,000 and $35,000 respectively. They agree to admit Chu as a partner. After the assets of the partnership are revalued, Chu will have a 10% interest in capital and profits for an investment of $15,000. What amount should be recorded as goodwill to the original partners?

A. $0
B. $65,000
C. $15,000
D. $55,000

378. Desimone and Jeffrey are partners in the Strat-o-Matic Partnership. During the current year, Desimone and Jeffrey maintained average capital balances in their partnership of $140,000 and $80,000, respectively. They share profit and loss equally, and each received interest of 5% on capital balances. Partnership profit before interest was $5,000. How much is ending capital for Desimone's partnership interest?

A. $140,000
B. $147,000
C. $150,000
D. $144,000

379. Barry and Saralee formed the Twin Brooks partnership in Year 13. The partnership agreement provides for annual salary allowances of $40,000 for Barry and $30,000 for Saralee. Barry and Saralee share profits equally, and they split losses 80/20. The partnership had earnings of $54,000 in Year 13 before any allowance to partners. What amount of earnings should be credited to Barry's capital account for Year 13?

A. $26,800
B. $27,200
C. $27,000
D. $28,300

Use the following facts to answer **Questions 380–381:**

Rochelle and Bob form a partnership and contribute the assets as follows: Rochelle contributes cash of $80,000. Bob contributes land with a carrying amount of $10,000, a fair value of $70,000, and subject to a mortgage of $20,000. Rochelle and Bob agree to share profits and losses 60/40.

380. Rochelle's capital account on the date of formation is equal to:

A. $70,000
B. $10,000
C. $50,000
D. $80,000

381. Bob's capital account on the date of formation is equal to:

A. $70,000
B. $10,000
C. $50,000
D. $80,000

Use the following facts to answer **Questions 382–383:**

Griffin and Owen are partners with capital balances of $50,000 and $30,000 respectively. Profits and losses are divided in the ratio of 60:40. Griffin and Owen decided to admit Tatum to the partnership, who invested equipment valued at $25,000 for a 30% capital interest in the new partnership. Tatum's cost of the equipment was $22,000. The partnership elected to use the bonus method to record the admission of Tatum into the partnership.

382. Tatum's capital account should be credited for:

A. $31,500
B. $22,000
C. $25,000
D. None of the above

383. After Tatum's admission, the balance in Griffin's capital account is:

A. $56,500
B. $53,900
C. $52,600
D. $46,100

384. Rukke and Murray share profits in the ratio of 70:30. On December 31, Year 13, they decide to liquidate the partnership. On that date, the partnership has assets of $420,000. Their only liabilities are accrued taxes of $100,000. Their capital accounts on the date of liquidation are as follows:

Rukke	$170,000
Murray	$150,000

If the assets are sold for $360,000, what amount of the available cash should be distributed to Rukke?

A. $212,000
B. $182,000
C. $128,000
D. $132,000

Use the following facts to answer **Questions 385–388:**

On November 1, Year 13, Chumley began a sole proprietorship with an initial cash investment of $3,000. The proprietorship provided $10,000 worth of services in November and received full payment in December. The proprietorship incurred expenses of $7,000 in December that were paid in January, Year 14. During December, Chumley withdrew $2,000 for personal use.

385. How much would Chumley's ending capital be on the cash basis at December 31, Year 13?

    A. $13,000
    B. $11,000
    C. $10,000
    D. $4,000

386. How much is the sole proprietorship's net income on the accrual basis for Year 13?

    A. $3,000
    B. $7,000
    C. $10,000
    D. $1,000

387. How much is the sole proprietorship's net income on the cash basis for Year 13?

    A. $3,000
    B. $13,000
    C. $10,000
    D. $11,000

388. How much is Chumley's ending capital on the accrual basis at December 31, Year 13?

    A. $3,000
    B. $6,000
    C. $7,000
    D. $4,000

389. With regard to fair value measurement (FVM), US GAAP regards fair value as:
    I. the price to sell an asset
    II. the price to transfer a liability

    A. I only
    B. II only
    C. Both I and II
    D. Neither I nor II

390. Which of the following is correct regarding FVM of an asset?
    I. It includes transportation costs if location is an attribute of the asset.
    II. Fair value is an entity-based measure rather than a market-based measure.

    A. I only
    B. II only
    C. Both I and II
    D. Neither I nor II

391. In FVM of financial assets, the most advantageous market is the market with the:

    A. greatest volume or level of activity
    B. best price without considering transaction costs
    C. lowest transaction costs
    D. best price after considering transaction costs

392. Under fair value reporting, when there is no principal market for a financial asset, which of the following is correct?
    I. Transaction costs are considered when determining the most advantageous market.
    II. Transaction costs are NOT included in the final FVM.

    A. I only
    B. II only
    C. Both I and II
    D. Neither I nor II

393. Which of the following statements is correct regarding the inputs that can be used to measure fair value?
    I. A fair value measurement based on management assumptions only (no market data) would NOT be acceptable per US GAAP.
    II. Level 1 measurements are quoted prices in active markets for similar assets or liabilities.

    A. I only
    B. II only
    C. Both I and II
    D. Neither I nor II

394. Which of the following would be considered a Level 2 input for a financial asset?
    I. Quoted market price on a stock exchange for an identical asset
    II. Historical performance and return on the investment
    III. Quoted market prices available from a business broker for a similar asset

    A. I and II
    B. II and III
    C. III only
    D. I, II, and III

395. Which of the following would be considered a Level 3 input?
  I. A warehouse whose price per square foot is derived from prices in observed transactions involving similar warehouses in similar locations
  II. A quoted stock price in an active market

  A. I only
  B. II only
  C. Both I and II
  D. Neither I nor II

396. Which of the following measures of fair value uses prices and other relevant information from identical or comparable transactions?
  I. Market
  II. Income

  A. I only
  B. II only
  C. Both I and II
  D. Neither I nor II

CHAPTER 34

BUSINESS COMBINATIONS AND CONSOLIDATIONS

QUESTIONS 397–421

397. On December 30, Year 4, Policastro Inc. paid $960,000 for all of the issued and outstanding common stock of Salva Corp. On that date, the book value of Salva's assets and liabilities were $900,000 and $280,000 respectively. The fair values of Salva's assets and liabilities were $940,000 and $240,000 respectively. On Policastro's December 31, Year 4, balance sheet, what amount should be recorded as goodwill?

A. $340,000
B. $260,000
C. $80,000
D. None of the above

398. When a subsidiary is acquired with an acquisition cost that is less than the fair value of the underlying assets, which of the following is correct?
   I. The balance sheet is adjusted to fair value.
   II. Negative goodwill is recorded.

A. I only
B. II only
C. Both I and II
D. Neither I nor II

399. In a business combination accounted for properly as an acquisition, which of the following costs should be expensed in the period incurred by the combined corporation?
   I. Registration and issuance costs
   II. Consulting fees

A. I only
B. II only
C. Both I and II
D. Neither I nor II

400. On February 14, Year 11, Heart Corp. acquired 25% of Flower Corp.'s common stock. On October 1, Year 13, Heart acquires 65% of Flower's outstanding common stock. Flower Inc. continues in existence as Heart's subsidiary. How much of Flower's Year 13 net income should be reported as accruing to Heart?

A. 90% of Flower's net income
B. 25% of Flower's net income from January 1 to September 30, and then all of Flower Inc.'s net income from October 1 through December 31
C. All of Flower's net income
D. 25% of Flower's net income from January 1 to September 30 and then 95% of Flower Inc.'s net income from October 1 through December 31

Use the following facts to answer **Questions 401–402:**

Corporation A buys 80% of B Corporation for $500,000 on December 31, Year 1. The fair value of B Corporation's assets is $400,000. The fair value of B Corporation's liabilities is $50,000, and the book value of the net assets of B Corporation is $300,000 on December 31, Year 1.

401. How much is the implied value of B Corporation based on purchase price?

A. $350,000
B. $400,000
C. $500,000
D. $625,000

402. How much goodwill should be recorded by Corporation A on the consolidated financial statements dated December 31, Year 1?

  A. $150,000
  B. $275,000
  C. $200,000
  D. $50,000

403. A 90%-owned subsidiary declares and pays a cash dividend. What effect does this transaction have on the noncontrolling interest and retained earnings balances in the consolidated balance sheet?

Noncontrolling interest	Retained earnings
A. No effect	Decrease
B. Decrease	Decrease
C. Decrease	No effect
D. No effect	No effect

404. Prunty Corp. owns all of the outstanding common stock of Shelly, Inc. On January 1, Year 2, Prunty sells a machine with a carrying value of $30,000 to Shelly for $40,000. Shelly uses straight line depreciation and intends to use the machine for five years. The net adjustments required to compute consolidation net income for Year 2 and Year 3 are:

  A. $(10,000), Year 2; $0, Year 3
  B. $(10,000), Year 2; $2,000, Year 3
  C. $(8,000), Year 2; $0, Year 3
  D. $(8,000), Year 2; $2,000, Year 3

405. Paul Co. owns 75% of Sal Co's common stock. During the third quarter of the current year, Sal sold inventory to Paul for $200,000. At December 31 of the current year, 50% of this inventory remained in Paul's ending inventory. For the current year, Paul's gross profit was 30%, while Sal's gross profit was 40%. How much unrealized profit should be eliminated from the December 31 ending inventory?

  A. $30,000
  B. $32,000
  C. $40,000
  D. $80,000

Use the following facts to answer **Questions 406–408:**

On January 1, Year 1, Poplar Corp. acquired 80% of Sienna Corp's 100,000 outstanding common shares for $2,800,000. On the date of acquisition, the book value of Sienna Corp's net assets was $2,750,000. Book value equaled fair value for all assets and liabilities of Sienna Corp., except land that had a fair value of $100,000 greater than book value and furniture and fixtures that had a fair value greater than book value of $50,000. On January 1, Year 1, Sienna Corp. had an intangible asset, unpatented technology, with a fair value of $525,000.

406. How much is the implied value of Sienna Corp. based on purchase price?

  A. $2,800,000
  B. $3,500,000
  C. $2,750,000
  D. $3,425,000

407. What is the goodwill to be reported on Poplar Corp's December 31, Year 1, balance sheet under US GAAP?

  A. $0
  B. $75,000
  C. $600,000
  D. $750,000

408. In the eliminating journal entry made just after the acquisition, how would noncontrolling interest be recorded?

  A. Debit of $560,000
  B. Credit of 560,000
  C. Credit of $700,000
  D. Debit of $700,000

Use the following facts to answer **Questions 409–411:**

On January 1, Year 13, Peyton Corp. acquired 90% of Shore Corp's outstanding common stock for $180,000. On that date, the carrying value of Shore Corp's assets and liabilities approximated their fair values. During Year 13, Shore earned $18,000 of net income and paid $4,000 cash dividends to its stockholders.

409. Using the acquisition method, calculate the amount of noncontrolling interest at the date of acquisition on January 1, Year 13.

A. $0
B. $20,000
C. $18,000
D. $14,000

410. Calculate the noncontrolling interest at December 31, Year 13.

A. $20,000
B. $18,600
C. $21,400
D. $22,200

411. On the December 31, Year 13, consolidated balance sheet, stockholders' equity is equal to Peyton Corp.'s stockholders' equity:

A. plus Shore Corp.'s stockholders' equity
B. plus Shore Corp.'s stockholders' equity plus the fair value of the noncontrolling interest
C. plus the fair value of the noncontrolling interest
D. less the fair value of the noncontrolling interest

Use the following facts to answer **Questions 412–413:**

On January 1, Year 12, Parsons Corp. acquired 100% of Stines Corp. by issuing 20,000 shares of Parsons Corp. common stock. The acquisition was announced on April 30, Year 12, when Parsons Corp. stock was selling for $35 per share and finalized on September 22, Year 12, when Parsons stock was selling for $40 per share. During Year 12, Parsons stock had an average selling price of $36 per share and a par value of $10 per share.

412. How much is the debit to investment in subsidiary on September 22, Year 12?

A. $800,000
B. $700,000
C. $720,000
D. $200,000

413. The journal entry to record the investment in subsidiary would include a credit to:

A. common stock for $800,000
B. additional paid-in capital for $600,000
C. common stock for $600,000
D. additional paid-in capital for $200,000

414. On November 1, Year 3, Plato Corp. acquired 100% of Socrates Corp. for $375,000. The carrying value of Socrates assets was $550,000, and the fair value was $750,000 at the date of acquisition. The book and fair value of Socrates liabilities on November 1, Year 3, was $300,000. Additionally, Socrates had identifiable intangible assets at the date of acquisition with a fair value of $165,000. How much goodwill or gain is to be reported on Plato's December 31, Year 3, consolidated income statement?

A. $75,000 gain
B. $75,000 goodwill
C. $240,000 goodwill
D. $240,000 gain

Use the following facts to answer **Questions 415–417:**

Prince Corp. issues $100,000 shares of its $1 par value common stock to acquire Simmons Inc. in a business combination accounted for as an acquisition. The market value of Prince's common stock is $14 per share. Legal and consulting fees incurred in relationship to the purchase are $80,000. Registration and issuance costs for the common stock are $15,000.

415. How much should be expensed immediately in connection with this combination?

A. $0
B. $15,000
C. $80,000
D. $95,000

416. What should be recorded in Prince Corp.'s additional paid-in capital for this business combination?

A. $1,315,000
B. $1,300,000
C. $1,400,000
D. $1,285,000

417. The journal entry to record the business combination would include a debit to investment in subsidiary in the amount of:

A. $1,400,000
B. $1,305,000
C. $1,385,000
D. $1,320,000

418. Pie Corp. buys 80% of Slice Corp. stock in a business combination accounted for as an acquisition on January 2, Year 1. At the date of acquisition, Pie Corp.'s common stock is $140,000 and Slice Corp. common stock is $30,000. Both Pie and Slice have additional paid-in capital of $120,000. Slice Corp. has retained earnings of $50,000 at the date of acquisition. Which of the following is correct?

    I. 80% of Slice's total equity is eliminated as of the date of acquisition.
    II. Consolidated common stock will be $140,000.

    A. I only
    B. II only
    C. Both I and II
    D. Neither I nor II

419. On January 1, Year 1, Peter Co. paid $250,000 for 70% of the outstanding common stock of Sally Co. At that time, Sally reported the following balance sheet amounts: Current assets $30,000; Property, plant, and equipment $270,000; Liabilities $120,000; and Stockholders' equity $180,000. On January 1, the fair value of the property, plant, and equipment was $30,000 more than its book value. Fair values approximated the book values for all other assets and liabilities. What amount of goodwill should Peter report on its acquisition date balance sheet under the IFRS partial goodwill method?

    A. $40,000
    B. $49,000
    C. $70,000
    D. $103,000

Use the following facts to answer **Questions 420–421:**

On December 31, Year 13, Potomac Corp. acquired a 100% interest in Seltzer Corp. by exchanging 25,000 shares of its common stock for 200,000 shares of Seltzer Corp.'s common stock. The fair value of Potomac's common stock on the date of acquisition was $10 per share, and the fair value of Seltzer Corp.'s common stock was $1.50 per share. Seltzer Corp. had current assets with a book and fair value of $150,000, and property plant and equipment with a book value of $175,000 and a fair value of $250,000. Potomac Corp.'s property plant and equipment had a book value of $1,200,000 and a fair value of $1,400,000.

420. On the consolidated financial statements dated December 31, Year 13, consolidated property plant and equipment would be reported at

    A. $1,450,000
    B. $1,200,000
    C. $1,375,000
    D. $1,650,000

421. How much goodwill or gain should be recorded by Potomac Corp. on the consolidated financial statements dated December 31, Year 13?

    A. Goodwill of $250,000
    B. Goodwill of $150,000
    C. Gain of $250,000
    D. Gain of $150,000

CHAPTER 35

STATEMENT OF CASH FLOWS

QUESTIONS 422–446

422. Required disclosures of a statement of cash flows prepared using the direct method under US GAAP includes a reconciliation of net income to net cash flow from:
  I. operating activities
  II. financing activities
  III. investing activities

A. I only
B. Both I and II
C. Both I and III
D. I, II, and III

423. Under US GAAP, a reconciliation is needed from ending retained earnings to cash flows from operating activities when preparing the statement of cash flows using which of the following methods?
  I. Direct method
  II. Indirect method

A. I only
B. II only
C. Both I and II
D. Neither I nor II

424. The purchase of a three-month US Treasury bill, when an entity's policy is to treat investment with maturities of three months or less as cash equivalents, would be reported in the entity's cash flow statement as:

A. a financial activity outflow
B. an operating activity outflow
C. an investing activity outflow
D. neither an operating, investing, nor financing outflow

425. On April 23, Year 4, Anderson, Inc. sold a building and received cash proceeds of $650,000. At the time of sale, the building had a net book value of $700,000. Anderson prepares its statement of cash flows using the indirect method. How should Anderson report the results of this transaction in its Year 4 statement of cash flows?

A. $50,000 addition in operating activities; $650,000 addition in investing activities
B. $50,000 subtraction in operating activities; $650,000 addition in investing activities
C. $0 in operating activities; $700,000 addition in investing activities
D. $650,000 addition in operating activities; $0 in investing activities

426. Which of the following would be included in the investing activities section of a statement of cash flows?
  I. Making loans
  II. Repaying amounts borrowed (principal)

A. I only
B. II only
C. Both I and II
D. Neither I nor II

427. Supplemental information in the cash flow statement should be reported for which of the following?
  I. Conversion of preferred stock
  II. Cash flow per share

A. I only
B. II only
C. Both I and II
D. Neither I nor II

428. The direct method will provide a larger amount of net cash provided from operating activities compared to the indirect method when:

    I. accelerated depreciation is used for book purposes rather than straight line

    II. bonds were issued at par rather than at a discount or premium

A. I only
B. II only
C. Both I and II
D. Neither I nor II

429. The statement of cash flows provides relevant information about which of the following?

    I. The cash receipts and disbursements of an enterprise during an accounting period

    II. A company's ability to meet cash operating needs in the future

A. I only
B. II only
C. Both I and II
D. Neither I nor II

430. Jenkins Inc. is preparing its statement of cash flows for Year 5. The following information pertains.

	12/31/Yr5	1/1/Yr5
Accounts receivable	$28,000	$21,000
Allowance for doubtful accts	$1,200	$700
Prepaid insurance	$10,000	$13,000
Payroll taxes payable	$9,600	$7,000

Net income for Year 5 is $190,000.

What amount should Jenkins Inc. include as net cash provided by operating activities using the indirect method?

A. $190,000
B. $189,100
C. $190,900
D. $183,900

431. Which of the following is correct regarding the statement of cash flows prepared using the indirect method?

    I. A loss from the sale of used equipment should be reported as a decrease to net income in the operating activities section.

    II. The entire amount of cash proceeds from the sale of equipment (including the loss) should be shown in the investing section of the statement of cash flows.

A. I only
B. II only
C. Both I and II
D. Neither I nor II

432. Which of the following items is included in the financing activities section of the statement of cash flows?

    I. Cash effects of acquiring and disposing of property, plant, and equipment

    II. Cash effects of transactions obtaining resources from owners and providing them with a return on their investment

A. I only
B. II only
C. Both I and II
D. Neither I nor II

433. During Year 13, Gulbin Corp. had the following activities related to its financial operations:

Payment for the early extinguishment of debt (carrying amount, $400,000)	$425,000
Payment of Year 13 dividend, declared in Year 12	$50,000
Purchase of fixed assets	$30,000
Proceeds from the sale of treasury stock	$20,000

Under US GAAP, how much should Gulbin Corp. report its net cash used in financing activities?

A. $495,000
B. $475,000
C. $425,000
D. $455,000

434. Dividends paid are reported under what section of the statement of cash flows for both IFRS and US GAAP?

	IFRS	US GAAP
A.	Financing	Financing
B.	Operating	Financing
C.	Operating or financing	Financing
D.	Operating or financing	Operating

435. Which of the following statements is true regarding the cash flow reporting of interest (whether paid or received) under both IFRS and US GAAP?

A. Interest received must be reported as an investing activity inflow for IFRS and an operating activity inflow for US GAAP.

B. Interest paid may be reported as either an operating or financing activity outflow for IFRS, but must be reported as an operating activity outflow for US GAAP.

C. Interest paid may be reported as either an operating or financing activity outflow for IFRS, but must be reporting as a financing activity outflow for US GAAP.

D. Both IFRS and US GAAP require that interest received be reported as an operating inflow.

436. Stewart Corp. acquired a building through the issuance of 25,000 shares of the corporation's common stock. How should this transaction be reported in Stewart's statement of cash flows if Stewart is preparing its statement in accordance with IFRS?

A. As a significant noncash transaction presented at the bottom of the cash flow statement

B. In the financial statement footnotes as a significant noncash transaction

C. As an investing activities outflow, and financing activities inflow

D. The transaction does not need to be reported, since there is both an operating inflow and outflow impact of the same amount

437. Dividends received may be reported as an investing or operating activity on the statement of cash flows under which of the following standards?
  I. US GAAP
  II. IFRS

A. I only

B. II only

C. Both I and II

D. Neither I nor II

438. If a debt repayment includes both principal and interest, how are the payments reported in a statement of cash flows prepared under US GAAP?

A. Entire payment is presented as a financing outflow.

B. Entire payment is presented as an operating outflow.

C. The interest portion is presented as an operating outflow and the principal portion as an investing outflow.

D. The interest portion is presented as an operating outflow and the principal portion as a financing outflow.

439. Under the indirect method, which of the following would be added back to net income to arrive at net cash flows from operating activities?
  I. Depreciation expense
  II. Bond premium amortization
  III. Gain on the early extinguishment of long-term debt

A. I only

B. II only

C. I and II only

D. I, II, and III

440. Dickinson Corp. prepares its statement of cash flows using the indirect method. Dickinson's unamortized bond premium account decreased by $18,000 during Year 10. How should Dickinson Corp. report the change in unamortized bond premium in its statement of cash flows for Year 10?

A. financing cash outflow

B. not an increase or decrease in net income to arrive at net cash flows from operating activities

C. decrease to net income in arriving at net cash flows from operating activities

D. increase to net income in arriving at net cash flows from operating activities

441. In its current year income statement, Micki Corp. reported cost of goods sold of $350,000. Changes occurred for the year in certain current asset and current liability accounts as follows:

Accounts payable	$20,000 decrease
Inventory	$100,000 decrease

What amount should Micki Corp. report as cash paid to suppliers in its current year cash flow statement prepared under the direct method?

A. $350,000

B. $470,000

C. $430,000

D. $270,000

442. Salinger Corp. prepared its statement of cash flows at December 31, Year 13, using the direct method. The following amounts were used in the computation of cash flows from operating activities:

Beginning inventory	$300,000
Ending inventory	$250,000
Cost of goods sold	$1,000,000
Beginning accounts payable	$200,000
Ending accounts payable	$100,000

What amount should Salinger Corp. report as cash paid to suppliers?

A. $850,000
B. $1,000,000
C. $1,150,000
D. $1,050,000

443. Pry Corp. prepares its statement of cash flows under the direct method. For Year 13, Pry Corp. had revenue under accrual accounting of $200,000. Additional information is as follows from beginning to the end of Year 13:

Accounts receivable	increased by $8,000
Unearned fees	decreased by $6,000

How much is cash received from customers for Year 13?

A. $214,000
B. $186,000
C. $202,000
D. $198,000

444. Calhoun Corp. had a beginning cash balance in Year 12 of $20,000. They had net cash provided by operating activities of $320,000 for Year 12, net cash used by investing activities of $402,000, and cash provided by financing activities of $262,000. During the year, there was a sale of a fixed asset that resulted in a loss of $10,000 and proceeds of $42,000 were received from the sale. What was Calhoun Corp.'s cash balance at the end of Year 12?

A. $200,000
B. $232,000
C. $168,000
D. $148,000

445. Traficante Corp. had the following equity transactions at December 31, Year 8:

Cash proceeds from the sale of Price Corp. stock (carrying amount $30,000)	$25,000
Dividends received on common stock of Aragona Corp.	$8,500
Common stock purchased from Wingnut Corp.	$13,000
Interest income received on County of Union Bonds	$2,000

What amount should Traficante Corp. recognize as net cash from investing activities in its statement of cash flows dated December 31, Year 8?

A. $25,000
B. $12,000
C. $14,000
D. None of the above

446. Which of the following items is included in the financing activities section of the statement of cash flows?

I. Cash effects of acquiring and disposing of property, plant, and equipment
II. Cash effects of transactions obtaining resources from owners and providing them with a return on their investment

A. I only
B. II only
C. Both I and II
D. Neither I nor II

CHAPTER 36

FINANCIAL INSTRUMENTS, FOREIGN CURRENCY, AND PRICE LEVEL ACCOUNTING

QUESTIONS 447–465

447. Which of the following is among the criteria that need to be met for a derivative to be designated a fair value hedge?
  I. There is formal documentation of the hedging relationship between the derivative and the hedged item.
  II. The hedged item is specifically identified.

  A. I only
  B. II only
  C. Both I and II
  D. Neither I nor II

448. Which of the following is among the criteria that need to be met for a derivative to be designated a fair value hedge?
  I. The hedge must be expected to be highly effective in offsetting changes in the fair value of the hedged item, and the effectiveness is assessed at least every 3 months.
  II. The hedged item presents exposure to changes in fair value that could affect income.

  A. I only
  B. II only
  C. Both I and II
  D. Neither I nor II

449. In a perfect hedge, which of the following would have NO possibility of occurrence?
  I. Gain on the derivative instrument
  II. Loss on the item being hedged

  A. I only
  B. II only
  C. Both I and II
  D. Neither I nor II

450. The risk that the other party to a financial instrument will NOT perform:
  I. need NOT be disclosed unless the risk is considered above average
  II. is known as market risk

  A. I only
  B. II only
  C. Both I and II
  D. Neither I nor II

451. The risk of a significant number of unsecured accounts receivable with companies in the same industry is referred to as:
  I. concentration of market risk
  II. concentration of credit risk

  A. I only
  B. II only
  C. Both I and II
  D. Neither I nor II

452. Which of the following is correct regarding a concentration of credit risk?
  I. It is the risk that a counterparty will partially or completely fail to perform per the terms of the contract.
  II. It exists if a number of counterparties are engaged in similar activities and if the industry they are in experiences economic disaster or ceases to exist.

  A. I only
  B. II only
  C. Both I and II
  D. Neither I nor II

453. Which of the following is correct regarding fair value hedges?

 A. Fair value hedge gains are recorded on the statement of comprehensive income.
 B. Fair value hedge losses are NOT recorded on the income statement.
 C. Fair value hedge gains are NOT recorded in the financial statements.
 D. Fair value hedge gains are recorded on the income statement.

454. Which of the following fair value hedge transactions are reported on the income statement?
   I. Losses
   II. Gains

 A. I only
 B. II only
 C. Both I and II
 D. Neither I nor II

455. Which of the following cash flow hedge transactions are reported on the income statement?
   I. Gains, to the extent they are effective
   II. Losses

 A. I only
 B. II only
 C. Both I and II
 D. Neither I nor II

456. A contract that conveys to a second entity a right to future collections on accounts receivable from a first entity is a:
   I. financial instrument
   II. derivative instrument

 A. I only
 B. II only
 C. Both I and II
 D. Neither I nor II

457. With regard to foreign currency accounting, which of the following are included in the determination of net income for the period?
   I. Remeasurement adjustments
   II. Translation adjustments

 A. I only
 B. II only
 C. Both I and II
 D. Neither I nor II

458. Quirk Company's wholly owned subsidiary Larue Corp. maintains its accounting records in Swiss francs. Because all of Larue's branch offices are in France, its functional currency is the euro. Remeasurement of Larue's Year 13 financial statements resulted in a $10,500 gain. Subsequent translation of those remeasured statements resulted in a $3,300 gain. What amount should Quirk (parent company) report as a foreign exchange gain in its income statement for the year ended December 31, Year 13?

 A. $0
 B. $3,300
 C. $10,500
 D. $13,800

459. Su Industries has international subsidiaries in Asia. These subsidiaries enter into contracts in both the US dollar and local currencies. In Year 13, Su Industries experienced a remeasurement loss of $55,000 and a translation gain of $36,000. As a result of these conversions, what would Su Industries report in accumulated other comprehensive income in Year 13?

 A. $0
 B. Loss of $55,000
 C. Loss of $19,000
 D. Gain of $36,000

460. Salazar is a subsidiary of Padre Corp. If Salazar's functional currency is its local currency, Salazar's financial statements are:
   I. *translated* to the reporting currency
   II. *remeasured* into the functional currency, the result of which is a gain or loss reported in the consolidated income statement

 A. I only
 B. II only
 C. Both I and II
 D. Neither I nor II

461. On October 5, Year 13, Griffin Corp. purchased merchandise from an unaffiliated company in Taiwan for 20,000 Taiwan dollars when the spot rate was $0.65. Griffin Corp. paid the bill in full in February of Year 14 when the spot rate was $0.74. The spot rate was $0.80 on December 31, Year 13. What amount should Griffin Corp. report as a foreign currency transaction gain/loss in its income statement for the year ended December 31, Year 13?

 A. $3,000 gain
 B. $3,000 loss
 C. $1,800 loss
 D. $0

462. Which of the following would result in a purchasing power decline?

A. Holding monetary assets in a period of deflation

B. Holding monetary assets in a period of inflation

C. Holding monetary liabilities in a period of inflation

D. None of the above

463. Under US GAAP, certain large publicly held companies may disclose information concerning the effect of changing prices. Which of the following methods of measuring prices and price changes ignores asset appreciation but adjusts for changes in the purchasing power of the dollar?

A. Historical cost/constant dollar

B. Historical cost/nominal dollar

C. Current cost/nominal dollar

D. Current cost/constant dollar

464. Which of the following methods of measuring prices and the effects of price changes involves adjustments for both purchasing power and appreciation of assets?

A. Historical cost/constant dollar

B. Historical cost/nominal dollar

C. Current cost/nominal dollar

D. Current cost/constant dollar

465. Which of the following statements regarding foreign exchange gains and losses is true?

I. An exchange gain occurs when the exchange rate increases between the date a payable is recorded and the date the payable is paid.

II. An exchange loss occurs when the exchange rate increases between the date a receivable is recorded and the date of cash receipt.

A. I only

B. II only

C. Both I and II

D. Neither I nor II

CHAPTER 37

GOVERNMENT ACCOUNTING AND REPORTING

QUESTIONS 466–490

466. Under modified accrual accounting, which of the following is NOT correct regarding the general fund of a governmental unit?

A. Budgetary accounting is emphasized in order to control spending.
B. Encumbrance accounting is used to record purchase orders.
C. Activity emphasizes flow of current financial resources.
D. A statement of cash flows is prepared as part of the fund-based financial statements.

467. With regard to the dual objectives of governmental reporting, the idea that government agreement should be accountable to its public by demonstrating that resources allocated for a specific purpose are used for that purpose is described as:

I. operational accountability
II. fiscal accountability

A. I only
B. II only
C. Both I and II
D. Neither I nor II

468. Which of the following is the most authoritative source for government accounting standards?

A. Financial Accounting Standards Board (FASB)
B. statements issued by the Governmental Accounting Standards Board (GASB)
C. American Institute of CPAs (AICPA) Practice Bulletins
D. GASB Implementation Guides

469. Which of the following regarding funds and fund accounting is correct?

I. Fund accounting supports financial control by helping prevent overspending.
II. A fund is a sum of money set aside to accomplish a specific goal.

A. I only
B. II only
C. Both I and II
D. Neither I nor II

470. All funds of a state or local government unit must be categorized as one of three separate classifications. Which of the following is NOT one of those classifications?

A. Proprietary fund
B. Fiduciary fund
C. Governmental fund
D. Permanent fund

471. Which of the following funds is a proprietary fund?

A. General fund
B. Permanent fund
C. Enterprise fund
D. Special revenue fund

472. Which of the following correctly describes an internal service fund?

   A. Same basis of accounting as the general fund

   B. A type of proprietary fund in which the services are open to the general public

   C. A type of proprietary fund in which the services are open to other agencies of the local government rather than to the public

   D. Same basis of accounting as the debt service fund

Use the following facts to answer **Questions 473–475:**

The following revenues were among those reported by Reading Township in Year 13:

Interest earned on investments held for employees' retirement benefits	$110,000
Property taxes available and measurable in Year 13	$6,100,000
Net rental revenue (after depreciation) from a parking garage owned by Reading Township	$47,000

473. Reading Township should account for how much revenue in governmental-type funds in Year 13?

   A. $6,210,000

   B. $6,100,000

   C. $6,257,000

   D. $47,000

474. How much revenue should Reading Township account for in proprietary-type funds in Year 13?

   A. $47,000

   B. $110,000

   C. $157,000

   D. $0

475. How much revenue should Reading Township account for in fiduciary type funds in Year 13?

   A. $6,100,000

   B. $110,000

   C. $47,000

   D. $0

476. The city of Wildwood is looking to rebuild Convention Hall. In Year 13, the state of New Jersey sent an unrestricted grant to the city for $2,000,000 that the city council plans to use in the construction. The remainder of the proceeds came from a 6% bond issuance in the amount of 10,000,000 issued at par on January 1 of Year 13. The bonds pay interest annually on June 30 and December 31. If the City of Wildwood accounts for the construction of City Hall in the capital projects fund, the City of Wildwood should credit other financing sources in Year 13 in the amount of:

   A. $12,000,000

   B. $10,000,000

   C. $2,000,000

   D. $0

477. Which of the following describes the basis of accounting used and measurement focus for all governmental-type funds?

   A. Accrual basis of accounting, flow of financial resources focus

   B. Modified accrual basis of accounting, flow of economic resources focus

   C. Accrual basis of accounting, flow of economic resources focus

   D. Modified accrual basis of accounting, flow of financial resources focus

478. The city of Morgan spent $50,000 on a new fire truck in Year 13. They also paid the 10 firemen their salaries of $60,000 each for Year 13. In addition they paid $12,000 to paint and maintain the firehouse during that year. Assume the fire department is accounted for as part of a governmental-type fund for the city of Morgan. How much represents expenditures for the Year 13 in the fund-based financial statements?

   A. $600,000

   B. $650,000

   C. $662,000

   D. $612,000

479. The City of Spanktown accounts for its public utility in an enterprise fund. On June 15, Year 13, the general fund for the City of Spanktown sent a check to the enterprise fund in the amount of $50,000. The general fund will debit "other financing uses" in Year 13 if the $50,000 sent to the enterprise fund was to:
    I. pay the electric bill for City Hall
    II. cover a cash shortfall in the enterprise fund resulting from storm-related damage
    A. I only
    B. II only
    C. Both I and II
    D. Neither I nor II

Use the following facts to answer **Questions 480–481:**

City of Spring Lake's Year 2 budget entry includes estimated revenues of $40,000,000, appropriations of $37,000,000, and an estimated transfer to capital projects fund of $600,000.

480. When Spring Lake's budget is adopted and recorded, the budgetary control account would include:
    A. $3,000,000 credit balance
    B. $3,000,000 debit balance
    C. $2,400,000 credit balance
    D. $2,400,000 debit balance

481. When Spring Lake's budget is closed at the end of the fiscal year:
    A. appropriations is credited for $3,000,000
    B. estimated revenues is debited for $40,000,000
    C. appropriations is credited for $37,000,000
    D. estimated revenues is credited for $40,000,000

Use the following information to answer **Questions 482–484:**

The City of East Hanover Township purchases a backup generator for the police department on February 3, Year 14, at an estimated cost of $40,000. The generator arrives on March 10, Year 14, with an invoice attached of $40,650. The vendor is paid in full by the township on April 5.

482. The journal entry to record the encumbrance on February 3 would include a:
    A. debit to encumbrance for $40,000
    B. credit to encumbrance for $40,000
    C. debit to budgetary control for $40,000
    D. credit to budgetary control for $40,650

483. The journal entry to record the receipt of the backup generator on March 10 would include a:
    A. debit to budgetary control for $40,650
    B. credit to encumbrance for $40,650
    C. credit to encumbrance for $40,000
    D. credit to budgetary control for $40,000

484. On April 5, the journal entry would include a $40,650:
    A. debit to expenditures
    B. debit to vouchers payable
    C. credit to vouchers payable
    D. credit to budgetary control

485. The City of Saddle Brook levied property taxes of $6,000,000 for the current year and estimated that $250,000 would be uncollectible. The journal entry for the property tax levy in the general fund would include:
    A. credit to allowance for uncollectible property taxes—current $250,000
    B. debit to property tax receivable $5,750,000
    C. debit to allowance for uncollectible property taxes—current $250,000
    D. credit to property tax revenue $6,000,000

486. The Township of Woodbridge prepares which of the following as part of its government-wide financial statements?
    I. Statement of activities
    II. Statement of net assets
    III. Statement of cash flows
    A. Both I and II
    B. Both I and III
    C. Both II and III
    D. I, II, and III

487. The Township of Smyrna should report the construction in progress for a senior center as an asset in the:
    I. government-wide statement of net assets
    II. capital projects fund
    A. I only
    B. II only
    C. Both I and II
    D. Neither I nor II

488. On the government-wide financial statements for the City of White Plains, which of the following are normally shown as business-type activities rather than governmental activities on the statement of net assets?

   I. Internal service funds

   II. Enterprise funds

A. I only

B. II only

C. Both I and II

D. Neither I nor II

489. For a governmental entity, which of the following is an example of a derived revenue?

   I. Sales tax

   II. Income tax

   III. Property tax

A. Both I and II

B. Both I and III

C. Both II and III

D. I, II, and III

490. The Township of Edison is preparing general purpose financial statements for Year 13. The question has arisen as to whether the school system should be viewed as a primary government so that separate financial statements are appropriate. Which of the following would need to be shown for the school system to qualify as a separate primary government?

A. The school system's board is appointed by Edison's city council.

B. The school system serves the City of Edison exclusively.

C. The school system is NOT fiscally independent of the city.

D. The school system is a legally separate entity.

CHAPTER 38
NOT-FOR-PROFIT ENTITIES

491. Not-for-profit (NFP) organizations include a wide array of organizations such as private colleges, hospitals, voluntary health and welfare organizations, and churches. Which of the following is the basis of accounting used for external reporting purposes for not-for-profit entities?

- **A.** Modified accrual basis
- **B.** Accrual basis
- **C.** Modified cash basis
- **D.** Cash basis

492. In the statement of financial position for a not-for-profit entity, how many categories of net assets (equity) appear?

- **A.** 2
- **B.** 3
- **C.** 4
- **D.** 5

493. How should the financial resources of a not-for-profit entity that are currently expendable at the discretion of the governing board and that have not been restricted externally be reported in the balance sheet of a not-for-profit?

- **A.** Temporarily restricted for a specific use
- **B.** Temporarily restricted until the passage of a certain amount of time
- **C.** Restricted by board designation
- **D.** Unrestricted

494. The Pisces Project is a nongovernmental not-for-profit that provides training and education to convicted felons who are near their release date. In Year 13 the Pisces Project received the following support:

- I. a cash contribution of $125,000 to be used at the discretion of the board of directors
- II. a promise to contribute $40,000 in Year 14 from a supporter who had made similar contributions in prior periods
- III. accounting services with a value of $35,000 that Pisces would have otherwise had to pay for
- IV. a building worth $300,000 with no stipulation as to use, which the Pisces board of directors plans to sell and use the proceeds for educational purposes

How much would the Pisces Project classify as unrestricted support in Year 13?

- **A.** $500,000
- **B.** $420,000
- **C.** $125,000
- **D.** $460,000

Use the following facts to answer **Questions 495–497:**

Spotted Owl Park, a private not-for-profit zoological society, received contributions temporarily restricted for research totaling $150,000 in Year 13. None of the contributions were spent on research in Year 13. In Year 14, $135,000 of the $150,000 was used to support the research activities of the society.

495. Which of the following is correct regarding the statement of activities for Spotted Owl Park in Year 13?

A. Temporarily restricted net assets decrease by $135,000.

B. Unrestricted net assets increase by $135,000.

C. Unrestricted net assets increase by $150,000.

D. Temporarily restricted net assets increase by $150,000.

496. Which of the following is correct regarding the statement of activities for Spotted Owl Park in Year 14?

A. Temporarily restricted net assets decrease by $135,000.

B. Unrestricted net assets increase by $150,000.

C. Unrestricted net assets decrease by $150,000.

D. Temporarily restricted net assets increase by $135,000.

497. Which of the following is NOT correct regarding Spotted Owl Park for Year 13 and Year 14?

A. In Year 13, there is no impact on unrestricted net assets when the $150,000 is received.

B. In Year 14, unrestricted net assets increase, then decrease to reflect the amount released from temporary restriction, $135,000.

C. Total unrestricted net assets do not change in Year 13 or Year 14.

D. In Year 13, unrestricted net assets increase by $135,000.

498. A private, not-for-profit organization prepares each of the following financial statements EXCEPT:

A. statement of activities

B. statement of cash flows

C. statement of restricted net assets

D. statement of financial position

499. Dartam Center is a private not-for-profit educational organization in support of homeschooled kids. How should Dartam Center report contributions of $1,000,000 in cash in the statement of cash flows if the money is donor-restricted for 5 years and then can be spent at the discretion of the governing body?

A. Operating activity inflow

B. Investing activity inflow

C. Financing activity inflow

D. Either operating or investing inflow

500. Reporting expenses by function and by natural classification:

A. is required for most not-for-profits

B. is not allowed for most not-for-profits

C. is not allowed for voluntary health and welfare organizations

D. is required for voluntary health and welfare organizations

Bonus Questions

501. For a not-for-profit entity, conditional pledges are considered unconditional when:

I. the possibility that the condition will NOT be met is remote

II. the donor-imposed conditions have been met

A. I only

B. II only

C. Both I and II

D. Neither I nor II

502. In Year 9, Sonia Walton promised Orange College that she would provide 75% of the funds needed to construct a new parking deck if the not-for-profit could get the remaining 25% of the funds needed from other donors by April 1, Year 11. At December 31, Year 10, the board of directors had received donations from other donors for 20% of the cost of the new parking deck and believed that the probability of NOT getting the remaining 5% was remote. For the year ended December 31, Year 10, Walton's promise would:

A. be reported as an increase in permanently restricted net assets

B. not be reported on the statement of activities since she has not made the contribution yet

C. not be reported on the statement of activities since the college has not raised the full 25% yet

D. be reported as an increase in temporarily restricted net assets

503. For a not-for-profit entity, *restricted* and *unrestricted* refer to:
I. the timing of revenue recognition
II. the net asset classes

A. I only
B. II only
C. Both I and II
D. Neither I nor II

504. In July of Year 12, a storm damaged the roof of Homeless Shelters, a not-for-profit voluntary health and welfare organization. One supporter of Homeless Shelters, a one time homeless man himself, now a trained professional roofer, repaired the roof at no charge. In the statement of activities for Year 12, the damage and repair of the roof should be reported as:

A. note disclosure only
B. increase in net assets and contributions
C. increase in both expenses and contributions
D. nothing—not be reported at all

505. The Jersey Shore Free School is a calendar year, nongovernmental not-for-profit. On February 3 of Year 13, they received unconditional promises of $60,000 expected to be collected within 1 year. Based on past experience, the Jersey Shore Free School anticipates that 85% of unconditional pledges are actually received. By December 31, Year 13, $20,000 was actually received. What amount should Jersey Shore Free School record as contribution revenue in Year 13?

A. $60,000
B. $51,000
C. $20,000
D. $0

506. PALS is a private not-for-profit to educate and benefit autistic children and their families. The functional expense categories used by PALS on the statement of activities are generally listed under the two main classifications of program expenses and which of the following?

A. General and administrative expenses
B. Support services
C. Fund-raising
D. Membership development

507. Desert Samaritan Hospital, a not-for-profit medical facility, would include which of the following as "nonoperating" revenue in the statement of activities?
I. Recovery room fees after spinal surgery
II. Parking fees and cafeteria income
III. Donated medicines and supplies
IV. Unrestricted gifts

A. Both I and IV
B. Both II and III
C. IV only
D. II, III, and IV

508. For the spring semester Year 13, Stellar University, a nongovernmental not-for-profit university, assessed its students $5,000,000 for tuition and fees. The net amount realized was only $4,500,000 because refunds in the amount of $200,000 had to be given when certain low-enrollment classes had to be cancelled and scholarships were granted in the amount of $300,000. What amount should Stellar University report as gross revenue from tuition and fees?

A. $5,000,000
B. $4,800,000
C. $4,500,000
D. $4,700,000

■■■ PART III ANSWERS AND EXPLANATIONS

Chapter 23: Accounting Theory and Financial Reporting

1. **A.** I is correct. The FASB statements of financial accounting standards are included in the Accounting Standards Codification. Prior to 2009, searching for generally accepted accounting principles (GAAP) was often difficult because GAAP existed in a variety of places. Since 2009, GAAP is contained in a single place known as the Codification. The Codification makes it easier to research US GAAP and find general and industry-specific accounting standards that are generally accepted. Since 2009, the FASB Accounting Standards Codification is the single source of authoritative nongovernmental US GAAP. Since the adoption of the Codification, accounting and reporting practices that are *not* found in the Codification are *not* generally accepted in the United States.

2. **C.** Accordingly to the FASB conceptual framework, the objectives of financial reporting of business enterprises are based on providing information that is useful to existing and potential investors and creditors (collectively financial statement "users") in making investment decisions. The objectives are not based on SEC reporting requirements (which govern, among other things, specific reports to be filed by publicly-traded entities, and the content of, and timing for, filing those reports), or GAAP, which govern the manner in which items are accounted for in the financial statements. And, while the reporting of useful information may be influenced by materiality, materiality is not the primary objective of financial reporting of business enterprises.

3. **C.** I is correct. According to the FASB and IASB conceptual framework, for financial information to be relevant it must have predictive value, that is, contain information used to predict future outcomes. For information to be relevant, it must be helpful to people making decisions about the entity. Therefore, relevance includes the qualitative characteristic of predictive value. II is correct. According to the FASB and IASB conceptual framework, for information to be relevant, it must have confirmatory value as well as predictive value. Confirmatory value is used to provide information about evaluations previously made. For information to be relevant, it must be helpful to people making decisions about the entity. Therefore, relevance includes the qualitative characteristic of confirmatory value.

4. **A.** I is correct. According to the FASB and IASB conceptual framework, neutrality refers to the need for financial information to be free from bias in selection or presentation. For example, estimates made by management need to be without bias if financial information is to be considered faithfully represented. Therefore, neutrality is an ingredient of faithful representation.

5. **C.** I is correct. According to the FASB and IASB conceptual framework, relevance is a fundamental characteristic of financial reporting. Financial information is considered relevant only if it's capable of making a difference in the decision-making process. *Relevant* means that the financial information must be material and provide predictive and confirming value. For information to be relevant, it must be helpful to people making decisions about the entity. II is correct. According to the FASB and IASB conceptual framework, faithful representation is also a fundamental characteristic of financial reporting. Financial information is faithfully represented when it's complete, without bias, and free from error. Although perfection is not achievable, completeness, neutrality, and freedom from error must be maximized if financial information is to be considered faithfully represented. For example, the independent auditor will test management estimates to determine if they are indeed neutral, or without bias. Only if the estimates are without bias can the financial information be viewed as faithfully represented.

6. **C.** I is correct. According to the FASB and IASB conceptual framework, comparability is an enhancing, rather than a fundamental, characteristic of financial reporting. An enhancing qualitative characteristic of financial information is that financial information can be compared. Comparability enhances the user's experience with financial information by allowing current year to prior year comparisons. The user can compare one entity with another over the same time period. II is correct. According to the FASB and IASB conceptual framework, verifiability is an enhancing, rather than a fundamental, characteristic of financial reporting. Verifiability enhances the user's experience with

financial information when different knowledgeable observers are able to reach consensus that a particular depiction is faithfully represented.

7. **A.** According to the FASB and IASB conceptual framework, timeliness is a characteristic that enhances the usefulness of financial information. An example of timeliness is the fact that although there is an annual report, the investor wants more timely information. Quarterly reports, although they are unaudited, enhance the usefulness of financial information because they are more timely. According to the FASB and IASB conceptual framework, understandability is an enhancing qualitative characteristic of financial reporting. Information is understandable if it is classified, characterized, and presented clearly and concisely. Thus, both timeliness and understandability are enhancing (rather than fundamental) characteristics of useful financial reporting. When it comes to *enhancing* qualitative characteristics of useful financial information, remember that a VCUT could be very enhancing!

Verify
Compare
Understand
Timeliness

8. **A.** Revenues are inflows (increases) of assets or settlements (decreases) of liabilities and arise from an entity's primary operating (not ancillary) activities. Outflows (decreases) of assets, or incurrences (increases) of liabilities as a result of primary operating (not ancillary) activities, would give rise to expenses. Therefore, revenues would arise from a decrease in liability from primary operations.

9. **C.** Deferred revenue refers to advance payments received that have not yet been earned (e.g., services have not yet been performed, goods have not yet been delivered) and is reported on the balance sheet as a liability. Services that have been performed but not yet billed represent accrued revenue and are reported with a corresponding receivable. Similarly amounts that have not yet been received in cash but have been earned would be reported as receivables (with revenue having been reported). Deferred revenue reported on the books of one company to a transaction would mirror a prepaid asset (or deferred expense), not accrued expenses, on the books of the other company.

10. **B.** III is correct. According to the FASB's conceptual framework, assets are probable future economic benefits obtained or controlled by a particular entity as a result of past transactions and events. I

is incorrect. An asset can be tangible (such as property, plant, and equipment) or intangible (such as goodwill). II is incorrect. In some cases, claims to an asset's benefits may not be legally enforceable (goodwill, again, being an example).

11. **A.** The rationale for accounting for contingencies according to Accounting Standards Codification (ASC) Topic 450, *Contingencies*, includes reflecting conservatism in the reporting of transactions. This means that losses should be recognized immediately (if probable and reasonably estimable), but gains recognized only when realized. Applying conservatism in the reporting of transactions prevents assets and/or net income from being overstated. Thus, when selecting accounting principles in accordance with US GAAP, the method that is less likely to overstate assets and understate liabilities should be chosen according to the rule of conservatism. Consistency includes applying similar accounting practices from period to period. Materiality is an entity-specific aspect of reporting relevant accounting information, which relates to the capacity of that information to influence a user's decision. Faithful representation is a fundamental qualitative characteristic of accounting information that is concerned with reporting information that is complete, neutral, free from error, and depicts what it purports to represent.

12. **B.** Comprehensive income is an element of the financial statements that includes all differences between beginning and ending equity other than transactions between an entity and its owners (e.g., investments from and distributions to owners). It includes all components of net income and other comprehensive income. Other comprehensive income includes unrealized holding gains or losses on available-for-sale securities, the effective portion of gains and losses on certain derivatives (e.g., those that are designated and qualifying as cash flow hedges), gains and losses on foreign currency transactions that are designated and effective as economic hedges of a net investment in a foreign entity, adjustments necessary to recognize the funded status of postretirement defined benefit pension plans, and foreign currency translation adjustments. Thus, administrative expenses, which are included in net income, would be an element of comprehensive income. Prepayments (deferred assets or liabilities) are balance sheet items. Shareholder investments and dividends, which are transactions that occur between an entity and its owners, are specifically excluded from comprehensive income.

13. **B.** $600,000 loss × (1 − the tax rate of 30%) = loss of $420,000. The Year 3 operating losses of the segment would be reported in the Year 3 income statement. Since the other transactions relating to the segment occurred in Year 4, the operating losses of the segment for Year 4 as well as the gain on disposal of the segment would be netted and reported in the Year 4 income statement, net of tax. These items would not be recorded in Year 3. Each amount should be reported in the period it occurs.

14. **C.** In the year of sale (Year 4), the loss from operating the segment in the amount of $50,000 must be recognized as well as the gain from the actual sale of the division. The amount is calculated as follows:

Gain on sale	$900,000
Operating loss	− $50,000
	$850,000
	$850,000 × 0.7 = $595,000

The Year 4 operating loss and the gain on disposal would be netted and reported in the Year 4 income statement, after tax. Since the tax rate is 30%, the gain of $850,000 is reported net of tax as $595,000 because discontinued operations of a segment are reported in the income statement just below income from continuing operations and shown net of tax.

15. **D.** I, II, and III are correct. All three of these items would be included in income from continuing operations, whether being reported under US GAAP or IFRS. Note that US GAAP no longer permits the reporting of extraordinary items in a separate extraordinary item classification on the income statement.

16. **C.** I is correct. A change in depreciation method is treated as a change in estimate and, therefore, receives prospective treatment in the income statement. If a company changed from the double declining balance to straight line method, this would qualify as a change in "accounting estimate," which affects only the current and subsequent periods. Prior periods would *not* be restated, nor would retained earnings require adjustment, as no accounting principle is being changed. II is correct. A change in the useful life of an asset is also treated as a change in estimate, and would receive prospective treatment in the income statement. For example, if a company changed an asset's useful life from 10 years to 4 years, this would qualify as a change in "accounting estimate," and impacts only the current and subsequent periods. As with a change in depreciation method, prior periods would *not* be restated,

and retained earnings would not be adjusted as no accounting principle is being changed.

17. **A.** I is correct. A change from FIFO inventory valuation to average cost is a change in accounting principle. An entity may change accounting principles if GAAP requires the change or, in this question, if the alternative accounting principle average cost more fairly presents the information. The entity will report this change in accounting principle by adjusting the beginning balance of retained earnings, net of tax, to show what the cumulative profit or loss would have been had the entity always used average cost rather than FIFO. If comparative financial statements are being shown, current and prior year, adjust the beginning retained earnings for the prior year, net of tax, and for the current year, use the new method for inventory. II is not correct. A change from the direct write-off method of recognizing bad debt expense to the allowance method is a change from a non-US GAAP to a US GAAP method, and, therefore, would not qualify for treatment as a change in accounting principle.

18. **D.** The cumulative effect adjustment is recognized by adjusting beginning retained earnings, net of tax. The difference between the pretax accounting income under the old method, $600,000, and the pretax accounting under the new method, $900,000, results in a higher profit of $300,000 prior to January 1, Year 8. With a tax rate of 30%, Ashbrook Corp. will adjust the beginning balance of Year 8 retained earnings for $210,000.

19. **B.** An accounting change whose cumulative effect on prior periods is impracticable to determine is treated as a change in estimate and should, therefore, be accounted for on a prospective basis. A change from any other inventory valuation method to the LIFO method would be an example of this type of change. Accounting changes are no longer treated as prior period adjustments, nor is it any longer acceptable, under US GAAP, to report the cumulative effect of those changes on the income statement. An adjustment to retained earnings for the earliest period presented would be required for an accounting change that qualifies as a change in accounting principle, which would also require restatement of prior period financial statements.

20. **C.** I is correct. Correction of an error from a prior period is reported as a prior period adjustment, and as a result, an adjustment is made to the opening balance of retained earnings for the earliest period presented. II is correct. The cumulative effect of

a change in accounting principle is shown as an adjustment to beginning retained earnings for the earliest period presented.

21. **B.** II is correct. The correction of a failure to accrue bad debt expense is treated as a correction of an error, and thus as a prior period adjustment, it results in the amount of $30,000.

22. **D.** This situation exhibits one in which there was a change in reporting entity. A change in reporting entity is accounted for in a similar manner to a change in accounting principle and must be retrospectively applied to all prior periods presented. Note only disclosure would not be appropriate, as this is a reportable transaction that requires recognition in the financial statements. Current and prospective treatment applies to changes in accounting estimate, not changes in a reporting entity.

23. **D.** I is incorrect. A change in the amount of mineral expected to be recoverable from an underground mine is a change in accounting estimate. A change in accounting estimate is handled prospectively; current and future income statements are affected. No cumulative effect adjustment is made for a change in estimate, and no separate line item presentation is made on any financial statement. II is incorrect. A change in the expected useful life of a machine from 7 years to 4 years is a change in estimate. A change in accounting estimate is handled prospectively; current and future income statements are affected. No cumulative effect adjustment is made for a change in estimate, and no separate line item presentation is made on any financial statement.

24. **B.** A change from the completed contract method to the percentage of completion method is treated as a change in accounting principle. The cumulative effect of a change in accounting principle equals the difference between retained earnings at the beginning of the period and what the retained earnings would have been if retained earnings were applied to all affected prior periods. Since comparative financial statements are not being shown, beginning retained earnings is adjusted. Therefore, retained earnings as of January 1, Year 9, is adjusted. Note: if comparative financial statements were shown, beginning retained earnings of the earliest period presented would be adjusted for the cumulative effect of the change. The other year presented would be handled using the new method.

25. **C.** I and II are correct. Comprehensive income can be presented on a single financial statement with net income. Comprehensive income also may be shown separately on its own financial statement. Comprehensive income is an element of the financial statements that includes all differences between beginning and ending equity other than transactions between a firm and its owners.

26. **C.** I and II are correct. Both US GAAP and IFRS require that a description of all significant policies be included as an integral part of the financial statements. To comply, most companies that report under US GAAP include a "summary of significant accounting policies" as the first or second footnote to the financial statements. Accounting policies commonly described as significant include basis of consolidation, depreciation methods, amortization of intangibles, inventory pricing, accounting for recognition of profit on long-term construction, and recognition of revenue from franchising or leasing operations.

27. **C.** I is correct. The summary of significant accounting policies should identify and describe the policies, accounting principles, and methods used in preparing the financial statements. The "basis" of profit recognition on long-term construction contracts is an accounting policy and should be disclosed in the footnote known as the summary of significant accounting policies. II is correct. The summary of significant accounting policies should identify and describe the criteria used to measure items for financial statement reporting. The criteria for measuring cash equivalents is an accounting policy and should be disclosed in the footnote known as the summary of significant accounting policies.

28. **B.** II is correct. IFRS requires disclosures of significant judgments and significant estimates.

29. **A.** While interim financial reporting should be viewed as an integral part of an annual period, the fact that the financial statements cover shortened periods (e.g., quarter versus year) and, therefore, require the increased use of estimates and allocations of costs and expenses, and incorporate business seasonality as well as other factors, can limit the reliability of the information provided. Even publicly traded companies, which must report quarterly (interim) financial statements to the US Securities and Exchange Commission (SEC), are not required to have those statement audited—rather they are reviewed. This, too, can impact reliability of the reported information. Consequently, it is the timeliness of reporting the information that is emphasized over the information's reliability.

30. **B.** II is correct. IFRS requires in the footnotes a statement that the financial statements are presented in accordance with IFRS.

31. **D.** Other comprehensive income includes unrealized holding gains or losses on available-for-sale securities, the effective portion of gains and losses on certain derivatives (e.g., those that are designated and qualifying as cash flow hedges), gains and losses on foreign currency transactions that are designated and effective as economic hedges of a net investment in a foreign entity, adjustments necessary to recognize the funded status of postretirement defined benefit pension plans, and foreign currency translation adjustments. Thus, Cimmino would report a comprehensive loss of $5,000 for Year 2, computed as follows:

Foreign currency translation loss	($2,000)
Unamortized prior service cost on pension plan	($15,000)
Deferred gain on effective cash-flow hedge	$12,000
Other comprehensive loss	($5,000)

Note that while net income is included in total comprehensive income, it is not a component of other comprehensive income. Distribution to owners, which is a transaction engaged in between an entity and its owners, is specifically excluded from comprehensive income.

32. **A.** I is correct. Interim reporting is *not* required under GAAP. Interim reporting is required by the US SEC for publicly traded companies under the Federal Securities Act of 1934. A report comes out every quarter to provide timely information to the users, but the information is only reviewed, not audited, so reliability may be affected. Interim reporting emphasizes timeliness over reliability. Each statement must be marked "unaudited" so the users are put on notice. Interim financial reporting should be viewed as reporting for an integral part of an annual period. II is incorrect. Permanent inventory losses from market declines should be reflected in the interim period in which they occur. Market increases in subsequent interim periods should be recognized in the recovery interim period not to exceed the losses included in prior interim periods. Quarterly reporting requires the use of the same accounting methods as annual reporting. III is incorrect. Revenues should be recognized as earned during an interim period in the same manner as they are for a full year. Costs and expenses that benefit more than one period should be allocated among interim periods, for example, property taxes. Costs and expenses incurred and benefiting only that period, should be expensed as incurred.

33. **B.** II is correct. A registered company that is considered a large accelerated filer must file Form 10-Q (quarterly report) within 40 days of the close of the entity's fiscal quarter. Registered companies that are considered accelerated filers but not "large" still must file their quarterly reports within 40 days. Other registrants not considered accelerated have 45 days to file their quarterly report. Quarterly reports and Form 10-Q contain unaudited financial statements. I is incorrect since large accelerated filers must file their Form 10-K within 60 days, not 90 days, of the close of the fiscal year.

34. **A.** US registered companies required to file both the Form 10-K annual report and Form 10-Q quarterly reports must file those reports using US GAAP. Foreign entities registered with the SEC file Forms 20-F and 40-F. Forms 20-F and 40-F are similar but not identical to Form 10-K, as they require audited financial statements and disclosures of important financial information. A big difference is that forms 20-F and 40-F can be filed using US GAAP or IFRS.

35. **C.** I is correct. Privately held companies are exempt from reporting EPS unless, of course, they have made a filing to become public. Publicly traded companies must report EPS on the face of the income statement. II is correct. Privately held companies are exempt from reporting segment information. Only publicly traded companies must report business segment information. For a publicly traded company, a segment is considered reportable if segment revenue represents 10% or more of the combined revenue of all operating segments. To determine whether the segment is reportable using the 10% test, sales to unaffiliated companies as well as intercompany sales are included. If a segment is deemed a reportable segment, separate disclosures are required for the amount of intercompany sales and unaffiliated sales. Using the 10% test, segment information is reported until sales representing 75% of total sales (to unaffiliated customers) have been disclosed. When 75% of sales to unaffiliated customers have been separately shown, at that point no additional reportable segments need to be identified.

36. **B.** II is correct. Lead would not be a reportable segment for Year 13, because its combined revenue of $5,000 is less than 10% of total combined revenue for all segments. Revenue for all combined

segments is $92,000, 10% would be $9,200. Since lead revenue was only $5,000, lead would *not* qualify as a reportable segment.

37. **D.** For publicly traded companies, there must be enough segments reported so that at least 75% of unaffiliated revenue is shown by reportable segments. In Year 12, sales to external customers total $40,000,000, so unaffiliated revenue (external revenues reported by operating segments) must be at least $30,000,000.

Chapter 24: Revenue and Expense Recognition

38. **B.** I is correct. For revenue to be recognized under US GAAP, persuasive evidence of an arrangement or contract must exist. II is correct. For revenue to be recognized under US GAAP, goods must have been delivered or services must have been performed.

39. **C.** I is correct. Under normal GAAP rules, revenue is not recognized until the earnings process is substantially complete. However, in a multiple deliverable arrangement, the company can recognize the revenue from each element if the delivered item has a value on a stand-alone basis. If the hardware and software installation has a value on a stand-alone basis, the revenue from the installation can be recognized upon delivery without having to wait until the contract is substantially complete. Although the customer support element of this contract carries over into Year 3 and is not complete until December 31 of Year 3, it is reasonable to believe that management of Advantage would want to recognize revenue at each deliverable element. Therefore, if the installation of the hardware and software and the training of the customer staff have a value on a stand-alone basis, Advantage would recognize that portion of revenue in Year 2 since that part of the contract has been completed. II is correct. Under normal GAAP rules, revenue is not recognized until the earnings process is substantially complete. However, in a multiple deliverable arrangement, the company can recognize the revenue from each element if the delivered item can be sold separately. If the hardware and software and the training of the staff can be sold separately, Advantage can recognize those elements of the multiple deliverable arrangement as they are completed.

40. **C.** I is correct. A deferral of revenues will occur when cash is received but is not recognizable for financial statement purposes, because it has not been earned. II is correct. Deferral typically results in the recognition of a liability when cash is received before the revenue is earned. A deferral results in a prepaid expense when cash is paid before the expense is incurred, such as prepaid insurance or prepaid rent.

41. **B.** Under accrual accounting, revenues are recognized when earned, rather than when cash is received, and expenses are recognized when incurred, rather than when cash is paid. Several expense recognition principles underlie the concept of expense incurrence. Some costs are recognized as expenses on the basis of a direct matching to specific revenue (e.g., cost of goods sold is recognized in the same period as the related sale). This is known as associated cause and effect (or the matching principle). In the absence of a direct matching to specific revenues, some costs are associated with specific accounting periods (deemed incurred in those periods) on the basis of an attempt to allocate those costs in a systematic and rational manner among the periods in which benefits are provided (e.g., depreciation and/or amortization expense). This principle is known as systematic and rational allocation. Finally, some costs fall under the expense recognition principle of immediate recognition and are associated with just the current period when they cannot be directly related to specific revenues; they are deemed to have no future economic benefit, or the period to which they relate may not be feasibly determinable (utilities expense, as an example). Abel should, therefore, recognize royalty expense as it is incurred in connection with these principles.

42. **A.** A 1-year insurance policy with a cost of $3,000 expires at a rate of $250 per month. For Year 10, 5 months expired and need to be expensed: $250 × 5 months = $1,250 that has expired. When assets expire and lose their economic benefit, they are expensed. $3,000 − $1,250 expired = $1,750 still considered prepaid at year end. Journal entry to record the adjustment at December 31, Year 10 is a debit to insurance expense and a credit to prepaid insurance for $1,250.

43. **B.** When cash is received in advance, deferred revenue is recorded for the full amount received. The entry on November 1, Year 12, includes a debit to cash and credit to deferred revenue for $6,000. Deferred revenue is a liability account, not a revenue account.

44. **C.** Both I and II are correct. When the certificates lapse, the company has no further liability and revenue is earned. Deferred revenue is decreased. The journal entry upon expiration would be a debit to deferred revenue and a credit to revenue. II is correct. When the certificates are redeemed, the revenue is earned and shown in the income statement. Deferred revenue is decreased. The journal entry upon expiration of the certificates would be a debit to deferred revenue and credit to revenue. Deferred revenue represents future income collected in advance. When the gift certificates are sold, deferred revenue is increased, not revenue.

45. **A.** I is correct. A decrease in accounts receivable from the beginning of the year to the end of the year generally represents cash collections. As cash is collected, the accounts receivable balance decreases. As a result, cash basis revenue exceeds accrual basis revenue whenever accounts receivable decreases from beginning of the year to the end of the year.

46. **A.** I is correct. When adjusting from cash basis revenue to accrual basis revenue, the ending balance of accounts receivable is added to cash basis revenue as additional accrual basis revenue when earned.

47. **B.** Under IFRS, if the outcome of services rendered cannot be measured reliably, the cost recovery method is required for recognizing revenues. The installment sales method is a US GAAP method, not an IFRS method. The completed contract method is a permissible method to recognize revenue in connection with long-term construction contracts under US GAAP, but it is not permissible under IFRS. The percentage of completion method is used when reliable estimates can be made.

48. **A.** I is correct. Unearned fees is a liability resulting from collecting money in advance. The ending balance of unearned fees represents cash received but not earned during the period.

49. **A.** At December 31, Year 2, Evanko would report $4,000 as prepaid expense on its balance sheet, and $2,700 in expense on its income statement for the year ended December 31, Year 2. Further details are provided below:

	Prepaid	Expense
$1,500 from $3,000 annual policy paid on July 1, Year 1		$1,500
$2,000 advance rent payment paid on November 1, Year 1	$2,000	
$3,200 of supplies prepaid on October 15, Year 2	$2,000	$1,200
	$4,000	$2,700

Because the annual insurance policy paid on July 1, Year 1, would be fully expired by December 31, Year 2, the $1,500 balance sitting in prepaid expense, should be fully expensed by December 31, Year 2. The $2,000 advanced rent payment paid on November 1, Year 1, is in payment for a new building lease that is to commence on January 1, Year 3, and is, therefore, still appropriately prepaid at December 31, Year 2. The supplies inventory count noted only $2,000 of supplies still on hand, which should be included as part of prepaid expense at December 31, Year 2. The difference between that amount and the $3,200 October 15, Year 2, supplies prepayment ($1,200) is expensed as used and consumed as of December 31, Year 2.

50. **B.** This question involves the recognition of deferred compensation, which is to be recognized over the executive's employment period from the date the agreement commences (January 2, Year 1) to the date the executive is fully eligible for the deferred compensation (December 31, Year 3). The total deferred compensation is $150,000 ($50,000 × 3 for Years 4, 5, and 6), which is then recognized over the eligibility period (3 years—Years 1, 2, and 3). Maximus Corporation would, therefore, recognize $50,000 in each of Years 1, 2, and 3. The deferred compensation should not be amortized after the eligibility date, nor should it be expensed immediately upon execution of the agreement or fully deferred until the eligibility date. Thus, answers A, C, and D would be incorrect.

51. **A.** I is correct. Beginning unearned fees must be added to cash fees collected to arrive at accrual basis revenue so that what was unearned at the beginning of the year and actually earned during the period don't get subtracted when the ending balance of unearned fees gets subtracted. For example, assume cash of $100,000 is collected in advance during the year. Assume that the beginning balance of unearned fees is $5,000 and the ending balance

of unearned fees is $15,000. To go from cash basis revenue to accrual, do the following:

Cash collected	$100,000
Ending balance of unearned fees	– $15,000
Beginning balance of unearned fees	+ $5,000
Accrual basis revenue for the year	$90,000

52. C. The following can be used to convert cash basis revenue to accrual basis revenue beginning with cash fees collected:

Cash fees collected

+ Ending accounts receivable
– Beginning accounts receivable
Accrual basis revenue

Cash fees collected

+ Beginning unearned fees
– Ending unearned fees
Accrual basis revenue

Using the facts from the question:

Cash basis revenue	$100,000
Ending accounts receivable	+ $60,000
Beginning accounts receivable	– $40,000
Subtotal	$120,000
Beginning unearned fees	+ 0
Ending unearned fees	– $4,000
Accrual basis revenue	$116,000

53. B.

Cash basis collections	$60,000
Rent receivable, ending	+ 8,200
Rent receivable, beginning	– 7,600
Unearned revenue	↓
Beginning	+ $28,000
Ending	–$21,000
Accrual basis rent revenue	$67,600

54. B. The percentage of completion method is the generally accepted method to recognize profit from a long-term construction contract. The percentage of completion method recognizes profit from a long-term construction contract on the basis of costs incurred. Under the percentage of completion method, the costs incurred to date are the rationale for determining the profit to recognize. The costs incurred to date are divided by the total estimated costs to determine the percentage of completion. For Year 12 the profit to date is $100,000, which is determined as follows using the costs incurred:

Costs incurred to date $300,000 / $1,500,000 total estimated costs = 20%

20% complete × total estimated profit of $500,000 = current profit to date of $100,000

Notice that the cash collected is not a basis for recognizing profit under the percentage of completion method.

55. D. Under the percentage of completion method, each year the cost *to date* is compared to the estimated *total cost* to determine the degree of completion. This percentage is multiplied by the expected total profit to determine the *profit to date*. The costs incurred to date in Year 13 are up to $1,200,000. The $1,200,000 of costs incurred to date in Year 13 includes the $900,000 spent in Year 13 plus the $300,000 spent in Year 12. Because an additional $400,000 of cost is estimated to be spent beyond Year 13, total estimated costs under this contract have risen from the initial estimate of $1,500,000 to $1,600,000. Since total costs have increased, a lower profit than previously expected is now anticipated. Since the contract price is $2,000,000, the old profit estimate was $500,000 based on expected total costs of $1,500,000. The new profit estimate is $400,000 based on expected total costs of $1,600,000. To calculate profit in Year 13, the second year of the contract, the costs incurred to date will be divided into the total estimated costs as follows:

Costs incurred to date in Year 13 ($300,000 + $900,000)	$1,200,000
Total estimated costs ($300,000 + $900,000 + $400,000)	÷ $1,600,000
Percentage completed after Year 13	75%

75% × profit now expected of $400,000 = $300,000 cumulative profit

Cumulative profit	$300,000
Less profit recognized in Year 12	– $100,000
Year 13 profit	$200,000

56. C. I is correct. For a long-term construction contract being accounted for using the percentage of completion method, the construction in progress account is debited for construction costs incurred. When costs are incurred, the construction in progress account is debited and cash or accounts payable is credited. II is correct. For a long-term construction contract being accounted for using the percentage of completion method, the construction progress account is debited for profit recognized to date. When profit is recognized, the construction in progress account is debited and revenue is credited.

57. D. In long-term construction projects, the contractor often will bill the customer to help finance the cost of construction. Such billings are recorded by the contractor on the balance sheet, but these billings do not impact the recognition of profit. The account "progress billings" is used to account for billings sent to customers during the contract. The journal entry when the bill is sent to the customer is a debit to accounts receivable and a credit to progress billings. When the customer pays, the debit is to cash and the credit to accounts receivable. The progress billings account is netted against the construction in progress account. If more billings have been sent out than costs incurred, the progress billings account is recorded as a liability. If construction costs incurred exceed billings, an asset is recorded.

58. **D.** With regard to profit recognition from long-term construction contracts accounted for on the percentage of completion method, progress billings and cash collections have no impact on profit. Profit is recognized under the percentage of completion method in proportion to monies spent, not monies received. Under the percentage of completion method, the costs incurred to date are divided into total estimated costs to determine the percentage completed. That percentage is then multiplied by profit anticipated to arrive at profit recognized to date. Any profit previously recognized would then need to be subtracted to arrive at current year profit.

59. **C.** Under the completed contract method, profit recognition is delayed until the project is substantially completed. However, in the event of a loss, conservatism says to recognize the loss in the year it becomes apparent.

60. **C.** I is correct. A construction company must apply the percentage of completion method to account for long-term construction contract revenue if the buyer can fulfill its obligations and the contractor has the ability to estimate the degree of completion with reasonable accuracy. Since the state of Arizona is the buyer and should certainly be able to pay, Olney Corp. would be expected to use the percentage of completion method. II is correct. A construction company must apply the percentage of completion method to account for long-term construction contract revenue if the buyer can fulfill its obligations and the contractor has the ability to complete the job. There were no uncertainties given in the facts regarding Olney's ability to complete the job. If on the exam the facts mentioned that this was the first time Olney Corp. had ever built a highway and they were not sure they could finish, it would be an example of a possibility that would allow Olney Corp. to choose between the completed contract method and percentage of completion.

61. **B.** The installment sales method is allowable for certain sales of property at a gain. The installment method is used when cash is received in installments rather than one lump sum. If the company is unable to make a reasonable estimation of the cash to be collected, the installment sales method, rather than accrual accounting, must be applied. Under the installment method, recognition of profit is delayed and it is recognized only when cash is collected. The first step in connection with profit recognition under the installment method is the computation of the gross profit from the sale and the gross profit percentage. The final step is to multiply the cash collected by the gross profit percentage to determine the realized gross profit. The gross profit from the sale is $100,000 − $60,000 cost = $40,000 gross profit.

Gross profit	$40,000
Divided by sale price	÷ $100,000
Gross profit percentage	40%
Cash collected in Year 13	× $20,000
Gross profit realized in Year 13	$8,000

62. **A.** Deferred gross profit from installment sales is the amount of cash not yet collected multiplied by the gross profit percentage. For Year 13, $20,000 of the $100,000 was collected, leaving a receivable balance of $80,000. The $80,000 represents the cash not yet collected. The profit on the $80,000 not yet collected is all deferred as of December 31, Year 13. Therefore, the deferred gross profit on December 31, Year 13, is calculated as

Accounts receivable balance from the installment sale	$80,000
Gross profit percentage	× 40%
Deferred gross profit	$32,000

Another way to determine deferred gross profit would be to simply subtract the amount of realized gross profit for Year 13, $8,000, from the total gross profit of $40,000.

Total gross profit from the installment sale	$40,000
Realized gross profit in Year 13	− $8,000
Deferred gross profit at December 31, Year 13	$32,000

63. **B.** III is correct. The installment method is considered a cash basis rather than accrual basis method of revenue recognition. As cash is collected, revenue is recognized based on the gross profit percentage calculated on the sale.

64. **D.** The cost recovery method is a cash basis method similar to the installment method but used when there is significant uncertainty as to whether cash will even be collected. The buyer, for example, might be on the verge of bankruptcy. The cost recovery method does not recognize a profit until an amount of cash is collected that equals the cost of the asset sold. Since $2,000 was collected in Year 13 but the asset cost $2,500, $500 of cost of goods sold have yet to be collected. So no profit is recognized in Year 13.

65. **B.** In Year 14, $3,000 is collected, but the first $500 collected in Year 14 is still a recovery of cost. Therefore, under the cost recovery method, gross profit in Year 14 is reported as follows:

Cash collected in Year 14	$3,000
Remaining recovery of cost	− $500
Gross profit in Year 14	$2,500

66. **D.** Had Russell Inc. used the installment method rather than cost recovery, Russell would have realized gross profit for Year 13 as follows:

Sales price	$5,000
Less cost	− $2,500
Total gross profit	$2,500
Gross profit on sale	50%
Cash collected in Year 13	× $2,000
Realized gross profit under the installment method	$1,000

67. **B.** Denni Stevens, Ltd. would report royalty revenue in the amount of $300,000. The question states that Denni Stevens will receive royalties of 30% on future album sales. Future album sales amounted to $1,000,000; therefore, $1,000,000 × 30% = $300,000. The information about royalties receivable and royalty payments received has no bearing on the computations in this question. It should be noted, however, that in recognizing the total royalty revenue of $300,000 for Year 3, Denni Stevens would report a total royalty receivable at December 31, Year 3, in the amount of $100,000 (a $25,000 increase to the existing royalty receivable balance of $75,000), since $200,000 had already been received.

68. **C.** This question requires a reconciliation of cash paid for royalties to royalty expense that should be reported/recognized in the income statement (accrual-based royalty expense). In the reconciliation process, decreases/increases in operating assets (e.g., prepaid royalties) are added back/subtracted to derive accrual-based royalty expense, and decreases/increases in operating liabilities (royalties payable) are subtracted/added back in determining accrual-based royalty expense. The opposite would hold true if royalty expense were given and cash paid for royalties was the unknown (e.g., decreases/increases in operating assets would be subtracted/added back in determining cash paid for royalties, and decreases/increases in operating liabilities would be added back/subtracted in determining cash paid for royalties). Mann would, therefore, report royalty expense of $305,000 in its Year 2 income statement, computed as follows:

Cash paid for royalties	$300,000
Decrease in prepaid royalties	+ $10,000
Decrease in royalties payable	− $5,000
Royalty expense recognized (reported in income statement)	$305,000

69. **A.** Royalty revenue is recognized on the accrual basis, not the cash basis. The first check received on September 30, Year 4, for $10,000 is for the period January through June, Year 4, and should be included in Year 4 revenue. The second check received on March 31, Year 5, for $20,000 would also be for Year 4 revenue for the second half of Year 4 sales from July 1 through December 31, Year 4. The check received on September 30, Year 5, for $30,000 is for the sales from January 1, Year 5, to June 30, Year 5, so all $30,000 belongs in Year 5 revenue. The estimated sales for the second half of Year 5 in the amount of $180,000 × the 10% royalty = $18,000 more revenue for Year 5, even though it won't be received until March 31, Year 6. Therefore, total Year 5 revenue for royalties is $48,000. Remember that royalties are on the accrual basis, not cash basis.

Chapter 25: Cash, Receivables, and Inventory

70. **B.** The gross method means recording the sale at the gross amount without taking the cash discount into consideration. The journal entry would include a debit to accounts receivable and a credit to sales of $49,000. The $49,000 is determined as follows:

List price	$70,000
Subtract 30% trade discount	− $21,000
Balance	$49,000

71. **C.** If the buyer pays within the discount period, the debit to sales discounts taken would be for $980: Accounts receivable $49,000 × 0.02 = $980. The journal entry would be a debit to cash for $48,020, a debit to sales discounts taken for $980, and a credit to accounts receivable for $49,000.

72. **C.** If the customer pays after the discount period, the entry would be a debit to cash for $49,000 and a credit to accounts receivable for $49,000. Notice that accounts receivable is debited for $49,000 whether the buyer pays within 10 days or after 10 days. The speed of the collection only affects how much cash is collected; accounts receivable needs to be removed for the entire amount that it was set up for, in this case, $49,000.

73. **B.** II is correct. The allowance method is consistent with US GAAP because it provides for matching of current year credit sales with the estimated uncollectible expenses from those sales.

74. **D.** Current assets are assets that are reasonably expected to convert into cash, be sold, or be consumed within 1 year or one operating cycle, whichever is longer. Current assets include cash, accounts receivable, trading securities, inventories, and prepaid expenses.

75. **A.** I is correct. Besides cash, demand deposits, and money market accounts, highly liquid investments that are readily convertible into cash can be shown on the balance sheet as cash or cash equivalent if the investments have a maturity of 90 days or less from the date the investment is acquired.

76. **D.** Compensating balances are not included as cash or cash equivalents if the deposit is legally restricted. Compensating balances may be included as a cash or cash equivalent if the deposit is not restricted. Compensating balances are often required by lenders so that a debtor can borrow from the institution but must leave some amount behind as collateral. If the amount left behind is legally restricted, it would be reported separately as a current asset but not part of cash or cash equivalents.

77. **B.** II is correct. A US Treasury bill in the amount of $1,000 purchased December 1, Year 13, that matures February 15, Year 14, has an original maturity of 90 days or less; therefore, it is included in cash or cash equivalents on December 31, Year 13.

78. **C.** The $1,800 check written to Snell Corp. is still cash that legally belongs to Early Corp. on December 31, Year 13. Although the check was dated December 31, Year 13, it was not mailed out until Year 14. No adjustment should be made regarding the $1,800 check written out to Snell Corp. The $500 check that was returned for insufficient funds should be subtracted out of the cash balance on December 31, Year 13. As of

December 31, Year 13, not only did the check bounce but there was no way of knowing on that date if it would ever clear. Therefore, $15,000 − $500 = an adjusted cash balance of $14,500.

79. **D.** I is incorrect. Factoring without recourse transfers the risk of uncollectible receivables to the buyer. Factoring with recourse leaves the risk of uncollectible receivables with the seller. II is incorrect. Factoring receivables without recourse is a sale of receivables, not a loan. If A had assigned or pledged the receivables in exchange for the $250,000, that would be, in effect, a loan for A rather than a sale of receivables.

80. **D.** Under the percentage of credit sales approach, uncollectible accounts expense would be debited and allowance for uncollectible accounts would be credited for $160,000 (2% × $8,000,000). For accounts written off, allowance for uncollectible accounts would be debited and accounts receivable would be credited for $315,000. The December 31, Year 6, allowance for uncollectible accounts balance would be $95,000 ($250,000 + $160,000 − $315,000).

81. **C.** III is correct. An entry to write off an account receivable under the allowance method (accrual basis) involves a debit to the allowance account and a credit to accounts receivable. The effect of that entry is a decrease in allowance for doubtful accounts and a decrease in accounts receivable.

82. **B.** II is correct. In Year 13 when Costas Corp. recovers 40% of the receivable from the bankruptcy trustee, this results in two journal entries. The first entry reverses the write-off of 40% of the amount previously written off ($15,000). Accounts receivable would be debited for $6,000 and allowance for doubtful accounts would be credited for $6,000, resulting in an increase to both the allowance account and to accounts receivable. The simultaneous increase in $6,000 results in an increase to cash and a decrease to accounts receivable in the amount of $6,000. The net effect of the recovery is an increase in cash, increase in allowance, no effect on net income, and no effect on accounts receivable, since accounts receivable first goes up for the reversal and then down by the amount of cash recovered.

83. **A.** Face amount of note, $400,000 × 10% interest = $40,000. Maturity value of the note is therefore equal to $440,000. This means that if Hondo held the note to maturity, he would receive $440,000 from the customer.

84. **D.** $411,400 is computed as follows:

Maturity value of note	$440,000
Discount by bank: 13% × $440,000 = $57,200 × 6 months held by bank	− $28,600
Proceeds received by Hondo from the bank	$411,400

85. **A.** The results of the aging schedule will determine the ending balance in the allowance account. The aging schedule results in a balance of $4,600 determined as follows: $50,000 × 0.03 = $1,500; plus $10,000 × 0.06 = $600; plus $2,500 = $4,600. Therefore, the ending balance in the allowance for doubtful accounts equals $4,600 credit. Notice that when using the aging schedule approach, what results is the ending balance of the allowance for doubtful accounts. This is known as a balance sheet approach. Under this approach, any prior balance in the allowance account is ignored for purposes of determining the ending balance in the allowance account. For this reason, the $700 credit balance is not taken into consideration for determining the ending balance in the allowance account.

86. **B.** The ending balance in the allowance account of $4,600, minus the previous balance in the allowance account of $700 credit results in the need for an adjustment to the allowance account of $3,900 credit. The journal entry involved in bringing the allowance account from $700 credit up to $4,600 credit involves a debit to bad debt expense of $3,900 and a credit to the allowance for doubtful accounts of $3,900.

87. **B.** Even if the prior balance in the allowance account had a balance of $500 debit rather than $700 credit, the allowance account would still need to have an ending balance of $4,600. The results of the aging schedule will always determine the ending balance in the allowance account. Once again, when using the aging schedule approach, what results is the ending balance of the allowance for doubtful accounts. Under this approach, any prior balance in the allowance account is ignored for purposes of determining the ending balance in the allowance account. Thus the $500 debit balance is ignored, and the ending balance of the allowance account is still $4,600 determined as follows: $50,000 × 0.03 = $1,500; plus $10,000 × 0.06 = $600; plus $2,500 = $4,600.

88. **C.** If the prior balance in the allowance account had a balance of $500 debit rather than $700 credit, the allowance account would still need to have an ending balance of $4,600. To get the allowance account

to $4,600, the prior balance of $500 debit would result in the need for an adjustment to the allowance account for $5,100. The adjustment would involve a debit to bad debt expense for $5,100 and a credit to the allowance account in the amount of $5,100.

89. **A.** When an account is written off under the allowance method, both allowance for doubtful accounts and accounts receivable are decreased (allowance for doubtful accounts would be debited, and accounts receivable would be credited). When that account is then subsequently collected, the prior entry to write off the account is reversed; therefore, accounts receivable and allowance for doubtful accounts are increased with a debit to accounts receivable and a credit to allowance for doubtful accounts. Collection of the receivable must also be recorded and is facilitated by debiting cash and crediting accounts receivable. Bad debt expense is not impacted in this transaction.

90. **A.** $5,000 is calculated as follows: Using the balance sheet approach, accounts receivable of $2,000,000 × 0.04 = $80,000, which represents the ending balance in the allowance account. $75,000 represents the prior balance in the allowance account. Therefore, the adjustment to the allowance account would be a credit of $5,000. The journal entry would be to debit bad debt expense and credit allowance for doubtful accounts for $5,000. Notice that the credit sales are ignored since Miller uses the balance sheet approach to estimating bad debt expense.

91. **B.** Under the income statement approach to estimating bad debt expense, the income statement accounts are used to estimate the bad debt expense without any regard for balance sheet accounts. Using the income statement accounts, the net credit sales of $1,800,000 is multiplied by 2% and the bad debt expense for Year 13 is $36,000. The journal entry is a debit to bad debt expense for $36,000 and a credit to the allowance for doubtful accounts in the amount of $36,000.

92. **A.** I is correct. At year-end, when using the income statement approach to estimating bad debt expense, the previous balance in the allowance account is ignored for the purposes of determining bad debt expense. Under the income statement approach, bad debt expense is calculated based on a percentage of net sales. The result is the amount of bad debt expense for the year without regard to any prior balance in the allowance account.

93. **C.** The beginning balance of $55,000 less the amount written off of $15,000 brings the allowance account down to $40,000. Since the ending balance is given at $45,000, an adjustment for $5,000 is needed at year-end. This adjustment increases the allowance account and increases bad debt expense in the amount of $5,000.

94. **C.** I is correct. Cash in checking accounts is included in cash and cash equivalents. If any bank accounts are overdrawn, they should be netted and offset by the accounts with positive balances. II is correct. Petty cash is included in cash and cash equivalents. Petty cash includes cash on hand.

95. **D.** I is incorrect. A check from a customer dated after the balance sheet date should not be part of unrestricted cash. Cash is defined as unrestricted cash. A postdated check is not unrestricted. In fact, there is no guarantee that the postdated check will even clear the bank. II is incorrect. A check dated after the balance sheet date should not be a part of cash equivalents. A cash equivalent is a short-term highly liquid investment that is near maturity (within 3 months) at the time of purchase.

96. **A.** I is correct. Factoring involves a company converting its receivables into cash by assigning them to a factor, in this case without recourse. When a company factors receivables without recourse in exchange for cash, title to the receivables is transferred to the factor and the transaction is treated as a sale of receivables. Factoring without recourse means the sale is final and the factor assumes the risk of any losses. Without recourse refers to the fact that if customers do not pay, the factor has no recourse against the entity that sold the receivables. For this reason, the factor often charges fees up front to allow for returns and uncollectible accounts.

97. **D.** When a company factors receivables without recourse in exchange for cash, title to the receivables is transferred to the factor and the transaction is treated as a sale of receivables. Without recourse refers to the fact that if customers do not pay, the factor has no recourse against the entity who sold the receivables. For this reason, the factor often charges fees up front to allow for returns and uncollectible accounts. Of the $100,000 factored, 15% is charged as an allowance for returns, $15,000. Another 5% commission is taken off the $100,000. $5,000 + $15,000 = $20,000 deducted. The total received by Barnes Corp. is therefore $80,000.

98. **D.** If prices are falling, FIFO would produce the highest costs of goods sold since FIFO cost of goods sold consists of the oldest units, which, under this scenario, would be priced the highest. LIFO, on the other hand would produce the highest inventory valuation under this scenario (falling prices) since LIFO inventory consists of the oldest units, and those are the higher-priced units.

99. **A.** I is correct. In a period of rising prices, cost of goods sold would be higher under LIFO as compared to FIFO. Under LIFO, the more recent purchases are expensed through cost of goods sold, and those are the higher priced items in a period of inflation. II is incorrect. Since LIFO cost of goods sold would be higher in periods of rising prices, net income would be lower than FIFO. III is incorrect. LIFO inventory consists of the oldest units, which in periods of rising prices would be the lower-priced units. Thus, under this scenario (rising prices) LIFO inventory would be lower than FIFO.

100. **D.** Currently, under US GAAP, inventory is valued at the lower of cost or market. Market is defined as the median value between the market "ceiling" (net realizable value), the market "floor" (net realizable value less a normal profit margin), and the replacement cost. Whichever value is in the middle of those three is the market. The designated market price in this question would, therefore, be $16,545, which is the median value between net realizable value ("ceiling") of $16,850, net realizable value less a normal profit margin ("floor") of $16,545, and replacement cost of $16,490. Since the cost ($16,730) is higher than designated market ($16,545), Olympic should report the ending inventory at $16,545, the lower of cost or market. Accounting Standards Update No. 2015-11, which was issued in July 2015 and is effective for fiscal years beginning after December 31, 2016, requires that inventory measured under the FIFO or average cost methods be valued at the lower of cost or net realizable value. Inventory measured under the LIFO or retail inventory methods remains unchanged. It should be noted that under IFRS, all inventory (with the exception of biological inventory items) is valued at the lower of cost or net realizable value. Biological inventory items are valued at fair value less the cost to sell at the point of harvest. Therefore, if this question had asked at what amount Olympic would have reported the ending inventory if it had used IFRS in the preparation of its financial statements, the answer would have been $16,730, FIFO cost, since that is less than net realizable value of $16,850.

101. A. Cost of goods sold is calculated as follows:

Beginning inventory	$41,875
Purchases	+ $112,800
Purchase returns	− $20,200
Freight in	+ $24,360
Total available for sale	$158,835
Ending inventory	− $32,109
Cost of goods sold	$126,726

102. A. I is correct. In a period of rising prices, LIFO can be advantageous on a tax return to show lower ending inventory and therefore lower net income. However, if LIFO is used for tax purposes, it must also be used for financial statement purposes under the LIFO conformity rule under US GAAP.

103. B. Cost of goods available for sale under FIFO is the total of the beginning inventory plus the purchases. The first step to doing inventory valuation is to get the cost of goods available. Prior to any units being sold, the cost of goods available for sale amounts to $113,200, calculated as follows:

Beginning inventory 10,000 units at $1	$10,000
Purchase on 2/10/13 11,200 units at $3	+ $33,600
Purchase on 12/30/13 11,600 units at $6	+ $69,600
32,800 units	$113,200
Total cost of goods available for sale	$113,200

Note that cost of goods available for sale would be identical regardless of using LIFO, FIFO, or average cost. Cost of goods available for sale would be identical using perpetual or periodic inventory.

104. A. Under FIFO, cost of goods sold consists of the oldest units. In this question, prices are rising, so the oldest units sold are the cheap units. Of the 32,800 units available, 11,800 were sold. Of the 11,800 units sold, the first 10,000 come from beginning inventory at a cost of $1. The other 1,800 units sold come from the oldest purchase, in this case 2/10/13 at a cost of $3. Therefore, cost of goods sold under FIFO, assuming a periodic system for the 11,800 units sold, would be calculated as follows:

10,000 units sold at $1	$10,000
1,800 units sold at $3	+ $5,400
Cost of goods sold	$15,400

105. D. Ending inventory consists of the 21,000 units not sold. Under FIFO, ending inventory will consist of the most recent purchases, since the oldest is sold first. Therefore, of the 21,000 units not sold and still in ending inventory, the first 11,600 were from the $6 purchase. The other units not sold, 9,400, are priced at $3. Ending inventory at FIFO:

11,600 units at $6	$69,600
9,400 units at $3	+ $28,200
Ending inventory	$97,800

Another way to determine the ending inventory under FIFO involves subtracting cost of goods sold from cost of goods available for sale. Using information already determined in the prior questions, cost of goods available for sale is $113,200 minus cost of goods sold of $15,400. Ending inventory must therefore be $97,800.

Cost of goods available for sale (from prior question)	$113,200
Minus cost of goods sold (from prior question)	− $15,400
Ending inventory	$97,800

106. A.

Beginning inventory, 10,000 units at $1	$10,000
Purchase on 2/10/13, 11,200 units at $3	+ $33,600
Purchase on 12/30/13, 11,600 units at $6	+ $69,600
Total available for sale	$113,200

Note that cost of goods available for sale would be identical regardless of using LIFO, FIFO, or average cost. Cost of goods available for sale would be identical using perpetual or periodic inventory.

107. B. Under periodic LIFO, cost of goods sold consists of the most recently purchased items without regard for whether they were even on hand at the time of sale. Therefore, the most recent purchase at December 30, Year 13, is expensed first, followed by the next most recent purchase on 2/10/13. Under periodic LIFO, cost of goods sold for the 11,800 units sold is calculated as follows:

11,600 units sold that cost $6	$69,600
200 units sold that cost $3	+ $600
Total cost of goods sold	$70,200

108. B. Ending inventory under periodic LIFO consists of the oldest units, since the first in are also the first out. Therefore, ending inventory under periodic LIFO is made up of the oldest 21,000 units. The 21,000 units are accounted for as follows: 10,000 units of beginning inventory and 11,000 units from the purchase on 2/10/13. Under periodic LIFO, the oldest 21,000 units are accounted for as follows:

From beginning inventory, 10,000 units at $1	$10,000
From the purchase on 2/10/13, 11,000 units at $3	$33,000
Ending inventory	$43,000

Another way to determine ending inventory is to subtract cost of goods sold from the cost of goods available for sale. Ending inventory can be calculated as follows:

Beginning inventory, 10,000 units at $1	$10,000
Purchase on 2/10/13, 11,200 units at $3	+ $33,600
Purchase on 12/30/13, 11,600 units at $6	+ $69,600
Total available for sale	$113,200
Less cost of goods sold	
(determined in the prior question)	– $70,200
Ending inventory	$43,000

109. C. Under perpetual LIFO, ending inventory consists of the oldest units, as the most recent purchases are charged to cost of goods sold. The sale on 3/20/13 could not have come from the most recent purchase on 12/30, since the 11,600 units purchased on 12/30 had not been acquired as of 3/20/13 and therefore could not have been sold yet. As a result, the units sold on 3/20/13 had to have consisted of the next most recent purchase on 2/10/13. Thus the 11,800 units sold consisted of the following:

Purchase on 2/10/13, 11,200 units at $3	$33,600
Beginning inventory, 600 units at $1	+ $600
Total cost of goods sold	$34,200

110. B. Ending inventory under perpetual LIFO consists of the oldest units, since the purchases made just before the sale were charged to cost of goods sold. Therefore, under perpetual LIFO, the 9,400 units of beginning inventory that were not sold are still on hand at year-end, for a total of $9,400. In addition, the entire end of year purchase of 11,600 units at $6, $69,600, would still be on hand under perpetual LIFO, since it could not have been sold on 3/20/13 as it had not been acquired yet. Therefore, ending inventory under perpetual LIFO could be calculated as follows:

Beginning inventory units not sold	
on 3/20/13, 9,400 units at $1	$9,400
Purchase on 12/30/13	+ $69,600
Total ending inventory	$79,000

An easier way to determine ending inventory under perpetual LIFO is to subtract cost of goods sold (already calculated in the prior question) from cost of goods available for sale as follows:

Beginning inventory, 10,000 units at $1	$10,000
Purchase on 2/10/13, 11,200 units at $3	+ $33,600
Purchase on 12/30/13, 11,600 units at $6	+ $69,600
Total available for sale	$113,200
Less cost of goods sold	
(calculated in the prior question)	– $34,200
Ending inventory	$79,000

It is important to note that calculation of cost of goods available for sale is the same regardless of periodic or perpetual inventory, LIFO or FIFO.

111. A. The first step in determining average cost per unit is to determine cost of goods available for sale.

Beginning inventory, 10,000 units at $1	$10,000
Purchase on January 14, 4,000 units at $3	+ $12,000
Purchase December 22, 6,000 units at $6	+ $36,000
Cost of goods available for sale =	
20,000 total units	$58,000
Average cost per unit = $58,000 /	
20,000 units	$2.90

112. D. When determining cost of goods sold using the weighted average method, the average cost per unit is multiplied by the number of units sold. In this question, cost of goods sold under the weighted average method is calculated as follows: average cost per unit $2.90 × 8,000 units sold = $23,200.

113. B. When determining ending inventory under weighted average, the first step is to determine the average cost per unit, $2.90 (see prior answer). Once the average cost per unit is determined, the next step is to multiply the ending inventory units of 12,000 by the average cost per unit of $2.90.

Average cost per unit	$2.90
Units in ending inventory	× 12,000
(20,000 units available minus	
8,000 units sold)	
Ending inventory	$34,800

Another way to determine ending inventory under weighted average would be to subtract the cost of goods sold figure from the total available for sale in dollars.

Total available for sale	$58,000
Less cost of goods sold	– $23,200
(calculated in previous question)	
Ending inventory	$34,800

114. D. I is incorrect. Under FOB shipping point, the seller's last point of responsibility is the place of shipment, as the seller, Shula Corp., no longer owns the goods sold to Langer Corp. on December 31. II is incorrect. Under FOB destination, the seller's last point of responsibility is the tendering of the goods at their destination, which had not occurred yet as of December 31, Year 13. Therefore, as the buyer, Shula Corp., does not have title yet at year-end in regard to the goods purchased from Mandich Corp.

115. A. The consignor of goods, not the consignee, must include consigned goods in his or her own inventory at year-end. Shipping costs incurred by the consignor in transferring the goods to the consignee is an inventoriable cost that is included in the consignor's inventory. It is not an expense. The consignor should also report (as part of his or her inventory) warehousing costs associated with the consigned goods.

116. **C.** I is correct. An understatement of beginning inventory of $1,000 causes an understatement of total available for sale of $1,000. With beginning inventory given incorrectly at $13,000 and with purchases of $5,000, total available for sale would be $18,000 instead of the correct amount of $19,000. Total available for sale minus ending inventory equals cost of goods sold; therefore, the understatement of beginning inventory also leads to an understatement of cost of goods sold for $1,000. II is correct. Since cost of goods available for sale minus ending inventory equals cost of goods sold, an overstatement of ending inventory also leads to an understatement of cost of goods sold. If ending inventory is overstated by $2,000, then cost of goods sold is understated by $2,000. The net effect of the two errors is an overstatement of cost of goods sold by $3,000, determined as follows:

Incorrectly Stated

Beginning inventory	$13,000
Purchases	+ $5,000
Total available for sale	$18,000
Ending inventory	– $10,000
Cost of goods sold (incorrectly stated)	$8,000

Correctly Stated

Beginning inventory	$14,000
Purchases	+ $5,000
Total available for sale	$19,000
Ending inventory	– $8,000
Cost of goods sold (correctly stated)	$11,000

Net effect of the two errors on cost of goods sold is $3,000 understatement.

117. **B.** Identifying an appropriate price index is crucial to dollar-value LIFO accounting, which measures changes in inventory in terms of dollars of constant purchasing power rather than units of physical inventory. An entity can choose to use published indexes or generate them internally for each year. In this example, the current year price index of 1.10 can be computed by dividing ending inventory at current-year cost ($660,000) by inventory at base-year cost ($600,000). This index is then applied to the current-year inventory layer stated at base-year cost in determining dollar value LIFO inventory and can be computed as follows: {$575,000 (base layer) + [($600,000 (base year cost) – $575,000) × 1.10]} = $602,500. A is wrong since $600,000 is the base-year cost. C is wrong since it incorrectly uses $600,000 as the base layer, versus $575,000. D is wrong since this is the amount of inventory at current cost at year-end.

118. **B.** In determining the presumed missing inventory in this question, it is necessary to apply the gross profit method, which is a method used to compute an estimated of ending inventory value. This method is often used when preparing interim financial statements and may also be used to determine an estimated inventory loss when inventory is destroyed or missing, as a check and balance on perpetual inventory records, or as an analytical procedure (to be used by external auditors) when attempting to determine the fairness of an entity's ending inventory balance. In applying the gross profit method, an estimate of cost of goods sold is first derived, and then that amount is subtracted from cost of goods available for sale (beginning inventory plus net purchases) in determining the ending inventory balance. In this question, since the gross profit percentage is given (20%), the cost of goods sold percentage is equal to 80% (100% – 20%). Cost of goods sold can then be computed as: $2,500,000 (sales) × 80% = $2,000,000. This amount is then subtracted from cost of goods available for sale to derive an estimate of the ending inventory value. That computation follows below:

Beginning inventory	$400,000
Purchases	+ $3,100,000
Cost of goods available for sale	$3,500,000
Cost of goods sold	– $2,000,000 (estimated)
Ending inventory	$1,500,000 (estimated)

Because the physical inventory resulted in a $1,400,000 balance, missing inventory is estimated to be $100,000 [$1,500,000 (estimated inventory) – $1,400,000 (per physical count)].

119. **A.** Under FOB shipping terms, legal title transfers to the buyer (Kenney) when the seller (Mann) tenders delivery of the goods to a carrier. The goods, while in transit, are in included in the buyer's (Kenney's) inventory. Any costs incurred that are necessary to prepare the goods for sale (which would include getting the goods to their destination, Kenney) are considered inventoriable costs and added to the

inventory balance. Therefore, all costs listed herein, the freight-in: $3,000 + the special handling costs: $2,000 + the insurance on the shipment: $500, or a total of $5,500, would be considered inventoriable costs, and would be reported by Kenney. B is incorrect as the $2,500 fails to include the freight-in, and the costs would be reported by Kenney, not Mann. C is incorrect since the special handling and insurance costs are excluded. D is incorrect since the freight-in and insurance costs are excluded and the costs are not to be reported by Mann.

120. **D.** As the name implies, the moving average inventory method requires that a new weighted average be computed after each purchase of inventory. Ending inventory is priced at the latest weighted average cost.

	Units	Unit Cost	Total Cost
Balance 1/1	1,200	$1	$1,200
Purchase 1/11	800	$3	$2,400
Balance	2,000	$1.80	$3,600
Sold 1/19	1,000	$1.80	$1,800
Balance	1,000	$1.80	$1,800
Purchase 1/30	600	$5	$3,000
Balance	1,600	$3.00	$4,800

121. **B.** Under the moving average method, Sanchez Corp. would price the next units sold at $3.00 per unit, the new weighted average.

122. **A.** With an estimated gross profit of 20%, cost of goods sold must be 80% of sales. Cost of goods sold is therefore $160,000 and can be added to the ending inventory of $10,000 to calculate the total available for sale at $170,000. With the total available for sale now known at $170,000, purchases can be backed into as follows:

Ending inventory	$10,000
Add cost of goods sold	+ $160,000
Total available for sale	$170,000
Minus beginning inventory	– $25,000
Purchases	$145,000

This calculation is used when purchases are not known. Sometimes the exam makes you work backward. If purchases were given, cost of goods sold would have been calculated the normal way as follows:

Beginning inventory	$25,000
Purchases	+ $145,000
Total available for sale	$170,000
Minus ending inventory	– $10,000
Cost of goods sold	$160,000

Chapter 26: Marketable Securities and Investments

123. **C.** I is correct. Under US GAAP, securities can be categorized as available for sale. Both debt and equity securities may be classified as available for sale if they do not meet the definition of either trading or held to maturity. III is correct. Under US GAAP, securities can be categorized as trading. Trading securities are those securities, both debt and equity, that are bought and held principally for the purpose of selling them in the near future. IV is correct. Under US GAAP, securities can be categorized as held to maturity. Investments in debt securities are classified as "held to maturity" only if the corporation has the positive intent and ability to hold these securities to maturity.

124. **B.** I is correct. Both debt and equity securities may be classified as available for sale. If the equity securities are not purchased for a quick resale and if the debt securities are not to be held to maturity, they will be classified as available for sale. II is correct. Both debt and equity securities may be classified as trading. If the securities are purchased for immediate resale, they are classified as trading securities.

125. **C.** Unrealized holding gains or losses reported in the income statement result from mark-to-market changes of trading securities from one period to the next. Changes in the market value of available-for-sale securities are reported in accumulated other comprehensive income. For Year 1, Tilly Company would report an unrealized holding loss of $50,000 computed as follows: Year 1 market value: $100,000 – cost: $150,000. The trading securities themselves would be marked to market and reported on the Year 1 balance sheet in the amount of $100,000. For Year 2, the $100,000 balance would be marked to market again, and increased to $155,000, the market value of the trading securities as of the end of Year 2. Therefore, Tilly would report a $55,000 unrealized gain in its income statement for Year 2.

126. **B.** The bonds will be marked to market and valued by Fords Inc. at $1,030,000. Although the bonds cost $800,000 and have a fair value of $1,000,000, the bonds are classified as trading securities because

the facts indicate that the bonds are held for the purpose of selling them within the operating cycle. Therefore, the bonds are considered trading securities. Trading securities are reported at fair value on the balance sheet.

127. **B.** II is correct. Losses on available-for-sale securities are reported in other comprehensive income. Unless the loss on available-for-sale securities is permanent, it should not be reported on the income statement.

128. **D.** Since the loss on an available-for-sale security was considered temporary in Year 1, the security would be written down to fair value. The unrealized holding loss would be reported in other comprehensive income and not on the income statement.

129. **B.** In Year 1, the security would have been written down to fair value. The unrealized holding loss would be reported in other comprehensive income. In Year 2, the unrealized holding loss would be removed from accumulated other comprehensive income and recognized in earnings as a realized loss on the Year 2 income statement, since the decline is classified as other than temporary in Year 2. This Year 2 entry has no effect on available-for-sale assets but decreases net income by the amount of the loss now considered permanent.

130. **B.** I is correct. With regard to securities classified as available for sale, unrealized losses considered temporary are reported in other comprehensive income. III is correct. With regard to securities classified as available for sale, unrealized gains are reported in other comprehensive income rather than the income statement. II is incorrect. With regard to securities classified as available for sale, unrealized losses considered other than temporary are reported on the income statement.

131. **D.** Loss on early extinguishment of bonds would be reported on the income statement, not comprehensive income, as a component of continuing operations. Realized gains on available-for-sale securities are reported on the income statement. Unrealized losses on available-for-sale securities are reported in other comprehensive income.

132. **B.** II is correct. The investment in investee is adjusted to fair value, marked to market at the end of the accounting period.

133. **B.** The cost (adjusted for fair value) method is used when accounting for investments in which the investor does not have the ability to exercise significant influence over the operating and financial policies of the investee. This is assumed to be the case when the investor own less than 20% of the outstanding voting stock of the investee. Under this method, the investment account is not adjusted, except for "marking to market" the investment at the end of the accounting period. Dividends received by the investor are reported as dividend income. Any income earned, or loss incurred by the investee company, has no impact on the investor's investment account. The equity method is used when the investor is able to exercise significant influence over the investee, which is assumed when the investor has between a 20% and 50% ownership of the investee company. Under this method, the investment account is adjusted for the investor's pro-rata share of the investee's net income or loss, pro-rata share of dividends declared/distributed by the investee, and for other adjustments that may be necessary to account for differentials in the cost of the investment versus the book value of the underlying net assets of the investee company (e.g. depreciation of fixed asset fair value excesses included in the investment cost). In this question, Koontz initially had a 15% ownership in Lamme, which would otherwise require use of the cost (adjusted for fair value) method to account for the Lamme investment. However, on December 31, Year 5, Koontz purchased an additional 10,000 shares of Lamme, which, at that time, gave Koontz a cumulative 35% investment in Lamme (15% of Lamme's 50,000 shares = 7,500 + 10,000 additional shares purchased = cumulative 17,500 shares, which divided by the total 50,000 shares outstanding equals a 35% investment). Thus, this additional purchase of shares triggers use of the equity method effective December 31, Year 5. Current accounting standards (in accordance with ASC Topic 323, "Investments – Equity Method and Joint Ventures"), state that when an investment qualifies for use of the equity method as a result of an increase in the level of ownership interest or degree of influence, the equity method investor should add the cost of acquiring the additional interest in the investee to the current basis of the investor's previously held interest and adopt the equity method of accounting as of the date the investment becomes qualified for equity method accounting. Retroactive adjustment of the investment is no longer required. And, if the investment (prior to qualifying for equity method accounting) had been reported as an available-for-sale equity security, any unrealized holding gain or loss previously recognized for that investment (in other comprehensive income) must be recognized through

earnings at the date the investment becomes qualified for equity method accounting treatment. Since Koontz would not be required to apply equity method accounting until December 31 (when its investment in Lamme increased from 15% to 35%), Koontz would not recognize any of Lamme's $80,000, Year 5 reported earnings in its investment account. Additionally, since there was no unrealized holding gain or loss previously reported (for this investment) in other comprehensive income, no investment or earnings adjustments would need to be made. Accordingly, in its December 31, Year 5 balance sheet, Koontz would report an investment account balance of $275,000 ($100,000, January 2, Year 5 purchase + $175,000, December 31, Year 5 purchase).

134. **D.** I is incorrect. Cash dividend received under the equity method is not income, but it reduces the carrying value of the investment account. II is incorrect. Stock dividends are never income under either the cost or equity method. Stock dividends received by the investee result in a memo entry only. No journal entry is made for the receipt of additional shares of stock under the equity (or cost) method. The new shares will serve to reduce the basis per share.

135. **B.** As a 4% owner, Woodley would use the cost method to account for its investment in Jensen. Under the cost method, dividend income is equal to the number of shares times the cash dividend per share. At the time the cash dividend is paid, Woodley has 6,000 shares × $3 per share = $18,000.

136. **C.** Under the equity method, adjustments to the investment account result from the differences between the price paid for the investment and the book value of the investee's net assets acquired. The premium paid for the investment is calculated as follows:

Total book value of the investee's net assets	$900,000
Percent acquired	× 40%
Book value of the 40% of the investee's net assets acquired	$360,000
Cost to acquire the 40% of the investee's net assets	− $400,000
Premium paid above book value for the 40% ownership	($40,000)

The $40,000 premium paid needs to be amortized based on what caused the premium in the first place. The facts indicate that there is undervalued equipment on the books of Clark Corp. and that alone is

the rationale for the premium paid of $40,000 for the investment. Therefore:

Undervalued equipment	
$100,000 × 40% acquired	$40,000
5-year life of equipment	÷ 5 years
Annual amortization for 5 years	$8,000

The $8,000 of amortization relating to the undervalued equipment needs to recorded each year for 5 years and will serve to reduce investee earnings of Clark Corp. each year. Therefore, for the next 5 years, each time Clark Corp. reports earnings, Rochelle Corp. will recognize 40% of those earnings but then subtract $8,000 of amortization. The calculation of investee earnings net of amortization for Year 13 for Rochelle Corp. is as follows:

Investee earnings	
$150,000 × 40% ownership	$60,000
Less annual amortization of undervalued equipment	−$8,000
Equity method investment income	$52,000

137. **A.** I is correct. Singer would record the additional cost of goods sold associated with the undervalued beginning inventory by debiting investment income and crediting the investment in the Kaufman account.

138. **B.** Transfers of securities between investment categories are accounted for at market (fair) value. If market (fair) value is less than the security's carrying amount at the date of transfer, it does not matter whether the decline was temporary or permanent.

139. **C.** Typically investor ownership of an investee company of less than 20% requires use of the cost (adjusted for fair value) method to account for the investment, unless evidence regarding the ability to exercise significant influence over the investee's operating and financial policies exists. In cases where evidence supports the investor's ability to exercise significant influence over the investee company, the investor would forgo use of the cost (adjusted for fair value) method and, instead, use the equity method to account for its investment in the investee company. Use of equity method accounting (and the ability to exercise significant influence) is typically implied when the investor company has a more than 20% but less than 50% ownership interest in the investee company. However, the ability to exercise significant influence is the overriding criterion in determining whether or not to use the equity method. In this question, even though Henry only has a 10% interest in Einhorn, evidence pointing to

Henry's ability to exercise significant influence over Einhorn's operating and financial policies is apparent in that Henry is the single largest shareholder in Einhorn, and Henry's officers represent a majority of Einhorn's board of directors. Thus, Henry would use the equity method to account for its investment in Einhorn. Under this method, the investor's initial investment is adjusted for its pro-rate share of investee net income or loss, its pro-rata share of dividends declared and/or paid by the investee company, and for other adjustments that may be necessary to account for differentials in the cost of the investment versus the book value of the underlying net assets of the investee company (e.g., depreciation of fixed asset fair value excesses included in the investment cost). Thus, Henry's computation of its investment in Einhorn as of December 31, Year 5, is as follows:

Initial investment:	$400,000
Pro-rata share of Einhorn's net income	
	+ $50,000 ($500,000 × 10%)
Pro-rata share of dividends paid by Einhorn	− $15,000 ($150,000 × 10%)
	$435,000

Henry would, therefore, report a $435,000 balance in its investment in Einhorn account at December 31, Year 5. Note that under the equity method, increases/decreases in the investment account mirror changes in the investee's equity (retained earnings), at the investor's pro-rata share of those changes.

Chapter 27: Fixed Assets, Intangibles, and Nonmonetary Exchanges

140. B.

$4,000 × present value of annuity 4.18	$16,720
Cash down payment	+ $2,000
Installation cost	+ $1,000
Total	$19,720

141. C. Under IFRS, when an asset is acquired that consists of major components, and those major components provide significantly different economic benefits, or have varying estimated useful lives that differ from the asset as a whole, the cost of the asset must be allocated to the components and those components depreciated separately. Accordingly, annual depreciation under IFRS would be equal to $9,125,000, computed as follows:

Component	Allocable Cost	Useful Life	Depreciation
Frame	$80,000,000	20 years	$4,000,000
Engine	$50,000,000	16 years	$3,125,000
Interior	$20,000,000	10 years	$2,000,000
			$9,125,000

142. C. I is correct. The cost of shipping the machine to Lavroff's plant should be capitalized since the capitalized cost of the asset should include all costs that are reasonable and necessary to get the asset in the condition for its intended use. II is correct. The cost of readying the machine for its intended use should be capitalized since the cost of the machine should include all costs that are reasonable and necessary to get the asset in the condition or location for its intended use.

143. D. When the buildings were revalued in Year 1, the $150,000 revaluation gain was booked to other comprehensive income as a revaluation surplus. Under IFRS, if a revalued asset becomes impaired, the impairment is recorded by first reducing any revaluation surplus to zero, with further impairment losses reported on the income statement. In this problem, the buildings were impaired on December 31, Year 2, because the $900,000 carrying value of the buildings exceeded the $720,000 recoverable amount. The $180,000 impairment loss is recorded by first reducing to zero the $150,000 revaluation surplus from the Year 1 revaluation and then recording the $30,000 remaining impairment loss on the income statement.

144. B. The original acquisition price of the land was $80,000 in Year 3. At the end of Year 3, the carrying amount was revalued to $70,000. This would result in a loss on the income statement of $10,000. Under the revaluation model of IFRS, the reversal of a revaluation is recognized in profit or loss. For this reason, $10,000 represents an increase in profit. If a revaluation results in an increase in value, however, it should be credited to other comprehensive income. For this reason, the increase in value of $5,000 ($85,000 − $80,000) will be recognized as other comprehensive income.

145. B. II is correct. Fixed assets can be revalued upward from the asset's carrying amount if the reporting framework is IFRS. Under IFRS, if an individual fixed asset is revalued, then the entire class of fixed assets to which that asset belongs must be revalued. Individual fixed assets cannot be revalued alone.

146. **A.** I is correct. When replacing an asset in which the cost of the old asset is known, replace the old carrying value with the capitalized cost of the new asset.

147. **A.** I is correct. When the cost of the old asset is unknown *and* the asset's life is extended rather than improved, reduce accumulated depreciation rather than capitalize the cost. Reducing accumulated depreciation will increase the book value of the asset class; remember, in the question, the carrying value of the specific asset was unknown.

148. **B.** II is correct. When extraordinary repairs merely extend the life of an asset without increasing the usefulness, the preferred treatment is to reduce accumulated depreciation.

149. **D.** I is correct. When acquiring land to be held as a future plant site, the cost of title insurance is capitalized, not charged to expense. II is correct. When acquiring land to be held as a future plant site, legal fees paid for recording ownership (recording the deed) are capitalized rather than expensed. III is correct. When acquiring land to be held as a future plant site, the cost of tearing down (razing) the old structure to clear the land for future development is capitalized rather than expensed. The amount to capitalize would be the cost to remove the old structure less any proceeds received from selling the scrap.

150. **B.** II is correct. Excavating costs are not land costs but building costs. While sometimes it's enough to know whether a cost is capitalized or expensed, in this question the candidate needs to know where to capitalize the cost. Therefore, excavating costs (costs of digging a hole) is a building cost and should be capitalized to the new building and will eventually be depreciated as part of the building.

151. **C.** I is correct. Land improvements are recorded as a separate asset from land and can include fence, water systems, sidewalks, landscaping, and paving. II is correct. While costs that are capitalized as part of the asset "land" cannot be depreciated, improvements to land such as sidewalks and fences are capitalized in the land improvements account and can be depreciated.

152. **D.** III is correct. The cost of the installation of a septic system is a land improvement. The septic system can then be depreciated (the land itself cannot be depreciated).

153. **B.** A gain or loss on the sale of an asset is the difference between the proceeds received from the sale less the asset's net book value (also referred to as its net carrying value). If the proceeds exceed the net

book value, a gain results; if the proceeds are less than the net book value, then a loss results. Thus, the higher the net book value, the lower the gain or the higher the loss. Conversely, the lower the net book value, the higher the gain or the lower the loss. An asset's net book value is equal to its cost less accumulated depreciation. In the second year of a 5-year useful life asset (which is when the asset is sold in this question), the sum of the years' digits method would have produced a lower amount of accumulated depreciation than the double declining balance method and, therefore, a higher net book value. Consequently, with a higher net book value, the sum of the years' digits method would produce a lower gain (have a decreasing effect on a gain) and a higher loss (have an increasing effect on a loss).

154. **A.** The corporation spent $100,000 for land and building. The land was recently appraised for $20,000, but the building was appraised for $120,000. Since only $100,000 is spent, pro rating is needed as follows:

Land	$20,000 / $140,000	14.28%
Building	$120,000 / $140,000	85.71%
Land	14.28% × $100,000	$14,280
Building	85.71 × 100,000	$85,710

155. **D.** The $1,000,000 total cost ($800,000 cash + $200,000 mortgage) should be allocated to the building and the land separately. There is no other information with which to perform this allocation other than the property tax assessment. So 65% of the $1,000,000, or $650,000, is allocated to the building.

156. **C.** I is correct. Under IFRS, property where the intent is to earn income on the property through renting it out should be classified as investment property. II is correct. Under IFRS, property where the intent is to sell the property and make income should be classified as investment property.

157. **B.** Under IFRS, investment property is defined as land and buildings held by an entity to earn rentals or for capital appreciation. Therefore, the amount of total investment property is $4,000,000 land held for rental + $3,000,000 buildings held for capital appreciation = $7,000,000.

158. **C.** I is correct. Under IFRS, if the entity elects the fair value method, no depreciation expense will be taken. II is correct. Gains and losses from fair value adjustments on assets classified as investment property are reported on the income statement. However, under IFRS, revaluation gains on fixed assets *not* classified as investment property are reported in other comprehensive income.

159. **A.** I is correct. Under IFRS, gains from investment property resulting from fair value adjustments are reported on the income statement. Note that US GAAP does *not* have a separate classification for assets known as investment property.

160. **B.** II is correct. Delays related to permit processing or inspections are ordinary delays and interest cost would be capitalized.

161. **A.** I is correct. Interest costs incurred during the construction period of machinery to be used by a firm as a fixed asset should be capitalized as part of the cost of acquiring the fixed asset.

162. **D.** I is incorrect. Do *not* capitalize interest on loans to construct inventory. II is incorrect. Do *not* capitalize interest on loans to buy inventory. Only capitalize interest if you are borrowing money to construct a building for use in the business, a factory, a warehouse, or an office building.

163. **D.** I is incorrect. Do *not* capitalize interest (before or) after construction if the asset is built to use. Only capitalize the interest during construction. II is incorrect. Do *not* capitalize interest before or after construction if the asset is built to sell. Only capitalize interest during construction.

164. **B.** If borrowings are not tied specifically to the construction of an asset, the weighted average interest rate for the other borrowings of the company should be used. The weighted average interest rate is calculated as follows:

($5,000,000 / $12,000,000) × 7%	2.9%
($7,000,000 / $12,000,000) × 10%	+ 5.8%
Weighted average interest rate	8.7%

If there was debt tied to the specific construction loan, the rate of that construction loan would be used.

165. **C.** I is correct. Total interest cost for the period is a required disclosure. II is correct. The amount of capitalized interest for the period, if any, is a required disclosure.

166. **B.** II is correct. The amount of capitalized interest is the lower of actual interest cost incurred or computed capitalized interest. Compute the capitalized interest by multiplying the appropriate interest rate by the weighted average accumulated expenditures. If the weighted average calculated amount does not exceed the total interest cost incurred, the amount calculated is capitalized.

167. **A.** Capitalized interest equals the smaller of the total interest cost incurred versus interest computed on the weighted average amount of accumulated expenditures. In this case, total interest incurred is $62,000 from the construction loan plus $22,000 from other sources, a total of $84,000. The capitalized interest is limited to the lower of the $84,000 total interest cost incurred versus the $37,000 interest calculated based on the weighted average of accumulated expenditures.

168. **B.** For straight line depreciation:

Step 1: Calculate depreciable base	$75,000 cost − $5,000 salvage = $70,000 depreciable base
Step 2: Divide	$70,000 / 7 years = $10,000 per year
Step 3: Multiply	annual depreciation × 9/12 = $7,500 (April 1 through December 31)

For US GAAP purposes, ignore the asset's useful life for tax purposes when given in the problem.

169. **B.** If the asset is purchased in January, a full year of depreciation is taken. Using sum of the years' digits, an asset with a 5-year life, simply add 5 + 4 + 3 + 2 + 1 = 15 years. In Year 1, 5/15 × $45,000 = depreciation expense for Year 1 of $15,000. Remember to deduct the salvage value from the cost when using SYD.

170. **D.** Using sum of the years' digits, an asset with a 5-year life, add 5 + 4 + 3 + 2 + 1 = 15 years. In Year 1, 5/15 × $45,000 = depreciation expense for Year 1 of $15,000. At the end of Year 1, the carrying value is $35,000. Cost minus accumulated depreciation equals carrying value. In Year 2, depreciation expense is 4/15 × $45,000 or $12,000. $12,000 plus $15,000 = $27,000 total accumulated depreciation thus far in Year 2. Carrying value on December 31, Year 2, is calculated as follows:

Cost	$50,000
Accumulated depreciation	− $27,000
Carrying value	$23,000

171. **D.** Additions made to existing assets are capitalized; therefore, the cost of the dispersing component that was added and attached to the existing assembly line machinery would be capitalized. The cost of installing the dispersing component is also capitalized because it was necessary to get the component ready for its intended use. Costs that increase the quality or quantity of machinery output should also be capitalized, even if those costs do not increase

the useful life of the asset. Thus, the $16,000 cost incurred to rearrange and overhaul the assembly line would also be capitalized as it helped increase the productivity and efficiency of the assembly line. Accordingly, a total of $152,000 would be capitalized: $110,000 (dispersing component addition) + $26,000 (installation cost) + $16,000 (rearrange and overhaul cost).

172. **D.** Depreciable assets should not be depreciated below salvage value under any depreciation method. I is incorrect. Under the sum of the years' digits depreciation method, salvage value is subtracted in the first year to arrive at the asset's depreciable base. II is incorrect. Under the double declining balance method, the salvage value is *not* subtracted in the first year to arrive at depreciable base, but instead the asset is depreciated using the full cost as the depreciable base. The double declining balance method is unique because each year's depreciation expense serves to decline the asset's depreciable base. When the asset's depreciable base declines low enough to equal the salvage value, the salvage value limits the amount of depreciation taken in the *final* year. III is incorrect. Under the straight line method (similar in this regard to the sum of the years' digits depreciation method), salvage value is subtracted in the first year to arrive at the asset's depreciable base.

173. **B.** The units of production method of depreciation is calculated based on usage rather than time. Total estimated usage is 200,000 miles. The rate of depreciation is $0.30 per mile and is calculated as follows:

cost of $70,000 – $10,000 salvage value = $60,000 depreciable base

depreciable base amount of $60,000 ÷ total estimated usage of 200,000 miles = 0.30 per mile

Depreciation every year will therefore be 30 cents per mile driven under the units of production method. For Year 1, 12,000 miles were driven, so depreciation for Year 1 is calculated as follows:

12,000 miles driven × 0.30 = $3,600 of depreciation expense should be taken for Year 1

Year 2 depreciation will be 0.30 times the number of miles driven in Year 2.

174. **A.** I is correct. When calculating depletion, the asset's depletion base is the cost to purchase the property minus the estimated net residual value.

175. **D.** I is incorrect. Under US GAAP, an impairment loss is reported as a component of income from continuing operations before income taxes unless

the impairment loss is related to discontinued operations. In the event that the impairment loss is related to discontinued operations, the impairment loss would *not* be shown before tax but rather after tax. II is incorrect. Impairment losses reduce the carrying value of an asset due to a decline in the asset's fair value below book value, *not* due to a decline in book value below fair value. When an asset declines in value below carrying or book value, an impairment loss occurs and needs to be recorded in the income statement.

176. **D.** I is incorrect. Fees to acquire a patent and other intangible assets from third parties are capitalized and amortized over the shorter of the patent's remaining legal life or estimated life using the straight line amortization method. Legal fees and registration fees associated with patents are also capitalized. II is correct. Under US GAAP, costs incurred to internally develop a patent are expensed as research and development. US GAAP requires research and development costs to be expensed although certain costs like consulting fees, design costs, and registration fees associated with an internally generated patent are capitalized. Notice that the manner of acquisition of intangible assets (e.g., patents) is a factor in determining whether the intangible asset is capitalized or expensed. Intangible assets that are purchased from third parties are capitalized. Intangible assets that are internally developed are expensed as research and development. III is incorrect. Only costs associated with a successful patent defense are capitalized. Costs associated with an unsuccessful patent defense are expensed.

177. **A.** As of the current year, it has been determined that cash flows will be derived from the trademark indefinitely. Intangible assets with indefinite useful lives are not amortized, but rather are assessed and tested for impairment at least annually. If the asset is determined to be impaired (e.g., its carrying value > its fair value), the difference is reported/recognized as an impairment loss.

178. **A.** I is correct. All research and development costs are expensed as incurred under US GAAP, unless they have an alternate future use outside of the research and development. In that case capitalization of the cost may be appropriate. II in incorrect. Under IFRS, research-related costs are expensed, but costs that qualify as development costs are capitalized.

179. **A.** I is correct. Costs incurred for developing and maintaining goodwill are expensed.

180. C. I is correct. Intangible assets with infinite lives such as acquired goodwill should be capitalized but not amortized, because under US GAAP assets with infinite lives such as goodwill are not amortized but tested for impairment. II is correct. Intangible assets with finite lives such as patents, franchises, and covenants not to compete should be capitalized and amortized. To amortize an intangible asset, it must have a finite life. US GAAP recognizes the fact that the value of intangible assets eventually disappears. Therefore, the cost of each type of intangible asset with a finite life is amortized over the period estimated to be benefited.

181. B. II is correct. Under IFRS, intangible assets can be reported under either the cost or revaluation (fair value) model. Under the revaluation method, intangible assets are initially recognized at cost, and then marked to market, and revalued to fair value each reporting period. It is important to note that only intangible assets that are traded with active market prices may be valued using the revaluation model. This model requires that gains and losses on revaluation be recorded in other comprehensive income. I is incorrect. US GAAP does not permit the revaluation of intangible assets under any circumstances.

182 A. Legal fees and other costs associated with registering a patent are capitalized. Research and development costs are expensed under US GAAP. If later on costs are incurred to successfully defend the patent, those costs would be capitalized as well.

183. D. I is incorrect. With regard to software that is to be used internally, all costs incurred up to the preliminary project state are expensed. Capitalize costs incurred after the "preliminary project state." Therefore, not all costs associated with the development of internal use software are expensed. II is incorrect. With regard to software that is to be sold, leased, or licensed before technological feasibility is established, computer software development costs are expensed as research and development. Once technological feasibility is established, computer software costs are capitalized; therefore, not all costs of computer software to be sold to customers are expensed.

184. C. While the early costs associated with computer software development are expensed as research and development, once technological feasibility is established, computer software costs are capitalized. Therefore, the costs that would not be expensed as research and development would include the production and packaging costs for the first month's

sales and producing product masters after technological feasibility has been established. The costs that would not be considered research and development would include the following:

Production and packaging costs for the first month's sales	$72,000
Producing product masters after technological feasibility	+ $180,000
Total	$252,000

185. D. Software development costs are expensed as research and development even if contracted out to a third party. The costs incurred in connection with preproduction prototypes are expensed as research and development. In addition, testing in search for new products is expensed as research and development under US GAAP. Quality control is not considered research and development, but would be capitalized rather than expensed. The amounts charged to research and development would include the following:

Research and development costs contracted out to third parties	$40,000
Design production and testing of preproduction prototypes	+ $120,000
Testing in search for new products	+ $25,000
Total research and development expense	$185,000

186. B. The intangible asset franchise is initially recorded as a debit to franchise in the amount of $90,000. The cost will be amortized over 20 years on a straight line basis, $4,500 per year. Scotti reports the 4% of sales paid to Subway annually as an operating expense each year. On December 31, Year 13, the intangible asset franchise has a balance of:

Cost	$90,000
Less amortization	– $4,500
Carrying amount at December 31, Year 13	$85,500

187. A. Step 1 is to compare the carrying value, $500,000, with the undiscounted cash flows of $498,000. Step 1 results in an impairment loss because the current carrying amount of $500,000 is higher than the undiscounted cash flows of $498,000. Step 2 takes place once impairment is imminent; the impairment loss is based on discounted cash flows (fair value):

Discounted or present value of future cash flows	$485,000
Carrying value of asset	– $500,000
Dollar amount of impairment loss	($15,000)

The dollar amount of the impairment is based on the discounted cash flows. Notice that both the undiscounted cash flows and the discounted cash flows need to be known. For an impairment loss to be determined and recorded, the undiscounted cash flows are used first to determine if there even is an impairment. Then if there is an impairment (based on comparing the undiscounted cash flows to the carrying amount), the discounted cash flows are used to determine the amount of impairment. Note that using the discounted cash flows to compare with the carrying amount will make the impairment loss larger than when the undiscounted cash flows are used.

188. **C.** Under Accounting Standards Codification (ASC) Topic 985, which addresses the accounting for costs of computer software to be sold, leased, or otherwise marketed, software costs are capitalized from the time technological feasibility has been established for the software product until the product is available for general release to customers. Technological feasibility is deemed to be established when either a detailed program design is complete or a working model has been created. Amortization of these costs begins when the product is available for general market release. The amortization rate is the *greater of*: (1) the ratio of current gross software product revenues to total current and anticipated future gross software product revenues, *or* (2) the straight line rate using the estimated economic life of the software product (computed as: 1/economic life × 100%). At the balance sheet date, capitalized software costs must be reported at the *lower of* unamortized cost or net realizable value. In order to determine the percentage of original capitalized cost Plant should report in its December 31, Year 5, balance sheet, the appropriate amortization rate must first be determined. The ratio of current revenues to expected or anticipated current and future revenues is given in the question as 20%, and the straight line rate can be computed as 10% (1/10 × 100%). Therefore, Plant's amortization rate for the capitalized software costs would be 20%, the greater of the two. The percentage of these costs unamortized can then be calculated as: 100% − 20% = 80%. Since the net realizable value (60%) is lower than the unamortized percentage (80%), the percentage of the original capitalized cost that Plant would report as the net amount on its December 31, Year 5, balance is 60%.

189. **C.** I is correct. Accounts receivable is a monetary asset. Monetary assets include cash and receivables. II is correct. A contra account is classified as monetary or nonmonetary based upon the classification of the related account. Allowance for doubtful accounts is an example of a contra account and is considered monetary because the asset that its contra to, accounts receivable, is monetary.

190. **C.** I is correct. Equipment is a nonmonetary asset. Nonmonetary assets fluctuate in value; they are not fixed like cash and receivables are. Nonmonetary assets include equipment, buildings, inventory, common and preferred stock investments, patents, and trademarks. II is correct. A contra account is classified as monetary or nonmonetary based upon the classification of the related account. Equipment is nonmonetary; therefore, accumulated depreciation-equipment is nonmonetary also. A contra account is classified as monetary or nonmonetary based upon the classification of the related account.

191. **B.** Under US GAAP, a nonmonetary exchange is recognized at fair value of the assets exchanged unless fair value is not determinable.

192. **B.** In nonmonetary exchanges that have commercial substance, gain is recognized for the difference in value between the fair value and book value of the asset given up. Since the exchange has commercial substance, Drexel's gain is calculated as follows:

Fair value of the asset given up	$60,000
Book value of the asset given up	− $52,000
Gain on nonmonetary exchange	$8,000

193. **C.** When a nonmonetary transaction has commercial substance, gains and losses are recognized immediately based on the difference between the asset's fair value and book value at the time of exchange. Since the exchange has commercial substance, the entire gain is recognized by Hayley Corp. despite the payment of $5,000 in cash to Dylan Corp. For Hayley Corp., gain on the asset given up is calculated as follows:

Fair value	$95,000
Subtract book value	
(cost $130,000 − accumulated	
depreciation $75,000)	− $55,000
Gain	$40,000

194. **D.** I is incorrect. Under US GAAP, losses on nonmonetary exchanges are recognized immediately even if the transaction lacks commercial substance, the rule of conservatism. II is incorrect. Under US GAAP, losses on nonmonetary exchanges are recognized immediately whether or not the exchange has commercial substance, the rule of conservatism. An

exchange is said to have commercial substance if the amount and timing of future cash flows change as a result of the exchange.

195. B. II is correct. Under US GAAP, nonmonetary exchanges that lack commercial substance could possibly result in a portion of the gain being deferred. If the exchange is said to lack commercial substance and the amount of cash received in the transaction is less than 25% of the total consideration received, then a proportional amount of the gain is recognized.

196. D. Since the cash flows will significantly change, the exchange has commercial substance; therefore, the fair value method is used to calculate gain or loss. The fair value of the equipment is $380,000 less the equipment's book value of $400,000, which equals a loss of $20,000. The payment of cash of $5,000 does not enter into the calculation of gain or loss.

197. C. Under US GAAP, the equipment's fair value of $380,000 plus the cash paid of $5,000 equals the basis of the new warehouse $385,000. Exchanges that have commercial substance use the fair value method.

198. A. I is correct. Under IFRS, nonmonetary exchanges are characterized as exchanges of similar assets and exchanges of dissimilar assets. Under IFRS, exchanges of dissimilar assets are treated in the same manner as exchanges having commercial substance under US GAAP. Exchanges of dissimilar assets under IFRS are regarded as exchanges that generate revenue. Exchanges of similar assets under IFRS are not regarded as exchanges that generate revenue and no gains are recognized.

199. A. I is correct. The test for impairment of long-lived assets with finite lives consists of two steps. First, the asset is assessed for recoverability. If the asset's carrying amount is not recoverable (e.g., the sum of the undiscounted cash flows to be derived from future use or disposition of the asset is less than the asset's carrying amount), an impairment loss may be recognized, and the second step of the test needs to be conducted. In this test, the carrying amount of the asset is compared to its fair value. If the fair value is less than the carrying amount, an impairment loss is recognized for the difference. However, if the fair value exceeds the carrying amount (or if the carrying amount is less than the fair value), no impairment loss is recognized. Therefore, II is not correct. It is important to note that if in the first step of the test, the asset is determined to be recoverable (e.g., the sum of the undiscounted cash flows derived from

future use or disposition of the asset is greater than the asset's carrying amount), no potential impairment exists and, therefore, the second step in the test is irrelevant and does not need to be conducted.

200. C. I is correct. When testing an asset for impairment that is held for disposal as a part of a discontinued operation, the asset's carrying amount is first compared to the undiscounted cash flows to see if any impairment has occurred. II is correct. When testing an asset for impairment that is held for disposal as part of a discontinued operation, if an impairment has occurred, the discounted cash flows (fair value) is compared to the asset's carrying amount. The calculation of impairment loss on assets held for disposal is the same as the calculation of impairment loss on assets held for use.

201. C. The impairment loss to be recognized on long-lived assets with finite lives consists of two steps. First, the asset is assessed for recoverability. If the asset's carrying value is not recoverable (e.g., the sum of the *undiscounted* cash flows to be derived from future use or disposition of the asset is less than the asset's carrying value), an impairment loss may be recognized, and the second step of the test needs to be conducted. In this test, the carrying value of the asset is compared to its fair value (or market value). If the fair value (market value) is less than the carrying value, an impairment loss is recognized for the difference. In this question, the *undiscounted* expected future cash flows = $150,000, which is less than the asset's carrying value of $160,000. This evidences a potential impairment, which now requires comparison of the asset's carrying value to its fair (market) value. Since the asset's fair (market) value of $135,000 is less than its carrying value ($160,000), the difference, or a $25,000 impairment loss, should be recognized/reported.

202. A. I is correct. Under US GAAP, no reversal of a fixed asset impairment loss is permitted when the asset is held for use. Under US GAAP, the reversal of impairment loss would be permitted only when the asset is held for sale.

Chapter 28: Payables, Contingencies, and Income Taxes

203. C. Current liabilities are obligations with maturities within 1 year or one operating cycle, whichever is longer.

204. B. II is correct. Under the matching principle, expenses are recognized when an entity's assets have no future economic benefit. The executive bonus of $25,000 to be paid in Year 6 was clearly earned in Year 5 and should be accrued as a current liability in Year 5.

205. **A.** I is correct. Under the net method, if payment is made after the discount period, a purchase discount lost account is debited. II is incorrect. Under the gross method, not the net method, would a purchase discount be debited if the buyer pays within the discount period.

206. **C.** Under the net method, the purchase is originally recorded net of the discount, so no actual account called "purchase discount" is ever recorded. Later, if payment is made within the discount period, no adjustment is made. If payment is made after the discount period, purchase discounts lost is debited. Under the gross method, accounts payable is recorded at the gross amount without regard to the discount.

207. **B.** Under the gross method, record the purchase and payable at the gross amount, without regard to the discount. When invoices are paid within the discount period, a purchase discount is recorded.

208. **A.** $10,000 base amount × 0.03 = $300; $300 × 3 employees = $900.

209. **C.** Since the note calls for quarterly payments, the first step is to compute annual interest and then divide by 4. Annual interest on $1,000,000 note × 0.09 = $90,000 interest annually. Divide $90,000 annual interest by 4 quarters, and quarterly interest is $22,500. The payment itself is $264,200. The next step is to subtract the quarterly interest from the payment, and the difference is the principal reduction for the first payment. The principal reduction is $241,700. Therefore, the new liability after the first payment is $758,300.

210. **A.** Normally, interest is imputed when no or an unreasonably low rate is stated. An exception exists for receivables and payables arising from transactions with customers or suppliers in the normal course of business when the trade terms do not exceed 1 year.

211. **B.** II is correct. The note payable is reported on the balance sheet at the net of the note payable face value less the unamortized discount.

212. **B.** II is correct. Loan origination fees deducted from the proceeds of the loan would be deferred and recognized over the life of the loan as additional

interest revenue similar to the treatment of bond discount amortization.

213. **C.** I is correct. Common debt covenants include limitations on how the borrowed money can be used. II is correct. Common debt covenants include minimum working capital requirements so there is always cash available to pay bondholders.

214. **B.** II is correct. Violation of a debt covenant results in technical default of the loan, and the lender could call the entire loan due and payable immediately. Normally the two sides get together to work out new terms and avoid default.

215. **C.** In order to compute the bonus amount, an equation must first be set up considering the facts contained in the question. Those facts state that the bonus (designated as B) equals 10% of income *after* deducting the bonus ($75,000 − B), but *before* considering income taxes. The income tax rate is, therefore, irrelevant, to this question's computation. Accordingly, the equation follows: B = 0.10 × ($75,000 − B). Solving for B, Hall should accrue a bonus for the CEO in the amount of $6,818.

216. **B.** Manufacturers or distributors who issue redeemable coupons with merchandise sold establish a liability for the coupons they *expect* to be redeemed in the future. This liability is established *at the time of sale* with the following journal entry: debit to promotion expense, credit to unredeemed coupon liability. Reimbursable handling costs for redeemable coupons adds to the promotion expense and liability. The liability is reduced when the manufacturer or distributor makes payments for the redeemable coupons with the following journal entry: debit to unredeemed coupon liability, credit to cash (or whatever has been liquidated to settle the obligation). In this question, Victor issues coupons in the amount of $550,000, but expects that 80% of those coupons will be redeemed. Victor, therefore, reports a liability for coupons to be redeemed in the amount of $440,000 ($550,000 × 80%). Victor also incurs a 5% handling cost in connection with the coupon redemption; thus, Victor incurs an additional liability of $22,000 ($440,000 × 5%). Victor also made payments for coupon redemption in the amount of $225,000. This reduces the liability for unredeemed coupons. Consequently, Victor should report a liability for unredeemed coupons at December 31, Year 1 in the amount of $237,000 ($440,000 + $22,000 − $225,000).

217. **C.** Manufacturers or distributors who extend warranty protection to their customers must establish

a warranty liability for the warranty costs they esti- mate or expect to incur in the future. The liability is established at the time of sale in accordance with the matching principle. The following journal entry is made when the warranty liability is established: debit to warranty expense, credit to warranty lia- bility. At the time the manufacturer or distributor settles warranty claims, it reduced the warranty liability, making the following journal entry: debit to warranty liability, credit to cash (or whatever has been liquidated to settle the warranty obligation). Blacker estimates warranty costs to be 3% within 12 months following the sale, and 6% in the sec- ond 12 months following the sale. Therefore, at December 31, Year 2, Blacker would have accrued warranty costs in connection with the Year 1 sales in the amount of $67,500 [750,000 × (3% first 12 months following the sale + 6% second 12 months following the sale)]. Additionally, as it relates to the Year 2 sales, Blacker would have accrued (at December 31, Year 2) an additional liability in the amount of $90,000 [$1,000,000 × (3% first 12 months following sale + 6% second 12 months following the sale)]. Blacker would also have reduced the warranty liability account for the $10,000 and $30,000 paid for actual warranty expenditures in Year 1 and Year 2, respectively. Thus, Blacker would report an estimated warranty liability at December 31, Year 2, in the amount of $117,500 ($67,500 + $90,000 − $10,000 − $30,000).

218. **A.** Accrued interest payable at December 31, Year 2, is interest that has been incurred by December 31, Year 2, that has not yet been paid by that date. Weis borrowed the $125,000 on November 1, Year 1, and the total interest payable is not due until March 31, Year 3, the note matu- rity date. Therefore, at December 31, Year 2, there should be 14 months (November 1, Year 1, to December 31, Year 2) of interest payable (accrued). Interest for Year 1 can be computed as follows: $125,000 × 10% × 2/12 (November 1, Year 1 through December 31, Year 1) = $2,083. Since inter- est is compounded annually, this unpaid (accrued) interest must be added to the $125,000 note prin- cipal when computing interest for Year 2. Accrued interest for Year 2 can, therefore, be calculated as ($125,000 + $2,083) × 10% = $12,708. Thus, at December 31, Year 2, Weis should have a liability for accrued interest reported on its balance sheet in the total amount of $14,791 ($2,083 from Year 1 + $12,708 from Year 2).

219. **D.** Catalina's liability for payroll taxes as of, and for the month ended, January, Year 1, is equal to $6,300 and includes amounts withheld from gross wages—federal income tax of $3,500 + employee FICA of $1,400 (7% × $20,000)—and also includes the employer (Catalina Corp.) FICA match of $1,400 (7% × $20,000). The employer FICA match ($1,400) is the only amount reported as payroll tax expense by Catalina Corp. It should be noted that if the question included amounts due for unemploy- ment taxes, those too, would be included in payroll tax expense and liability for payroll taxes.

220. **D.** The $450,000 accounts payable balance reported by Martinez at December 31, Year 1, is net of the $60,000 debit related to the advance payment for goods to be manufactured. That advance pay- ment should be reported as a current asset (not a reduction of a liability) and needs to be reclassified as such. Doing so would add $60,000 back to the accounts payable balance. The $50,000 of checks written to vendors on December 30, Year 1, but not mailed until January 10, Year 2, incorrectly reduced the accounts payable balance and should also be added back. That $50,000 reduction should not have been recorded until the checks were mailed on January 10, Year 2. Therefore, Martinez should report $560,000 ($450,000 + $60,000 + $50,000) as accounts payable in its December 31, Year 1, bal- ance sheet.

221. **B.** II is correct. Under US GAAP, provision for a loss contingency relating to pending or threatened litigation is recorded if the loss can be reasonably estimated.

222. **A.** I is correct. In the event that a range of proba- ble losses is given ($50,000 to $150,000), US GAAP requires that the best estimate of the loss be accrued.

223. **C.** I and II are correct. IFRS and US GAAP agree that a contingent liability should be recorded when the loss is probable and can be reasonably estimated.

224. **A.** I is correct. Under US GAAP, if no amount in the range is a better estimate than any other amount, the minimum amount in the range should be accrued, in this case $75,000, and a note describing the possibility of an additional $75,000 loss should be presented.

225. **B.** A contingent liability that is probable and esti- mable must be recognized. If all amounts within a range of values are equally likely, then the lowest amount in the range is the measurement amount. The final settlement was unknown prior to the

issuance of the financial statements, so a contingent liability of $400,000 should have been recorded.

226. **A.** I is correct. A contingent liability must be disclosed in its financial statements if sold with recourse. Stabler Corp. would need to disclose the contingency for the note at its face amount.

227. **C.** I is correct. Under US GAAP, an example of a loss contingency that would be recorded if probable would include a note discounted with recourse. A note endorsed "with recourse" means the endorser is liable if the maker of the note does not pay. This contingent liability should be disclosed. The amount of the loss contingency would include the full maturity value of the note. II is correct. Under US GAAP, an example of a loss contingency that would be recorded if probable would include tax disputes with a state taxing agency. If a range of losses is known, the best estimate should be accrued. If no estimate is better than any other, the minimum loss in the range should be accrued.

228. **D.** For a contingent loss to be accrued, the loss must be probable. This loss is only reasonably possible, so no loss is accrued but the possibility is disclosed. The disclosure should include the range of between $150,000 and $300,000 and indicate that the best estimate is $220,000. No amount should be accrued for losses that are only "reasonably possible."

229. **A.** I is correct. Under US GAAP, a gain contingency should be disclosed in the notes unless the likelihood of the gain being realized is remote. If there is a range, the full range of gain contingencies should be disclosed in the notes.

230. **D.** Gain contingencies are not reported as revenue until realized. Since the out-of-court settlement had not been accepted by the date of the issuance of the Year 2 financial statements, the gain should not be reported in Year 2. However, there should be adequate disclosure in the notes to the financial statements.

231. **B.** The likelihood of loss is reasonably possible and is disclosed on the financial statement notes, but it is not accrued on the financial statements, because it's not reasonably probable. The false claims lawsuit is a gain contingency, and gain contingencies are not recorded (conservatism), because to do so may cause recognition of revenue prior to its realization.

232. **C.** As of February 22, Year 5, Triano Corp.'s financial statements have not been issued and the actual amount of the final settlement is known. Therefore, the known amount should be accrued and disclosed

in Triano Corp.'s December 31, Year 4, financial statements as a "subsequent event." This is a recognized subsequent event because it relates to litigation that originated in Year 4.

233. **B.** II is correct. Using the installment method for tax purposes allows the deferral of taxable income until cash is collected. When cash is collected under the installment method, some of the cash collected represents profit from the sale and is taxed each year as it's collected (cash basis). For US GAAP, under the accrual basis the income would already be on the financial statements in the year of sale, but the income would not all be taxed in the year of sale, thus creating a future tax liability.

234. **D.** I is incorrect. Warranty expense results in deferred tax assets because with warranty expense, the expense is taken on the income statement first, when estimated, but warranty costs are not deductible on the tax return until paid in later years. II is incorrect. Bad debt expense results in a deferred tax asset rather than a deferred tax liability, because the expense for bad debts is taken on the income statement when first estimated, by the matching principle, in the year of sale. For tax purposes, however, the deduction cannot be taken until the debt is worthless.

235. **B.** IFRS provides that the netting of deferred tax assets and liabilities may only occur if the accounts relate to the same taxing authority and the entity has a legal right to offset taxes. A is incorrect. US GAAP currently requires that deferred tax assets and liabilities be classified as either current or noncurrent based on the classification of the related asset or liability for financial reporting. Accounting Standards Update (ASU) No. 2015-17, issued in November 2015, which is effective for annual periods beginning after December 31, 2016, for public business entities and after December 31, 2017, for all other business entities, requires that all deferred tax assets and liabilities be classified as noncurrent. C is incorrect. IFRS does permit the netting of deferred tax assets and liabilities as long as the accounts related to the same taxing authority and a legal right to offset taxes exists. D is incorrect. Deferred tax assets and liabilities currently require reporting as either current or noncurrent depending on the classification of the related asset or liability for financial reporting. However, ASU No. 2015-17, issued in November 2015 (and effective for annual periods beginning after December 31, 2016 and 2017, for public and other business entities, respectively), requires noncurrent classification.

236. C. I is correct. For tax purposes, prepaid insurance would be deducted in full in the year in which the policy was paid, Year 13. For financial statement purposes, the entire cost associated with prepaying the policy is recorded as an asset when paid in Year 13 and charged to expense at the end of Year 13, but only for those months that have expired in Year 13. The remaining insurance expense for book purposes is taken in Year 14. Therefore, the cost associated with prepaying an insurance policy in Year 13 would result in a deferred tax liability at December 31, Year 13. II is correct. Rent receivable represents income earned but not yet received in cash. While all the increase in rent receivable during Year 13 will be an increase to financial statement income, taxable income will increase in the following years when the receivables are collected. For the tax return, this will result in more taxable income in years subsequent to Year 13. Therefore, an increase in rent receivable during Year 13 results in a deferred tax liability at December 31, Year 13.

237. C. I is correct. Deferred income tax expense is equal to the change in deferred tax liability (or asset) on the balance sheet from the beginning of the year to the end of the year. II is correct. Current income tax expense is equal to the taxable income per the tax return multiplied by the current year tax rate. Current income tax payable represents the amount of taxes owed at the end of the current year. If no estimated tax payments were made, current income tax expense and the current income tax payable would be the same.

238. C. IFRS permits the netting of deferred tax assets and liabilities if those accounts relate to the same taxing authority/jurisdiction and the company has the legal right to offset taxes. Ginger has a $25,000 deferred tax asset related to Greece and in that same jurisdiction/taxing authority has a deferred tax liability of $15,000. Because Ginger also has the legal right to offset taxes, the company would report a net deferred tax asset of $10,000 in its December 31, Year 2, financial statements. The $10,000 deferred tax liability related to Italy cannot be netted and is presented as a deferred tax liability in the December 31, Year 2, financial statements. A is incorrect as it fails to offset the deferred tax asset and liability related to Greece. B is incorrect as it offsets a deferred tax asset and deferred tax liability related to two different taxing jurisdictions/authorities (Greece and Italy), and IFRS only permits netting/offsetting within the same taxing authority/jurisdiction. D is incorrect as there is reporting of a net deferred tax asset (related to Greece) and a deferred tax liability (related to Italy) in Ginger's December 31, Year 2, financial statements.

239. D. Fusco did not elect to forgo the carryback of its Year 2 operating loss. Thus, under net operating loss (NOL) carryback/carryforward rules, Fusco can carry back the NOL 2 years (earlier year first), and carry forward 20 years. Year 1 taxable income was $100,000, so Fusco can carry back $100,000 of the $200,000 Year 2 operating loss and claim an income tax refund/receivable in the amount of $40,000 ($100,000 × 40%). The remaining Year 2 $100,000 NOL can be carried forward to reduce Year 3 taxable income. Fusco, therefore, has a future tax benefit that should be reported in Year 2 as a deferred tax asset in the amount of $40,000 ($100,000 × 40%). No valuation of this deferred tax asset is required, since the question states that Fusco has determined it is more likely than not that it will realize the full benefit of any loss carryforward. In Year 3, after carrying forward the remaining $100,000 NOL from Year 2, Fusco has $300,000 of current taxable income (Year 3 income $400,000 − Year 2 NOL carryforward $100,000). Thus, Fusco has current income tax expense and liability for Year 3 in the amount of $120,000 ($300,000 × 40%). To that Fusco must add $40,000 of deferred tax expense since the deferred tax benefit is realized in Year 3 as a result of the $100,000 NOL carryforward. Consequently, Fusco would report total income tax expense for Year 3 in the amount of $160,000 ($120,000 current portion + $40,000 deferred portion). Journal entries Fusco would make in both Years 2 and 3 follow:

Year 2:

Debit to income tax refund/receivable	$40,000
Debit to deferred tax asset	$40,000
Credit to income tax benefit (expense)	$80,000

Year 3:

Debit to income tax expense (current)	$120,000
Credit to income taxes payable (current)	$120,000
Debit to income tax expense (deferred)	$40,000
Credit deferred tax asset	$40,000

240. A. Taxable income is calculated as follows:

Pretax financial statement income	$400,000
Add warranty costs	+ $35,000
Subtract revenue taxed in later year	− $60,000
Taxable income	$375,000
Current year tax rate	30%

241. B. The current portion of income tax expense is calculated by multiplying the taxable income of $375,000 calculated in the previous question times the current year tax rate of 30%. Therefore, the current year tax expense is:

taxable income × current year tax rate = current year tax expense

↓

$375,000 × 30% = $112,500

Note: The four estimated tax payments of $25,000 reduce the current income tax payable figure, but do not impact the current income tax expense. If the question had asked how much is the current income tax payable, the answer would have been $12,500, since the estimated payments reduce the current tax liability but not the current tax expense.

242. **B.** Deferred income tax expense is a plug figure and is calculated as the difference between the deferred tax asset and the deferred tax liability. The deduction in the future for warranty costs of $35,000 creates a deferred tax asset of $14,000 based on a 40% tax rate. Notice that the tax rate for Year 14 is used. The revenue of $60,000 to be taxed in the future creates a deferred tax liability in the amount of $24,000 based on the enacted 40% future tax rate. Creating both the $14,000 deferred tax asset and the $24,000 deferred tax liability results in a $10,000 deferred tax expense for Aragona Corp. at December 31, Year 13.

243. **C.** Total income tax expense on the income statement for Year 13 would include the current income tax expense of $112,500 plus the deferred income tax expense of $10,000 for a total income tax expense of $122,500.

244. **D.** The answer is $0 deferred income tax liability. The premium on the officer's life insurance (when the company is the beneficiary) as well as interest income on municipal bonds are permanent differences. Deferred taxes are not affected by permanent differences. Therefore, when the differences between financial statement income and taxable income are caused by permanent differences, deferred taxes will not result. Deferred taxes will be impacted only when the differences between financial statement income and taxable income are the result of temporary differences.

245. **B.** The only permanent difference between book income and taxable income is the interest income on state of Florida bonds. Municipal bond interest income is not taxable but is included in the financial statements as income. Therefore, the difference will never reverse, making municipal bond interest a permanent difference. The excess tax depreciation

of $8,000 is considered a deferred tax liability because it results in more tax later. The rent received in advance is taxable now, so it results in a deferred tax asset.

246. **D.** Since the financial statement income is provided, taxable income will need to be determined. The $125,000 financial statement income includes municipal bond interest that will never be taxable, so the $18,000 is subtracted. The excess tax depreciation of $8,000 is subtracted from the $125,000 financial statement income because although depreciation was taken, the facts indicate that an additional $8,000 of depreciation can be taken this year on the tax return. The rent received in advance was not includable in the $125,000 financial statement income, because it has not been earned yet. But rent received in advance is taxable when received. Therefore, the $14,000 gets added to financial statement income to arrive at the taxable income for Year 13. Taxable income for Year 13 is computed as follows:

Financial statement income	$125,000
Add rent received in advance	+ $14,000
Subtract excess depreciation	− $8,000
Subtract municipal bond interest income	− $18,000
Taxable income	$113,000

247. **A.** The current tax expense is computed by multiplying the current year's tax rate times the corporation's taxable income. Taxable income was determined in the prior question to be $113,000. Therefore, current year tax expense is calculated as follows: taxable income $113,000 × 35% tax rate = $39,550.

248. **D.** The current tax payable is computed by multiplying the current year's tax rate times the corporation's taxable income and then subtracting the estimated tax payments made during the year. Taxable income and current income tax expense were determined in the prior question to be $113,000 and $39,550 respectively. Therefore, current year tax payable is calculated as follows:

Current income tax expense	$39,550
Subtract estimated tax payments	− $36,000
Current income tax payable at December 31, Year 13	$3,550

249. **D.** At the end of Year 1, the deferred tax liability shown as a noncurrent deferred liability is based on the enacted tax rate (40%) expected to apply to annual income for Years 2, 3, and 4 (the years when the liability is expected to reverse).

250. D. Neither I nor II is correct. Recently issued Accounting Standards Update (ASU) No. 2015-17 requires that, for reporting purposes, all deferred income tax assets and liabilities be classified and presented as noncurrent. Therefore, neither the depreciation nor warranty expense differences should be reported as current.

251. B. Deferred tax liabilities (and/or assets) are recognized for the estimated future tax effects of temporary differences. A temporary difference results when the GAAP basis and the tax basis of an asset or liability differ. Differences in these two bases arise when items of income and/or expense are recognized in different periods under GAAP and under the tax code. In this question, Trevellyan received $20,000 cash in Year 1 that was recognized as income for book purposes, but $12,000 of that will not be recognized for tax purposes (and taxed) until Year 2 (this means that only $8,000 was recognized as taxable income and taxes in Year 1). Therefore, the $12,000 represents a taxable temporary difference, the effect of which must be recognized (as a deferred tax liability) and reported in Trevellyan's Year 1 financial statements. The deferred tax liability is computed by multiplying the future enacted tax rate (in this question that would be the Year 2 tax rate of 25%) by the $12,000 temporary difference. Thus, $12,000 × 25% = $3,000, and Trevellyan would report a $3,000 deferred tax liability in its Year 1 balance sheet. If the question had asked for the current tax liability, or taxes payable, the current taxable amount of $8,000 would have to be multiplied by the current tax rate of 30% to derive $2,400. Total income tax expense would be equal to $5,400. The transaction would be journalized as follows:

Debit to income tax expense	$5,400
Credit to (current) taxes payable	$2,400
Credit to deferred tax liability	$3,000

252. B. Deferred tax assets (and/or liabilities) are recognized for the estimated future tax effects of temporary differences. A temporary difference results when the GAAP basis and the tax basis of an asset or liability differ. Differences in these two bases arise when items of income and/or expense are recognized in different periods under GAAP and under the tax code. In this question, Benson received a rental payment in the amount of $42,000 in Year 1. Under the tax code, this amount is entirely taxable in the year received (Year 1). However, for GAAP or book purposes, only 6/12 or one-half (representing the period from July 1, Year 1, to December 31, Year 1) of that payment ($21,000) is recognized in

Year 1 since the payment is for the one-year period beginning July 1, Year 1, and ending on July 1, Year 2. The other 6/12 or one-half ($21,000) (representing the period January 1, Year 2, to July 1, Year 2) would be recognized for GAAP/book purposes in Year 2. Thus, this $21,000 represents a deductible temporary difference, the effect of which must be recognized (as a deferred tax asset) and reported in Benson's Year 1 financial statements. Essentially, Benson will receive a tax benefit in Year 2, since the company will recognize $21,000 of income for book purposes but have no tax obligation associated with the receipt of the rental payment in Year 2. The deferred tax asset is computed by multiplying the future enacted tax rate (in this question that would be the Year 2 tax rate of 30%) by the $21,000 temporary difference. Thus, $21,000 × 30% = $6,300, and Benson would report a $6,300 deferred tax asset in its Year 1 balance sheet. If the question had asked for the current tax liability, or taxes payable, the current taxable amount of $42,000 would have been multiplied by the current tax rate of 25% to derive $10,500. Total income tax expense would be equal to $4,200. The transaction would be journalized as follows:

Debit to income tax expense	$4,200
Debit to deferred tax asset	$6,300
Credit to (current) taxes payable	$10,500

253. C. The estimate for bad debt expense and estimate for warranty expense are both temporary differences. Bad debt expense and warranty expense will both reverse in later years. For bad debt expense, the reversal will impact the tax return in a year that the receivable is worthless. For warranty expenses, the reversal will impact the tax return in a later year when money is spent for warranty costs. Life insurance proceeds are not taxable; therefore, life insurance proceeds are permanent differences between financial statement income and taxable income.

Chapter 29: Accounting for Leases and Pensions

254. D. US GAAP and IFRS prefer that leases be accounted for as capital leases; therefore, if any one of the given criteria are met, the lease should be accounted for as a debit to an asset and a credit to a liability. The alternative, if none of the given criteria are met, is to account for the lease as an operating lease. But that would involve the lessee not recording a lease liability (or asset) on its books. Operating leases are a form of off-balance-sheet financing, and entities can use that to hide legal obligations such as monthly lease payments. Therefore, GAAP and IFRS prefer capital lease accounting for a lessee.

255. B. Since there is no title transfer and no bargain purchase option, the lessee will only have use of the asset during the period of the lease. Thus 8 years is used for depreciation purposes in this question.

256. B. The portion of the minimum lease payment in the 6th year applicable to the reduction of the net lease liability should be more than in the 5th year. A lease is a sophisticated loan, and all loans work essentially the same way. A typical loan payment includes both principal and interest. The principal portion of the loan payment reduces the obligation. The interest portion is the expense incurred to use other people's money. In a lease or loan payment, the interest portion of the payment is always higher in the early years compared to the principal portion, although the monthly payment never changes. Each lease payment is allocated between a reduction of the lease obligation and interest expense so as to produce a constant periodic rate of interest on the remaining balance of the liability. Since the interest will be computed based on a declining lease obligation balance, the interest component of each payment will also be declining. The result will be a relatively larger portion of the lease payment allocated to the reduction of the lease obligation in the later years of the lease term. In the early years of any loan repayment, much of the payment represents interest. Therefore, the portion of the minimum lease payment in the 6th year applicable to the reduction of the net lease liability should be more than in the 5th year.

257. B. II is correct. If the lessor is either a manufacturer or dealer, the lessor would record the lease as a sales type lease rather than direct financing lease.

258. A. The lease is "minor" because it will be classified as an operating lease (it fails all the tests for capital lease based on the given information). In minor sale-leasebacks, there is no deferral. Leaseback is considered minor because the lease life is less than 10% of its useful life. Therefore, all gain is recognized. Proceeds of $1,000,000 − $350,000 book value = $650,000 gain.

259. D. There is no deferred gain, because under US GAAP, when the seller-lessee retains only a minor portion (present value of leaseback is 10% or less of fair value of the asset sold), any gain should be recognized immediately and none deferred.

260. C. Since free rent is part of the lease arrangement, the tenant must calculate net cost for the entire lease term and divide it evenly over each period. The question involved a 5-year lease with the first 6 months free rent. Therefore, total rent to be paid is not $90,000 but rather $81,000. The net cost of $81,000 is divided over the 60 months, because US GAAP normally requires the same amount of rent expense each month regardless whether cash was paid that month. Although only $6,000 was collected in Year 13, an expense equal to all 12 months is recognized as follows:

$1,500 per month × 60 months $90,000
Subtract 6 months free   − $9,000
Net cost for 5 years $81,000
                 ↓
Divide by 60 months $1,350 per month
                 ↓
$1,350 multiplied by 12 months $16,200

261. C. I is correct. If sales for the month were $800,000, rent expense for the month would be $16,000. If sales are $800,000 in a single month, $300,000 above base, the rent is $10,000 (base) plus 2% of the excess, $300,000. Total rent would be $16,000 for the month recognized in full. Notice that the additional $6,000 is recognized immediately as expense. II is correct. In months with no contingent rent, the base rent of $10,000 is recognized.

262. D. The lease bonus should be recognized on the straight line basis over the 10-year lease term:

Lease bonus of $20,000 / 10 years $2,000 per year
Excess sales of $100,000 result in
     additional rent expense   + $5,000
Base rent   + $80,000
Total rent expense $87,000

263. D. I is incorrect. If a lease contains a bargain purchase option, the lease would automatically be accounted for by the lessee as a capital lease rather than an operating lease. Therefore, if a lease contains a bargain purchase option, this is not evidence that the lease should be accounted for as an operating lease. II is incorrect. If the lease is for 8 years and the asset's life is 10 years, the lease would automatically be accounted for by the lessee as a capital lease. The rule is that if the lease life is equal to or greater than 75% of the asset's life, the lease should be capitalized. In this case, the lease life represents 80% of the asset's life; therefore, this is not evidence of an operating lease.

264. A. I is correct. In an operating lease, no asset or liability is shown on the balance sheet; however, disclosures are required in footnotes. The full amount of remaining lease obligation is required.

265. D. Since the lease is an operating lease, Bowman Inc., the lessee, must disclose in the footnotes the entire remaining balance of the lease obligation, but the amount does not appear anywhere on the balance sheet. For this reason, operating leases are sometimes referred to as off-balance-sheet financing. Also in the footnotes Bowman must show a schedule disclosing the annual minimum lease payments for each of the next 5 years. The schedule would appear as follows:

Year 12	$23,000
Year 13	$23,000
Year 14	$23,000
Year 15	$23,000
Year 16	$23,000

266. C. I is correct. The lessee must capitalize leasehold improvements even if the tenant is accounting for the lease as an operating lease. Leasehold improvements are then amortized over the shorter of the term of the lease or the life of the assets. Leasehold improvements are not expensed in the year incurred even if the lessee accounts for the lease as an operating lease. II is correct. The lessee would capitalize leasehold improvements if accounting for the lease as a capital lease (or operating lease). Leasehold improvements are then amortized over the shorter of the term of the lease or the life of the assets.

267. A. I is correct. Leasehold improvements is capitalized even if the lessee reports the lease as an operating lease. The capitalized amount of leasehold improvements is $60,000 determined as follows:

Installation of drop ceilings	$20,000
Installation of new walls	+ $30,000
Installation of flooring and lighting	+ $10,000
Total leasehold improvements	$60,000

268. B. II is correct. The $25,000 for last month's rent is recorded as an asset, prepaid rent. When rent is paid in advance, the asset prepaid rent should be debited and rent expense would represent the amount of cost incurred that has no future benefit. The $25,000 for last month's rent has a future benefit and thereby would not be expensed in Year 11.

269. A. The total expense for Year 11 includes both the amortization of the leasehold improvements for Year 11 plus the lease payment. The security deposit of $63,000 and the last month's rent of $25,000 are recorded as assets. The total expense for Year 11 is determined as follows:

Leasehold improvements of $60,000 / 15 years = $4,000 multiplied by 1/12	$333
Lease payment for the month of December, Year 11	+ $25,000
Total expense	$25,333

270. D. The lease term began January 2, Year 13, on a lease valued at $371,600. Since the first lease payment was not made immediately, interest accrued on the entire balance for all of Year 13. Therefore, the calculation of interest expense is as follows:

Present value of the initial lease obligation at January 2, Year 13 × interest rate = interest expense for Year 13

↓

$371,600 × 10\% = $37,160$

271. C. The lease term began January 2, Year 13, on a lease valued at $371,600. Since the first lease payment was not made immediately, interest accrued on the entire balance for all of Year 13. Therefore, interest expense was calculated (prior question) to be $37,160. The remaining $62,840 of the $100,000 payment serves to reduce the liability balance down to $308,769, calculated as follows:

Balance at January 2, Year 13	$371,600
Principal reduction from payment on December 31, Year 13	− $62,840
Lease liability balance at December 31, Year 13	$308,760

272. B. The lease term began January 2, Year 13, on a lease valued at $371,600. Since the first lease payment was made immediately, the initial payment of $100,000 reduces the principal amount by $100,000. All of the first payment applies to principal since no interest accrued yet. The principal balance becomes $271,600, and the calculation of interest expense at December 31, Year 13, is as follows:

Present value of the initial lease obligation at January 2, Year 13, $271,600 × interest rate = interest expense for Year 13

↓

$271,600 × 10\% = $27,160$

273. A. The lease term began January 2, Year 13, on a lease valued at $371,600. Since the first lease payment of $100,000 was made immediately, no interest had accrued yet and all of the initial payment represented principal. The initial payment reduced the principal to $271,600. Therefore, interest expense was calculated (prior question) to be $27,160. The remaining $72,840 of the $100,000 payment serves to reduce the liability balance down to $198,760, calculated as follows:

Balance at January 2, Year 13	$271,600
Principal reduction from payment on December 31, Year 13	– $72,840
Lease liability balance at December 31, Year 13	$198,760

274. **A.** The fair value of the equipment, $125,000, is equal to the present value of the future cash flows. Since the first payment is due immediately, annual payments equal $25,000, determined as follows:

Present value = annual rents × annuity due factor (5 years, 7%)

↓

$105,000 / 4.2 = $25,000 annual lease payments

275. **C.** The fair value of the equipment is equal to the present value of the future cash flows determined as follows:

Present value = annual rents × annuity due factor (5 years, 7%)

↓

$105,000 / 4.2 = $25,000 annual lease payments

Total annual interest payments include principal and interest, so the interest portion is the amount received minus the present value of the principal given at $105,000.

$25,000 annual payment × 5 payments	$125,000
Subtract present value of equipment	– $105,000
Interest income over life of lease	$20,000

276. **B.** In a lease that is accounted for by the lessor as a sales type lease, there are two income statement components: interest income and profit on sale. Although the Golf Corp. is not selling the equipment but rather leasing it, accounting for the lease as a sales type lease leads to recognition of profit from sale just as if the equipment was being sold. Profit from the sale is recognized as the excess of the present value of the selling price over its cost. The present value of the lease payments is used as the proceeds. If the present value of the lease payments were not given, the cash selling price would be used if that were given. On the CPA exam, one or the other will be given. The list price is irrelevant and is not to be used as a present value or fair value to determine the profit. In this question, the profit on sale is calculated as follows:

Present value of payments	$1,700,000
Subtract cost basis of equipment	– $1,100,000
Profit on sale of equipment	$600,000

277. **D.** I is incorrect. The pay-as-you-go method expenses pension costs from the date the employee retires up until the date of the employee's death. The pay-as-you-go method does not properly match the expense for employee pension costs to the periods benefited. With regard to pension expense, the Financial Accounting Standards Board (FASB) believes that the periods benefited are the years of service that the employee worked for the company. Therefore, those years of employee service should have expenses recorded for pension cost even though the employee is not collecting any retirement benefits in those working years. Since the pay-as-you-go method doesn't begin recognizing pension expense until the employee stops working, the pay-as-you-go method is not generally accepted under US GAAP. II is incorrect. Under the terminal funding method, similar to pay-as-you-go, the company does not record expense during the service period of the employee. Once the employee retires, the company incurs the expense all at once, usually by purchasing an annuity for the employee that is expected to furnish income to that employee over the next many years. The annuity is expensed as incurred and thus does a poor job of matching pension expense with the periods benefited. Therefore, the terminal funding method is not considered generally accepted under US GAAP.

278. **A.** Under US GAAP, amortization of unrecognized prior service cost is calculated by assigning an equal amount of the cost to the future periods of service of each employee at the date of amendment to the plan. The average service life of the four employees is 8 years. Calculate the average service life as follows:

6 years + 8 years + 10 years = 24 years

↓

24 / 3 = 8-year average service life for the four employees

↓

$64,000 / 8 years = $8,000

279. **A.** To calculate the $108,300 projected benefit obligation at year-end, start with the beginning projected benefit obligation of $93,000 and add 10% interest of $9,300. Then add the service cost of $11,000 and subtract the pension benefits paid during the year of $5,000. The calculation appears as follows:

Beginning projected benefit obligation	$93,000
10% interest	$9,300
Service cost	+ $11,000
Pension benefits paid	− $5,000
Ending projected benefit obligation	$108,300

280. **D.** Under US GAAP, all the components of net periodic pension cost must be aggregated and presented as one amount on the income statement. Therefore, the interest cost on the projected benefit obligation, the current service cost, the return on plan assets, the amortization of prior service cost, actuarial gains and losses, and amortization of existing net obligation are all combined and shown as one amount known as net periodic pension cost, pension expense, on the income statement. The separate components of net periodic pension cost is a required footnote disclosure. Other key pension disclosures include detailed description of the plan, including employee groups covered, the fair value of plan assets, and the funded status of the plan, either overfunded or underfunded.

281. **B.** The actual return on plan assets is calculated as follows: $1,000,000 beginning fair value + $50,000 in contributions − benefits paid to retirees of $20,000 = $1,030,000. If ending fair value of plan assets were $1,300,000, then $270,000 must have been the actual return on plan assets.

282. **A.** The funded status of the pension plan at December 31, Year 7, is the projected benefit obligation minus the fair value of the plan assets at the end of Year 7 or $18,500,000 − $9,000,000 = $9,500,000. The pension plan is underfunded since the liability is greater than the fair value of the plan assets. This amount of underfunded status, $9,500,000, must be reported on the balance sheet at year-end as a liability. If the pension plan status had been overfunded rather than underfunded, the overfunded amount would be reported on the balance sheet as an asset.

283. **D.** When calculating the present value of future retirement payments, the projected benefit obligation (by definition) is a projection, an estimate of what future salaries may be. This inclusion of future salaries (in its calculation of benefit obligation) serves to increase the pension obligation compared to taking into account only past and current salary levels. Therefore, the projected benefit obligation is used for most pension calculations because of conservatism. The projected benefit obligation is the present value of future retirement payments attributed to the pension benefit formula to employee services rendered *prior* to a date, based

on *current, past, and (an assumption about) future compensation levels.* The only difference between the accumulated benefit obligation and the projected benefit obligation is the assumption of future compensation levels.

284. **C.** I is correct. Under US GAAP, interest cost included in the net pension cost recognized for a period by an employer sponsoring a defined benefit pension plan represents the increase in the projected benefit obligation due to the passage of time. The interest cost will probably need to be calculated by the candidate on the CPA exam. II is correct. The current service cost is the present value of all benefits earned in the current period. Current service cost represents the increase in the projected benefit obligation resulting from employee services in the current period. The actuary provides the current service cost. Current service cost will always be given on the CPA exam.

285. **D.** The funded status of Century Corp.'s pension plan at December 31, Year 13, is the difference between the ending fair value of plan assets and the ending projected benefit obligation of $450,000. The ending fair value of plan assets is calculated as follows:

Beginning fair value	$350,000
Add contributions	+ $35,000
Add return on plan assets $350,000 × 12%	+ $42,000
Subtract benefits paid	− $40,000
Fair value at 12/31/13	$387,000

Ending projected benefit obligation of $450,000 − the ending fair value of plan assets of $387,000 = $63,000 underfunded. This underfunded status of $63,000 appears on the balance sheet at year-end.

286. **C.** The amount of unrecognized prior service cost that is amortized to pension expense in Year 13 = $240,000 / 15 years = $16,000 amortized to pension expense in Year 13.

Chapter 30: Bonds and Other Noncurrent Liabilities

287. **B.** If the market rate of interest (6%) is higher than the stated or coupon rate (5%), the bonds will sell at a discount. A comparison of coupon rate and market rate is always done on the issue date to determine what the bonds will sell for.

288. **D.** I is incorrect. The market rate would have to be below 5% for Anna Inc. bonds to sell at a premium,

above par. II is incorrect. Whether the bonds pay interest annually or semiannually will not determine discount or premium.

289. **A.** With regard to a $1,000 bond issued at a premium of 102 on January 1, Year 10, that pays interest semiannually on June 30 and December 31, the stated interest rate is used to calculate the amount of interest payment. If the stated interest rate was 8%, the amount of interest payment would be $1,000 times 8%, or $80 per year. Since the bond pays interest twice per year, the investor would receive $40 on June 30 and $40 on December 31 for a total of $80 per year.

290. **A.** $500,000 × 0.98 = $490,000 bond proceeds plus accrued interest of $12,500 = $502,500. Accrued interest is calculated as follows: $500,000 × 10% = $50,000 interest for one year divided by 12 months equals interest each month of $4,166.67. Accrued interest must be collected for May 1 to Aug 1. Multiply 3 by $4,166.67 = $12,500.

Since the amount of interest, $25,000, is legally obligated to be paid every 6 months, accrued interest is calculated from the previous interest date of May 1 to the bond issue date of August 1. Since the amount of interest, $25,000, is legally obligated on November 1, Blue must pay $12,500 for 3 months of interest (from May 1 to August 1). That way, Blue may receive 6 months' interest of $25,000 on November 1 and come out even, since Blue held the bonds for only 3 months prior to the November 1 interest date.

291. **B.** Under the straight line method of amortizing the discount, the same amount is amortized each period. The amount of cash paid for interest is added to the amortization, and the total of the two represents the interest expense for the period. The interest expense is a plug figure and is determined last. Also, under the straight line method, the interest expense and the amortization do not vary from period to period. The same amount is amortized each period. The amount of amortization is added to the carrying value of the bonds and increases the carrying amount of the bonds, but it does not affect the interest expense or amortization of future periods. Finally, under the straight line method, the bonds carrying value increases by the same amount each period. By the maturity date, the carrying amount will equal the par value.

292. **C.** Under the effective interest method, the interest expense is determined first and the amortization is a plug figure. The interest expense is determined

by multiplying the carrying amount of the bonds at the beginning of the period by the market rate of interest. The amount of *cash interest paid* is then subtracted from the interest expense, and the difference is the amount of discount amortization for the period. The amount of amortization is then added to the carrying value of the bonds and increases the carrying value of the bonds. The increase in the carrying value of the bonds will increase the interest expense in the following period. Also under the effective interest method, the bonds carrying value increases by a different amount each period. By the maturity date, the carrying amount will equal the par value. Note that when bonds are issued at a discount, interest expense is always greater than cash interest paid.

293. **D.** Under the effective interest method, the amount of interest expense is determined by multiplying the carrying amount of the bonds at the beginning of the period by the effective rate of interest. $468,500 × 10% = $46,850, *but* the bonds were outstanding for only 6 months from July 1, Year 1, to December 31, Year 1. Therefore, the interest expense for Year 1 is for the 6 months, or half of the $46,850: $23,425. Interest expense is recognized for the period from bond issuance, July 1 through the end of the year, December 31.

294. **A.** Under the effective interest method, the interest expense is determined first. The interest expense was computed in the previous question as $23,425. The interest payable at December 31, Year 1, is $20,000, resulting in a discount amortization of $3,425. Under the effective interest method, the amortization is a plug figure and determined last. The $3,425 is then added to the carrying amount at the beginning of the period, which was $468,500. Therefore, the carrying amount of December 31, Year 1, is $471,925.

295. **C.** At December 31, interest would be accrued from September 1 through December 31. At year-end, accrued interest needs to be recorded from the most recent payment date to the end of the year.

296. **A.** Accrued interest at September 30, Year 5, is the interest owed at year-end since the June 30, Year 5, interest payment. Accrued interest is calculated as $200,000 × 11% × 3/12 = $5,500. The period of time from June 30 through September 30, 3 months, needs to be accrued on the September 30 balance sheet. The journal entry at September 30 (end of year) would include a debit to interest expense of $5,500 and a credit to interest payable of $5,500.

297. D. II is correct. Serial bonds mature on different dates rather than all maturing on the same day. Serial bonds are prenumbered bonds that the issuer may call and redeem a portion by serial number. III is correct. Debentures are unsecured bonds issued by a corporation. Debentures are unsecured because they are not secured by any specific assets of the corporation in the event of default.

298. C. $9,333 is calculated as follows: $800,000 × 7% = $56,000; $56,000 × 1/2 = $28,000; $28,000 × 2/6 = $9,333. Since $28,000 of interest is legally obligated to be paid on the next interest payment date of December 1, Year 13, accrued interest is calculated for 2 months, from the previous interest date of June 1 to the bond issue date of August 1. Since the amount of interest, $28,000, is legally obligated to be paid by Tucker on December 1, Tucker collects 2 months of interest on August 1 (from June 1 to August 1) so that Tucker may pay 6 months' interest on December 1 and come out even, because Tucker issued the bonds only 4 months prior to the December 1 interest date.

299. B. $4,667 is calculated as follows: Accrued interest at December 31, Year 13, is the amount of interest owed since the last payment date on December 1. Accrued interest at December 31, Year 13, is calculated as follows: $800,000 × 0.07 = $56,000 × 1/12 = $4,667. The journal entry would include a debit to interest expense of $4,667 and a credit to interest payable for $4,667.

300. B. Interest expense is calculated from the date the bonds were issued. Interest would be calculated from August 1 through December 31, 5 months: $800,000 × 0.07 = $56,000; $56,000 × 5/12 = $23,333.

301. D. The entry to record the bond premium would be a debit to cash of $1,020,000, a credit to bonds payable for $1,000,000, and a credit to bond premium for $20,000.

302. B. Amortization of a bond premium always results in more cash interest than interest expense. This is because when bonds are originally issued at a premium, the issuer gets to keep the premium but only has to pay back the par. In this case, the company raises $1,020,000, keeps the excess $20,000, and only has to pay back the $1,000,000. This serves to reduce overall borrowing cost. The entry to record the amortization of the premium will include two debits, one to amortize the premium and the other to record the interest expense. The credit will be to cash for the total of the two. Therefore, interest

expense will always be less than cash paid when bonds are sold for a premium due to the amortization of the premium each period. Conversely, when bonds are sold for a discount, interest expense will always be greater than cash paid.

303. C. I is correct. Under US GAAP, no value is assigned to the conversion feature of convertible bonds, because the conversion feature cannot be sold separately from the bonds. Under US GAAP, the theory is that the entire amount should be allocated to the bonds because the conversion feature has no value on a stand-alone basis. II is correct. Under IFRS, both a liability and an equity component should be recognized when convertible bonds are issued. IFRS recognizes the bond as a liability and the conversion feature as an equity component. Under IFRS, the bond liability is valued at fair value with the difference between the actual proceeds received and the fair value of the bond liability being recorded as a component of equity.

304. C. All costs associated with the issuance of a bond are capitalized as a deferred charge and amortized over the outstanding term of the bonds. The unamortized portion of these costs are to be presented as a direct deduction from the carrying amount of the bond, similar to the presentation of a bond discount. Capitalized costs of a bond issuance include commissions paid to an underwriter, legal fees, registration fees, printing, and engraving.

305. B. II is correct. A conversion feature that is separate from a security should be accounted for separately, and a value should be assigned to it at the time of issuance of the bonds. Detachable warrants are option contracts that are issued with and are detachable from the bond. The warrant gives the bondholder the right to buy stock, within a certain time period. If the warrants are detachable, then the fair value of the warrants is credited to APIC-Warrants at the time the bonds are issued. Since the bonds were issued at par, the remainder of the bond proceeds would be credited to bonds payable. Because they are detachable, the warrants are traded separately and are considered to be a separate financial instrument.

306. D. Stockholders' equity is increased by the value of the warrants. There are 500 bonds with 20 warrants worth $5 each: 500 × 20 × $5 = $50,000.

307. C. I is correct. While the entire balance in the sinking fund account is generally considered to be a noncurrent asset, sinking fund accounts that are considered to offset current bond liabilities can be included within current assets. II is correct. A bond sinking fund is basically an appropriation of retained earnings to indicate to the shareholders that certain retained earnings are being accumulated for the purposes of repaying debt.

308. **B.** II is correct. Concessions made by the creditor normally include reduced interest rates.

309. **C.** I is correct. With regard to troubled debt restructuring, creditors typically will extend maturity dates to minimize the risk of bad debt write-off. II is correct. With regard to troubled debt restructuring, creditors typically will reduce accrued interest to minimize the risk of bad debt write-off. Reducing or eliminating accrued interest would result in a fresh start for the debtor and is a good faith gesture by the creditor.

310. **A.** When assets are transferred in a troubled debt restructuring, the asset (land) is adjusted to fair value and an ordinary gain or loss is recorded.

Carrying amount	$140,000
Fair value of land	− $80,000
Ordinary loss	($60,000)

311. **D.** When assets are transferred in a troubled debt restructuring, the asset (land) is first adjusted to fair value and an ordinary gain or loss is recorded. The $60,000 loss was recorded in the prior question. Then the gain or loss on restructuring is recorded as the difference between the debt and fair value of asset transferred. Liability $165,000 − the fair value of land (80,000) = debt forgiven gain $85,000.

312. **A.** I is correct. Under US GAAP, if a current liability is expected to be refinanced on a long-term basis, the liability may be reclassified as long term on the balance sheet. For the entity to reclassify the liability as long term under US GAAP, the company must have both the intent and ability to refinance. The actual refinancing may be done after year-end, and the liability may still be reclassified to long term. If the current liability has not been refinanced prior to the issuance of the financial statements, the liability would likely be listed on the balance sheet as current, unless the entity has a signed noncancelable agreement with a solvent lender to refinance the short-term debt on a long-term basis. If such an agreement with a lender is in place prior to the issuance of the financial statements, the liability may be presented as long term even though it has not been refinanced yet.

313. **A.** Under US GAAP, if a company intends to refinance a short-term obligation and has the ability

to do so, the liability can be recorded as long term rather than current. The requirements are that the entity has a signed commitment from a solvent financial institution to refinance the debt or the debt is refinanced prior to the date the financial statements are issued. Since both conditions have been met, the obligation should be recorded as a long-term liability rather than short term.

314. **A.** $500,000 accounts payable + $150,000 current portion of mortgage = $650,000. The bank loan was refinanced long term prior to the financial statements being issued.

Chapter 31: Stockholders' Equity and Ratio Analysis

315. **D.** I is incorrect. The issuer would credit, not debit, common stock for $10. When new stock is issued, common stock is credited for the par value of the shares. II is incorrect. The issuer would debit cash for $13, credit common stock for $10, and credit additional paid-in capital for $3. A corporation is not allowed to have a gain or loss on sale of its own stock.

316. **D.** The land will be recorded at the fair market value (FMV) of the shares being surrendered by the company. If the FMV of these shares is not available, the FMV of the land will be used for reporting purposes. The journal entry includes a debit to land for $15,000, a credit to common stock for $10,000, and a credit to additional paid-in capital for $5,000.

317. **B.** II is correct. The additional paid-in capital would increase on March 1, Year 6. The journal entry on February 1, Year 6, would include a debit to cash of $20 and a credit to common stock at par, $20. The journal entry on March 1, Year 6, would include a debit to legal fees of $60,000, a credit to common stock for $50,000, and a credit to additional paid-in capital of $10,000. I is incorrect. On February 1, Year 6, there is no increase to the additional paid-in capital account since the shares were issued at par on that date.

318. **C.** I is correct. The credit to common stock would be for the 2,000 shares multiplied by the $5 par or $10,000. II is correct. The credit to additional paid-in capital would include the 2,000 shares multiplied by $95, $190,000. The $95 represents the excess of the current market value over par at the date of issuance. Notice that the value of the services is ignored since the stock has a ready market price. The value of the services would have been used for valuation if no other information was available.

319. **B.** II is correct. The additional $12 per share ($12,000) that will be received is recorded as additional paid-in capital at the date of subscription. In addition, cash of $4,000 is recorded along with a subscription receivable of $18,000. The journal entry at the subscription date is a debit to cash for $4,000 and a debit to subscription receivable for $18,000. The credits are to common stock subscribed for $10,000 and additional paid-in capital for $12,000. I is incorrect. On the date of subscription, the additional paid-in capital account is increased in the amount of $12,000 not $4,000.

320. **C.** I is correct. Preferred stock has no set rights other than the rights defined in the stock certificate. Preferred stock rights usually include a set dividend that takes precedence over the rights of the common stockholders dividend. Preferred stock may also contain rights to convert the preferred shares to common (convertible preferred) and may also contain rights to unpaid dividends in arrears (cumulative preferred). Preferred stock may also contain rights to participate with the common stockholder on dividends paid after both preferred and common receive a set dividend (participating preferred). II is correct. All common stock issued by companies incorporated within a state typically will have the same legal rights because the rights of common stockholders are established by the laws of that particular state.

321. **A.** I is correct. *Cumulative* means that if the preferred stock dividend is not paid when due, the preferred dividend will have to be paid before holders of common stock can receive any dividend payment. If no dividend is ever paid to the owners of the common stock, then no dividend has to be paid to the preferred stockholders, even if the preferred stock dividend is cumulative.

322. **A.** When the preferred stock is issued, the preferred stock is credited for par value of $500,000. The excess $10 over par is credited to additional paid-in capital from preferred stock. Therefore, $50,000 is credited to additional paid-in capital from preferred stock on February 1, Year 13. The journal entry on February 1 would include a debit to cash of $550,000 and a credit to preferred stock for $500,000 and a credit to APIC-preferred stock for the excess of $50,000 above par.

323. **D.** On December 31, Year 14, when all the preferred shares are converted, preferred stock must be debited by $500,000 and additional paid-in capital preferred stock must be debited by $50,000. Total debits are $550,000. As for the credits, when the 5,000 shares of preferred stock are converted into 10,000 shares of common stock, the 10,000 shares of common stock need to be recorded with a par value of $10—$100,000. To balance the entry, the additional paid-in capital from common stock must be credited for $450,000.

324. **C.** With regard to dividends paid by a corporation, retained earnings is debited on the date of declaration. The date of declaration is the date that the board of directors formally approves a dividend. The journal entry on the declaration date is a debit to retained earnings and credit to dividends payable. On the record date, no entry is needed, just a determination of who owns the stock. On the payment date, the dividends payable is reduced and cash is credited.

325. **C.** I is correct. Cash dividends result in a reduction of retained earnings at the declaration date. II is correct. Property dividends result in a reduction of retained earnings for the market value of the property at the date of declaration.

326. **D.** The journal entry on January 14, Year 13, to record the issuance of 20,000 shares is a debit to cash for $220,000 and a credit to common stock for the par value of $100,000, and the remainder of $120,000 is a credit to additional paid-in capital.

327. **B.** Under the cost method of accounting for treasury stock transactions, treasury stock is debited for the cost of repurchasing the shares at the time the shares are reacquired. Therefore, the entry Stefano would make to record the treasury stock transaction on July 28, Year 13, would be to debit treasury stock for $80,000 and credit cash for $80,000.

328. **C.** Under the cost method, the entry to reissue the treasury stock on December 5 would include a debit to cash in the amount of $95,000, a credit to treasury stock for cost of $80,000, and a credit to additional paid-in capital from treasury stock of $15,000. Reissuing treasury stock cannot increase retained earnings or net income. A corporation is not allowed to record a gain or loss from the sale or purchase of its own stock.

329. **D.** The journal entry on January 2, Year 13, to record the issuance of 20,000 shares at $15 is a debit to cash for $300,000 and a credit to common stock for the par value of $200,000, and the remainder of $100,000 is a credit to additional paid-in capital. The $5 excess over par is credited at issuance to additional paid-in capital.

330. A. Under the par value method of accounting for treasury stock, treasury stock is debited for the par value of the shares reacquired. Therefore, the debit to treasury stock is for 5,000 shares multiplied by $10 par, $50,000.

331. C. Under the par value method of accounting for treasury stock transactions, when the treasury shares are repurchased, the original amount recorded as additional paid-in capital must be reduced. The 5,000 treasury shares were originally issued for $5 above par back in January of Year 13. This $5 per share above par must be eliminated from the books under the par value method. The 5,000 shares times the $5 per share original excess over par is debited to additional paid-in capital to remove that original APIC from the books, since those shares are no longer outstanding. The reduction of additional paid-in capital on June 7, Year 13, is calculated as follows:

Excess over par	$5
Shares reacquired	× 5,000
Reduction of additional paid-in capital	$25,000

332. B. The journal entry on June 7, Year 13, would be as follows: Cash is credited for $90,000. The debits include treasury stock for $50,000, additional paid-in capital for $25,000, and the difference of $15,000 is a debit to retained earnings for $15,000. Notice that retained earnings can be debited, never credited, with regard to treasury stock transactions.

333. D. Under the par value method of accounting for treasury stock transactions, the treasury shares are credited for the par value at the date of reissue. Therefore, on December 29, Year 13, treasury stock is credited for 5,000 shares multiplied by $10 par, $50,000.

334. A. Under the par value method of accounting for treasury stock, the reissuance of the 5,000 treasury shares on December 29, Year 13, for $30 per share would involve an increase to cash for $150,000 and a credit to treasury stock for the par value of $50,000, and the excess would be a credit to additional paid-in capital in the amount of $100,000.

335. C. Under the par value method of accounting for treasury stock transactions, the entry on January 2, Year 13, increased additional paid-in capital by $100,000. The second entry on June 7, Year 13, decreased additional paid-in capital by $25,000, dropping the balance to $75,000. The third entry on December 29, Year 13, increased additional paid-in

capital by $100,000, bringing the ending balance up to $175,000.

336. D. When accounting for stock dividends, the most important factor is the size of the stock dividend in proportion to the total number of shares outstanding before the dividend. When a corporation pays its dividend in shares of stock, it distributes additional shares of its own stock to investors of record as of a certain date. The stock dividend is accounted for as a small stock dividend if less than 20% of the total shares are being distributed. In a stock dividend accounted for as a small stock dividend, not enough shares are being issued to affect the market price of the stock. Therefore, in a small stock dividend, the company will debit retained earnings for the market value of the stock. Common stock is credited for the par value of the new shares distributed, and additional paid-in capital is credited for the difference. Conversely, if more than 25% of the total shares are distributed in the stock dividend, the stock dividend is accounted for as a large stock dividend, as it may be expected to reduce the market value of the stock. Therefore, a large stock dividend is recorded as a debit to retained earnings for the par value of the shares and a credit to common stock distributable on the declaration date. On the date of payment, the shares are issued and the common stock distributable account is debited and common stock is credited. No entry is made to additional paid-in capital for a large stock dividend.

337. B. When recording the journal entry for the stock dividend, retained earnings is debited for the market value of the shares on the date of declaration, $18, because the stock dividend is considered small. The stock dividend is considered small because the total shares distributed, 10,000, is only 5% of the total shares prior to the stock dividend. The debit to retained earnings is $18 multiplied by 10,000 shares, $180,000.

338. A. The journal entry to record the new shares issued as a result of a small stock dividend will include a debit to retained earnings and credit to common stock for the par value of the shares. The excess is credited to additional paid-in capital. Since common stock is always credited for par, when the journal entry to distribute the shares from a stock dividend is recorded, additional paid-in capital is credited for $80,000, calculated as follows:

Retained earnings	$180,000
Less credit to common stock	− $100,000
Additional paid-in capital	$80,000

339. **A.** When more than 25% of the total shares prior to the dividend are distributed, the stock dividend qualifies as large. In a large stock dividend, retained earnings is debited for the par value of the shares, not the fair market value. The reason for debiting retained earnings for the par value of the shares is because the number of shares being distributed is large enough to affect the market price of the stock, similar to a stock split. As a result of debiting retained earnings at par, retained earnings is recorded as follows: $60,000 new shares distributed × $10 par = $600,000.

340. **C.** The journal entry to record the declaration of the 30% stock dividend will include a debit to retained earnings and credit to common stock distributable for $600,000.

341. **D.** Since retained earnings is debited for the par value of the shares, the full amount of $600,000 is first credited to common stock distributable and ultimately will be transferred to the common stock account. Nothing will affect additional paid-in capital, since the market price of the stock in the large stock dividend is being ignored.

342. **C.** II is correct. In a cash dividend, retained earnings is reduced and cash is paid out, which serves to reduce both stockholders' equity and current assets.

343. **D.** In connection with a stock split, there is no journal entry. Additional shares will be issued, but the reduction in par value will offset the new shares outstanding, so there is no effect on any accounts. The result of the 2:1 stock split will be that the original 10,000 shares of $20 par common stock were $200,000 and will remain at $200,000 after the split. After the split, 20,000 shares are outstanding with a $10 par; total is the same $200,000:

Before the split, 10,000 shares × $20 par = $200,000 stated capital.

After the split, 20,000 shares × $10 par = $200,000 stated capital.

344. **C.** III is correct. A reverse stock split reduces the number of shares outstanding and increases the par value proportionately. The result of a reverse stock split is an increase in the market price of the stock. Companies will sometimes use the reverse stock split to reverse the embarrassment of an extremely low stock price as compared to its historical price.

345. **D.** When stock options are issued to employees, the most relevant factor in determining the accounting treatment under US GAAP is whether the stock is being issued to employees as part of their compensation (compensatory stock options) or whether the stock options are not part of compensation (noncompensatory). Under a noncompensatory stock option plan, no journal entry is made for the stock options until the employees exercise their rights and purchase the shares. Noncompensatory stock options tend to allow employees to purchase shares at a small discount below market price. Conversely, compensatory stock options are valued at the time of issuance. Therefore, knowing whether the stock options are issued in lieu of salary is the most relevant factor of the given options in determining the accounting treatment under US GAAP.

346. **C.** Under compensatory stock options, both US GAAP and IFRS agree that the expense is determined based on fair value when the options are granted. However, this expense is not booked on the grant date. Instead, under the matching principle the expense must be recognized over the vesting period that the person must work to earn the options.

347. **B.** I and II are correct. When accounting for the expense related to compensatory stock options, the journal entry includes a debit to compensation expense and a credit to additional paid-in capital-stock options. The debit to compensation expense reduces net income; therefore, retained earnings as net income is closed out to retained earnings.

348. **D.** When accounting for compensatory stock options, when the employees exercise their options and purchase the shares for an amount above par but below the market price, the journal entry will include a debit to cash for the amount received and another debit to close out the additional paid-in capital-stock options. The credits will include a credit to common stock for par and a credit to additional paid-in capital for the amount in excess of par.

349. **A.** I is correct. Under US GAAP losses from writedown of assets under quasi-reorganization would affect retained earnings.

350. **C.** Working capital can be defined as current assets minus current liabilities. Working capital is a measure of solvency. Working capital is an assessment of an entity's ability to pay debts as they become due.

351. **C.** I is correct. The numerator for the quick ratio includes cash, net receivables, and marketable securities. II is correct. The numerator for the quick ratio includes cash, net receivables, and marketable securities.

352. C. I is correct. Total current liabilities is used as the denominator in determining the current ratio. The current ratio is expressed as current assets divided by current liabilities. II is correct. Total current liabilities is used as the denominator in determining the quick ratio. The quick ratio is expressed as cash plus marketable securities plus net receivables divided by current liabilities.

Chapter 32: Earnings Per Share

353. A. I is correct. A private entity that has yet to make such a filing is exempt from reporting EPS.

354. D. I and II are incorrect. A company can report basic EPS and not have to report diluted EPS if it has common stock and no debt or equity securities that are convertible into common stock. If the company has options or debt securities that are convertible into common stock, it must report basic and diluted EPS.

355. C. I is correct. Income available to common shareholders is determined by deducting dividends declared in the period on noncumulative preferred stock (regardless of whether they have been paid). II is correct. Income available to common stockholders is determined by deducting dividends accumulated in the period on cumulative preferred stock (regardless of whether they have been declared).

356. B. The preferred stock dividend was not paid in Year 11. Therefore, the Year 11 preferred dividend needs to be subtracted from the $1,400,000. The preferred dividend is calculated as follows:

10,000 preferred shares × 5% = $500 × $100 par	$50,000
Net income	$1,400,000
Less preferred dividend	− $50,000
	$1,350,000
($1,350,000 / 60,000) shares of common stock outstanding	$22.5

357. A. I is correct. When calculating the weighted average number of shares to be used in the EPS calculation, stock dividends and stock splits are treated as if they occurred at the beginning of the period, and those shares are counted as if they had been outstanding all year.

358. C. In determining the number of shares to be used in Sadie's computation of diluted EPS for Year 3, Sadie first needs to compute the weighted average shares that would be used in computing basic EPS:

Date	Shares	*Pro-rata weighting	Weighted average shares
1/1	300,000 ×	12/12 =	300,000
7/1	50,000 ×	6/12 =	25,000
			325,000

The stock options must then be considered. Options are potentially dilutive securities that factor into the weighted average shares used in the diluted EPS computation only if they are deemed to be dilutive. Options are dilutive if the average market price of the stock is greater than the exercise price of the options. If the market value is less than the exercise price, then the options are considered antidilutive (they will have the effect of increasing, rather than decreasing, the basic EPS computation) and are excluded from weighted average shares used in the diluted EPS computation. In this question, the market price ($20) exceeds the option exercise price ($15) and, therefore, the stock options would have a dilutive effect on EPS. In order to calculate how many shares from the options should be used in the diluted EPS calculation, use of the treasury stock method is required. Under this method, the stock options are "assumed" to be exercised, and "assumed" proceeds received from that exercise. Those "assumed" proceeds are then used to buy back shares into "treasury," and the remaining shares not bought back are deemed to be the "incremental" shares issued in connection with the "assumed" exercise. The incremental shares are then added to the weighted shares outstanding in determining the total shares to be used in the diluted EPS computation. Calculation of the incremental shares is presented below:

Assumed proceeds (40,000 options × $15)	$600,000
Shares assumed issued from exercise	40,000
Shares bought back ($600,000/$20 per share)	(30,000)
Incremental shares issued	10,000

Adding these incremental shares to the 325,000 weighted average shares computed in connection with the basic EPS calculation above, results in 335,000 used in the diluted EPS computation for Year 3.

359. C. I is correct. When calculating basic EPS, include the convertible preferred shares that were converted during the period in the calculation of weighted average common shares outstanding and

---

*The pro-rata weighting fraction is determined by the length of time the group (tranche) of shares is outstanding for the year.

time-weight them based on the number of months that those shares were outstanding as common shares. II is correct. When calculating basic EPS, if convertible preferred shares are not converted into common shares during the period, ignore convertible preferred shares in the calculation of weighted average common shares outstanding.

360. **D.** I is incorrect. If the preferred stock is cumulative, only the current year undeclared dividend is subtracted from net income to arrive at net income available for common shareholders. Dividends in arrears were subtracted from income in Year 1, the year that they first were an obligation of the company. II is incorrect. Only the current period dividends, and not the dividends in arrears from Year 1, on the cumulative preferred stock are added to the net loss. Dividends in arrears were subtracted from income in the year that they first were an obligation of the company.

361. **C.** When convertible bonds are outstanding, the computation of diluted EPS incorporates the assumed conversion of those bonds into common stock as long as doing so provides a dilutive effect on the earnings per share computation. The assumed conversion of the bonds requires adjustments to the basic earnings per share computation, which includes adding back interest expense, net of tax, to net income in the numerator, and increasing the common shares issued and outstanding in the denominator. Interest expense is added back since bonds converted would no longer pay interest and, therefore, net income would increase, net of tax, as a result. Common shares issued and outstanding would increase since converting the bonds to common stock adds to the common stock issued and outstanding. Frenzy's diluted earnings per share for Year 1 can, therefore, be calculated as follows:

Net income – preferred dividends + interest expense, net of tax /
Weighted common shares outstanding + shares issued in connection with bond conversion
$500,000 – $60,000 + ($7 × 10,000 bonds)
   (1 – 0.30) /
100,000 shares + (2 shares × 10,000 bonds)
Diluted EPS = $4.08

362. **C.** I is correct. In the event of a net loss for the period, declared dividends on noncumulative preferred stock are added to the net loss even if the dividend was not yet paid. This is because dividends on noncumulative preferred stock are added to the net loss or subtracted from net income the moment they are declared. II is correct. In the event of a net loss for the period, current year dividends on cumulative preferred stock are added to the net loss regardless of whether the dividends have been declared, because the company is obligated to pay these dividends before distributions are made to common shareholders. Note that only the current year dividends not declared would be added to the net loss, not the dividends in arrears.

363. **A.** Diluted EPS incorporates the effects of all potentially dilutive securities (those that have the effect of reducing the basic EPS computation in deriving diluted EPS), but excludes any antidilutive securities (those that have the effect of increasing the EPS computation). In doing so, the concept of conservatism is applied. Because assumed conversion of the convertible preferred stock would have the effect of reducing earnings per share by $0.75, it is included in computing diluted earnings per share. However, the stock options have an antidilutive effect since conversion of those options would increase earnings per share by $0.10. They are, therefore, excluded from the diluted earnings per share computation. Thus, Everest would report diluted earnings per share in the amount of $14.25 ($15.00 – $0.75).

364. **C.** I is correct. If the debt is converted during the period, then it's not convertible any longer. So the shares have already been issued and should be time-weighted as part of basic EPS. II is correct. The starting point for diluted EPS is basic EPS, so debt already converted during the period would be included and time-weighted as part of basic and diluted EPS. Note that if the convertible debt were dilutive but not yet converted, only diluted EPS would be impacted. In this case, because the debt was converted, both basic and diluted EPS are impacted. The if-converted method of computing EPS data assumes conversion of convertible securities as of the beginning of the earliest period reported or at time of issuance if later.

365. **C.** 65,000 shares of common stock is the weighted average for EPS. The year starts with 60,000 shares. The 10,000 shares issued on July 1, Year 13, must be time-weighted for the 6 months of the year (6/12) that they were outstanding. The calculation is as follows:

1/1/Year 13, outstanding all year	60,000
7/1/Year 13, 10,000 issued × 6/12	+ 5,000
Weighted average	65,000

366. B. A 3% stock dividend equals 2,100 shares with a total of 72,100 shares outstanding after the distribution of the dividend. A stock dividend would be treated as if it had occurred at the beginning of the fiscal year. The net income figure given in the question was not relevant.

367. C.

Beginning of year 10,000 shares × 12/12	10,000
2:1 stock split given full-year treatment	+ 10,000
Shares issued 10/1 (5,000 × 3/12)	+ 1,250
Weighted average common shares	21,250

368. A. Since no additional common shares were issued in Year 13, weighted average number of shares outstanding equals the beginning balance of 360,000 shares. As for the numerator, net income available to common shareholders is $270,000 after subtracting the preferred dividend of $20,000 from the net income of $290,000. The additional preferred shares of 100,000 issued during Year 13 were not relevant.

Net income available to common shareholders ($290,000 − $20,000)	$270,000
Weighted average number of shares outstanding	360,000
Earnings per common share ($270,000 / 360,000)	$0.75

369. A. I is correct. For basic EPS, income available to common shareholders is determined by deducting preferred dividends from net income to arrive at net income available to common stockholders.

370. C.

Net income	$750,000
Less preferred dividends	− $30,000
Net income available to common stockholders	$720,000
Divided by weighted average common shares outstanding	÷ 100,000
Basic EPS	$7.2

371. A. To calculate the numerator:

Add interest expense not incurred $1,000,000 × 0.09	$90,000
Less tax deduction eliminated 30%	− $27,000
Interest saved from conversion net of tax	$63,000
Net income	+ $750,000
Adjusted net income	$813,000

To calculate the denominator:

Adjusted common shares outstanding	100,000
Conversion of preferred shares	+ 20,000
Conversion of debt	+ 30,000
Adjusted shares outstanding	150,000

↓

Diluted EPS $813,000 / 150,000 shares　　$5.42

Chapter 33: Partnerships and Fair Value Accounting

372. C. I is correct. Upon the formation of a partnership, tangible assets such as equipment would be recorded at fair value at the date of the investment. II is correct. Upon the formation of a partnership, tangible assets such as real estate would be recorded at fair market value at the date of the investment.

373. C. Assets contributed by partners to a partnership are valued at fair value of the assets, net of any related liabilities. Zuckerman's land was worth $60,000 subject to a mortgage of $25,000, so Zuckerman's capital is $35,000 on November 13, Year 1.

374. A. To add a new partner with an interest of one-fifth, use the following shortcut: Subtract 1 from 5, which equals 4. Take the 4 and divide it into the old partnership capital of $180,000. The result is $45,000. Therefore, Tim must contribute $45,000 to the partnership to receive an exact one-fifth interest. The $45,000 contributed by Tim will add to the $180,000 capital already there. The new total partnership capital will be $225,000 and Tim will receive one-fifth, or exactly, $45,000.

Tim's contribution for a one-fifth interest	$45,000
Partnership capital before Tim's admission	+ $180,000
Partnership capital after Tim's admission	$225,000

↓

Tim's capital account (20% of $225,000)　　$45,000

375. B. II is correct. Under the goodwill method, the incoming partner's capital account is his or her actual contribution. Goodwill is then determined based on the incoming partner's contribution and shared by the existing partners only; therefore, the incoming partner's capital account is credited for the exact amount of the new partner's contribution.

376. B. II is correct. The bonus method of accounting for Broskie's retirement increases (or decreases) the individual partners' capital accounts without changing total net assets of the partnership. Under the bonus method of accounting for retirement, any premium paid to the retiring partner is allocated to the remaining partners' capital accounts based on the profit and loss ratios of the remaining partners. Therefore, the bonus method of accounting for Broskie's retirement could increase partners' capital without increasing total assets of the partnership.

377. **D.** If Chu will be admitted with 10% of total capital for an investment of $15,000 after revaluing partnership assets, then 10% of total capital equals $15,000. If 10% of total partnership capital equals $15,000, then total partnership capital must be equal to $150,000 and goodwill must be equal to $55,000, calculated as follows:

Total partnership capital equals $15,000 / 10%	$150,000
Subtract existing capital balances ($45,000 + $35,000 + $15,000 = $95,000)	– $95,000
Goodwill to original partners	$55,000

378. **D.**

	Desimone	Jeffrey	Profit
Capital	$140,000	$80,000	$5,000
Interest	+ 7,000	+ 4,000	– 11,000
	147,000	84,000	(6,000)
Loss allocation	– 3,000	– 3,000	(6,000)
Total	144,000	81,000	

379. **B.** The salary is allocated first, which results in a loss that needs to be distributed. The loss gets allocated based on a loss ratio of 80% to Barry / 20% to Saralee.

	Barry	Saralee	Total
Earnings			$54,000
Salary	$40,000	$30,000	– $70,000
Net loss to distribute			($16,000)
Distribution 80/20	– $12,800	– 3,200	($16,000)
Total	$27,200	$26,800	

380. **D.** Rochelle's basis is equal to the cash contributed of $80,000. The fact that the partners agree to share profits 60/40 does not affect their partnership capital accounts at the date of formation.

381. **C.** Bob's capital account is equal to the fair value of the land less the mortgage assumed by the partnership. Assets contributed by partners to a partnership are valued at the FMV of the assets net of any related liabilities.

Fair value of land	$70,000
Subtract mortgage	– $20,000
Basis to Bob	$50,000

382. **A.**

Capital balances prior to Tatum's admission $50,000 + $30,000	$80,000
Fair value of Tatum's equipment investment	+ $25,000
New partnership capital balances	$105,000
↓	
Tatum's capital interest 30%	$31,500

383. **B.** After Tatum's admission, the difference between the fair value of the equipment contributed by Tatum of $25,000 and the $31,500 credit to Tatum's capital account of $6,500 is debited to Griffin and Owen's capital accounts based on the prior profit and loss ratio of 60:40.

Tatum's capital account credit	$31,500
Fair value of equipment contributed by Tatum	– $25,000
Bonus to Tatum	– $6,500
60% of $6,500 bonus allocated to Griffin	+ $3,900
Griffin's beginning capital	+ $50,000
Griffin's ending capital	$53,900

384. **C.** Begin accounting for the liquidation by selling the other assets and realize cash of $360,000. A loss of $60,000 is recorded as the difference between the proceeds and carrying amount of the assets, $420,000. The $360,000 cash is first used to pay off the accrued taxes of $100,000. Cash of $260,000 remains. Before any cash can be distributed, the loss of $60,000 from the asset sale must be allocated based on profit and loss ratios of 70:30. Therefore, Rukke receives $42,000 of the loss and Murray receives $18,000 of the loss. Allocate the remaining cash to Rukke and Murray based on remaining capital balances.

Rukke capital prior to liquidation	$170,000
Subtract share of loss	– $42,000
Total cash paid to Rukke	$128,000

385. **B.** The capital account for a sole proprietor begins with the initial investment of $3,000. Under the cash basis, the cash received for revenue in December of $10,000 increases capital and the withdrawal in December decreases capital. The expenses were not paid until January Year 13, so they have no effect on capital under the cash basis. Therefore, ending capital on the cash basis is $11,000 determined as follows:

Initial investment	$3,000
Add revenue	+ $10,000
Subtract withdrawal of	– $2,000
Ending capital on December 31 under the cash basis	$11,000

386. **A.** The owner's initial investment of $3,000 and withdrawal of $2,000 do not affect the income statement. Therefore, on the accrual basis, net income is $3,000 calculated as follows:

Revenue earned in November	$10,000
Subtract expenses incurred in December	− $7,000
Accrual basis net income	$3,000

387. **C.** On the cash basis, net income includes only the cash collected for revenue in December. Expenses were not paid until January, so net income in Year 13 under the cash basis is $10,000. The owner's initial investment of $3,000 and withdrawal of $2,000 do not affect the income statement.

388. **D.** For a sole proprietorship, capital begins with the owner's initial investment of $3,000 and increases by the accrual basis net income of $3,000. The withdrawal of $2,000 does not affect the income statement but does result in a decrease in Chumley's capital account. Therefore, on the accrual basis, ending capital is calculated as follows:

Investment	$3,000
Accrual basis net income	+ $3,000*
Drawings	− $2,000
Ending capital accrual basis	$4,000
*Revenue earned in November	$10,000
Subtract expenses incurred in December	− $7,000
Accrual basis net income	$3,000

389. **C.** I is correct. With regard to fair value measurement, US GAAP considers fair value as the price to sell an asset, which is sometimes known as "exit price." II is correct. With regard to fair value measurement, US GAAP considers fair value as the price to transfer a liability.

390. **A.** I is correct. Fair value includes transportation costs if location is an attribute of an asset. If an asset has to be moved to be sold, fair value includes the cost of the transportation of the asset to the location in which it can be sold.

391. **D.** In FVM of financial assets, the most advantageous market is the market with the best price after considering transaction costs. Note: transaction costs are not included in final fair value. Only include transaction costs when determining the most advantageous market.

392. **C.** I is correct. Transaction costs are considered when determining the most advantageous market. II is correct. Transaction costs are *not* included in the final fair value measurement.

393. **D.** I is incorrect. A FVM based on management assumptions only is a level 3 measurement and is acceptable when there are no Level 1 or Level 2 inputs or when undue cost or effort is required to obtain Level 1 or Level 2 inputs. II is incorrect. Level 1 measurements are quoted prices in active markets for *identical* assets or liabilities only. Quoted prices in active markets for similar assets or liabilities are Level 2 inputs.

394. **C.** III is correct. Quoted market prices available from a business broker for a similar asset are considered to be a Level 2 input, not as reliable as those coming from a stock exchange for an identical asset.

395. **D.** I is incorrect. Prices from observed transactions involving similar assets are Level 2 inputs. II is incorrect. Quoted stock prices in active stock markets are Level 1 inputs.

396. **A.** I is correct. The market approach uses prices and other relevant information from identical or comparable market transactions to measure fair value.

Chapter 34: Business Combinations and Consolidations

397. **B.** When 100% of the subsidiary is acquired, goodwill is equal to the cash paid of $960,000 minus the fair value of the net assets of the subsidiary. $940,000 assets − $240,000 liabilities = fair value of the net assets of $700,000. $960,000 − $700,000 = $260,000 goodwill.

398. **A.** I is correct. When a subsidiary is acquired with an acquisition cost that is less than the fair value of the underlying assets, the balance sheet is adjusted to fair value, which creates a negative balance in the acquisition account. If there are any identifiable intangible assets, they are recognized at fair value and this would increase the negative balance in the investment account. The total negative balance in the investment account is recorded as a gain.

399. **B.** II is correct. Consulting fees as well as finder's fees associated with combining two or more corporations are expensed as incurred. If a corporation hires Goldman Sachs to consult or find them a company for takeover, the direct costs paid to Goldman Sachs are expensed as incurred.

400. **D.** The net income of the subsidiary will only be included in consolidated net income from the date of acquisition. Therefore, for Year 13, 25% of Flower's net income until September 30 would be

reported by Heart. From October 1 to the end of the year, 95% of Flower's income belongs to Heart.

401. D. The implied value of B Corporation is based on the purchase price of $500,000 and the percentage acquired by Corporation A, 80%. The amount paid by Corporation A of $500,000 divided by the percentage acquired, 80%, equals $625,000. If Corporation A is willing to pay $500,000 for an 80% ownership of B Corporation, the implied value of B Corporation must be $625,000. $625,000 × 80% = $500,000. Notice that although the fair value of B Corporation's net assets were $350,000, the implied fair value of B Corporation is $625,000 based on the amount paid by Corporation A and the percentage acquired by Corporation A.

402. B. $625,000 − $350,000 = $275,000. When less than 100% of the subsidiary is acquired, goodwill is calculated as the excess of the implied fair value of the subsidiary based on purchase price, $625,000, minus the fair value of the net assets acquired, $350,000. Notice that regardless of the amount acquired, 100% of the net assets, $350,000, are adjusted to fair value and the difference is reported as goodwill.

403. C. When consolidated financial statements are prepared, transactions that have occurred between the parent and subsidiary company must be eliminated. For one, the parent's investment in the subsidiary account is eliminated against the subsidiary's equity accounts, which include retained earnings. Subsidiary equity not attributable to the parent company is reported separately in consolidated equity as noncontrolling interest. The subsidiary's retained earnings include dividends it paid to its owners/shareholders. Those owners/shareholders include the parent company (which reports the receipt of its share of the dividend distribution) and any noncontrolling interest if less than 100% of the subsidiary company is owned by the parent. Thus, in the consolidated financial statements (e.g., consolidated retaining earnings), the portion of the dividend paid to the parent company is fully eliminated and has no effect on consolidated retained earnings. However, the portion of the dividend attributable to the noncontrolling interest has the effect of decreasing the noncontrolling interest balance. It should be noted that changes in the subsidiary company retained earnings (e.g., decrease in retained earnings as a result of a dividend payment) have the same effect on the noncontrolling interest balance, as attributable to the noncontrolling interest in the subsidiary. A

is wrong, as the noncontrolling interest balance is affected (decreased) by the dividend payment. B is wrong, as there is no effect on consolidated retained earnings. D is wrong, as the noncontrolling interest balance is affected by the payment of the dividend.

404. D. When preparing consolidated financial statements, transactions that have occurred between the parent and subsidiary company must be eliminated. In this question, Prunty (parent company) sold a machine to Shelly. When eliminating this transaction, all relevant accounts (e.g., asset net book value, gain on transaction, and depreciation expense) need to be restored to their initial amounts "as if" the intraentity transaction never took place. This requires first understanding how relevant accounts have changed as a result of the intraentity transaction. First, Prunty recognized a $10,000 gain from the sale of the machinery (proceeds from sale: $40,000 − asset carrying value: $30,000 = $10,000). This gain needs to be eliminated in the period of sale (Year 2). A gain can only be recognized by the consolidated entity after the machinery is sold to a party outside of that entity. Second, currently, Shelly is holding the machinery at an inflated cost of $40,000, since Prunty sold the machinery to Shelly for $40,000. Thus, the carrying value of the asset needs to be restored to $30,000, which was the initial carrying amount on Prunty's books. Finally, since Shelly purchased the asset for $40,000 from Prunty, depreciation expense needs to be adjusted in the consolidation. If it is assumed that this transaction never took place, Prunty would have continued to recognized $6,000 of annual depreciation expense ($30,000/5-year life = $6,000). However, with the asset now on Shelly's books at the inflated $40,000 amount, depreciation expense is overstated by $2,000 ($40,000/5-year life = $8,000; $8,000 − $6,000 = $2,000) and must be adjusted down to $6,000 in the consolidation process. This $2,000 adjustment will take place each year over the asset's 5-year life. In summary, the net book value of the machinery will be adjusted down from $40,000 to $30,000 (a $10,000 decline), the $10,000 gain will be eliminated and reduced to zero in Year 2 (this reduces consolidated income in Year 2), and depreciation expense will be adjusted down from $8,000 to $6,000 (a $2,000 decline) over the 5-year period starting with Year 2. A reduction in depreciation expense has the effect of increasing consolidated net income by $2,000. Thus, in Year 2 the net adjustments necessary to compute consolidated net income would include an $8,000 decline

($10,000 decrease resulting from the elimination of the gain, and $2,000 increase resulting from elimination of excess depreciation expense). In Year 3, the only adjustment in computing consolidated net income would be the $2,000 increase resulting from the elimination of the excess depreciation expense. A is wrong as it fails to include the depreciation expense adjustment in both Years 2 and 3. B is wrong as it fails to include the depreciation expense adjustment in Year 2. C is wrong as it fails to include the depreciation adjustment in Year 3.

405. **C.** When preparing consolidated financial statements, transactions that have occurred between the parent and subsidiary company must be eliminated. In this question, Sal sold inventory to Paul at a 40% gross profit. Because 50% of the inventory remains in Paul's ending inventory at December 31, this remaining inventory has been inflated by the 40% gross profit earned by Sal from the sale. Thus, this profit is deemed unrealized and must be eliminated in the consolidation. If Paul had sold all of the inventory to parties outside of the consolidated entity by December 31, then all of the profit would be realized, and no elimination of unrealized profit would be necessary. This elimination process requires a three-step process: (1) determine the gross profit percentage on the inventory sale (given in this question as 40%—Sal was the seller, so use Sal's gross profit; (2) determine the amount that still remains in ending inventory of the purchasing party (Paul is the purchaser, and 50% of the sale still remains in ending inventory: $200,000 × 50% = $100,00); (3) apply the gross profit percentage to the amount remaining in ending inventory and that represents the unrealized profit to be eliminated: $100,000 × 40% = $40,000. Thus, $40,000 should be eliminated from the $100,000 ending inventory balance.

406. **B.** On the acquisition date, the fair value of Sienna Corp. is calculated as follows: $2,800,000 / 0.80 = $3,500,000. The implied fair value of Sienna Corp. based on purchase price is therefore $3,500,000.

407. **B.** On the acquisition date, the fair value of Sienna Corp. is calculated as follows:$2,800,000 / 0.80 = $3,500,000. The implied fair value of Sienna Corp. based on purchase price is therefore $3,500,000. The $750,000 difference between the fair value of the subsidiary of $3,500,000 and the $2,750,000 book value of the net assets acquired must be allocated first by adjusting 100% of Sienna's net assets to fair value. The $750,000 difference minus the $100,000

land adjustment minus the $50,000 furniture and fixtures adjustment leaves $600,000. The next step is to allocate $525,000 of the remaining $600,000 to the unpatented technology. This leaves a balance for goodwill in the amount of $75,000.

408. **C.** As part of the eliminating entry on the consolidated work papers, the fair value of any portion of the subsidiary that is *not* acquired by the parent must be reported as noncontrolling interest in the equity section of the consolidated financial statements, separate from the parent's equity. On the acquisition date, the fair value of Sienna Corp. is calculated as follows: $2,800,000 / 0.80 = $3,500,000. The implied fair value of Sienna Corp. is therefore $3,500,000. $700,000 is the noncontrolling interest (equity account with normal credit balance) calculated as 20% of the fair value of $3,500,000.

409. **B.** Since Peyton Corp. acquired 90% of Shore but not 100%, a noncontrolling interest account will need to be created. To calculate the noncontrolling interest at the date of acquisition, the first step is to determine the total fair value of the net assets of the subsidiary. As part of the eliminating entry on the consolidated work papers, the fair value of any portion of the subsidiary that is *not* acquired by the parent must be reported as noncontrolling interest in the equity section of the consolidated financial statements, separate from the parent's equity. Although Peyton is acquiring only 90%, 100% of the net assets needs to be adjusted to fair value. $180,000 / 0.9 = $200,000. $200,000 is the total fair value of all the net assets of Shore. $200,000 fair value multiplied by 10% not acquired equals the noncontrolling interest of $20,000 at January 1, Year 13. Under the acquisition method, 100% of the subsidiary's net assets are adjusted to fair value regardless of percentage of stock acquired by the parent. Therefore, the noncontrolling interest at the beginning of Year 1, $20,000, represents the percentage of the fair value of the net assets of Shore that were *not* acquired by Peyton Corp.

410. **C.** Since Peyton Corp. acquired 90% of Shore but not 100%, the noncontrolling interest amount starts out at $20,000 but then will increase by 10% of the net income earned by Shore Inc. and will decrease by 10% of the dividends paid by Shore Inc. $20,000 + $1,800 − $400 = $21,400.

411. **C.** Consolidated equity is equal to the parent company's equity plus the fair value of any noncontrolling interest. The subsidiary company's equity accounts are eliminated.

412. A. The debit to investment in subsidiary is equal to the market price of the stock issued on the closing date, not the average selling price or the market price on the announcement date. The acquisition price is calculated on the date the acquisition is finalized: 20,000 shares × $40 per share = $800,000.

413. B. The journal entry to record the investment in subsidiary would include a debit to investment in subsidiary of $800,000, a credit to common stock for $200,000, and a credit to additional paid-in capital for $600,000.

414. D.

Fair value of net assets (assets minus liabilities)	$450,000
Acquisition price	– $375,000
Excess of fair value over acquisition price	$75,000
Intangible asset acquired	+ $165,000
Gain	$240,000

When Plato acquired the assets with a net fair value of $450,000 upon paying only $375,000, that resulted in a bargain of $75,000. The deal got even better for Plato when they determined that an intangible asset was also being acquired with a fair value of $165,000. The total excess of fair value acquired, $615,000, minus the acquisition price of $375,000 equals a gain of $240,000.

415. C. In a business combination accounted for as an acquisition, legal and consulting fees are expensed. Thus $80,000 is expensed immediately. The registration costs of $15,000 will serve to reduce the additional paid-in capital account.

416. D. In a business combination accounted for as an acquisition, the registration costs of $15,000 will serve to reduce the additional paid-in capital account. When the stock is issued to acquire the subsidiary, common stock is credited for the par value of $100,000. The additional $13 per share, or $1,300,000, would have been recorded as additional paid-in capital but for the stock issuance costs of $15,000, which serve to reduce additional paid-in capital to $1,285,000.

417. C. In the journal entry to record the acquisition, cash is credited for $95,000, common stock is credited for $100,000, and additional paid-in capital is credited for $1,285,000. The credits add up to $1,480,000. The only other debit besides the investment account is a debit to legal and consulting expense in the amount of $95,000. Thus the debit to the investment in subsidiary account is (plugged) $1,385,000.

418. B. II is correct. Consolidated common stock will consist of Pie Corp.'s common stock only. Therefore, consolidated common stock will be $140,000.

419. D. Under IFRS, goodwill can be calculated using either the "partial goodwill" or "full goodwill" method. These methods will derive different amounts for goodwill only when the parent company owns less than 100% of the subsidiary company. Under the IFRS partial goodwill method, goodwill is computed as follows:

Goodwill = acquisition cost – fair value of subsidiary's net assets acquired

In this question, the fair value of the subsidiary's net assets is: $30,000 (current assets) + $270,000 (property, plant, and equipment) + $30,000 (fair valuation adjustment for property, plant, and equipment) – $120,000 (liabilities) = $210,000. Goodwill under the IFRS partial goodwill method is therefore, equal to $103,000, calculated as follows: Acquisition cost: $250,000 – Fair value of subsidiary's net assets acquired: ($210,000 × 70%) = $103,000.

420. A. The acquisition method requires that 100% of the subsidiary's assets be adjusted to fair value (regardless of the percentage acquired). For that reason, consolidated property plant and equipment should be reported at $250,000 for Seltzer Corp. plus $1,200,000 for Potomac Corp., total of $1,450,000. Under US GAAP, property plant and equipment (of the parent) is not written up above book value even if fair value is higher.

421. D. Assets and liabilities acquired in a business combination must be valued at their fair value. When a parent acquires a subsidiary with an acquisition cost that is less than the fair value of the net assets acquired, the excess is recognized as a gain by the acquirer at the time of acquisition. Calculation of gain:

Fair value of the net assets acquired	$400,000
Less cost to acquire subsidiary	– $250,000*
Gain	$150,000

Chapter 35: Statement of Cash Flows

422. A. Under US GAAP, there are three sections to the statement of cash flows. The three sections are cash flows from operating activities, cash flows from investing activities, and cash flows from financing

---

*25,000 shares × $10 per share

activities. I is correct. Under US GAAP, a statement of cash flows operating activities section prepared under the direct method requires disclosures, including a reconciliation of net income to net cash flow from operating activities. This reconciliation of net income to net cash flow from operating activities is essentially the cash flows from operating activities prepared under the indirect method. Companies choose the indirect method of presenting the statement of cash flows from operating activities (rather than the direct method) because if they use the direct method, they still have to show the reconciliation from net income to net cash flows from operating activities, which is essentially presenting the indirect method anyway.

423. **D.** I is incorrect. Under US GAAP, a statement of cash flows prepared under the direct method requires reconciliation, but the reconciliation is from net income (not retained earnings) to net cash flow from operating activities. The direct method is prepared showing the major sources and uses of cash starting with cash received from customers. II is incorrect. Under US GAAP, a statement of cash flows prepared under the indirect method does not require a disclosure from retained earnings to cash flows from operating activities. A statement of cash flows prepared using the indirect method begins with net income and then reconciles net income to cash flows from operating activities, avoiding the need for any reconciliation.

424. **D.** This transaction would not be reported in either operating, investing, or financing activities. A cash equivalent (3-month US Treasury bill) was purchased for cash and is simply a reallocation of the cash and cash equivalents balance (cash moved to cash equivalents). Therefore, this purchase transaction would not be reported in the body of the statement of cash flows, and would simply appear in the cash and cash equivalents balance, which the statement of cash flows computes and presents.

425. **A.** Selling (and/or buying) property, plant, and equipment represents an investing activity. However, when the property, plant, and equipment is sold at a gain or loss, that gain/loss increases/decreases net income, which, under the indirect method, is a component of operating activities on the statement of cash flows. The gain or loss must, therefore, be subtracted (if a gain)/added back (if a loss) to net income in order to remove it from operating activities. Additionally, since the proceeds from the sale of the property, plant, and equipment is reported at its gross amount in the investing activities section of the statement of cash flows, and the proceeds include the gain or loss on the sale, double counting of the gain or loss is avoided by removing it from operating activities. In this question, Anderson recognized a $50,000 loss on the building sale transaction (proceeds from sale: $650,000 − net book value of building: $700,000). Therefore, the $50,000 loss gets added back to net income in the operating activities section of the cash flow statement, and the $650,000 gross proceeds received is reported as an inflow to investing activities. B is wrong as the $50,000 loss needs to be added back, not subtracted from net income. If a gain resulted from the transaction, the gain would have been subtracted. C is wrong as it fails to account for the loss, which is embedded in net income and, consequently, incorrectly captured in operating activities. D is wrong as this transaction represents an inflow to investing activities, not operating activities.

426. **A.** I is correct. Making loans to others is an investing activity and would be shown in the investing activities section of the statement of cash flows. II is incorrect. Repaying the principal amounts of debt (borrowings) is a cash outflow associated with financing activities and should be reported in the financing activities, not investing activities, section of the statement of cash flows.

427. **A.** I is correct. Supplemental cash flow information includes the reporting of information associated with noncash investing and financing activities. These activities are excluded from the statement of cash flows because they do not involve cash inflows or outflows. They do, however, impact future cash flows and, therefore, must either be reported in a separate schedule or in the footnotes to the financial statements (they are often reported in a separate schedule at the bottom of the statement of cash flows). The conversion of preferred stock (converting preferred stock to common stock) is an example of a noncash financing activity, and would be reported as part of supplemental information in the statement of cash flows. Other examples would include acquiring property, plant, and equipment through the assumption of directly related liabilities (e.g., a mortgage) or via a capital lease arrangement, and converting debt to equity (e.g., convertible debt to common stock). II is incorrect. Cash flow per share is not a required disclosure when preparing the statement of cash flows. Cash flow per share is not a required disclosure in financial statements and should not even be disclosed. To disclose cash

flow per share would imply that cash flow per share is somehow indicative of an entity's performance like EPS.

428. D. I and II are incorrect. Regardless whether the direct or indirect method is used, the cash provided by operating activities will be the same, only the presentation is different.

429. A. I is correct. The primary purpose of the statement of cash flows is to provide relevant information about the cash receipts and cash disbursements of an enterprise during an accounting period.

430. B.

Net income	$190,000
Increase in accounts receivable	– $7,000
Increase in allowance for doubtful accounts	+ $500
Decrease in prepaid insurance	+ $3,000
Increase in payroll taxes payable	+ $2,600
Net cash provided by operating activities	$189,100

Net income is $190,000. The increase in accounts receivable means that accrual net income is higher than cash basis net income, so subtract $7,000 from net income to arrive at cash flows from operating activities. Whenever current assets go up, subtract the increase from net income. The allowance account works the opposite way of accounts receivable, since it's a contra asset. Add the increase in the allowance account of $500 to net income. The decrease in prepaid insurance is added to net income, so add $3,000. Whenever current assets decrease, add the decrease to net income. Finally, payroll taxes payable increased by $2,600. Anytime a current liability increases, add the increase to net income.

431. B. II is correct. The entire amount of cash proceeds from the sale of equipment (including the loss) should be shown in the investing section of the statement of cash flows. Cash flows related to fixed asset sales (and purchases) are shown in the investing section. The loss on sale of equipment reduced net income but should not be included in operating cash flows, so it must be added to net income to compute cash flows from operating activities.

432. B. II is correct. Financing activities include the cash effects of transactions obtaining resources from owners and providing them with a return on their investment.

433. D.

Payment for early extinguishment of debt is a financing cash outflow of	– $425,000
Payment of Year 13 dividend is a financing cash outflow of	– $50,000
Proceeds from the sale of treasury stock is a financing inflow of	+ $20,000
Net cash used by financing activities	($455,000)

434. C. Under IFRS, dividends paid may be reported as an operating or financing cash outflow on the statement of cash flows. Dividends paid are reported as a financing outflow, unless paying dividends is part of the company's core business, in which case dividends are reported as an operating outflow. Under US GAAP, dividends paid are reported as a financing outflow on the statement of cash flows. There is no option to report dividends paid as an operating activity.

435. B. Under IFRS, paying interest may be reported as an outflow in financing activities or operating activities on the statement of cash flows. Interest paid is reported as a financing outflow, unless paying interest is part of core operations, in which case it would be reported as an operating outflow. Banks, for example, will report interest paid as an operating outflow on the statement of cash flows, since paying interest to customers on deposited funds is part of a bank's core operations. Under US GAAP, interest paid must be reported as an operating outflow on the statement of cash flows. A is wrong because interest received, under IFRS, may also be reported as part of operating activities. C is wrong, because US GAAP requires that interest paid be reported as part of operating activities on the statement of cash flows. D is wrong because IFRS does not require that interest received be reported as part of operating activities. Interest received may also be reported as part of investing activities.

436. B. Acquiring a building through the issuance of equity is an example of a noncash investing and financing transaction. The transaction does not inflow a cash exchange and, therefore, is not reported on the statement of cash flows. IFRS requires these types of transactions to be reported in the financial statement footnotes. Note that US GAAP permits noncash investing and financing transactions (supplemental cash flow information) to be reported at the bottom of the statement of cash flows if there are only a few transactions, but if there are a more significant number of these transactions, they should be reported in a separate schedule in the notes to the financial statements. A is wrong as IFRS requires noncash investing and financing transactions to be reported in the financial statement footnotes. C is wrong since the transaction does not require a cash exchange and, therefore, would not be reported in the statement of cash flows. D is wrong since the transaction does need to be reported in the financial statement footnotes.

437. **B.** II is correct. Under IFRS, dividends received may be reported as an investing or operating activity on the statement of cash flows.

438. **D.** Under US GAAP, cash payments made to reduce debt principal are financing outflow. The interest portion would be reported as an operating outflow.

439. **A.** I is correct. Recording depreciation decreases net income and because it is a non-cash expense, it must be added back to net income in deriving cash flows from operating activities under the indirect method. II is incorrect. Bond premium amortization reduces interest expense, and therefore, increases net income. And because it is a non-cash item, it needs to be subtracted from (not added back to) net income in determining cash flows from operating activities under the indirect method. III is incorrect. A gain on the early extinguishment of long-term debt increases net income. And, since it is associated with a financing activity, the gain is subtracted from, not added back to, net income in computing cash flows from operating activities under the indirect method.

440. **C.** Amortization of bond premium reduces interest expense and makes net income higher. But because no cash is received, the amortization of the premium should be subtracted from net income to arrive at net cash provided by operating activities under the indirect method. So in this question, $18,000 would be subtracted from net income to arrive at cash flows from operating activities.

441. **D.** The decrease in inventory represents a cash inflow of $100,000. The decrease in accounts payable represents a cash outflow of $20,000. The net cash inflow is $80,000. Reducing cost of goods sold, $350,000, by the amount of net cash inflow of $80,000 would result in cash paid to suppliers of $270,000.

442. **D.** The decrease in inventory from $300,000 to $250,000 represents a cash inflow of $50,000. The decrease in accounts payable represents a cash outflow of $100,000. The net cash outflow is $50,000. Therefore, the $50,000 net cash outflow is added to

cost of goods sold to get $1,050,000 as cash paid to suppliers under the direct method.

443. **B.** An increase in accounts receivable of $8,000 represents less cash collected than revenue recorded. Therefore, cash basis revenue is less than accrual basis revenue by $8,000, because under the cash basis, revenue is not recorded until the $8,000 cash is received. The decrease in unearned fees represents the amount earned during the period but is collected in a prior period. Therefore, cash basis revenue would be less than accrual basis revenue by $6,000. If accrual basis revenue is $200,000, then cash basis revenue must $186,000.

444. **A.**

Beginning cash balance	$20,000
Net cash provided by operating activities	+ $320,000
Net cash used by investing activities	– $402,000
Net cash provided by financing activities	+ $262,000
Ending cash balance	$200,000

The loss on sale of the fixed asset was already included as part of cash flows from investing activities and does not get considered separately.

445. **B.** Net cash from investing activities should include the total proceeds received from the sale of investment, $25,000, minus the common stock purchase of $13,000, for a total of $12,000. The dividends and interest income are both considered cash flows from operating activities.

446. **B.** II is correct. Financing activities include the cash effects of transactions obtaining resources from owners and providing them with a return on their investment.

Chapter 36: Financial Instruments, Foreign Currency, and Price Level Accounting

447. **C.** I is correct. A derivative may be designated and qualify as a fair value hedge if there is formal documentation of the hedging relationship between the derivative and the hedged item. II is correct. A derivative may be designated and qualify as a fair value hedge if the hedged item is specifically identified.

448. **C.** I is correct. The hedge must be expected to be highly effective in offsetting changes in the fair value of the hedged item, and the effectiveness is assessed at least every 3 months. II is correct. The

hedged item presents exposure to changes in fair value that could affect income.

449. **C.** I is correct. A perfect hedge results in no possibility of a gain on the derivative instrument, because the gain would exactly offset the loss on the item or transaction being hedged. II is correct. A perfect hedge results in no possibility of a loss on the item being hedged, because in a perfect hedge, the loss on the item being hedged would be offset by the gain on the derivative instrument.

450. **D.** I is incorrect. The risk that the other party to the instrument will not perform must be disclosed. II is incorrect. The risk that the other party to the instrument will not perform is known as concentration of credit risk, not market risk.

451. **B.** II is correct. The risk of a significant number of unsecured accounts receivable with companies in the same industry is referred to as "concentration of credit risk."

452. **C.** I is correct. Concentration of credit risk is the risk that a counterparty will partially or completely fail to perform per the terms of the contract. II is correct. Concentration of credit risk exists if a number of counterparties are engaged in similar activities and the industry in which they are involved experiences economic disaster, technological obsolescence, or ceases to exist.

453. **D.** Fair value hedge *gains and losses* are recorded on the income statement. Conversely, *cash flow hedge* gains and losses, to the extent they are effective, are recorded as a component of other comprehensive income. Unrealized gains and losses on the effective portion of derivatives used as cash flow hedges are included in other comprehensive income until the future cash flows associated with the hedged item are realized.

454. **C.** I is correct. Fair value hedge losses are recorded on the income statement, while cash flow hedge gains and losses, to the extent they are effective (which is assumed in this fact pattern), are recorded as a component of other comprehensive income. II is correct. Fair value hedge gains are recorded on the income statement. It is important for candidates to know that fair value hedges are not the same as cash flow hedges. Unrealized gains and losses on the effective portion of derivatives used as cash flow hedges are included in other comprehensive income until the future cash flows associated with the hedged item are realized.

455. **D.** I and II are incorrect. Cash flow hedge gains and losses are not reported on the income statement. Only fair value hedge gains and losses should be reported within the income statement, not cash flow hedge gains and losses. Unrealized cash flow hedge gains and losses should be reported as a component of other comprehensive income. Unrealized gains and losses on the effective portion of derivatives used as cash flow hedges are included in other comprehensive income until the future cash flows associated with the hedged item are realized.

456. **A.** I is correct. A contract that conveys to a second entity a right to receive future collections on accounts receivable or cash from a first entity is a financial instrument but not a derivative. A derivative is an instrument that derives its value from the value of some other instrument.

457. **A.** I is correct. Gains or losses from remeasuring the foreign subsidiary's financial statements from the local currency to the functional currency should be included on the income statement in "income from continuing operations" of the parent company.

458. **C.** Gains or losses from remeasuring a foreign subsidiary's financial statements from the local currency to the functional currency should be included on the income statement in "income from continuing operations" of the parent company. Gains or losses resulting from translating a foreign subsidiary's remeasured financial statements into the parent company's reporting currency (e.g., US dollar) are reported as a foreign currency translation adjustment in stockholder's equity through the accumulated other comprehensive income account.

459. **D.** Conversion adjustments associated with translation of financial statements are displayed in accumulated other comprehensive income. As a result, the $36,000 translation gain is included in accumulated other comprehensive income.

460. **A.** I is correct. A subsidiary's financial statements are usually maintained in its local currency. If the subsidiary's functional currency is its local currency, the subsidiary's financial statements are simply translated to the reporting currency. The resulting adjustment is reported as other comprehensive income.

461. **B.** On October 5, the contract date, 20,000 Taiwan dollars equals $13,000 US dollars (20,000 units × the spot rate of $0.65). On December 31, the liability for Griffin Corp. increases because it became more expensive ($0.80) to convert US dollars to Taiwan

dollars. On December 31, the liability denominated in dollars rises to $16,000. Therefore, at year-end the foreign currency transaction loss is the difference between the exchange rate at the contract date and the exchange rate at year-end. The journal entry at year-end would include a debit to foreign exchange transaction loss for $3,000 and a credit to accounts payable. The loss of $3,000 is determined as follows:

Original liability (20,000 × 0.65)	$13,000
Liability at 12/31/13 (20,000 × 0.8)	– $16,000
Loss on foreign currency	($3,000)

462. **B.** Holding monetary assets in a period of inflation would result in a purchasing power decline because the dollars lose buying power during a period of rising prices. Holding monetary assets during periods of inflation will result in less purchasing power compared to when a person first started holding the cash.

463. **A.** Under US GAAP, certain large publicly held companies may disclose information concerning the effect of changing prices. Historical cost/constant dollar disclosures ignore asset appreciation. Instead, the disclosures are based on historical cost but are adjusted for changes in the general purchasing power of the dollar due to inflation. Historical cost/constant dollar disclosures use a general price index to adjust historical cost based on the rate of inflation. Thus historical cost disclosures ignore appreciation of the asset over its original cost. Constant dollar disclosures adjust for inflation based on the consumer price index. Therefore, historical cost/constant dollar disclosures ignore asset appreciation but adjust for changes in the purchasing power of the dollar.

464. **D.** Under US GAAP, certain large publicly held companies may disclose information concerning the effect of changing prices. Current cost/constant dollar disclosures involve adjustments for both purchasing power and appreciation. Current cost/constant dollar disclosures are based on current cost rather than historical cost and are adjusted for changes in the purchasing power of the dollar. Current cost/constant dollar may use specific price indexes or direct pricing to determine current cost and will use a general price index to measure general purchasing power effects. Therefore, current cost/constant dollar disclosures adjust for both purchasing power and inflation.

465. **D.** I and II are incorrect. When the exchange rate increases between the date a payable is recorded and the date of its cash payment, the foreign currency becomes more expensive and results in a loss. An exchange gain would occur when the exchange rate decreases between the date the payable is recorded and the payable is subsequently paid. When the exchange rate increases between the date a receivable is recorded and the cash receipt date, an exchange gain, not a loss, results, since the foreign currency is worth more and converts to more US dollars in the exchange.

Chapter 37: Government Accounting and Reporting

466. **D.** As part of the fund-based financial statements of the general fund, a balance sheet is prepared on the modified accrual basis as well as a statement of revenue, expenditures, and changes in fund balance. No statement of cash flows is prepared for the general fund as part of the fund-based financial statements.

467. **B.** II is correct. With regard to the dual objective of governmental reporting, the idea that government should be accountable to its public by demonstrating that resources allocated for a specific purpose are used for that purpose is described as fiscal accountability. A government attempts to demonstrate fiscal accountability with the use of fund accounting. Fund accounting is how a government attempts to show that it used legally restricted monies for the purpose intended. Through fiscal accountability, the government attempts to demonstrate that the government's actions have complied with public decisions concerning the raising and spending of public funds in the short term, usually one budgetary period. I is incorrect. Operational accountability is one of the dual objectives to government reporting standards but does *not* relate to the idea that government should be accountable to its public by demonstrating that resources allocated for a specific purpose are used for that purpose. Instead, operational accountability deals with the extent to which the government has met its objectives using all resources available and the extent to which it can continue to meet its objectives for the future. Operational accountability deals with the financial statement objectives of timeliness, consistency, and comparability. With operational accountability, the government entity seeks to demonstrate its accountability for the entity taken as a whole. Therefore, fiscal, not operational, accountability relates to the government being accountable to its public for the

money being spent as designated. Note: state and local government units gather and report financial information through the use of fund accounting. At the end of the fiscal year, funds prepare financial statements *and* the government as a whole prepares financial statements. This results in two sets of financial reporting.

468. **B.** The GASB establishes accounting and reporting standards for governments. GASB statements and interpretations are the most authoritative source of government accounting standards. The GASB is the equivalent of the FASB, and its statements and interpretations are considered the most authoritative.

469. **C.** I is correct. Fund accounting supports financial control by helping prevent overspending and making sure that legally restricted and designated monies are spent as intended. Fund accounting makes it easier to monitor compliance with legal restrictions and spending limits. By using fund accounting, the governing body attempts to demonstrate fiscal accountability. II is correct. A fund is a sum of money set aside to accomplish a specific goal. The purpose of fund accounting is to isolate the recording of each activity or group of activities. With fund accounting used by governmental units, resources are segregated for the purpose of carrying on specific activities and attaining certain objectives. Therefore, a self-balancing set of accounts is established for the fire department, the community pool, the subway system, and so on. Each of these sets of accounts is known as a fund.

470. **D.** All funds of a state or local government unit must be categorized as one of three separate classifications: proprietary, fiduciary, and governmental type funds. Permanent funds are a type of governmental fund.

471. **C.** An enterprise fund is one of the proprietary funds. Proprietary funds include activities of a government that have a user charge (such as a bus system or a municipal airport). If an activity has a user charge (or at least a user charge that is a reasonably significant amount), the activity is recorded and reported by the government within the proprietary funds. A proprietary fund such as an enterprise fund uses fund accounting but also uses accrual accounting, almost like a for-profit business. A fund set up as a proprietary fund has an actual profit motive. Net income is a measurement focus of a proprietary fund. Other than the fact that they use fund accounting and for-profit companies do not, proprietary funds are accounted for much like

a for-profit business using the full accrual method of accounting. Under accrual accounting, all assets and liabilities appear on the balance sheet for proprietary funds. This is different than accounting for governmental type funds, which follow modified accrual accounting. Under modified accrual accounting, only current assets and current liabilities appear on the balance sheet for governmental funds in the fund-based financial statements.

472. **C.** An internal service fund is a type of proprietary fund in which the services are provided to other agencies of the local government for a fee on a cost reimbursement basis, but the internal service fund typically does not offer those same services to the public. An example of an internal service fund would be a motor pool to store township cars. Proprietary funds use the full accrual basis of accounting and the economic resource focus, as opposed to the financial resource focus. All assets and liabilities are included in the fund-based financial statements of an internal service fund, not just the current assets and current liabilities.

473. **B.** Property tax revenue is accounted for in a governmental-type fund, the general fund. Property taxes are recorded in the period in which they are available and measurable. Available under modified accrual accounting means that the property taxes are collectible within the current period or 60 days after year end. *Measurable* simply means "quantifiable in monetary terms."

474. **A.** Since the parking garage revenue is shown net of depreciation, that must mean that the parking garage is being accounted for in a proprietary fund and not a governmental fund. Proprietary funds carry all their own assets and liabilities and record depreciation. Governmental funds carry only current assets and current liabilities in their fund-based financial statements. Governmental funds do not record depreciation, since no property plant and equipment exist on the balance sheet. Therefore, the $47,000 of garage rental income must be accounted for in a proprietary fund.

475. **B.** Fiduciary funds include assets that the government must monitor and then give to a third party. Only the interest income on employee retirement benefits of $110,000 qualifies as a fiduciary fund, since the money is not available to the government.

476. **B.** Money received for the construction of government-owned assets is recorded in the capital projects fund. Of the $12,000,000 raised, a $2,000,000 unrestricted grant from the state of New Jersey

represents revenue for the City of Wildwood. The journal entry would include a debit to cash and a credit to revenue in the amount of $2,000,000. The $10,000,000 from the bond issuance is accounted for as other financing sources. The journal entry to record the bond issue is a debit to cash and credit to other financing sources for $10,000,000 on January 1, Year 13, when the bonds are issued. Notice that the account "other financing sources" is credited and not "bonds payable," since the City of Wildwood is going to account for the construction using a capital projects fund. A capital projects fund is a governmental-type fund and uses the modified accrual basis of accounting, and the measurement focus is on current financial resources. As such, the capital projects fund cannot carry long-term debt on the fund-based financial statements. Therefore, the journal entry in the capital projects fund for the City of Wildwood would include a credit to other financing sources. The new convention center will not even appear on the balance sheet in the fund-based financial statements of the capital projects fund, because only current assets and current liabilities can be shown. Convention hall will appear only on the government-wide financial statements. In the capital projects fund, all costs of construction will be shown as expenditures.

477. **D.** For all governmental-type funds, including the general fund, capital projects fund, special revenue fund, debt service fund, and permanent funds, the basis of accounting is modified accrual and the measurement focus is the flow of financial resources. The modified accrual basis refers to recognizing revenue when available and measurable. The financial resource focus refers to carrying only the current assets and current liabilities in the fund-based financial statements. The flow of financial resources answers the question, "Where did the monies come from and where did they go?" Net income is not a measurement focus of governmental-type funds.

478. **C.** For governmental-type funds, expenditures include capital outlay for large acquisitions as well as expense type costs. Since no property plant and equipment get included on the fund-based financial statements, all the given costs will be recorded as expenditures. Notice that the term *expenditures* is used rather than *expenses* for all governmental type funds when they incur these costs. The term *expense* would be used rather than the term *expenditure* if the fund was a proprietary or fiduciary type fund.

479. **B.** II is correct. If the enterprise fund is short of cash and needs $50,000 from the general fund to stay afloat after a storm damages equipment, the $50,000 transfer of cash by the general fund to the enterprise fund is recorded by the general fund as a credit to cash and a debit to other financing uses. Although not an expenditure, transfers from one fund to another fund represent the use of financial resources. While the general fund records this as an "other financing use" the enterprise fund records the receipt of the cash transfer as a credit to "other financing sources" and a debit to cash.

480. **C.** Only a governmental-type fund like the general fund would record budget entries into the books at the start of the fiscal year. The entry to record the budget includes a debit to estimated revenues of $40,000,000, and a credit to estimated expenditures (known as appropriations) in the amount of $37,000,000. The expected transfer of $600,000 to the capital projects fund is credited in the budget entry to show that this amount is already assigned or committed. The remaining amount, $2,400,000, is credited to budgetary control, which basically represents budgetary equity at the time the budget is adopted. A credit to budgetary control indicates an expectation that enough revenues will cover expenditures. The estimated revenues could be an estimate of property tax revenues from homeowners. If conditions change, this may affect the government's ability to collect the property taxes. For example, the economy could turn and citizens could lose jobs. A loss of jobs could lead to homeowners going into default and eventual foreclosure, and if so, less property tax revenue would be collected. Although the budget entry is just an estimate, it's still required of every governmental-type fund at the start of the fiscal year because of accountability and control.

481. **D.** After the budgetary accounts are recorded at the beginning of the year, no other entries are made to estimated revenues or to appropriations during the year. Budgeted accounts are closed against the budget accounts at year end. For example, to close estimated revenues, credit estimated revenues, and to close appropriations, debit appropriations. The budget closing entry is for the same accounts and same amounts as the budget opening entry, but the debits and credits are reversed. Therefore, in the budget closing entry, estimated revenues is credited in the amount of $40,000,000, appropriations is debited for $37,000,000, other financing uses are debited for $600,000, and budgetary control is debited for $2,400,000.

482. A. To avoid overspending, purchase orders are recorded as encumbrances when a commitment is made. The assumption is that the encumbrances plus expenditures cannot exceed appropriations. Government accounting systems must reflect not only the expenditures but also the obligations to spend (purchase orders). Encumbrances represent obligations to spend. The encumbrance is debited on February 3 in the amount of $40,000 for control purposes to prevent overspending of appropriations. The credit is to budgetary control. The encumbrance is *not* an expenditure nor is the budgetary control account a liability. The budgetary control account acts as a constraint that reduces available fund balance.

483. C. On March 10 when the backup generator arrives, the commitment becomes a liability. The original encumbrance is removed and replaced by the actual expenditure. Two journal entries are needed on March 10. The first entry reverses the encumbrance by the actual amount encumbered, $40,000. The first entry is a debit to budgetary control and a credit to encumbrance for $40,000. The second journal entry would involve a debit to expenditures in the amount of $40,650 and a credit to vouchers payable for the same amount.

484. B. On April 5 when the invoice is paid, the journal entry would include a debit to vouchers payable for $40,650 and a credit to cash of 40,650. The expenditure was booked when the generator and invoice arrived on March 10. When the bill is paid, the liability is reduced and the cash is paid.

485. A. The journal entry to record property taxes receivable and revenue occurs when the property tax levy takes place. The amount estimated to be uncollectible is $250,000 and that allowance reduces the amount of revenue recognized to the measurable and available amount of $5,750,000. Along with the $250,000 credit to the allowance, the journal entry to record the property tax levy includes a debit to accounts receivable for the full amount levied of $6,000,000. The difference of $5,750,000 is a credit to property tax revenue at the time of levy.

486. A. I is correct. The government-wide statement of activities is like the income statement for the township. The government-wide statement of activities is prepared using the accrual basis, and the measurement focus is on the flow of economic resources. II is correct. The government-wide statement of net assets is much like a balance sheet. The government-wide statement of net assets is prepared on the accrual basis, and the measurement focus is on the flow of economic resources. Both fixed assets and long-term debt are reported in the government-wide statement of net assets. Infrastructure assets, like roads and bridges, tunnels, and storm sewers are included also. The government-wide statement of net assets reports all assets and liabilities of the primary government except the fiduciary funds. Fiduciary activities are *not* reported in the government-wide financial statements (GWFS) since the net assets of fiduciary funds do not belong to the government. Reporting fiduciary funds in the GWFS would be misleading.

487. A. I is correct. Assets like a senior center would appear in the government-wide statement of net assets prepared on the accrual basis. The construction in progress prior to completion would also be reported as an asset until the project is complete.

488. B. II is correct. On the government-wide statement of net assets, enterprise funds are shown as business-type activities, since enterprise funds conduct business activities on behalf of the government and serve the needs of the general public for a fee.

489. A. I and II are correct. Sales tax and income tax are examples of derived revenue for a governmental entity. Derived revenue is where the underlying event is being taxed.

490. D. For the school system to qualify as a separate primary government, several criteria must be established, including the fact that the school system is a legally separate entity from the city. For a school system to qualify as a separate primary government and file its own financial statements, the following conditions need to be met: the school board would have to be a legally separate entity from the city, have a separately elected governing board (not city council members), and be fiscally independent of other state and local governments. If these criteria can be established, then the school board qualifies as a special purpose local government and would need to report its own government-wide financial statements. Note: a component unit of a primary government such as a school system is blended into the primary government if the board of directors of the component unit is basically the same as the board of the primary government. Also, if the component unit serves the primary government almost exclusively and the debts of the component unit are to be repaid by the primary government, then the component unit should be blended with the primary government on the government-wide statement of activities. In addition, if the component unit is *not* a separate legal entity, then once again, the component unit is blended with the primary government. When the criteria for blending is *not* met and the component unit does not qualify as a separate primary government either, then the activities of the component unit would have to be shown in its own column on the government-wide statement of activities, discrete presentation.

Chapter 38: Not-for-Profit Entities

491. B. Not-for-profit (NFP) organizations include a wide array of organizations such as private colleges, hospitals, charities, voluntary health and welfare organizations, and churches. Not-for-profit entities use accrual accounting, similar but not identical to for-profit accounting. Accrual accounting is used by all not-for-profit organizations for external reporting purposes. For all not-for-profits, revenue is recognized when earned, and expenses (not expenditures) are recognized as incurred. Resources are received primarily from providers that do not expect repayment or economic returns. Although the operating purpose is other than to provide goods or services at a profit, accrual accounting is nevertheless used. Without a single indicator of performance, the measurement focus of reporting for nonprofits is on the organization "taken as a whole." Accrual accounting is used to determine whether management is performing well in its role as custodian of resources. The Financial Accounting Standards Board (FASB) is the primary source of literature regarding not-for-profit accounting.

492. B. In the statement of financial position for a not-for-profit, there are three categories of net assets (equity). The categories of net assets are based on whether any restriction has been placed on the net assets by an external donor. The three categories of net assets for a not-for-profit are as follows: unrestricted net assets (governing body can use for any purpose), temporarily restricted net assets (time restriction or use restriction exists), and permanently restricted net assets (only the income can be used, principal must be retained).

493. D. Financial resources of a not-for-profit entity that are currently expendable at the discretion of the governing board and that have not been restricted externally should be reported in the balance sheet of a not-for-profit entity as unrestricted

net assets. When assets are contributed to a not-for-profit, always look to the donor. A building received by a not-for-profit would be shown as unrestricted if the donor placed no restrictions on its use, thus allowing the governing body of the not-for-profit to do whatever it wishes with the structure. If restrictions were placed on the building's use by the external donor, the building would be shown as restricted, either temporarily restricted or permanently restricted based upon the donor's instructions. Assets that are donated to the not-for-profit without an external restriction but later become restricted by the governing board must still be shown as unrestricted. Regardless of the type of asset, if no external restriction exists, the asset is shown in the financial statements as unrestricted. Board-designated restrictions are not the same as donor-imposed restrictions. All board-designated assets are to be shown as unrestricted.

494. D. Unrestricted support amounts to $460,000 in Year 13. The $125,000 cash contribution is considered unrestricted support, since it can be used at the board of director's discretion and no restrictions were imposed by external donors. Services of $35,000 that are donated would be included as unrestricted support to the extent that they represent skilled services that the not-for-profit would otherwise have to pay for. Since the facts suggest the services were accounting related and that they would otherwise have to pay, all $35,000 of the accounting services are considered unrestricted. Finally, the building worth $300,000 is shown as unrestricted. A building received by a not-for-profit would be shown as unrestricted if the donor placed no restrictions on its use, thus allowing the governing body of the not-for-profit to do whatever it wishes with the structure. If restrictions were placed on the building's use by the external donor, the building would be shown as restricted, either temporarily restricted or permanently restricted based upon the donor's instructions. Assets, such as a building, that are donated to the not-for-profit without an external restriction, but later become restricted by the governing board, must still be shown as unrestricted. Regardless of the type of asset, if no external restriction exists, the asset is shown in the financial statements as unrestricted. Board-designated restrictions are not the same as donor-imposed restrictions. All board-designated assets are to be shown as unrestricted.

495. D. In Year 13 the contributions are received of $150,000, but they have strings attached. The donor restricted the $150,000, indicating that it can only be used for research. In Year 13 none of the $150,000 was used yet; therefore, in Year 13 all the $150,000 is considered temporarily restricted revenue on the statement of activities (income statement).

496. **A.** In Year 13 the contributions received were $150,000, but they had strings attached. The donor (temporarily) restricted the $150,000, indicating that it can only be used for research. By the end of Year 13, none of the $150,000 was used yet; so in Year 13 all of the $150,000 was considered temporarily restricted revenue on the statement of activities (income statement). In Year 14, $135,000 of the temporarily restricted net assets were spent on research. This involves a reclassification of net assets from temporarily restricted to unrestricted. The reclassification involves reducing temporarily restricted net assets by $135,000 and simultaneously increasing unrestricted net assets for the same amount. Just as the unrestricted net assets are going to increase by $135,000, they will also decrease by $135,000 to reflect the spending of the $135,000 that has been released from restriction. If a temporarily restricted net asset is released from restriction, it reflects a decrease in temporarily restricted net assets by the amount released, in this case, $135,000.

497. **D.** In Year 13 unrestricted net assets increase by $150,000, not $135,000. In Year 13 the contributions received were $150,000, but the donor restricted the $150,000, indicating that it can be used only for research. By the end of Year 13, none of the $150,000 was used yet; so in Year 13 all of the $150,000 was considered temporarily restricted revenue on the statement of activities (income statement). In Year 14, $135,000 of the temporarily restricted net assets was spent on research. This involves a reclassification of net assets from temporarily restricted to unrestricted. The reclassification involves reducing temporarily restricted net assets by $135,000 and simultaneously increasing unrestricted net assets for $135,000. Just as the unrestricted net assets are going to increase by $135,000, unrestricted net assets will also decrease by $135,000 to reflect the spending of the $135,000 that has been released from restriction.

498. **C.** A private, not-for-profit organization prepares all of the given except a statement of restricted net assets. Instead, the not-for-profit prepares a statement of financial position. The statement of financial position (balance sheet) is prepared under accrual accounting, but since there are no owners of a not-for-profit, there is no owner's equity. Instead, the statement of financial position presents: assets – liabilities = the organization's net assets taken as a whole. Instead of having owner's equity, a private not-for-profit must classify all of its net assets into one of three categories on the statement of financial position: unrestricted net assets, temporarily restricted net assets, and permanently restricted net assets. Therefore, a private not-for-profit organization does prepare a statement of financial position.

499. **C.** Contributions of cash that are donor-restricted for 5 years represent temporarily restricted net assets. Proceeds received from restricted contributions are included in the financing section of the statement of cash flows whether permanently or temporarily restricted. Also included as financing inflows are cash flows related to borrowing. Interest and dividend income restricted to reinvestment are classified as financing inflows as well.

500. **D.** Reporting expenses by function and by natural classification are very different ways to report expenses. Reporting by natural classification refers to listing each expense: salary expense, rent expense, and depreciation expense. For-profit companies show expenses by natural classification. Not-for-profits can also show expenses by natural classification but must show a statement of functional expenses either on the face of the financial statements or as a separate disclosure. Showing expenses by function refers to listing each program of the not-for-profit and showing the income and the expense from each program. While not-for-profits are encouraged to report expenses by function on the face of the financial statements, they can choose to present expenses by natural classification instead of by function. If not-for-profits don't present expenses by function on the face of the financial statements, they must do so in a separate disclosure and include a statement of functional expenses. That being the general rule, an exception exists for voluntary health and welfare organizations. The reason that voluntary health and welfare organizations must report expenses by function in the statement of activities *and* report expenses by natural classification is because voluntary health and welfare organizations typically raise large amounts of money through contributions. Donors are interested in knowing how their money is being utilized; therefore, voluntary health and welfare organizations must present expenses both by function and by natural classification.

501. C. I is correct. Conditional pledges are considered unconditional (earned) when the possibility that the condition will *not* be met is remote. The exam question will indicate whether the possibility that the condition will not be met is remote. II is correct. Conditional pledges are considered unconditional (earned) when donor-imposed conditions have been substantially met. For example, if the donor places a condition on the pledge, such as a matching contribution, then the donor-imposed conditions expire when the matching funds are received by the not-for-profit. Until that point the promise is said to be unconditional, unless the possibility that the matching contributions won't be received is remote.

502. D. A conditional promise is considered unconditional if the possibility that the condition will not be met is remote. Since the college believed that the possibility of not receiving the remaining 5% was remote on December 31, Year 10, Walton's promise is treated as unconditional and revenue is recorded. The revenue is considered temporarily restricted since it must be used for the new parking deck. Although the promise is unconditional, the money is temporarily restricted.

503. B. II is correct. *Restricted* and *unrestricted* are net asset concepts. When assets are donated to a not-for-profit, they often have strings attached by the donor. Only if the asset has no strings attached can the assets be designated as unrestricted when received.

504. C. The general rule regarding services donated to a not-for-profit is that no entry is made unless the services require specialized skill donated by experts in their field, such as doctors, lawyers, CPAs, and professional contractors like electricians, roofers, and craftsmen, that would need to be purchased if not donated. Donated professional services such as the preceding are *not* capitalized but are recorded as *both* expense and revenue on the statement of activities. Thus homeless shelters would increase both expenditures and contributions in Year 12. The journal entry would involve a debit to expense and a credit to nonoperating revenue. Had the roof been repaired by a group of amateur volunteers without specialized roofing skills, Homeless Shelters would not have made any entry in the statement of activities.

505. B. A not-for-profit entity such as the Jersey Shore Free School would recognize contribution revenue based on the net realizable value of the pledges receivable at the time the pledges are made. Therefore, the contribution revenue should be recognized on February 3, Year 13, as follows:

Unconditional pledges	$60,000
(Multiplied by uncollectible percentage	×15%)
Allowance for doubtful accounts	− $9,000
Net realizable value	$51,000

The journal entry to record the pledge on February 3 would include a debit to pledge receivable for $60,000. The credits would be to allowance for doubtful accounts in the amount of $9,000, and $51,000 is credited to contribution revenue. Notice that the actual amount received in Year 13 of $20,000 does not enter into the calculation of contribution revenue.

506. B. The functional expense categories used by not-for-profit organizations are generally listed under the two main classifications of program expenses and *support services*. Included in the main classification of support services are three subcategories: general and administrative expenses, membership development, and fund-raising. While program expenses directly relate to the mission of the not-for-profit such as a teacher's salary, support services include all other costs involved in maintaining a not-for-profit.

507. C. IV is correct. Revenues for a not-for-profit hospital arise from activities associated with the providing of health care services, since the providing of health care constitutes the ongoing major or central operations of providers of health care services. There are three categories of revenue for a not-for-profit hospital: patient service revenue, other operating revenue, and nonoperating revenue. Unrestricted gifts to a not-for-profit hospital would be considered nonoperating revenue. Nonoperating revenues would represent incidental earnings unrelated to the central operations of the hospital. Unrestricted gifts would represent nonoperating revenue but would nevertheless be reported as revenue. Therefore, unrestricted gifts would be reported by a not-for-profit hospital as nonoperating revenue.

509. B. For not-for-profit colleges and universities, gross revenues for tuition are reported net of refunds for cancelled classes. The scholarships are presented as an expense rather than netted against tuition on the statement of activities. Therefore, tuition should be reported at $4,800,000 for the spring semester, Year 13, calculated as follows:

Gross tuition revenue assessed	$5,000,000
Less refunds for cancelled classes	− $200,000
Gross tuition revenue	$4,800,000

The journal entry would be a debit to cash for $4,500,000, a debit to expenses-scholarships for $300,000, and a credit to revenue-tuition and fees for $4,800,000.

PART IV

REGULATION

QUESTIONS 1–140

1. Theresa and John were single for all of Year 12 and lived mostly apart until December 31 when they flew to Las Vegas and were married shortly before midnight. What is Theresa and John's filing status for Year 12?

   A. Married filing jointly
   B. Head of household
   C. Single
   D. Married filing separately

2. Gil Gallon's wife died in Year 1. Gil Gallon did not remarry. He continued to maintain a home for himself and his dependent infant child during Year 1 and Year 2, providing full support for himself and his child during these years. Gil Gallon's filing status for Year 2 is:

   A. single
   B. head of household
   C. married filing jointly
   D. qualifying widower with dependent child

3. Bonnie's husband died in Year 1. She did not remarry. She continued to maintain a home for herself and her dependent infant child during Year 2, Year 3, and Year 4, providing full support for herself and her child during these three years. For Year 4, Bonnie's filing status is:

   A. single
   B. head of household
   C. qualifying widow with dependent child
   D. married filing jointly

4. In Year 8, Kathleen and Lee were married and had four dependent children. On May 1, Year 8, Lee packed his bags and abruptly deserted his family. His whereabouts were still unknown to Kathleen at the time she filed her Year 8 income tax return in February of Year 9. What is the most advantageous filing status that Kathleen is legally allowed for Year 8?

   A. Single
   B. Married filing separately
   C. Head of household
   D. Qualifying widow with dependent child

5. For which of the following potential dependents would taxpayers NOT have to demonstrate that they provided more than one-half of the support?
   I. Taxpayer's qualifying child
   II. Taxpayer's parent

   A. I only
   B. II only
   C. Both I and II
   D. Neither I nor II

6. Ben and Freeda, both age 62, filed a joint return for Year 7. They provided all the support for their daughter Susan, who is 19, legally blind, mostly deaf, and has no income. Their son, Harold, age 21 and a full-time university student, had $6,200 in income during Year 7. Ben and Freeda can claim how many exemptions on their Year 7 joint tax return?

   A. 2
   B. 3
   C. 4
   D. 5

7. Walter is 86 years old but still files an income tax return because he works part-time at a nearby amusement park. Which of the following is true?

   A. Because of his age, Walter receives an additional amount if he claims itemized deductions.
   B. Because of his age, Walter receives an additional amount of personal exemptions.
   C. Because of his age, the first $6,200 of Walter's salary is nontaxable.
   D. Because of his age, Walter receives an additional amount for his standard deduction.

8. Erin and Mars are married cash-basis taxpayers. The couple had interest income as follows:

   $500 interest on federal income tax refund
   $600 interest on state income tax refund
   $800 interest on US Treasury (i.e., federal government) obligations
   $300 interest on Puerto Rico government obligations
   $700 interest on state government obligations

   What amount of interest income is taxable on the couple's joint income tax return?

   A. $500
   B. $1,100
   C. $1,900
   D. $2,900

9. Griffin received the following interest payments during the current year:

   Interest of $500 on a refund of federal income tax for last year
   Interest of $400 on an award for personal injuries sustained in a car accident three years ago
   Interest of $1,600 on municipal bonds
   Interest of $1,100 on US savings bonds (Series HH)

   What amount, if any, should be reported as interest income on Griffin's current year tax return?

   A. $3,600
   B. $2,000
   C. $900
   D. $0

10. Which of the following is a condition required for accumulated interest on Series EE US savings bonds to be exempt from tax?
    I. The bonds must have been purchased by the taxpayer or taxpayer's spouse and put in the name of a dependent child.
    II. Redemption proceeds from the bonds are used to fix up the taxpayer's home.

    A. I only
    B. II only
    C. Both I and II
    D. Neither I nor II

11. Kleinman bought Series EE US savings bonds. Redemption proceeds from the bonds will be used to pay for the college tuition of his dependent daughter. One of the conditions that must be met for tax exemption of accumulated interest on these bonds is that:
    I. Kleinman must be the sole owner of the bonds (or joint owner with his spouse)
    II. the bonds must have been purchased by Kleinman before Kleinman reached the age of 24
    III. the bonds must be transferred to the college for redemption by the college rather than by Kleinman

    A. I only
    B. II only
    C. I and III only
    D. II and III only

12. Which of the following dividends are taxable?
    I. Dividend on a listed stock where the taxpayer reinvests the dividend into additional shares
    II. Dividend on a life insurance policy
    III. Dividend of a Chinese corporation listed on a foreign stock exchange

    A. I and III only
    B. I, II, and III
    C. I and II only
    D. II and III only

13. Tatum owned 1,000 shares of common stock in Cyrus Corp. for which she paid $50 per share. The company distributed a 5% common stock dividend to all holders of common stock. The fair market value (FMV) of the stock on the date of distribution was $60. With respect to this dividend, what amount must be included in Tatum's gross income?

    A. $0
    B. $1,000
    C. $2,500
    D. $3,000

14. On Form 1040, which of the following schedules are used to report interest and dividend income?

Interest Income	Dividend Income
A. Schedule B	Schedule D
B. Schedule D	Schedule B
C. Schedule B	Schedule E
D. Schedule B	Schedule B

15. In Year 2, Stegman had a passive gain of $1,000 and a passive loss of $5,000. Stegman also earned a salary of $50,000 from her employer in Year 2 and had interest income of $100 on a certificate of deposit. What is Stegman's net passive income or loss for Year 2?

A. loss of $4,000
B. $0
C. loss of $3,900
D. income of $46,100

16. Adrian, an unmarried individual, had an adjusted gross income (AGI) of $190,000 for Year 6. Adrian incurred a loss of $29,000 from rental real estate activity she participated in during Year 6. What amount of the $29,000 loss can be used (in Year 6) to offset income from nonpassive sources?

A. $0
B. $12,500
C. $25,000
D. $30,000

17. Cindy, an unmarried individual, had an AGI of $75,000 for Year 9. Cindy incurred a loss of $30,000 from a rental real estate activity in which she actively participated during Year 9. What amount of loss attributable to this rental activity can Cindy use in Year 9 to offset income earned from nonpassive sources?

A. $0
B. $12,500
C. $25,000
D. $30,000

18. In Year 10, Shan, a single taxpayer, received $160,000 in salary from his employer; received $15,000 in income from an S corporation in which he did not actively participate during Year 10; and incurred a $35,000 loss from a rental real estate activity in which he did actively participate during Year 10. Shan's AGI amounted to $165,000 for Year 10. What amount of the $35,000 loss associated with the rental real estate activity was deductible in Year 10?

A. $0
B. $15,000
C. $20,000
D. $25,000

19. Skorecki owns a two-family house that has two identical apartments. He lives in one unit and rents out the other. In Year 4, the rental apartment was fully occupied and Skorecki received $10,000 in rent. Skorecki owned no other real estate during Year 4 and paid the following:

Mortgage interest	$3,000
Real estate taxes	$5,000
Repairs of rental apartment	$800

Skorecki is preparing his Year 4 income tax return. Depreciation for the entire house was determined to be $2,000. What amount should Skorecki include in his income for the rental property for Year 4?

A. ($800)
B. $4,200
C. $3,800
D. $1,000

20. Rudnick became a general partner in Wolinsky Associates partnership on January 1, Year 6, with a 5% interest in profits, losses, and capital. Wolinsky Associates is a distributor of test prep software. Rudnick does not actively participate in the partnership business. For the year ended December 31, Year 6, Wolinsky had an operating loss of $50,000. In addition, Wolinsky earned interest of $20,000 on US Treasury obligations. Rudnick's passive loss for Year 6 is:

A. $0
B. $1,500
C. $2,500
D. $5,000

21. Benson, an individual taxpayer, reported the following items for Year 7: $70,000 of ordinary income from partnership A: operating a bowling alley in which she materially participates; $9,000 passive loss from partnership B: operating an equipment rental business in which she does not materially participate; $7,000 of rental income from a building rented to a third party; and $4,000 of interest and dividend income. What is Benson's AGI for Year 7?

    A. $70,000
    B. $72,000
    C. $74,000
    D. $77,000

22. Shapiro, an individual taxpayer, reports the following items for Year 9:

    $40,000 of ordinary income from partnership A: operating a pinball arcade in which Shapiro materially participates

    $9,000 net gain from partnership B: operating a bike rental business in which Shapiro does not materially participate

    $17,000 loss from Shapiro's rental of a building to a third party

    How much of Shapiro's $17,000 building rental loss is deductible in Year 9?

    A. $0
    B. $9,000
    C. $8,000
    D. $17,000

23. Jonathan, age 22, is a full-time student at Randolph College and a candidate for a bachelor's degree. During Year 9, he received the following payments:

State scholarship for tuition	$4,200
Loan—college financial aid	$1,000
Cash support from parents	$2,000
Cash dividends on stocks	$500
Cash prize awarded in contest	$300
Unemployment compensation	$1,000
Interest income on tax refund	$10

    Jonathan's AGI for Year 9 is

    A. $700
    B. $800
    C. $810
    D. $1,810

24. During Year 5, Tammy accepted and received a $10,000 humanitarian award. Tammy was selected to win this award without any action on her part, and no future services are expected of her as a condition of receiving the award. Which of the following is correct?

    I. If Tammy never took possession of the $10,000 but instead had the amount sent directly to a charity, the $10,000 would be excluded from gross income.
    II. If Tammy first took the $10,000 check and later donated it to a charity, the $10,000 would be included in gross income.

    A. I only
    B. II only
    C. Both I and II
    D. Neither I or II

25. Carl owns a machine shop and provides life insurance for each of his employees. The amount of life insurance provided is equal to the employee's annual salary (under a qualified plan). Bob works for Carl and is covered by the life insurance policy. How much of the premium (paid by Carl to the insurance company) is taxable to Bob as income?

    A. None
    B. All of the premium
    C. An amount equal to the premium paid for the first $50,000 of coverage provided
    D. An amount equal to the premium paid for coverage provided in excess of $50,000

26. Cobbs works for the Johnson Regional Bank. He is covered by a $90,000 group-term life insurance policy, which lists his brothers as the beneficiaries. Johnson Regional Bank pays the entire cost of the policy, for which the uniform annual premium is $8 per $1,000 of coverage. How much of this premium is taxable to Cobbs?

    A. $0
    B. $360
    C. $320
    D. $720

27. Olney, an accrual basis taxpayer, operates an office building. He received the following payments during the current year:

Current rents	$30,000
Rents for next year	$10,000
Security deposits held in a segregated account	$5,000
Lease cancellation payments	$15,000

What amount can be included in Olney's current gross income?

A. $60,000
B. $55,000
C. $40,000
D. $30,000

28. Jay, a dentist, billed Lou $600 for dental services. Lou paid Jay $200 cash for these services and catered a party for Jay's office staff in full settlement of the bill. Lou caters comparable parties for $350 and makes a profit of approximately $250 per party. What amount should Jay include in taxable income as a result of this transaction?

A. $200
B. $450
C. $550
D. $600

29. Which of the following conditions must be present in a divorce agreement for a payment to qualify as deductible alimony?
   I. Payments must be in cash or property.
   II. Payments can be made to a third party on behalf of a spouse.

A. I only
B. II only
C. Both I and II
D. Neither I or II

30. Karen and Terry were divorced in Year 3. The divorce decree provides that beginning in Year 4, Terry pay alimony of $20,000 per year, to be reduced by 30% on their child's 18th birthday. Karen and Terry's child is currently 13 years old. During Year 4, Terry paid $9,000 to Karen's landlord, $6,000 directly to Karen, and $5,000 to Wildwood College for Karen's college tuition. What amount of these payments should be reported as income in Karen's Year 4 income tax return?

A. $6,000
B. $14,000
C. $15,000
D. $20,000

31. Buddy is a cash-basis, self-employed handyman. He files Schedule C as a sole proprietor. His cash receipts and disbursements for Year 2 were as follows:

Gross income	$30,000
Plumbing supplies	$2,500
Web page hosting	$300
Depreciation of business equipment	$400
Advertising	$1,700
Estimated federal income tax	$4,000
Charitable contribution to Red Cross	$500
Buddys' regular weekly salary— $100 per week	$5,200

What amount can Buddy deduct on his Form 1040 Schedule C for Year 2?

A. $4,900
B. $8,900
C. $9,400
D. $14,600

32. Dr. Bernstein is a cash-basis taxpayer. The following items pertain to Dr. Bernstein's medical practice in Year 4:

Cash received from patients in Year 4	$270,000
Cash received in Year 4 from insurance companies for services provided by Dr. Bernstein in Year 3	$30,000
Salaries paid to employees in Year 4	$50,000
Year 4 bonuses paid to employees in Year 5	$4,000
Other expenses paid in Year 4	$25,000

What amount of taxable net income should Dr. Bernstein report from his medical practice for Year 4?

A. $255,000
B. $216,000
C. $221,000
D. $225,000

Use the following facts to answer **Questions 33–34.**

Anita earned consulting fees of $8,000 and directors' fees of $1,800 last year. Also last year, Anita had a net profit on her gift business of $1,000, which she reported on Form 1040 Schedule C. Anita also had interest income of $2,400 from PNC Bank and she received alimony of $1,500.

33. Anita's income from self-employment last year was:

A. $10,800
B. $10,000
C. $9,800
D. $0

34. Will Anita pay federal income or self-employment tax on her net earnings from self-employment?

Federal Income Tax	Self-Employment Tax
A. Yes	No
B. No	Yes
C. Yes	Yes
D. No	No

35. Freedson is a self-employed literary agent and is required to pay self-employment tax as a result. On Freedson's current year tax return, the self-employment tax is:

A. one-half deductible from gross income in arriving at AGI

B. not deductible

C. fully deductible as an itemized deduction

D. fully deductible in determining net income from self-employment

36. Truncale is a landlord with an AGI of $75,000 for the current year. What taxes would Truncale pay if he shows a profit from net rental activities on Form 1040 Schedule E?

A. Federal income tax only

B. Self-employment tax only

C. Both federal income tax and self-employment tax

D. Neither federal income tax nor self-employment tax, because rental income is passive

37. Which of the following would be considered a capital asset?

   I. Land operated as a small outdoor marketplace

  II. A large shed on the land used for table storage when the marketplace is not open

A. I only

B. II only

C. Both I and II

D. Neither I nor II

38. Ratner recently purchased land to be held as a long-term investment. On that land was an abandoned building that will soon need to be torn down. Should Ratner classify the land and the building as Section 1231 assets?

Land	Building
A. No	Yes
B. Yes	No
C. Yes	Yes
D. No	No

39. Rocky owns the following assets: recreational skis and a limousine that is used in her personal limousine service business for transporting passengers to and from airports. Which of these assets should Rocky classify as part of capital assets?

A. The recreational skis only

B. The limousine only

C. Both the recreational skis and the limousine

D. Neither the recreational skis or the limousine

40. During Year 6, Angie sold a painting for $25,000 that she had bought for her personal use in Year 1 at a cost of $10,000. Angie sold the painting in Year 6 and had a gain on the sale. In Angie's Year 6 income tax return, Angie should treat the sale of the painting as a transaction resulting in:

A. ordinary gain

B. long-term capital gain

C. Section 1231 gain

D. short-term capital gain

41. Andrea and Ken are a married couple filing a joint return. A current year capital loss incurred by them:

A. can be deducted only to the extent of capital gains

B. may be carried forward up to a maximum of three years

C. cannot be deducted unless the capital loss is from an asset held for personal use

D. can be deducted to the extent of capital gains, plus to $3,000 of ordinary income

42. Which of the following statements is TRUE with respect to capital assets for individual taxpayers?

A. Gains and losses for both investment and personal property are reported on Form 1040, Schedule D.

B. The taxpayer must report gains and losses on investment property, but should report only gains on personal property.

C. Losses on personal property are deductible only to the extent of gains on personal property.

D. Losses on investment property are deductible only to the extent of gains on investment property.

43. When exchanging "like-kind" property, which of the following terms has essentially the same meaning as "realized gain"?
    I. Recognized gain
    II. Accounting gain
    III. Economic gain

    A. I only
    B. II only
    C. II and III only
    D. III only

44. Saralee exchanged commercial real estate that she owned for other commercial real estate. Saralee also received $50,000 cash as part of the exchange. The following additional information pertains to this transaction:

    Property Given Up by Saralee
    Fair market value $500,000
    Cost basis $300,000

    Property Received by Saralee
    Fair market value $450,000
    Cost basis $50,000

    Based on these facts and additional information, what is Saralee's recognized gain?

    A. $200,000
    B. $50,000
    C. $100,000
    D. $0

    Use the following facts to answer **Questions 45–46.**

    Pollack exchanged an apartment building having an adjusted cost basis of $375,000 and subject to a mortgage of $100,000 for $25,000 cash and another apartment building with an FMV of $550,000 and subject to a mortgage of $125,000. The property transfers were made subject to the outstanding mortgages.

45. What amount of gain would Pollack **realize** on this exchange?

    A. $25,000
    B. $100,000
    C. $125,000
    D. $175,000

46. What amount of gain should Pollack **recognize** on this exchange?

    A. $25,000
    B. $100,000
    C. $125,000
    D. $175,000

47. Hymanson exchanged investment real property with an adjusted cost basis of $160,000, which was subject to a mortgage of $70,000, and received (from Poppel) $30,000 cash and other investment real property having an FMV of $250,000. Poppel assumed Hymanson's old mortgage in this exchange. What is Hymanson's recognized gain on this exchange?

    A. $100,000
    B. $90,000
    C. $70,000
    D. $30,000

    Use the following facts to answer **Questions 48–49.**

    In Year 7, Jerry paid $15,000 for shares of ABC stock. In Year 9, Jerry sold all of the ABC stock shares to his son, Evan, for $11,000.

48. Considering these facts, which of the following is a correct statement?
    I. Jerry may NOT deduct any of the $4,000 loss on the sale to Evan, since it is a related-party loss.
    II. Evan may use Jerry's previously disallowed loss if Evan sells the ABC stock shares at a gain to an unrelated party.

    A. I only
    B. II only
    C. Both I and II
    D. Neither I or II

49. Now assume in Year 9 that Evan sells the ABC company shares to an unrelated party for $16,000. As a result, what amount of gain (from the sale of these shares) should Evan recognize in his Year 9 income tax return?

    A. $0
    B. $1,000
    C. $4,000
    D. $5,000

50. On July 1 of Year 4, Mitch owned stock (held for investment) having an FMV of $7,000 that had been purchased two years earlier at a cost of $10,000. On this date (July 1, Year 4), Mitch sold the stock to his brother Glen for $7,000. Glen then sold the stock for $6,000 to an unrelated party on November 1, Year 4. Glen should report the effects of this stock sale on his Year 4 tax return as a:

    A. short-term capital loss of $1,000
    B. long-term capital loss of $1,000
    C. short-term capital loss of $4,000
    D. long-term capital loss of $4,000

51. Phil died on December 31, Year 2, bequeathing shares of stock to his son, Jeff. All of the stock was distributed to Jeff on March 31, Year 3. Phil's estate executor elected the alternative valuation date (AVD) for Phil's estate. The value of the stock on December 31, Year 2, was $210,000. The value on March 31, Year 3, was $240,000. The value on June 30, Year 3, was $270,000. Jeff's basis for this stock is:

    A. $210,000
    B. $240,000
    C. $270,000
    D. $300,000

52. Fanny died on April 1, Year 1. Because of the size of Fanny's estate, no distributions were made until after July 1, Year 2. For estate valuation purposes, the executor of the estate selected the AVD. On what date must the estate assets be valued?

    A. April 1, Year 1
    B. October 1, Year 1
    C. December 31, Year 1
    D. April 1, Year 2

53. Andy sold 500 shares of XYZ Corp. stock on June 1, Year 2. He had received this stock on June 1, Year 1, as a bequest from the estate of his uncle Bart, who died on March 1, Year 1. Andy's basis was determined by reference to the stock's FMV on March 1, Year 1. Andy's holding period for this stock was:

    A. long-term
    B. short-term
    C. short-term if sold at a gain; long-term if sold at a loss
    D. long-term if sold at a gain; short-term if sold at a loss

54. Denise, a single individual, sold her personal residence in Year 15 for $390,000. She had purchased the home in Year 12 for $105,000. In Year 13, she added a patio to the home at a cost of $25,000. She has always used the home as her principal residence. Back in Year 8, she sold a different personal residence and excluded $100,000 of gain earned on that sale from her tax return in that year. What amount of gain must Denise recognize on her Year 15 tax return from the Year 15 sale of her personal residence?

    A. $10,000
    B. $110,000
    C. $250,000
    D. $260,000

55. Which of the following is a requirement for a taxpayer filing single to exclude (from income) up to $250,000 of realized gain on the sale of a home?
    I. The home must be considered a vacation home.
    II. The taxpayer must buy another residence for an amount in excess of the proceeds the taxpayer received from the sale of the current residence.

    A. I only
    B. II only
    C. Both I and II
    D. Neither I nor II

56. Barry and Saralee are a married couple filing jointly for Year 12. They purchased their principal residence for $300,000 back in Year 2. The couple spent $40,000 on improvements to the home. After living in the home for 10 years, Barry and Saralee sold the home for $650,000 and paid $36,000 in real estate commissions. What amount of gain should the couple recognize on their Year 12 joint return?

    A. $0
    B. $60,000
    C. $274,000
    D. $500,000

Use the following facts to answer Questions 57–58.

Koshefsky owned a building condemned by the state. The building had a tax basis of $200,000, but was worth $250,000. The state paid him $260,000 for the condemned property.

57. If Koshefsky bought similar replacement property for $170,000, what was Koshefsky's taxable gain?

    A. $10,000
    B. $30,000
    C. $60,000
    D. $90,000

58. If Koshefsky bought similar replacement property for $230,000, what amount of gain would Koshefsky be required to recognize on this transaction?

    A. $0
    B. $30,000
    C. $60,000
    D. $90,000

59. An office building owned by Brad was condemned by the state on January 2, Year 2. Brad received proceeds for the condemnation, from the state, on March 1, Year 2. In order to qualify for nonrecognition of gain on this involuntary conversion, what is the last date for Brad to acquire qualified replacement property?

A. December 31, Year 4
B. January 2, Year 4
C. December 31, Year 5
D. March 1, Year 5

60. In Year 4, Frank gave a painting to his friend Stan. Frank originally paid $200 for the painting. At the time of the gift, the painting was worth $150. Stan sold the painting in Year 5 to Rizzo for $360, its FMV at that time. Which of the following is correct?

I. Stan's basis in the painting is NOT determinable until he sells the painting.
II. At the time of sale, Stan recognizes a $160 gain.

A. I only
B. II only
C. Both I and II
D. Neither I nor II

61. Property is purchased by Harry for $150,000 and later gifted to Barry when the value of the property is $147,000. If Barry then sells the property to Larry, an unrelated party, for $144,000, which of the following is correct?

I. Barry's basis in the property is NOT determinable until he sells the property.
II. Barry is precluded from reporting a loss on the sale of the property to Larry since Barry had originally received the property as a gift.

A. I only
B. II only
C. Both I and II
D. Neither I nor II

62. Property is purchased by Keri for $150,000 and later gifted to Jeri when the value of the property is $147,000. Jeri then sells the property to Meri, an unrelated party, for $149,000. What amount of gain or loss should Jeri report on this transaction?

A. $0
B. $1,000 loss
C. $2,000 gain
D. $3,000 gain

63. In June, Year 4, Debbie gifted her grandson, Craig, 100 shares of a listed stock. Debbie's basis for this stock, which she bought in Year 2, was $4,000 and the FMV of the stock on the date of the gift was $3,000. Craig sold this stock in July Year 4 to an unrelated party for $3,500. What was Craig's basis when he sold the 100 shares in Year 4?

A. $4,000
B. $3,500
C. $3,000
D. $0

Use the following facts to answer **Questions 64–65.**

Grace bought a diamond necklace in Year 1 for her own use at a cost of $10,000. In Year 9, when the FMV was $12,000, she gave this necklace to her daughter, Rochelle.

64. Assuming that Rochelle sells the diamond necklace in Year 9 for $13,000, Rochelle's recognized gain would be:

A. $3,000
B. $2,000
C. $1,000
D. $0

65. For tax purposes, Rochelle's diamond necklace and the sale thereof are considered a(n):

A. Section 1231 asset
B. capital asset
C. involuntary conversion
D. passive activity

66. During the current year, Lois, an unmarried US citizen, made a $5,000 cash gift to an only child and also paid $25,000 in tuition expenses directly to a grandchild's university on the grandchild's behalf. Lois made no other lifetime transfers. For gift tax purposes, what was Lois's taxable gift?

A. $30,000
B. $25,000
C. $17,000
D. $0

67. Micki, a single taxpayer, gave the following outright gifts during the current year: $16,000 cash to her grandson for a down payment on a house, $14,000 cash to her friend's son for his college tuition, and $6,000 cash to her cousin for a vacation trip. What amount of the gifts Micki gave would be excluded from the gift tax?

    A. $28,000
    B. $34,000
    C. $14,000
    D. $2,000

68. Jeffrey and Alice have been married for 25 years. Alice inherited $1,000,000 from her father. What amount of the $1,000,000 can Alice give to Jeffrey without incurring a gift tax liability?

    A. $0
    B. $26,000
    C. $500,000
    D. $1,000,000

69. During the holiday season, Luchentos Restaurant gave business gifts to 16 customers. The value of the gifts, which were not of an advertising nature, were as follows: four customers at $10; four customers at $20; four customers at $60; four customers at $80. What amount of these gifts can Luchentos deduct as a business expense?

    A. $0
    B. $340
    C. $320
    D. $400

70. For which of the following asset sales would the seller's tax basis NOT be known until the time of actual sale?
    I. Sale in Year 3 of property received by gift back in Year 1
    II. Sale in Year 3 of property received as an inheritance back in Year 1

    A. I only
    B. II only
    C. Both I and II
    D. Neither I nor II

71. Which of the following are deductible to arrive at AGI?
    I. Moving expenses
    II. Student loan interest

    A. I only
    B. II only
    C. Both I and II
    D. Neither I nor II

72. Which of the following are deductible to arrive at AGI?
    I. Alimony paid
    II. Child support paid
    III. Contribution to a health savings account

    A. I only
    B. I and II only
    C. I and III only
    D. II and III only

73. Which of the following penalties can a taxpayer deduct from gross income to arrive at AGI?
    I. Penalty on early withdrawal of savings
    II. Penalty for late payment of federal income tax

    A. I only
    B. II only
    C. Both I and II
    D. Neither I nor II

74. Corey was transferred from New Jersey to Massachusetts by his employer. In connection with this transfer, Corey incurred the following moving expenses: moving his household goods: $2,000; temporary living expenses in Massachusetts: $400; lodging on the way to Massachusetts: $100; meals on the way to Massachusetts: $40; and a penalty for breaking his lease on his residence in New Jersey: $50. What amount of these moving expenses can Corey deduct on his tax return if his employer reimburses him $2,000 for these expenses?

    A. $0
    B. $100
    C. $150
    D. $500

75. A single taxpayer, age 42, wishes to contribute and deduct $5,500 into a traditional IRA for the current year. Which of the following types of income combinations would enable the taxpayer to qualify for the full $5,500 deduction?

    A. Alimony received of $2,000 and wages earned of $3,500
    B. Self-employment income (Schedule C profit) of $2,000, alimony of $1,000, and interest income of $2,500
    C. Interest income of $3,000 and dividend income of $2,500
    D. Wages earned of $4,500 and rental income of $1,000

Use the following facts to answer **Questions 76–77.**

Koslow is 45 years old and has a dependent daughter, Lily. During Year 2, Koslow took three premature distributions from his IRA account. The first distribution was $6,000 and was used to pay medical expenses. The second distribution was $10,000 and was used to pay off his credit card balances. The third distribution was $8,000 and was used to pay for tuition for his daughter, Lily, who is attending Western City University.

76. How much is the 10% penalty tax that Koslow will be subject to?

   A. $0
   B. $1,000
   C. $1,600
   D. $2,400

77. How much increase in **taxable income** will Koslow have as a result of the three premature IRA distributions?

   A. $6,000
   B. $8,000
   C. $16,000
   D. $24,000

78. Which of the following is correct regarding IRA limits in the current year?
   I. The maximum IRA deduction is $5,500 for those under age 50.
   II. The maximum IRA deduction is $6,500 for those ages 50 or older.

   A. I only
   B. II only
   C. Both I and II
   D. Neither I nor II

79. Audrey takes a qualifying distribution from her **Roth IRA**. Such distributions are:

   A. fully taxable
   B. taxable only to the extent of the income element distributed
   C. not taxable
   D. not taxable, but subject to the alternative minimum tax

80. By what age must a taxpayer begin to withdraw at least minimum distributions from a retirement account such as a traditional IRA?

   A. 59½
   B. 65
   C. 70½
   D. Whatever age the taxpayer first begins to collect social security benefits

81. Contributions to a health savings account (HSA) are:

   A. deductible as an itemized medical expense deduction if made by the employee
   B. not available to self-employed individuals
   C. excluded from the employee's income if made by the employer
   D. not available to employees

82. Anzalone, a self-employed taxpayer, had a gross income of $57,000. Anzalone made a contribution of $4,000 to an HSA, paid health insurance premiums of $6,000, and paid $5,000 of alimony and $3,000 in child support. Anzalone also contributed $2,000 to a traditional IRA and contributed $1,000 to an educational IRA for his nephew, age 10. What is Anzalone's adjusted gross income?

   A. $55,000
   B. $50,000
   C. $46,000
   D. $40,000

83. Cindy and Dan are married and file a joint income tax return. Both were employed during the year and earned the following salaries: Dan: $128,000; Cindy: $134,000. In order to enable Cindy to work, she incurred at-home child care expenses of $16,000 for their two-year-old daughter and elderly grandfather. Cindy and Dan can claim what amount of the dependent care credit?

   A. $1,200
   B. $600
   C. $960
   D. 0

84. Mike qualified for the earned income credit in Year 2. This credit could result in a:

   A. refund only if Mike had tax withheld from wages
   B. carry back or carry forward for any unused portion
   C. refund even if Mike had no tax withheld from wages
   D. refund provided Mike had at least one child

85. Which is correct regarding tax credits?
    I. Most credits will reduce tax dollar for dollar and then provide a tax refund if the remaining credit is greater than the total tax.
    II. The earned income credit is a refundable credit.

    A. I only
    B. II only
    C. Both I and II
    D. Neither I nor II

86. Ziga is single with no dependents. He showed a loss on his Schedule C of $8,000. He has dividend income of $200 and interest income of $100. He also has a profit of $500 from a rental activity on Schedule E. Which is correct?
    I. Because Ziga's income is very low, he should qualify for the earned income credit.
    II. Ziga's income from rental activities of $500 is considered passive income.

    A. I only
    B. II only
    C. Both I and II
    D. Neither I nor II

87. Michael and Joan, married filing jointly, have a tax liability prior to the American Opportunity Credit of $2,000. Their only son in college, Paul, is a full-time student in his junior year. If Michael and Joan qualify for the full American Opportunity Credit, what is the amount of their tax refund?

    A. $0
    B. $500
    C. $1,000
    D. $1,500

88. The American Opportunity Credit:
    I. can be taken for the first four years of postsecondary education
    II. can be taken regardless of a taxpayer's AGI, but the student must be enrolled on at least a half-time basis

    A. I only
    B. II only
    C. Both I and II
    D. Neither I nor II

89. Benny is single and has a modified AGI of $64,000. He paid $8,000 in tuition for his daughter Melissa to attend Richmond University. What is the amount of Benny's Lifetime Learning Credit for the year?

    A. $2,500
    B. $1,800
    C. $1,600
    D. $0

90. "Student must be enrolled on a half-time basis at least" is a characteristic of the:
    I. American Opportunity Credit
    II. Lifetime Learning Credit

    A. I only
    B. II only
    C. Both I and II
    D. Neither I nor II

91. In the current year, Joe and Jean Riley, married and filing jointly, paid a solar contractor $80,000 to have solar panels installed on their roof. Their state of residence gave them a $20,000 instant rebate toward the purchase. If their AGI is $150,000, how much is their solar energy tax credit for the current year?

    A. $18,000
    B. $45,000
    C. $12,000
    D. $40,000

92. Which of the following personal tax credits are **refundable**?
    I. Lifetime Learning Credit
    II. Foreign Tax Credit

    A. I only
    B. II only
    C. Both I and II
    D. Neither I nor II

93. Which of the following costs do NOT qualify as deductible costs for purposes of the adoption credit?
    I. Legal fees
    II. Costs associated with adopting the child of a spouse
    III. Agency fees

    A. I and II
    B. II and III
    C. I and III
    D. II only

94. Which of the following statements is correct regarding tax credits and tax deductions?
    I. Student loan interest can be taken as a deduction or a credit.
    II. In order to qualify for the retirement savings contribution credit, the taxpayer must NOT be a full-time student.
    A. I only
    B. II only
    C. Both I and II
    D. Neither I nor II

95. Foreign taxes paid by US taxpayers may be taken on Form 1040 as:
    I. a credit against the taxpayer's US tax
    II. an adjustment to arrive at adjusted gross income (AGI)
    A. I only
    B. II only
    C. Both I and II
    D. Neither I nor II

96. Luke made the following expenditures this year. Which of the following qualifies as a deductible medical expense for tax purposes?
    I. Vitamins for general health NOT prescribed by a physician
    II. Health club dues
    III. Transportation to a physician's office for required medical care
    A. I and II only
    B. I, II, and III
    C. III only
    D. II and III only

97. Scotti, an individual, paid the following expenses:

Premiums on an insurance policy against loss of earnings due to sickness or accident	$1,000
Physical therapy after surgery	$2,000
Premium on an insurance policy that covers reimbursement for the cost of prescription drugs	$600

Scotti recovered $1,500 of the $2,000 that she paid for physical therapy through an insurance reimbursement from a group medical policy paid for by her employer. Disregarding the AGI percentage threshold, what amount could be claimed on Scotti's income tax return for medical expenses?
    A. $2,100
    B. $2,600
    C. $600
    D. $1,100

98. Which of the following is correct regarding medical expenses?
    I. For taxpayers under age 65, medical expenses must exceed 10% of the taxpayer's AGI in order to be deductible.
    II. For taxpayers 65 and older, medical expenses must exceed 7.5% of the taxpayer's AGI in order to be deductible.
    A. I only
    B. II only
    C. Both I and II
    D. Neither I nor II

99. Which of the following is correct regarding medical expenses in 2014?
    I. If a taxpayer swipes her credit card for medical expenses in early December of Year 15, she must pay the credit card company by December 31, Year 15, in order to claim the deduction in Year 15.
    II. Taxpayers may NOT deduct the medical costs paid on behalf of elderly parents unless the elderly parent qualifies as a dependent of the taxpayer.
    A. I only
    B. II only
    C. Both I and II
    D. Neither I nor II

100. Imhoff, a 67-year-old cash-basis taxpayer, had an AGI of $40,000 in Year 5. During the year, he incurred and paid the following medical expenses:

Medicines prescribed	$300
Health insurance premiums	$500
Dental surgery	$4,000

Imhoff received $1,000 as reimbursement for a portion of the dental surgery. If Imhoff were to itemize his deductions, what is his allowable net medical expense deduction in Year 5?
    A. $0
    B. $800
    C. $900
    D. $1,200

101. Keith, a 35-year-old unmarried taxpayer with an (AGI of $70,000, incurred and paid the following unreimbursed medical expenses for the year:

Doctor bills resulting from a serious fall	$3,500
Eyeglasses	$500
Cosmetic surgery that was necessary to correct a birth defect considered a congenital deformity	$16,000

For regular income tax purposes, what is Keith's maximum allowable medical expense deduction, after the applicable AGI threshold limitation, for the year?

A. $20,000
B. $4,000
C. $0
D. $13,000

102. O'Connor was a single taxpayer, age 72, with an income of $95,000 reported on his W-2 form for Year 3. He was not covered by an employer-sponsored retirement plan but contributed $5,000 to his own traditional IRA in June of Year 3. His medical costs for Year 3 include two surgeries: September Year 3, surgery to correct hearing loss, $10,000; November Year 3, hair transplant, $8,000. How much is O'Connor's medical deduction in Year 3?

A. $0
B. $1,000
C. $2,250
D. $3,250

103. Labuono was a cash-basis taxpayer whose records show the following:

Year 1 state income taxes withheld	$1,500
Year 1 city taxes withheld	$200
Year 1 state and local income taxes paid April 17, Year 2	$300

Labuono is entitled to claim what amount for taxes on his Year 1 Schedule A of Form 1040?

A. $0
B. $1,700
C. $2,000
D. $1,500

104. Superak is a cash-basis taxpayer whose records show the following:

Year 1 federal income tax withheld	$4,000
Year 1 state and local income taxes withheld	$1,500
Year 1 state and local estimated income taxes paid September 15th, Year 1	$400
Year 1 state and local estimated income taxes paid January 15th, Year 2	$200

Superak is entitled to claim what amount for taxes on her Year 1 Schedule A of Form 1040?

A. $1,500
B. $1,900
C. $2,100
D. $5,900

105. Which of the following is a Schedule A itemized deduction?
   I. Real estate taxes paid on a vacation home that is not rented out
   II. Personal property tax paid on an automobile

A. I only
B. II only
C. Both I and II
D. Neither I nor II

106. In Year 10, Ben pays real estate taxes and medical expenses out of his own funds for his elderly mother, Sabina, who has very little income and slightly more income than the exemption amount, but who would otherwise qualify as Ben's dependent. Sabina, however, is NOT Ben's dependent. Which of the following is deductible by Ben in Year 10?
   I. The medical expenses
   II. The real estate taxes

A. I only
B. II only
C. Both I and II
D. Neither I nor II

107. Simberg, a self-employed individual, paid the following taxes this year:

Personal property tax on value of car	$10
State income tax	$2,000
Real estate tax on land in the Netherlands	$900
State unincorporated business tax	$300
Real estate taxes on his mother's house	$400

Simberg can claim what amount as an itemized deduction for taxes paid?

A. $7,500
B. $4,400
C. $2,930
D. $2,910

108. If a taxpayer owns four houses and does not rent out any, on how many of the homes can the taxpayer deduct the real estate taxes?

A. 4
B. 3
C. 2
D. 1

109. If a taxpayer owns three houses and does not rent out any, on how many of the homes can the taxpayer deduct the mortgage interest?

A. 4
B. 3
C. 2
D. 1

110. Which of the following interest payments are deductible on Form 1040 Schedule A itemized deductions?
  I. Interest paid in connection with acquiring a taxpayer's main home or second home
  II. Interest paid on a home equity loan where the loan proceeds are used to buy a car

A. I only
B. II only
C. Both I and II
D. Neither I nor II

111. On January 2, Year 5, Briscese paid $40,000 cash and obtained a $300,000 mortgage to purchase a home. In Year 8, he borrowed $10,000 secured by his home, and used the cash to add a new pool to the residence. That same year, he took out a $25,000 auto loan from GMAC Finance. Briscese paid credit card interest in Year 8 and also was assessed by the Internal Revenue Service (IRS) and had to pay interest in regard to late payment of federal income taxes from Year 7. The following information pertains to interest paid by Briscese in Year 8:

Mortgage interest	$15,000
Interest on home equity loan	$1,500
Auto loan interest	$500
Credit card interest	$2,000
Interest on late paid Year 7 federal income tax	$200

How much interest is deductible in Year 8, prior to any itemized deduction limitations?

A. $16,500
B. $17,000
C. $19,000
D. $19,200

112. Fein earned $120,000 in investment income, $100,000 in noninterest investment expenses, and $50,000 in investment interest expense. What amount can Fein deduct on his current year's tax return for investment interest expenses?

A. $0
B. $20,000
C. $30,000
D. $50,000

113. Jerry and Elaine Newman made the following payments during the tax year:

Interest on bank loan (loan proceeds were used to purchase taxable US Treasury bonds)	$4,000
Interest on home mortgage	$5,000

During the year, income of $4,300 was received on savings bonds. What is the maximum amount of interest expense that the Newmans can utilize in calculating their current year's itemized deductions?

A. $4,000
B. $5,000
C. $5,300
D. $9,000

114. Kyle and Ann made the following payments during the tax year:

Interest on bank loan (loan proceeds were used to purchase taxable US Treasury bonds)	$4,000
Interest on home mortgage	$5,000
Points to obtain mortgage	$2,500
Interest on credit cards	$100

During the year, income of $4,300 was received on savings bonds. What is the maximum amount of interest expense that Kyle and Ann can utilize in calculating their current year's itemized deductions?

A. $7,500
B. $9,000
C. $11,500
D. $11,600

115. Donna and Jeff made the following payments during this taxable year:

Interest on home mortgage	$3,600
Late payment penalty for mortgage	$2,100
10% penalty on IRA distribution	$1,000
Personal property tax	$500

What amount of these expenses can Donna and Jeff utilize in calculating their current year's itemized deductions?

A. $3,600
B. $4,100
C. $5,100
D. $7,200

116. Pollack, who itemizes deductions, had an AGI of $70,000 in Year 5. He made a contribution to his church in the amount of $4,000 and a cash contribution to a friend's son in the amount of $1,300. He made a donation of his used car to charity (FMV evidenced by receipt received: $600). What is the maximum amount Pollack can claim as a deduction for charitable contributions in Year 5?

A. $5,900
B. $5,200
C. $5,000
D. $4,600

117. Foltz itemizes his deductions and had an AGI of $60,000 in Year 5. That same year he donated $4,000 to his church. His church has a tradition: all members who donate over $3,000 in one single donation receive tickets to a ballgame. Foltz's tickets were worth $200 when he received them in Year 5. Also that same year, Foltz purchased jewelry at the church bazaar for $1,900. The fair value of the jewelry was $1,500 on the date of purchase. Foltz had no other charitable deductions or carryovers in Year 5. What is the maximum amount Foltz can claim as a deduction for charitable contributions in Year 5?

A. $4,200
B. $4,400
C. $5,700
D. $5,900

118. Naomi, a single taxpayer, had $50,000 in AGI for Year 2. During the year, she contributed $18,000 to her church. She had a $10,000 charitable contribution carryover from her Year 1 church contribution. What is the maximum amount of properly substantiated charitable contributions that Naomi could claim as an itemized deduction for Year 2?

A. $10,000
B. $18,000
C. $25,000
D. $28,000

119. O'Keefe, an unmarried taxpayer, qualified to itemize Year 3 deductions. O'Keefe's Year 3 AGI was $20,000. In Year 3, O'Keefe donated stock, valued at $3,000, to her church. O'Keefe had purchased the stock **seven months** earlier for $1,400. What was the maximum amount of the charitable contribution allowable as an itemized deduction on O'Keefe's Year 3 income tax return?

A. $0
B. $1,400
C. $1,600
D. $3,000

120. Berman, an unmarried taxpayer, qualified to itemize Year 3 deductions. Berman's Year 3 AGI was $40,000. Berman donated art in Year 3, valued at $11,000, to a local art museum. Berman had purchased the artwork two years earlier for $2,000. What was the maximum amount of the charitable contribution allowable as an itemized deduction on Berman's Year 3 income tax return?

A. $2,000
B. $9,000
C. $11,000
D. $12,000

121. Brian, an unmarried taxpayer, qualified to itemize Year 3 deductions. His Year 3 AGI was $20,000. He donated art in Year 3, valued at $15,000, to a local art museum. He had purchased the artwork two years earlier for $6,000. What was the maximum amount of the charitable contribution allowable as an itemized deduction on Brian's Year 3 income tax return?

A. $2,000
B. $6,000
C. $9,000
D. $15,000

122. Teri, an unmarried taxpayer, qualified to itemize Year 3 deductions. Teri's Year 3 AGI was $25,000. Teri donated art in Year 3, valued at $11,000, to a local art museum. Teri had purchased the artwork two years earlier for $2,000. She also gave a cash contribution of $7,000 to her temple. What was the maximum amount of the charitable contribution allowable as an itemized deduction on Teri's Year 3 income tax return?

    A. $7,500
    B. $12,500
    C. $14,500
    D. $18,000

123. Harold had AGI of $60,000 in the current year, donated artwork to a museum held for five years worth $20,000, and also donated $5,000 in cash to a recognized charity. How much is Harold's total deduction in the current year for charitable contributions?

    A. $5,000
    B. $18,000
    C. $23,000
    D. $25,000

124. Casualty losses are deductible if they exceed what percentage of an individual taxpayer's AGI?

    A. 2%
    B. 7.5%
    C. 10%
    D. 30%

125. In Year 2, Boniguen's residence was totally destroyed by fire. The property had an adjusted basis and an FMV of $130,000 before the fire. During Year 2, she received an insurance reimbursement of $120,000 for the destruction of her home. Boniguen's Year 2 AGI was $70,000. Boniguen is entitled to claim what amount of the fire loss as an itemized deduction on her Year 2 tax return?

    A. $2,900
    B. $8,500
    C. $8,600
    D. $10,000

126. In Year 8, Grande's AGI is $50,000, including $3,000 in gambling winnings. Grande has gambling losses totaling $7,000 in the current year and had gambling losses from last year that he could NOT deduct on his Year 7 tax return of $1,000. Grande can itemize the deductions. What amount of gambling losses is deductible by Grande in Year 8?

    A. $0
    B. $4,000
    C. $3,000
    D. $7,000

127. Which of the following unreimbursed employee expenses are considered miscellaneous itemized deductions subject to 2% of AGI?
    I. Small tools
    II. Nurse's uniforms
    III. Unreimbursed business car expense

    A. I and III only
    B. I, II, and III
    C. I and II only
    D. II and III only

128. Which of the following is included in the category of miscellaneous itemized deductions that are deductible only to the extent that the aggregate amount of such expenses exceeds 2% of the taxpayer's AGI?

    A. Funeral expenses
    B. Union dues
    C. Preparation of a will
    D. Credit card interest expense

129. Which of the following are deductible subject to 2% of AGI?
    I. Preparation of a will
    II. Gambling losses
    III. Safe-deposit box rental

    A. I, II, and III
    B. I and III only
    C. II and III only
    D. III only

130. Which item can be claimed as an itemized deduction subject to the 2% of AGI floor?
    I. Tax return preparation fee
    II. Foreign taxes paid
    III. Penalty on early withdrawal of savings (from a non-retirement account)
    IV. Penalty for late payment of mortgage

    A. I, II, and III only
    B. I, II, and IV only
    C. I only
    D. I and III only

131. Wes, 49 years of age, incurred the following expenses in the current year: $500 for the preparation of a personal income tax return, $100 for custodial fees on an IRA, $150 for professional publications, and $2,000 for union dues. His current year AGI is $85,500 before consideration of a $5,500 IRA contribution. Wes, who is NOT covered by any retirement plan at work, NOT self-employed, and NOT married, itemizes deductions. What will Wes's deduction be for miscellaneous itemized deductions after any limitations in the current year?

    A. $0
    B. $850
    C. $1,150
    D. $2,250

132. Landi earned $6,000 in wages, incurred $1,000 in unreimbursed employee business expenses, paid $400 in interest on a student loan, contributed $100 to a charity, and received $10 in jury duty pay. What is Landi's AGI?

    A. $6,010
    B. $4,600
    C. $5,600
    D. $5,610

133. During the current year, Pelosi was assessed a deficiency on a prior year's federal income tax return. As a result of this assessment, he was required to pay $2,750 determined as follows:

Additional federal income tax	$2,350
Late filing penalty	$150
Negligence penalty	$50
Interest on late paid taxes	$200

What portion of the $2,750 paid by Pelosi would qualify as an itemized deduction on Schedule A?

    A. $0
    B. $200
    C. $350
    D. $2,750

134. For an individual taxpayer, which of the following is includable in income?
    I. Damages awarded for breach of contract
    II. Fees received for jury duty services
    III. Workers' compensation monies received
    IV. Forgiveness of debt

    A. I, III, and IV only
    B. I, II, and IV only
    C. I and II only
    D. I, II, and III only

135. The calculation of alternative minimum tax (AMT):

    A. begins with taxable income, then adds back adjustments, and subtracts out preferences
    B. begins with taxable income, then adds back adjustments and preferences, and subtracts an AMT exemption
    C. does not involve the addition or subtraction of itemized deductions, except for charitable contributions and miscellaneous itemized deductions that exceed 2% of AGI
    D. does not involve the addition or subtraction of municipal bond interest income from private activity bonds

136. In Year 4, Reynolds, a single taxpayer, had $70,000 in taxable income. Her itemized deductions were as follows:

State income tax	$3,500
Local income tax	$1,500
Home mortgage interest on loan to acquire a residence	$6,000
Miscellaneous deductions in excess of 2% of AGI	$2,000
Gambling losses	$1,000

What amount should Reynolds report as alternative minimum taxable income before the AMT exemption?

    A. $72,000
    B. $75,000
    C. $77,000
    D. $83,000

137. Shirley, a single taxpayer, reported the following items in her regular federal income tax for Year 6:

Personal exemption	$3,100
Interest on a home equity loan, the proceeds of which were used for son's college expenses	$1,200
Cash charitable contribution	$1,250
Net long-term capital gain	$700

What amount of the preceding items represents AMT adjustments for Shirley?

A. $4,300
B. $5,000
C. $6,250
D. $3,100

138. Betty has the following items:

Straight line depreciation	$600
Tax-exempt interest income on private activity bonds	$400
Personal exemption	$3,100
Itemized deduction for state income taxes	$1,500
Cash charitable contributions	$1,250
Net long-term capital gain	$1,000

What amount of tax preference items should be added back to Betty's regular income in determining AMT?

A. $400
B. $1,000
C. $1,900
D. $3,700

139. For an individual computing his or her AMT, which of the following are considered AMT adjustments?
    I. Standard deduction
    II. Personal exemption

A. I only
B. II only
C. Both I and II
D. Neither I nor II

140. For an individual taxpayer, interest income from which of the following bond investments is considered a tax preference item for the computation of the AMT?
    I. Private activity bonds issued by the State of Arizona
    II. General obligation bonds issued by the State of Florida

A. I only
B. II only
C. Both I and II
D. Neither I nor II

CHAPTER 40

QUESTIONS 141–283

---

141. During March of Year 8, Steelman and Schechter contribute cash equally to form the Glenwood Partnership. Steelman and Schechter share profits and losses of 75% and 25%, respectively. The Glenwood Partnership's ordinary income was $60,000 in Year 8. A distribution of $5,000 was made to Steelman. No distribution was made to Schechter. What is Steelman's share of taxable income from the Glenwood Partnership in Year 8?

A. $5,000
B. $30,000
C. $45,000
D. $50,000

142. The Daltrey Partnership has sales revenues of $450,000, operating expenses of $350,000, dividend revenue of $8,000, charitable contributions of $6,000, and a $12,000 capital loss. Therefore, the partnership has a net income of $90,000. What is the Daltrey Partnership's ordinary income for tax purposes?

A. $90,000
B. $100,000
C. $102,000
D. $104,000

143. Which is correct regarding partnership tax returns?
  I. A partnership tax return is due March 15th, or two and a half months after year end.
  II. Each partner in a partnership is given a Schedule K-1 to report all items of income and loss on their personal tax returns.

A. I only
B. II only
C. Both I and II
D. Neither I nor II

144. Which of the following is correct regarding partnership tax returns?
  I. No tax is due with the filing of a partnership tax return even if the partnership earned profits in excess of $50,000.
  II. A partnership tax return is filed on Form 1065.

A. I only
B. II only
C. Both I and II
D. Neither I nor II

145. In a partnership, a fixed payment made to a partner for services provided to the partnership is known as a:
  I. normal distribution
  II. guaranteed payment

A. I only
B. II only
C. Both I and II
D. Neither I nor II

146. A guaranteed payment by a partnership to a partner for services rendered may include an agreement to pay:
  I. a salary of $15,000 monthly without regard to partnership income
  II. a 17% interest in partnership profits

A. I only
B. II only
C. Both I and II
D. Neither I nor II

147. Barry, CPA, is computing the ordinary income of a client's partnership. A deduction is allowed for:
    I. contributions to recognized charities
    II. short-term capital losses
    III. guaranteed payments to partners

    A. I and III only
    B. II and III only
    C. III only
    D. I and II only

Use the following facts to answer **Questions 148–149.**

Disston, a 25% partner in Witness Partnership, received a $40,000 guaranteed payment for deductible services rendered to the partnership. Guaranteed payments were not made to any other partner. Witness Partnership income consisted of:

Net business income *before* guaranteed payments	$100,000
Net long-term capital gains	$10,000

148. How much is ordinary income of the Witness Partnership?

    A. $40,000
    B. $60,000
    C. $100,000
    D. $140,000

149. Disston should report how much income from the Witness Partnership on his Form 1040?

    A. $20,000
    B. $67,500
    C. $55,000
    D. $57,500

150. The partnership of Marty and Walter sustained an ordinary loss of $104,000. The partners share profits and losses equally. Walter had an adjusted basis of $36,000 on December 31, before consideration of the loss. Walter can deduct what amount on his individual tax return?

    A. Ordinary loss of $36,000
    B. Ordinary loss of $52,000
    C. Ordinary loss of $36,000 and a capital loss of $16,000
    D. Capital loss of $52,000

Use the following facts to answer **Questions 151–152.**

Norris is a 25% partner in Clark Partnership. Norris's tax basis in Clark on January 1 was $20,000. At the end of the year, Norris received a cash distribution of $8,000 from Clark Partnership. The partnership reported ordinary income of $40,000.

151. Norris's basis in Clark on December 31 is:

    A. $15,000
    B. $22,000
    C. $25,000
    D. $30,000

Assume the same fact as in Question 151 but that, in addition, Clark Partnership also received a municipal bond interest income of $12,000 during the year.

152. As a result of the municipal bond interest income addition, how much is Norris's basis in Clark Partnership on December 31?

    A. $15,000
    B. $23,000
    C. $25,000
    D. $30,000

153. Tax-exempt interest income received by a partnership will have what effect on the basis of each partner in the partnership?

    A. Increase the basis, thereby making the tax-exempt income taxable
    B. Decrease the basis
    C. Have no effect on the basis
    D. Increase the basis although the tax-exempt income is not taxable

154. Krin is a partner in Prager Partnership. Which of the following represents a **decrease** in Krin's partnership basis?
    I. Distributions of cash from Prager Partnership to Krin
    II. Loans made to the partnership from Krin

    A. I only
    B. II only
    C. Both I and II
    D. Neither I nor II

155. Cuciti and Lussier Partnership had a $10,000 increase in partnership liabilities. The partnership will treat that increase in which of the following ways?

    A. Increases each partner's basis in the partnership by $5,000
    B. Increases the partner's basis only if the liability is nonrecourse
    C. Increases each partner's basis in proportion to his or her ownership
    D. Does not change any partner's basis in the partnership, regardless of whether the liabilities are recourse or nonrecourse

156. Andy is a 50% partner in the London Ale House, a US partnership. Andy's tax basis on January 1, Year 2, was $5,000. London Ale House recorded the following:

Ordinary income	$20,000
Tax exempt income	$8,000
Taxable interest income	$4,000
Cash distribution	$1,000

What is Andy's tax basis in the London Ale House Partnership on December 31, Year 2?

    A. $21,000
    B. $20,000
    C. $10,000
    D. $12,000

Use the following facts to answer **Questions 157–159.**

Mike and Luke formed Stratomatic Partnership as equal partners by contributing the following assets: Mike contributed cash of $45,000. Luke contributed land with a basis of $30,000 and a fair value of $53,000. The land was held by Luke as a capital asset.

157. Luke's initial basis in his partnership was:

    A. $30,000
    B. $45,000
    C. $37,500
    D. $15,000

158. Assume that the land was subject to a $12,000 mortgage, which was assumed by Stratomatic Partnership. Because of the mortgage, Luke's initial basis would be:

    A. $53,000
    B. $30,000
    C. $24,000
    D. $18,000

159. Assuming the $12,000 mortgage on the land is assumed by Stratomatic Partnership, what was Mike's initial basis in this partnership?

    A. $51,000
    B. $45,000
    C. $39,000
    D. $33,000

160. In 2012, Adimak, Singer, and Klein formed Olympic General Partnership by contributing the assets that follow:

Adimak contributed cash of $40,000 for a 50% partnership interest.

Singer contributed land with a $12,000 basis and a $21,000 fair market value (FMV) for a 20% partnership interest. The land was a capital asset to Singer, subject to a $5,000 mortgage, which was assumed by the partnership.

Klein contributed inventory with both a $24,000 basis and FMV for a 30% partnership interest.

Klein's initial basis in Olympic Partnership is:

    A. $25,000
    B. $24,000
    C. $25,500
    D. $29,000

161. The adjusted basis of Chris's interest in Dean Partnership was $240,000 immediately before receiving two distributions in complete liquidation of Dean Partnership. One distribution was a cash amount of $150,000. The other distribution was real estate with an FMV of $110,000 and basis of $91,000. What is Chris's basis in the real estate?

    A. $0
    B. $150,000
    C. $91,000
    D. $90,000

162. In Year 1, Anita acquired a one-third interest in Party Basket Associates, a partnership. In Year 12, when Anita's entire interest in the partnership was liquidated, Anita's adjusted basis for her one-third interest was $52,000. Anita received cash of $50,000 in liquidation of her entire interest. What was Anita's recognized loss in Year 12 on the liquidation of her interest in Party Basket Associates?

    A. $2,000 long-term capital loss
    B. $0
    C. $2,000 short-term capital loss
    D. $2,000 ordinary loss

163. If a partnership is being liquidated, which of the following is correct?

A. A partner may report a gain but not a loss on liquidation.

B. A partner may report a loss but not a gain on liquidation.

C. The partnership may report a gain but not a loss on liquidation.

D. The partnership may report neither a gain nor a loss on liquidation.

164. Carol received $30,000 in cash and an automobile with an adjusted basis and market value of $20,000 in a proportionate liquidating distribution from Zeta Partnership. Carol's basis in the partnership interest was $70,000 before the distribution. What is Carol's basis in the automobile received in the liquidation?

A. $70,000

B. $40,000

C. $30,000

D. $20,000

Use the following facts to answer **Questions 165–166.**

Ryan's basis in Bruder Partnership was $70,000 at the time he received a nonliquidating distribution of partnership capital assets. These capital assets had an adjusted basis of $65,000 to the Bruder Partnership and an FMV of $83,000.

165. Ryan would value the capital assets when received from the partnership at what amount?

A. $65,000

B. $70,000

C. $83,000

D. $0

166. Assuming Ryan's basis was $40,000 prior to the distribution of the capital assets, what would Ryan's basis be in the capital assets distributed to him?

A. $40,000

B. $65,000

C. $70,000

D. $83,000

167. Tyler's basis in Aero Partnership was $80,000 at the time he received a nonliquidating distribution of partnership capital assets. These capital assets had an adjusted basis of $75,000 to the partnership and an FMV of $93,000. What is Tyler's recognized gain or loss on the distribution?

A. $18,000 ordinary income

B. $13,000 capital gain

C. $0

D. $5,000 capital gain

Use the following facts to answer **Questions 168–169.**

Yimeny is a 50% partner is Victoria Partnership. Yimeny's basis in the partnership is $50,000 immediately before Yimeny received a current nonliquidating distribution of $20,000 cash and property with an adjusted basis to the partnership of $40,000 and an FMV of $35,000.

168. What is the amount of taxable gain that Yimeny must report as a result of this distribution?

A. $0

B. $5,000

C. $10,000

D. $20,000

169. Based on the same facts, what is Yimeny's basis in the distributed property?

A. $0

B. $30,000

C. $35,000

D. $40,000

Use the following facts to answer **Questions 170–171.**

Robyn is a partner in the Seena Partnership. Her basis in the partnership at the time she received a nonliquidating distribution of land was $5,000. The land had an adjusted basis of $6,000 and a fair value of $9,000 to Seena Partnership.

170. What is Robyn's basis in the land?

A. $9,000

B. $6,000

C. $5,000

D. $1,000

171. How much gain will Robyn recognize on the distribution?

    A. $0
    B. $1,000
    C. $5,000
    D. $9,000

172. Kelvin's basis in his KB Partnership interest is $50,000 at the beginning of the current year. During the current year Kelvin received a nonliquidating distribution of $25,000 cash plus land with an adjusted basis of $15,000 to KB and an FMV of $20,000. Kelvin's basis in the land is:

    A. $10,000
    B. $15,000
    C. $20,000
    D. $25,000

173. Lesnik, a 50% partner in Lesnik and Condon, received a distribution of $12,500 in the current year. The partnership's income for the year was $25,000. What is the character of the payment that Lesnik received?

    A. Partial liquidating distribution
    B. Full liquidating distribution
    C. Disproportionate distribution
    D. Current distribution

174. Which of the following are generally includable as income by a partner in a partnership?

    I. Partnership distributions of cash that are NOT in excess of basis
    II. Guaranteed payments to partners

    A. I only
    B. II only
    C. Both I and II
    D. Neither I nor II

175. Which of the following items does a partnership entity pay taxes on?

    I. Ordinary business income
    II. Municipal bond interest income

    A. I only
    B. II only
    C. Both I and II
    D. Neither I nor II

176. Which of the following cash distributions from partnership to partner would require a partner to recognize a gain for tax purposes?

    I. A liquidating distribution that is NOT in excess of basis
    II. A nonliquidating distribution that is NOT in excess of basis

    A. I only
    B. II only
    C. Both I and II
    D. Neither I nor II

177. On February 1, Year 4, Stefano Corp. was formed. Stefano Corp. met all eligibility requirements for S corporation status during the pre-election portion of the year. What is the last date that Stefano Corp. can file their S election and be recognized as an S corporation in Year 4?

    A. December 31, Year 4
    B. April 15th, Year 4
    C. March 15th, Year 4
    D. February 1, Year 4

178. Hanson Corp., a calendar-year corporation, began business in Year 2. Hanson made a valid S corporation election on August 25th, Year 5, with the unanimous consent of all shareholders. The eligibility requirements for S corporation status continued to be met throughout Year 5. On what date did Hanson's S corporation status become effective?

    A. January 1, Year 5
    B. January 1, Year 6
    C. August 25, Year 5
    D. August 25, Year 6

179. Capell Corp., a calendar-year S corporation, has two equal shareholders. For the year ended December 31, Year 1, Capell Corp. had income of $90,000, which included $60,000 from operations, $20,000 from investment interest income, and $10,000 from municipal bond interest income. There were no other transactions that year. Basis in the stock of Capell Corp. for each shareholder will increase by:

    A. $90,000
    B. $45,000
    C. $40,000
    D. $15,000

180. If an S corporation receives municipal bond interest income of $50,000 and has two equal shareholders:

    A. each shareholder would increase their basis by $25,000 and report $25,000 each in taxable income

    B. since interest income is municipal, the S corporation rather than the individual shareholders would recognize all the tax on the interest

    C. each shareholder will report a basis decrease of $25,000

    D. each shareholder will report a basis increase of $25,000

181. Morgan is the sole shareholder of Corinthos, Inc., an S corporation. Morgan's adjusted basis in Corinthos, Inc., stock is $60,000 at the beginning of the year. During the year, Corinthos, Inc., reports the following income items:

Ordinary income	$30,000
Tax-exempt income	$5,000
Capital gains	$10,000

    In addition, Corinthos makes a nontaxable distribution to Morgan of $20,000 cash during the year. What is Morgan's adjusted basis in the Corinthos stock at the end of the year?

    A. $105,000
    B. $125,000
    C. $80,000
    D. $85,000

182. Crellin is considering forming an S corporation. Which of the following conditions will prevent a corporation from qualifying as an S corporation?

    A. The corporation has one class of stock with different voting rights.
    B. The corporation has 75 shareholders.
    C. The corporation was formed before 1991.
    D. The corporation has both common and preferred stock.

183. Bagel Bazaar, Inc., has been an S corporation since inception. In each of Year 1, Year 2, and Year 3, Bagel Bazaar, Inc., made distributions in excess of each shareholder's basis. Which of the following statements is correct concerning these three years?

    A. In Year 1 and Year 2 only, the excess distributions are taxed as a capital gain.
    B. In Year 1 only, the excess distributions are tax free.
    C. In Year 3 only, the excess distributions are taxed as a capital gain.
    D. In all three years, the excess distributions are taxed as capital gains.

Use the following facts to answer **Questions 184–185.**

Wilson owns 100% of an S corporation and materially participates in its operations. The stock's basis at the beginning of Year 7 is $5,000. During Year 7, the S corporation makes a distribution of $3,500 and passes through a loss from operations of $2,000 for the year.

184. How much of the $3,500 distribution will be taxable to Wilson in Year 7?

    A. $3,500
    B. $2,000
    C. $1,500
    D. $0

185. How much loss can Wilson deduct on Wilson's personal tax return in Year 7?

    A. $0
    B. $1,500
    C. $2,000
    D. $5,500

186. Wolfson, Inc., an S corporation, reported in Year 1 $50,000 of income from operations and a $20,000 long-term capital gain for a total profit of $70,000. The corporation has 10 equal shareholders, and each one received a cash distribution during the year of $4,000. Wolfson shareholders report what with respect to ownership of the S corporation for tax purposes?

    A. $5,000 ordinary income and $2,000 long-term capital gain
    B. $4,000 ordinary income
    C. $5,000 ordinary income
    D. $4,000 ordinary income and $7,000 long-term capital gain

187. An S corporation is NOT permitted to take a deduction for:
    I. charitable contributions
    II. compensation of officers
    III. short-term capital losses

    A. I and II only
    B. III only
    C. I and III only
    D. II and III only

188. Dauber, Inc., a calendar-year S corporation, reported the following items of income and expense in the current year:

Revenue	$44,000
Operating expenses	$20,000
Long-term capital loss	$6,000
Charitable contributions	$1,000

What is the amount of Dauber's ordinary income?

A. $17,000
B. $18,000
C. $24,000
D. $28,000

189. Which of the following is correct regarding the due date of a partnership tax return?
   I. Partnership tax returns are currently due 3.5 months after the close of the business year.
   II. Partnership tax returns will be due 2.5 months after the close of the business year starting in 2017.

A. I only
B. II only
C. Both I and II
D. Neither I nor II

190. What are the requirements to form an S corporation?
   I. Must have at least two shareholders
   II. Must adopt a calendar year (December 31) as its year end

A. I only
B. II only
C. Both I and II
D. Neither I nor II

191. For the taxable year ended December 31, Rothstein, Inc., an S corporation, had net income per books of $80,000, which included $62,000 from operations and a $18,000 net long-term capital gain. During the year, $9,000 was distributed to Rothstein's three equal stockholders, all of whom are on a calendar-year basis. On what amounts should Rothstein, Inc., compute its income tax and capital gain taxes?

A. Income tax of $31,500, capital gain tax of $0
B. Income tax of $0, capital gain tax of $0
C. Income tax of $22,500, capital gain tax of $0
D. Income tax of $0, capital gain tax of $9,000

192. Lonegan Corp. was a C corporation until it elected S corporation status on January 1, Year 3. Lonegan Corp had accumulated earnings and profits of $20,000 at December 31, Year 2. From Year 3 through Year 5, Lonegan Corp had ordinary income of $130,000 and made shareholder distributions of $90,000. Therefore, its accumulated adjustments account balance at December 31, Year 5, was $40,000. In Year 6, Lonegan Corp had ordinary income of $40,000 and made distributions of $110,000. How much distribution is taxable as a dividend to shareholders in Year 6?

A. $0
B. $20,000
C. $40,000
D. $110,000

193. With regard to S corporations, unanimous consent of all shareholders is required to:
   I. elect S corporation status
   II. voluntarily revoke the S corporation election

A. I only
B. II only
C. Both I and II
D. Neither I nor II

194. Krepps owns 100% of RK Incorporated, which is an S corporation for income tax purposes. Krepps's basis in the company at the beginning of the year is $60,000. During the year the company had ordinary income of $39,500, municipal bond interest income of $10,000, and short-term capital losses of $17,000. Krepps also received a dividend distribution of $20,000. What is his basis in this corporation at year end?

A. $92,500
B. $82,500
C. $72,500
D. $62,500

195. Owen incorporated a sole proprietorship by exchanging all the proprietorship's assets for the stock of Millstone Corp., a new corporation. To qualify for tax-free incorporation, Owen must be in control of Millstone Corp. immediately after the exchange. What percentage of Millstone Corp.'s stock must he own to qualify as control for this purpose?

A. 50%
B. 51%
C. 100%
D. 80%

196. In the current year, Hametz decides to form a corporation. Cash of $120,000 is transferred to the business along with equipment having a tax basis of $100,000 but a fair value of $165,000. Hametz received all of the stock of this new corporation. What is his tax basis in this new business, and what tax basis does the new business use for this equipment?

    A. $220,000 and $100,000
    B. $270,000 and $165,000
    C. $220,000 and $165,000
    D. $270,000 and $100,000

Use the following facts to answer **Questions 197–202.**

Laura and Micki organized the Minder Binder Corp., which issued voting common stock with a fair market value (FMV) of $120,000. Laura transferred a building with a basis of $40,000 and an FMV of $82,000 for 60% of the stock. Micki contributed equipment with a basis of $45,000 and an FMV of $48,000 in exchange for 40% of the stock.

197. How much is Laura's basis in Minder Binder Corp. stock?

    A. $35,000
    B. $40,000
    C. $30,000
    D. $50,000

198. Now assume that Laura's building had a mortgage of $10,000, and Minder Binder Corp. assumed the $10,000 mortgage. What is Laura's basis in Minder Binder Corp. stock?

    A. $35,000
    B. $40,000
    C. $30,000
    D. $50,000

199. Assume the same fact as Question 198 and that the Minder Binder Corp. assumed the $10,000 mortgage remaining on Laura's building. What gain did Laura recognize on the exchange?

    A. $0
    B. $10,000
    C. $42,000
    D. $52,000

200. Assume the same fact regarding the assumption of the $10,000 mortgage noted in Questions 198 and 199, what was the newly formed corporation's basis in the building transferred by Laura?

    A. $30,000
    B. $40,000
    C. $72,000
    D. $82,000

201. Assume that Laura's building had a mortgage of $10,000 and the mortgage is being assumed by Minder Binder Corp.. What is Micki's basis in her stock?

    A. $45,000
    B. $48,000
    C. $50,000
    D. $53,000

202. How much is the newly formed corporation's basis in the equipment transferred by Micki?

    A. $45,000
    B. $48,000
    C. $60,000
    D. none of the above

Use the following facts to answer **Questions 203–204.**

During Year 5, Adrian, Barry, and Corey formed David Corp. Pursuant to the incorporation agreement, Adrian transfers property with a basis of $30,000 and an FMV of $45,000 for 40% of David Corp. stock. Barry transfers cash of $35,000 in exchange for 30% of the stock, and Corey performed legal services valued at $25,000 (exchanged no property) and received 30% of the stock.

203. How much does David Corp. value the property received from Adrian?

    A. $0
    B. $30,000
    C. $45,000
    D. $65,000

204. Adrian would recognize a gain of:

    A. $0
    B. $15,000
    C. $10,000
    D. $5,000

Use the following facts to answer **Questions 205–206.**

Parker, Broussard, and Monti organized Kenpo Corp. Parker received 10% of the capital stock in payment for the organizational services that he rendered for the benefit of the newly formed corporation. Parker did not contribute property and was not receiving payment for the services. Broussard and Monti contributed property as follows:

Broussard contributed assets with a basis of $5,000 and an FMV of $20,000 for 20% of the stock.
Monti contributed assets with a basis of $60,000 and FMV of $70,000 for 70% of the stock.

205. What amount of gain did Monti recognize from this transaction?

A. $0
B. $5,000
C. $10,000
D. $3,333

206. How much does Kenpo Corp. value the asset contributed by Broussard?

A. $65,000
B. $20,000
C. $5,000
D. $0

Use the following facts to answer **Questions 207 and 208.**

The Ashbrook Corp. is an accrual-based taxpayer. The company generates credit revenues in Year 1 of $400,000 and estimates that 4%, or $16,000, of these accounts will prove to be uncollectible. In Year 2, $23,000 of these accounts turn out to be uncollectible and are written off the company's records.

207. For tax purposes, how much is bad debt expense for Year 1?

A. $16,000
B. $0
C. $23,000
D. $7,000

208. For tax purposes, how much is bad debt expense for Year 2?

A. $16,000
B. $0
C. $23,000
D. $7,000

209. Fascination Corp. is a small fashion-consulting firm. The company operates as a cash-basis taxpayer. In January of the current year, the firm did work for a client, Twin Spin, Inc., and accepted a note for $40,000 plus interest at a 10% annual rate in lieu of immediate payment. After exactly one month, Twin Spin, Inc., went bankrupt and the note was judged to be worthless. What is the amount of the bad debt expense deduction that Fascination Corp. is entitled to report?

A. $0
B. $40,000
C. $42,000
D. $44,000

Use the following facts to answer **Questions 210–211.**

In October of Year 1, Solar Express Corp. sells 100,000 solar panels with a warranty to fix any that break. Based on Year 1 sales, the company expects 1,500 to break in the first two years and cost $100 each to fix. None break in Year 1. During Year 2, 800 panels break and cost $120 each to fix.

210. What amount can Solar Express deduct for tax purposes for warranty expenses in Year 1?

A. $150,000
B. $96,000
C. $0
D. $12,000

211. What amount can Solar Express deduct for tax purposes for warranty expenses in Year 2?

A. $150,000
B. $96,000
C. $0
D. $12,000

212. Life insurance premiums paid by a corporation on behalf of its employees:
   I. are deductible for financial reporting purposes to arrive at book income, regardless of who the beneficiary of the policy is
   II. are NOT deductible for tax purposes if the corporation pays the premiums on behalf of employees and the employees can name the beneficiary of the policy

A. I only
B. II only
C. Both I and II
D. Neither I nor II

213. Marlboro Freedom, Inc., had book income of $200,000. $5,000 was deducted to arrive at book income to pay for life insurance to cover the lives of key employees. The face amount of the policy, $500,000, gets paid to the family members of the employees. No employees died during the year. In addition, the company incurred warranty costs of $10,000. An estimated $4,000 was expensed for warranty costs on the financial statements. How much is taxable income for this year?

    A. $194,000
    B. $199,000
    C. $203,000
    D. $205,000

214. Spence Corp. has sales revenues of $400,000, normal and necessary operating expenses of $300,000, short-term capital gain of $7,000, and a long-term capital loss of $10,000. What is the amount of capital loss that can be deducted by Spence Corp. for this year?

    A. $0
    B. $3,000
    C. $7,000
    D. $10,000

215. Blue Chip Industries is a C corporation. How does Blue Chip, Inc., treat its net capital losses for federal income tax purposes?

    A. Deducted from the corporation's ordinary income only to the extent of $3,000 per year
    B. Carried back 3 years and carried forward 5 years
    C. Deductible in full from the corporation's ordinary income
    D. Carried forward 15 years

216. Drake Corp., a calendar-year C (regular) corporation, had the following capital gains and capital losses during Year 5:

Short-term capital gain	$7,500
Short-term capital loss	$5,000
Long-term capital gain	$2,500
Long-term capital loss	$2,500

    In addition, Drake realized taxable income of $56,000 from its regular business operations for calendar Year 5. What is Drake Corp.'s total taxable income for Year 5?

    A. $56,000
    B. $62,000
    C. $60,500
    D. $58,500

217. Linden Corp., a calendar-year C (regular) corporation, realized taxable income of $66,000 from its regular business operations for calendar Year 5. In addition, the corporation had the following capital gains and capital losses during Year 5:

Short-term capital gain	$5,000
Short-term capital loss	($4,000)
Long-term capital gain	$1,000
Long-term capital loss	($9,000)

    With $66,000 in ordinary income before capital gains and losses, what is Linden Corp.'s taxable income for Year 5?

    A. $59,000
    B. $66,000
    C. $72,000
    D. $53,000

218. For the year ended December 31, Year 8, Breitbart Corp. had book net income of $227,000. Included in the computation of net income were the following items:

Net long-term capital loss	$5,000
Utility expense	$4,000
Key-person life insurance premiums (company is beneficiary)	$3,000

    Breitbart Corp.'s Year 8 taxable income was:

    A. $227,000
    B. $230,000
    C. $232,000
    D. $235,000

219. In Year 4, Adams Corp., an accrual-basis, calendar-year C corporation, reported book income of $480,000. Included in that amount were:

$5,000	rent expense
$50,000	municipal bond interest income
$170,000	federal income tax expense
$2,000	interest expense on the debt incurred to carry the municipal bonds

    How much is Adams Corp.'s taxable income as reconciled on Schedule M-1 of Form 1120, US corporation income tax return?

    A. $607,000
    B. $600,000
    C. $602,000
    D. $650,000

220. On December 31, Year 5, Hampton Corp. reported book income (financial accounting) of $240,000 for the year. Included in that amount was $50,000 for meals and entertainment expense, $11,000 for advertising expense, and $40,000 for federal income tax expense. In Hampton Corp.'s Schedule M-1 of Form 1120, which reconciles book income and taxable income, what amount should Hampton Corp. report as taxable income?

    A. $240,000
    B. $265,000
    C. $280,000
    D. $305,000

221. Tailgate Studios, Inc., is a C corporation and has the two expense items listed. Which of the two items will be reported on Schedule M-1 of Tailgate's corporation income tax return in order to reconcile book income to taxable income?

    I. Interest incurred on a loan to carry municipal bonds

    II. Provision for federal income tax

    A. I only
    B. II only
    C. Both I and II
    D. Neither I nor II

222. Which of the following items are reportable on a corporation's Schedule M-1 book to taxable income reconciliation?

    I. Interest expense on a loan to carry US savings bonds

    II. State income tax provision

    A. I only
    B. II only
    C. Both I and II
    D. Neither I nor II

223. Which of the following costs incurred to organize a corporation are considered amortizable organizational expenditures?

    A. Professional fees to issue the corporate stock
    B. Printing costs to issue the corporate stock
    C. Legal fees for drafting the corporate charter
    D. Commissions paid by the corporation to an underwriter

224. Mobile Tech was organized and began doing business on July 1 of Year 6. Amounts that Mobile Tech paid for organizational costs included $3,000 to Barry Surett & Co. CPAs for services the firm provided to assess which business structure was most advantageous for Mobile Tech and then to file various documents needed to incorporate Mobile Tech. Mobile Tech also paid the State of New Jersey $7,500 in fees to incorporate. In additions Mobile Tech paid the law firm of Gerald S. Hymanson $3,500 to draft the corporate charter. Other organization costs in Year 6 included $2,000 to print the stock certificates and $5,000 to sell the initial shares. For tax purposes, Mobile Tech would like to take as much of a deduction for these costs as possible. How much can Mobile Tech deduct in Year 6 for organizational expenditures?

    A. $5,300
    B. $5,000
    C. $5,534
    D. $14,000

225. A company is filing its Year 2 income tax return. The company bought another company in Year 1, and $300,000 of the purchase price was allocated to goodwill. For financial reporting (book) purposes, that amount was not amortized nor viewed as impaired. Which of the following is correct?

    I. The goodwill should be recorded as a capital asset and amortized over 15 years for tax purposes.

    II. For Year 2, a deduction of $20,000 should be reported on the company's corporate tax return.

    A. I only
    B. II only
    C. Both I and II
    D. Neither I nor II

226. Which of the following assets are amortized for tax purposes over a 15-year life (180 months)?

    I. Trademarks and trade names that are purchased

    II. Covenants NOT to compete

    III. Goodwill

    A. I and II only
    B. II and III only
    C. I and III only
    D. I, II, and III

227. Davis owns land that is operated as a parking lot. A shed was erected on the lot for the purpose of conducting business with customers. How should the land and shed be classified?

    A. Land and shed both as capital assets
    B. Land as a capital asset, shed as a Section 1231 asset
    C. Shed as a capital asset, land as a Section 1231 asset
    D. Land and shed both as Section 1231 assets

228. For a corporation, which of the following is a capital asset?

    A. A machine used in the business
    B. Land used in the business
    C. Goodwill
    D. Treasury stock

229. Which of the following is correct?

    I. Since land does not depreciate, land cannot be a Section 1231 asset.
    II. For a corporation, capital assets are assets used in the production of ordinary income.

    A. I only
    B. II only
    C. Both I and II
    D. Neither I nor II

230. Regina Corp. sells treasury stock to an unrelated broker in Year 9 and receives proceeds of $50,000. The treasury stock cost Regina Corp. $30,000 to acquire. The total par value of the treasury shares sold is $9,000. What amount of capital gain should Regina Corp. recognize on the sale of the treasury stock in Year 9?

    A. $0
    B. $8,000
    C. $20,000
    D. $30,500

231. On May 1, Year 1, Laughlin, Inc., purchased and placed into service an office building costing $304,000, including $70,000 for the land. What was Laughlin, Inc.'s Modified Accelerated Cost Recovery System (MACRS) depreciation deduction for Year 1?

    A. $3,750
    B. $6,000
    C. $4,000
    D. $2,250

232. On August 1, Year 1, Bachman, Inc., purchased and placed into service an apartment building costing $225,000, including $25,000 for the land. What was Bachman, Inc.'s MACRS deduction for Year 2?

    A. $7,273
    B. $8,182
    C. $2,727
    D. $5,128

Use the following facts to answer **Questions 233–235.**

On February 1, Year 1, Griffin Corp. buys an asset considered a "light truck" for tax purposes on that has a cost of $40,000 and an expected salvage value of $6,000. Griffin Corp. estimates that the truck will last eight years.

233. What method of depreciation should be used for tax purposes according to the MACRS?

    A. Double declining balance over eight years
    B. Double declining balance over five years with half year taken in Year 1
    C. Straight line method over eight years
    D. Straight line method over five years with depreciation for Year 1 starting on February 15th of Year 1

234. What amount of depreciation should be recognized by Griffin Corp. for Year 2 based on the MACRS?

    A. $16,000
    B. $12,800
    C. $8,000
    D. $6,800

235. What amount of depreciation should be recognized for Year 3 based on the MACRS?

    A. $7,680
    B. $12,800
    C. $19,200
    D. $8,000

236. The Carson Company bought a piece of equipment on September 4 of the current year. The company's tax return is filed on a calendar-year basis. The MACRS is used to determine depreciation for income tax purposes. Which of the following is true as to the amount of depreciation that can be recognized in this initial year?

A. Carson should take depreciation for four-twelfths of the year.

B. Carson should take a full year of depreciation.

C. Carson can take depreciation for three-twelfths of the year.

D. Carson can take depreciation for one-half of the year.

237. The allowable depreciation deduction taken in Year 3 for a commercial building that was placed in service in Year 1:

A. is calculated based on a 27.5-year straight line

B. depends upon the amount of depreciation taken in Year 1

C. depends upon what month in Year 1 the building was originally purchased

D. is calculated based on a 39-year straight line

238. Which of the following statements is NOT true in connection with Section 179 asset acquisitions and the immediate expense thereof?

A. The cost spent for off-the-shelf computer software qualifies for Section 179 expense as long as the software has a useful life of more than one year.

B. There is a maximum amount that can be taken as a Section 179 expense.

C. If the company buys a large quantity of qualifying Section 179 property, the immediate expense is reduced, eventually to zero.

D. Buildings are qualifying property for Section 179 expense, but land is not.

239. Ashley sold a truck used for business for $11,000. The truck cost $20,000 three years ago, and $14,000 depreciation was taken. What is the appropriate classification of the $5,000 gain for tax purposes?

A. Short-term capital gain

B. Ordinary gain

C. Section 1231 gain

D. Long-term capital gain

240. For the year ended December 31, Year 1, Bentley, Inc., had gross business income of $160,000 and dividend income of $100,000 from unaffiliated domestic corporations that are at least 20% owned. Business operating expenses for Year 1 amounted to $170,000. How much is Bentley's dividends received deduction (DRD) for Year 1?

A. $0

B. $72,000

C. $80,000

D. $90,000

241. Jandersit Corp., in the current year, had sales revenues of $380,000 and normal and necessary operating expenses of $390,000. In addition, the company received a $50,000 cash dividend from another domestic corporation, a company in which it held a 17% ownership. What is Jandersit Corp.'s taxable income?

A. $0

B. $5,000

C. $8,000

D. $12,000

242. Belfer Corp., a calendar-year C corporation, contributed $80,000 to a qualified charitable organization. Belfer had taxable income of $820,000 before the deduction for current year charitable contributions and after a $40,000 DRD. Belfer Corp. also had carryover charitable contributions of $10,000 from the prior year. What amount can Belfer Corp. deduct as charitable contributions?

A. $90,000

B. $86,000

C. $82,000

D. $80,000

243. Markware Corp. contributed $40,000 to a qualified charitable organization in the current year. Markware Corp.'s taxable income before the deduction for charitable contributions was $410,000. Included in that amount was a $20,000 DRD. Markware Corp. also had carryover charitable contributions of $5,000 from the prior year. What amount can Markware Corp. deduct as charitable contributions in the current year?

A. $40,000

B. $41,000

C. $43,000

D. $45,000

244. Christie Corp., an accrual-basis, calendar-year corporation, was organized on January 2, Year 4. The following information pertains:

Taxable income before charitable
  contributions for the year ended
  December 31, Year 4 $419,000
Gifts in Year 4 directly to families in
  need following hurricane disaster $20,000
Contributions to recognized charities
  after hurricane disaster $10,000
Board of directors' authorized
  contribution to a qualified charity
  (authorized December 1, Year 4,
  made February 1, Year 5) $30,000

What is the maximum allowable deduction that Christie Corp. may take as a charitable contribution on its tax return for the year ended December 31, Year 4?

   A. $30,000
   B. $40,000
   C. $41,900
   D. $60,000

245. Czonka, Inc., is preparing its consolidated tax return. Which of the following statements is correct?
   I. The common parent must directly own 51% or more of the total voting power of all corporations included in the consolidated return.
   II. Operating losses of one group member may be used to offset operating profits of the other members included in the consolidated return.

   A. I only
   B. II only
   C. Both I and II
   D. Neither I nor II

246. The accumulated earnings tax can be avoided by:
   I. paying dividends late where the calendar-year corporation pays the dividend by March 15th of the following year
   II. consent dividends where the taxpayer (stockholder) agrees to include the dividend on his or her Form 1040 even though he or she never received the money
   III. demonstrating that the reasonable needs of the business include retention of all or part of the earnings

   A. I and II only
   B. II and III only
   C. I and III only
   D. I, II, and III

247. The personal holding company tax can be imposed:
   A. regardless of the number of shareholders in a corporation
   B. on companies that make distributions in excess of accumulated earnings
   C. on corporations that have paid the accumulated earnings tax in the same year
   D. on small C corporations that do not pay sufficient dividends

248. An accumulated earnings tax can be imposed:
   A. regardless of the number of shareholders in a corporation
   B. on companies that make distributions in excess of accumulated earnings
   C. on personal holding companies
   D. on both partnerships and corporations

249. For a corporation, removing which of the following benefits would be considered an alternative minimum tax (AMT) adjustment?
   I. Installment sales method
   II. Completed contract method

   A. I only
   B. II only
   C. Both I and II
   D. Neither I nor II

250. For a corporation, which of the following represents an AMT preference item?
   A. Municipal bond interest income from private activity bonds
   B. The 80% dividends received deduction
   C. The 70% dividends received deduction
   D. All of the above

251. For a corporation that invests in municipal bonds, which of the following is true regarding the AMT and municipal bond interest income?
   I. Interest income from general obligation municipal bonds is considered a tax preference item for a corporation when computing their alternative minimum taxable income prior to the adjusted current earnings (ACE) adjustment.
   II. Interest income from private activity municipal bonds is considered a tax preference item for a corporation when computing their alternative minimum taxable income prior to the ACE adjustment.

   A. I only
   B. II only
   C. Both I and II
   D. Neither I nor II

252. In computing the AMT for a corporation, which of the following is true?

    A. If the corporation has any tax-exempt private activity bond interest, taxable income will be increased in arriving at the alternative minimum taxable income.

    B. If the corporation has any municipal bond interest, that interest must be added to taxable income in arriving at the alternative minimum taxable income.

    C. All corporations are allowed to subtract an exemption.

    D. If the corporation has any life insurance proceeds, taxable income will be increased by that amount in arriving at the alternative minimum taxable income.

253. Which of the following is part of the calculation of the ACE adjustment used to calculate a corporation's AMT?

    I. Interest income from general obligation municipal bonds
    II. Life insurance proceeds received by the corporation
    III. The 70% dividends received deduction

    A. I and III only
    B. I, II, and III
    C. I and II only
    D. II and III only

254. The number of shareholders in a corporation is a factor in determining whether a corporation is subject to which of the following?

    I. The AMT
    II. The accumulated earnings tax
    III. The personal holding company tax

    A. I, II, and III
    B. II and III only
    C. I and III only
    D. III only

255. Which of the following is subject to the AMT ACE adjustment?

    I. C corporations
    II. S corporations
    III. Individuals
    IV. Partnerships

    A. I and III only
    B. I and II only
    C. I and IV only
    D. I only

Use the following facts to answer **Questions 256–257.**

Lemoi, a single individual, had a $60,000 investment in qualified Section 1244 stock that became worthless in Year 7. He had no other capital gains or losses in Year 7.

256. How much total loss can Lemoi deduct in Year 7?

    A. $50,000
    B. $53,000
    C. $60,000
    D. $3,000

257. Assuming Lemoi were married filing jointly, how much total loss could he deduct in Year 7?

    A. $50,000
    B. $53,000
    C. $60,000
    D. $3,000

Use the following facts to answer **Questions 258–260.**

Aquilino, married filing jointly, sells 2,000 shares of his qualified Section 1244 small business stock for a loss of $110,000 in Year 5 and sells his remaining 600 shares for a loss of $35,000 in Year 6. Aquilino had no other capital gains or losses in either year.

258. How much total loss can Aquilino deduct in Year 5?

    A. $100,000
    B. $103,000
    C. $50,000
    D. $53,000

259. How much total loss can Aquilino deduct in Year 6?

    A. $100,000
    B. $35,000
    C. $3,000
    D. $38,000

260. How much total loss can Aquilino deduct in Year 7?

    A. $0
    B. $30,000
    C. $100,000
    D. $3,000

261. Junior, a single individual, inherited Rainbow Corp. common stock from his parents. Rainbow is a qualified small business corporation under code Section 1244. The stock cost Junior's parents $120,000 and had an FMV of $225,000 at the parents' date of death. During the year, Rainbow Corp. declared bankruptcy and Junior was informed that the stock was worthless. What amount may Junior deduct as an **ordinary loss** in the current year?

   A. $0
   B. $3,000
   C. $120,000
   D. $225,000

262. Which of the following entities may operate on a fiscal year rather than a calendar year?

   I. C corporation
   II. S corporation
   III. Partnership

   A. I, II, and III
   B. I and II only
   C. I and III only
   D. II and III only

263. An income tax return for a trust is filed on Form:

   A. 990
   B. 1040
   C. 1041
   D. 706

264. The party who creates the trust and funds the trust with assets is known as the:

   A. trustee
   B. beneficiary
   C. grantor
   D. remainderman

265. If NOT expressly granted, which of the following implied powers would a trustee have?
   I. Power to sell trust property
   II. Power to borrow from the trust
   III. Power to pay trust expenses

   A. I and III only
   B. I and II only
   C. II and III only
   D. I, II, and III

266. Grace is the creator of an inter vivos trust naming Rochelle as beneficiary. Which of the following would generally be allocated to trust principal rather than to Rochelle?
   I. Cash dividend
   II. Stock dividend

   A. I only
   B. II only
   C. Both I and II
   D. Neither I nor II

267. Aragona transferred assets into a trust under which Cain is entitled to receive the income for life. After Cain's death, the remaining assets are to be given to Clark. In Year 1, the trust received rent of $1,000, stock dividends of $6,000, interest on certificates of deposit of $3,000, municipal bond interest of $4,000, and proceeds of $7,000 from the sale of bonds. Both Cain and Clark are still alive. What amount of the Year 1 receipts should be allocated to the trust principal?

   A. $15,000
   B. $8,000
   C. $13,000
   D. $7,000

268. Haley is the grantor of a trust over which Haley has retained a discretionary power to receive income. Blanche, Haley's child, receives all taxable income from the trust, unless Haley exercises the discretionary power. To whom is the income earned by the trust taxable?

   A. To the trust to the extent it remains in the trust
   B. To Haley because she has retained a discretionary power
   C. To Blanche as the beneficiary of the trust
   D. To Blanche and Haley in proportion to the distributions paid to them from the trust

269. Generally, which of the following parties would have the first priority to receive the estate of a person who dies without a will?

   A. The state
   B. A parent of the deceased
   C. A spouse of the deceased
   D. A child of the deceased

270. Which of the following is correct regarding a trust?
    I. A trust that begins upon the creator's death is known as a testamentary trust.
    II. Assets held in trust are known as trust corpus or trust res.

    A. I only
    B. II only
    C. Both I and II
    D. Neither I nor II

271. Which of the following types of trusts are allowed to distribute more than their current earnings for the year?
    I. Complex trusts
    II. Simple trusts

    A. I only
    B. II only
    C. Both I and II
    D. Neither I nor II

272. The standard deduction for a simple trust in the fiduciary income tax return (Form 1041) is:

    A. $800
    B. $300
    C. $0
    D. $750

273. Which of the following is correct regarding a simple trust?
    I. If a simple trust properly distributes all its income for a year, the simple trust will pay no tax for that year.
    II. A simple trust receives an exemption of $300.
    III. A simple trust can use a fiscal year or calendar year.

    A. I and II only
    B. II and III only
    C. I and III only
    D. I, II, and III

274. For an estate, the income distribution deduction equals the:

    A. actual distribution to the beneficiary
    B. amount of distributable net income (DNI)
    C. lesser of actual distribution to beneficiary or DNI
    D. greater of actual distribution to the beneficiary or DNI

275. The following are the fair market values of Richard's assets at the date of his death:

Personal effects and jewelry	$150,000
Land bought by Richard's funds five years prior to his death and held with Rita	$800,000

    If Rita was Richard's spouse, the amount includable in Richard's gross estate in the federal estate tax return (Form 706) would be:

    A. $950,000
    B. $550,000
    C. $475,000
    D. $800,000

276. An estate distributed $10,000 to its sole beneficiary as directed by the will. The estate's current year records were as follows:

    Estate income
    $32,000 taxable interest

    Estate disbursements
    $28,000 expenses attributable to taxable interest

    What amount of the distribution was taxable to the beneficiary?

    A. $0
    B. $4,000
    C. $6,000
    D. $10,000

277. Castellano died on March 1 of Year 1. He had total assets of $2 million and liabilities of $400,000. He had funeral expenses of $30,000. In the will, he donated $290,000 to a charitable organization and gave his spouse another $400,000. The remaining amount is divided evenly between his daughter and his father. Without regard for any exclusion, what is the taxable amount of Castellano's estate?

    A. $880,000
    B. $440,000
    C. $460,000
    D. $900,000

278. Sylvia died early in Year 1 with an estate that had a considerable value. The executor of her estate is currently determining the value of her estate for taxation purposes. Which of the following CANNOT be deducted in arriving at the estate value?

    A. Debts owed at death
    B. A bequest made to her only daughter
    C. Funeral expenses
    D. Charitable bequests

279. Gordon died early in Year 1 with an estate valued at several million dollars. In his will, he left a considerable amount of money (approximately 72% of his asset value) to his spouse, Grace. In determining the amount of his taxable estate for federal estate tax purposes, what amount is subtracted in connection with this bequest to his spouse?

    A. $600,000
    B. $1 million
    C. 50% of the value of the estate assets
    D. No limitation

280. Within how many months after the date of a decedent's death is the federal estate tax return (Form 706) due if no time extension for filing is granted?

    A. 9
    B. 6
    C. 4.5
    D. 3.5

281. Which of the following is correct regarding estates?
    I. Estates may adopt a fiscal year or calendar year.
    II. Estates are exempt from paying estimated tax during the estate's first two taxable years.

    A. I only
    B. II only
    C. Both I and II
    D. Neither I nor II

282. An executor of a decedent's estate that has only US citizens as beneficiaries is required to file a fiduciary income tax return if the estate's gross income for the year is at least:

    A. $100
    B. $600
    C. $300
    D. $1,000

283. Which of the following is a valid deduction from a decedent's gross estate?
    I. Federal estate taxes
    II. Unpaid income taxes on income received by the decedent before death

    A. I only
    B. II only
    C. Both I and II
    D. Neither I nor II

CHAPTER 41

OTHER TAXATION AREAS

QUESTIONS 284–316

284. Mac opened a brokerage account with Vanguard Bank in Year 1. Mac was instructed to provide his social security number on the application. Mac failed to provide the social security number to the financial institution. The investment earned interest and dividend income of $2,000 in Year 1.
   I. Mac will be limited to receiving only $500 of the interest income since he failed to provide his social security number to the bank.
   II. Mac will be subject to backup withholding tax on any investment income earned in this new brokerage account until he provides his social security number to the brokerage company.

   A. I only
   B. II only
   C. Both I and II
   D. Neither I nor II

285. Stefano Inc., has sales of inventory in excess of $10,000,000 for the past three tax years. Which of the following costs are subject to uniform capitalization?
   I. Repackaging
   II. Research
   III. Advertising and marketing

   A. I and II only
   B. I and III only
   C. I only
   D. II and III only

286. Which of the following is correct regarding uniform capitalization rules?
   I. Officers' compensation NOT attributed to production would be expensed even if a company were subject to uniform capitalization.
   II. Service companies, like accounting and law firms, are NOT subject to uniform capitalization.

   A. I only
   B. II only
   C. Both I and II
   D. Neither I nor II

287. Maskell, an individual taxpayer, had Year 2 taxable income of $195,000 with a corresponding tax liability of $40,000. For Year 3, Maskell expects taxable income of $264,000 and a tax liability of $50,000. In order to avoid a penalty for underpayment of estimated tax, what is the minimum amount of Year 3 estimated tax payments that Maskell can make?

   A. $40,000
   B. $44,000
   C. $45,000
   D. $50,000

288. Selzer Corp.'s taxable income for the year ended December 31, Year 7, was $2,000,000, on which its tax liability was $680,000. In order for Selzer to escape the estimated tax underpayment penalty for the year ending December 31, Year 8, Selzer's Year 8 estimated tax payments must equal at least:

   A. 90% of the Year 8 tax liability
   B. 93% of the Year 8 tax liability
   C. 100% of the Year 8 tax liability
   D. the Year 7 tax liability of $680,000

289. Which of the following entities must make their final payment of Year 4 taxes by December 15, Year 4?
    I.   C corporations
    II. Individuals
    III. S corporations

    A. II only
    B. I and II only
    C. I only
    D. I, II, and III

290. Quirk filed his Year 1 tax return on March 12, Year 2, and paid a small tax due for the prior year. What is the statute of limitation for this return?

    A. Three years from the date filed because it was filed on time
    B. Three years from the due date for the return
    C. Three years from the date filed regardless of whether it was filed on time or not
    D. Three years from December 31, Year 1

291. Gabriel, a self-employed individual, had income for Year 4 as follows:

$436,000	gross receipts
$(316,000)	deductions
$120,000	net business income

    In March of Year 6, Gabriel discovers that he had inadvertently omitted some income on his Year 4 return and retains Rutherford and Banks CPAs to determine his position under the statute of limitations. Rutherford and Banks CPAs should advise Gabriel that the six-year statute of limitations would apply to his Year 4 return only if he omitted from gross income an amount in excess of:

    A. $109,000
    B. $30,000
    C. $29,000
    D. $120,000

292. A calendar-year taxpayer files an individual tax return for Year 9 on March 20, Year 10. The taxpayer neither committed fraud nor omitted amounts in excess of 25% of gross income on the tax return. What is the latest date that the Internal Revenue Service (IRS) can assess tax and assert a notice of deficiency?

    A. April 15, Year 13
    B. March 20, Year 13
    C. March 20, Year 12
    D. April 15, Year 12

293. Strauss, a sole practitioner CPA, prepares individual income tax returns. According to the IRS Circular 230, approximately how long is Strauss required to keep copies of the tax returns that he prepared?

    A. 2 years
    B. 3 years
    C. 5 years
    D. permanently

294. Which of the following is correct regarding Circular 230?
    I.   A dispute over fees does NOT generally relieve the practitioner of responsibility to return the client's records.
    II. A contingent fee is allowed in connection with the filing of a client's **amended** tax return but not when filing an original tax return.
    III. A paid preparer is required to sign a tax return and include their preparer tax identification number (PTIN) on the client's return.

    A. I and II only
    B. I and III only
    C. II and III only
    D. I, II, and III

295. According to the AICPA's "Statements on Standards for Tax Services" and IRS Circular 230, which of the following is correct?
    I.   When considering whether to give oral or written advice to a client, a CPA should consider the tax sophistication of the client and whether the client will seek a second opinion.
    II. If new legislation will have an impact on advice previously given a year ago, a tax preparer need NOT advise the client of the new legislation even if the original advice was given in writing.
    III. A tax return preparer is NOT permitted to endorse a taxpayer's refund check.

    A. I and II only
    B. II and III only
    C. I and III only
    D. I, II, and III

296. According to Circular 230, which of the following individuals may represent taxpayers before the IRS?
    I.   Registered tax return preparers
    II. Attorneys
    III. CPAs and enrolled agents

    A. I, II, and III
    B. I and III only
    C. II and III only
    D. I and II only

297. When representing a client in an uncertain tax position, arrange the following standards in order from least likely to be upheld to most likely to be upheld.

A. More likely than not, reasonable basis, substantial authority

B. Substantial authority, reasonable basis, more likely than not

C. Reasonable basis, more likely than not, substantial authority

D. Reasonable basis, substantial authority, more likely than not

298. Which of the following is correct regarding the State Board of Accountancy?

I. Ultimately grants the successful CPA candidate a license to practice public accounting

II. Has the power to suspend but not the power to revoke the CPA license

A. I only

B. II only

C. Both I and II

D. Neither I nor II

299. Brenner, a CPA, discovers material noncompliance with a specific Internal Revenue Code (IRC) requirement in the prior-year return of a new client. Which of the following actions should Brenner take?

I. Contact the prior CPA and discuss the client's exposure.

II. Contact the IRS and discuss courses of action.

A. I only

B. II only

C. Both I and II

D. Neither I nor II

300. If a tax preparer knowingly deducted the expenses of the taxpayer's personal domestic help as wages paid in the taxpayer's business on the taxpayer's income tax return:

A. the IRS will examine the facts and circumstances to determine whether the reasonable cause exception applies

B. the IRS will examine the facts and circumstances to determine whether the good faith exception applies

C. the tax preparer's action does not constitute an act of tax preparer misconduct

D. the tax preparer's action constitutes an act of tax preparer misconduct subject to the IRC penalty

301. Before a tax preparer is assessed a penalty, the IRS will sometimes examine the facts and circumstances to determine whether the reasonable cause or the good faith exception applies. In which of the following situations would the IRS examine the facts further to determine whether the good faith or reasonable cause exception applies?

I. The tax preparer relied on the advice of an advisory preparer to calculate the taxpayer's tax liability. The tax preparer believed that the advisory preparer was competent and that the advice was reasonable. Based on the advice, the taxpayer had understated income tax liability.

II. The tax preparer endorses and cashes the taxpayer's refund check and within 24 hours then gives the taxpayer the remainder of the refund after deducting the tax preparer's fee.

III. The tax preparer reveals confidential client information while being evaluated by a quality or peer review team from the state society of CPAs.

A. I only

B. I and III only

C. I, II, and III

D. III only

302. The Perry Corp. sells inventory costing $15,000 to a customer for $20,000. Because of significant uncertainties surrounding the transaction, the installment sales method is viewed as proper. In the first year, Perry Corp. collects $5,700. In the second year, Perry Corp. collects another $8,000. What amount of profit should the Perry Corp. recognize in the second year?

A. $2,000

B. $3,000

C. $4,000

D. $5,000

303. Desimone Corp. began operations on January 1, Year 1 and appropriately uses the installment method of accounting for financial reporting purposes. The following information pertains to operations for Year 1:

Installment sales	$1,200,000
Collections on installment sales	$500,000
General and administration expenses	$180,000
Cost of goods sold minus installment sales	$720,000

The balance in Desimone's deferred gross profit account at December 31, Year 1, should be:

A. $160,000

B. $175,000

C. $200,000

D. $280,000

304. In Year 1 Krohn, Inc., sells $5,000 of goods with a total cost of $2,500 on installment. During Year 1, Krohn, Inc., collects $2,000 and then collects $3,000 in Year 2. Using the cost recovery method, how much will Krohn, Inc., report as gross profit in Year 1 and Year 2 respectively?

	Year 1	Year 2
A.	$0	$2,500
B.	$1,500	$1,000
C.	$1,000	$1,500
D.	$1,250	$1,250

305. Mitchell, Inc., has a contract to build a building for $1,000,000, with an estimated completion time of three years. A reliable cost estimate for the project will be $600,000. In the first year, Mitchell, Inc., incurred costs totaling $240,000. No cash was received from the customer in Year 1. Under the percentage of completion method, in the first year, Mitchell, Inc., will report a profit of:

A. $0
B. $160,000
C. $400,000
D. $760,000

306. Binstock Construction Co. has consistently used the percentage of completion method. On January 10, Year 1, Binstock began work on a $3,000,000 construction contract. At the inception date, the estimated cost of construction was $2,250,000. The following data relate to the progress of the contract:

Income recognized at December 31, Year 1	$300,000
Costs incurred January 10, Year 1 through December 31, Year 2	$1,800,000
Estimated costs to complete at December 31, Year 2	$600,000

In its income statement for the year ended December 31, Year 2, what amount of gross profit should Binstock Co. report?

A. $450,000
B. $300,000
C. $262,500
D. $150,000

307. Cash collection is a critical event for income recognition in the:
  I. percentage of completion method
  II. installment method
  III. cost recovery method

A. II only
B. II and III only
C. I, II, and III
D. III only

308. In October 1 of Year 4, Everlast Builders receives $250,000 as an advance payment from the State of New Jersey for a contract to build an express roadway connecting the interstate highway to a section of the Jersey Shore. The contract is for $4,000,000 and expected to last three years. Total costs incurred over the life of the contract are expected to be $3,500,000. No costs have yet been expended by Everlast by December 31, Year 4. Everlast will recognize at least some of the $250,000 as profit in Year 4 if they use which of the following methods to account for the long-term construction contract?
  I. Percentage of completion method
  II. Completed contract method

A. I only
B. II only
C. Both I and II
D. Neither I nor II

309. Which of the following tax-exempt organizations must file annual information returns (Form 990)?

A. Those with gross receipts of less than $10,000 in each taxable year
B. Private foundations
C. Internally supported auxiliaries of churches
D. Churches

310. Which of the following is required information of a not-for-profit that files Form 990-N?

A. Name and address of major contributors
B. Highest employee salaries
C. Name and address of a principal officer
D. All of the above

311. Most tax-exempt organizations are required to file an annual return. Which form an organization must file generally depends on its:
  I. gross receipts for the year
  II. total assets at year end

A. I only
B. II only
C. Both I and II
D. Neither I nor II

312. The Olney Group is a not-for-profit organization formed under Section 501c of the IRC. Total assets are $350,000 for the current year. Barnes, CPA, and a director of the Olney Group are wondering whether he needs to file Form 990 on behalf of the Olney Group and if so, which Form 990 to file. The following are the figures for the current year.

Revenues	$350,000
Cost of sales	$200,000
Gross profit	$150,000
Salary expenses	$70,000
Net income	$80,000

Assuming these figures closely approximate the most recent three prior years, which 990 form is Barnes likely to file on behalf of the Olney Group?

A. Form 990-N
B. Form 990-EZ
C. Form 990 (long form)
D. Even if the Olney Group was a church, they would have to file Form 990.

313. A tax-exempt organization must still pay income taxes on any unrelated business income in excess of:

A. $1,000
B. $5,000
C. $10,000, after allowing for three prohibited transactions
D. $25,000

Use the following facts to answer **Questions 314–316.**

The Benning Museum, a not-for-profit art gallery, offers art appreciation summer courses to high school students for a fee.

314. Since the museum's mission involves the education of the public about art, the proceeds from such courses are:

A. fully taxable
B. tax exempt
C. taxable for the amount in excess of $1,000 per student
D. tax exempt if the high school students receive high school credit, otherwise taxable

315. Assume that the Benning Museum maintains a website that sells advertising to restaurants and hotels located near the museum. The income from advertising on its website is:

  I. taxable at the corporate tax rate after a $1,000 exemption
  II. considered unrelated business income

A. I only
B. II only
C. Both I and II
D. Neither I nor II

316. The time for filing Form 990-N for a not-for-profit (NFP) organization is normally:

A. two and a half months after the close of the tax year
B. three and a half months after the close of the tax year
C. four and a half months after the close of the tax year
D. five and a half months after the close of the tax year

CHAPTER 42

BUSINESS LAW, ETHICS, AND PROFESSIONAL RESPONSIBILITIES

QUESTIONS 317–468

317. Which is correct regarding contract law?
   I. A legally enforceable agreement can result even if an offer is not accepted.
   II. A contract can be for any legal purpose.

   A. I only
   B. II only
   C. Both I and II
   D. Neither I nor II

318. On November 20, Sheran, Inc., an appliance dealer, placed a television advertisement stating that Sheran would sell 300 high-end smartphones at its store for a special discount only on November 25, Year 13. On November 22, Ragofsky called Sheran and expressed an interest in buying one of the advertised phones.

Ragofsky was told that there will probably be long lines and to come to the store as early as possible.

Ragofsky went to Sheran's store on November 25 and demanded the right to buy the phone at the special discount.

Sheran had sold the 300 phones and refused Ragofsky's demand.

Ragofsky sued Sheran for breach of contract.

Sheran's best defense to Ragofsky's suit would be that Sheran's:

   A. offer was unenforceable
   B. advertisement was not an offer
   C. mentioning of the long lines in the phone call effectively revoked the offer
   D. offer had not been accepted

319. Which of the following communications sent by an offeree must be received to be effective?
   I. Counteroffers
   II. Rejections

   A. I only
   B. II only
   C. Both I and II
   D. Neither I nor II

320. An offer that is irrevocable for an agreed time and is supported by consideration:
   I. is called an option or an option contract
   II. is NOT allowed in a real estate contract

   A. I only
   B. II only
   C. Both I and II
   D. Neither I nor II

321. Poznok offers to sell Lavroff his pizza place for $50,000. Lavroff would like to think about it for a while and offers Poznok $500 for a 30-day option. If Poznok takes Lavroff's $500 check:
   I. Lavroff has 30 days to make offers to Poznok but does not have to buy the store
   II. then on day 18, Lavroff offers Poznok less than $50,000 and Poznok refuses, the option contract has been terminated by counteroffer and Poznok could immediately place the store back on the open market

   A. I only
   B. II only
   C. Both I and II
   D. Neither I nor II

322. The mailbox rule generally makes acceptance of an offer effective at the time the acceptance is dispatched. The mailbox rule does not apply if:

A. both the offeror and offeree are merchants

B. the offer provides that an acceptance should not be effective until actually received

C. the offer proposes a sale of real estate

D. the duration of the offer is not in excess of three months

323. An offer is made on July 2 that calls for acceptance to be in writing and received by August 10. Which of the following is correct regarding the acceptance of this offer?

  I. An acceptance that is mailed August 3 and is received on August 6 is valid on August 3.

  II. An acceptance that is mailed July 8 and received on August 12 is considered a counteroffer and not an acceptance.

A. I only

B. II only

C. Both I and II

D. Neither I nor II

324. Micki received an offer from Clark, Inc., that contained the following specific instructions: "We need to know soon whether you can agree to the terms of this proposal; you must accept by September 22 or we will assume you cannot meet our terms." If Micki's letter of acceptance is mailed by September 21 and arrives on September 25:

A. no contract exists since the acceptance was received after September 22

B. the attempted acceptance letter is a counteroffer

C. a contract is formed on September 21

D. a contract is formed on September 25

325. Rick promises to pay anyone in his office $150 if they pick his son Ricky up at school on April 8 and drive him home. Allison, a coworker, promises to be parked at the school waiting for little Ricky. Brad, another coworker, tells Rick that he may be available and will know more the day before. Which of the following is correct?

A. The contract is bilateral because Rick promised to pay and Allison promised to perform.

B. The contract is unilateral because Rick's promise needs to be accepted by performance, not by promising to perform.

C. If Brad picks up Ricky and drives him home, he would not be entitled to the $150, because Allison promised to perform and Brad did not.

D. None of the above

326. To prevail in a common law action for fraud, a plaintiff must prove that the:

  I. plaintiff is justified in relying on the misrepresentations

  II. defendant made the misrepresentations with knowledge of their falsity and with an intention to deceive

A. I only

B. II only

C. Both I and II

D. Neither I nor II

327. To prevail in a contract for a common law action for fraud, a plaintiff must prove that the:

  I. misrepresentations were material

  II. defendant was an expert with regard to the misrepresentations

A. I only

B. II only

C. Both I and II

D. Neither I nor II

328. Dave negotiated the sale of his bagel store to Ed. Ed asked to see the prior year's financial statements. Using the store's checkbook, Dave prepared a balance sheet and profit and loss (P&L) statement as well as he could. Dave told Ed to go have an accountant examine it, as Dave is not an accountant. Ed later learned that the financial statements contained several errors that resulted in material overstatement of assets and net income. Dave was not aware of the errors. Ed sued Dave for fraud claiming that Ed relied on the financial statements in making the decision to buy the bagel store. Which is correct?

A. Ed will prevail, if the errors in the financial statements are material.

B. Ed will not prevail because his reliance on the financial statements was not justifiable.

C. Ed would be able to prove duress and cancel the contract.

D. Ed would be able to cancel the contract even if the errors were not material.

329. If one party to a contract makes a material unilateral mistake:

  I. the contract could still exist unless the other party knows it's a mistake and is just trying to take advantage

  II. the contract is voidable by the party who made the mistake

A. I only

B. II only

C. Both I and II

D. Neither I nor II

330. Contracts made under which of the following conditions are voidable?

   I. Duress

   II. Undue influence

   A. I only

   B. II only

   C. Both I and II

   D. Neither I nor II

331. Which is correct regarding consideration as an element of a contract?

   I. Consideration can involve money or goods but not services.

   II. Consideration is something that is bargained for and exchanged in a contract.

   A. I only

   B. II only

   C. Both I and II

   D. Neither I nor II

332. Mirro has almost completed the renovation of a building that he owns. Mirro urgently needs the plumbing inspector to inspect the property so that Mirro's new tenants can move in on time. Mirro promises a $125 bonus to the plumbing inspector if the plumbing inspector will come the following morning. Mirro's promise:

   A. qualifies as consideration if the plumbing inspector conducts the inspection the following morning

   B. does not qualify as consideration, because the plumbing inspector already has a pre-existing legal duty to perform inspections

   C. does not qualify as consideration if the plumbing inspector conducts the inspection the following morning and Mirro fails the inspection

   D. qualifies as consideration if the plumbing inspector conducts the inspection the following morning and Mirro passes the inspection

333. Todd Winger, 15 years old, signs a contract to receive flying lessons at a local airport. It's legal in Todd's state for a minor to take flying lessons as early as age 14. Todd's parents drive him to the weekly lesson, the flight school gets paid each month, and Todd continues to show up for the weekly lessons for an entire year. Which of the following is correct?

   A. Todd can cancel the contract at any time while still a minor, but not after reaching the age of majority.

   B. Todd can cancel the contract at any time while still a minor and even within a reasonable time after reaching the age of majority.

   C. The flight school, after learning it just did business with a minor, can cancel the contract at any time.

   D. Todd may cancel the contract at any time while still a minor but would have to pay for the flight lessons that he already received.

334. Darrel is a minor who attends college and lives 900 miles from his parents. Darrel entered into the following contracts and has already received some of the benefits of both contracts. Darrel must pay for what has already been received but can cancel the remainder of which of the following contracts?

   I. Guitar lessons

   II. Campus housing

   A. I only

   B. II only

   C. Both I and II

   D. Neither I nor II

335. Phil, who has not yet reached the age of majority, purchased a motorcycle from Whiting Cycles, Inc. Seven months later, the bike was stolen and never recovered. Which of the following statements is correct?

   I. Phil may rescind the purchase because Phil is a minor.

   II. Phil effectively ratified the purchase because Phil used the bike for more than six months.

   A. I only

   B. II only

   C. Both I and II

   D. Neither I nor II

336. Mona works as the secretary for Amazing Amusements for 13 years. Upon her retirement, Brian, the owner of Amazing Amusements, promises to pay Mona $500 per month for the next six years because of the wonderful job she has done for his company. Which of the following statements is correct?

    I. Brian's promise is based on past consideration, and his promise is NOT a legal obligation.
    II. If Amazing Amusements pays Mona the $500 for more than six months, they would have to continue to pay her.

    A. I only
    B. II only
    C. Both I and II
    D. Neither I nor II

337. Black Bear, Inc., made a contract in writing to hire Ditka for five years for $150,000 per year. After two years, Ditka asked Black Bear, Inc., for a raise of $20,000 per year. Black Bear, Inc., at first refused but then agreed after Ditka put on some pressure. After the fifth year, Ditka left and Black Bear, Inc., sued to get back the extra $20,000 per year for the last three years. Who wins?

    A. Ditka, because Black Bear, Inc., agreed to the raise
    B. Ditka, if the raise was agreed to in writing
    C. Black Bear, Inc., even though Black Bear, Inc., agreed to the raise
    D. Black Bear, Inc., because Ditka had applied some pressure to get the raise

338. Which of the following is legally binding despite lack of consideration?

    I. Modification of a signed contract to purchase a parcel of land
    II. A promise to donate money to a charity, which the charity relied on in incurring large expenditures

    A. I only
    B. II only
    C. Both I and II
    D. Neither I nor II

339. In contract law, which of the following correctly relates to the terms *valid*, *void*, and *voidable*?

    A. Once a party has been declared legally insane by a court with proper jurisdiction, all contracts entered into by that person would be voidable at the other party's option.
    B. Void contracts are otherwise valid, but one of the parties has the power to set the contract aside.
    C. Voidable contracts are agreements that are void from the start.
    D. Once a party has been declared legally insane by a court with proper jurisdiction, all contracts entered into by that person would be void.

340. Which of the following contracts are voidable?

    I. Contracts entered into by a minor
    II. Contracts entered into by an individual who is drunk every day

    A. I only
    B. II only
    C. Both I and II
    D. Neither I nor II

341. Under the law governing service contracts, if A hired B to kidnap C, which of the following is correct?

    I. If A already paid B, the court would force B to refund A's money but would not force B to kidnap C.
    II. This would be an example of a voidable contract.

    A. I only
    B. II only
    C. Both I and II
    D. Neither I nor II

342. Which is correct as it relates to licensing statutes?

    I. A revenue license is not required in order to collect for real estate services rendered in most states.
    II. A regulatory license is required in order to collect for legal services rendered in most states.

    A. I only
    B. II only
    C. Both I and II
    D. Neither I nor II

343. Which of the following contracts ordinarily needs to be in writing to be enforceable?
    I. Contracts for the sale of real estate
    II. Contracts for services that are impossible to complete within one year
    III. Contracts for services with consideration of $500 or more

    A. I, II, and III
    B. I and II only
    C. I and III only
    D. II and III only

344. On September 18, Juan, a salesperson, orally contracted to service a piece of equipment owned by Genarro, Inc. The contract provided that for a period of 36 months, Juan would provide routine service for the equipment at a fixed price of $30,000 payable in three annual installments of $10,000 each. Which of the following is correct?
    I. On October 29, Genarro, Inc.'s president could decide that Genarro does not have to honor the service agreement, because there is no written contract between Juan and Genarro, Inc.
    II. This agreement need not be in writing if both parties have already fully performed their agreement.

    A. I only
    B. II only
    C. Both I and II
    D. Neither I nor II

345. Hayes agreed orally to repair Patterson's rare guitar for $389. Before the work was started, Patterson asked Hayes to perform additional repairs to the instrument and agreed to increase the contract price to $625. After Hayes completed the work, Patterson refused to pay and Hayes sued. Patterson's defense was based on the statute of frauds (the contract was oral). What total amount will Hayes recover?

    A. $389
    B. $625
    C. $0
    D. $500

346. Which of the following contracts if not fully performed must be in writing to be enforceable?
    I. Sale of goods for a price of $1,500
    II. Executor of a will
    III. A contract to cosign the debts of another

    A. I and III only
    B. II and III only
    C. I and II only
    D. I, II, and III

347. Which of the following is correct regarding the parol evidence rule?
    I. It allows for the admission of evidence of oral agreements that existed prior to the written contract if the oral agreements contradict the written contract.
    II. It does not apply if the contract did not have to be in writing.

    A. I only
    B. II only
    C. Both I and II
    D. Neither I nor II

348. Which of the following would NOT be prohibited by the parol evidence rule?
    I. Oral evidence that existed prior to the writing that could prove fraud
    II. Written evidence that existed prior to the writing that could prove fraud

    A. I only
    B. II only
    C. Both I and II
    D. Neither I nor II

349. Which of the following is correct regarding assignment of rights in a contract?
    I. Assignment must be in writing and signed by the assignor.
    II. Most contract rights are NOT assignable as a matter of law.

    A. I only
    B. II only
    C. Both I and II
    D. Neither I nor II

350. Conisha contracted with White for Conisha to buy certain real property. If the contract is otherwise silent, Conisha's rights under the contract are:

    A. assignable only with White's consent
    B. generally assignable
    C. not assignable, because they were meant only for Conisha; therefore, they would be considered highly personal contract rights
    D. not assignable as a matter of law

351. On December 19, Cutrone contracted in writing with Bonacorso Landscaping Corp. The contract provided Cutrone to deliver certain specified new equipment to Bonacorso by December 31. On December 23, Cutrone determined that he would not be able to deliver the equipment to Bonacorso by December 31 because of an inventory shortage. Therefore, Cutrone made a written assignment to Ricci Equipment, Inc. When Ricci attempted to deliver the equipment on December 31, Bonacorso refused to accept it, claiming that Cutrone could not properly delegate its duties under the December 19 contract to another party without the consent of Bonacorso. Which of the following statements is correct?

   I. Since the contract is silent with regard to assignment, assignment is NOT allowed as the goods are considered inventory.

   II. The rights under this contract would be considered too "personal" to freely assign without permission.

   III. Assignment is generally allowed unless it is prohibited by the contract, would substantially increase someone's risk, or contains highly personal contract rights.

   A. I and II only

   B. III only

   C. I only

   D. II only

352. Fisk, Inc., is a creditor beneficiary of a contract between Larkin and Donner Industries, Inc. Donner is indebted to Fisk. The contract between Larkin and Donner provides that Larkin is to purchase goods from Donner and pay the purchase price directly to Fisk until Donner's obligation is satisfied. Without justification, Larkin failed to pay Fisk, and Fisk sued Larkin. Which is correct?

   I. Fisk is an incidental beneficiary of the contract between Larkin and Donner.

   II. Fisk is a third-party donee beneficiary.

   A. I only

   B. II only

   C. Both I and II

   D. Neither I nor II

353. Which of the following third parties can sue to enforce a contract?

   I. Incidental beneficiaries

   II. Intended creditor beneficiaries

   III. Intended donee beneficiaries

   A. I and III only

   B. II and III only

   C. I, II, and III

   D. II only

354. Which of the following describes an anticipatory repudiation?

   I. One party announces in advance that they will not perform a contractual obligation.

   II. One party reasonably demands an assurance of performance and does not receive one.

   A. I only

   B. II only

   C. Both I and II

   D. Neither I nor II

355. Which of the following represent actual dollar losses that when recovered would restore the parties to the position they would have been in had there been no breach?

   I. Liquidated damages

   II. Compensatory damages

   A. I only

   B. II only

   C. Both I and II

   D. Neither I nor II

356. In 1998 the American Institute of CPAs (AICPA) decided to computerize what had always been a paper-and-pencil CPA exam. After several vendors were interviewed, the AICPA contracted with Prometric, a technology company, to computerize the CPA exam and make it available on demand. The contract between the AICPA and Prometric contained a damages clause that said in the event that Prometric did not finish by a certain date, Prometric owed the AICPA a predetermined amount of money. This predetermined amount in the event of breach is referred to as:

   A. liquidated damages

   B. specific performance

   C. compensatory damages

   D. punitive damages

357. Regarding breach of contracts and remedies, specific performance is an available remedy when which of the following contracts are breached?

   I. Contract for services where one party refuses to perform

   II. Sale of goods where the goods are unique

   III. Sale of real estate

   A. II and III only

   B. I and III only

   C. I, II, and III

   D. III only

358. Murray and Rukke purchased a dog-grooming business from Eichmann. The agreement contained a covenant prohibiting Eichmann from competing with Murray and Rukke in the dog-grooming business. Which of the following is correct regarding the covenant not to compete?
   I. For the covenant not to compete to be enforceable, the time period for which it is to be effective must be reasonable.
   II. For the covenant not to compete to be enforceable, the geographic area covered by the agreement must be reasonable.

   A. I only
   B. II only
   C. Both I and II
   D. Neither I nor II

359. Naomi contracted to sell May a building for $310,000. The contract required May to pay the entire amount at closing. Naomi refused to close the sale of the building. May sued Naomi. To what relief is May entitled?

   A. Specific performance and compensatory damages
   B. Compensatory damages or specific performance
   C. Punitive damages and compensatory damages
   D. Specific performance only

360. Which of the following is correct regarding common law and the Uniform Commercial Code (UCC)?
   I. Whether the UCC sales article is applicable does not depend on the price of the goods involved.
   II. The common law rules apply to contracts for the sale of a business but NOT to contracts for real estate.

   A. I only
   B. II only
   C. Both I and II
   D. Neither I nor II

361. The UCC sales article applies:

   A. to a contract for personal services
   B. to the sale of specially manufactured goods
   C. to the sale of real estate
   D. to the sale of goods only if the buyer and seller are merchants

362. Under the sales article of the UCC, a firm offer will be created only if the:
   I. offeree and offeror are both merchants
   II. offeree gives some form of consideration
   III. offer is made by a merchant in a signed writing

   A. I, II, and III
   B. I and III only
   C. II and III only
   D. III only

363. Carrabel Breads, Inc., offered to sell Shop and Cart Market's 20,000 pounds of Plantation Bread at $1.00 per pound, subject to certain specified terms for delivery. Shop and Cart replied in writing as follows: "We accept your offer for 20,000 pounds of Plantation Bread at $1.00 per pound, terms 2/10 net 30." In accordance with the sales article of the UCC:

   A. a contract will be formed only if Carrabel Bread agrees to the 2% off
   B. a contract was formed between the parties
   C. no contract was formed, because Shop and Cart included the 2/10 net 30 in its reply
   D. no contract was formed, because Shop and Cart's reply was a counteroffer

364. With regard to contract law, the price of the contract is sometimes considered too material to leave out and at other times can be left open. Which of the following contracts would fail if the price were left open?
   I. Sale of goods
   II. Sale of real estate
   III. Services

   A. I only
   B. II and III only
   C. I, II, and III
   D. II only

365. Which of the following would require additional consideration to both parties in the event that the original contract is modified?
   I. Contract for personal services
   II. Contract for the sale of goods

   A. I only
   B. II only
   C. Both I and II
   D. Neither I nor II

366. Under the UCC sales article, which of the following statements is correct concerning a contract for the sale of goods involving a merchant seller and a merchant buyer for a price of $10,000?
    I. If the contract is oral, and the seller sends the buyer a written confirmation, that confirmation could substitute for a signed contract.
    II. The contract would follow the common law rules rather than the UCC rules.

    A. I only
    B. II only
    C. Both I and II
    D. Neither I nor II

367. Collins, Inc., and Hackett Corp. agreed orally that Hackett would custom manufacture a piece of equipment for Collins at a price of $130,000. After Hackett completed the work at a cost of $95,000, Collins notified Hackett that the item was no longer needed. Hackett is holding the equipment and has requested payment from Collins. Hackett has been unable to resell the item for any price. Hackett incurred storage fees of $1,000. If Collins refuses to pay Hackett and Hackett sues Collins, the most Hackett will be entitled to recover is:

    A. $95,000
    B. $96,000
    C. $130,000
    D. $131,000

368. In which of the following trial sales would title pass to the buyer before the expiration of the trial period?
    I. Sale on approval
    II. Sale or return

    A. I only
    B. II only
    C. Both I and II
    D. Neither I nor II

369. Under the sales article of the UCC, which of the following statements is CORRECT concerning a contract involving a merchant seller and a non-merchant buyer?

    A. The contract may not involve the sale of personal property with a price of more than $500.
    B. The contract will be either a sale or return or sale on approval contract.
    C. Only the seller is obligated to perform the contract in good faith.
    D. Whether the UCC sales article is applicable does not depend on the price of the goods involved.

370. Under the sales article of the Uniform Commercial Code (UCC), unless otherwise agreed to, the seller's obligation to the buyer is to:
    A. deliver all the goods called for in the contract to a common carrier
    B. set aside conforming goods for inspection by the buyer before delivery
    C. hold conforming goods and give the buyer whatever notification is reasonably necessary to enable the buyer to take delivery
    D. deliver the goods to the buyer's place of business

371. Giant Retail Corp. agreed to purchase 20,000 phone systems from VoiceNext Telecom. VoiceNext is a wholesaler of phone systems, and Giant is a large technology retailer. The contract required VoiceNext to ship the phones by common carrier, free on board (FOB) VoiceNext, Inc., loading dock. Which of the parties bears the risk of loss during shipment?

    A. VoiceNext because the risk of loss passes only when Giant receives the goods
    B. VoiceNext because both parties are merchants
    C. Giant because the risk of loss passes when the goods are delivered to the carrier
    D. Giant because this is an example of a sale on approval

372. Under the UCC, risk of loss passes to the buyer:
    A. when the goods are delivered to the carrier if the terms are FOB destination
    B. when the goods are placed on the seller's loading dock if the terms are FOB destination
    C. when the goods are placed on the seller's loading dock if the terms are FOB shipping point
    D. when the goods are delivered to the carrier if the terms are FOB shipping point

373. If a seller ships nonconforming goods to a buyer in a sale of goods contract under the UCC:
    I. risk of loss would remain with the seller even if the terms were FOB shipping point and the goods were already delivered to the carrier
    II. the buyer could reject the entire shipment and would NOT be able to accept a partial shipment and reject the rest
    III. the seller has breached the contract, but the buyer must follow reasonable instructions from the seller as to what to do with the nonconforming goods

    A. I, II, and III
    B. I and III only
    C. I and II only
    D. III only

374. Your client buys a guitar from a seller. Rather than take the instrument home, your client leaves the instrument at the place he bought it for a few days. Thieves break in and steal the guitar. Your client would NOT bear the risk of loss if the guitar was sold by and ultimately stolen from a:
    I. merchant seller
    II. nonmerchant seller

    A. I only
    B. II only
    C. Both I and II
    D. Neither I nor II

375. Which of the following events will release the buyer from all its obligations under a sales contract?
    I. The goods are destroyed after the risk of loss had already passed to the buyer.
    II. The seller refuses to give written assurance of performance when reasonably demanded by the buyer.

    A. I only
    B. II only
    C. Both I and II
    D. Neither I nor II

376. Which of the following correctly describes a seller's right to cure?
    I. As long as the time for performance has not passed, the seller has the right to correct defects in shipments made.
    II. The seller must give timely notice of intent to cure before the buyer secures goods elsewhere.

    A. I only
    B. II only
    C. Both I and II
    D. Neither I nor II

377. Under the UCC sales article, which of the following legal remedies would a buyer NOT have when a seller fails to transfer and deliver unique goods identified to the contract?
    A. Recover the identified goods
    B. Suit for specific performance
    C. Purchase substitute goods (cover)
    D. Suit for punitive damages

378. Fessler contracted in writing to sell Fishman a portable generator for $600. The contract did not specifically address the time for payment, place of delivery, or Fishman's right to inspect the generator. Which of the following statements is correct?
    I. Fessler is obligated to deliver the generator to Fishman's home.
    II. Fishman is entitled to inspect the generator before paying for it.

    A. I only
    B. II only
    C. Both I and II
    D. Neither I nor II

379. Which of the following warranties are given only by a **merchant** seller?
    I. Express warranty
    II. Implied warranty of title
    III. Implied warranty of merchantability

    A. I and III only
    B. II and III only
    C. III only
    D. I, II, and III

380. Which of the following warranties would arise only by the buyer making known his needs to the seller and the seller selecting an item to fit the buyer's specific needs?
    I. Implied warranty of fitness for a particular purpose
    II. Implied warranty of merchantability

    A. I only
    B. II only
    C. Both I and II
    D. Neither I nor II

381. A merchant who attempts to disclaim "any and all warranties" has NOT adequately disclaimed the warranty of:
  I. title
  II. merchantability
  III. fitness for a particular purpose

  A. I only
  B. I and II only
  C. I and III only
  D. I, II, and III

382. Which of the following must be proven by an injured party looking to recover damages from a seller of defective merchandise after being injured by the defective product?
  I. Negligence on the part of the manufacturer
  II. The product was sold in a defective condition
  III. Privity of contract with the seller

  A. I, II, and III
  B. II only
  C. I only
  D. II and III only

383. Traficante sues the manufacturer, wholesaler, and retailer for bodily injuries caused by a rechargeable battery system she purchased. Which of the following statements is correct?

  A. The manufacturer will avoid liability if it can show it followed the custom of the industry.
  B. Traficante may recover even if she cannot show any negligence was involved.
  C. Privity will be a bar to recovery insofar as Traficante did not purchase from the wholesaler.
  D. Contributory negligence on Traficante's part will always be a bar to recovery.

384. Which of the following is correct regarding a contract for the sale of goods?
  I. For the UCC rules to apply, the contract must be for a price of more than $500.
  II. Acceptance of the offer can be valid prior to receipt unless the offer requires the acceptance to be received by a particular date to be effective.

  A. I only
  B. II only
  C. Both I and II
  D. Neither I nor II

385. Which of the following is correct regarding a written contract for the sale of goods in order for the agreement to be enforceable under the UCC?
  I. The written contract must contain the quantity of the goods to be sold.
  II. The written contract must contain the signature of the party seeking to enforce the contract.

  A. I only
  B. II only
  C. Both I and II
  D. Neither I nor II

386. Your client takes his guitar to Loria Music, a merchant seller, for repairs and is given a repair receipt. Your client leaves the instrument with Loria Music and is told to come back in a few weeks with the repair receipt. While the guitar was with Loria Music, Pete, a salesman at Loria Music, accidentally sells the instrument to Cace, a customer in the ordinary course of business. Pete and Loria Music know the identity of all parties but are refusing to reveal the identity of Cace to your client, who insists on getting the guitar back. What is the likely outcome?

  A. If Pete were the owner of the store rather than a salesman, Pete would have to get the guitar back from Cace at his own expense.
  B. Your client would have the option of Loria Music paying your client a sum of money in damages, or your client can choose to have Loria Music get the guitar back from Cace.
  C. The guitar now belongs to Cace; Loria Music owes money damages to your client.
  D. If the guitar were unique, Cace would have to return it to your client.

387. Which of the following is correct regarding the sales article of the UCC?

  A. Merchants and nonmerchants are treated alike.
  B. None of the contract terms may be omitted or the contract would fail.
  C. None of the provisions of the UCC may be disclaimed by agreement.
  D. The obligations of the parties to the contract must be performed in good faith.

388. Under the UCC, commercial paper can be described as a:
- I. substitute for money
- II. means of providing credit

  A. I only
  B. II only
  C. Both I and II
  D. Neither I nor II

389. According to the (UCC, which of the following are commercial paper?
- I. Note
- II. Draft
- III. Warehouse receipt

  A. I, II, and III
  B. I and III only
  C. I and II only
  D. II only

390. According to the commercial paper article of the UCC, which of the following would be considered a promise to pay rather than an order to pay?
- I. Certificate of deposit
- II. Installment note
- III. Check

  A. I and II only
  B. II and III only
  C. I, II, and III
  D. I and III only

391. Russell is the payee of a note and Diane is the maker. Which of the following, if found on the front of the instrument, would cause the note to be non-negotiable?

  A. "Pay to the order of Russell"
  B. "Pay to Russell or bearer"
  C. "Pay to Russell or his order"
  D. "Pay to Russell"

392. According to the commercial paper article of the UCC, a note would be negotiable if the note was payable in:

  A. money only, payable in a foreign currency
  B. money or goods
  C. money or services
  D. money, goods, or services

393. With regard to negotiability, what do you focus on to see whether or not the commercial paper is negotiable?

  A. Back of the instrument only
  B. Front and back of the instrument
  C. Front of the instrument only
  D. Commercial paper is always negotiable

394. Which of the following would destroy negotiability if found on the front of an otherwise negotiable instrument payable for $5,000?

  A. An extension clause, extending out the time for payment to a date specified in the note
  B. An acceleration clause, accelerating the time for payment in the event of default
  C. A contingency that must occur before the note was payable
  D. A different amount of interest, before and after default

395. Trixie holds a check that is written out to her. The check has the amount in words as "four hundred dollars." The amount in figures on this check states $450.

  A. The check is cashable for $400.
  B. The check is cashable for $450.
  C. The check is not cashable, because the amounts differ.
  D. The check is not cashable, because the amounts differ by more than 5%.

396. In order to negotiate **bearer** paper, one must:

  A. endorse the paper
  B. endorse and deliver the paper with consideration
  C. deliver the paper to the next party without the need for endorsement
  D. deliver and endorse the paper

397. To negotiate order paper, one must:

  A. endorse the paper
  B. deliver the paper with consideration
  C. deliver the paper to the next party without the need for endorsement
  D. deliver and endorse the paper

398. Which of the following is a type of endorsement regarding negotiable instruments?
  I. Qualified
  II. Special
  III. Blank
  IV. Restrictive

  A. I, II, and IV only
  B. I, II, III, and IV
  C. I and IV only
  D. I, II, and III only

399. Advantage Telecom LLC received a check that was originally made payable to the order of one of its customers, Roy Hobbs. The following endorsement was written on the back of the check: Roy Hobbs, "for collection only." Which of the following describes the endorsement?
  I. Blank
  II. Restrictive
  III. Qualified

  A. II and III only
  B. I, II, and III
  C. I and III only
  D. I and II only

400. The front of an instrument is order paper and reads "Pay to the order of Mark Davis." Which type of endorsement on the back of that instrument would turn the order paper on the front into bearer paper on the back?
  I. Blank endorsement
  II. Special endorsement

  A. I only
  B. II only
  C. Both I and II
  D. Neither I nor II

401. Which of the following is correct regarding commercial paper?
  I. If commercial paper is determined to be negotiable, it remains negotiable unless a blank endorsement appears on the back.
  II. If commercial paper is determined to be order paper, it remains order paper even if a blank endorsement appears on the back.

  A. I only
  B. II only
  C. Both I and II
  D. Neither I nor II

402. Corey is the holder of a note made payable to his order. He turns the instrument over and signs "without recourse," and then he signs his name and writes "pay to Stuart Sheldon." Which of the following describes the endorsement and the type of paper the instrument is after the endorsement?

  A. Qualified and special endorsement, instrument becomes bearer paper
  B. Qualified and special endorsement, instrument remains order paper
  C. Qualified and blank endorsement, instrument becomes bearer paper
  D. Qualified and blank endorsement, instrument remains order paper

403. Under the UCC commercial paper article, which of the following is a requirement to become a *holder in due course*?
  I. The instrument must be negotiable.
  II. The holder must give value for the instrument and in good faith.
  III. The holder must have knowledge that the instrument is past due or dishonored at the time the instrument is acquired.

  A. I, II, and III
  B. I and II only
  C. II and III only
  D. I and III only

404. Boyle is the purchaser of a negotiable note from Jordan. Boyle would still be a holder in due course even if, at the time of purchase:
  I. Boyle purchased the instrument at a 30% discount
  II. Boyle knew that the maker was three months behind on the payments

  A. I only
  B. II only
  C. Both I and II
  D. Neither I nor II

405. Capell, a holder in due course, is seeking to collect on a note where Sussman is the maker. Sussman would have a real defense and NOT have to pay Capell if:
  I. Sussman was a minor
  II. Sussman's signature was a forgery

  A. I only
  B. II only
  C. Both I and II
  D. Neither I nor II

406. Rusty, a holder in due course of a $2,000 note, negotiates the note to your client Salas. At the time Salas acquires the instrument for value from Rusty, Salas notices that it was overdue by five weeks. Which of the following best describes Salas?

    A. Salas has the standing of a holder in due course.

    B. Salas has the standing of a holder through a holder in due course.

    C. Salas is unable to acquire the rights under the shelter provision since the instrument was overdue.

    D. none of the above

407. With regard to the commercial paper article of the UCC and the rights of a holder in due course, which of the following are real defenses?

    I. Material alteration

    II. Lack of consideration

    III. Discharge in bankruptcy

    A. I and II only

    B. I and III only

    C. I, II, and III

    D. II and III only

408. Grace Gordon is a holder in due course of a promissory note. Therefore, she will take a note free of which of the following defenses?

    A. Discharge of the maker in bankruptcy

    B. Negligence of the maker

    C. Extreme duress placed upon the maker at the time the maker signed the note

    D. The maker not yet having reached the age of majority

409. Which of the following parties has primary liability on a negotiable instrument?

    I. Maker of a note

    II. Drawer of a draft after the draft has been accepted

    III. Drawee of a draft before the draft has been accepted

    A. I and III only

    B. I and II only

    C. I only

    D. None of the above

410. Under the UCC, which of the following are considered commercial paper?

    I. Bills of lading

    II. Warehouse receipts

    A. I only

    B. II only

    C. Both I and II

    D. Neither I nor II

411. According to the UCC, documents of title and investment securities:

    A. are NOT commercial paper unless they are negotiable

    B. are commercial paper if they are NOT negotiable

    C. are NOT commercial paper because they are NOT payable in money only

    D. are commercial paper because they are payable in money only

412. A document of title, like a warehouse receipt or bill of lading:

    A. can be negotiable if payable to "the order of Owen Michaels"

    B. cannot be negotiable if payable to "Owen Michaels or bearer"

    C. is NOT negotiable unless payable to bearer

    D. cannot be negotiable

413. According to the UCC, warehouse receipts and bills of lading:

    A. are NOT commercial paper

    B. cannot be negotiable unless they are payable to a named payee

    C. can be negotiable only if they are considered commercial paper

    D. cannot be negotiable unless they are payable to bearer

414. A bill of lading payable "to Billy Spence or bearer":

    A. can be negotiated by delivery alone without the need for endorsement

    B. is NOT negotiable, because bills of lading are NOT commercial paper

    C. can be negotiated but would require the endorsement of Billy Spence

    D. is considered order paper rather than bearer paper since it's payable to a named payee

415. Under the UCC governing transactions involving debtor/creditor relationships, which of the following is correct regarding the terms *attachment* and *perfection*?

    I. Attachment relates to the creditor's rights against the debtor.

    II. Perfection relates to the creditor's rights against third parties.

    A. I only

    B. II only

    C. Both I and II

    D. Neither I nor II

416. Under the UCC governing transactions involving debtor/creditor relationships, which of the following is correct regarding the security agreement?

    I. It is an agreement to grant a security interest in certain personal property.

    II. It is an attempt to protect a creditor or lender.

    A. I only

    B. II only

    C. Both I and II

    D. Neither I nor II

417. Under the UCC governing transactions involving debtor/creditor relationships, which of the following is correct regarding the attachment of the security interest?

    I. The security interest is enforceable once the security agreement has been signed.

    II. The security interest is intended to give the creditor rights against the debtor in the event of default.

    A. I only

    B. II only

    C. Both I and II

    D. Neither I nor II

418. Frazier goes to Lester-Glenn Auto dealership late Saturday afternoon. Frazier takes test drives and talks financing with the salespeople. Frazier ultimately selects a special order car that is not currently at the dealership. Frazier is promised by Lester-Glenn that they would deliver the car to Frazier's house by Friday (within five business days) if he signs the contract, the note, and security agreement while still at the Lester-Glenn dealership. Frazier agrees and signs all the papers Saturday while still at the dealership. The car is delivered to Frazier's house on Friday just as promised by Lester-Glenn. According to the UCC secured transactions article, when did attachment take place?

    A. Attachment took place Saturday night in the dealership when Frazier signed the security agreement.

    B. Attachment took place Saturday night in the dealership when Frazier signed the contract and promissory note.

    C. Attachment took place Friday afternoon when the car was delivered to Frazier's house.

    D. Attachment took place Saturday night at the dealership because the car arrived at Frazier's house within five business days of Frazier signing all the papers.

419. Which of the following transactions would illustrate a secured party perfecting its security interest by taking possession of collateral?

    I. When the collateral is a stack of negotiable notes and the creditor takes possession of the negotiable instruments

    II. When a pawnbroker lends money

    A. I only

    B. II only

    C. Both I and II

    D. Neither I nor II

420. According to the UCC secured transactions article, attachment and perfection will occur simultaneously when:

    I. a pawnbroker lends money

    II. a financing statement is filed

    A. I only

    B. II only

    C. Both I and II

    D. Neither I nor II

421. Ivy is a former professional athlete. Retired, broke, and unable to qualify for a loan, Ivy decides to pawn a piece of valuable jewelry. Ivy pawns his League Championship Ring at the Tenderloin Pawn Shop, borrowing $15,000 from Tenderloin. Ivy takes the $15,000 from the Tenderloin Pawn Shop and purchases a used automobile outright for cash. Which of the following is correctv?

   I. Once Tenderloin Pawn Shop takes possession of Ivy's championship ring, Tenderloin Pawn Shop automatically receives a nonpossessory interest in the used automobile.

   II. Once Tenderloin Pawn Shop takes possession of Ivy's ring, Tenderloin Pawn Shop has a possessory interest in the piece of jewelry.

   III. Once Tenderloin Pawn Shop takes possession of Ivy's ring, Tenderloin does NOT need to file a financing statement to perfect its interest in the piece of jewelry.

A. I only
B. II and III only
C. I and III only
D. I, II, and III

422. Which of the following is correct regarding a financing statement?

   I. A typical financing statement filing lasts for five years.

   II. If the debtor moves to a new state, the creditor need not file a financing statement in the new state, because the original filing is good for five years.

A. I only
B. II only
C. Both I and II
D. Neither I nor II

423. Salika is a buyer in the ordinary course of business. If Salika purchases goods from a merchant seller,

   I. Salika purchases the goods free and clear of any security interest that she was NOT aware of at the time of purchase

   II. Salika purchases the goods free and clear of any security interest that she was aware of at the time of purchase

A. I only
B. II only
C. Both I and II
D. Neither I nor II

Use the following facts to answer **Questions 424–425.**

Stacey is behind on the payments on her convertible, and the creditor has already attempted to repossess the car.

424. Which of the following rights does Stacey have after the convertible has been repossessed but before it has been sold?

   I. Redemption

   II. Right to be notified of the sale

A. I only
B. II only
C. Both I and II
D. Neither I nor II

425. Assume that Stacey's creditor has repossessed the convertible. Which of the following is correct?

   I. If the car is repossessed and sold for less than the balance due, Stacey could not be sued for a deficiency, since she paid more than 60% of the purchase price.

   II. Once the car is repossessed by the creditor, Stacey could force the creditor to sell the car.

A. I only
B. II only
C. Both I and II
D. Neither I nor II

Use the following facts to answer **Questions 426–427.**

Cliff bought a smart device for personal use from DC Appliance Corp. for $3,000. Cliff paid $2,000 in cash and signed a security agreement for the balance. DC Appliance properly filed the security agreement. Cliff defaulted in paying the balance of the purchase price. DC Appliance asked Cliff to pay the balance. When Cliff politely refused, DC Appliance peacefully repossessed the smart device.

426. As this transaction is covered by the UCC secured transactions article, which of the following is correct?

   I. DC Appliance may retain the smart device over Cliff's objection.

   II. DC Appliance may sell the smart device without notifying Cliff.

A. I only
B. II only
C. Both I and II
D. Neither I nor II

427. Assume the smart device is sold at auction. Which of the following is correct?
    I. If the smart device sells at auction for less than the amount owed, DC Appliance can obtain a judgment against Cliff for the deficiency.
    II. If the smart device sells at auction for more than the amount owed, DC Appliance could keep the surplus.

    A. I only
    B. II only
    C. Both I and II
    D. Neither I nor II

428. Which of the following is correct regarding an agency relationship?
    I. An agency relationship must be in writing if the agent will earn more than $500.
    II. An agent owes a duty of loyalty to the principal, but no such duty of loyalty is owed from principal to agent.
    III. An agent for a disclosed principal would NOT be held liable to a third party if the principal backs out of the agreement.

    A. I and II only
    B. I, II, and III
    C. I and III only
    D. II and III only

429. Stump works as an agent for the New York Bombers, a major-league baseball team. Stump is paid to scout amateur baseball players and report information back to the Bombers' general manager. The Bombers send Stump from New York to Tokyo to follow a Japanese prospect named Hito, whom the Bombers are interested in signing for the upcoming major-league season. It is not uncommon for Stump to travel to other countries to follow a player for the Bombers. Which of the following is correct?
    I. Stump would be liable to the Bombers for disclosing information about Hito to other major-league baseball teams without the consent of the Bombers.
    II. The Bombers would be liable to Stump if they sent additional agents to Japan to follow Hito without the knowledge and consent of Stump.

    A. I only
    B. II only
    C. Both I and II
    D. Neither I nor II

430. If a principal wishes to no longer be obligated on any new contracts made by a recently dismissed agent, which of the following actions need be taken?
    I. Actual notice needs to be given to third parties with whom the agent had prior dealings.
    II. Constructive notice needs be given to potential third parties, even though it's not possible to ensure that all potential third parties would become aware of the agent's dismissal.

    A. I only
    B. II only
    C. Both I and II
    D. Neither I nor II

431. Which of the following is required for a surety contract?
    I. Principal debtor, creditor, and surety
    II. Written agreement between the surety and the principal debtor
    III. Written agreement between the surety and the creditor

    A. I and III only
    B. I, II, and III
    C. I and II only
    D. II and III only

432. If a debtor defaults and one surety is left to pay the entire obligation, which of the following rights does that surety have after payment in full?

    A. Contribution
    B. Exoneration
    C. Subrogation
    D. Attachment

433. If a surety is asked by the creditor to pay for the default of a principal debtor's car loan, which of the following best describes a surety's rights?
    I. Exoneration refers to the surety's rights prior to payment.
    II. Subrogation refers to the surety's rights after payment in full.

    A. I only
    B. II only
    C. Both I and II
    D. Neither I nor II

434. Levon holds several credit cards from various banks. The federal Credit Card Fraud Act protects Levon from loss by:

- **A.** restricting the interest rate charged by the credit card company
- **B.** requiring credit card companies to issue cards to qualified persons
- **C.** allowing the card holder to defer payment of the balance due on the card
- **D.** limiting the card holder's liability for unauthorized use

435. The Equal Credit Opportunity Act prohibits creditors from discriminating in consumer credit transactions on the basis of:

  I. marital status
  II. race and gender

- **A.** I only
- **B.** II only
- **C.** Both I and II
- **D.** Neither I nor II

436. Liquidation is a key element in which of the following bankruptcy cases?

  I. Chapter 7
  II. Chapter 11
  III. Chapter 13

- **A.** I only
- **B.** II and III only
- **C.** III only
- **D.** I, II, and III

437. Green owes unsecured debts of $310,000 to nine creditors. Green owes each creditor more than $20,000. Which of the following is a requirement for these creditors to file involuntary bankruptcy against Green?

  I. Three or more creditors must file the petition.
  II. Green must be insolvent.
  III. Creditors must prove that Green is not paying her bona fide debts as they become due.

- **A.** I and III only
- **B.** III only
- **C.** I, II, and III
- **D.** II and III only

438. A debtor who declares bankruptcy is still entitled to which of the following assets if they are to be received by the debtor within 180 days of filing for relief?

  I. Life insurance proceeds
  II. Alimony
  III. Inheritance

- **A.** I and II only
- **B.** II only
- **C.** I, II, and III
- **D.** Neither I, II, nor III

439. Which of the following transfers could be set aside by the bankruptcy trustee and made property of the debtor's bankruptcy estate for the purposes of paying creditors?

  I. Fraudulent conveyances
  II. Preferential transfers in the course of the debtor's business

- **A.** I only
- **B.** II only
- **C.** Both I and II
- **D.** Neither I nor II

440. Based on the reorganization provisions of Chapter 11 of the Federal Bankruptcy Code, which of the following statements is correct?

  I. A trustee always needs to be appointed.
  II. The commencement of a bankruptcy case may be voluntary or involuntary.

- **A.** I only
- **B.** II only
- **C.** Both I and II
- **D.** Neither I nor II

441. Based on the reorganization provisions of Chapter 11 of the Federal Bankruptcy Code, which of the following statements is correct?

  I. Creditors could force a debtor into bankruptcy under Chapter 11, even if the debtor's total assets were greater than total liabilities.
  II. A reorganization plan may be filed by creditors.

- **A.** I only
- **B.** II only
- **C.** Both I and II
- **D.** Neither I nor II

442. In a bankruptcy estate, which of the following creditors would be paid first?

   A. Alimony and child support owed for seven months

   B. Federal income taxes due no more than two years

   C. Employees of the debtor who have not been paid in two months

   D. Secured creditors who filed a financing statement on the debtor's inventory

443. Assuming a voluntary bankruptcy proceeding under the Federal Bankruptcy Code, which of the following claims incurred within 180 days prior to filing will be paid first?

   A. Employee vacation and sick pay

   B. Customer deposits

   C. Secured creditors who were paid the value of their security but remain unsatisfied with a balance owed them

   D. Unsecured federal taxes

444. Acts by a debtor could result in a bankruptcy court revoking the debtor's discharge. Which of the following acts will revoke the discharge?

   I. Failure to list one creditor

   II. Fraudulent conveyances

   A. I only

   B. II only

   C. Both I and II

   D. Neither I nor II

445. Which of the following events will follow the filing of a Chapter 7 involuntary petition?

   I. A stay against creditor collection proceedings goes into effect.

   II. A trustee is appointed.

   A. I only

   B. II only

   C. Both I and II

   D. Neither I nor II

446. Under the Federal Securities Act of 1933, which of the following relates to how the Securities and Exchange Commission (SEC) registration requirements affect an investor?

   I. The investor is NOT guaranteed by the SEC that the facts contained in the registration statement are accurate.

   II. The investor is provided with financial and nonfinancial information regarding the company seeking to raise capital.

   A. I only

   B. II only

   C. Both I and II

   D. Neither I nor II

447. If a Texas corporation were to issue securities for sale only to Texas residents, which of the following securities laws would the issuing corporation have to follow?

   I. Federal Securities Act of 1933

   II. State of Texas securities laws

   A. I only

   B. II only

   C. Both I and II

   D. Neither I nor II

448. Under the Federal Securities Act of 1933, which of the following is defined as a security and therefore would require registration with the SEC prior to issuance unless an exemption applies?

   I. Preferred stock

   II. Corporate bonds

   A. I only

   B. II only

   C. Both I and II

   D. Neither I nor II

449. Certain exemptions from registration are allowed under the Federal Securities Act of 1933. Which of the following securities are allowed such an exemption?

   I. Bonds issued by a not-for-profit charitable organization

   II. Debenture bonds issued by a publicly traded company

   A. I only

   B. II only

   C. Both I and II

   D. Neither I nor II

450. Cramer, Inc., intends to make a $775,000 common stock offering under Rule 504 of Regulation D of the Federal Securities Act of 1933. Cramer, Inc.:

A. may sell the stock to an unlimited number of investors

B. may not make the offering through a general advertising

C. must register the offering with the SEC

D. must provide all investors with a prospectus

451. In general, which of the following is part of Rule 505 of Regulation D of the 1933 act?

A. No more than 35 investors and no advertising are allowed.

B. No more than 35 accredited investors and advertising are allowed.

C. No more than 35 nonaccredited investors and no advertising are allowed.

D. The dollar limit is $1,000,000 and advertising is allowed.

452. Under Regulation D of the Securities Act of 1933, Rules 505 and 506 each require that:

A. the offering needs to be made without general advertising

B. the dollar limit is $5,000,000

C. immediate resale is unrestricted

D. there will be a maximum of 35 total investors

453. Under Regulation D of the 1933 act, what do Rules 504, 505, and 506 all have in common?

A. Must report each sale to the SEC within 15 days after each sale

B. Must report the first sale to the SEC within 15 days after the first sale

C. Must be totally sold out within 12 months

D. No advertising or immediate resale to the general public

454. By itself, which of the following factors requires a corporation to comply with the reporting requirements of the Securities Exchange Act of 1934?

A. 600 employees

B. Shares listed on a national securities exchange

C. Total assets of $2 million

D. 200 holders of equity securities

455. Which of the following events must be reported to the SEC under the reporting provisions of the Securities Exchange Act of 1934?

   I. Unusual events not in the ordinary course of business

   II. Unaudited quarterly earnings reports

   III. Proxy solicitations

A. I, II, and III

B. I and II only

C. I and III only

D. II and III only

456. The annual report Form 10-K must be filed by a large reporting company within 60 days after the end of the fourth quarter of the fiscal year according to which of the following rules issued by the SEC?

   I. Federal Securities Act of 1933

   II. Securities Exchange Act of 1934

A. I only

B. II only

C. Both I and II

D. Neither I nor II

457. Horizons, Inc., is a smaller reporting company under the Securities Exchange Act of 1934. The maximum number of days that Horizons, Inc., has to file its quarterly report Form 10-Q is:

A. 40

B. 45

C. 60

D. 90

458. A party making a tender offer to purchase at least what amount of the shares of a class of securities registered under the 1934 act must file a report with the SEC?

A. 2% of the shares

B. 5% of the shares

C. 10% of the shares

D. An amount considered material to the individual purchaser's net worth

459. Which of the following services would the Sarbanes-Oxley Act of 2002 permit a registered firm to perform for an audit client?

   I. Tax services

   II. Bookkeeping services

A. I only

B. II only

C. Both I and II

D. Neither I nor II

460. Two areas of the Sarbanes-Oxley Act of 2002 involve auditor *rotation* and auditor *retention*. Which of the following is correct?

    I. The lead or coordinating partner and the reviewing partner must be *rotated* off an audit engagement for a publicly traded company every three years.

    II. *Retention* of the auditing firm is the responsibility of the audit committee.

    III. *Retention* of the audit documentation must be for a period of at least seven years.

    A. I and II only
    B. II and III only
    C. I, II, and III
    D. II only

461. According to the Sarbanes-Oxley Act, in order to enhance independence, the audit firm cannot have employed the issuer's CEO or CFO for how long a period preceding the audit?

    A. Four years
    B. Three years
    C. Two years
    D. One year

462. Audit firms whose clients issue securities to the public must undergo routine periodic audits by the PCAOB based on how many audits of issuers they conduct annually. Which of the following is correct?

    A. A firm that audits mostly privately held entities and audits just a few issuers annually would be inspected by the PCAOB every six years.

    B. A firm that regularly audits no issuers would still be inspected by the PCAOB every seven years.

    C. A firm that audits more than 25 issuers annually but less than 100 issuers annually would be inspected by the PCAOB every two years.

    D. A firm that audits more than 100 issuers annually would be inspected by the PCAOB every year.

463. If a CPA is found to have breached a duty of professional care and competence by lacking reasonable care in the conduct of the engagement, which of the following will the CPA most likely be sued for?

    A. Gross negligence
    B. Ordinary negligence
    C. Constructive fraud
    D. Actual or common law fraud

464. Which is correct regarding accountants' liability under the federal securities laws?

    I. If a plaintiff is suing a CPA under the 1934 act, the plaintiff would have to prove that material misstatements were included in a filed document.

    II. If a plaintiff is suing a CPA under the 1934 act, the plaintiff would have to prove reliance on the financial statements.

    III. If a plaintiff is suing a CPA under the 1933 act, the plaintiff would have to prove reliance on the financial statements.

    A. I and II only
    B. II and III only
    C. I and III only
    D. I, II, and III

465. Which of the following statements is generally correct regarding the liability of a CPA who negligently gives an opinion on an audit of a client's financial statements?

    A. The CPA is liable only to the client.
    B. The CPA is liable only to those third parties who are in privity of contract with the CPA.
    C. The CPA is liable to anyone in a class of third parties whom the CPA knows will rely on the opinion.
    D. none of the above

466. Which of the following would support a finding of common law fraud (actual fraud) on the part of a CPA?

    I. Material misrepresentation of fact
    II. Intent to deceive
    III. Justifiable reliance and damages

    A. I, II, and III
    B. I and II only
    C. I and III only
    D. I only

467. Under common law, which of the following statements most accurately reflects the liability of a CPA who fraudulently gives an opinion on an audit of a client's financial statements?

A. The CPA probably is liable to the client even if the client was aware of the fraud and did not rely on the opinion.

B. The CPA probably is liable to any person who suffered a loss as a result of the fraud.

C. The CPA is liable only to known users of the financial statements.

D. The CPA is liable only to third parties in privity of contract with the CPA.

468. Which of the following would support a finding of constructive fraud on the part of a CPA?
I. CPA acting "recklessly"
II. Intent to deceive
III. Justifiable reliance and damages

A. I only

B. I and II only

C. I, II, and III

D. I and III only

CHAPTER 43

BUSINESS STRUCTURES AND OTHER REGULATORY AREAS

QUESTIONS 469–503

469. Under the Revised Model Business Corporation Act, which of the following statements regarding a corporation's bylaws is correct?

  I. A corporation's initial bylaws shall be adopted by either the incorporators or the board of directors.

  II. A corporation's bylaws are contained in the articles of incorporation.

  A. I only

  B. II only

  C. Both I and II

  D. Neither I nor II

470. Noll is a promoter of a corporation to be known as Rotondo Corp. On January 1, Year 5, Noll signed a nine-month contract with Clark, a CPA, which provided that Clark would perform certain accounting services for Rotondo Corp. Noll did not disclose to Clark that Rotondo Corp. had not been formed.

Prior to the incorporation of Rotondo Corp. on February 1, Year 5, Clark rendered accounting services pursuant to the contract. After rendering accounting services for an additional period of six months pursuant to the contract, Clark was discharged without cause by the board of directors of Rotondo. In the absence of any agreements to the contrary, who will be liable to Clark for breach of contract?

  A. Noll only

  B. Both Noll and Rotondo

  C. Rotondo only

  D. Neither Noll nor Rotondo

471. Under the Revised Model Business Corporation Act, corporate directors are authorized to rely on information provided by the:

  I. appropriate corporate officer

  II. independent auditor's report

  A. I only

  B. II only

  C. Both I and II

  D. Neither I nor II

472. Lucas owns 200 shares of Shea Corp. cumulative preferred stock. In the absence of any specific contrary provisions in Shea's articles of incorporation, which of the following statements is correct?

  A. If Shea declares a dividend on its common stock, Lucas will be entitled to participate with the common stock shareholders in any dividend distribution made after preferred dividends are paid.

  B. Lucas will be entitled to vote if dividend payments are in arrears.

  C. Lucas is entitled to convert the 200 shares of preferred stock to a like number of shares of common stock.

  D. If Shea declares a cash dividend on its preferred stock, Lucas becomes an unsecured creditor of Shea.

473. Eco Environmental Services, Inc., is a C corporation. Which of the following is a characteristic of a C corporation?

    A. Is the business structure of choice for most privately held businesses

    B. Is allowed to deduct dividends paid prior to paying taxes

    C. Is subject to double taxation on profits if dividends are paid

    D. Must have only one class of stock

474. In the absence of fraud, the corporate veil is most likely to be pierced and the shareholders held personally liable if:

    I. a partnership incorporates its business solely to limit the liability of its partners

    II. the shareholders have commingled their personal funds with those of the corporation

    A. I only

    B. II only

    C. Both I and II

    D. Neither I nor II

475. Which of the following is a corporate equity security?

    I. A callable bond

    II. A share of convertible preferred stock

    A. I only

    B. II only

    C. Both I and II

    D. Neither I nor II

476. For what purpose will a stockholder of a publicly held corporation be permitted to file a shareholder's derivative lawsuit in the name of the corporation?

    I. To compel payment of a properly declared dividend

    II. To recover damages from corporate management for an ultra vires management act

    A. I only

    B. II only

    C. Both I and II

    D. Neither I nor II

477. In a corporation, which of the following rights does a shareholder typically have?

    I. Right to vote on fundamental changes in corporate structure such as a merger

    II. Right to reasonable inspection of corporate records

    A. I only

    B. II only

    C. Both I and II

    D. Neither I nor II

478. Which of the following is correct regarding an agreement to form a general partnership?

    I. Must be filed with the state government

    II. Must be in writing

    III. may be oral, or implied by conduct

    A. I and II only

    B. I and III only

    C. II only

    D. III only

479. Under the Uniform Partnership Act, which of the following statements concerning the powers and duties of partners in a general partnership are correct?

    I. Each partner is an agent of every other partner and acts as both a principal and an agent in any business transaction within the scope of the partnership agreement.

    II. Each partner is subject to joint and several liability on partnership debts and contracts.

    A. I only

    B. II only

    C. Both I and II

    D. Neither I nor II

480. When a new partner is admitted to an existing partnership to replace an outgoing partner, the liability of the newly admitted partner for *existing partnership* debts is:

    A. normally limited to the amount of his or her capital contribution to the partnership

    B. normally unlimited, and the newly admitted partner's personal property may be seized to satisfy the existing debts

    C. joint and several, as well as personal

    D. limited to whatever liability the outgoing partner had

481. Which of the following actions of a partnership require unanimous consent of all partners?

    I. Submitting a claim to arbitration

    II. Admission of a new partner

    A. I only

    B. II only

    C. Both I and II

    D. Neither I nor II

482. A, B, C, and D are partners in the ABCD partnership. If Partner A retires from the partnership, then for Partner A to avoid liability for future debts of the partnership, actual notice needs to be given to existing creditors of Partner A's retirement and:

A. Partner A needs to give actual notice to existing partnership creditors or Partner A will remain liable for existing firm debts

B. constructive notice needs to be given to existing creditors for Partner A to avoid liability on existing firm debts

C. actual notice needs to be given to potential creditors for Partner A to avoid liability for future partnership debts

D. constructive notice needs to be given to potential creditors for Partner A to avoid liability on future partnership debts

483. In which of the following respects do general partnerships and limited liability partnerships (LLPs) differ?

   I. In the level of personal liability for torts that partners themselves commit

   II. In the level of liability for torts committed by other partners of the same firm

A. I only

B. II only

C. Both I and II

D. Neither I nor II

484. A key advantage of the limited liability company (LLC) is that:

   I. the entity is treated as a partnership for liability purposes

   II. the liability of members is limited to the amount of their investments

A. I only

B. II only

C. Both I and II

D. Neither I nor II

485. Harry, Ben, and Chico want to form a new business and be taxed as a partnership, yet have the same liability protection as shareholders in a corporation. If they carry on as co-owners of a business for profit but never file an LLP application or articles of incorporation with their state government:

   I. they will be double taxed on all profits

   II. they will have unlimited personal liability for business debts

A. I only

B. II only

C. Both I and II

D. Neither I nor II

486. Which of the following characteristics apply to an LLP?

   I. Profits and losses flow through to partners.

   II. Partners may agree to have the entity managed by one or more of the partners.

   III. A partner may be another entity.

A. I, II, and III

B. I and III only

C. I and II only

D. I only

487. Which of the following types of businesses may generally be formed without filing an organizational document with a state agency?

   I. Proprietorship

   II. General partnership

   III. Limited liability partnership (LLP)

   IV. Limited liability company (LLC)

A. I and II only

B. I, II, and III

C. I only

D. I, II, and IV

488. Which of the following tax returns are due within three and a half months of the end of the business year?

   I. Trusts

   II. Individual tax returns

   III. Partnership tax returns

A. I, II, and III

B. II and III only

C. I and III only

D. I and II only

489. Larry, an employee of Hanson Manufacturing, Inc., was injured in the course of employment while operating a forklift manufactured and sold to Hanson by Suzy Wong, Inc. Under the state's mandatory workers' compensation statute, Larry will be successful in obtaining:

   I. workers' compensation even if Larry was negligent

   II. legal action against Hanson, Inc.

   III. legal action against Suzy Wong, Inc.

A. I and III

B. I, II, and III

C. II and III

D. I and II

490. Which of the following gets deducted from an employee's salary?

   I. Federal unemployment tax

   II. Social security tax

   III. Workers' compensation insurance

A. I and III only

B. I and II only

C. I, II, and III

D. II only

491. Based on the Americans with Disabilities Act of 1990, which of the following is correct?

   I. The act does NOT require companies to set up a specified plan to hire people with disabilities.

   II. The act requires companies to make reasonable accommodations for disabled persons unless this results in undue hardship.

A. I only

B. II only

C. Both I and II

D. Neither I nor II

492. Which of the following agencies is likely to enforce the law against an act of sexual discrimination in the workplace?

A. Occupational Safety and Health Administration (OSHA)

B. Federal Trade Commission (FTC)

C. Internal Revenue Service (IRS)

D. Equal Employment Opportunity Commission (EEOC)

493. According to the Employee Retirement Income Security Act (ERISA), which of the following agencies is empowered to regulate pension plans?

   I. Internal Revenue Service (IRS)

   II. US Department of Labor

A. I only

B. II only

C. Both I and II

D. Neither I nor II

494. According to the Bank Secrecy Act, financial institutions must file a currency transaction report (CTR) for each transaction in excess of:

A. $2,500

B. $5,000

C. $7,500

D. $10,000

495. According to the Sherman Antitrust Act, which of the following would be considered evidence of a monopoly?

   I. A firm's ability to control prices

   II. A firm's ability to exclude competition

   III. A firm's market share of above 70%

A. I, II, and III

B. I and III only

C. I and II only

D. II and III only

496. Surett wrote a personal finance autobiography called *Million Dollars Later*. He wishes to copyright the book and protect his rights. Which of the following is correct?

   I. A copyright would protect Surett's rights for Surett's natural life plus 70 years.

   II. The Fair Use Doctrine would allow for certain classroom uses of the book for educational purposes without Surett's permission.

A. I only

B. II only

C. Both I and II

D. Neither I nor II

497. Which of the following are rights included with the owner of a copyright?

   I. Fair use

   II. License the copyright to others

A. I only

B. II only

C. Both I and II

D. Neither I nor II

498. The length of the creator's life is NOT a factor in determining the years of protection for a:
  I. copyright
  II. patent

  A. I only
  B. II only
  C. Both I and II
  D. Neither I nor II

499. Which of the following are attributes that must be shown in order to obtain a patent for an invention?
  I. The invention is novel and useful.
  II. The invention is NOT obvious to others who work in the field.
  III. The invention is in a tangible medium of expression.

  A. I, II, and III
  B. I and II only
  C. I and III only
  D. II and III only

500. The Bank Secrecy Act requires:
  I. the filing of a currency transaction report for any deposit, withdrawal, or exchange of currency of $5,000 or more
  II. a report to be filed within 30 days of a currency transaction in excess of $10,000

  A. I only
  B. II only
  C. Both I and II
  D. Neither I nor II

Bonus Questions

501. In connection with the Orderly Liquidation Authority established under Title II of the Dodd-Frank Act, which of the following is correct before the FDIC can liquidate a banking institution?
  I. The banking institution must have more than $50 billion in assets.
  II. The banking institution must have paid into the Orderly Liquidation Fund for at least two years.

  A. I only
  B. II only
  C. Both I and II
  D. Neither I nor II

502. Nonqualified stock options are granted to employees on February 3, Year 1. Ordinary income is paid by the employees based on the options having a readily ascertainable value. Which of the following is correct?
  I. If the options are exercised, the holding period for the shares begins with the date the options are granted.
  II. If the options expire without being exercised, the employees have a capital loss based on the ordinary income already recognized.

  A. I only
  B. II only
  C. Both I and II
  D. Neither I nor II

503. Assessment of the $100 preparer penalty for failure to employ due diligence in connection with the earned income credit applies to:
  I. determining the client's eligibility for the earned income credit
  II. determining the amount of the client's earned income credit

  A. I only
  B. II only
  C. Both I and II
  D. Neither I nor II

Chapter 39: Taxation of Individuals

1. **A.** Filing status is determined on the last day of the year, not by a majority of days in the year. Although Theresa and John were both single for nearly the entire year, the only day that counts for filing status is the last day of the year.

2. **D.** Usually, filing status is determined on the last day of the year, but in the case of death, filing status is determined on the date of death. For this reason, in the year a spouse dies (Year 1), the surviving spouse is permitted to file a joint return. In Years 2 and 3 following the spouse's death, the surviving spouse could qualify to file as a qualifying widower (or widow) and would therefore be able to use the same tax rates as those applied to a joint return. In this question, Gil Gallon had a qualifying child and could therefore file as a qualifying widower in Year 2 (and Year 3 as well, but the question only asked about Year 2). If the question had asked about Year 4, the answer would have been head of household because the qualifying widower (widow) filing status is available only for the two immediate years following a spouse's death, and Gil Gallon has met the requirements for head of household status.

3. **B.** Normally, filing status is determined on the last day of the year, but in the case of death, filing status is determined at the date of death. Accordingly, in the year a spouse dies (Year 1), the surviving spouse is permitted to file a joint return. In Years 2 and 3 following the spouse's death, the surviving spouse could qualify to file as a qualifying widower (widow) and would therefore be able to use the same tax rates as those applied to a joint return. This status, however, is available only for the two years immediately following a spouse's death. Afterward, the surviving spouse would either file as head of household (if meeting the requirements for head of household filing status) or single. Since the question asks about Year 4, Bonnie would file as head of household as she otherwise meets the head of household requirements (i.e., she has a dependent child for whom she provides full support).

4. **C.** Kathleen, as an abandoned spouse providing sole support for her four dependent children, would be permitted to file under the head of household filing status, provided that she were truly abandoned for the last six months (or more) of Year 8.

5. **A.** I is correct. For a qualifying child, the support test has been modified to show that as long as the child does *not* support himself over 50%, the parent presumably does even though the income is over the exemption amount. II is wrong. For a relative other than a qualifying child, taxpayers must demonstrate that they furnish more than 50% of a potential dependent's support.

6. **C.** Ben and Freeda furnished more than 50% of Harold's support, and since he is under the age of 24 and is a full-time student, they can claim him even though his income was more than the exemption amount ($4,000 for 2015). Ben and Freeda can also claim Susan, who is blind, is mostly deaf, and has no income, and for whom they provide full support. However, Susan's disabilities do not qualify the taxpayers for any additional exemption. If on the CPA examination, however, the *taxpayer* himself is blind (i.e., Ben, Freeda), a higher *standard deduction* is available. But nothing additional is available for having a blind *dependent*. Thus Ben and Freeda would claim four exemptions on their tax return: one for Ben, one for Freeda, one for Harold, and one for Susan.

7. **D.** The tax laws provide a few tax benefits for the elderly. One of those is an increased standard deduction. If Walter does not itemize his deductions, he will take the standard deduction, which will be at an increased level because of his age.

8. **C.** While interest income on obligations of a state or a possession of the United States (i.e., Puerto Rico, Guam, or Virgin Islands bonds or obligations) are tax-exempt, most other interest income is taxable. Thus the interest on both the federal and state income tax returns would be taxable, as well as the interest on US Treasury (federal government) obligations. Consequently, a total of $1,900 would be reported as taxable income on Erin and Mars's joint income tax return.

9. **B.** The general rule is that most interest income is taxable with the exception of interest income on obligations of a state (i.e., municipal bonds) or a possession of the United States (i.e., Puerto Rico, Guam, or the Virgin Islands). Accordingly, from the items listed, only the municipal bond interest of $1,600 is tax free. The interest income received on the federal income tax refund, personal injury award, and US savings bonds would all be taxable.

Griffin would therefore report $2,000 as interest income on his current year tax return.

10. **D.** I is wrong. Accumulated interest on Series EE US savings bonds may be exempt from tax but *only if* certain conditions are met: (1) the bonds have been issued to the taxpayer after December 31, 1989, (2) the bonds must be purchased by the taxpayer or taxpayer's spouse and kept in the taxpayer's name (i.e., the taxpayer must be the sole owner of the bonds or joint owner with his or her spouse), (3) the taxpayer (owner) must be 24 years or older before the bond's issue date (i.e., the taxpayer or owner must be 24 years old when purchasing the bonds), and (4) redemption proceeds from the bonds must be used to pay for higher education costs (usually college costs) for the taxpayer, taxpayer's spouse, or taxpayer's dependents. II is wrong. Redemption proceeds from the bonds must be used to pay for higher education costs (usually college costs) for the taxpayer, taxpayer's spouse, or taxpayer's dependents. If proceeds are used for any other purpose, like home improvement, the interest would be taxable.

11. **A.** Accumulated interest on Series EE US savings bonds may be exempt from tax but *only if* certain conditions are met: (1) the bonds have been issued to the taxpayer after December 31, 1989, (2) the bonds must be purchased by the taxpayer or taxpayer's spouse and kept in the taxpayer's name (i.e., the taxpayer must be the sole owner of the bonds or joint owner with his or her spouse), (3) the taxpayer (owner) must be 24 years or older before the bond's issue date (i.e., the taxpayer or owner must be 24 years old when purchasing the bonds), and (4) redemption proceeds from the bonds must be used to pay for higher education costs (usually college costs) for the taxpayer, taxpayer's spouse, or taxpayer's dependents.

12. **A.** Most dividends are taxable. Sometimes the taxpayer reinvests the monies earned from the dividend receipt into additional shares. This in and of itself does not make the dividend tax exempt. Reinvested dividends are treated as if the cash received was used to immediately purchase new shares. If, however, an examination question stated that the dividend was paid in shares of the corporation's stock with no opportunity for the taxpayer to receive cash, then the dividend would be tax free. Dividends received on unmatured life insurance policies are generally tax exempt (provided those dividends do not exceed cumulative premiums paid). Dividends received on foreign corporations are taxable.

13. **A.** Stock dividends issued on common stock are normally not taxable. Instead, the cost of the original shares must be spread over all shares owned (old and new) because that is the taxpayer's actual total cost. Tatum's original basis per share was $50 and is now:

$$\frac{\$50,000^*}{1,050 \text{ shares}^{**}} = \$47.62$$

Any gain or loss on the stock will be included on Tatum's tax return when the stock is eventually sold. Further, since there was no opportunity to receive cash, none of the stock dividend is taxable.

14. **D.** Although interest income is taxed at ordinary income tax rates, and dividends (depending on how they are classified) may or may not be taxed at ordinary income tax rates, both interest and dividend income are reported on Schedule B. Schedule D is used to report capital gains and losses, and Schedule E is used to report supplemental income and loss (i.e., passive income and loss) such as rental real estate income or loss, income or loss derived from investments in partnerships or S corporations, and income or loss from estates and trusts.

15. **A.** The question asked for the amount of net passive income or loss in Year 2. There were only two passive activities, a passive gain of $1,000 and a passive loss of $5,000. All passive activity gains and losses are netted to arrive at a single number. The two passive activities for Stegman net out to a $4,000 passive loss. Had the question then asked how much passive loss is deductible in the current year against nonpassive income, all $4,000 passive loss would be carried forward. A passive loss cannot be deducted in the current year against nonpassive income unless the passive loss is from a rental real estate activity. The deductibility of any potential rental real estate loss is further subject to an adjusted gross income threshold and active participation in the rental real estate activity. The salary of $50,000 earned from Stegman's employer does not qualify as a passive activity and therefore would not result in any passive gain or loss. The interest income of $100 is considered portfolio income, not passive income. Be careful on the CPA exam not to net passive and portfolio activities. If the question asks for passive income or loss, leave the portfolio income aside.

---

*1,000 original shares × $50 per share

**1,000 original shares + additional 50 shares issued in connection with the stock dividend (i.e., 1,000 shares × 5%)

16. **A.** Income or loss derived from a rental real estate activity is deemed passive income or loss. Passive losses up to $25,000 can be deducted against ordinary income if the taxpayer actively participates in the passive activity *and* does not have an AGI that exceeds $150,000 for the tax year. Because Adrian's AGI exceeded the $150,000 threshold, no deduction for the rental loss can be taken in Year 6. However, the entire $29,000 can be carried over to her Year 7 next tax year and beyond (indefinitely) until fully utilized. If Adrian's AGI had been $150,000 or less, she would have been able to deduct $25,000 of the loss and the remaining $4,000 would be carried over to her Year 7 tax return and beyond (indefinitely) until fully utilized.

17. **C.** Income or loss derived from a rental real estate activity is deemed passive income or loss. Passive losses up to $25,000 can be deducted against ordinary income if the taxpayer actively participates in the passive activity *and* does not have an AGI that exceeds $150,000 for the tax year. In this case, since Cindy's Year 9 AGI is less than $150,000, and the $30,000 loss she incurred was derived from a passive activity in which she actively participated, she can deduct $25,000 of that loss against her ordinary income of $75,000 in Year 9 and the remaining $5,000 can be carried over to her Year 10 tax year and beyond (indefinitely) until fully utilized.

18. **B.** All passive activity gains and losses are netted to arrive at a single number. If this net number is a gain, it is taxable; if it is a loss, that loss cannot be deducted unless it is from a rental real estate activity. Losses from such activities (up to $25,000) can be deducted against ordinary income if the taxpayer actively participates in the passive activity and does not have AGI that exceeds $150,000 for the tax year. In this case, Shan had two sources of passive income and loss: the S corporation investment and the rental real estate activity. Regardless of whether or not Shan had actively participated in the S corporate or rental real estate activity, he would net the income and loss from these activities, leaving him with a $20,000 net loss. Because Shan's AGI exceeded the $150,000 threshold, Shan would *not* be able to deduct the remaining $20,000 against his ordinary income in Year 10 and would have to carry over this amount to Year 11 and beyond (indefinitely) until the $20,000 loss was fully utilized. Thus Shan is able to deduct only $15,000 of the $35,000 loss against the $15,000 of passive income he earned from the

S corporation investment. If Shan's AGI had been less than $150,000, Shan would have been able to deduct the entire remaining $20,000 loss against his ordinary income in Year 10, as this net loss was derived from a rental real estate activity.

19. **B.** The answer is $4,200. The question expects you to be somewhat familiar with rental activities reported on Form 1040 Schedule E. Only the portion of expenses that applies to the tenant can be deducted on Schedule E. Skorecki can deduct on Schedule E half the mortgage interest, $1,500; half the real estate taxes, $2,500; and half the depreciation, $1,000. The rental apartment repairs, $800, can be 100% deducted because it was the tenant's apartment that was repaired. Skorecki did not perform repairs on the other apartment where he lives. Note: the other half of the real estate taxes and mortgage interest can be deducted on Schedule A if Skorecki itemizes.

Rent income	$10,000
Deductions:	
Mortgage interest	$1,500
Real estate taxes	$2,500
Depreciation	$1,000
Painting of rental	$800
	↓
Total deductions	$5,800
Net rental income	$4,200

20. **C.** Rudnick's passive loss for Year 6 amounts to $2,500, or 5% of the partnership's operating loss. The $20,000 of interest earned on the US Treasury obligations is considered portfolio or investment income and does not qualify as passive income, so while Rudnick's share of this portfolio income is $1,000 (or 5% of $20,000), it would not be netted against Rudnick's passive loss of $2,500. Note: the passive loss of $2,500 would *not* be tax deductible, unless there was another source of passive income to offset it.

21. **C.** All income items presented in this question comprise Benson's AGI. The passive loss can be netted against, and up to, the amount of any passive income. The only passive income included in her reported income items is the $7,000 of rental income. Thus the $9,000 passive loss from partnership B can be offset against this income, with a remaining $2,000 loss that cannot be offset or deducted in Year 7 (as it was derived from an equipment rental business, and

not a rental real estate activity) and must be carried over to Year 8 and beyond (indefinitely) until fully utilized. Accordingly, Benson's AGI consists of:

$70,000	ordinary income from partnership A
+ $7,000	rental income
− $7,000	passive loss from partnership B (with $2,000 remaining loss carried over to Year 8)
+ 4,000	interest and dividends
$74,000	

22. **D.** All $17,000 of the building rental loss is deductible by Shapiro in Year 9. That loss (a passive loss) is first offset against any passive income and gains. There is one passive gain presented in this question (i.e., the net gain from partnership B, a gain from a bike rental business without active participation). That passive gain amounted to $9,000, and therefore, $9,000 of the building rental loss (passive loss) is first used to offset against the $9,000 passive gain from bike rentals. The $8,000 passive loss remaining can be offset against Shapiro's ordinary income since the passive loss relates to a rental real estate activity and Shapiro's AGI (as can be derived from the data presented) is less than $150,000. Net passive losses are generally not deductible and are carried over indefinitely (until utilized), unless they are associated with a rental real estate activity and the taxpayer materially participates in the activity and his or her AGI does not exceed $150,000 for the tax year.

Passive loss from rental real estate	$17,000
Passive income	9,000
Passive loss from rental real estate in excess of passive income	8,000

The excess passive rental loss of $8,000 is deductible against ordinary income from the pinball arcade since AGI is under $150,000 and the passive loss is from real estate rental. Therefore, the total passive loss deduction for Shapiro in Year 9 is $17,000.

23. **D.** Unemployment compensation is taxable as are cash dividends on stocks, cash prizes awarded in a contest (unless the winner or recipient doesn't accept the check and has it sent directly to a charitable organization), and interest income on tax refunds. A college loan must be repaid and therefore would not be taxable. Neither a state scholarship awarded for tuition nor cash support received from parents is taxable. Therefore, his AGI for Year 9 amounts to $1,810 computed as follows:

$500	cash dividends on stocks
+ $300	cash prize awarded in contest
+ $1,000	unemployment compensation
+ $10	interest income on tax refund
= $1,810	AGI

24. **C.** The general rule for prizes is that prizes are taxable, except when the winner, recipient, or taxpayer doesn't accept the check but has it sent directly to a charity. If the taxpayer accepts the check and later donates it to a charity, the prize is taxable as other income on Form 1040. The taxpayer can then deduct the charitable contribution as an itemized deduction on Form 1040 Schedule A. The only way to avoid paying tax on the prize is to never take possession of the check.

25. **D.** If an employer offers life insurance as part of a qualified plan, the premium paid (by the employer) on the first $50,000 of coverage is not included in the employee's gross income. That amount is viewed as a nontaxable fringe benefit. However, the employer must include (in the employee's taxable wages) the amount of premium paid for any life insurance coverage in excess of $50,000.

26. **C.** If an employer offers life insurance (to its employees) as part of a qualified plan (i.e., group-term life insurance), the premium paid (by the employer) in excess of $50,000 of coverage, for an employee, is a taxable fringe benefit that must be included in the employee's taxable income. In this question, Cobbs is covered by a $90,000 policy, and therefore, the premium paid on the excess $40,000 of coverage ($90,000 − $50,000) would be taxable and computed as follows:

$$\frac{\$40,000 \text{ excess}}{\$1,000} = 40 \times \$8 = \$320$$

Although the $320 is taxable, it is not subject to social security tax.

27. **B.** Even for an accrual basis taxpayer, all cash received is taxable when received. In this example, the only exception would be for the security deposits, since they are placed into a segregated account and will eventually be returned to the tenant. Thus these amounts do not represent income to Olney. Olney will, therefore, include $55,000 in his current gross income computed as follows:

$30,000	current rents
+ $10,000	rents for next year—i.e., advance rents, which are taxable when received
+ $15,000	lease cancellation payments, which represent an additional source of rental income from the tenant
$55,000	total to be included in Olney's current gross income

28. **C.** In performing a service, if a taxpayer receives an asset other than cash, the FMV of the asset received is taxable as ordinary income. In this case, Jay received $200 cash plus a catered party that had an FMV of $350; thus Jay would report $550 as taxable income from this transaction. Note that the $250 that Lou earns as profit on these types of parties does not impact the taxable income attributable to Jay.

$200	cash
$350	fair value of the party
$550	total income

29. **B.** I is wrong. Alimony must be paid in cash (it cannot be paid in property or any other form for that matter). II is correct. Alimony can be paid directly to a spouse or a third party on behalf of the spouse.

30. **B.** Alimony can be paid directly to one's spouse or to a third party on behalf of one's spouse. Accordingly, the $6,000 cash paid directly to Karen, the $9,000 paid to her landlord, and the $5,000 paid to Wildwood College on behalf of Karen would all qualify as alimony. Payments that are deemed to be alimony are deductible by the paying party and taxable to the recipient. However, in this example, since the total $20,000 payment will be reduced by 30% (or $6,000) when Karen and Terry's child reaches 18 years of age, the $6,000 piece of the total $20,000 payment implicitly represents child support (since the required payment of child support ceases when a child reaches 18 years of age). Child support is not deductible to the paying party (i.e., Terry) and consequently, not taxable to the recipient (i.e., Karen). Thus the amount of payments that Karen should include in her Year 4 income includes:

$6,000	cash paid to spouse
$14,000	payments on behalf of spouse
($6,000)	30% of the total payment that represents child support
$14,000	taxable as alimony

31. **A.** The plumbing supplies, web hosting, depreciation, and advertising ($4,900 total) are all expenses incurred that pertain to Buddy's business. Thus these expenses are deductible on Buddy's Schedule C. Buddy's salary of $5,200 is not deductible. The owner's salary is not a tax deduction for a sole proprietorship. Thus the $5,200 taken by Buddy is treated as drawings, not a deductible expense. The estimated federal tax of $4,000 is given the status of a tax credit on Buddy's return (tax credits are not included in Schedule C business deductions), and the charitable contribution to the Red Cross of $500 is an itemized deduction that gets reported on Schedule A.

Plumbing supplies	$2,500
Web page hosting	$300
Depreciation	$400
Advertising	$1,700
Total deductions	$4,900

32. **D.** All cash is taxable when received. Thus the cash received from patients in Year 4 would be part of taxable net income for Year 4, as would the cash received from insurance companies for services provided in Year 3. Deductions in Year 4 would include salaries paid in Year 4 and other expenses paid in Year 4. The Year 4 bonuses of $4,000 that were paid to employees in Year 5 would be deductible in Year 5. Accordingly, Dr. Bernstein would report a taxable net income of $225,000 ($270,000 + $30,000 − $50,000 − $25,000).

33. **A.** Alimony and interest are not subject to self-employment tax, as they are not derived from self-employment and providing consultative services. Thus only the consulting fees, the directors' fees, and the net profit Anita reported on her Form 1040 Schedule C would be subject to self-employment tax: $8,000 + $1,800 + $1,000 = $10,800.

34. **C.** While all of the amounts Anita received in this question would be subject to federal income tax, only the consulting fees, directors' fees, and the net profit she reported on her Form 1040 Schedule C (collectively, her self-employment income) would be subject to self-employment tax. Thus Anita would pay both federal income tax and self-employment tax on her self-employment income.

35. **A.** A portion of the self-employment tax Freedson must pay on her self-employment income is deductible from gross income in arriving at AGI. One-half of the self-employment tax is deductible to arrive at AGI. B is not correct, because a portion of the self-employment tax is deductible. Both C and D are not correct, because only a portion of the self-employment tax is deductible and it is

deductible for AGI, not as an itemized deduction or in determining net income from self-employment.

36. **A.** Income from net rental activities is subject to regular income tax but not self-employment tax. Rental income is passive, not active; consequently, it is not subject to self-employment tax.

37. **D.** I is wrong. The land is being used as an outdoor marketplace; therefore, the land would be considered a Section 1231 asset, not a capital asset. Section 1231 assets include those assets held for more than one year and *used in the business* to generate revenue. Capital assets, on the other hand, are assets used for personal enjoyment or held for investment. The land cited in this question, for instance, could be classified as a capital asset if it was *not* being used in business and was instead being held for long-term appreciation (investment). It is the manner in which the asset is being used that determines its classification as a capital asset or a Section 1231 asset—not the asset itself.

   II is wrong. The large shed used for table storage is also being used in the business; therefore, the shed would be considered a Section 1231 asset.

38. **D.** Section 1231 assets include "business assets," or *assets used in the business* to generate revenue, which are held for more than one year. Capital assets are those assets held for investment or used for personal enjoyment. In this question, neither the land nor the building is being used in the business, so both would be classified as capital assets. It is not the asset itself that determines its classification as a capital asset or Section 1231 asset; rather, it is the manner in which the asset is being used that determines its classification.

39. **A.** Capital assets are assets used for personal enjoyment or held for investment. Section 1231 assets, on the other hand, include "business assets" used in the business to generate revenue, which are held for more than one year. In the question, the limousine is being used in the limousine service business to transport passengers to and from airports (i.e., it is being used in the business to generate revenues) and therefore would be classified as a Section 1231 asset, not a capital asset. The recreational skis are assets Rocky is using for personal enjoyment and consequently would be classified as a capital asset.

40. **B.** The painting is considered a capital asset to Angie. Capital assets include investment property and property held for personal use. The question herein explicitly states that Angie had bought the painting for personal use. The gain from the sale should therefore be classified as a capital gain, which must be further classified as either long-term or short-term based on the asset's holding period. Long-term classification is required for assets held in excess of one year, while short-term classification is appropriate for holding periods of one year or less. Since Angie bought the painting in Year 1 and sold it in Year 6, the gain she experienced on the sale would be classified as a long-term capital gain.

41. **D.** A married couple filing jointly, as well as an individual filing as single or head of household, can deduct capital losses to the extent of capital gains. Any excess capital loss deductions are limited to $3,000 of ordinary income, with any remainder carried forward to future periods indefinitely. For married couples filing separately, excess capital loss deductions are limited to $1,500 of ordinary income (for each taxpayer), with any remainder carried forward to future periods indefinitely.

42. **B.** Individual taxpayers must report gains and losses on investment property (i.e., individual stock and bond investments), but only gains should be reported on personal property transactions. For example, if a taxpayer sells personal furniture at a gain, that gain must be reported (and would be reported as a capital gain). However, if the same personal property is sold at a loss, no deduction is allowed.

43. **C.** *Accounting gain*, *economic gain*, or *realized gain* is synonymous terminology in the context of exchanges of like-kind property. Essentially a realized gain means the taxpayer has transacted (i.e., sold or exchanged) an asset (property) for a profit. Use of these terms does not necessarily mean that the gain is recognized for tax purposes.

44. **B.** The general rule in a like-kind exchange is that no gain is recognized. However, when a taxpayer receives "boot" (cash or unlike property) in connection with a like-kind exchange, the boot results in a recognized gain to the extent of the lesser of the realized gain or the boot received. In this question, the realized gain is computed as follows:

FMV of new property	$450,000
Boot received	+ $50,000
Total amount realized	$500,000
Cost basis of property given up	− $300,000
Realized gain	$200,000

The gain recognized is limited to the lesser of the realized gain ($200,000) or the boot received ($50,000). The boot is the lesser amount, and therefore Saralee would recognize a $50,000 gain.

45. D. Pollack would realize a gain in the amount of $175,000 computed as follows:

FMV of building received	$550,000
Mortgage on the apartment building given up	+ $100,000*
Cash/"boot" received	+ $25,000
Total amount realized	$675,000

From this amount subtract total cost basis:

Basis of old apartment building	$375,000
Mortgage on new apartment building assumed by Pollack	+ $125,000
Total basis	$500,000

Total amount realized: $675,000. Total basis $500,000 = $175,000 (realized gain).

46. A. Pollack would recognize a gain on this exchange in the amount of $25,000. The general rule in a like-kind exchange is that no gain is recognized. However, when a taxpayer receives "boot" (cash or unlike property) in connection with a like-kind exchange, the boot results in a recognized gain to the extent of the lesser of the realized gain or the boot received. The realized gain on this transaction is $175,000 computed as follows:

FMV of building received	$550,000
Mortgage on the apartment building given up	+ $100,000
Cash received	+ $25,000
Basis of old apartment building	– $375,000
Mortgage on new apartment building assumed by Pollack	– $125,000

Since Pollack assumed a mortgage ($125,000), which is greater than that of which he was relieved ($100,000), the release of the mortgage is not considered boot. Thus the gain recognized in this transaction would be limited to the amount of cash boot received (i.e., $25,000), as that was less than the realized gain of $175,000.

47. A. The general rule in a like-kind exchange is that no gain is recognized. However, when a taxpayer receives "boot" (cash or unlike property) in connection with a like-kind exchange, the boot results in a recognized gain to the extent of the lesser of the realized gain or the boot received. In this question, the total boot received is equal to the $30,000 cash received + the $70,000 of debt that Hymanson was relieved of, or $100,000. Hymanson's realized gain, on the other hand, is equal to $190,000:

FMV of real property received	$250,000
Cash received	+ $30,000
Debt relief	+ $70,000
Adjusted cost basis of investment real property given up	– $160,000

Since the total boot received is less than the realized gain, Hymanson will recognize a $100,000 gain on the exchange transaction.

48. C. I is correct. Losses are disallowed on the sale or exchange of property to a related-party taxpayer. Examples of related-party taxpayers include, but are not limited to, members of the family (i.e., spouse, brothers, sisters, ancestors, and lineal descendants), a corporation and a more than 50% shareholder, two corporations that are members of the same controlled group, and so on. In this question, Evan is Jerry's son (a related-party taxpayer or transferee); thus Jerry is not permitted to deduct the $4,000 loss he incurs on the sale of ABC stock shares to Evan. II is correct. If the stock is later sold by the related-party taxpayer (i.e., the transferee), any gain that may be recognized is reduced by the previously disallowed loss. However, when Evan resells the stock (and provided he does so at a gain), Evan can reduce his gain by Jerry's previously disallowed loss. Therefore, both statements presented in this question are correct statements.

49. B. Losses are disallowed on the sale or exchange of property to a related-party taxpayer. However, when the property is later sold by the related-party taxpayer (i.e., the transferee), any gain that may be recognized is reduced by the previously disallowed loss. In this question, when Jerry initially sold the shares of ABC company stock to Evan, he experienced a loss of $4,000 (i.e., sell price: $11,000 – cost/basis: $15,000). Because Evan was his son (and therefore considered a related-party taxpayer), Jerry was disallowed a deduction for the $4,000. However, because Evan resold the shares to an unrelated party at a $5,000 gain (sell price: $16,000 – cost/basis: $11,000), he is permitted to use the previously disallowed loss of $4,000 to reduce his gain. Evan would therefore report a $1,000 gain on his Year 9 income tax return ($5,000 gain – previous $4,000 disallowed loss).

---

*This is considered a form of boot received since Pollack is being relieved of this mortgage.

50. **A.** Losses are disallowed on the sale or exchange of property to a related-party taxpayer. However, when the property is later sold by the related-party taxpayer (i.e., the transferee) *any gain that may be recognized* is reduced by the previously disallowed loss. In this question, although Mitch and Glen are related parties, Glen is unable to use the $3,000 disallowed loss experienced by Mitch; therefore, Glen would report a short-term capital loss of $1,000. Note that the classification of the loss is short-term since Glen bought the stock from Mitch on July 1, Year 4, and resold it on November 1, Year 4. The two sales are illustrated as follows:

    Related-party sale from Mitch to Glen

Selling price	$7,000
Cost basis	– $10,000
Related-party loss disallowed	– $3,000

    Sale from Glen to unrelated party

Selling price	$6,000
Cost basis	– $7,000
Loss from sale to unrelated party	– $1,000

51. **B.** The general rule for valuation of assets received through an inheritance is that those assets are valued at their FMV on the date of death. An exception to this general rule occurs when the executor of the estate chooses to value all assets on the alternative valuation date (AVD), which is six months after the date of death or the date of conveyance of the estate assets, whichever comes first. In this case, because Jeff was distributed the stock prior to the AVD, the stock would be valued on the date of conveyance (i.e., March 31, Year 3); hence, Jeff's basis for the stock would be $240,000, the stock's value on March 31, Year 3.

52. **B.** Normally, estate assets are valued as of the date of death. However, the executor does have the right to elect to value the assets at an alternative date. The AVD is six months after the date of death or the date of conveyance of the estate assets, whichever comes first. Since no estate assets or property were conveyed until July 1, Year 2 (which was over a year from the date of Fanny's death), the assets should be valued at the AVD, or October 1, Year 1, six months after the date of Fanny's death.

53. **A.** When assets are inherited, the beneficiary automatically inherits the assets under a long-term holding period. Even assets, which may only be held for a short-term period after the inheritance, can still qualify for long-term capital gain or loss treatment when sold.

54. **A.** Denise must recognize a $10,000 gain on the sale of her personal residence in Year 15 computed as follows:

Proceeds from sale	$390,000
Cost basis of residence	– $105,000 (purchase price)
Patio addition	– $25,000
Realized gain	$260,000

    Out of the $260,000 realized gain, the first $250,000 of gain from the sale of a primary residence is exempt from tax for a taxpayer filing as a single filer; $500,000 is exempt from tax for taxpayers filing as married filing jointly. Since Denise is single and would therefore be filing as such, she would be able to exclude $250,000 of the gain on her Year 15 tax return. Consequently, Denise would report a recognized gain of $10,000:

Realized gain	$260,000
Less gain exclusion	– $250,000
Taxable gain	$10,000

    Note that a taxpayer can take advantage of this exclusion every two years. Several years had passed since Denise sold her last personal residence in Year 8.

55. **D.** I is wrong. In order for a single taxpayer to exclude (from income) up to $250,000 of gain realized on the sale or exchange of a home or residence, the taxpayer must have owned and occupied the residence as a principal residence for an aggregate of at least two of the five years preceding the sale or exchange. A $500,000 exclusion is afforded married couples filing jointly provided they meet the same requirements. The home cannot be a vacation home; it must be a principal residence and used as such. II is wrong. There is no requirement that the taxpayer buy another residence in order to qualify for this gain exclusion.

56. **A.** For married couples filing jointly, a gain realized on the sale of a personal (primary or principal) residence of up to $500,000 is excludable from income if the taxpayers jointly owned and used the property as a principal residence for an aggregate of at least two of the five years preceding the sale or exchange of the property. Taxpayers filing single may exclude up to $250,000 of realized gain provided they meet these same requirements. In this question, Barry and Saralee may exclude all of the gain realized on the home sale as they have met the

requirements for gain exclusion and the gain does not exceed $500,000, computed as follows:

Net proceeds from sale of home

Selling price	$650,000
Real estate commissions paid on sale	– $36,000
Net proceeds from sale of home	$614,000

↓

Less: Cost basis of home (Purchase price + improvements)	$340,000

Realized gain of $274,000 is less than $500,000, so none of the $274,000 of the realized gain would be recognized. The entire $274,000 realized gain is tax free.

57. **C.** Koshefsky's taxable gain would be $60,000. The condemnation of the building by the state qualifies as an involuntary conversion. In such cases, the taxpayer must recognize the gain realized on the conversion or the amount of cash remaining after replacement of the condemned property, whichever is less.

Proceeds received from the state	$260,000
Less the building's tax basis	– $200,000
Realized gain	$60,000

Proceeds received from the state	$260,000
Less cost to replace	– $170,000
Excess proceeds received	$90,000

Since the realized gain was $60,000, and this amount was less than the $90,000 of excess proceeds received, Koshefsky would report a taxable gain on the involuntary conversion transaction in the amount of $60,000.

58. **B.** Koshefsky would be required to recognize a $30,000 gain on this transaction, which qualifies as an involuntary conversion. When a transaction qualifies as an involuntary conversion, the taxpayer must report the gain realized on the conversion, or the proceeds remaining after replacement of the condemned property, whichever is less. In this case, the $30,000 excess proceeds received after replacement of the property is computed as follows:

Proceeds received from the state	$260,000
Less cost to replace	– $230,000
Excess proceeds received	$30,000

This was less than the $60,000 realized gain on the conversion:

Proceeds from the state	$260,000
Less building's tax basis	– $200,000
Realized gain	$60,000

59. **C.** In order to qualify for nonrecognition of gain on a real property involuntary conversion transaction, the taxpayer must replace the property within three years from the date the cash proceeds are received from the condemnation. The taxpayer is given until *the end of the calendar year in which that three-year term falls.* For instance, in this case, the three-year term would technically elapse on March 1, Year 5, but a taxpayer is actually given until December 31 of Year 5. In the case of personal property (such as a car versus a building), the taxpayer is permitted a two-year period from the date the cash proceeds are received from the condemnation to replace the property (with extension to December 31 of that second year if that two-year period elapses within the second year). For any involuntary conversion question on the exam that asks when the last day to replace the property is, the correct answer is December 31. The correct answer of December 31 is either December 31 two years after proceeds are received (for personal property) or December 31 three years after proceeds are received (for real estate).

60. **C.** Both I and II are correct. When property is received as a gift, the basis is not determinable until the property is sold, because the basis is dependent on the final selling price of the gifted property. When gifted property is sold for an amount above the prior owner's basis in the property, the prior owner's basis should be used as the gifted property's basis and a gain recognized in an amount equal to the difference between the final selling price and the prior owner's basis. On the other hand, when gifted property is sold for an amount below the prior owner's basis, then the basis in determining a loss is the lower of the prior owner's basis or the value of the gifted property at the date of the gift. In this case, the selling price of $360 is above the prior owner's basis of $200, so Stan would report a gain in the amount of $160.

61. **A.** I is correct but II is wrong. When property is received as a gift, the basis is not determinable until the property is sold, because the basis is dependent on the final selling price of the gifted property. When gifted property is sold for an amount above the prior owner's basis in the property, the prior owner's basis should be used as the gifted property's basis and a gain recognized in an amount equal to the difference between the final selling price and the prior owner's basis. On the other hand, when gifted property is sold for an amount below the prior owner's basis, then the basis in determining a loss is the

lower of the prior owner's basis or the value of the gifted property at the date of the gift. In this case, Barry would not be precluded from reporting a loss, since the final selling price ($144,000) was less than Harry's (the prior owner's) basis of $150,000. However, in determining the loss, Barry should use the value of the property at the date he received the gift from Harry ($147,000) as the basis in the property, since it is less than Harry's original basis of $150,000. Consequently, Barry would report a loss of $3,000 computed as follows:

Selling price to Larry: $144,000
Basis in gifted property – $147,000, which is lower than Harry's (prior owner's) basis of $150,000

62. **A.** When property is received as a gift, the basis is not determinable until the property is sold, because the basis is dependent on the final selling price of the gifted property. When gifted property is sold for an amount above the prior owner's basis in the property, the prior owner's basis should be used as the gifted property's basis and a gain recognized in an amount equal to the difference between the final selling price and the prior owner's basis. On the other hand, when gifted property is sold for an amount below the prior owner's basis, then the basis in determining a loss is the lower of the prior owner's basis or the value of the gifted property at the date of the gift. In this question, the property is sold for $149,000, which is below the previous owner's basis, and would typically present a loss situation. When this type of situation occurs, the basis in determining the loss is the lower of the previous owner's basis (in this case, $150,000) or the value at the time of the gift ($147,000). Since the value at the time of the gift is lower, this amount would normally be used as the basis in determining the loss. However, when using $147,000 as the basis, a $2,000 gain (not a loss) results ($149,000 selling price – $147,000 basis). *Since this transaction should produce a loss, not a gain, NO taxable gain or loss is recognized on this transaction.*

63. **D.** In this situation, the stock was initially bought by Debbie for $4,000. It then declined in value to $3,000 at the time it was gifted to Craig. Subsequent thereto and at the time Craig later sold the stock to an unrelated party, the stock's value had increased to $3,500, but did not increase to the amount of Debbie's (previous owner's) initial purchase price or basis. Thus in this type of situation, *there is neither a taxable gain nor taxable loss, and consequently, no defined basis.* This is so since computing a gain would arrive at a $500 loss (selling price: $3,500 – $4,000, which would be the basis used for computing a gain [the previous owner's basis]), and computing a loss would result in a $500 gain (selling price: $3,500 – $3,000, which would be the basis used for computing a loss [the lesser of the value of the stock at the time of the gift or the previous owner's basis]).

64. **A.** When gifted property is sold for an amount above the prior owner's basis in the property, the prior owner's basis should be used as the gifted property's basis and a gain recognized in an amount equal to the difference between the final selling price and the prior owner's basis. In this question, Rochelle sold the diamond necklace that was gifted to her for $13,000, which exceeded the prior owner's basis of $10,000 by $3,000. Rochelle would therefore use the prior owner's (Grace's) basis of $10,000 when calculating her (Rochelle's) gain. Consequently, Rochelle's recognized gain would be $3,000, calculated as follows:

Proceeds from sale $13,000
Cost basis (which is equal to prior owner's basis) – $10,000
$3,000 gain

65. **B.** Capital assets are those assets held for investment or used for personal enjoyment. The diamond necklace would therefore qualify as a capital asset. A is not correct. Section 1231 assets include "business assets," or assets used in the business to generate revenue, which are held for more than one year. The diamond necklace is not being used for business purposes to generate revenue and therefore would not qualify as a Section 1231 asset. C is not correct. Rochelle sold the necklace. It was not involuntarily converted or lost due to theft or some other damage. D is not correct. A passive activity is either a rental activity or a trade or business in which the individual does not materially participate.

66. **D.** Although no tax is paid by the recipient of a gift, the donor or taxpayer may have a gift tax to pay if the gift is greater than $14,000 (exemption limitation) to any one person. A taxpayer can gift up to $14,000 cash to any number of individuals without paying a gift tax. Married couples can gift up to $28,000 without a gift tax if both individuals consent to the gift. In this question, Lois gave a $5,000 cash gift to her child, which is below the $14,000 threshold, and she gave another gift of $25,000 to her grandchild for college tuition; however, that gift

was paid directly to the university. An individual is permitted to gift more than the $14,000 exemption amount by paying another's medical bills or college tuition (not room and board) directly to the provider. Additionally, gifts between spouses are tax free, and the amounts between spouses are unlimited. Any other cash gifts given directly to the recipient that exceed the $14,000 exclusion limit will trigger a gift tax.

67. **B.** Micki would be able to exclude an aggregate total of $34,000 on the three gifts. For 2015, a taxpayer or donor can exclude up to $14,000 for each cash gift given. Married couples can gift up to $28,000 without a gift tax if both individuals consent to the gift. In this question, Micki can exclude $14,000 on the cash gift to her grandson for the home down payment; $14,000 on the cash gift to her friend's son for his college tuition (note that the tuition was not paid directly to the college, which could have provided Micki with even more of an exclusion if the gift was in excess of $14,000); and the entire $6,000 cash gift to her cousin for the vacation trip because this gift was less than the $14,000 gift exclusion limitation. Thus Micki would be subject to tax only on $2,000 of the $16,000 cash gift she gave to her grandson.

68. **D.** Alice can gift the entire $1,000,000 to Jeffrey without incurring any gift tax liability. There is no gift tax on gifts made between spouses. Gifts between spouses are unlimited, and no gift tax would ever apply.

69. **C.** Luchentos can deduct an aggregate $320 of these gifts as follows:

4 gifts at $10 each = $40
4 gifts at $20 each = $80
4 gifts at $60 each = $100
   ($25 limit for each individual gift)
4 gifts at $80 = $100
   ($25 limit for each individual gift)
   ↓
$40 + $80 + $100 + $100 = $320

The deduction for business gifts is limited to $25 per customer. When the exam indicates that the gift is "not of an advertising nature," this means that the amount paid or given is not to be considered an advertising expense, but rather a gift.

70. **A.** I is correct. The sale of property received as a gift has no basis until it is sold. If the property is sold for an amount that exceeds the prior owner's (donor's) basis, the prior owner's (donor's) basis is used in computing and reporting a gain on the sale. If the property is sold for an amount below the prior owner's (donor's) basis, a loss could result. II is incorrect. Unlike gifted property, property received as an inheritance has a basis that is usually known to the taxpayer before the time of sale. The general rule for inherited property is that the basis of the property is equal to the property's fair value at the date of death, *or* its fair value six months after the date of death, or the date of conveyance of the property, whichever comes first, *if* the alternative valuation date is elected by the executor of the estate.

71. **C.** I is correct. Moving expenses are deductible to arrive at AGI. II is correct. Student loan interest is deductible to arrive at AGI. Other expenses that are deductible for AGI include educator expenses, health savings account deductions, self-employment costs (i.e., portion of self-employment tax; self-employed retirement plan contributions—SEP IRA, SIMPLE IRA, and other qualified plans; self-employed health insurance deduction), penalty on early withdrawal of savings, alimony paid, and tuition and fees.

72. **C.** I is correct. Alimony is deductible to arrive at AGI by the spouse who pays the alimony and is includable in income by the spouse who receives it. III is correct. Contributions to a health savings account are deductible to arrive at AGI. Health savings accounts allow a taxpayer to pay for copays with pretax dollars. II is wrong. Child support is not deductible nor is it includable in income.

73. **A.** I is correct. The only penalty deductible for AGI on a tax return is the penalty for early withdrawal of a savings account (i.e., certificate of deposit). If the savings account or CD was part of a retirement plan account, however, the penalty on the early withdrawal would *not* be deductible. II is wrong. Penalties assessed for late payment of income taxes are *not* deductible.

74. **B.** Corey would be able to deduct $100 of the moving expenses. The only moving expenses (noted in this question) that would qualify for deductibility are the moving of Corey's household goods ($2,000) and the lodging costs he incurred on the way to Massachusetts ($100). Meals, temporary living expenses, and the penalty for breaking the New Jersey residence lease do not qualify as deductible moving expenses. However, since Corey is being reimbursed $2,000 from his employer, he would be permitted to deduct only $100 of the $2,100 total deductible moving costs.

Moving household goods	$2,000
Lodging while moving	+ $100
Reimbursement	− $2,000
Moving expense deduction	$100

75. **A.** In order to qualify for the maximum IRA contribution of $5,500, a single taxpayer needs to have earned income of at least $5,500. Earned income for the purposes of an IRA includes wages, Schedule C business profits, and alimony. Alimony is not really earned income, but for purposes of qualifying for an IRA deduction, it counts toward the $5,500. B is wrong. The IRA deduction would be limited to the self-employment income of $2,000 and the alimony received of $1,000, since interest income is considered portfolio income. The $2,500 doesn't qualify. C is wrong. There would be no IRA deduction, since interest and dividends are portfolio income and do not qualify for IRA deduction. D is wrong. The IRA deduction would be limited to the wages earned of $4,500, since rental income is passive and does not qualify as earned income.

76. **B.** The tax is $1,000. The 10% premature distribution tax will only be assessed on the $10,000 withdrawal used to pay off credit card balances. Withdrawals for qualified education expenses and qualified medical expenses are not subject to the 10% premature distribution tax.

77. **D.** Whenever money is distributed to a taxpayer from a traditional IRA, there is an increase in taxable income unless the money is rolled over into another IRA. Regardless of the age of the taxpayer or what the money is spent on, distributions from traditional IRAs result in taxable income. This question did not ask about the penalty but about the increase in taxable income. Thus, all of the distributions presented, totaling $24,000, would increase Koslow's taxable income.

78. **C.** I is correct. The maximum IRA deduction is $5,500 for those under age 50. II is correct. The maximum IRA deduction is $6,500 for those ages 50 or older.

79. **C.** The advantage of Roth IRAs is that the qualifying distributions from Roth IRAs result in no tax. Distributions from Roth IRAs are tax free after five years as long as the taxpayer is 59½ years old. The disadvantage of a Roth IRA is that contributions to a Roth IRA are not tax deductible. CPA exam candidates need to understand the theory behind the traditional and Roth IRA as well as the advantages and disadvantages of each. The Roth IRA results in a tax-free distribution upon retirement but contributions are not tax deductible as they are made to the IRA. That can be contrasted to traditional IRAs that do not result in tax deductions as contributions are made but result in taxable distributions upon retirement.

80. **C.** By age 70½, a taxpayer must begin to take at least minimum distributions from his or her traditional IRA. At 70½ an actuarial calculation is performed, and minimum distribution from the IRA must be taken from that year on. A is wrong. When a taxpayer reaches age 59½, the taxpayer *may* begin to take distributions from a traditional IRA without penalty, but when a taxpayer reaches age 70½, he or she must begin taking minimum distributions. B is wrong. Age 65 is not the age that a taxpayer must begin to withdraw from an IRA. A taxpayer can actually wait until age 70½. D is wrong. The age that a taxpayer begins to collect social security is not related to the age that he or she must begin taking minimum distributions from a traditional IRA.

81. **C.** Health savings accounts (HSAs) are used by taxpayers to help pay for deductibles and copays. If a taxpayer has a health insurance plan with high deductibles, a health savings account makes sense because deductibles and copays would be paid from pretax dollars. When taxpayers put money into a health savings account, they receive a *deduction in arriving at AGI*. Money is not taxable when removed from the HSA as long as it is used to cover medical expenses. If money is left over, it remains in the HSA into the following year. HSAs originally began for the self-employed taxpayer because the only health insurance that many self-employed taxpayers can afford is a high-deductible plan. Employees, on the other hand, originally did not require a high-deductible plan because their employer was paying most of the cost. Recently, employer health costs have become so expensive that employers have found that it's actually cheaper for an employer to drop the old employee health plan and instead get a high-deductible plan for each employee *and* put money in each employee's HSA to pay for deductibles. If the employer puts money into the HSA of an employee, that money is not taxed.

82. **D.**

Gross income	$57,000
Health savings account contribution	– $4,000
Health insurance premiums	– $6,000
Alimony paid	– $5,000
Traditional IRA contributions	– $2,000
AGI	$40,000

The child support of $3,000 and education IRA contribution of $1,000 are not deductible.

83. **A.** Assuming their AGI will exceed $43,000, their dependent care credit percentage is 20%. Qualifying expenditures cannot exceed $3,000 per dependent. With two or more dependents, a max of $6,000 is the base amount even though they spent $16,000. Multiplying the $6,000 base amount times the rate of 20% will produce a credit of $1,200. This credit is nonrefundable, and there is no AGI limit or threshold that might otherwise disallow the credit entirely: $6,000 base amount multiplied by 20% = $1,200 dependent care credit.

84. **C.** The benefit of most credits cease if a taxpayer's income tax payable is reduced to zero. However, the earned income credit can further reduce a taxpayer's tax obligation, thereby creating a refund. For example, if a taxpayer's income taxes are reduced to zero even before factoring in an earned income credit of $490, the taxpayer will actually receive a $490 refund. Having more children in a low-income home would normally qualify for the maximum earned income credit, but a reduced earned income credit is also available even without having a child in the taxpayer's home.

85. **B.** II is correct. While most credits are nonrefundable, the earned income credit is a refundable tax credit. I is wrong. Most credits are nonrefundable, like the dependent care credit. For example, if the tax was $800 but the dependent care credit was $1,200, total tax would be reduced to zero and there would be *no* refund of $400, because the dependent care credit is nonrefundable.

86. **B.** I is wrong. In order to qualify for earned income credit, the taxpayer must have some earned income. Ziga had income but no earned income, so he would *not* qualify for the earned income credit. II is correct. The rental income is considered passive income; the interest and dividends are portfolio income. Neither the rental income nor the interest and dividends would qualify Ziga for the earned income credit.

87. **B.** The American Opportunity Credit is limited to $2,500 per student and is available for the first *four* years of college. Credit is taken by multiplying 100% of the first $2,000 and 25% of the next $2,000 spent for a maximum of $2,500, and up to $1,000 is refundable Therefore, if their tax is $2,000, the first $1,500 of the $2,500 credit would reduce tax of $2,000 down to tax of $500. The remaining $1,000 of the $2,500 credit would reduce the $500 tax to a $500 refund.

88. **A.** I is correct. The American Opportunity Credit can be taken for four years of college. II is wrong. Adjusted gross income limits do apply to the American Opportunity Credit. Phaseouts begin with AGI of $80,000 single and $160,000 married filing jointly. The student doesn't have to be a full-time student to qualify, but "must be enrolled on a half-time basis" or more. Taking just "a few courses" will *not* qualify for the American Opportunity Credit. The CPA exam will say whether the student is enrolled at least "half time."

89. **C.** The Lifetime Learning Credit is another credit that is meant to benefit students taking courses. Different from the American Opportunity Credit, the student does *not* need to be full time or even part time. The amount spent for courses (up to a maximum of $10,000) is multiplied by 20%. In this question, $8,000 spent × 20% = $1,600 Lifetime Learning Credit.

90. **A.** I is correct. The American Opportunity Credit requires the student to be enrolled on a half-time status or more. II is wrong. The Lifetime Learning Credit can be used by a student who is enrolled only in a single course or even for an adult taking continuing education courses.

91. **A.** A taxpayer is entitled to a tax credit of 30% of the cost for amounts invested in property that uses solar, geothermal, or ocean thermal energy; the solar panel industry took off when this credit began. The solar credit is nonrefundable, but carries forward if not used up. There is no AGI limit on the credit. $80,000 – $20,000 instant state rebate = $60,000 actual cost × 30% tax credit = $18,000.

92. **D.** I is wrong. The Lifetime Learning Credit is nonrefundable as are most tax credits. The Lifetime Learning Credit, maximum $2,000, can reduce taxes to zero but would not create a refund should the credit exceed the tax. II is wrong. The foreign tax credit is nonrefundable as are most tax credits. The foreign tax credit can reduce the tax to zero but

would *not* create a refund should the credit exceed the tax.

93. **D.** II is correct. Costs associated with adopting the child of a spouse do *not* qualify for the adoption credit. I is wrong. Legal fees paid to adopt a child qualify for the adoption credit. III is wrong. Fees paid to an adoption agency qualify for the adoption credit.

94. **B.** II is correct. The retirement savings contribution credit is meant to help young newly working taxpayers save and contribute to an IRA. The taxpayer not only receives a deduction for contributing money to an IRA, but may also qualify to receive a credit for that contribution as well. One of the conditions for the credit is that the taxpayer *not* be a full-time student. I is wrong, student loan interest can be taken as a deduction to arrive at AGI, not as a tax credit.

95. **A.** I is correct. A taxpayer may claim a credit against US taxes due for foreign income taxes paid to a foreign country or a US possession. There is a limitation on the amount of the foreign tax credit an individual can obtain. II is wrong. Foreign taxes may be taken as a deduction rather than a credit but not as an adjustment to arrive at adjusted gross income (AGI). Instead, the deduction for foreign taxes paid would be a miscellaneous itemized deduction, not subject to 2% of AGI. Since the credit for foreign taxes paid is limited, an individual might find it better to deduct the taxes as an itemized deduction (*not* subject to the 2% floor) instead of taking the foreign tax paid as a credit.

96. **C.** III is correct. Transportation to a physician's office for required medical care is a qualifying medical expense. II is wrong. Health club dues are *not* deductible for medical expenses. I is wrong. Vitamins are generally *not* deductible for medical expenses.

97. **D.** Deductible expenses include

Physical therapy, net of reimbursement	$500
Insurance for prescription medicines	+ $600
Total deductible medical expenses	$1,100

The insurance policy that protects against the loss of earnings due to sickness or accident (i.e., a disability policy) of $1,000 provides income should the taxpayer become disabled. It does not pay for medical expenses; therefore, it does not qualify for a medical deduction.

98. **C.** I is correct. You actually have to know the taxpayer's AGI before you can deduct medical expense. Medical expenses in excess of 10% of AGI can be deducted for taxpayers under age 65. II is correct. Medical expenses in excess of 7.5% of AGI can be deducted for taxpayers age 65 and older.

99. **D.** I is wrong. With medical expenses, its common to swipe a credit card in December and pay the balance in the following year. Take the deduction in the year of the swipe for the taxpayer's or dependent's medical care. II is wrong. Taxpayers are allowed to deduct medical costs paid on behalf of elderly parents even if the elderly parent had a little too much income to qualify as the taxpayer's dependent.

100. **B.**

Medicines prescribed	$300
Health insurance premiums	+ $500
Dental surgery	+ $4,000
Total	$4,800
Less insurance reimbursement	− 1,000
Medical expenses before AGI limit	$3,800

↓

Qualifying medical expenses before AGI limit	$3,800
7.5% of AGI	− $3,000
Deductible portion	$800

While Imhoff has qualifying medical expenses of $3,800, he gets only a $800 deduction because $3,800 net medical expenses exceed 7.5% of his AGI ($3,000) by $800.

Note: Taxpayers over 65 years old can deduct medical expenses in excess of 7.5% of AGI. Anyone under 65 can deduct medical costs only in excess of 10% of AGI.

101. **D.** All three medical expenses are includable. The cosmetic surgery is not elective, since it was necessary to correct a congenital deformity. The AGI limit is 10% since the taxpayer is under age 65.

Doctor bills from fall	$3,500
Eyeglasses	+ $500
Surgery	+ $16,000
Total	$20,000

↓

AGI limitation ($70,000 × 10%)	− $7,000 (threshold)
Deduction	$13,000

102. **D.** $3,250 is deductible for medical expenses after the 7.5% AGI limit. AGI is calculated as follows:

$95,000 W-2 – $5,000 IRA contribution = $90,000 AGI

$90,000 × 0.075 = $6,750

(AGI threshold is 7.5% since taxpayer is over 65)

Only the ear surgery is deductible, so $10,000 – $6,750 = $3,250. Hair transplant is considered cosmetic surgery and is not deductible.

103. **B.** $1,700 is a Year 1 itemized deduction; $300 is a Year 2 itemized deduction. The amount paid during the tax year for state and local income taxes is deductible. Payments can be through employee withholding, through state estimated tax payments, or with the filing of a return. Since a return is always filed after the tax year, the $300 paid in April of Year 2 is a Year 2 itemized deduction for state taxes. Note: each year, the taxpayer has the option of taking a deduction for state and local sales taxes rather than state and local income taxes.

104. **B.** The state taxes withheld in Year 1 of $1,500 plus the estimated state taxes of $400 paid in September of Year 1 are added together to become the state and local tax deduction of $1,900 on Schedule A for Year 1. Although $200 paid in January Year 2 relates to Year 1, it was paid in Year 2 and will be a Year 2 itemized deduction. The federal income tax withheld of $4,000 is taken as a credit, not an itemized deduction.

105. **C.** I is correct. Real estate taxes paid on a vacation home are deductible as an itemized deduction; however, if the property was rented out, the deduction would likely appear on Schedule E versus Schedule A. II is correct. Personal property taxes are deductible as an itemized deduction if they are based on the value of the personal property. Some states, for example, tax the value of an automobile every year. This tax would be deductible on Schedule A.

106. **A.** I is correct. A taxpayer can deduct the medical expenses paid for someone who would be a qualifiable dependent but who may not be a dependent and is earning slightly more income than the exemption amount.

II is wrong. In order for the real estate taxes to be deductible, the property must belong to the individual who pays the real estate tax bill; otherwise the payment for real estate taxes is viewed as a gift and is not deductible by that individual, who in this case, is Ben.

107. **D.** Only the state income tax, real estate taxes in the Netherlands, and personal property taxes are deductible. Taxes paid on the mother's house would be considered a gift and would not be deductible by Simberg, since Simberg is not the owner of the home. In some states like Connecticut, personal property taxes are paid every year on the value of a car. These personal property taxes are includable as an itemized deduction for state and local taxes on Schedule A. The $300 state unincorporated business tax is *not* deductible on Schedule A but is deductible on Schedule C for a small business owner. Notice that the real estate taxes are deductible even though the property is located outside of the United States.

State income tax	$2,000
Personal property tax	+ $10
Real estate tax	+ $900
Total	$2,910

108. **A.** Real estate taxes are deductible on all the houses that a taxpayer owns. Since the question said the taxpayer is *not* renting any of the houses, the real estate tax would be deducted on Schedule A.

109. **C.** When a taxpayer owns a home, it's common to have both real estate taxes and mortgage interest. Although both are deductible on Schedule A as an itemized deduction, real estate taxes deduction is different than mortgage interest deduction. Mortgage interest can be deducted on two of the taxpayer's homes; the real estate taxes however can be deducted on *all* the real estate the taxpayer owns. If a taxpayer owned three homes, the real estate taxes would be deductible on all three, but the mortgage interest would be deductible only on two of the three homes. The taxpayer would need to rent out the third home to get a mortgage interest deduction on the third home.

110. **C.** I is correct. Interest is deductible in connection with a taxpayer's main home or second home. Even if the second home is a vacation home, the mortgage interest can be deducted on both homes. Taxpayers are allowed to deduct the mortgage interest on two homes, not just one. II is correct. With regard to a home equity loan, interest on a home equity loan is deductible regardless of what the taxpayer decides to do with the loan proceeds. Interest on home equity loans (proceeds of up to $100,000) can be deducted. A home equity loan is where the loan is secured by the residence, but the money does not have to be used to buy, build, or substantially improve the home. For example, proceeds from a home equity

loan could be used to buy a car or send a son or daughter to college.

111. **A.** Only the mortgage interest of $15,000 and the interest on the home equity loan of $1,500 qualifies as an interest deduction. The remaining interest is all considered personal interest and is *not* deductible. No deduction is allowed for credit card interest, interest on auto loans, or interest on late tax payments.

$15,000	mortgage interest
+ $1,500	home equity loan interest
$16,500	total interest deduction on Schedule A, itemized deductions

112. **B.** If money was borrowed to finance investments, the interest expense can be deducted up to the amount reported as net investment income. Investment interest is deductible against net investment income.

Gross investment income	$120,000
Less investment expenses (unrelated to interest expense)	– $100,000
Net investment income	$20,000

The limit of $20,000 net investment income is deductible for investment interest on Schedule A itemized deductions.

113. **D.** If money is borrowed to finance investments, the interest paid can be deducted up to the amount reported as net investment income. Since the net investment income of $4,300 exceeds the investment interest paid of $4,000, the $4,000 paid is deductible.

$5,000	mortgage interest
+ $4,000	net investment interest
$9,000	interest expense deductible on Schedule A as an itemized deduction

114. **C.** If money is borrowed to finance investments, the interest paid can be deducted up to the amount reported as net investment income. Since the net investment income of $4,300 exceeds the investment interest paid of $4,000, the $4,000 investment interest paid is deductible. Interest on credit cards is not deductible. Points are deductible in full when paid in connection with obtaining a mortgage. Each point is 1% of the loan. For example, a $100,000 mortgage that costs 1 point means that the taxpayer must pay $1,000 up front to obtain a $100,000 mortgage. Points are normally deductible in the year paid unless the taxpayer is refinancing, in which case the points are amortized over the life of the new loan.

$2,500	points
+ $5,000	mortgage interest
+ $4,000	investment interest
$11,500	total interest deduction on Schedule A

115. **B.** Home mortgage interest of $3,600 and $500 personal property tax paid are deductible as an itemized deduction. Late payment penalties are not deductible, and neither is the 10% penalty on premature IRA distribution.

116. **D.** $4,000 cash to church + $600 car = $4,600. Cash contributions to individuals are gifts and *not* tax deductible; only contributions to recognized charitable organizations are tax deductible.

117. **A.** There are two separate donations; The cash of $4,000 to the church nets Foltz a $3,800 deduction because of the tickets received with a fair value of $200. The jewelry purchased for $1,900 is above the fair value of $1,500, so the jewelry purchased at the church actually benefits the church by $400.

$400	jewelry
+ $3,800	cash
$4,200	total

118. **C.** The cash contributed of $18,000 qualifies, plus the $10,000 carryover equals $28,000. However, the total contribution deduction is limited to 50% of AGI. AGI is $50,000, so the deduction is limited to $25,000. The other $3,000 carries over to next year.

Total contributions including carryover from prior year	$28,000
Limit	AGI of $50,000 × 50% = $25,000

119. **B.** O'Keefe's deduction would be limited to cost basis, $1,400, since she did not own the asset for more than a year. If she had held the stock for more than one year, the FMV of $3,000 would be deductible. Since she held the stock for only seven months, her deduction is limited to lower of fair value or cost basis, in this case, $1,400.

120. **C.** Since Berman held the artwork for longer than one year, he is entitled to the full FMV, $11,000, as a deduction. The built-in gain of $9,000 is not taxable. The next step is to compare the $11,000 deduction to 30% of AGI: $12,000. The deduction for any long-term capital gain property is limited to 30% of

AGI each year. The deduction for property contributions is not allowed to exceed 30% of AGI.

AGI $40,000 × 30% limit = $12,000

Therefore, the $11,000 charitable deduction is allowed in full.

121. B. Since Brian held the artwork for longer than one year, he may be entitled to the full FMV, $15,000, as a deduction. The built-in gain of $9,000 is not taxable. The first step is to compare the $15,000 potential deduction to 30% of AGI: $6,000. The deduction for any long-term capital gain property is limited to 30% of AGI each year. The deduction for property contributions is not allowed to exceed 30% of AGI.

Total potential charitable contribution before limit $15,000

AGI $20,000 × 30% = $6,000 limit

The amount of property contribution that carries over to the next year is $9,000.

122. B. Since Teri held the artwork for longer than one year, she may be entitled to the full FMV, $11,000, as a deduction. The built-in gain of $9,000 is not taxable, since the art was donated to a charity. The first step is to compare the $11,000 potential deduction to 30% of AGI: $7,500. The deduction for any long-term capital gain property is limited to 30% of AGI each year. The deduction for property contributions is not allowed to exceed 30% of AGI. Since AGI is $25,000 and 30% = $7,500, only $7,500 of the $11,000 charitable contribution is allowed this year; the other $3,500 carries over to the next year. The next step is to add the cash contribution of $7,000 to the $7,500 property contribution deduction. The total of $14,500 is compared to 50% of her AGI: $12,500. $12,500 is the maximum deduction because charity is limited to an overall 50% of AGI maximum. The total charitable contribution deduction in the current year for Teri is $12,500.

Property contribution allowed this year	$7,500
Cash contribution allowed this year	$7,000
Total potential contribution before	
50% of AGI limit	$14,500
50% of AGI limit	$12,500
	(maximum deduction)
Amount that carries over to next year	$2,000

123. C. The donation for the artwork is limited to 30% of AGI: $60,000 × 0.3 = $18,000. Although the artwork

is worth $20,000 and was held for more than one year, $20,000 exceeds the AGI limit for property contributions of 30%. Harold's deduction for the artwork is limited to $18,000, and the other $2,000 carries over for a maximum of five years. The cash contribution of $5,000 is deductible in full, since the available total from long-term capital gain property plus all other contributions for the year is limited to 50% of AGI.

Property contribution limited	
to 30% of AGI	$18,000
Cash contribution	+ $5,000
Total potential contribution before	
AGI limit	$23,000

Harold would be allowed to deduct $23,000 since his AGI is $60,000 and his overall 50% limit is $30,000.

124. C. A personal casualty loss deduction is allowed only where it exceeds a $100 floor for each separate loss and then 10% of a taxpayer's AGI.

125. A. The personal casualty loss deduction is determined by taking the lesser of the decrease in the FMV of the property or its basis, less the insurance reimbursement, subject to a $100 floor, and then subject to 10% of the taxpayer's AGI. With the FMV and basis being identical, the computations are

$130,000 decline − $120,000 reimbursement = $10,000 potential loss

$10,000 potential loss − $100 floor = $9,900 loss

$9,900 loss − 10% of AGI ($7,000) = $2,900 deduction

126. C. Gambling losses are miscellaneous itemized deductions *not* subject to the 2% AGI limitation. The deductions for gambling losses are, however, limited to gambling winnings. Unused gambling losses do *not* carry over.

127. B. Unreimbursed expenses such as small tools and supplies, protective clothing, required uniforms not suitable for ordinary use, and business car expense are deductible subject to 2% of AGI. The separate amounts would be added and the amount in excess of 2% of the taxpayer's AGI would be deducted.

128. B. Unreimbursed expenses such as small tools and supplies, protective clothing, required uniforms not suitable for ordinary use, and employee business car expense are deductible subject to 2% of AGI. Also included in the category of miscellaneous itemized deductions subject to the 2% of AGI floor are dues to professional organizations, subscriptions to professional journals, tax preparation fees, and union dues. The list is quite large and also includes rent on a safe-deposit box and certain investment expenses like the annual custodial fee for an IRA. Preparation of a will, funeral expenses, and credit card interest are not miscellaneous deductions but are often asked about on the exam.

129. **D.** Preparation of a will and funeral expenses are not miscellaneous itemized deductions. Gambling losses are *not* subject to 2% of AGI, although gambling losses *are* considered miscellaneous itemized deductions. Safe-deposit box rental is the only one listed in the question that qualifies as a miscellaneous itemized deduction subject to 2% of AGI.

130. **C.** I is correct. Among the items listed, only tax return preparation fees are miscellaneous itemized deductions subject to 2% of AGI. II is wrong. Foreign taxes paid may be taken as a credit or deduction. A credit is usually better than a deduction, but the foreign tax credit is limited so it's sometimes advantageous to take foreign taxes paid as a deduction. Foreign taxes paid taken as a deduction is a miscellaneous itemized deduction *not* subject to 2% of AGI. III is wrong. A penalty on early withdrawal of savings from a non-retirement account certificate of deposit (breaking a CD early) is deductible as an adjustment to arrive at AGI, *not* as an itemized deduction. IV is wrong. Penalty for late payment of mortgage is *not* deductible.

131. **C.** Miscellaneous itemized deductions are deductible to the extent that they in total exceed 2% of AGI.

$85,500 – $5,500 IRA contribution	$80,000 AGI
Tax preparation	$500
Custodial fees	+ $100
Publications	+ $150
Union dues	+ $2,000
Total misc. deductions	$2,750
	↓
AGI $80,000 × 2%	– $1,600
Allowable deduction	$1,150

132. **D.** Adjusted gross income (AGI) is gross income less adjustments or deductions. $6,000 in wages is part of gross income. Jury duty pay is taxable, so add $10 to gross income. Gross income is $6,010. The only adjustment listed is $400 in student loan interest, resulting in an AGI of $5,610. Charitable contributions and unreimbursed employee business expense are *not* deductions subtracted to arrive at AGI.

Wages	$6,000
Jury duty pay	+ $10
Less student loan interest	– $400
Total AGI	$5,610

133. **A.** Federal income tax is *not* deductible. Penalties and interest related to federal income tax matters are not deductible.

134. **B.** I is correct. Unique items of income that are taxable and sometimes tested on the CPA exam include damages awarded for a breach of contract. II is correct. Fees received for jury duty service are also sometimes tested on the CPA exam and are included in taxable income. IV is correct. Also sometimes tested on the CPA exam is the forgiveness of debt, which is an income-includable item and benefit received by a taxpayer. III is wrong. Workers' compensation awards are tax free.

135. **B.** The calculation of AMT begins with taxable income, then adds back adjustments and preferences, and subtracts an AMT exemption. Common adjustments for the AMT include:

Personal exemption
State and local taxes
Miscellaneous itemized deductions *in excess of* 2% of AGI
Home mortgage interest where the loan proceeds are not used to buy, build, or improve a home

Private activity bond interest is considered a preference item (rather than an adjustment) for AMT and is added to taxable income to arrive at alternative minimum taxable income. Another preference item for AMT is percentage depletion. The excess of percentage depletion over cost depletion gets added back to arrive at the taxpayer's alternative minimum taxable income. An AMT exemption is then subtracted out to reduce the taxable income, but that exemption is lost by taxpayers with relatively high levels of income. What remains after adding back the adjustments and preference items and subtracting the exemption is alternative minimum taxable income. The alternative minimum taxable income is then multiplied by the AMT tax rate, and the additional amount must be paid in addition to the regular income tax.

136. **C.** Alternative minimum taxable income starts with taxable income. Then certain items are added back to taxable income because they are not deductible for AMT. The items in this question that need to be added back include the state and local income taxes and the miscellaneous itemized deductions in

excess of 2% of AGI. While these items are deductible to arrive at taxable income for normal tax rules, they are considered AMT adjustments and must be added back to arrive at alternative minimum taxable income. Gambling losses are not an AMT adjustment. Home mortgage interest on a loan to acquire a residence is *not* an AMT adjustment. Note: in a question about the AMT, watch out for a home equity loan. If the home equity loan proceeds are *not* used to fix up the house, the home equity loan interest cannot be deducted for AMT purposes. In this question, the calculation of reportable alternative minimum taxable income is as follows:

$70,000	taxable income
+ $5,000	state and local income taxes
+ $2,000	miscellaneous itemized deductions in excess of 2% of AGI
$77,000	AMT income

137. **A.** Shirley's AMT adjustments include:

Personal exemption	$3,100
Home equity loan interest	$1,200
Total AMT adjustments	$4,300

Common adjustments for AMT include:

Personal exemption
State and local income taxes
Miscellaneous itemized deductions *in excess of* 2% of AGI
Home mortgage interest where the loan proceeds are not used to buy, build, or improve a home

138. **A.** Only the $400 tax-exempt interest income on private activity bonds should be added back as a tax preference item. The personal exemption and state income taxes are not added back, because the question asked about preference items, not adjustments. The only preference item here is interest income from private activity bonds. Another common preference item is percentage depletion. The excess of percentage depletion over cost depletion is a preference item. While interest income from municipal bonds is exempt from regular income tax, for AMT purposes, municipal bond interest income is divided into two categories: general obligation bond interest and private activity bond interest. General obligation bonds are sold by the government, and the government can do whatever it wants with the money since the bonds are sold as "general obligation." Private activity bonds, on the other hand, are sold by the government, but the government must use the money for the specific private activity. If an investor buys private activity bonds, the interest

income is taxable for AMT. If the investor buys general obligation bonds, the interest income is not a preference item and is *not* added to taxable income.

139. **C.** I is correct. The standard deduction is an AMT adjustment for an individual taxpayer. The individual taxpayer begins with taxable income and then adds the impact of removing the standard deduction and other AMT adjustments. II is correct. The personal exemption is an AMT adjustment for an individual taxpayer. The individual taxpayer begins with taxable income and then adds the impact of removing the personal exemption and other AMT adjustments.

140. **A.** I is correct. For an individual taxpayer, private activity bonds issued by a state or local government are a preference item for AMT and will result in the taxpayer paying additional AMT. While the interest from private activity bonds is not includable for regular tax purposes, for AMT purposes the amount is considered a preference item.

II is wrong. For an individual taxpayer, general obligation bonds issued by a state or local government are *not* taxable for regular tax or AMT.

Chapter 40: Taxation of Entities

141. **C.** Steelman's share of the ordinary income is 75% of the $60,000 partnership ordinary income. To tax the $5,000 distribution would result in double taxation. Partners pay tax on the income, or the profits, from the partnership. Since tax is being paid by the partners based on the income earned by the business, profit *distributions* to the partners are normally tax free. A profit distribution is a payment of partnership profits to the partner. The profits are already being taxed at the partner level; therefore, the profit distribution would *not* be taxed to the partner—to tax it would result in double taxation.

142. **B.** Ordinary income of a partnership is sales less ordinary business expenses (page 1 of Form 1065, partnership return). The dividend revenue, the charitable contributions, and the capital loss are pass-through items, which are separately allocated to the individual partners. Only the remaining $100,000 is the ordinary income of the partnership.

Sales	$450,000
Operating expenses	− $350,000
Partnership ordinary income	$100,000

143. **B.** II is correct. Since a partnership is a pass-through entity, no tax is paid by the partnership. So all items of income and loss must eventually appear on the

partner's tax returns. Schedule K-1 is the missing link between the partnership tax return and the 1040 tax return of each partner. Each partner receives the Schedule K-1, which lists the amounts of income and loss that need to be reported by each partner on their 1040. All items of income and loss, including ordinary income, capital gains and losses, charitable contributions, and interest and dividends, must be reported by each partner on Schedule K-1. The Schedule K-1 is filed with the 1065 partnership tax return so the IRS knows how much each partner should include on their Form 1040. I is wrong. A partnership tax return is due to be filed on April 15th, three and a half months after year end.

144. **C.** I is correct. Partnership tax returns are informational only. No tax is due with the filing of a partnership tax return, because partnerships do not pay any tax. All tax is paid by the individual partners when they file their 1040. II is correct. Partnership tax returns are filed on Form 1065.

145. **B.** II is correct. In a partnership, a fixed payment made to a partner for work that is done is known as a guaranteed payment. Payment is made regardless of whether the business is profitable. A guaranteed payment, sometimes known as guaranteed salary, is deductible by the partnership on Form 1065 as an ordinary business expense and then includable in taxable income by the recipient partner. It is quite common to see partnerships in the CPA exam where one partner receives a guaranteed payment but the other partners do not. I is wrong. A normal distribution is *not* the same as a guaranteed payment. A normal distribution is *not* deducted by the partnership *and* is *not* a normal distribution included in taxable income by the recipient partner. On the CPA exam it is quite common to see a partnership where one partner receives a normal distribution and the other partners do not. Candidates must be able to distinguish between a guaranteed payment and a normal distribution.

146. **A.** I is correct. A salary that is "without regard to profits" is evidence that the payment to the partner is guaranteed. II is incorrect. A 17% interest in partnership profits is not guaranteed, because if there are no profits, there will be no payment to that partner.

147. **C.** III is correct. Guaranteed payments to partners are an ordinary business deduction for a partnership. I is wrong. Charitable contributions made by a partnership are *not* deductible by the partnership

but are deductible by the partners on their individual tax returns if they itemize. Each partner would receive Schedule K-1 from the partnership listing their share of the charitable contribution. II is wrong. Short-term capital losses are *not* deductible by the partnership but are deductible by the partners on their individual tax returns. On the K-1 form received from the partnership, the amount of short-term capital loss would be reported for each partner.

148. **B.** Guaranteed payments are deducted to arrive at ordinary income of a partnership. Ordinary income before guaranteed payments: $100,000 less $40,000 guaranteed payment = $60,000 ordinary income.

149. **D.** In determining the amount of ordinary income to allocate to the partners, guaranteed payments must first be subtracted and allocated to that partner. The balance is then allocated according to the partnership agreement. Disston gets 25% of all income and 100% of the guaranteed payment. Any distributions or withdrawals generally have no impact on the amount of taxable income recognized by the partner. Disston will be taxed on

100% of the guaranteed payment	$40,000
25% of $60,000 in partnership net income (after guaranteed payment)	+ $15,000
25% of 10,000 capital gain	+ $2,500
Total	$57,500

150. **A.** The loss is limited to a basis of $36,000. Deductible loss is always limited to the amount at risk. Walter's basis balance prior to loss is $36,000.

151. **B.**

Beginning basis	$20,000
Income	+ $10,000
Distribution	− $8,000
Ending balance	$22,000

152. **C.** First, tax basis must be updated for activity incurred during the year. Basis begins at $20,000 and is increased by $13,000 for Norris's 25% share of the municipal interest and ordinary income. Then basis is reduced by the $8,000 cash distribution, leaving a December 31 basis of $25,000. The municipal bond interest income increases basis even though it's not taxable. Note that the question did not ask how much is taxable to Norris.

Beginning basis	$20,000
25% of all income	+ $13,000
Distribution	− $8,000
Ending basis	$25,000

153. **D.** Whether taxable or not, each partner's basis goes up for all income earned by the partnership. The tax-exempt interest income will *not* be taxed, but each partner's basis will increase by their proportionate share of the tax-exempt income.

154. **A.** I is correct. Distributions are a decrease in basis. II is wrong. Loans made to a partnership from a partner are an increase in basis, not decrease. In the event of a total loss, the deductible loss for Krin would include the loan made to the partnership.

155. **C.** Anytime the partnership borrows money from a third party, each partner's basis will increase by their share of the debt. If they were 50/50, the answer could have been A, but there is no indication what their percentage of ownership is. B is wrong because all general partnership loans are considered recourse. Recourse means that the creditor can collect from the partner personally if the partnership fails to pay and the partnership has no funds of its own.

156. **B.** Andy's tax basis starts with his beginning basis of $5,000 and includes his proportionate share of all items of income. Note that a partner's tax basis is affected by items that are nontaxable as well as taxable.

Beginning basis January 1, Year 2	$5,000
Ordinary income	+ $10,000
Tax exempt income	+ $4,000
Taxable interest	+ $2,000
Cash distribution	− $1,000
Ending basis December 31, Year 2	$20,000

157. **A.** The basis rolls over from partner to partnership, so the land has a basis of $30,000 to the partnership and Luke has a $30,000 basis in the partnership as a result of his contribution of the asset.

158. **C.** A partner's basis of an interest in the partnership is the basis of the property transferred less the debt relief. The basis is determined as follows: $30,000 original basis less debt transferred of $18,000 plus debt assumed of $6,000 by being 50% partner = $24,000.

159. **A.** A partner's basis of an interest in the partnership is the basis of the property transferred plus any liabilities assumed. As a 50% partner, Mike assumes 50% of the mortgage transferred by Luke. The basis is determined as follows: $45,000 + $6,000 liability assumed by being a partner = $51,000.

160. **C.** Klein's $24,000 basis is increased by Klein's share of the mortgage, which is 30% of $5,000, or $1,500. Klein's basis is equal to $24,000 + 1,500 = $25,500.

161. **D.** $240,000 original basis less $150,000 cash distribution = $90,000 basis remaining for the real estate. When a partnership is liquidated, the partner removes his or her entire investment in partnership balance. Always distribute the cash to the partner *before* whatever other assets are received in liquidation. What remains after the cash is distributed will be the value of the real estate, because when the distribution is considered liquidating, the partner's basis must be reduced to zero.

162. **A.** Since Anita received a liquidating cash distribution of $50,000 in exchange for her partnership $52,000 interest and no other assets were being distributed, the loss is $2,000. At the time of the cash distribution, Anita's adjusted basis of her interest was $52,000. Anita must zero out her entire basis since the distribution is considered liquidating. Since she held her interest longer than one year, she recognizes a $2,000 long-term capital loss determined as follows:

Basis prior to liquidation	$52,000
Cash received to zero out basis	− $50,000
Loss on liquidation	$2,000

163. **D.** In liquidation, the partner's basis must be closed out. Cash received by the partner in liquidation is always recorded before any other assets. The first step is to use the cash received to reduce the partner's basis. If no other assets are distributed to the partner in liquidation, the remaining partner's basis is considered a loss from liquidation for tax purposes. A gain could result if more cash than basis is distributed. The partnership, on the other hand, doesn't pay tax, so the partnership itself would have no gain or loss from liquidation.

164. **B.** $70,000 less $30,000 cash = $40,000. Always subtract the cash first. Since it's a liquidating distribution, all remaining basis must be closed out. Since Carol's basis stands at $40,000 after receiving the cash, to zero out her basis, Carol would need a basis of $40,000 for the car.

Basis prior to liquidation	$70,000
Cash received	− $30,000
Remaining basis	$40,000

165. **A.** The general rule is that assets come out of a partnership at basis. Any partnership property distributed by the partnership to the partner decreases that partner's basis by the adjusted basis of that

property, but only to the extent of the partner's remaining basis. Since this distribution is nonliquidating, Ryan's basis does *not* have to be zero after the distribution. Therefore, Ryan's basis in the capital assets is limited to $65,000, and Ryan would have a remaining basis in the Bruder Partnership of $5,000.

Basis prior to distribution	$70,000
Less assets distributed	– $65,000
Remaining basis	$5,000

166. **A.** Any partnership property distributed by the partnership to the partner decreases that partner's basis by the adjusted basis of that property—but only to the extent of the partner's remaining basis. In this case, Ryan would value the capital assets at $40,000, and he would have a zero basis remaining in the Bruder partnership.

167. **C.** The general rule is that no gain is recognized on a nonliquidating distribution, unless cash is being distributed in excess of basis. There is no possibility of loss on a nonliquidating distribution. In a *nonliquidating* distribution to a partner, any cash received is first used to reduce that partner's basis. Prior to the distribution, Tyler's basis was $80,000. There was no cash distributed. The capital assets received by Tyler would have the same basis of $75,000 that they had in the partnership, because Tyler had sufficient basis ($80,000) to allocate to the capital assets. The general rule is that assets come out of a partnership at basis and no gain or loss is recognized.

Basis prior to distribution	$80,000
Capital assets distributed	– $75,000
Tyler's remaining basis in the partnership	$5,000

168. **A.** The general rule is that no gain is recognized on a nonliquidating distribution, unless cash is being distributed in excess of basis. In this problem, Yimeny's basis was $50,000 immediately before the distribution. Because the cash distributed of $20,000 was less than her basis, no gain is recognized.

169. **B.** In a nonliquidating distribution to a partner, any cash received is first used to reduce that partner's basis. Then any in-kind property distributed by the partnership to the partner decreases that partner's basis by the adjusted basis of that property, but *only to the extent of the partner's remaining basis.* Yimeny's basis prior to the distribution was $50,000, as just described. After the $20,000 cash distribution, Yimeny's partnership basis was $30,000. Even though the basis and FMV of the property in the partnership was $40,000 and $35,000 respectively,

Yimeny's basis in the property will be limited to her remaining basis in the partnership of $30,000. No gain or loss is recognized on this transaction. Yimeny's eventual sale of the property in the future will trigger the gain due to the low basis allocated at this time.

Basis prior to distribution	$50,000
Less cash distributed	– $20,000
Remaining basis prior to receiving other assets	$30,000
Basis in other assets when received	$30,000

170. **C.** In a nonliquidating distribution to a partner involving only in-kind property, the adjusted basis of the property distributed by the partnership to the partner decreases that partner's basis by the adjusted basis of that property, but only to the extent of the partner's remaining basis. Since Robyn's basis cannot go below zero, her basis in the land is limited to her basis remaining in the partnership, $5,000.

171. **A.** Only cash received in excess of basis can cause a gain. Since no cash was received, there can be no gain. Robyn's basis prior to the distribution was $5,000. Even though the adjusted basis of the land was $6,000 and the FMV of the land was $9,000, Robyn's basis in the land will be limited to the remaining basis in the partnership, or $5,000.

172. **B.** The general rule is that assets come out of a partnership at basis. The exception is when the partner does *not* have enough basis. Here, Kelvin starts with a basis of $50,000, and after subtracting the cash of $25,000, he still has a basis remaining of $25,000. The land would then be transferred to Kelvin at its existing basis of $15,000. Note: had the distribution been liquidating, the basis in the land would have been $25,000, since Kelvin's basis would have needed to be zeroed out.

Basis	$50,000
Less cash distributed	– $25,000
Basis available prior to the distribution of other assets	$25,000
Basis of land distributed	$15,000

173. **D.** The distribution is current because nothing in the question indicated that the partnership is being liquidated. The distribution seems rather proportionate since Lesnik is a 50% partner receiving 50% of the income as a distribution.

174. **B.** II is correct. Guaranteed payments to partners are deductible by the partnership and includable in income by the recipient partners. I is wrong. Normal partnership distributions of cash are not

includable in income by the recipient partners or it would result in double taxation. However, if the cash distribution ever exceeds basis, the excess would be taxable.

175. **D.** Partnerships pay no tax! All tax is paid by the partners. Any answer choice that says a partnership pays tax is the wrong answer. If the question asked about basis, *both* taxable interest and tax-exempt interest would increase the partner basis.

176. **D.** Distributions of cash that exceed basis are taxable, whether liquidating or nonliquidating. Distributions of cash that are *not* in excess of basis are *not* taxable.

177. **B.** Corporations that wish to file as S corporations must make a timely election. Many small corporations file the S election (Form 2553) because S corporations get taxed like a partnership and thus avoid double taxation. All of the shareholders of the S corporation must consent to the election or it's not valid. If filed timely (two and a half months after incorporation date), the election reverts back to the first day of the year and there will be no double taxation for the entire year.

178. **B.** If the S election is made after March 15, it takes effect January 1 of the following year. If a corporation is formed in Year 2 and doesn't file an S election, it is taxed as a corporation and is subject to double taxation each year until it files an S election. If the C corporation is formed in Year 2 and decides in Year 5 to become an S corporation, the S election would have to be filed before March 15th of Year 5. If it's filed late, the election for S status would be effective January 1, Year 6.

179. **B.** All income, whether taxable or not, increases the basis of an S corporation stockholder.

$90,000 of income/2 stockholders = basis increase of $45,000 per stockholder

180. **D.** Since municipal bond interest is tax exempt, each shareholder will report a basis increase of $25,000 of the $50,000, even though none of the interest will be taxable. This is because all income earned by an S corporation or partnership increases basis, even tax-exempt income.

181. **D.** All income, even tax-exempt income, will increase basis:

Beginning basis	$60,000
Ordinary income	+ $30,000
Tax-exempt income	+ $5,000
Capital gains	+ $10,000
Cash distribution	− $20,000
Ending basis	$85,000

182. **D.** An S corporation is allowed a maximum of 100 shareholders—minimum of 1 shareholder, max of 100. Having 101 shareholders would lose the eligibility. An S corporation is allowed to have only one class of stock: common stock. If an S corporation adds preferred stock, it loses its eligibility for S status. S corporations cannot have preferred stock. Note: an S corporation can have both common stock with voting rights and common stock with no voting rights, because that is still considered one class.

183. **D.** In each of the three years, Bagel Bazaar, Inc., made distributions to the shareholders in excess of basis. Any distribution of cash in excess of basis would result in a capital gain to a shareholder.

184. **D.** Wilson's basis is $5,000, so none of the $3,500 distribution is taxable to Wilson. Only when cash distributed exceeds basis does the partner have a taxable situation. For example, if the distribution was over $5,500, the capital gain would be $500.

185. **B.** An S corporation shareholder's basis or amount "at risk" is reduced by distributions to the shareholders as well as loss or expense items. However, loss deductions are limited to a shareholder's adjusted basis in S corporation stock plus direct shareholder loans to the corporation. Any losses disallowed may be carried forward indefinitely and will be deductible as the shareholder's basis is increased. The total loss of $2,000 exceeds the amount "at risk," so only the amount "at risk" of $1,500 is deductible this year. The remaining $500 loss carries forward.

Beginning basis	$5,000
Less distribution of	− $3,500
Basis available	$1,500 (amount at risk)
	↓
Total loss	$2,000
Excess loss over amount at risk	$500

186. **A.** Wolfson shareholders report $5,000 ordinary income and $2,000 long-term capital gain. The cash distribution is not taxable. Taxing the cash distribution of $4,000 would result in double taxation. The $4,000 distribution is considered a distribution of profits, and the profits are being taxed once already.

10% of $50,000 is $5,000 ordinary income.
10% of $20,000 is $2,000 long-term capital gain.

187. **C.** An S corporation can take a tax deduction for ordinary business expenses, like compensation of officers. Charitable contributions and capital losses are not ordinary business deductions. Charitable contributions and capital losses pass through to the shareholders separately on the K-1 form the same way as for a partnership.

188. **C.** Dauber's ordinary income is calculated as follows:

Revenue	$44,000
Operating expenses	– $20,000
Ordinary income	$24,000

Note: the long-term capital loss and charitable contributions are not considered "ordinary" and would *not* affect ordinary income of an S corporation (or partnership).

189. **C.** Partnership tax returns have historically been due 3.5 months after year-end, April 15th, for a calendar-year partnership. A new law goes into effect in 2017 that will change the due date for a partnership tax return to be due one month earlier, March 15th, for a calendar-year partnership.

190. **B.** II is correct. An S corporation must adopt a calendar year. I is wrong. S corporations need only a minimum of one shareholder. Partnerships require a minimum of two owners; corporations require only one.

191. **B.** An S corporation is a pass-through entity. The S corporation pays no federal income tax. The ordinary income and long-term capital gains flow through to its shareholders. Any answer choice on the exam that says an S corporation or partnership pays federal taxes is the wrong answer.

192. **D.** To the extent that an S corporation has accumulated earnings and profits from its days as a C corporation, those earnings as a C corporation, $20,000, will be taxable as a dividend to shareholders when distributions exceed S corporation earnings and profits. Therefore:

Distributions	$110,000
S corporation earnings and profits, tax free	($80,000)
C corporation earnings and profits, taxable as a dividend	($20,000)
Excess distribution	$10,000

The excess distribution reduces basis in shareholders' stock. If it is in excess of basis, then it is capital gain.

193. **A.** I is correct. For a corporation to elect S corporation status, unanimous consent of all shareholders is required. If all shareholders approve, the corporation would then file Form 2553 with the IRS in order to elect S corporation status and be treated as a pass-through entity for tax purposes. II is wrong. *Revocation* of an S election does *not* require unanimous consent of shareholders. A revocation of S election may be filed by shareholders owning more than 50% of an S corporation's outstanding stock. If the S corporation has both common voting and nonvoting shares, for this purpose both voting and nonvoting shares are counted. It's not important how many shareholders consent—more important is how many shares they own. A majority of total S corporation shares is needed to vote in favor of revoking an S election. Therefore, unanimous consent is not required to revoke an S election.

194. **C.** The basis of an S corporation for a shareholder is increased by all income items, including tax-exempt income, and decreased by all loss and deduction items, including nondeductible expenses and distributions.

Beginning basis	$60,000
Ordinary income	+ $39,500
Municipal bond interest income	+ $10,000
Capital loss	– $17,000
Distribution	– $20,000
Ending basis	$72,500

195. **D.** If property is exchanged for voting stock and the owner winds up with 80% or more, the exchange is viewed for tax purposes in the same way as for a partnership. That is, the tax basis of the property is retained by both parties so that no taxable gain or loss is recognized.

196. A. When an owner transfers property to a corporation and winds up with 80% or more of the outstanding stock, the transfer is handled like a partnership rather than a corporation. That is, the tax basis is retained by both parties, and no income effect results. Hametz gave up two assets with a tax basis of $220,000 ($100,000 + $120,000). He keeps that original basis amount as his tax basis for his investment. The business picks up the equipment at the same tax basis of $100,000.

197. B. The general rule to incorporate is that property is transferred to the corporation at the same basis that previously existed, $40,000, if those who transferred the property came away with at least 80% of the new shares. Since Micki and Laura both transferred property in exchange for stock and together came away with more than 80% of the total shares, the incorporation is handled as a tax-free incorporation.

198. C. If those who transferred the property came away with at least 80% of the new shares, the basis in the stock is equal to the basis of the transferred asset, and there is no gain or loss. Since Micki and Laura both transferred property in exchange for stock and together came away with more than 80% of the total shares, the incorporation is handled as a tax-free incorporation. That is, the tax basis of the property is retained by both parties so that no taxable gain or loss is recognized. The only difference here is that Laura had debt relief of $10,000, so her basis in the stock is $40,000 less $10,000 debt relief = $30,000 basis.

199. A. If property is exchanged for voting stock and the owner winds up with 80% or more, the exchange is viewed for tax purposes as a tax-free incorporation. The tax basis of the property is retained by both parties so that no taxable gain or loss is recognized.

200. B. The corporation's basis in the building is the greater of the debt assumed, $10,000, or the net book value of the asset contributed, $40,000.

201. A. If property is exchanged for voting stock and the owner winds up with 80% or more, the tax basis of the property is retained by both parties so that no taxable gain or loss is recognized. The property is transferred to the corporation and retains the same basis that previously existed, $45,000. Micki's basis in the stock is $45,000.

202. A. If property is exchanged for voting stock and the owner winds up with 80% or more, the exchange is viewed for tax purposes in the same way as for a partnership. That is, the tax basis of the property is retained by both parties so that no taxable gain or loss is recognized. Micki's basis of $45,000 for the equipment rolls over into the corporation.

203. C. If property is exchanged for voting stock and the owner winds up with 80% or more, the exchange is viewed for tax purposes in the same way as for a partnership. That is, the tax basis of the property is retained by both parties so that no taxable gain or loss is recognized. Although Adrian did contribute property and so did Barry, *together they came home with only 70% of the stock of the new corporation.* As a result, the asset contributed by Adrian will be adjusted to the FMV, $45,000.

204. B. Adrian and Barry are the only transferors of *property* (Corey exchanged only services). Together, Adrian and Barry (who exchanged property) own less than 80% of the stock; therefore, Adrian is taxed on her built-in gain of $15,000. The transfer is treated as if Adrian sold the property to the corporation rather than transferred it. Adrian's gain is calculated as follows:

FMV of $45,000 – basis of $30,000 =
$15,000 gain to Adrian

205. A. Although Parker contributed no property, Broussard and Monti, who did contribute property, end up with 80% or more of the stock. So no gain is recognized by Monti, because the assets do *not* get raised to FMV.

206. C. Although Parker contributed no property, Broussard and Monti, who did contribute property, end up with 80% or more of the stock. So the assets basis simply rolls over into the newly formed corporation, and there is no gain or loss. Since the asset had a basis to Broussard of $5,000, Kenpo Corp. picks up the asset at $5,000.

207. B. For tax purposes, a company cannot anticipate its bad debts and can only recognize, for tax purposes, a bad debt expense when the account proves to be uncollectible. Ashbrook will recognize no bad expense for tax purposes in Year 1.

208. C. For tax purposes, a company cannot anticipate its bad debts and can only recognize, for tax purposes, a bad debt expense when the account proves to be uncollectible. Ashbrook will recognize a bad expense for tax purposes in Year 2 of $23,000.

209. A. Cash-basis taxpayers do not record bad debt expense. Since Fascination operates as a cash-basis taxpayer, it has not included any revenue for tax purposes, either for the original work that was done or the interest on the note. A bad debt can only be deducted to the extent that it was included in income. Bad debt expense is actually the removal of a previously recognized income that was never received. No income was recognized here, so no expense can be reported.

210. **C.** Warranties arise when there is a sale of products and the manufacturer gives a promise to fix product defects for a period of time. The manufacturer knows that they will incur some cost to repair and ship the panels. The amount is unknown at the time of sale. For financial reporting, both bad debt and warranty expenses are accrued based on estimations. For tax purposes, warranties can only be deducted when an actual cost is incurred. Since no panels broke in Year 1, there is no warranty expense for tax purposes.

211. **B.** For financial reporting, both bad debt and warranty expenses are accrued based on estimations. For tax purposes, warranties can only be deducted when an actual cost is incurred. Since no panels broke in Year 1, there is no warranty expense for tax purposes in Year 1. But in Year 2 the actual warranty cost incurred equals the deduction in the year the money is spent. The warranty expense for Year 2 is calculated as follows:

800 panels broke × $120 spent to fix each = $96,000

212. **A.** I is correct. Life insurance premiums paid by a corporation on behalf of employees are expensed in full for financial reporting regardless of who the beneficiary of the policy is. II is wrong. If a company pays insurance premiums to cover the lives of its employees, the deductibility of those expenses depends on the identity of the beneficiary. If the company is *not* the beneficiary (the employee can name the beneficiary), the cost is tax deductible to the corporation. If the corporation were the beneficiary of the policy, no corporate tax deduction would have been allowed. Life insurance settlements are tax free; the IRS would not allow a deduction for something that will never be taxable.

213. **A.** The starting point is book income of $200,000. The $5,000 for life insurance premiums was already expensed on the books and is also a tax deduction, also since the employee can name the beneficiary. Don't do anything with the $5,000. The warranty expense already deducted for book purposes of

$4,000 needs to be added back, and $10,000 actual warranty costs paid should be deducted.

$200,000 + $4,000 − $10,000 = $194,000 taxable income

214. **A.** The net capital loss of $3,000 is not deducted from the $100,000 of ordinary income in the current year. The $3,000 capital loss carryover can either be carried back three years or forward five years to reduce capital gains in those years. For corporations, all capital gains and losses are netted to a single gain or loss. Stocks may be sold at a gain and bonds at a loss, and it all nets out to one final figure. If that net figure is a gain, it is taxed at *ordinary income rules*. If the figure is a loss, no deduction is allowed in the current year. A corporation is not permitted to take a tax deduction in the current year for capital losses. Unlike for an individual, there is no $3,000 deduction for a corporation.

215. **B.** If a net capital loss results from all of the capital asset transactions of a corporation, that loss cannot be deducted in the current year. Instead, the net capital loss can be carried back for three years to reduce previous capital gains and then forward for five years.

216. **D.** The net capital gains of $2,500 are added to taxable income from operations of $56,000 to determine total taxable income of $58,500. There is no difference in the tax rates for capital gains, unlike an individual. Drake Corp. must first net its capital transactions together as follows: the net capital gain simply gets added to the ordinary income of $56,000.

Total capital gains of $10,000 ($7,500 short-term capital gain + $2,500 long-term capital gain) − capital losses of $7,500 ($5,000 short-term capital loss + $2,500 long-term capital loss) = $2,500 net capital gain

217. **B.** Taxable income remains at $66,000. Although there is a capital loss of $13,000 and a capital gain of $6,000 netting out to a loss of $7,000, that loss cannot be deducted in the current year. Instead, the $7,000 carries over as a short-term capital loss for a maximum of five years, which is available to reduce future capital gains.

218. **D.** Book income is $227,000. The long-term capital loss of $5,000 gets added back since, for tax purposes, the capital loss is *not* deductible in the current year against ordinary income. The $3,000 premium for key-person life insurance is also added back since the company is the beneficiary. When the company is the beneficiary of a key-person life

insurance policy, the company gets no deduction for the premium it pays for that insurance. Utility expense is deductible for both tax and book purposes; therefore, no reconciling adjustment needs to be made for it. Therefore, taxable income is computed as follows:

$227,000 + $5,000 + $3,000 = $235,000

219. C.

Start with book income	$480,000
Subtract municipal bond interest income	− $50,000
Add municipal bond interest expense	+ $2,000
Add back federal income tax provision	+ $170,000
Taxable income	$602,000

The rent expense of $5,000 is handled the same way for books and tax purposes, so no reconciling adjustment needs to be made for rent expense.

220. D. Start with book income of $240,000. Add back the $40,000 for federal income tax expense and the $25,000 for meals and entertainment since the tax code only allows a 50% deduction for meals and entertainment. The advertising expense is deductible for both book and tax purposes so no reconciling is adjustment needs to be made for the advertising expense. Therefore, Hampton Corp.'s taxable income can be computed as follows: $240,000 + $40,000 + $25,000 = $305,000.

221. C. I is correct. Interest incurred on loan to carry municipal bonds is included as a reconciling item on the Schedule M-1 because it's included in income on the books, but not on the corporate tax return. This is because municipal bond interest is tax free. II is correct. The provision for federal income tax is an expense for book purposes but is not deductible for tax purposes. An item is includable on the Schedule M-1 reconciliation only if it's handled differently for book and tax purposes.

222. D. An item only makes the M-1 reconciliation if it's treated differently for tax purposes and book purposes. Interest on US savings bonds is considered income for both books and taxes. State income tax is an expense on the books *and* a deduction for taxes. State income tax expense on the books is a tax deduction, but federal income tax expense on the books is not a tax deduction.

223. C. Legal and professional fees to file incorporation documents and state filing fees plus any other fees necessary to incorporate a business are deductible as organization costs. Stock issuance costs, printing of stock certificates, underwriter fees, and commissions to the broker are not deductible as organization costs.

224. A. Deductible organizational costs include the accounting fees of $3,000, the state incorporation fees of $7,500, and the legal fees of $3,500, for a total of $14,000. Of that $14,000, the first $5,000 can be deducted immediately (without being amortized), which will reduce the remaining amount to $9,000. The $9,000 can then be amortized over 180 months, $50 per month. In Year 6, the company began doing business on July 1, so multiply $50 × 6 months = $300 and add that to the immediate deduction of $5,000. Therefore, the total deduction in Year 6 for organization costs is $5,300. Note that the $2,000 to print the stock certificates and the $5,000 to sell the initial shares cannot be expensed. Instead of a deduction, they are a reduction in the capital stock account.

Immediate deduction of	$5,000
$9,000/180 months = $50 per month	
for 6 months	+ $300
Total deduction for organization costs	
in Year 6	$5,300

225. C. I is correct. The goodwill is referred to as a Section 197 cost. Even though not amortized for financial reporting purposes, goodwill should be written off over 15 years for tax purposes. When one company acquires another, some amount of the purchase price is usually assigned to goodwill (capital asset) or acquired intangible assets. Although goodwill is not expensed for financial statement purposes, for tax purposes these assets are amortized to expense over a 15-year period of time. II is correct. In Year 2, an expense of $20,000 can be deducted ($300,000/15 years).

226. D. Acquisitions of goodwill, trademarks, trade names, and covenants not to compete are amortized on a straight line basis for tax purposes over a 15-year life, or 180 months.

227. D. Business assets such as equipment, machinery, and buildings are known, in general, as Section 1231 assets. It is not the land itself that makes it a 1231 asset; it's what the land is being used for. Since the land is being used in the business right now, it's Section 1231. If the land was being held for long-term appreciation, then the land would be considered a capital asset. This is true for the shed as well. Classify assets as Section 1231 or capital assets based on what they are being used for.

228. **C.** Goodwill is a capital asset and for tax purposes is amortized over 180 months. Treasury stock is not an asset, so it could not possibly be a capital asset. Assets used in the business, such as is the case here in this question with the machinery and land, are Section 1231 assets, not capital assets.

229. **D.** I is wrong. Although land does not depreciate, if the land is being used in business, the land qualifies as a Section 1231 asset. Section 1231 assets tend to be fixed assets used in the production of ordinary income. II is wrong. Capital assets are *not* used in business to generate ordinary income. For a corporation, capital assets are investments in stocks and bonds.

230. **A.** A corporation will never recognize a gain or loss on the receipt of money or other property in exchange for its own stock.

231. **A.** In the assets first year, begin depreciating real estate as of the 15th of the month of purchase. This is called the mid-month convention. This mid-month adjustment is only for Year 1 and only for real estate depreciation. Since the building was bought May 1, depreciation starts May 15th and only 7.5 months of depreciation will be taken for the first year. In Year 2 and beyond, depreciate all 12 months using the straight line method. Depreciation for Year 2 would be $6,000. Remember not to depreciate the land.

$$\$304,000 - \$70,000 \text{ for the land} = \$234,000/$$
$$39 \text{ years} = \$6,000 \text{ depreciation per year}$$
$$(\$6,000 \text{ annual depreciation} \times 7.5 \text{ months})/$$
$$12 \text{ months} = \$3,750$$

232. **A.** In Year 2, a full year of depreciation is taken using the straight line method for real estate. Residential real estate is depreciated using a 27.5-year straight line. Only depreciate a partial year in the first year of real estate depreciation. Depreciation for Year 2 is equal to

$$\$225,000 - \$25,000 \text{ land} = \$200,000/27.5 \text{ years} =$$
$$\$7,273$$

233. **B.** While real estate is depreciated using the straight line method, personal property is depreciated using double declining balance. Five-year personal property such as computers would be depreciated 40% per year rather than 20% per year, since the double declining balance method is used rather than straight line. For personal property used for a partial year, the half-year convention is utilized in the first year. Do not subtract the salvage value. Two-fifths equals 200% of straight line, since straight line for

a 5-year life would be one-fifth. Autos, light trucks, and computers have a 5-year life for tax purposes; furniture, fixtures, and equipment have a 7-year life. Notice that management's expected useful life of 8 years is *not* used for tax depreciation purposes. For personal property: Year 1 depreciation equals $8,000, calculated as follows:

$$(\$40,000 \times 2)/5 = \$16,000 \times \text{half year} = \$8,000$$

234. **B.** The question asked about Year 2, but for personal property you have to calculate Year 1 depreciation first and then decline the balance. Remember to subtract the depreciation taken in the prior year from the carrying amount. Do *not* take half-year depreciation in the asset's second year.

Year 1 depreciation: ($40,000 × 2)/5 = $16,000 × half year = $8,000
Year 2 depreciation: $40,000 − $8,000 = $32,000; ($32,000 × 2)/5 = $12,800 in depreciation for Year 2

235. **A.** For personal property used for a partial year, the half-year convention is utilized in the first year.

Year 1 equals $8,000 of depreciation
Year 2 $40,000 − $8,000 = $32,000; ($32,000 × 2)/5 = $12,800
Year 3 $32,000 − $12,800 = $19,200; ($19,200 × 2)/5 = $7,680

236. **D.** According to the rules of MACRS, personal property is treated as placed in service or disposed of at the midpoint of the taxable year, resulting in a half year of depreciation for the year in which the property is placed in service or disposed of by the company.

237. **D.** The allowable depreciation deduction taken in Year 3 for a commercial building that was placed in service in Year 1 is based on calculating the asset's depreciable basis over 39 years. A is wrong. A 27.5-year straight line is used to depreciate residential rental property. B and C are wrong. For real estate depreciation, the adjustment for midmonth depreciation is done only in the year of purchase, Year 1, and does *not* affect the amount of depreciation for future years.

238. **D.** Real estate does *not* qualify for Section 179 deduction. To encourage the growth of smaller companies, the tax laws provide for the immediate expensing of the cost of tangible personal property used in a business as well as off-the-shelf computer software (as long as it has a life of more than one year). Real property (such as land and buildings) does

not qualify. Because this deduction is for smaller companies, the amount of the expense is limited. That number has changed numerous times over the years. However, if the company buys a significant amount of such assets, the immediate expense deduction begins to be lost dollar for dollar after a limit is reached.

239. **B.** The truck is a depreciable asset used in a trade or business. Therefore, it qualifies as a Section 1231 asset. A truck qualifies as personal property (not real property), so the recapture rules of Section 1245 will apply to any gains. The truck was sold for a gain of $5,000, but the gain ($11,000 less basis of $6,000) is less than the accumulated depreciation taken of $14,000. Under the Section 1245 rules of depreciation recapture, the gain is all recaptured as ordinary income. Had the gain been greater than the accumulated depreciation taken, the excess gain over and above accumulated depreciation would have been a Section 1245 gain.

240. **B.** In an attempt to avoid triple taxation for corporations, there is a unique deduction that involves no outlay of expenditure. This is called the DRD. To determine the DRD, the first step is to determine the taxable income before the DRD, sometimes referred to as the base amount:

Gross business income	$160,000
Dividend income	+ $100,000
Total income	$260,000
↓	
Less operating expenses of	− $170,000
Taxable income before DRD	$90,000

The actual DRD is the lesser of 80% of the DRD: (1) dividends received of $100,000, or (2) taxable income of 90,000. Therefore, the DRD is 80% of the $90,000, or $72,000, for Year 1. The DRD is 80% of the dividends if less than 80%, but at least 20% of the stock is owned. The DRD is 70% of the dividends if less than 20% of the stock is owned. The DRD is 100% if 80% or more of the stock is owned. When 80% or more is owned, the companies are viewed as an affiliated group.

241. **D.** Prior to the dividends received deduction (DRD), the company has a tentative taxable income of $40,000. The DRD for a 17% ownership is 70%. The DRD is 70% of the dividends collected, unless the income before the deduction is lower than the dividends received. Here, the $40,000 tentative taxable income is less than the $50,000 in dividends. So the DRD is $28,000 (70% of

$40,000), which reduces the income from $40,000 down to $12,000. The tentative taxable income and DRD are calculated as follows:

Sales revenue	$380,000
Add dividend income	+ $50,000
Less operating expenses	− $390,000
Taxable income before DRD	$40,000
↓	
70% of dividends received	− $28,000
Taxable income	$12,000

242. **B.** Subchapter C corporations can deduct the amount donated up to 10% of the total of all revenues less all ordinary and necessary expenses. The DRD is not an ordinary and necessary expense, so it gets added back before the charitable contribution is computed. To determine the allowable charitable deduction, the base amount must be determined. The base is taxable income, without regard to the charitable contribution itself and the DRD. The contributions available for use total $90,000. This comprises the current-year contribution of $80,000 plus the carryover of $10,000. Since $86,000 is the limit for contributions, $4,000 gets carried forward for five years. The $86,000 contribution limit is calculated as follows:

Taxable income	$820,000
Add DRD	+ 40,000
Base amount for charitable contribution deduction	$860,000
↓	
Multiply by 10% of the base amount ($860,000)	$86,000

243. **C.** The contributions available for deduction total $45,000. This comprises the current year contribution of $40,000 plus the carryover contributions of $5,000. To determine the allowable portion, the base amount must be determined. The base is equal to taxable income, without regard to the charitable contributions, plus the DRD.

$410,000 + $20,000 = $430,000 (Base amount)
10% of $430,000 = $43,000

244. **B.** In order for a gift to qualify for a deduction, the gift must be to a recognized charity. Thus, the $20,000 given to directly needy families (and not to a recognized charity) after a hurricane disaster, does not qualify. The $10,000 given to recognized charities does qualify as a charitable contribution.

Additionally, a contribution authorized to be paid to a recognized charity by a board of directors in one year, which will be paid within two and a half months subsequent there to and in the following year, is deductible in the year of authorization. Since Christie Corp. is an accrual-based taxpayer, and the authorization of the contribution payment was made by the board of directors within two and a half months of the payment date (i.e. authorization made on December 1, Year 4, payment made on February 1, Year 5), the $30,000 qualifies for deduction in Year 4. Christie can, therefore, take a $40,000 charitable contribution deduction in Year 4 ($10,000 + $30,000), since that amount falls below the 10% of taxable income limitation of $41,900 (i.e., $419,000 × 10% = $41,900).

245. B. II is correct. A subsidiary may have one or more attractive tax attributes. Tax attributes refer to a company's ability to use a tax deduction simply because they are entitled to it from a previous year, such as a charitable contributions carryover or a capital loss carryover. These tax attributes make a company more attractive to a parent company looking to save taxes. A parent company can file a consolidated tax return with the subsidiary who has these tax attributes and save money. Operating losses of one subsidiary could reduce the profits of another subsidiary. I is wrong. A parent must own 80% or more of the subsidiary to file a consolidated tax return, but the decision to file consolidated is always optional.

246. D. I is correct. The accumulated earnings tax is a penalty for not paying enough dividends. The IRS assesses this tax because double taxation is avoided. An alternative to paying the accumulated earnings tax is for the corporation to pay the dividends late, by March 15th, the date the tax return is due for a calendar-year corporation. If a calendar-year C corporation pays the dividends to the shareholders but pays them after the end of the year, that would avoid the accumulated earnings tax. II is correct. The accumulated earnings tax is a penalty for not paying enough dividends. Once again, the IRS assesses this tax because double taxation is avoided. Another alternative to paying the accumulated earnings tax is "consent dividends." Consent dividends involve the corporation not actually paying the dividend but the stockholder consenting to paying the tax on the dividend. In a small C corporation, the individual taxpayers may consent to the dividends because the individual tax on the dividends is lower than the accumulated earnings tax. III is correct. The accumulated earnings tax is a penalty for not paying enough dividends. The IRS assesses this tax

because double taxation is avoided. Accumulated earnings tax is based on the amount of the corporation's accumulated (retained) earnings that is in excess of the "reasonable needs" of the business. The primary way for a corporation to avoid the accumulated earnings tax is to pay enough dividends to shareholders. A corporation is allowed to argue that they reasonably need the earnings to grow; thus the term *reasonable needs argument*. The accumulated earnings tax can be imposed on C corporations regardless of the number of shareholders. An S corporation or partnership would never be subject to the accumulated earnings tax, since those entities pay no tax and there is no double taxation to worry about. Note that even a publicly traded company can be hit with the accumulated earnings tax. The IRS would send a letter.

247. D. Small C corporations that do not pay sufficient dividends can be liable for the personal holding company tax. A is wrong. Personal holding companies are based on a stock ownership test. For example, if there are only a few owners, five or less owners hold half or more of the stock at any time in the last half of the year; this would be evidence of a personal holding company. B is wrong. If a company makes distributions in excess of earnings, no penalty (no personal holding company tax) will be paid. The whole idea of the personal holding company tax and the accumulated earnings tax is to compel C corporations to pay sufficient dividends to force double taxation upon the corporate entity and its shareholders. C is wrong. Corporations cannot get hit with both the accumulated earnings tax and the personal holding company tax in the same year.

248. A. The accumulated earnings tax can be imposed on C corporations regardless of the number of shareholders. B is wrong. The personal holding company tax, like the accumulated earnings tax, is imposed on C corporations to compel them to pay sufficient dividends. If distributions are paid in excess of earnings, then it's clear that sufficient dividends have been paid so no personal holding company tax or accumulated earnings tax would be imposed. C is wrong. A company is not subject to both the personal holding company tax and the accumulated earnings tax, but it can be subject to one or the other. D is wrong, because partnerships do not pay tax.

249. C. I is correct. Adjustments used in the corporate AMT computation include removing the benefit of using the installment sales method for inventory sales. II is correct. Adjustments used in the corporate AMT computation include removing the benefit of using the completed contract method for construction contracts. As with individual taxpayers, corporations have to compute their AMT and pay any amount in excess of the regular income tax. The AMT is designed to prevent taxpayers from receiving too much benefit from specific tax breaks. The computation is similar but not identical to that of an individual taxpayer.

250. **A.** Municipal bond interest income from private activity bonds is an AMT preference item. B is wrong. The 80% dividends received deduction is not added back at all for AMT. C is wrong. Although the 70% dividends received deduction is added back for AMT, the 70% dividends received deduction is called an AMT adjusted current earnings (ACE) adjustment, not an AMT preference item. The ACE adjustments are a third round of add-backs that only corporations have to worry about for AMT. Individuals have to add back only adjustments and preference items, but corporations have to add back the ACE adjustment as well.

251. **B.** II is correct. If a state or local government issues a bond for a "private activity" like an airport, a stadium, a bridge, or tunnel, the government must apply the proceeds to that activity. This is known as a *private activity bond*. The interest income from the bond is tax free to the investor for regular tax purposes. *But* for AMT, the interest income is a tax preference item and added back to arrive at alternative minimum taxable income, prior to another round of add-backs known as the ACE adjustment. I is wrong. If a state or local government issues a bond and the government can do whatever it chooses with the money raised, that bond is considered a *general obligation bond*. The interest income from general obligation municipal bonds is tax free to the investor for regular tax purposes and is *not* a tax preference item for corporate AMT.

252. **A.** In computing the AMT for a corporation, municipal bond interest that is from private activity bonds is converted from tax exempt to taxable. Interest income from private activity bonds issued by a state or local government is considered a tax preference item for AMT. B and D are both wrong, since not all of municipal bond interest and not all of life insurance proceeds are added back in this same determination. There is a big difference between investing in private activity bonds and investing general obligation bonds. For AMT, 100% of the private activity bond interest income is an

AMT preference item. Besides AMT adjustments and AMT preference items, there is another round of AMT add-backs for corporations, known as the ACE adjustment. If the municipal bond interest is from investing in general obligation bonds, only a percentage of the interest income, *not all*, of the general obligation bond interest is added back for the ACE adjustment. Note: general obligation bond interest income is *not* a tax preference item, although a percentage is added back for the ACE adjustment. C is wrong. Only relatively small companies receive an exemption for AMT, because the AMT exemption phases out as income gets to a certain level.

253. **B.** I is correct. Interest income from general obligation municipal bonds is part of the ACE adjustment for corporate AMT. 75% of the benefit of having general obligation bonds is removed. The net effect is that much of the interest income from general obligation bonds becomes taxable, not for regular tax but for AMT. II is correct. Life insurance proceeds received by a corporation upon the death of the officer are not taxable for regular corporate income tax. However, the ACE adjustment adds back 75% of the proceeds from the death benefit. The result of the ACE adjustment is that only 25% of the death benefit is tax free for AMT. III is correct. The 70% DRD is part of the ACE adjustment. This means that 75% of the benefit of the DRD is lost due to the ACE adjustment. Only 25% of the DRD survives the AMT ACE adjustment. Note: although much of the benefit of the 70% DRD is lost to the ACE adjustment, the 80% DRD is not added back to the ACE adjustment. After the adjustments and preference items, the ACE adjustment is another series of add-backs designed to make corporations pay more tax. The ACE adjustment is not for individual taxpayers but for only corporations. The ACE adjustment removes 75% of the benefit of certain tax advantages, such as municipal bond interest on general obligation bonds, life insurance proceeds received by the corporation upon the death of an officer, and the 70% DRD.

254. **D.** III is correct. If a corporation has five or fewer shareholders at any time during the last six months of the year, the corporation may be subject to the personal holding company tax. Therefore, the number of shareholders is a factor in determining whether the corporation is subject to the personal holding company tax. I is wrong. The number of shareholders in a corporation is *not* a factor in determining whether a corporation is subject to

the AMT. While the number of shareholders is not a factor, a corporation would *not* be subject to the AMT in the first year of corporate existence. II is wrong. The number of shareholders in a corporation is *not* a factor in determining whether a corporation is subject to the accumulated earnings tax.

255. **D.** I is correct. C corporations are subject to the AMT ACE adjustment. The ACE adjustment results in a C corporation having to pay additional tax through the loss of 75% of common tax breaks. II is wrong. S corporations are not subject to AMT at all, since S corporations are pass-through entities that do not pay any tax. S corporations are not subject to corporate tax rules. Any answer choice that says that S corporations pay income tax is the wrong answer choice. III is wrong. Individuals are subject to the AMT but not the ACE adjustment. The ACE adjustment is only for C corporations. IV is wrong. Partnerships are not subject to AMT at all, since partnerships are pass-through entities that do not pay any tax. Any answer choice that says partnerships pay tax is the wrong answer choice.

256. **B.** Under Section 1244, a single taxpayer can deduct as an ordinary loss $50,000 per year and an additional $3,000 per year as a capital loss. The ordinary loss would go on other gains and losses, Form 4797. The excess would be reported on Schedule D capital gains and losses $3,000. Since Lemoi had no other capital gains, the limit for the capital loss deduction is $3,000 per year.

257. **C.** The entire $60,000 would be claimed as an ordinary loss in Year 7. Although the limit for Section 1244 loss for a single individual is $50,000 ordinary loss plus $3,000 capital loss, the limit for a married couple is $100,000 ordinary loss plus $3,000 capital loss.

258. **B.** If a stockholder sells Section 1244 stock over a two-year period, rather than all in one year, the deductible Section 1244 loss is $100,000 per year, not per security, which allows for far more than $100,000 total ordinary loss. Thus, sufficient stock can be sold in one year to obtain all ordinary loss, and then more can be sold the following year. In Year 5, $100,000 is the ordinary loss limit and then $3,000 capital loss—total of $103,000. The $7,000 carries over as a capital loss, not an ordinary loss.

259. **D.** If a stockholder sells Section 1244 stock over a two-year period, rather than all in one year, the deductible Section 1244 ordinary loss is $100,000 per year, not per security, which allows for far more than $100,000 total ordinary loss. Thus, sufficient

stock can be sold in one year to obtain all ordinary loss, and then more can be sold the following year. In this situation, $35,000 would qualify as an ordinary loss plus $3,000 capital loss.

260. **D.** Since Aquilino did not sell any Section 1244 stock in Year 7, his total loss is limited to a $3,000 capital loss, which carried over from Years 5 and 6.

261. **A.** Ordinary loss treatment is not available if the shareholder sustaining the loss was not the original holder of the stock. An individual who acquires by purchase, gift, or inheritance is not entitled to ordinary loss treatment; therefore, Junior cannot deduct any ordinary loss. The stock must have been issued in exchange for money or other property, and the stock must have been issued to the individual sustaining the loss.

262. **C.** I is correct. C corporations can choose calendar year or fiscal year. III is correct. Partnerships are generally on a calendar year, but partnerships may choose a fiscal year. II is wrong. S corporations must operate on a calendar year.

263. **C.** A trust must file Form 1041 by April 15th if it has any taxable income for the year or gross income of $600 or more for the year. A simple trust may report on the cash or accrual method. A trust may make estimated tax payments like individuals do. A trust must use the calendar year, and a trust is subject to the AMT.

264. **C.** The grantor creates the trust. A trust begins when a grantor conveys assets to a trustee to manage for the benefit of a third party, known as a beneficiary.

265. **A.** I is correct. The trustee has the power to sell trust property. A trustee is a fiduciary who has the duty to manage the trust and carry out the trust purpose according to its terms. III is correct. The trustee has the power to pay trust expenses. The trustee must use his or her own skill, prudence, and judgment as a reasonable person would in making trust decisions and must abide by the trust instrument. II is wrong. The trustee does not have the implied power to borrow from the trust. Trustees may not profit personally from the role as trustee other than to receive whatever compensation is called for. Trustees cannot comingle personal assets with that of the trust.

266. **B.** II is correct because stock dividends represent additional shares and would remain with the trust. The general rule is that proceeds from the sale of trust assets along with extraordinary expenses are charged to the trust itself. I is wrong. Cash dividends

are generally allocated to the income beneficiaries. The question asked which would be charged to the trust principal, and cash dividends are ordinary income items and would be available for distribution to the income beneficiaries. Cash dividends, interest, and rents are generally given to the income beneficiaries to spend as they see fit.

267. **C.** Stock dividends of $6,000 and proceeds from the sale of trust property of $7,000 for a total of $13,000 remain with the trust and are not distributed to the beneficiary. The rent income of $1,000 and the interest income of $3,000 are considered ordinary income and would be given to the income beneficiaries, unless the trust instrument specified otherwise.

268. **B.** When the grantor of the trust retains the beneficial enjoyment or substantial control over the trust property or income, the grantor is taxed on the trust income. The trust is disregarded for income tax purposes. The grantor is taxed on the income if he or she retains (1) the beneficial enjoyment of the corpus or (2) the power to dispose of the trust income without the approval or consent of any adverse party.

269. **C.** Someone making a will is known as a testator. Dying without a will is considered dying intestate (not interstate). State laws determine priority of someone who dies without a will after these general rules:

Priority	Family members
First	spouse
Second	children (if no living spouse)
Third	parents (if no living spouse or kids)
Fourth	siblings (if no living spouse, kids, or parents)

270. **C.** I is correct. A trust that begins upon the creator's death is known as a testamentary trust. A trust that begins while the creator is still alive is known as an inter vivos trust. II is correct. Assets held in trust are known as trust corpus or trust res.

271. **A.** I is correct. A complex trust is allowed to distribute less than its current earnings for the year, distribute more than its current earnings for the year, and make charitable contributions. II is wrong. A simple trust must distribute all of its current earnings to the beneficiary. A simple trust cannot distribute principal; therefore, a simple trust cannot distribute in excess of earnings or it would be effectively distributing principal. Complex trusts are subject to basically similar tax rules as simple trusts, except a complex trust is allowed only a $100 exemption, not

$300 as in a simple trust. No personal exemption is allowed on a final return of a simple or complex trust, and both simple and complex trusts must use calendar years.

272. **C.** A simple trust has an exemption of $300. Note: there is no standard deduction for a trust. Only an individual who does not qualify to itemize gets a standard deduction.

273. **A.** I is correct. If a simple trust properly distributes all its income for a year, the simple trust will pay no tax for that year. II is correct. A simple trust receives an exemption of $300, but no exemption is allowed on the final return of a simple trust. III is wrong. A trust must use a calendar year.

274. **C.** For an estate, the income distribution deduction equals the lesser of the actual distribution to the beneficiary or DNI. The DNI fixes the limit on the deduction allowed on the estate income tax return.

275. **C.** If property is co-owned by husband and wife, one-half of its value is automatically included in the deceased spouse's estate regardless of whose funds were used to purchase the property.

276. **B.** The amount of income an estate beneficiary reports from the estate is limited by the estate's distributable net income, $4,000 in this case. Therefore, the beneficiary is taxed on $4,000. Although the estate distributed $10,000 to the beneficiary, $4,000 (DNI) is taxed to the beneficiary and the estate will have no taxable income to report. The $6,000 ($10,000 − $4,000) that the beneficiary received in cash over the amount of taxable income is treated as a nontaxable distribution of principal.

277. **A.** Computing the taxable amount of Castellano's estate (when the tax-free exclusion is ignored) begins with its asset FMV of $2 million:

$2,000,000	
− $400,000	liabilities
− $30,000	funeral expenses
− $290,000	charitable bequests
− $400,000	amount given to spouse
$880,000	taxable amount of Castellano's estate

278. **B.** A gift to a child would not qualify as a deduction in arriving at the taxable estate. To determine the amount of a taxable estate, certain deductions are allowed for costs, such as funeral expenses, debts, administrative expenses, debts at death, and charitable bequests. Bequests to a spouse are deductible,

but no other personal bequests (even to a son or daughter) can be used as a deduction.

279. **D.** In determining the amount of a taxable estate, certain deductions are allowed for costs, such as funeral expenses, debts, administrative expenses, bequests to a spouse, and charitable bequests. There is no limitation to the amount that can be deducted because of a bequest to a spouse.

280. **A.** Form 706 is due nine months after death if no extension is filed. An estate may use a calendar year or any fiscal year, and estimated taxes are not required for the first two years. After the first two years, estimated taxes are required.

281. **C.** I is correct. Estates may adopt a fiscal year or calendar year.

    II is correct. Estates are required to pay estimated income tax if any tax is due on income earned by estate assets. However, an estate is exempt from paying estimated taxes for the first two years.

282. **B.** The threshold for filing a fiduciary return of an estate is the amount of the estate personal exemption of $600.

283. **B.** II is correct. Unpaid income taxes would be a liability of the estate, so it would be deductible by the gross estate to arrive at the taxable estate. I is wrong. The federal estate tax is *not* a deduction from the gross estate to arrive at the taxable estate. State inheritance taxes are deductible from the gross estate, but federal inheritance taxes are not.

Chapter 41: Other Taxation Areas

284. **B.** II is correct. This concept is known as backup withholding, and the purpose is to compel customers to provide their social security number to a financial institution when opening a new brokerage or bank account. The banks will withhold 31% of the portfolio income every year until Mac provides his social security number. Without the social security number, the Internal Revenue Service (IRS) is unable to tax the investment income. The bank or brokerage house is required to send the IRS a matching 1099 to report the income and is unable to do so without knowing the social security number of the investor. I is incorrect. Mac will *not* be limited to $500 of the portfolio income. Mac will be subject to backup withholding at the rate of 31%, until he furnishes a tax identification number or social security number to the brokerage firm.

285. **C.** I is correct. Repackaging costs are among costs required to be capitalized for companies subject to uniform capitalization. For those companies, other costs that require capitalization include direct materials, direct labor, and applicable indirect costs. Applicable indirect costs required to be capitalized under uniform capitalization include utilities, warehousing costs, repairs, maintenance, indirect labor, rents, storage, depreciation and amortization, insurance, pension contributions, engineering and design, spoilage and scrap, and administrative supplies. Only when sold are the items allowed to be expensed. II is wrong. Although Stefano, Inc., is subject to uniform capitalization rules, research costs are expensed and are not part of uniform capitalization. III is wrong. Although Stefano Inc., is subject to uniform capitalization rules, advertising and marketing expenses are expensed and not capitalized. The uniform capitalization rules do not apply to inventory acquired for resale if the taxpayer's average gross receipts for the preceding three tax years are less than $10,000,000. Even for a company that must comply with uniform capitalization rules, costs that are not required to be capitalized include selling, advertising and marketing expenses, certain general and administrative expenses, research, and officer compensation not attributed to production services.

286. **C.** I is correct. A company subject to uniform capitalization rules would still be able to expense officers' compensation that is *not* attributed to production. II is correct. Service companies, like accounting and law firms, are *not* subject to uniform capitalization rules. Companies would be subject to uniform capitalization if their average sales of inventory exceed $10,000,000 over a three-year period.

287. **B.** To avoid penalties, if a taxpayer owes $1,000 or more in tax payments beyond withholdings, that taxpayer will need to have paid in taxes the lesser of the following: 90% of the current year's tax ($50,000 × 90%) = $45,000, or 100% of the previous year's tax ($40,000 × 100%) = $40,000. However, if the taxpayer had an AGI in excess of $150,000 in the prior year, 110% of the prior year's tax liability is used to compute the safe harbor for estimated payments. (Previous year's tax $40,000 × 110% = $44,000.) A is wrong. $40,000 is 100% of last year's tax. This would be sufficient if the previous year's income were $150,000 or less. C is wrong. $45,000 is 90% of this year's tax, which is sufficient, but the question

is looking for the minimum amount. D is wrong. $50,000 is 100% of the current year's tax, which is sufficient, but more than required. The question asked for the minimum that would *not* result in a penalty: $44,000 is the minimum.

288. **C.** Because taxable income is in excess of $1,000,000, Selzer cannot use its tax for the preceding year as a safe estimate. To avoid a penalty, a corporation must pay estimated tax payments each quarter. If a company will have a taxable income of over $1 million, estimated tax payments must be based on estimated income for the *current year*; if taxable income is less than $1 million, then estimates can be based on the prior year. Note: the prior year cannot serve as the basis if the company had no tax liability in the prior year.

289. **C.** I is correct. C corporations must pay estimated tax each quarter. For Year 4, the payments due for a C corporation's estimated taxes are due April 15, June 15th, September 15th, and December 15th. The fourth installment for a corporation in Year 4 is due December 15, Year 4. II is wrong. Individuals get the holidays off; their final estimated tax payment for Year 4 is not due until January 15 of Year 5. For individuals, the first three estimated payments for Year 4 are due April 15th, June 15th, and September 15th. The final installment for Year 4 is due January 15th of Year 5. In this way, the IRS expects a self-employed taxpayer to have all Year 4 taxes paid by January 15th of Year 5. So when the taxpayer files his Year 4 1040 return, the taxes should have already been paid. Employee taxpayers don't pay estimated taxes, because most of their tax gets paid through a withholding each pay period. III is wrong. S corporations do not pay federal income taxes; therefore, they do not pay estimated taxes.

290. **B.** The general rule is that the statute of limitations runs for three years from the time the statute begins. The question is, when does the statute begin? The statute of limitations for individual tax returns begins to run from the due date of the return, if it is filed on or before the due date, April 15th. Since Quirk filed before the due date (March 12, Year 2), the statute of limitations begins on April 15th, Year 2, and expires on April 15th, Year 5. If the taxpayer files one or more extensions and files the return after the due date, the statute of limitations begins on the filing date.

291. **A.** The three-year statute of limitations is extended to six years if there is a substantial understatement of gross income. If *gross* income is underreported by 25% or more, the three-year rule is extended to six years. Gross income represents $436,000 × 0.25 = $109,000.

292. **A.** Since there was no fraud or substantial underpayment of gross income in excess of 25%, the three-year statute applies. Statute of limitations would begin April 15th if you file early or by the due date. Only if you file after April 15th does the statute begin on the date you file.

293. **B.** According to IRS Circular 230, a tax preparer is charged a $50 penalty for failing to keep a copy of prepared returns for three years. The penalty is $50 for each tax return copy not maintained, up to a maximum of $25,000. Keeping a listing of just the name and ID number of each taxpayer for whom the preparer prepared a return is an adequate substitute for keeping a completed copy of the return. Other tax preparer penalties tested on the CPA exam include:

$50 preparer penalty for failure to sign the client's tax return

$50 preparer penalty for failure to report the tax preparer's identification number (PTIN) on the return

$50 preparer penalty for failure to give the taxpayer a completed copy of the return

294. **D.** I is correct. A practitioner must return all client records at the request of the client; a dispute over fees does *not* relieve the practitioner of the responsibility to return the client's records. II is correct. A contingent fee is allowed in connection with the filing of a client's *amended* tax return but not when filing an original tax return. III is correct. A paid preparer is required to sign a tax return and include his or her PTIN on the client's return. A PTIN is a number that identifies the preparer, much like a social security number. In the past, paid preparers were allowed to include either their PTIN or social security number on the client's return. With Circular 230, only the PTIN is allowed.

295. **B.** II is correct. If new legislation will have an impact on tax advice previously given, a practitioner has no obligation to advise the client of the new legislation even if the original advice was given in writing. III is correct. According to Circular 230, a tax return preparer is *not* permitted to endorse a taxpayer's

refund check. I is incorrect because the statement is not entirely correct. When considering whether to give oral or written advice to a client, a CPA should consider the tax sophistication of the client but *not* whether the client will seek a second opinion.

296. **A.** I is correct. According to Circular 230, registered tax return preparers may represent taxpayers before the IRS. II is correct. According to Circular 230, attorneys may represent taxpayers before the IRS. III is correct. According to Circular 230, CPAs as well as enrolled agents may represent taxpayers before the IRS.

297. **D.** From least likely to be upheld to most likely, if a preparer thinks that there is at least a 20% chance of an uncertain tax position being upheld, this is the standard known as reasonable basis. If the preparer thinks that there is at least a 1 in 3 chance to being upheld to a 50% chance of being upheld, this would be described as substantial authority for the position. Finally, if a tax preparer feels that there is more than a 50% chance of being upheld, the standard is described as more likely than not that the uncertain position will be upheld.

298. **A.** I is correct. The State Board of Accountancy is the party that ultimately grants a successful CPA candidate a license to practice public accounting. II is wrong. The State Board of Accountancy is also the party with the power to suspend and revoke a CPA's license to practice. The state board must provide due process of law before revoking a license. The state board may conduct a formal hearing regarding the licensee. If the state board determines, by preponderance of the evidence, that the CPA's actions constituted professional misconduct, the license may be suspended. The decisions made by the State Board of Accountancy may be reviewed by the courts. Notice that the state board doesn't have to prove guilt beyond a reasonable doubt to revoke or suspend a license. It only needs to establish guilt by preponderance of the evidence.

299. **D.** I is wrong. The CPA has no right or obligation to contact the prior CPA without client permission. II is wrong. The CPA should notify the client concerning the noncompliance and recommend the proper course of action to the client. The CPA is not allowed to contact the IRS without the client's permission. Upon discovery of an error in a previously filed return involving the client's failure to file a required return, the CPA should promptly notify the client (either orally or in writing) of the error, noncompliance, or omission and advise the

client of the appropriate measures to be taken. In this case the CPA should advise the client to correct the error in the previously filed return. If the client does *not* correct the error, the CPA should consider withdrawing from the engagement.

300. **D.** When a tax preparer signs a taxpayer's return, the tax preparer's declaration on the tax return indicates that the information contained therein is true, correct, and complete to the best of the preparer's knowledge and belief. In this case, the tax preparer knowingly deducted nonbusiness expenses on a business return and will be subject to a penalty possibly as high as $1,000.

301. **A.** I is correct. If the tax preparer relied on the advice of an advisory preparer to calculate the taxpayer's tax liability and the tax preparer believed that the advisory preparer was competent and that the advice was reasonable, the IRS would examine the facts further to determine if a penalty applies, since the result was an understated income tax liability. II is wrong. Under Circular 230, there is an automatic penalty assessed if a tax preparer endorses and negotiates the client's refund check. The IRS would *not* have to examine the facts further, because the penalty automatically applies. There is no good faith exception to this rule. III is wrong. There is no penalty for revealing confidential client information during a peer review by the state society quality control team. While it's likely that confidential client information would be exposed, the IRS would *not* have to examine the facts further to see whether the good faith exception applies, because revealing client information is expected and appropriate in order to comply with peer review regulations. Tax preparer penalties may be assessed for improper use or disclosure of confidential client information. Acceptable circumstances for disclosure include peer review and also in response to a court order.

302. **A.** The installment method is used rather than the accrual method when collection is in doubt. Under the installment sales method, the profit from the sale must be recognized proportionally as the cash is collected. The key to applying the installment sales method correctly is the determination of the gross profit and the gross profit percentage. Using the installment method, the first step is to calculate the dollar amount of gross profit from the sale. The sale price of $20,000 less the $15,000 cost equals the gross profit of $5,000. The second step is to determine the gross profit percentage from the sale. The gross profit percentage is the gross profit on the

sale divided by the sales price. The third step is to multiply the cash collection times the gross profit percentage.

Step 1: gross profit from sale: $20,000 − $15,000 = $5,000 gross profit

Step 2: gross profit percentage from sale: $5,000/$20,000 sales price = 25%

Step 3: realized gross profit: cash collected $8,000 × 25% = $2,000

303. **D.** The gross profit is $480,000 ($1,200,000 − $720,000). Thus the gross profit percentage is 40% ($480,000/$1,200,000). The company still has $700,000 in receivables from the installment sales ($1,200,000 − collections of $500,000). Of that amount, 40% represents the gross profit that will not be recognized until the cash is collected. Deferred gross profit is $280,000 ($700,000 × 40%). Note: at any point in time, the deferred gross profit is the accounts receivable balance multiplied by the gross profit percentage. Deferred gross profit equals the amount not yet collected times the gross profit percentage. The first two steps to determine the deferred gross profit are the same as to calculate the realized gross profit.

Step 1: gross profit from sale is $1,200,000 − $720,000 = $480,000

Step 2: gross profit percentage: $480,000/$1,200,000 = 40% gross profit

Step 3: deferred gross profit: $700,000 × 40% = $280,000

304. **A.** The cost recovery method does not recognize profit until the entire cost of goods sold has been collected. In Year 1, $500 of cost of goods sold is yet to be collected, so no profit is recognized until Year 2. The cost recovery method is used if there is significant uncertainty about collection. When the cost recovery method is used, all profit is initially recorded as a deferred gross profit. Under the cost recovery method, no profit at all is recognized until *cash equal to the cost of the asset sold is collected.* After that point, each dollar collected is viewed as being equal to a dollar of profit. In Year 1 only $2,000 was collected, and that is not enough to equal the cost of goods sold amount of $2,500. Therefore, in Year 2 when $3,000 more is collected, the first $500 from Year 2 is still recovering cost. At that point enough cash has been collected to equal the cost of goods sold. Therefore, the remainder of cash collected in Year 2, $2,500, is recognized as profit.

305. **B.** The percentage of completion method involves three steps in order to determine profit recognition on a long-term contract. Step 1 involves estimating costs. For Year 1, dividing the $240,000 costs incurred to date by $600,000 total estimated costs means 40% of the project is estimated to be completed at the end of Year 1. Step 2 involves using that estimate of completion percentage to determine profit recognized to date. Since 40% of the project is estimated to be complete at the end of Year 1, 40% is multiplied by the $400,000 estimated total profit. Therefore, estimated total profit at the end of Year 1 equals $160,000. Step 3 involves subtracting any profit recognized in prior years under this contract. Since this is the first year, there is nothing to subtract and only the first two steps are relevant for Year 1. Notice that although no cash was received, profit is still recognized. The percentage of completion method is based on accrual accounting.

Step 1: costs incurred to date $240,000/$600,000 total estimated costs = 40% complete

Step 2: 40% × $400,000 expected profit equals $160,000 profit recognized to date

Step 3: subtract any profit recognized in the previous year; none, since this is the contract's first year

306. **D.** The percentage of completion method involves estimating costs in order to recognize revenue and profit. For Year 2, $1,800,000 cost incurred to date divided by $2,400,000 total estimated costs means that the job is 75% completed as of December 31, Year 2. Total estimated profit of $600,000 × 75% means $450,000 profit should be recognized to date. Since $450,000 profit should be recognized to date and $300,000 profit was recognized in Year 1, $150,000 profit should be recognized in Year 2. Total estimated profit for Year 2 of $600,000 is calculated by subtracting the total estimated costs as of December 31, Year 2 of $2,400,000 and subtracting that from the $3,000,000 contract price. Total estimated costs of $2,400,000 is calculated by adding the costs incurred through Year 2 of $1,800,000 and adding the estimated costs remaining at December 31, Year 2, of $600,000.

Step 1: costs incurred to date: $1,800,000/$2,400,000 = 75% complete after Year 2

Step 2: 75% times the expected profit of $600,000 = $450,000 profit to date

Step 3: Subtract $300,000 profit already recognized in Year 1 from the $450,000 profit to date = $150,000 profit to recognize in Year 2

307. B. II is correct. Cash received is the critical event for income recognition in the installment method because under the installment, the cash collected is multiplied by the gross profit percentage to equal the realized gross profit from the installment sale. III is correct. Cash received is the critical event for income recognition in the cost recovery method since the amount of cash collected must exceed the cost of the item sold in order to recognize any profit from the sale. I is wrong. Billings and cash collections have no impact on profit recognized in either the percentage of completion method or the completed contract method of accounting for long-term construction contracts. Under the percentage of completion method, the profit earned over a long-term construction contract is based on costs incurred already in proportion to total estimated costs remaining. Under the completed contract method, no revenue is recognized until the job is substantially complete.

308. D. I is wrong. Under the percentage of completion method, profit recognition is not based on cash received, but rather on costs incurred. The fact that no costs have yet been incurred by Everlast means that no profit will be recognized in Year 4. II is wrong. Under the completed contract method, profit recognition is delayed until the job is substantially complete. The completed contract method is *not* based upon cash received.

309. B. If a tax-exempt organization has gross receipts of $50,000 or more, it must file an informational return each year, Form 990 (due May 15th), listing major contributors and highest employee salaries. If the not-for-profit (NFP) has gross receipts of under $50,000, the filing requirement is much simpler: only Form 990-N would be filed, which does not include listing major contributors or employee salaries. Form 990-N includes only the basic information, NFP name, federal ID number, website address, and name and address of one principal officer of the NFP. Churches do not have to file 990 information returns; private foundations do.

310. C. A not-for-profit (NFP) files Form 990-N if its gross revenues are less than $50,000 per year. This would be considered a small NFP, and the filing requirements are simple compared to larger NFPs. The filing requirements for a small NFP, that files a Form 990-N would include the name and mailing address of the NFP; the federal employer identification; the number, name, and address of a principal officer; website address; and confirmation of the fact that the revenues are less than $50,000.

Information on major contributors and employee salaries are only included in a filing for larger NFPs with gross income exceeding $50,000.

311. C. Most organizations exempt from income tax must file an annual information return (Form 990 or 990-EZ) (due May 15th) or submit an annual electronic notice (Form 990-N), depending upon the organization's gross receipts for the year and total assets at year end. The simple Form 990-N electronic notice is permitted if the organization's average gross receipts are less than $50,000 per year. Form 990-EZ is permitted if average gross receipts are between $50,000 and $200,000 and total assets are less than $500,000.

Form 990, the long form, is the most sophisticated form of the three and applies to the larger not-for-profits. It is required if average gross receipts are greater than or equal to $200,000 or total assets are greater than or equal to $500,000 at the end of the tax year. Gross receipts include the total amounts the organization received from all sources during its three most recent tax years, without subtracting any costs or expenses for those years.

312. C. Since Olney's gross receipts are greater than $200,000 for the three most recent years, the long-form 990 must be filed. This is the case even though Olney's total assets were below $500,000. If total assets are above $500,000 or if average revenues are greater than or equal to $200,000, Form 990, the long form, must be filed. A is wrong. For a not-for-profit organization, if average gross revenues (for the past three years) are below $50,000, only Form 990-N needs to be filed. Form 990-N is sometimes called an E-postcard in that it contains only the entity name, employer ID number, name and address of a principal officer, and website address of the organization. B is wrong. Olney's gross receipts are too high to file 990-EZ. If average gross receipts were between $50,000 and $200,000, Form 990-EZ could have been filed as long as total assets were less than $500,000. D is wrong. Filing Form 990 is required of a not-for-profit, unless the entity is a church. Churches are exempt from filing Form 990.

313. A. A tax-exempt organization must pay income taxes on any unrelated business income in excess of $1,000. Some income activities are not taxable even though they are unrelated to the charitable purpose: sale of donations, operations run by volunteers or patients of the not-for-profit (NFP), and legal bingo at the church. Although the preceding represent unrelated business from the charitable purpose, income from these activities is exempt from tax.

314. **B.** Since the museum's mission involves the education of the public about art, the proceeds from such courses are tax exempt because they are related business income, which is tax exempt for a not-for-profit.

315. **C.** I is correct. Unrelated business income is taxable to the not-for-profit (NFP) after a $1,000 exemption. The tax is paid at the corporate tax rate. If this income were not taxed, then NFPs would directly compete with for-profit business and not have to pay tax, which would give the NFP a lower cost structure and an unfair advantage in the marketplace. II is correct. If an NFP carries advertising for business that has nothing to do with its mission, then the income from advertising on its website is considered unrelated business income.

316. **C.** The deadline for filing the Form 990-N is four and a half months after the close of the year. For a calendar year NFP, the E-filed postcard would be due May 15th of the following year.

Chapter 42: Business Law, Ethics, and Professional Responsibilities

317. **B.** II is correct. A contract can be for any legal purpose. A contract made for an illegal purpose is considered void. I is wrong. An offer would have to be accepted in order for a legally enforceable agreement to take effect. A contract (agreement) starts when one party makes an offer, but the other party would need to accept the offer to have an agreement. Silence does *not* normally act as acceptance.

318. **B.** Advertisements are *not* considered offers. Instead, advertisements are considered invitations for the customer to come in and make an offer. Therefore, no offer existed here at all. Exam hint: this question could have been answered without even reading the facts. Knowing the rule that advertisements are not offers would have made B the correct choice regardless of the facts.

319. **C.** I is correct. Counteroffers must be received to be effective. Once received, the counteroffer destroys the original offer. II is correct. Rejections must be received to be effective. Once received, rejections destroy the original offer. Other communications in contracts that must be received to be effective include offers and revocations of offers. Both must be received to be effective. Only acceptances can be valid prior to receipt. Although the general rule is that acceptance of an offer is valid upon dispatch (the mailbox rule), an offeror could require

acceptance to be received by a certain date in order to be effective. Therefore, it's essential to look to the offer to see if there are any specific instructions with regard to acceptance.

320. **A.** I is correct. An option or option contract is an offer that is irrevocable for an agreed time period and is supported by consideration. II is wrong. Option contracts are very common in real estate where the price is high and financing may need to be secured. The buyer may need time to qualify for a loan, and maybe the buyer wants some time to decide whether or not to proceed.

321. **A.** I is correct. An option is used when the dollar value of the deal is high and the financing may need to be secured, but the buyer isn't sure that he or she could even get the financing or whether he or she is 100% dedicated. Options give buyers time to think. II is incorrect. Generally a counteroffer like this would destroy the original offer, but not when there is an option contract in place. An option contract is when an offer is made in writing and supported by consideration (payment is made to keep the offer open). The option keeps the offer open and the offer cannot be terminated before the agreed-upon date, even by what looks like a counteroffer.

322. **B.** The general rule is that acceptances only have to be sent (they do not have to be received) to form a contract. This is known as the *mailbox rule* or the early acceptance rule. However, the mailbox rule *can be eliminated* by the parties. The offeror can state in the offer that acceptance must be received to be effective.

323. **B.** II is correct. A late-arriving acceptance is considered a counteroffer.

I is incorrect. While the general rule is that acceptance can be valid when mailed, the offer here requires acceptance to be received to be effective; therefore, acceptance is valid on August 6 not August 3.

324. **C.** The general rule for acceptance is that acceptance only has to be sent; it does not have to be received to be effective. Since the offer stated only that Micki must accept by a certain date, and not that Clark, Inc., must receive the acceptance by any particular date, then the mailing on September 21 is a valid date for acceptance.

325. **B.** This is an example of a unilateral contract, an offer for a reward. In a unilateral contract, one party (Rick) promises and the other party needs to perform in order to accept the contract. When deciding

whether a contract is bilateral or unilateral, look at the offer. Rick's offer stated that whoever picks up Ricky gets paid, not whoever promises to pick him up.

326. **C.** To prove common law fraud, the injured party must prove *all* of the following:

Material misrepresentation
Intent to deceive, scienter, bad faith
Justifiable reliance
Damages, usually money damages

327. **A.** I is correct. In order to prove fraud, the misrepresentations must be material. II is wrong. The defendant need not be an expert to commit fraud; experts and nonexperts can both potentially commit fraud. For example, a seller lying about an appraised value of a diamond ring is committing fraud. Although the appraiser was the expert, the one who lied about the appraised value committed fraud even though he himself was not an expert.

328. **B.** Just as you have to know what fraud is, sometimes you have to know what fraud is not. This is not an example of fraud, because all the elements of fraud cannot be proven. There is no intent to deceive and therefore no fraud. There is also no justifiable reliance. No one is justified in relying on accounting work done by a nonaccountant. Notice that all the elements of fraud need to be proven, not just one or two elements.

329. **C.** I is correct. For example, suppose I offer to sell you my accounting firm for $500,000, but you accept for $5,000,000! I am eager to close that deal, but you discover your mistake just before closing. Result: although you made the mistake, it's clear that I know it's a mistake and am just trying to take advantage. You will have a defense called a unilateral mistake and not have to pay me $5,000,000 for my $500,000 firm unless you want to. The contract would be voidable if you don't want to pay me $5,000,000. II is correct. The term *voidable* refers to an otherwise valid contract, but one party has the right to cancel—in this case because of the unilateral mistake. In the event of a unilateral mistake, the contract could still exist if both parties agree. On the CPA exam, the party who made the mistake will discover the mistake prior to performance. The mistake would be a defense, and the contract would be voidable since the other party knows it's a mistake and is simply trying to take advantage.

330. **C.** I is correct. Duress involves threatening someone and physically forcing that person to enter a contract against his or her will. Duress would result in a voidable agreement. II is correct. Undue influence involves using one's position to take unfair advantage of a person in a close personal relationship. Lawyers and accountants could easily influence an individual into making a contract that they would otherwise not make.

In addition to fraud and unilateral mistake, duress and undue influence are two additional situations where someone would have a defense and could back out of a contract.

331. **B.** II is correct. Consideration is something that is bargained for and exchanged in a contract. For example, if a person pays $50,000 for a used car, the $50,000 is consideration to one party and the car is consideration to the other. I is incorrect. Consideration can involve money, goods, or services.

332. **B.** Although Mirro promised the $125, if the plumbing inspector shows up the following morning, Mirro does *not* have to pay the plumbing inspector. This is because the plumbing inspector is *not* offering any additional consideration by showing up earlier than scheduled. The plumbing inspector already gets paid and is obligated to perform inspections. Mirro's promise is a moral obligation rather than a legal obligation.

333. **B.** As a minor, Todd can cancel the contract at any time while still a minor and even for a reasonable time after becoming an adult, thus, answer choice A is incorrect. C is incorrect. The flight school after learning it just did business with a minor cannot cancel the contract. Only the party who lacks capacity may cancel; the party with capacity cannot back out. A minor's contract is voidable at the minor's election. D is incorrect. If the contract was for necessaries, the minor must pay reasonable value for what has been already received, even though the minor is still allowed to void the remaining contract. This would be the case if the minor's parents were not able to provide the food and shelter, and so on. Necessaries include food, clothing, shelter, and medical attention.

334. **B.** II is correct. If the contract was for campus housing or other necessaries, the minor must pay reasonable value for what has been already received, even though the minor is still allowed to void the remaining contract. This would be the case if the minor's parents were not able to provide the campus housing. Necessaries include food, clothing, shelter, and medical attention. I is wrong. Guitar

lessons are not considered necessaries, so the minor could skip out on those services already received and could certainly cancel the remaining lessons while still a minor and even within a reasonable time after becoming an adult.

335. **A.** I is correct. Phil may rescind (cancel) while still a minor and even within a reasonable time after becoming an adult. Minors are allowed to cancel contracts even if the other contracting party (adult) suffers a financial loss. II is wrong. Ratification means acceptance. Ratification has nothing to do with how long the minor kept or used the item. A minor cannot ratify (accept) a contract while still a minor. Notice that even an item stolen from a minor can be the subject of a cancelled contract.

336. **A.** I is correct. Brian's promise is based on past consideration and is a moral obligation rather than a legal obligation. Mona would have to work or do something for Amazing Amusements to be entitled to the $500 per month, or there is no consideration to the company. Brian's promise is based on past consideration. Past consideration is not viewed as consideration. II is wrong. Even if Amazing Amusements began paying Mona each month, neither Amazing Amusements nor Brian would be required to continue the payments unless Mona came back to work or did something in return.

337. **C.** Modification of an existing services contract requires consideration. Since Black Bear, Inc., did not receive any consideration when they agreed to modify and give Ditka the raise, Black Bear, Inc., does not have to pay Ditka the increase and can sue him to recover it. It is important to know for the CPA exam that with regard to service contracts, modification requires consideration be given to both sides, not just one side.

338. **B.** II is correct. The general rule is that a promise needs to be supported by consideration for the promise to be legally enforceable. An exception is when a person makes a promise to donate money to a charity. This promise to the charity can be enforced by the charity even though the charity never promises anything in return to the donor. On the exam, look to see whether the charity already spent the money or incurred debt based on the expectations of the large donation. If the charity spent the money already or incurred debt with anticipation of the large donation, the donor's promise is enforceable. I is wrong. Modification of a real estate or services contract requires additional consideration be given (to both sides, not just one side). If the contract

to purchase the land is signed, both sides would need additional consideration for modification to take place. The question asked which of the given statements would be valid without consideration. Modification of a real estate agreement would need consideration to be valid.

339. **D.** The question asked which answer choice correctly relates to the terms *valid*, *void*, and *voidable*. Once a party has been declared legally insane by a court with proper jurisdiction, all contracts entered into by that person would be void. *Void* means without legal effect. Contracts require a party to have mental capacity and be competent in order for a contract to be valid and enforceable. A person having been declared mentally incompetent lacks such capacity, and all contracts would then be void, without legal effect. This is done to protect the mentally incompetent from being taken advantage of. A is wrong because once a party has been declared legally insane, all contracts entered into by that individual are *void*, not *voidable*. Voidable contracts are otherwise valid and enforceable, but if a contract is voidable then one party would have the power to set the contract aside. B is wrong because if a contract is otherwise valid, but one party has the power to set the contract aside, the contract would be *voidable*, not *void*. C is wrong because voidable contracts are not void from the start. *Void* means without legal effect. Voidable contracts are otherwise valid and enforceable, but if the contract is voidable, one party has the right to set the contract aside. An example of a voidable contract is a contract entered into by a minor (under age 18) is valid but may be set aside by the minor.

340. **A.** I is correct. A minor may cancel a contract anytime while still a minor and even within a reasonable time after becoming an adult. Therefore, a contract entered into by a minor is voidable by the minor. II is wrong. Contracts entered into by a person who is drunk every day are not voidable. Being drunk at the time of entering into a contract can sometimes be a defense to a contract but sometimes not. If a person who doesn't normally abuse alcohol had too much to drink and then enters into a contract, that person can avoid the contract because that person could say that he or she was "accidentally drunk." The court would likely have sympathy and release the "accidentally drunk" individual from the terms of the contract. However, if alcohol is part of that person's daily diet, if that same person drinks alcohol every day, then that person would *not* be able to say that he or she was "accidentally drunk."

Therefore contracts entered into by a person who is drunk every day are not voidable. Notice that with alcohol as a defense, it's not how much an individual had to drink, but how often he or she drinks.

341. **D.** I is wrong. In an illegal contract, the court will not help either party. The court would leave the parties where they stand. II is wrong. This would be an example of a void contract, not a voidable contract. Contracts that are illegal are void from the start. Voidable contracts, on the other hand, are valid contracts, but one or more parties have the power to set the contract aside, like a minor. Other examples of voidable contracts include where there is a mistake, fraud, duress, or undue influence.

342. **C.** I is correct. A revenue license is not required in order to collect for professional services rendered in most states. A revenue license is just a tax ID number. Someone can still get paid for services rendered if they are missing a tax ID number or what is sometimes known as a revenue license. Make sure you know the difference between a revenue license and a regulatory license. II is correct. A regulatory license is a competency license. A regulatory license is required in order to collect for professional services rendered in most states. If someone performs a service on the exam, look to see if they have the required competency (regulatory) license. If they don't have the required regulatory license, they are not entitled to getting paid even if they performed the services flawlessly.

343. **B.** I is correct. Contracts for the sale of real estate need to be in writing. II is correct. Contracts for services that are impossible to complete within one year need to be in writing. III is wrong. Sales of *goods* of $500 or more need to be in writing, but *not* all contracts over $500. Service contracts over $500 do not need to be in writing unless they are impossible to complete within one year.

344. **C.** I is correct. The statute of frauds applies to contracts that cannot be fully performed within one year. This means that the contract between Juan and Genarro should have been in writing and signed. The fact that Genarro, Inc., did not sign the contract means that Genarro, Inc., is not obligated to perform. II is correct. The statute of frauds applies to contracts that have not yet been fully performed and provides a defense—a reason to cancel. A fully performed contract is not subject to any writing requirement.

345. **B.** Hayes will recover $625 because a contract for services does not have to be in writing unless it is impossible to complete within one year. So even though the price is above $500, an oral contract for services is enforceable. The fact that this contract was not in writing is irrelevant since goods were not being sold.

346. **D.** I is correct. While most oral contracts are valid, certain contracts are required to be in writing, and if they are not signed, the party who did not sign is allowed to back out. An example of this would be a contract for the sale of goods with a price greater than $500. II is correct. If a contract that is required to be in writing is not signed, the party who did not sign the written agreement has the right to back out. An example of this would be an executor of a will. The party agreeing to be the executor must sign the will agreeing to the role of executor. III is correct. If a contract that is required to be in writing is not signed, the party who did not sign the written agreement has the right to back out. An example of this would be a co-signor. An oral promise to pay the debts of another would *not* be enforceable.

347. **D.** I is wrong. If a contract is in writing, the parol evidence rule states that the terms of the contract must be determined from the writing itself. Any evidence that existed prior to the written contract is not allowed to dispute the final written contract. II is wrong. If a contract is in writing, regardless of whether it needs to be in writing, the parol evidence rule states that the terms of the contract must be determined from the writing itself. The moral of the story of the parol evidence rule is to read and understand the contract before you sign it. If you don't like the contract after you sign it, it's often too late.

348. **C.** I and II are correct. While most evidence that exists prior to a written contract would be excluded by the parol evidence rule, both oral and written evidence that could prove fraud would not be prohibited by the parol evidence rule.

349. **D.** I is wrong. An assignment of rights in a contract to another party need not be in writing. The parties to the contract could agree orally on the rights to be assigned. Note that consideration is *not* required for assignment to be valid. II is wrong. Most contract rights are assignable, and the assignor is generally permitted to transfer the contract rights to a third party, provided the assignment of those contract rights are not prohibited by the contract itself. If a contract is silent with regard to assignment, assignment is usually permitted unless assignment would increase the other party's risk. An example of a

contract that cannot be freely assignable would be the following: a doctor cannot assign his or her malpractice insurance policy to another doctor without the consent of the insurance company, because it may increase the insurance company's risk.

350. **B.** The rule for assignment is that most contract rights are generally assignable. The only contract rights that are not assignable are when the contract prohibits assignment, if it increases the other party's risk, or if highly personal services are involved. Nothing in this question indicates that assignment would be prohibited.

351. **B.** III is correct. Most contract rights are assignable. Assignment is generally allowed, unless it is prohibited by the contract, would substantially increase someone's risk, or contains highly personal contract rights. I is wrong. Since the contract is silent with regard to the rights of assignment, assignment is allowed. II is wrong. The right to receive delivery of landscaping equipment would *not* be considered highly personal contract rights. An example of highly personal contract rights would be the right to receive an operation scheduled for surgery with the chief of staff. This would be an example of a highly personal contract and cannot be assigned without permission in advance.

352. **D.** I is wrong. Fisk is a third-party intended beneficiary, not an incidental beneficiary. As a third-party intended beneficiary, Fisk is able to sue to enforce the contract made to benefit him. II is wrong. While Fisk is a third-party intended beneficiary, Fisk is a creditor beneficiary rather than a donee beneficiary. As a creditor beneficiary, money is owed to Fisk and this contract was made to benefit Fisk—to help him get paid. Therefore, as an intended creditor beneficiary, Fisk has the rights to sue to enforce the contract. Had Fisk been a *donee* beneficiary rather than a creditor beneficiary, he would still have been able to sue. An example of a donee beneficiary would be a child in a life insurance policy contract. The child is a third party who is intended to benefit from the contract and has the rights to enforce the agreement as a third-party intended beneficiary. Note: had Fisk been only an *incidental* beneficiary, Fisk would *not* have been able to sue.

353. **B.** II is correct. When two parties make a contract intending to benefit a third-party beneficiary, the third-party beneficiary may have the right to sue to enforce the contract if the third party is an intended creditor beneficiary. Creditor beneficiaries are owed money from one of the parties in the contract, and the contract is entered into to facilitate the payment. The third-party creditor beneficiary has the right to sue to enforce the agreement because the creditor beneficiary is intended to benefit from the agreement. III is correct. When two parties make a contract intending to benefit a third-party beneficiary, the third-party beneficiary may have the right to sue to enforce the contract if the third party is an intended donee beneficiary. An example of an intended donee beneficiary would be a child in a life insurance contract. The contract is between the parents and the life insurance company, but the contract is intended to benefit the child. The contract gets donated to the child; thus the term *donee beneficiary*. I is wrong. Incidental beneficiaries cannot sue, as they were never named in the contract or intended to benefit from the original contract between the parties. An example of an incidental beneficiary is a party who buys land where a casino development contract is under way. The buyer of the land stands to benefit from the increased property values when the casino is developed. But if the casino never gets built, the buyer would have no rights to sue anyone, as he was never intended to benefit from the casino development contract.

354. **C.** I is correct. Anticipatory repudiation occurs if one party announces in advance that they will not perform as required. II is correct. Anticipatory repudiation occurs if one party reasonably demands an assurance of performance from the other and does not receive one. In either case, the threatened party may sue immediately and does not have to wait until performance is due.

355. **B.** II is correct. Compensatory damages represent actual dollar losses that when recovered would restore the parties to the position they would have been in had there been no breach. *Compensatory* means designed to compensate. I is wrong. Liquidated damages are an amount of general damages agreed to in advance when actual damages are difficult to determine. Liquidated damages are designed to alleviate litigation delays in seeking damage awards to contract breaches. Note that liquidated damages are not automatically awarded in contract breaches. If the court determines that the liquidated damage clause is too severe, it would be thrown out even though both parties agreed to it. Therefore, any answer choice to a multiple-choice question on the CPA exam that says a liquidated damage clause is automatically enforceable is the wrong answer. For the liquidated damages clause to survive a court challenge, the amount of

predetermined damages must bear a reasonable relationship to the probable loss.

356. **A.** Liquidated damages are damages that are agreed to (in amount) at the time the parties enter the contract. Liquidated damages will be enforced as long as they are not punitive. D is wrong. Punitive damages are designed to punish and are not granted in breach of contract cases. B is wrong. Specific performance does not involve money damages; rather, it is where the court orders the party to do what they agreed to do in the contract. C is wrong. Compensatory damages are actual dollar losses, and in the case of the AICPA contract with Prometric, actual damages were almost impossible to determine. So for that reason, the liquidated damages clause was inserted into the contract. It should be known that Prometric finished on time, but if they had not, Prometric would have paid the AICPA the liquidated damages, agreed to in advance, or would have gone to court in order to establish that the liquidated damages were too severe. Therefore, any answer choice to a multiple-choice question that says "liquidated damages are automatically awarded in a contract" is never the right answer, because liquidated damages are not awarded by the court if the court determines that the previously agreed to amount is nothing but a penalty.

357. **A.** II is correct. Specific performance is available where the contract calls for the sale of unique goods. Contracts that call for ordinary goods are not entitled to specific performance. III is correct. Specific performance is available where the contract calls for the sale of unique items like real estate. All real estate is considered unique; therefore, specific performance is available in real estate contracts. I is wrong. Specific performance is not a remedy when the subject matter is personal services. In the case of services when a party refuses to perform as contractually obligated, you can't force them. Instead, if you have to hire another at a higher price, you can sue for the difference. Specific performance is where there has been a breach and the injured party tells the court she would rather have the court enforce the contract rather than collect any money damages.

358. **C.** I is correct. With respect to a covenant not to compete, the agreement not to compete must be reasonable in time. The restraint must be no more extensive than is necessary to protect the goodwill purchased by Murray and Rukke. II is correct. With respect to a covenant not to compete, the agreement not to compete must be reasonable in geographical area. A covenant not to compete is very common where there is a sale of a business. Without a covenant not to compete, there is nothing to stop a seller of a business from opening a competing business across the street from the buyer. These restrictions on the seller must be reasonable to be enforceable. An example of a reasonable covenant not to compete that could be expected to go along with this sale would include that the seller cannot open a competing business for a term of five years within a radius of 20 miles.

359. **B.** In a real estate contract breach, both specific performance and compensatory damages are available, but the injured, non-breaching party, is only entitled to receive one or the other, not both. Specific performance would involve the nonbreaching party asking the court to force the breaching party to perform as contractually obligated.

360. **A.** I is correct. The UCC rules apply to contracts that involve the sale of goods. The minute goods are being sold, the UCC rules apply, regardless of the price of the goods and whether the seller is a merchant seller or nonmerchant seller. II is wrong. The common law rules apply to real estate contracts, contracts for the sale of a business, and personal services contracts.

361. **B.** The UCC rules apply to contracts that involve the sale of goods. The minute goods are being sold, the UCC rules apply, regardless of whether the goods are ordinary goods or custom made.

362. **D.** III is correct. A firm offer must be in writing, for the sale of goods, and signed by a merchant. The firm offer must contain some assurance that the offer will be held open. I is wrong. Under the sales article of the UCC, a firm offer will be created only if the offeror is a merchant. The offeree need not be a merchant for the offeror to create a firm offer. II is wrong. Under the sales article of the UCC, a firm offer does *not* require consideration to be given in exchange for the irrevocable offer. Note that this is different than the option contract under the common law that did require consideration to be exchanged. The option contract requires consideration; the firm offer does not.

363. **B.** In the sale of goods under the UCC, the acceptance need not always be a mirror image of the offer. Under the UCC, acceptance with additional terms acts as acceptance of the original offer. This is often tested on the CPA exam because it represents a difference between the common law rules and the UCC rules. Under common law rules, if the subject

matter was real estate, services, or the sale of a business, adding additional terms would be a counteroffer and *not* a valid acceptance. Under the UCC, when goods are sold, the acceptance of the offer will likely include additional terms on the CPA exam. The additional terms become part of the contract.

364. **B.** II is correct. If the contract were for real estate, the price would be considered material and the contract would fail if the price of a real estate contract were left open. III is correct. If the contract were for personal services, the price would be considered material and the contract would fail if the price of a services contract were left open. I is wrong. Under the UCC for the sale of goods, price can be left open and the contract would still exist. The buyer would simply pay the reasonable value for the goods. Under the UCC, terms may be left open, changed, deleted, or added by the acceptance and it will still create a valid agreement. While the *price* of a contract under the UCC is not considered material, quantity would be considered material and cannot be left open.

365. **A.** I is correct. Contracts under the common law rules, including services or sale of a business and real estate, require additional consideration to both sides for modification to be valid. II is incorrect. If a contract is for the sale of goods, consideration is not necessary for modifications to be valid. The only requirement for modification of a contract for the sale of goods is that the modification must be in good faith.

366. **A.** I is correct. Between merchants, a written confirmation of an oral agreement for the sale of goods can substitute for a signed contract if the confirmation is received and *not* disputed within 10 days. II is wrong. A contract for the sale of goods would follow the UCC rules rather than the common law rules regardless of whether the parties are merchants or nonmerchants.

367. **D.** The general rule is that contracts for sale of goods of $500 or more must be in writing and signed, setting forth the terms to be enforceable according to the statute of frauds. There is an important exception to that rule being tested in this question. With specially manufactured goods, if the goods are custom made to the buyer's specifications, the seller can recover full contract price plus storage fees if the buyer backs out, even if the contract is oral. Recoverable damages include the full contract price plus storage fees.

368. **B.** II is correct. In a trial sale known as a sale or return, the seller ships goods to a buyer to use or test for 10 days. In a sale or return, title and risk of loss pass to the buyer immediately. The buyer has the right to return the goods. In a sale or return, the buyer is not the ultimate consumer but instead is buying for resale. The buyer would have risk of loss during the trial period since the buyer is also a merchant. I is wrong. If the buyer is *not* a merchant buying for resale but rather the ultimate consumer, then the trial sale is considered a sale on approval rather than a sale or return. In a sale on approval, title and risk of loss will *not* pass during the trial period.

369. **D.** When goods are involved, the UCC rules apply. If a merchant is the seller, the UCC rules apply. If a nonmerchant is the seller, the UCC rules apply. The UCC rules apply regardless of the price of the goods. A is wrong because the price can be greater than $500 and the UCC would still apply regardless if the buyer and seller were merchants. B is wrong because there is no evidence that the contract is a trial sale. C is wrong. Both parties must always perform in good faith.

370. **C.** Unless the contract calls for delivery, the seller only has to set aside the goods called for in the contract, conforming goods, and hold those goods and give the buyer notification to take his or her own delivery.

371. **C.** The contract between VoiceNext and Giant is FOB shipping point. In FOB shipping point, the seller has no risk during shipment. In FOB shipping point the buyer bears all risk during shipment. Another term for FOB shipping point is FOB seller's loading dock, or a "shipping contract." Conversely, with FOB destination, the seller would bear all risk during shipment. When it's FOB buyer's loading dock, risk passes only upon tender of delivery at destination.

372. **D.** Under the UCC, risk of loss passes to the buyer when the goods are delivered to the carrier if the terms are FOB shipping point. In FOB shipping point, the seller is responsible only until the goods are delivered to the carrier.

373. **B.** I is correct. If a seller ships nonconforming goods, no title and no risk of loss passes to the buyer even if the shipping terms were FOB shipping point. In the event of nonconforming goods, the seller has breached the contract by shipping the wrong goods.

III is correct. Although the seller has breached the contract by shipping nonconforming goods, the buyer must follow reasonable instructions from the seller as to what to do with the nonconforming goods that have been rejected. The buyer must act in good faith as to what to do with the nonconforming goods. II is wrong. Example: If a seller ships *nonconforming* goods to a buyer, the buyer could reject the entire shipment or could accept a partial shipment. For example, if a seller ships 90 cases of bottled water and 10 cases of iced tea to a buyer, but the contract called for 100 bottles of water, the entire shipment is nonconforming. The buyer could accept or reject all or part. If partially accepted, the buyer must pay for what has been accepted but can send back the rest.

374. **A.** I is correct. If the item was purchased and ultimately stolen from a merchant seller, the store bears risk of loss because the risk of loss passes from a merchant seller to a buyer only when the buyer takes goods out of the store. II is wrong. If the item was purchased and ultimately stolen from a nonmerchant seller, your client bears risk of loss because risk of loss passes from a nonmerchant seller to a buyer upon tender. The word *tender* means to make available. Once the nonmerchant seller tenders the guitar, title and risk of loss pass.

375. **B.** II is correct. If the seller refuses the buyer's reasonable request for a written assurance of performance, that would result in a breach of contract known as an anticipatory repudiation, or breach in advance. I is wrong. If the risk of loss had already passed to the buyer, that would not release the buyer. Rather, that would be bad news for the buyer, because the buyer would have to pay for goods that were already destroyed.

376. **C.** I is correct. If the seller ships nonconforming goods, the seller may be able to cure and ship conforming goods and mitigate any losses suffered by the buyer. II is correct. As long as the time for performance has not passed, the seller has the right to correct defects in shipments made. The seller must give timely notice of intent to cure.

377. **D.** Regardless of the question, punitive damages are NOT available in contract breaches. The buyer's right to cover relates to the buyer's right to go into the market and purchase substitute goods. If the buyer has to pay more, the buyer could sue the seller for compensatory damages.

378. **B.** II is correct. A buyer has the right to inspect goods prior to payment unless the contract is COD (cash on delivery). There is no indication that this contract is COD. I is wrong. The seller has no obligation to deliver the goods to the buyer. Unless otherwise agreed to, the seller's obligation to the buyer is to hold conforming goods and give the buyer whatever notification is necessary for the buyer to take his or her own delivery. Unless you see that delivery is called for in the contract (FOB shipping point or FOB destination), no delivery is required.

379. **C.** III is correct. The implied warranty of merchantability warrants that the item must be fit and safe for normal use. Only a merchant seller gives this warranty. I is wrong. An express warranty is a statement of fact made by the seller that the buyer relies upon when making the purchase. An example of an express warranty would be the seller explaining to the buyer that the high price on the used baseball glove is because it "used to belong to Derek Jeter." Any seller, merchant or nonmerchant, would be liable for such an express warranty. II is wrong. Title means ownership: all sellers warrant good title and rightful transfer. Merchant and nonmerchants are responsible if they breach the warranty of title. If a neighbor sells a stolen baseball glove to your client, the client would have to surrender the glove to the rightful owner because the warranty of title has been breached. Even a merchant seller cannot pass stolen goods to a buyer in the ordinary course of business.

380. **A.** I is correct. Implied warranty of fitness for particular purpose arises where the seller knows the particular purpose for which goods are to be used and that the buyer is relying on the seller's skill or judgment—there is an implied warranty that the goods will be fit for such purpose. II is wrong. The implied warranty of merchantability would arise anytime goods are being sold by a merchant seller.

381. **A.** I is correct. The warranty of title can only be disclaimed with use of the word *title* in the disclaimer. For example, to properly disclaim the warranty of title, the seller should say, "There is no warranty of title for this sale." II is wrong. A merchant who attempts to disclaim "any and all warranties" has adequately disclaimed the warranty of merchantability. III is wrong. A merchant who attempts to disclaim "any and all warranties" has adequately disclaimed the warranty of fitness for a particular purpose.

382. B. II is correct. The following four items must be proven to collect damages for product liability injury:

1. The defendant was in the business of selling the defective product.
2. They sold the product in a defective condition.
3. The product was unreasonably dangerous.
4. Use of the product caused the injury (must be physical injury not mental).

I is wrong. Historically, a person who is injured because of a product defect could successfully sue the seller only if the injured party was the purchaser. This is because only these two parties were in privity of contract. Today, privity rules vary from state to state, but generally privity is not required if injury occurs. III is wrong. Negligence on the part of the seller or manufacturer need not be proven in order to collect damages in product liability cases.

383. B. Product liability lawsuits are difficult to defend since no negligence needs to be proven on the part of the seller or manufacturer, and the manufacturer is not allowed to hide behind the "we have been building it this way for 150 years and no one has ever gotten hurt before" defense. To collect on a product liability lawsuit, the injured party must prove all four of the following:

1. The defendant was in the business of selling the defective product.
2. They sold the product in a defective condition.
3. The product was unreasonably dangerous.
4. Use of the product caused the injury (must be physical injury not mental).

384. B. II is correct. The mailbox rule applies to the UCC contracts for the sale of goods just as it does to the common law contracts for services and sale of a business and real estate. I is wrong. The UCC rules apply to *all* contracts for the sale of goods, regardless of price. Note that the UCC applies to contracts for the sale of goods whether the contracts are oral or written.

385. A. I is correct. In a written contract under the UCC, the quantity is considered material to the contract and cannot be left open. Price would be allowed open but not quantity. II is wrong. To enforce a written contract against another party, the written contract must contain the signature of the party against whom enforcement is sought. If A wanted to hold B liable on a written contract, A would need to show the court B's signature. If A signed the contract but B didn't, that would not help A seeking to enforce the contract.

386. C. Under the entrustment rule, if a merchant seller sells goods entrusted to its care to a customer in the ordinary course of business, that customer gets good title. The store would have to pay your client a sum of money in damages, but that guitar, even if unique, would belong to the good faith purchaser. A customer who buys in the ordinary course of business from a merchant seller automatically gets good title. Otherwise, you would have to ask every time you bought something from a merchant seller whether the item actually belonged to the store or to someone else!

387. D. Regardless of the question, any answer that says, "the obligations of the parties to the contract must be performed in good faith" has to be the correct answer; no one is allowed to perform in bad faith.

388. C. I is correct. Commercial paper is a substitute for money and includes notes and drafts. II is correct. Commercial paper is a means of providing credit. The purpose of commercial paper, both notes and drafts, is to provide credit and facilitate commerce.

389. C. I is correct. A note is a type of commercial paper. Notes have two parties, maker and payee. The maker of the note is the debtor, and the payee is the party to whom the note is made payable. Notes are a substitute for money and a means of providing credit. II is correct. A draft is a type of commercial paper. A draft has three parties: drawer, drawee, and payee. An example of a draft is a check. In a check, a drawer orders a drawee bank to pay a payee. Drafts are substitutes for money and a means of providing credit. III is wrong. A warehouse receipt is not commercial paper, because commercial paper is payable in money and a warehouse receipt is payable in goods.

390. A. I is correct. A certificate of deposit is an example of a promise to pay made by a bank to pay its customer an amount borrowed plus interest on a specific date. II is correct. Installment notes are an example of a promise to pay often made by a customer in a consumer purchase where the note will be satisfied in installments (of principal and interest) rather than just a single payment. III is wrong. A draft is considered an order to pay rather than a promise to pay. In a check, the drawer *orders* a drawee bank to pay a payee. A check is the most common type of draft.

391. D. For an instrument to be negotiable, it must be payable to order or bearer. "Pay to Russell" on the front would make the instrument nonnegotiable, since in order to be negotiable, the instrument must show a willingness to pay more than just one party. If the note were payable only to Russell, it would not be a substitute for money, because Diane would only be agreeing to pay Russell. A is wrong. "Pay to the order of Russell" is negotiable because Diane is willing to pay Russell or anyone Russell orders her to pay. B is wrong. "Pay to Russell or bearer" is negotiable because Diane is willing to pay Russell or a bearer. *Bearer* means anyone in possession of the note. C is wrong. "Pay to Russell or his order" is negotiable because Diane is willing to pay Russell or anyone Russell orders her to pay. To be negotiable, the front of the note must show willingness to pay more than just one party.

392. **A.** According to the UCC, to be negotiable the instrument must be payable in money only. A note payable in a foreign currency satisfies the requirement for negotiability. B, C, and D are wrong. An instrument that allows for the payment of money or goods or the payment of money or services is non-negotiable.

393. **C.** To determine whether an instrument is negotiable, look only at the front of the instrument. The back of the instrument is only for the endorsements. By the time you get to the back of the instrument, you already know whether or not it's negotiable. The front determines negotiability. Only if an instrument is negotiable can it be a true substitute for money, or a means of providing credit. If it's negotiable on the front, then it's negotiable on the back. Remember this phrase, "once negotiable, always negotiable." Remember this phrase, "once non-negotiable, always non-negotiable."

394. **C.** If an instrument is conditional, it's non-negotiable. To be negotiable, the instrument must be unconditional. B is wrong. An acceleration clause would accelerate the time for payment in the event of default—making it so the lender would not have to sue the debtor separately over every missed payment. The acceleration clause allows the entire note to be due immediately upon default. Acceleration clauses are very common with installment notes and do *not* destroy negotiability. A is wrong. An extension clause is common also and allows the debtor an opportunity, for example, to renegotiate a five-year note to six years. Extension clauses are common with installment notes and do *not* destroy negotiability. D is wrong. Remember, commercial paper is a substitute for money and a means of providing credit. If the debtor defaults, it's common

to have the interest rate rise, and if specified in the note, the note would still be negotiable.

395. **A.** In case of a discrepancy, the words control figures but the instrument is still negotiable, in this case for $400.

396. **C.** Bearer paper is payable to no one in particular, possibly even payable to cash. The instrument can be negotiated without endorsement by delivery alone, simply by handing it off to the next person. Delivery is always required to negotiate commercial paper. Delivery refers to handing the paper to the new owner.

397. **D.** Order paper is made payable to someone in particular, and that special someone must sign his or her name on the back to further negotiate the instrument. For this reason, order paper requires endorsement and delivery.

398. **B.** I is correct. A qualified endorsement is "without recourse," which attempts to remove the liability to pay if the primary party defaults. II is correct. A special endorsement names the next party to receive the instrument, so as a result the instrument would need to be endorsed to be negotiated. If the instrument were order paper on the front, the special endorsement would allow the instrument to remain order paper on the back. III is correct. A blank endorsement does not name the next party, so the instrument could then be negotiated by delivery alone. If the instrument were order paper on the front, the blank endorsement on the back would convert the order paper on the front to bearer paper on the back. IV is correct. A restrictive endorsement would be "For Deposit Only," which locks the instrument into the banking system. Only a bank can become a holder, but the instrument would still be negotiable. Remember the phrase, "once negotiable, always negotiable."

399. **D.** I is correct. The endorsement is blank since Hobbs signed his name but failed to indicate the next party to whom the instrument is payable. As a result, the instrument becomes bearer paper. II is correct. The endorsement became restrictive when Hobbs added "for deposit only." A restrictive endorsement restricts what can be done with the instrument, although the instrument remains negotiable. III is wrong. Roy would need to endorse the instrument "without recourse" for the endorsement to be qualified. The general rule is that endorsers are at least secondarily liable for payment except for the party who endorses "without recourse."

400. A. I is correct. While the instrument is order paper on the front, it would become bearer paper after a blank endorsement. An example of a blank endorsement would be if Mark Davis turns the instrument over and signs his name "Mark Davis" and leaves the rest blank without naming the party he is about to negotiate the instrument to. Since a blank endorsement does not name the next party, the instrument could then be negotiated by delivery alone. II is wrong. A special endorsement on the back of an instrument names the next party to receive the instrument. As a result, the instrument would need to be endorsed again to be further negotiated; therefore, the instrument would remain order paper.

401. D. I is wrong. Once an instrument is negotiable on the front, no endorsement on the back could render the instrument non-negotiable. II is wrong. An instrument can start out as order paper on the front, but then become bearer paper on the back as a result of a blank endorsement. The instrument may remain bearer paper at that point or could flip back to order paper again with the use of a special endorsement.

402. B. The endorsement is both qualified and special. The endorsement is qualified because by Corey signing "without recourse," he is not obligated to pay if the primary party defaults. The endorsement is a special endorsement because by naming Stuart Sheldon, the instrument remains order paper. Since the instrument remains order paper, Stuart Sheldon would need to sign the instrument to further negotiate it.

403. B. I is correct. For the third party to qualify as a holder in due course, the instrument must be negotiable. There cannot be a holder in due course of a non-negotiable instrument. II is correct. For the third party to be a holder in due course, that party must give value for the instrument in good faith. The advantage of being a holder in due course, or sheltered party, is that these parties have greater rights to collect from the maker than the original payee had. III is wrong. For the third party to be a holder in due course, that party must have *no knowledge* of the instrument being dishonored or any payments being overdue. Note that the original payee is *not* a holder in due course. On the CPA exam, the original payee usually transfers the instrument to a third party who will probably qualify as a holder in due course. The next thing that will happen is that the holder in due course will negotiate the instrument to a fourth party who will *not* qualify (for whatever reason) to be a holder in due course. But it is important to know that the fourth party receives the same rights as a holder in due course under the "shelter rule."

404. A. I is correct. Boyle can purchase the note at a discount and still acquire the status of a holder in due course. Most instruments are acquired at a discount. The advantage of being a holder in due course, or sheltered party, is that these parties have greater rights to collect from the maker than the original payee had. II is wrong. Whether or not Boyle obtains the status of a holder in due course is determined at the time Boyle acquires the instrument. For a holder to receive the status of a holder in due course, he or she cannot be aware of the fact that the maker was behind on the payments. Since Boyle was aware of that fact, Boyle would *not* qualify as a holder in due course.

405. C. I is correct. If Sussman were a minor, he would *not* have to pay the holder in due course, Capell or anyone else. A minor can avoid any contract while still a minor and even within a reasonable time of becoming an adult. II is correct. If Sussman's signature on the note were a forgery, that would mean that someone else signed Sussman's name pretending to be Sussman. In the event of a forgery, Sussman would have a real defense to payment and *not* have to pay the holder in due course, Capell or anyone else.

The advantage of being a holder in due course, or sheltered party, is that these parties have greater rights to collect from the maker than the original payee had. The only ways that a holder in due course would not collect from the maker is if the maker, Sussman, has a real defense. Both forgery and infancy (minor) are real defenses. It would seem in both I and II that Sussman would avoid liability to the holder in due course. Other real defenses include discharge in bankruptcy of the maker, extreme duress, material alteration of the note, and fraud in the execution.

406. B. Rusty provides shelter to Salas, and Salas will have the same rights as a holder in due course. But Salas does not qualify as a holder in due course, since Salas knew that the instrument was overdue at the time Salas acquired the instrument. If Salas knows something is wrong, he cannot be a holder in due course. But he will have the same rights as a holder in due course under the shelter rule, which means Salas can collect from the primary party unless the maker has a real defense.

407. B. I is correct. A material alteration is an example of a real defense. If a $30,000 note is materially altered to read $300,000, the primary party does *not* have to pay the holder in due course (or sheltered party) the altered amount of $300,000. Rather the primary party pays *just* the original amount of $30,000, because material alteration is a real defense. III is correct. A discharge in bankruptcy is an example of a real defense. If the maker of a note declares bankruptcy, that will excuse the maker from having to pay a holder in due course (or sheltered party) any amount. II is wrong. Lack of consideration is a personal defense rather than a real defense. If the maker of a note has a personal defense, that personal defense is only good against the original payee, not good against a holder in due course or sheltered party. For example, if the maker was buying a car and the payee was a car dealer, once the car dealer negotiates the note to a holder in due course, a dispute between the maker of the note and car dealer would *not* affect the rights of a holder in due course to get paid from the maker. This is because the holder in due course gave value to the payee, in good faith and without knowledge of the dispute. The court would force the maker to pay the holder in due course (or sheltered party) the monthly payments.

408. B. As a holder in due course Grace would take the note free of all personal defenses. Personal defenses, such as negligence, would *not* stop Grace from collecting from the maker. The most popular personal defenses on the CPA exam include negligence. With negligence, the maker will have lacked reasonable care and left blank spaces so the amount was easily able to be altered. Rather than be considered a real defense, negligence is just a personal defense, good only against the party who raised the amount of the note. Negligence is *not* a valid defense against a holder in due course or sheltered party. The primary party would need a real defense (rather than a personal defense) to prevent a holder in due course or sheltered party from collecting. A is wrong, because discharge in bankruptcy is a real defense and the question is looking for a personal defense. C is wrong, because extreme duress is a real defense and the question is looking for a personal defense. D is wrong. Infancy is a real defense and the question is looking for a personal defense. If the primary party were a minor (infancy), the primary party would *not* have to pay.

409. C. I is correct. The maker of a note has primary liability. The maker of a note promises to pay the original payee or anyone that the original payee orders them to pay. II is wrong. The drawer of a draft has secondary liability, not primary liability. In the case of a check, the drawer draws up a check and has secondary liability in case the bank does *not* honor the check. III is wrong. The drawee of a draft has primary liability only after the drawee accepts the draft. In the case of a check, the drawer draws up the check and has secondary liability. The drawee bank has primary liability only after determining that the drawer has money in his or her bank account. Prior to accepting the draft, the drawee has no liability.

410. D. I is wrong. Bills of lading are shipping documents. Shipping documents are payable in goods. Commercial paper must be payable in money only. Therefore, shipping documents like bills of lading are *not* commercial paper. II is wrong. Warehouse receipts are payable in goods. Commercial paper must be payable in money only; therefore, warehouse receipts are not commercial paper. Note: although bills of lading and warehouse receipts are *not* commercial paper, they follow the same rules with regard to negotiability.

411. C. Documents of title are *not* commercial paper because they are *not* payable in money only. While documents of title like bills of lading and warehouse receipts may be negotiable, they are payable in goods rather than in money. Investment securities are *not* commercial paper under the UCC definition, because investment securities are payable in shares of stock.

412. A. Documents of title and investment securities are *not* commercial paper, but they follow similar rules as commercial paper when it comes to negotiability. If a document of title is payable "to the order of Owen Michaels," the document of title is negotiable (order paper). A document of title that is considered order paper requires a signature and delivery to further negotiate the document of title. B is wrong. If the same document of title were payable "to Owen Michaels or bearer," then the document of title would be negotiable (bearer paper). Bearer paper requires delivery alone to negotiate the document of title to the next party. It is important to remember for the CPA exam that documents of title and investment securities are not commercial paper, because they are not payable in money. But they follow similar rules regarding negotiability. C is wrong. If a document of title were made payable to bearer, then it would be negotiable by delivery alone without the need for endorsement. D is wrong. Documents of title and investment securities are *not* commercial paper, but they follow similar rules as commercial paper when it comes to negotiability.

413. **A.** Documents of title include warehouse receipts and bills of lading. Documents of title are *not* commercial paper but follow similar rules regarding negotiability. A document of title payable to bearer (bearer paper) can be negotiated by delivery alone. A document of title payable to the order of a named individual (order paper) can be negotiated by endorsement and delivery.

414. **A.** A bill of lading payable "to Billy Spence or bearer" is bearer paper and can be negotiated by delivery alone without the need for endorsement. B is wrong. Although documents of title are not commercial paper, they can still be negotiable if they are payable to a named payee or if they are payable to bearer. C is wrong. The bill of lading is bearer paper, and bearer paper does not require a signature to negotiate it. D is wrong. The instrument is bearer paper, rather than order paper. To be considered order paper, the bill of lading would have had to read, "pay to the order of Billy Spence." Documents of title are not commercial paper, but generally follow the same rules with regard to negotiability.

415. **C.** I is correct. With regard to debtor/creditor relationships governed by the UCC, attachment relates to the creditor's rights against the debtor. II is correct. With regard to debtor/creditor relationships governed by the UCC, perfection relates to the creditor's rights against third parties.

416. **C.** I is correct. A security agreement gives the creditor a security interest in the debtor's property. For example, without a security agreement, when a consumer buys a new car, the debtor would have to make all the payments first prior to being able to drive the car out of the showroom. The UCC refers to this security interest as either possessory or nonpossessory, depending on whether the creditor is in possession of the collateral while the payments are being made. In the case of a consumer buying a car, the creditor allows the consumer to drive off with a car that has not been fully paid for because of the security agreement that is in place. For this reason, the UCC considers the creditor's security interest to be nonpossessory. II is correct. While the security interest allows the debtor to drive off in a car while money is still owed, the security agreement is in place to protect the lender. In the event of default, the creditor

having a security agreement signed by the debtor will allow the creditor to repossess the car from the debtor should the debtor fail to make the payments. The creditor's right to repossession is written into the security agreement.

417. **B.** I is wrong. A security interest is *not* enforceable until the debtor has rights in the collateral. For a security interest to attach and be enforceable, there is often a written security agreement between the debtor and creditor. In the case of a consumer purchasing a car, the written security agreement is signed by the debtor at the dealership but is not enforceable until the debtor has the keys to the car. For example, if the security agreement is signed Saturday night at the dealership but the car is not delivered to the debtor until Monday morning, the security interest is not enforceable until Monday morning when the debtor gets behind the wheel. In this example, the CPA exam will ask which day attachment took place: Saturday night at the dealership when the security agreement was signed or Monday when the debtor had the rights to the car. The answer is that attachment took place Monday when the debtor got the car—the creditor would then have attachment of a nonpossessory security interest. The UCC considers the creditor's security interest to be nonpossessory in this example since the creditor is *not* in possession of the car during the term of the security interest. II is correct. In case of default, the security agreement allows the creditor to repossess the car and sell it to apply proceeds to satisfy the debt. In this way, the creditor has rights against the debtor. The term that describes the creditor's rights against the debtor is *attachment*.

418. **C.** Attachment took place the following Friday at Frazier's house, because that was the first moment that Frazier had any rights to the car. For attachment to take place, the debtor must have rights in the collateral. Frazier has rights in the car on Friday at his house when the car arrived, and not before even though Frazier signed the security agreement on Saturday night. Attachment refers to the creditor's rights against the debtor. The CPA exam will ask when attachment takes place. For a security interest to attach (in other words, for a security interest to be enforceable), three things must occur:

1. The debtor must have rights in the collateral.
2. The creditor must give value to the debtor.
3. There must be a signed security agreement.

The security agreement between Frazier and Lester-Glenn would be considered nonpossessory since

Lester-Glenn is not in possession of the car during the term of the agreement.

419. **C.** I is correct. An example of a possessory interest would be a creditor taking possession of negotiable instruments to be used as collateral for a loan. Once the creditor has possession of the stack of notes, the creditor would have attachment and perfection simultaneously. II is correct. An example of a possessory interest would be a pawnbroker accepting goods in exchange for a loan. Once the pawn shop has possession of the goods, they have attachment and perfection simultaneously.

420. **A.** I is correct. Attachment and perfection occur simultaneously when a pawnbroker lends money. The pawnbroker takes possession of the debtor's collateral, and at that moment attachment and perfection take place. Attachment refers to the pawnbroker's rights against the debtor. Perfection refers to the pawnbroker's rights against third parties whom the debtor may owe money to. A pawnbroker lending money is an example of a possessory interest rather than a nonpossessory interest. II is wrong. For a nonpossessory interest, the filing of a financing statement leads to perfection, not attachment. A financing statement is filed after the attachment has already taken place. The financing statement gives the world constructive notice of the financing arrangement between the debtor and creditor. The filing of a financing statement does *not* relate to attachment. The attachment takes place earlier when the security agreement is signed *and* the debtor has rights in the collateral.

421. **B.** II is correct. A pawn shop taking possession of collateral is what the UCC refers to as a possessory interest. A possessory interest accomplishes attachment and perfection at the same time. Once Tenderloin has possession of the ring, the Tenderloin Pawn Shop has rights against Ivy and rights against third-party creditors of Ivy. Before taking possession of the ring, Tenderloin has no such rights. III is correct. When perfecting by possession, neither a financing statement nor a written security agreement is needed. Once Tenderloin has possession of the jewelry, the pawn shop has rights against Ivy and rights against third-party creditors of Ivy without the need for a written security agreement or financing statement. Note that when the security interest is possessory, no financing statement is required to perfect the creditor's interest against third parties. I is wrong. Tenderloin would *not* automatically get a security interest in the automobile; the automobile is purchased outright for

cash. Tenderloin would have *no* security interest in Ivy's car.

422. **A.** I is correct. Once filed, a financing statement gives the world constructive notice for five years of the financing arrangement between the parties. If the financing were to last more than five years, a continuation statement could be filed afterward. II is wrong. If the debtor moves the collateral from the state where the financing statement was filed, the original filing is valid for four months, but after a four-month grace period, the creditor would have to file a financing statement in the new state that the debtor moved to.

423. **C.** I and II are both correct. A buyer in the ordinary course of business is free of any liens even if he or she knew about the liens. You don't have to ask when you go into a store whether the store finished paying for the item yet. Note: Salika would be considered a buyer in the ordinary course of business whether she was buying goods for consumer use or business use.

424. **C.** I is correct. After repossession but before sale, the debtor has the right of redemption. The right of redemption involves the debtor having the right to pay the obligation in full just prior to the sheriff's auction and get the collateral back. After the auction, it's too late. II is correct. The creditor must notify the debtor of imminent sale because the debtor has the right to bid at auction.

425. **B.** II is correct. There are special rules relating to consumer goods: if the consumer has paid 60% or more of the purchase price, retention by the creditor is not allowed after repossession. The creditor must sell the goods within 90 days of repossession or be liable for damages. This is because the debtor is hoping that the car sells for more than the balance owed, and if it does, the debtor would take home any surplus. I is wrong. If the car sells for less than the balance owed, Stacey would be liable for the deficiency.

426. **D.** I is wrong. Special rules relate to consumer goods: if the consumer has paid 60% or more of purchase price, retention by the creditor is not allowed. The creditor must sell repossessed goods within 90 days or be liable for damages, because this would give the debtor the best chance for a surplus and the least chance for a deficiency as items tend to depreciate quickly after repossession. II is wrong. Notice must be given to the debtor before the sale because the debtor is allowed to bid. The sale must be commercially reasonable.

427. **A.** I is correct. If the smart device sells for less than the amount owed, DC Appliance can obtain a judgment from Cliff for the deficiency because creditors have the right to get paid back what they are owed, provided they follow the rules relating to the collection process. II is wrong. If the smart device sells for a surplus, more than what is owed to DC Appliance, DC Appliance could *not* keep the surplus. The surplus would be given to Cliff minus any costs of collection and sale.

428. **D.** II is correct. An agent owes a fiduciary duty of loyalty to the principal, but the principal can have several agents all working at once without their being aware of it. III is correct. An agent for a disclosed principal has no contract liability to third parties if the principal backs out, but an agent for an undisclosed principal would have potential contract liability if the principal backs out. I is wrong. An agency contract does *not* need to be in writing, unless the agent is selling real estate for the principal or if the agency is impossible to complete within one year.

429. **A.** I is correct. An agent owes a fiduciary duty of loyalty to his principal. Stump, the agent, owes a duty of loyalty to the New York Bombers. Stump would be liable to the Bombers for breach of fiduciary duty of loyalty if he were to disclose information to any competing teams without the Bombers' consent because the Bombers are paying Stump for this information. II is wrong. While an agent owes a fiduciary duty of loyalty to his principal, a principal does *not* owe a fiduciary duty of loyalty to the agent. The Bombers could have more than one agent in Japan following Hito at the same time. The principal would owe the agent the right of compensation but not a duty of loyalty.

430. **C.** I is correct. If the principal no longer wishes to be associated with an agent, notice must be given to third parties. Actual notice needs to be given to all parties that the agent did business on behalf of the principal. Actual notice to current customers will terminate the agent's actual authority to bind the principal on any new contracts. II is correct. If the principal no longer wishes to be associated with an agent, constructive notice to potential customers is required also. Constructive notice may be accomplished by classified advertisements in trade journals, etc. This will terminate the agent's apparent authority even if the third party did not read the advertisement regarding the termination. Note: notice need *not* be given if the reason for termination was due to death, insanity, bankruptcy, or

destruction of the subject matter of the contract. Termination would be automatic.

431. **A.** I is correct. To have a surety agreement, three parties are needed. These three parties are known as creditor, principal debtor, and cosignor. The cosignor is known on the exam as a surety or guarantor. III is correct. The agreement of surety to pay the creditor if the principal debtor defaults must be in writing, because it is a promise to answer for the debt of another. This promise is one of the contracts that has to be in writing according to the statute of frauds. II is wrong. The agreement between the surety and principal debtor may or may not be in writing and would have no effect on the surety's obligation to pay the creditor.

432. **C.** Subrogation is the surety's right, after paying the creditor, to step into the shoes of a creditor against the principal debtor. If the debtor's father pays for the debtor's loan balance on a new car, the father has the right, after payment, to demand from the debtor either the money or the keys. Subrogation gives the surety the greatest chance of collecting from the debtor. A is wrong. Contribution would involve more than one surety contributing their share after one surety pays in full. B is wrong. A surety has different rights before and after payment. Prior to payment, a surety could attempt to be exonerated. If the surety was exonerated he would not have to pay, but the question is looking for a surety's right once payment has been made. D is wrong. *Attachment* is a term that refers to the creditor's rights, and the question asked about the surety's rights.

433. **C.** I is correct. Prior to payment, the surety hopes to be exonerated. Exoneration means to be found not liable. It's not easy to be exonerated, because once the surety cosigns, the surety has primary liability. II is correct. After payment, the surety stands in the shoes of the creditor against the principal debtor. The surety can demand payment from the debtor or can demand the car from the debtor.

434. **D.** The Credit Card Fraud Act deals with what happens if your card is used in an unauthorized situation, if it's stolen, and so on. If your credit card is stolen, your max liability is $50 per card if you promptly notify the credit card company upon receiving your statement balance or sooner. The debtor must act in good faith and report the issue promptly to minimize the overall damages.

435. **C.** I is correct. The Equal Credit Opportunity Act prohibits discrimination in credit granting on the basis of marital status. II is correct. The Equal

Credit Opportunity Act prohibits discrimination in credit granting on the basis of race and gender.

436. **A.** I is correct. Liquidation involves selling all non-cash assets in order to raise cash and pay all debts. Chapter 7 bankruptcy results in liquidation. In a Chapter 7 case, the debtor needs to sell all non-cash assets, pay creditors, and get a discharge for the remaining debts. The business is not meant to survive a Chapter 7 bankruptcy. II is wrong. Chapter 11 is reorganization. The debtor wants to keep the struggling business alive. In the absence of fraud, the debtor is allowed to remain in charge during bankruptcy. A creditors committee is composed of unsecured creditors, and a plan gets submitted that gives the debtor more time to pay. III is wrong. Chapter 13 is for a small business owner looking to save the equity in his home. Liquidation is the last thing on the debtor's mind in Chapter 13, but it could become reality if the creditors don't get paid under the debtor's promise of a new payment plan.

437. **B.** III is correct. For creditors to file involuntary bankruptcy against a debtor, unsecured creditors must prove that the debtor is not paying bona fide debts as they mature. I is wrong. If there are 12 or more unsecured creditors, then 3 or more creditors would need to file the bankruptcy petition. Since Green has only 9 creditors, only one needs to file. II is wrong. Insolvency refers to the fact that total liabilities exceed total assets. The creditors do not have to prove that Green is insolvent, but they do need to prove that Green is equitably insolvent, which is the inability to pay short-term debts as they become due.

438. **B.** II is correct. The debtor is still entitled to alimony. The debtor must agree to surrender certain property to which the debtor becomes entitled within the 180 days *after* the petition is filed, but alimony is not among that property. I is wrong. Among that property that must be surrendered for the bankruptcy is life insurance proceeds. III is wrong. Among that property that must be surrendered for the bankruptcy is inherited property.

439. **C.** I is correct. The trustee in bankruptcy can void any transfer made by the debtor during one year prior to bankruptcy *if* the transfer was considered a fraudulent conveyance. A conveyance would be viewed as fraudulent if it was made with the intent to hinder or delay creditors: for example, hiding assets or selling property for less than adequate consideration. Fraudulent conveyances

are considered an act of bad faith and could hurt the debtor's hopes of receiving a discharge in bankruptcy, or forgiveness of debt. II is correct. A preferential transfer is also voidable by the trustee even though these transfers happen in the course of business. An example of a preferential transfer is the debtor favoring one creditor over another with payments made to that favored creditor while the debtor is insolvent. The result of a preferential transfer is that the creditor favored by the debtor receives more than he or she would have had the favored creditor been forced to wait in line in bankruptcy.

440. **B.** II is correct. A Chapter 11 reorganization case may be filed voluntarily by the debtor or involuntarily by creditors. I is wrong. A trustee is *not* always appointed under a Chapter 11 bankruptcy case. Under Chapter 11 the business debtor sometimes remains in charge and other times a trustee is placed in charge of the debtor's assets. The court decides based on several factors, including the competency of the debtor.

441. **C.** I is correct. A debtor could have total assets greater than total liabilities and still be unable to pay current debts as they become due. A debtor does not have to be insolvent for creditors to force the debtor into Chapter 11 bankruptcy. II is correct. The reorganization plan could be filed by the creditors or filed by the debtor, and all plans must be in by a certain date set forth by the bankruptcy judge. The goal of Chapter 11 is to give the struggling debtor more time to pay debts without the need to sell off assets. A new repayment plan will be filed by the interested parties and ultimately approved by the court.

442. **D.** Secured creditors get theirs before the unsecured creditors. What happens on the CPA exam is that the secured creditors will get paid, but they won't get enough money to satisfy what was owed to them. So after they get theirs, they jump over to the unsecured creditor line. But when they get to the unsecured creditor line, they must wait at the end of that line, not the front of the line.

443. **A.** Employees are given a high priority in a bankruptcy case. Of the unsecured creditors listed in this question, employees have the highest priority. It is important to note that had one of the choices been alimony, child support, or administrative costs of the bankruptcy, such as lawyer and accounting fees, those costs would have been paid ahead of employees. C is wrong. When assets are distributed

in a bankruptcy case, certain creditors have priority over others. Secured creditors get paid the value of their security first, but if they are owed more than what their collateral sold for, they go to the end of the unsecured creditor line with no priority and wait until other unsecured creditors with a priority in that line get paid, such as employees. D is wrong. While unsecured taxes are given a priority, employees get paid before employer taxes get paid. B is wrong. In the event of bankruptcy, while customers are given a priority, employees get paid ahead of customers.

444. **B.** II is correct. If the debtor acts in bad faith while in bankruptcy, this could result in no discharges at all, or discharges obtained may be revoked. An example would be fraudulent conveyances or the debtor purposefully answering the questions on the bankruptcy petition incorrectly, such as failing to explain the whereabouts of assets. I is wrong. Any creditor that the debtor fails to list will result in the debtor not getting a discharge for that one unlisted creditor. Discharges would still be available for the remaining creditors, provided the debtor acted in good faith.

445. **C.** I is correct. Upon filing of a petition for involuntary bankruptcy under Chapter 7, the court will appoint an interim trustee. While a trustee was optional under Chapter 11 reorganization, a trustee is mandatory under Chapter 7 liquidation. II is correct. The bankruptcy filing will act as an automatic stay and stop all collection efforts with the exception of alimony, child support, and criminal actions.

446. **C.** I is correct. The SEC does not render any opinion regarding the facts contained in a registration statement. Instead, the SEC looks to see if the required information is complete. The SEC renders no opinion regarding the securities value as an investment. II is correct. The registration statement will contain the following information: names of issuer, directors, officers, underwriters, and large shareholders, and description of property, business, and capitalization; description of security to be offered; certified financial statements; a balance sheet not more than 90 days old; and a profit and loss statement for five years.

447. **B.** II is correct. The Federal Securities Act of 1933 states that if a corporation wants to issue securities in interstate commerce that have not previously been issued, then the securities must be registered. An exception would be when the buyers are in the same state as the seller, because no interstate commerce would apply and the federal government would have no jurisdiction. In this example, the Texas securities laws (known on the CPA exam as "blue sky" laws) would apply since all the potential purchasers live in the same state as the issuer. I is wrong. The securities would *not* need be registered with the Securities and Exchange Commission, because the purchasers live in the same state as the issuer; therefore, no interstate commerce is involved. This is known as the intrastate exemption, where the issuer and all purchasers or offerees are residents of the same state and the issuer does 80% of its business in that state.

448. **C.** I is correct. The Federal Securities Act of 1933 includes common and preferred stock in its definition of a security. Preferred stock would need to be registered if being sold to the public in interstate commerce by a firm looking to raise capital. II is correct. The Federal Securities Act of 1933 includes corporate bonds in its definition of a security. Corporate bonds would need to be registered if being sold to the public in interstate commerce by a firm looking to raise capital.

449. **A.** I is correct. Exemptions apply to securities issued by not-for-profit organizations. This means that a charity could issue bonds without first registering the bonds with the Securities and Exchange Commission (SEC). II is wrong. Corporate bonds, whether they are debentures or secured bonds, must be registered with the SEC prior to sale to the public in interstate commerce under the Federal Securities Act of 1933. Other exempt securities include government bonds, banks issuing securities, charities, railroads, and bankruptcy trustees. Commercial paper is exempt if it has an original maturity of less than nine months. Insurance policies and annuities are exempt.

450. **A.** Issuers under Regulation D, Rule 504, may sell the shares to an unlimited number of investors. While the general rule of the 1933 act says that new issues need to be registered with the SEC, exemptions do sometimes apply. The Regulation D exemption includes Rule 504. Rule 504 limits an offering to $1,000,000 within a 12-month period. If Cramer, Inc., follows Rule 504, Cramer could sell its shares to an unlimited number of investors without registering them with the SEC prior to sale. The important points to remember about the Rule 504 exemption under Regulation D are as follows: Issuers are allowed to sell to an unlimited number of investors; both accredited and nonaccredited investors are

unlimited and welcome to invest. Accredited investors include mutual fund managers, banks, hedge fund managers, and so on. Nonaccredited investors are members of the general public who want to invest and are not institutionally connected. Under Rule 504, the issuer could sell its stock to an unlimited number of both accredited and nonaccredited investors and still not have to register with the SEC, provided the dollar limit raised is $1,000,000 or less. Also under Rule 504, immediate resale of the securities is allowed. An investor who buys stock under Rule 504 can immediately sell it to another individual without violating Rule 504. B is wrong. If Cramer, Inc., follows Rule 504, Cramer could advertise the sale of its shares to an unlimited number of investors without registering them with the SEC prior to sale. Issuers are allowed to advertise their offering under Rule 504. C is wrong. If Cramer, Inc., follows Rule 504, Cramer could sell its shares to an unlimited number of investors without registering them with the SEC prior to sale. D is wrong. If Cramer, Inc., follows Rule 504, Cramer could sell its shares to an unlimited number of investors without registering the securities or providing the investors with a prospectus. The CPA exam often tests Rule 504 and its dollar limit of $1,000,000. If the issuer wants to raise more than $1,000,000, it cannot rely on Rule 504.

451. **C.** While the general rule of the 1933 act says that new issues need to be registered with the SEC, exemptions do sometimes apply. The Regulation D exemption includes Rule 505. Rule 505 allows a corporation to issue its stock to the public without registering with the SEC. The rules for Rule 505 are as follows: The dollar limitation of Rule 505 is $5,000,000. Up to $5,000,000 can be raised over a 12-month period. Because as much as $5,000,000 is being raised, Rule 505 has more restrictions than Rule 504. While the issuer could sell the stock to an unlimited number of accredited investors under Rule 505, no more than 35 nonaccredited investors are allowed to participate. Accredited investors include mutual fund managers, banks, hedge funds, and so on. Nonaccredited investors are members of the general public who want to invest and are not institutionally connected. Having zero nonaccredited investors would comply with the rule, but 36 nonaccredited investors would violate Rule 505. Unlike Rule 504, resale of stock purchased by investors under Rule 505 is restricted and must be held for two years. It's up to the issuer to disclose the restriction to the potential investors, usually done

by placing a notation or legend on the securities themselves. Unlike Rule 504, no general advertising is allowed.

452. **A.** Under the Federal Securities Act of 1933, Regulation D, Rules 505 and 506, the offering needs to be made without general advertising. Rule 505 and 506 offerings are sometimes referred to as private offerings, because advertising to the general public is prohibited under these two rules. Rule 505 and 506 have a few things in common:

No advertising
No more than 35 nonaccredited investors
No immediate resale to the public

It is important to note that while Rule 505 has a dollar limit of $5,000,000, Rule 506 has no dollar limit. While Rule 506 has no dollar limit, it's important to note that Rule 506 has a provision that any nonaccredited investor who wants to invest must show that he or she is financially sophisticated. Financial sophistication refers to the fact that the nonaccredited investor understands the risk and has other money in case this money is lost. This provision is unique to Rule 506.

453. **B.** Under Regulation D, Rules 504, 505, and 506 each require that the SEC be notified within 15 days after the first sale, not before the sale.

454. **B.** The following must register with the SEC per the 1934 act:

Any company that trades on a national securities exchange
Brokers and dealers doing business in interstate commerce

If not traded on a national exchange, large corporations with $10,000,000 in assets and at least 2,000 shareholders, or 500 shareholders who are nonaccredited, must also register under the 1934 act and file Form 10-K and Form 10-Q just like a large issuer.

455. **A.** I is correct. Unusual events not in the ordinary course of business must be reported using an 8-K report. 8-K reports are used to report material change of events by the publicly traded company to the SEC. For example, if a board member resigns, a company must release the news in an 8-K within four days. II is correct. 10-K annual reports are required to be audited by the 1934 act and filed within 60 to 90 days of the close of the fiscal year. 10-Q quarterly reports are unaudited but required to be released under the Securities Exchange Act of

1934 within 40 to 45 days after the end of the first three quarters. III is correct. A proxy is any matter subject to shareholder vote. Soliciting proxies by use of mail or interstate commerce requires following these rules: Whomever is soliciting the proxy must state whether the proxy is being solicited by management and, if so, include annual reports for two years. Proxy solicitations must include the matters to be voted on and the place to vote. Proxy solicitations must be filed with the SEC 10 days before sending to shareholders.

456. **B.** II is correct. The annual report Form 10-K must be filed by a large reporting company within 60 days after the end of the fiscal year according to the Securities Exchange Act of 1934. Certain smaller firms have 90 days to file their annual reports, but the larger companies get only 60 days. Prior to the Securities Exchange Act of 1934, corporations did not have to file an annual report. I is wrong. The Federal Securities Act of 1933 regulates initial public offerings of securities. The 1933 act does *not* regulate reporting once the shares are issued. The 1933 act regulates reporting of required disclosures for a corporation wishing to sell its stock to the public for the first time.

457. **B.** Depending upon the size of the corporation, Form 10-Q is due a maximum of 45 days after the end of the quarter. Form 10-Q is a quarterly report that must be filed with the SEC at the end of the first three quarters of the fiscal year. In the 10-Q, the company's financial statements are reviewed rather than audited. Since the question mentioned that Horizons, Inc., is a small reporting company rather than large, the 10-Q is due a maximum of 45 days after the close of the first three quarters. A is wrong. 40 days would be the maximum amount of time that a large corporation would have to file its 10-Q. C is wrong. 60 days is the maximum number of days that a large reporting company has to file its annual report, Form 10-K, after year end. D is wrong. 90 days is the maximum number of days that a small reporting company has to file its annual report, Form 10-K, after year end.

458. **B.** A party making a tender offer to purchase at least 5% of the shares of a class of securities registered under the 1934 act must file a report with the SEC. A report must also be filed by that same party to the issuer of those securities and to the exchange on which those shares trade. A tender offer is an offer to all shareholders to purchase stock at a specific price for a specified period of time. Note that the tender offer must be reported to the SEC by the party making the tender offer, not by the company being targeted.

459. **A.** I is correct. The Sarbanes-Oxley Act through its Public Company Accounting Oversight Board (PCAOB) permits a registered auditing firm to perform tax services for audit clients if the tax services are preapproved by the board of directors. II is wrong. The Sarbanes-Oxley Act of 2002 prohibits many services that audit firms had previously performed for their issuer audit clients prior to 2002. Among the many prohibited services are bookkeeping, financial information system design and implementation, and actuarial services. The goal of prohibiting these services is to enhance independence of the audit firm.

460. **B.** II is correct. To enhance oversight by the board of directors, the audit committee, rather than management, is directly responsible for the appointment compensation and oversight of the independent registered audit firm. The audit firm reports directly to the audit committee, and the audit committee decides whether or not to retain the independent registered CPA firm from one year to the next. III is correct. According to the Sarbanes-Oxley Act of 2002, documentation that relates to audits of publicly traded companies must be retained for seven years. I is wrong. The lead or coordinating partner and the reviewing partner must be rotated off an audit engagement every five years.

461. **D.** According to the Sarbanes-Oxley Act, the audit firm cannot have employed the issuer's CEO, CFO, controller, chief accounting officer, or any person serving in an equivalent position for a one-year period preceding the audit, in order to enhance independence.

462. **D.** A firm that audits more than 100 issuers annually would be inspected by the PCAOB every year. According to the Sarbanes-Oxley Act, the PCAOB must inspect registered CPA firms that regularly audit more than 100 issuers annually. A is wrong. According to the Sarbanes-Oxley Act, the PCAOB must inspect registered CPA firms every three years if those CPA firms regularly perform fewer than 100 audits of issuers annually. B is wrong. A firm that regularly performs no audits of issuers would *not* be inspected by the PCAOB. The Sarbanes-Oxley Act only has jurisdiction over publicly traded companies and their audit firms. C is wrong. A firm that audits more than 25 issuers annually but less than 100 issuers annually would be inspected by the PCAOB every three years.

463. **B.** The CPA will likely be sued for negligence. When a CPA lacks professional care and competence during the course of the engagement, the CPA has committed negligence. A and C are wrong. For the injured party to prove that the CPA acted with gross negligence and therefore committed constructive fraud would mean that the CPA would have acted "recklessly" with regard to the rights of others, and there was no indication that the CPA acted "recklessly" in the question. D is wrong. Actual or common law fraud would have required the injured party to prove that the CPA acted with scienter or bad faith, that is, with intent to deceive or cheat. There was no indication of that in the facts.

464. **A.** I is correct. For an injured party to sue a CPA under the 1934 act, the plaintiff would have to prove that a material misstatement or omission was included in a filed document. (This would also have to be proven if the plaintiff was suing the CPA under the 1933 act.) II is correct. For an injured party to sue a CPA under the 1934 act, the plaintiff would have to prove that they read and relied on the false financial statements. III is wrong. For an injured party to sue a CPA under the 1933 act, the plaintiff would *not* have to prove that they read or relied on the false financial statements. All they would have to prove under the 1933 act is that a material omission or misrepresentation was included in a filed document, that they bought the stock, and that they lost money.

465. **C.** When a CPA is liable for negligence, the CPA is liable to anyone in a class of third parties whom the CPA knows will rely or did rely on his opinion. Negligence means lack of reasonable care; a client could sue a negligent CPA because of the privity of contract between. A third party who suffers money damages by relying on the CPA's work can also sue the CPA for negligence.

466. **A.** I is correct. To support a finding of common law fraud against a CPA, the injured party must prove that the CPA materially misrepresented facts. II is correct. To support a finding of common law fraud against a CPA, the injured party must prove an intent to deceive (scienter) on the part of the CPA. III is correct. To support a finding of common law fraud against a CPA, the injured party must prove justifiable reliance on the CPA's work and that the injured party suffered money damages by relying on the CPA's work.

467. **B.** If the CPA is liable for fraud, the CPA can be sued for fraud by anyone who suffers a loss as a result of the fraud. To sue a CPA for fraud, the injured party must prove material misrepresentation of a fact, intent to deceive, scienter, bad faith, justifiable reliance, and damages.

468. **D.** I is correct. To support the finding of constructive fraud on the part of the CPA, the injured party must prove that the CPA acted recklessly. You will know constructive fraud or gross negligence when you see it on the exam; if the CPA acted "recklessly," that means "gross negligence" or "constructive fraud." III is correct. To support the finding of constructive fraud on the part of the CPA, the injured party must show reliance on the CPA's work and that they suffered money damages as a result of the justifiable reliance. II is wrong. To support the finding of constructive fraud on the part of the CPA, the injured party need not show intent to deceive. The difference between actual fraud and constructive fraud is that the intent to deceive is lacking with constructive fraud. With constructive fraud, either intent to deceive is lacking or cannot be proven. It's difficult to prove that the CPA acted in bad faith, but if all the other elements of fraud are present, a finding of constructive fraud or gross negligence is often the result. Notice that constructive fraud or gross negligence is more serious than negligence, but not as serious as common law or actual fraud.

Chapter 43: Business Structures and Other Regulatory Areas

469. **A.** I is correct. The bylaws of a corporation govern the corporation's internal management. The bylaws may be adopted by the incorporators or the board of directors. II is wrong. The bylaws are not filed with the state as part of the articles of incorporation. Corporate bylaws are *not* contained in the articles of incorporation.

470. **B.** Promoters are primarily liable on preincorporation contracts they make. They remain primarily liable, even if the corporation accepts the contract. Noll (the promoter) is primarily liable for the contract made with Clark. The corporation, by using Clark's services for six months after incorporation, had impliedly accepted the contract and would be liable also. The correct answer is that both Noll and Rotondo are liable.

471. **C.** I is correct. A corporate director is authorized to rely on information provided by the appropriate corporate officer. The financial statements that come from the officers of the corporation are an example of the corporate directors relying on

information provided by the officers. II is correct. A corporate director is authorized to rely on information provided by the independent auditor's report. The corporate directors rely on the independent auditor's report when the board decides whether or not to declare the dividend.

472. **D.** Once a dividend is duly declared by the board of directors, the stockholders become unsecured creditors of the corporation. Thus once Shea declares a cash dividend, Lucas became an unsecured creditor of Shea. C is wrong. A preferred stockholder is not entitled to convert preferred stock into common stock unless this right is specifically authorized. A is wrong. Lucas is a holder of cumulative preferred stock, not participating preferred stock. Only participating preferred stock shareholders may participate with common stock shareholders on dividend distributions. B is wrong. Cumulative preferred stock is usually nonvoting stock. Whether voting or nonvoting depends on the stock, not on whether dividend payments are in arrears.

473. **C.** Corporations are subject to double taxation if dividends are paid. Profits are taxed at the corporate level, and if the corporation pays dividends, the dividends are taxable income for the recipient. A is wrong. Most privately held businesses are sole proprietorships and partnerships, not C corporations. B is wrong. C corporations are *not* allowed to deduct dividends paid. D is wrong. C corporations are not limited to only one class of stock. They can have as many classes of stock as described in its articles of incorporation. S corporations are limited to one class of stock.

474. **B.** II is correct. If the shareholders have commingled their personal funds with those of the corporation, then in the event of bankruptcy, the court could hold the shareholder liable who commingled. This is common when there is one shareholder of a small C corporation who tries to run the corporation out of his personal checking account. I is incorrect. In the absence of fraud, a corporation can be formed for the sole purpose of limited liability. One of the principal reasons for choosing the corporate form over others is to obtain limited personal liability. If there was fraud involved, the court could pierce the corporate veil and hold the shareholders liable who participated in the fraud.

475. **B.** II is correct. Preferred stock is considered equity securities. I is wrong. All bonds represent debt securities, not equity securities.

476. **B.** II is correct. In a shareholder's derivative lawsuit, angry shareholders are suing on behalf of the corporation. The shareholder's derivative lawsuit is commonly brought against the director or officer who participated in an ultra vires act. If the corporation wins the shareholder's derivative lawsuit against the director or officer who participated in the ultra vires act, recovery of the money would belong to the corporation as an entity, not to any shareholders. I is wrong. A properly declared dividend becomes a claim against the corporation. The money from a dividend declaration is owed to the shareholders, not to the corporation. You will know a shareholder's derivative lawsuit when you see it, because the recovery would have to belong to the *corporation* and not to any individual shareholders or group of shareholders. Therefore, unpaid dividend declarations would not be the subject of a shareholder's derivative lawsuit.

477. **C.** I is correct. Shareholders have the right to vote on fundamental changes in structure like a merger or consolidation. II is correct. Shareholders have the right to a reasonable inspection of corporate records unless they themselves have abused that right in the past.

478. **D.** III is correct. The evidence that the parties are partners is often implied by the parties' everyday conduct. The fact that they are co-owning a business for profit will often substitute for a written partnership agreement. I is wrong. A partnership agreement need not be filed with the government. II is wrong. While you would think that all partnerships would insist on a written agreement, many partnerships begin without any agreement whatsoever and while risky, it is perfectly legal. If a dispute arises, the court asks to see the partnership agreement, and if there is none, the court then looks for evidence that the parties are partners.

479. **C.** I is correct because partners are agents of the partnership and agents of each other. Each partner owes a duty of loyalty to the partnership. Since partners are co-owners of the business, when a partner acts on behalf of the business, the partner is acting both as a principal and as an agent. II is correct because partners are jointly and severally (separately) liable on all partnership debts and contract obligations. This means all partners must be sued as a group, but then after partnership assets are exhausted, whichever partner still has money can be sued individually. The term *several* means "separate."

480. A. The liability of a new partner is normally limited to the amount of his or her capital contribution to the partnership. The outgoing partner is still liable for old partnership debts and would even be liable for new debts unless the partnership gave notice of that outgoing partner's retirement.

481. C. I is correct. Submitting to arbitration requires unanimous consent of all partners. II is correct. Admitting a new partner requires unanimous consent of all partners. Other acts requiring unanimous consent include confessing in court and disposing of partnership goodwill.

482. D. A partner who retires, withdraws, disassociates, and so on still has liability for existing partnership debts incurred while he was a partner. The retiring partner would also be liable for new debts of the partnership unless notice of retirement is given. Actual notice of retirement would need to be given to existing creditors, and constructive notice of retirement (classified ad) would need to be given to potential creditors for Partner A to avoid liability for future firm debts. Remember, the retiring partner is still fully liable for debts incurred while he was a partner until those debts are paid off. The only way the retiring partner would *not* be liable for existing partnership debts is if released by the creditor, an unlikely situation unless there is a novation. In the case of a novation, there would be a substitution of debtors with the creditor's consent. An example of a novation would involve the creditor agreeing to release the retiring partner from existing debts and holding only the remaining partners liable. The creditor would have the power to release the retiring partner, but would be unlikely to do so.

483. B. I is wrong. In an LLP, a partner would only be liable for torts that she herself committed and would *not* be liable for torts committed by other partners. In a general partnership, a general partner would be liable for torts committed by other partners as well as for torts that she committed herself. II is correct. In an LLP, a partner would *not* be liable for the torts committed by other partners but only for those she herself commits. In a general partnership, a partner would be liable for torts committed by other partners. LLPs are less risky than general partnerships.

484. B. II is correct. In an LLC, losses are limited to the amount of investment, much like a shareholder in a corporation. I is wrong. The key advantage to the LLC is that the entity is treated as a partnership for tax purposes, not liability purposes. Being treated as a general partnership for liability purposes is not an advantage but a disadvantage.

485. B. I is wrong. They will be taxed like a partnership, not a corporation, because they did *not* file articles of incorporation. II is correct. They will be taxed like a partnership because they are going to default to being a general partnership. The bottom line in an LLP or LLC is that the investor receives the tax benefits of a partnership and the liability protection of a shareholder in a corporation. This is why many new small business owners are choosing LLP and LLC over the general partnership or sole proprietorship. Since Harry, Ben, and Chico never filed with the state to be recognized as an LLP, LLC, or corporation, they would default to being a general partnership.

486. A. I is correct. In an LLP, no tax is paid at the partnership level; the tax return is informational only, and all profits and losses flow through to the partners. II is correct. The partners may agree to have the LLP managed by just one partner or by just a few partners. III is correct. An entity such as a corporation may be a partner in an LLP.

487. A. I is correct. A proprietorship needs no formal filing with the state. II is correct. A general partnership needs no formal filing with the state. III is wrong. LLPs do require a formal filing with the state in order to secure limited liability. IV is wrong. LLCs do require a formal filing with the state in order to secure limited liability.

488. A. I is correct. Trusts are three and a half months after death, April 15th. Trusts must use the calendar year. II is correct. Individual returns are due three and a half months after year end, April 15th. III is correct. Partnership returns are due three and a half months after year end, April 15th, for a calendar-year partnership.

489. A. I is correct. Workers' compensation is available even if the employee is negligent. III is correct. A negligence action could be brought against Suzy Wong, Inc., if Suzy Wong, Inc., were determined to be a third-party manufacturer of faulty equipment. II is incorrect. No negligence action can be brought against Hanson, the employer, since the employer carries the workers' compensation policy and the employee can immediately collect on the policy (even if the employee was negligent).

490. D. II is correct. Social security tax is paid one-half by the employee and one-half by the employer. The amount that the employer pays gets deducted by the employer as part of payroll tax expense. The amount that comes out of the employee's pay cannot be deducted by either the employee or employer. I is wrong. No money comes out of the employee's pay to go toward federal unemployment. Federal unemployment is paid for 100% by the employer. The employer then deducts the amount paid for federal unemployment. A portion of payroll tax expense for the employer includes the amount paid for federal unemployment. III is wrong. No money comes out of the employee's pay to go toward workers' compensation insurance. The employer pays the full workers' compensation premium. Workers' compensation is designed to compensate an employee for job-related injury or illness without suing the employer. If the employer did not carry a workers' compensation policy, then the employer would be exposed to lawsuits from employees who got hurt while working.

491. **C.** I is correct. The Americans with Disabilities Act of 1990 does *not* require companies to set up a plan to make sure they hire enough people with disabilities. II is correct. The Americans with Disabilities Act prohibits discrimination against persons with a disability in hiring, firing, compensation, or promotion. Unless the employer shows undue hardship (e.g., undue expense), the employer must make reasonable effort to accommodate someone who is handicapped, which may include modifying the facility, changing the job, or installing necessary equipment, like a wheelchair ramp or elevator. A qualified applicant with a disability is an individual who with or without reasonable accommodation can perform the essential functions of the job.

492. **D.** The EEOC enforces laws regarding workplace discrimination cases. A is wrong. OSHA requires employers to keep records of and report serious accidents. OSHA develops standards that it enforces in the workplace for employee safety and could force an employer to purchase safety equipment from a third-party manufacturer. B is wrong. The FTC deals with the sale of goods and its purpose is to protect consumers, not employees. C is wrong. The IRS does not get involved investigating workplace discrimination cases.

493. **C.** I and II are correct. ERISA allows for joint jurisdiction by the IRS and US Department of Labor with the purpose of pension regulation.

494. **D.** According to the Bank Secrecy Act, financial institutions must file a CTR for each transaction in excess of $10,000, to help detect and prevent money laundering.

495. **A.** I is correct. Evidence of an illegal monopoly includes the ability to control prices. II is correct. Evidence of an illegal monopoly includes the ability to exclude competition. III is correct. Evidence of an illegal monopoly includes the ability to control more than 70% market share. Market share of less than 40% will not be considered a monopoly. Market share between 40% and 70% may or may not be considered a monopoly.

496. **C.** I is correct. Copyrights are good for the author's natural life plus 70 years. II is correct. Under the fair use doctrine, teachers in the classroom can bring in pages from a copyrighted book and distribute them to the class without the author's permission for classroom use.

497. **B.** II is correct. The owner of the copyright can transfer ownership by sale, by rental, lease, licensing, or lending; the owner of a copyright has the exclusive right, in the case of literary, musical, and dramatic works, and motion pictures, to perform the work publicly. I is wrong. Fair use is a right that belongs to someone other than the owner of the copyright. Fair use includes using parts of the protected work without the owner's permission for purposes of teaching, criticism, news reporting, and so on: for example, a teacher making copies of a page of a copyrighted book to teach a class, and so on.

498. **B.** II is correct. Patents are awarded for machines, designs, and new drugs and are good for 20 years, unrelated to the creator's life. I is wrong. Copyrights are good for the author's natural life plus 70 years.

499. **B.** I is correct. To obtain a patent, an applicant must show that the invention is novel and useful. II is correct. To obtain a patent, an applicant must show that the invention is not obvious to a person who works in the field. III is wrong. There is no requirement that the invention be in a tangible medium. The work must be in a tangible medium of expression in order to obtain a copyright.

500. **D.** I is wrong. $10,000 is the threshold for reporting any deposit, withdrawal, or exchange of currency. II is wrong. 15 days is the time for filing the transaction report, not 30 days.

Bonus Questions

501. D. I is wrong. While much of the Dodd-Frank Act applies to institutions with greater than $50 billion in assets, liquidation can occur whenever the FDIC feels that the impact will hurt the economy. The institution may at one time have had assets of above $50 billion, but the banking institution may need to be liquidated now because its assets are quickly declining. II is wrong. While paying into the fund is required, no rule exists under the Dodd-Frank Act that a firm must pay into the fund for two years prior to being liquidated.

502. B. II is correct. If the employee allows the options to lapse (not exercised), there is a capital loss based on the value of the options previously taxed. If there is a readily ascertainable value, the employee recognizes ordinary income in that amount in the year granted. If there is a cost to the employee, then the ordinary income is the value of the option minus the cost. If the options lapse, that amount previously recognized can be taken as a capital loss. I is wrong. If the options are exercised, the holding period begins with the exercise date, not the grant date.

503. C. I is correct. A penalty of $100 may be assessed to the tax preparer who fails to be diligent with regard to whether the client is eligible for the earned income credit. The earned income credit has been widely abused for decades, and in recent years, the IRS has enlisted the tax preparer as something of a gatekeeper. The tax preparer must fill out a checklist that includes computational worksheets, with the goal of determining whether the client is eligible for the earned income credit. II is correct. A penalty of $100 may be assessed to the tax preparer who fails to be diligent with regard to the amount of the client's earned income credit. The requirements for due diligence with respect to the earned income credit include eligibility checklists, computational worksheets, record retention, and inquiry of the taxpayer. The penalty for failure to be diligent will not apply if the tax return preparer can demonstrate that the preparer's normal office procedures were reasonably designed and routinely followed to ensure due diligence compliance and the failure to meet the due diligence requirements was isolated and inadvertent.